Accounting Theory and Practice

Titles in the
Accounting Theory and Practice Series

Accounting in a Changing Environment
an introductory text
M. W. E. Glautier and B. Underdown
Pitman Books 1974

Accounting Theory and Practice
a student text
M. W. E. Glautier and B. Underdown
Pitman Books
First edition 1976, second impression 1978,
second edition 1982

Basic Accounting Practice
a workbook
M. W. E. Glautier, B. Underdown and A. C. Clark
Pitman Books
First edition 1978, revised edition 1980

Teacher's Guide to Basic Accounting Practice
M. W. E. Glautier, B. Underdown and A. C. Clark
Pitman Books
First edition 1978, revised edition 1980

Accounting Theory and Practice

Second edition

**M W E Glautier
and B Underdown**

Pitman

PITMAN PUBLISHING LIMITED
128 Long Acre, London WC2E 9AN

PITMAN PUBLISHING INC
1020 Plain Street, Marshfield, Massachusetts

Associated Companies
Pitman Publishing Pty Ltd, Melbourne
Pitman Publishing New Zealand Ltd, Wellington
Copp Clark Pitman, Toronto

© M W E Glautier and B Underdown 1976, 1982

First published in Great Britain 1976
Second edition 1982
Reprinted 1983, 1984

British Library Cataloguing in Publication Data
Glautier, M W E
    Accounting theory and practice.—2nd ed
    1. Accounting
    I. Title   II. Underdown, B
    657   HF5635

    ISBN 0-273-01541-9

Text set in 10/11 pt Linotron 202 Times
Printed in Great Britain at the Pitman Press, Bath

Contents

Preface

The tradition in accounting education has been to focus the teaching of accounting almost entirely upon procedures for processing financial data. The treatment of accounting as a skill, rather than as a body of knowledge, is based on the belief that 'accounting is what accountants do'. Whilst this assertion undoubtedly holds good as a statement of what accountants do, such a view of accounting has serious shortcomings as regards the educational qualities of accounting courses and the education of accountants. First, by restricting the nature and scope of accounting to an exposure of its procedures, it fails to provide an adequate understanding of these procedures in relation to the problems facing accountants. Second, it impedes the recognition of economic and social changes which bear directly on these problems. These changes have made many accounting practices redundant, and have called for a re-structuring of the accounting process. Third, it supports a conviction widespread among students and practitioners that what they have been taught is in the nature of an everlasting truth, or a collection of everlasting truths. Hence, it has hindered the development of accounting.

The most damaging factor as regards the teaching of accounting has been the absence of a theoretical framework to serve as a standard of reference for examining the validity of the assumptions held by accountants. As a result, accounting courses have sometimes tended to be virtually devoid of rigorous analysis, which is characterized by the uncritical acceptance of the assumptions reflected in accounting procedures. It is not surprising, therefore, that teachers of other subjects tend to regard accounting as being qualitatively inferior in the potential which it offers for the development of the mind and person.

This textbook is committed to a different view of accounting education in a number of important respects. First, as its title Accounting Theory and Practice implies, it attempts to provide a theoretical framework for the understanding of the nature of the accounting problem and an appreciation of the purpose of various accounting practices. This approach permits accounting practices to be exposed to critical analysis by means of which their usefulness and relevance may be assessed and their shortcomings exposed. Hence, it provides the teacher and the student with a means of overcoming the most serious criticism made about accounting education. Second, the nature and the scope of accounting is extended beyond accounting procedures by conceiving the essential function of accounting as facilitating socio-economic activities and decisions. Accordingly, we give a global and rounded view of accounting in which the emphasis is appropriately placed on the role of accounting as being the provision of information for decision making. We examine both traditional and new problems, and bring to our analysis developments in other subject areas which are important to accounting. In so doing, we provide for the interdisciplinary nature of accounting and hope to end its isolation as an esoteric collection of procedures. From this viewpoint, we believe that the traditional emphasis placed in first-year texts on the importance of financial accounting is misplaced.

We have emphasized the importance of the scientific method for the development of accounting. In terms of its ultimate objectives, accounting is as scientific as any other discipline. In terms of its ability to develop and apply empirically verified theories, it is far from being a mature science, but it is striving in this direction. We try to reflect this trend in this textbook.

Finally, we believe that accounting is a very important social science. We hope that our readers will develop insights into the social role of accounting at an early stage, and it is for this reason that we decided to adopt a global, rather than a narrow view of the accounting process.

We have interpreted the broad objectives of accounting as being to provide information for the following purposes:

(1) Decision-making regarding the use of limited resources, including the identification of crucial decision areas, and the determination of objectives and goals.
(2) Effectively directing and controlling human and material resources.
(3) Maintaining and reporting on the custodianship of resources.
(4) Facilitating social functions and controls.

The textbook is divided into five parts, as follows:

Part 1   A Theoretical Framework
Part 2   Financial Accounting—The Historical Cost Approach
Part 3   Financial Reporting—Alternative Valuation Approaches
Part 4   Financial Reporting—Extending The Disclosure of Information
Part 5   Planning and Control

In Part 1 we discuss the nature and the importance of theory covering every aspect of accounting knowledge and incorporating this knowledge into a unified whole, the purpose of which is the provision of information for decision making.

Part 2 examines the traditional nature of accounting information based on the historical cost approach which illustrates the way of thinking underlying financial accounting practices and looks at the development of financial accounting practice in the context of accounting conventions and standards.

Part 3 examines the problems of financial reporting in terms of alternative valuation methods to those employed in conventional financial accounting, which are based on historical cost.

Part 4 evaluates current financial reporting practices in terms of extending the disclosure of information to investors and employees as well as corporate social reporting.

Part 5 focuses on the role of information for management decision making and examines the needs of management relevant for planning and control.

We would emphasize that although this textbook is divided into five parts, each addressed to a special aspect of accounting, they are nevertheless linked by the provision of a theoretical framework which brings them together and establishes their purposes in the provision of information for decision making.

We believe that this book will be suitable for the following uses:

(1) University and Polytechnic first- and second-year degree courses in Accounting;
(2) First-year MBA courses in Business Schools;
(3) Professional examinations;
(4) Practising accountants who wish to acquire a broader viewpoint of the accounting process.

Acknowledgements

We wish to place on record our gratitude to colleagues and friends for the advice and help which they have given us in the course of writing this text. We owe a particular debt to Professor W. Rotch of the Colgate Darden Graduate School of Business Administration, University of Virginia, and Charles Clark, Principal Lecturer in Accounting, Manchester Polytechnic, who have both been closely associated with every aspect of the book and who have helped us unstintingly, as well as Professor T. A. Lee of Edinburgh University, Professor R. H. Parker of Exeter University, Dr Anthony Hopwood of the London Business School, C. P. Rickwood of Birmingham University, Geoffrey J. Harris of Melbourne University and Dr H. C. Dekker of Amsterdam University.

E. C. Johnson, Senior Lecturer in Accounting, University of Hull, contributed two chapters on Accounting for Acquisitions and Mergers, whilst C. Burke and O. A. Bello, both of Southampton University, and P. J. Taylor of the University College of North Wales read and commented in detail on several chapters. For help with the second edition, thanks are due to R. W. Wallis and M. H. C. Lunt of Preston Polytechnic, A. J. Naughton of Leeds Polytechnic, Michael Shearer and Alan Southworth of Manchester University and A. Chandiok of Kingston Polytechnic.

We have been privileged as authors to have had so much support from our publishers Pitman Books Ltd, and this book is indeed the outcome of a close partnership between authors and publishers. We wish to thank all those members of the Pitman staff who have worked with us, particularly Navin Sullivan, Vice Chairman, Martin Marix Evans, James Shepherd and Eric Dalton of the University and College Department. James Shepherd deserves special mention for his patience, tact and above all for the hard work which he put into the first edition of this book and thanks are due to Eric Dalton for his generous assistance and enthusiasm in planning the second.

Dr. Ken Watkins of Sheffield University was one of the original instigators of this book, and we owe much to his friendship.

We both are fortunate to have wives who have encouraged us to work, and who have made the many sacrifices which wives of authors have to make. We dedicate this book with our love to Christiane and Anne.

Part 1   A THEORETICAL FRAMEWORK

1 Scope of accounting

Accounting is in an age of rapid transition; its environment has undergone vast changes in the last two decades and an accelerating rate of change is in prospect for the future. Much of what is accepted as accounting today would not have been recognized as such 50 years ago, and one may safely predict that in 50 years' time the subject will bear little resemblance to what it is today.

Changing social attitudes combine with developments in information technology, quantitative methods and the behavioural sciences to affect radically the environment in which accounting operates today, thereby creating the need to re-evaluate the objectives of accounting in a wide perspective. Accounting is moving away from its traditional procedural base, encompassing record-keeping and such related work as the preparation of budgets and final accounts, towards the adoption of a role which emphasizes its social importance.

The changing environment has extended the boundaries of accounting and has created a problem in defining the scope of the subject. There is a need for a definition which is broad enough to delineate its boundaries, whilst at the same time being sufficiently precise as a statement of its essential nature. It is interesting to contrast definitions which were accepted a little time ago with more recent statements. According to a definition made in 1953, 'the central purpose of accounting is to make possible the periodic matching of costs (efforts) and revenues (accomplishments). This concept is the nucleus of accounting theory, and a benchmark that affords a fixed point of reference for accounting discussions' (Littleton, 1953).

The Committee on Terminology of the American Institute of Certified Public Accountants formulated the following definition in 1961: 'Accounting is the art of recording, classifying and summarizing in a significant manner and in terms of money, transactions and events which are, in part at least, of a financial character, and interpreting the result thereof'. (A.I.C.P.A., 1961.)

A more recent definition is less restrictive and interprets accounting as 'the process of identifying, measuring and communicating economic information to permit informed judgements and decisions by the users of the information'. (A.A.A., 1966.)

This definition comes closer to our own interpretation of the scope of accounting, and the manner in which we should like to treat its subject matter, but we would add the rider that accounting is moving rapidly now towards a consideration of social welfare objectives. Accordingly, the purpose of accounting has been re-defined as 'to provide information which is potentially useful for making economic decisions and which, if provided, will enhance social welfare'. (A.A.A., 1975.)

According to this viewpoint, the scope of accounting should not be restricted to the private use of information, which has the limited perspective of being concerned with the impact of information on the welfare of individuals as such. The social welfare viewpoint is concerned with the impact of information on all the individuals making up society.

The actions of individuals have what are known as 'externality effects' which affect the welfare of other members of society. Hence, the social value of information resides in knowledge of these 'externality effects'. The significance of such information may be seen in the context of the range of groups having vested interests in business organizations, for example shareholders, managers and employees. It is evident that the supply of information to one group may give them an unfair advantage over the other groups in the decisions which they subsequently make, resulting in changes in the allocation of social benefits. The social welfare viewpoint states that in considering the information accountants ought to be supplying and the groups to whom such information should be provided, judgements ought to be made on the basis of the extent to which improvements in the welfare of one group outweigh the sacrifices in welfare borne by other groups.

One aspect of the social welfare theory of accounting is reflected in the development of social responsibility accounting. In the past, the interests of shareholders, investors, creditors and managers have exerted a dominating influence on the development of accounting practices. The social welfare theory of accounting requires that the interests of employees, trade unions and consumers ought to be taken into account, and that the traditional imbalance existing in the supply of information should be corrected. Social responsibility accounting draws attention to the gulf existing between the sectarian interests represented in conventional business accounting and its focus on profit, and the need to see the entire social role of business organization in the context of all those affected by its activities.

The emerging role of accounting as a social science

The social sciences study man as a member of society; they share a concern about social processes, and the results and consequences of social relationships. In this respect, the usefulness of accounting as a social science depends on the benefits which it may bring to society, rather than on the advantages which it may confer to its individual members. We would say, therefore, that although an individual businessman may benefit from the availability of accounting information, what is much more important is that society as a whole should benefit from the fact that its individual members use accounting information for the solution of business problems.

The history of accounting reflects the evolutionary pattern of social developments and in this respect, illustrates how much accounting is a product of its environment and at the same time a force for changing it. There is, therefore, an evolutionary pattern which reflects changing socio-economic conditions and the changing purposes to which accounting is applied. From today's perspective, we may distinguish four phases which may be said to correspond with its developing social role.

(1) Stewardship accounting has its origins in the function which accounting served from the earliest times in the history of our society of providing the owners of wealth with a means of safeguarding it from theft and embezzlement. The title 'stewardship' accounting also has its origins in the fact that wealthy men employed 'stewards' to manage their property. These stewards rendered an account periodically of their stewardship, and this notion still lies at the root of financial reporting today. Essentially, stewardship accounting involved the orderly recording of business transactions, and although accounting records of this type date back to as early as 4500 B.C., the method of keeping these records, known as 'book-keeping', remained primitive until fairly recent times. Indeed, the accounting concepts and procedures in use today for the orderly recording of business transactions have their origin in the practices employed by the merchants of the Italian City States during the early part of the Renaissance. The main principles of the Italian Method, as it was then known, were set out by Luca Pacioli in his famous treatise *Summa de Arithmetica, Geometrica, Proportioni et Proportionalita* which was published in Venice in 1494. The Italian Method, which became known subsequently as 'double-entry book-keeping' was not generally used in Western Europe until the early part of the 19th century. Whether or not businessmen kept their accounts on the single-entry or the double-entry principle, stewardship accounting played an important social role during the period of commercial expansion in Western Europe, which followed the Renaissance and characterized that phase of Capitalism known as Commercial Capitalism. Stewardship accounting is associated, therefore, with the need of businessmen to keep records of their transactions, the manner in which they had invested their wealth and the debts owed to them and by them.

(2) Financial accounting has a much more recent origin, and dates from the development of large-scale businesses which were made possible by the Industrial Revolution. Indeed, the new technology not only destroyed the existing social framework, but altered completely the method by which business was to be financed. The industrial expansion in the early part of the 19th century necessitated access to large supplies of capital. This led to the advent of the Joint Stock Company, which is a form of business which enables the public to particpate in providing capital in return for 'shares' in the assets and the profits of the company. An earlier experience of the Joint Stock form of trading which had resulted in a frantic boom in company flotations, culminating in the South Sea Bubble of 1720, had instilled public suspicion of this form of trading. Reflecting this mood, Adam Smith, himself, questioned the ability of the directors of such companies to administer honestly and well any of the most routine and easily checked business, for

'. . . being the Managers rather of other people's money than of their own, it cannot well be expected that they should look over it with the same anxious vigilance with which the partners of a private copartnery frequently watch over their own . . . Negligence and profusion . . . must always prevail, more or less, in the management of the affairs of such a company'. (Smith, 1904 edition.)

Nevertheless, the Joint Stock Companies Act, 1844 permitted the incorporation of such companies by registration without the necessity of obtaining a Royal Charter or a special Act of Parliament. It was not until 1855, however, that the Limited Liability Act permitted such companies to limit the liability of their members to the nominal value of their shares. This meant that the liability of shareholders for the financial debts of the company was limited to the amount which they had agreed to subscribe. In effect, in subscribing for a £1 share, a shareholder agreed to pay £1, and once he had paid that £1, he was not liable to make any further contribution in the event of the company's insolvency.

The concept of limited liability was a contentious point in the politics of the mid-19th century. The Limited Liability Act 1855 was passed in the teeth of bitter opposition, and one Member of Parliament described the Act as a 'rogues' charter'. Mindful of the potential for abuse which lay within this legislation, and mindful too of the necessity to safeguard the interests of shareholders and investors in these companies, Parliament eventually re-stated the doctrine of stewardship in a legal form. It made the disclosure of information to shareholders a condition attached to the privilege of Joint Stock status and of Limited Liability. This information was required to be in the form of annual Income Statements and Balance Sheets. We may say briefly, however, that the former is a statement of the profit or loss made during the year of the report, and the balance sheet indicates the assets held by the firm and the monetary claims against the firm.

Financial accounting is concerned with the emergence of these two accounting statements as vehicles for the disclosure of information to shareholders in Joint Stock companies. The unwillingness of company directors to disclose more than the minimum information required by law, and growing public disquiet as to the usefulness of the information contained in financial accounts culminated in the extension of disclosure requirements in the United Kingdom by means of the Companies Act, 1976. It is evident that the 1976 Act will be but one step in the history of public involvement in this problem which effectively began in 1844, and which has conferred upon accounting information an important social role.

Parallel developments have taken place also in the United States, where since the early 1930s there has been a continuous discussion on ways to improve the disclosure of information. The Securities and Exchange Commission has been concerned with the problem of the sufficiency of information disclosed at the time when new issues are sold to the public, and together with the Stock Exchanges and the accounting profession via the Financial Accounting Standards Board, it has been concerned with the adequacy of financial information regularly disclosed by companies. For some years, also, the European Economic Community has been trying to move towards a standardization of accounting practices both as regards disclosure and consistency of practices. The Companies Act 1981 which implements the requirements of the EEC Fourth Directive is discussed in Chapter 13.

The legal importance attached to financial accounting statements stems directly from the need of a capitalist society to mobilize savings and direct them into profitable investments. Investors, be they large or small, must be provided with reliable and sufficient information in order to be able to make efficient investment decisions. Herein lies one of the most significant social purposes of financial accounting reports. In a changing society, increased recognition that employees have a legitimate right to financial information is evident in the legislation passed or proposed in several European countries.

A more important influence in the demand for the disclosure of financial information to employees stems from the growing strength of the worker participation or co-determination movement. This aspect of accounting will be examined in Part 4.

(3) Management accounting is also associated with the advent of Industrial Capitalism, for the Industrial Revolution of the 18th century presented a challenge to the development of accounting as a tool of industrial management. In isolated cases there were some, notably Josiah Wedgwood, who developed costing techniques as guides to management decisions. But the practice of using accounting information as a direct aid to management was not one of the achievements of the Industrial Revolution: this new role for accounting really belongs to the 20th century.

Certainly, the genesis of modern management with its emphasis on detailed information for decision making provided a tremendous impetus to the development of management accounting in the early decades of this century, and in so doing considerably extended the boundaries of accounting. Management accounting shifted the focus of accounting from recording and analysing financial transactions to using information for decisions affecting the future. In so doing, it represented the biggest surge forward in seven centuries.

The advent of management accounting demonstrated once more the ability and capacity of accounting to develop and meet changing socio-economic needs. Management accounting has contributed in a most significant way to the success with which modern capitalism has succeeded in expanding the scale of production and raising standards of living.

(4) Social responsibility accounting is an entirely new phase in accounting development which owes its birth to the social revolution which has been underway in the Western world in the last few years. Social responsibility accounting widens the scope of accounting by considering the social effects of business decisions as well as their economic effects. The demand for social responsibility accounting stems from an increasing social awareness of the undesirable by-products of economic activities, and in this connection, one may point to the public attention which has been given to environmental problems over the last few years. Increasingly, management is being held responsible not only for the efficient conduct of business as expressed in profitability, but also for what it does about an endless number of social problems. Hence, with changing attitudes, the time-honoured standards by which performance is measured have come into disrepute. There is a growing consensus that the concepts of growth and profit as measured in traditional Balance Sheets and Income Statements are too narrow to reflect what many companies are trying, or are supposed to be trying to achieve.

Accounting in a changing environment

The process of change has had a dramatic impact on accounting research and accounting practice in recent years. The factors which have affected accounting may be identified as follows:

(1) Developments in quantitative methods and the behavioural sciences

have shifted the focus of interest towards decision making. The increased importance of quantitative methods in the management of organizations has meant that the subject of management has become less descriptive and more analytical. Thus, it has become less concerned with describing management as a process and more concerned with the concepts and theoretical models associated with organizations and their decision-making activities. To these developments have been added advances in the behavioural sciences which have increased the level of knowledge existing about the organizational decision-making process.

(2) The emphasis on decision making in recent years has brought together disciplines which once were viewed as separate areas of knowledge. Since there are different aspects of decision making—economic, behavioural, sociological and quantitative, accounting has become an inter-disciplinary subject. The accountant has to be knowledgeable over a broad area if he is to be efficient in providing information which is relevant and useful for decision making. The education of the accountant has tended to be traditional and to have had a narrow focus on gaining a knowledge of accounting methods. Hence, many accountants were not educated to cope with the problems of change, and in particular were not able to integrate their own skills with the knowledge relevant to decision making.

(3) Traditional accounting areas are being invaded by experts in cognate areas, such as systems analysts, computer programmers and operations research specialists, who bring with them new knowledge and different skills. As a result, the traditional status and role of the accountant is changing.

(4) Accounting is not an exact science, though it is a social science. As in the case in other social sciences, accounting concepts do not rest on universal truths or general laws. Accounting concepts are rooted in the value system of the society in which they operate, and they are socially determined. Hence, value judgements are applied to the interpretation and significance of economic and social events. The subjective nature of these values implies that there is ample opportunity for controversy as to how events should be measured and to whom such measurements are intended.

(5) In particular, the nature of external financial reporting has caused much concern in recent years. The status of the accounting profession has depended to some extent on its monopoly of the auditing and external financial reporting function. In the 1960s much criticism was directed towards financial reporting practices, primarily on the grounds that the lack of uniformity made the comparison of financial reports difficult. Furthermore, the reluctance of the accounting profession to take account of changes in the value of the money standard of measurement when presenting financial information impaired the usefulness of financial reports.

(6) The role of business in society has come under greater scrutiny in recent years. Increasingly, business corporations are viewed as accountable to society in general for their actions, in addition to being answerable to shareholders in respect of profitability.

The major consequences which have resulted from the changing environment in which accounting operates may be stated as follows:

(1) There has been a dramatic effect on accounting research. Sophisticated statistical techniques are being used increasingly. There has been a movement

away from a concern with the processes of accounting to an interest in the analysis of its problems and to theoretical models relevant to these problems. Primarily, accounting is being viewed as influencing human behaviour. At the same time, the influence of economics on the development of accounting practice has increased. For example, it has become highly influential in the area of finance, whilst the inflation accounting debate has been concerned with issues which are addressed to analysis of the economic events affecting the enterprise. Some of the implications of these developments are considered in Parts 3 and 4.

(2) The accountant in management does not exist in isolation. He should be regarded as a member of the management team. We discuss this point further in the next chapter, and we suggest that this difficulty may be resolved by adopting a 'systems approach' to the study of accounting.

(3) In the United Kingdom, the need to improve accounting practice was recognized formally by the appointment of the Accounting Standards Committee in 1970. However, there is still a need to establish a theoretical framework for validating external financial reporting practices in terms of their perceived objectives, and to enable future development to take place in accordance with those objectives. In this regard, the existence of a theoretical framework would have promoted agreement on many of the specific issues which have caused controversies in financial reporting in recent years.

(4) Finally, the emergence of social responsibility accounting imposes new information objectives for accountants and these new objectives will require a new accounting methodology. At this point in time, we are able to discuss only the information objectives, though some countries, particularly France, are already legislating for this new accounting development.

Summary

In this chapter, we have examined the development of accounting from its earliest form as a recording activity to its present-day importance which stems from its objective of providing socio-economic information for decision making.

The history of accounting development reflects an ability to respond to changing social needs. Today, changing social attitudes combine with developments in information technology, quantitiative methods and the behavioural sciences to affect radically the environment in which accounting operates. These changes have created a number of problems for the accountant. It is with these problems that this book is concerned.

References

1. A.A.A. *A Statement of Basic Accounting Theory*, p. 1, 1966.
2. A.A.A. 'Report of the Committee on Concepts and Standards for External Financial Reports', *Accounting Review Supplement*, Vol. XLX, 1975.
3. A.I.C.P.A. *Committee on Terminology*, p. 9, American Institute Publishing Co., New York, 1961.

4. Littleton, A. C. *The Structure of Accounting Theory*, A.A.A. Monograph No. 5, p. 30, 1953.
5. Smith, A. *Wealth of Nations*, Cannon ed., Vol. 2, pp. 233, 246, 1904.

Questions

1. In what ways have the definitions of accounting changed over time?
2. Discuss the concepts of stewardship, financial, management and social responsibility accounting.
3. Examine the main factors which have affected the development of accounting in the last twenty years.
4. What do you consider to be the major challenges facing a new graduate entering the accounting profession?

2 Accounting as an information system

The term 'system' is commonly used today, and we read much about environmental systems, ecological systems, economic systems and political systems. Indeed, we live in the age of systems. Reduced to its utmost simplicity, a system is a set of elements which operate together in order to attain a goal. The following are examples of systems analysed in this manner:

System	Elements	Basic goal
Social club	Members	Recreation
School	Teachers, students, textbooks, buildings	Education
Police	Men, equipment, communication network, buildings	Crime control

From the foregoing illustrations, we may see that systems vary considerably in their appearance, their attributes, their elements and their basic goals. They have certain characteristics in common, however, for they consist of parts which interact together to achieve one or a number of objectives. Systems, therefore, do not consist of random sets of elements, but of elements which may be identified as belonging together because of a common goal.

A system may also be seen as consisting of three activities: input, processing of input, and output. Sometimes, one hears references to closed systems and open systems, and these terms refer to the nature of the relationship between these systems and their environment. An open system is one which interacts with its environment, and a closed system is one which does not. We may classify a business organization as an open system which has a dynamic interplay with its environment from which it draws resources and to which it consigns its products and services. An example of a closed system is a chemical reaction in a sealed container. The important distinction between an open and a closed system is that the former is constantly rejuvenated by its environment, whereas the latter tends to run down through loss of energy which is not replaced from the environment.

Accounting is often analysed as a series of activities which are linked and form a progression of steps, beginning with observing, then collecting, recording, analysing and finally communicating information to its users. We may say, therefore, that *accounting information* has a special meaning in that it is data organized for a special purpose, that is, decision making. The task of the accountant is to transform raw data into information. Of itself, data is simply a collection of facts expressed as symbols and characters which have no meaning, and are unable to influence decisions until transformed into information. We shall see in Part 2 how conventions existing among accountants for the treatment of data gives accounting information a distinctive character.

Accounting is a social science which lends itself easily to its analysis as an information system, for it has all the attributes of a system. It has a basic goal, which is to provide information, and it has clear and well-defined elements in the form of people and equipment. Moreover, accounting has the typical activities of systems, consisting of input, process and output, as shown in Fig. 1.1.

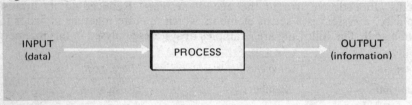

INPUT (data) → PROCESS → OUTPUT (information)

Fig. 1.1

The application of systems analysis to the treatment of accounting facilitates our study of accounting as a social science, and enables us to examine its various activities in terms of the relevance of its output for decision-making purposes.

The boundaries of an information system

An important aspect of the study of accounting as an information system is the definition of its boundaries. A system exists as an independent entity in an environment, and the nature of its relationship with that environment is clearly very important. We have already made reference to the distinction which exists between 'open' and 'closed' systems. We must now turn our attention to a closer examination of the boundaries of a system, by which we mean identifying a system in such a way that we are able to distinguish it from its environment.

In the previous section, we mentioned that the accountant selected from raw data that data which is relevant to his purpose. The filtering process by which he selects accounting data is provided by the conventions of accounting, which play a deterministic role in defining accounting information. This filtering process may be taken as one boundary between the accounting system and its environment; that point at which raw data becomes input data. The data which is so selected forms, as we have seen, the input into the processing system which produces accounting information. The information output is used by a group of decision makers, which we are able to identify, and it is evident that a decision-oriented information system should produce information which meets the needs of its users. Clearly, these needs should be specified in accordance with a theory of users' requirements. We may say, therefore, that the other boundary to an accounting information system is

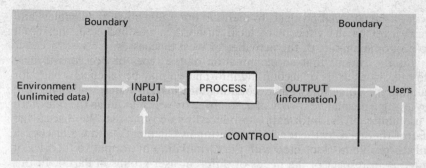

Fig. 1.2

established by the specific information needs of its users. We may establish these boundaries diagramatically as in Fig. 1.2.

This analysis of accounting as an information system enables us to make some important deductions. First, the goal of the system is to provide information which meets the needs of its users. If we can sufficiently and correctly identify these needs, we are then able to specify the nature and character of the output of the system. Second, the output requirements should determine, therefore, the type of data which is selected as the input for processing into information output. Third, welfare considerations may be taken into account in the selection of data, in accordance with the objective of accounting stated in Chapter 1.

In this connection, the idea of *control* which has been indicated on the diagram above shows that users' needs not only should determine the nature of data input but that the extent of the data input should be determined by a cost-benefit analysis related to users' needs and the impact of their decisions on society.

An important application of the concept of an information system's boundaries will be seen in Part 4, where we examine the problems of financial reporting in the context of investors' needs for information which is not really provided by the accountant. By ignoring users' needs, accounting information is deprived of the objectives which otherwise would enable us to validate accounting practices in the area in terms of the theoretical frameworks discussed in Chapter 3.

The output of an information system

The foregoing discussion has served to indicate how important are the needs of users of accounting information, for they determine the objectives of an accounting information system.

There are several groups of people who have vested interests in a business organization—managers, shareholders, employees, customers and creditors. Additionally, the community at large has economic and social interests in the activities of business organizations. This interest is expressed at national level by the concern of government in various aspects of firms' activities, such as their economic well-being, their contribution to welfare, their part in the growth of the national product, to mention but a few obvious examples; and at local level by the concern of local authorities and bodies in the direct socio-economic impact of the activities of local businesses.

It is quite evident that an examination of the types of decisions usually made by various users of accounting information may be taken as a basis for stipulating the objectives of an accounting information system and therefore, for evolving a normative theory of accounting by which to judge the relevance and usefulness of the information produced by accountants. We discuss the nature of theory construction in accounting in Chapter 3, and we discuss in detail the problems associated with the formulation of normative theories of accounting in respect of the needs of different user-groups in Part 4. In this chapter, we initiate these discussions by stating the general nature of the needs of different groups of information users.

In general terms, users of accounting information should be regarded as decision makers interested in determining the sacrifices which must be made for the benefits which are expected to flow from the decisions to which they commit themselves. Since all the sacrifices and the benefits necessarily materialize in the future, by reason of the nature of the decision-making process, uncertainty plays a critical role in assessing the sacrifices and benefits associated with particular decisions. It will be argued in Part 4, that rational decision makers will seek to maximize long-run returns consistent with the degree of risk which they are willing to accept.

The information needs of shareholders and investors

Historically, business accounting developed to supply information to those who had invested their wealth in business ventures. As we saw in Chapter 1, financial accounting, as it is now known, emerged in the 19th century as a result of the need to protect investors in Joint Stock Companies trading under limited liability. It has been evident for a long time that the information needs of investors are not adequately met by published balance sheets and income statements. In Part 2, we shall examine the nature of the information disclosed to shareholders and investors, and in Part 4, we shall subject traditional financial accounting practice considered in Part 2 to a critical analysis based on the question 'what information should be provided to investors'? To answer this question, we begin our discussion in Part 4 with an inquiry into the objectives of shareholders in business corporations. By stating that they are concerned with the value of their investment and the income which they expect to derive from their shareholding we are able to enquire into the nature of the information which they need in order to make rational decisions.

The information needs of management

Organizations may be considered as falling into two broad classes: those having profit or business objectives, and those having welfare objectives. In this book, we are concerned mainly with business organizations, but it should be remembered that many of the accounting methods employed in business organizations are equally employed by welfare or non-profit organizations. As regards the management of organizations, little difference exists between the information needs of managers of business organizations and those of welfare organizations.

The management process may be analysed into three major functions—planning, organizing and controlling the activities of the organization. Planning involves setting objectives for the organization, and devising strategies to attain those objectives. Organizing means establishing the administrative structure for implementing plans. Controlling is the process of observing and measuring actual performance so that it conforms with the planned and required performance. Thus, controlling means identifying deviations from planned performance, and taking such corrective action as may be necessary.

These various management functions have one thing in common: they are all concerned with making decisions, which have their own specific information requirements. Planning decisions, for example, are directed towards realizing broad goals which, in addition to the organization's survival and its profitability, usually include the intention to grow and to capture a large share of the market for its products. Other goals often include product leadership, increased productivity and improved industrial relations. There is an element of conflict between various organizational objectives, and it is the function of management to reconcile them through the planning process.

We devote Part 5 of this book to the examination of the accounting information needs of management, and the manner in which these needs are met. The scientific management of organizations has considerably extended the demand for accounting information, and the nature of the accounting problem. As we shall see, the influence of the behavioural sciences and the need for more information generally has created measurement problems as well.

The information needs of employees

It is a popular view that the interests of employees are in direct conflict with those of the firm, and in particular with those of management. Unless employees are able to share in the profits of business organizations, they are effectively dissociated from their activities if we suppose that the objective of business organizations is to maximize profits and maximize returns to shareholders. This classical concept of the objective of business enterprises is being replaced as a result of the social changes taking place in our society, and there is a broadening view of the social and economic responsibilities of management. It is recognized that employees have a vested interest in the outcome of management decisions of every kind. Improvements in industrial democracy through employee participation in management decisions have important implications for the supply of information to employees. A number of firms are already investigating this question. As regards the settlement of wage disputes, the question of profit sharing between employees, shareholders and management can only properly be settled on the basis of a full disclosure of the relevant facts.

The immense importance of good industrial relations, of harmony between management and employees, is acknowledged already in the literature of management science. It is quite evident that there must be eventually a symmetry of treatment between shareholders, management and employees in respect of the accounting information which each group requires and receives. We may say therefore, that the economic and social role of accounting in this particular context has not yet been properly explored. We touch upon these issues in Part 4.

The information needs of governments

To a greater or lesser degree, all Western governments intervene in the activities of business organizations in the process of managing what is known as a 'mixed economy', that is, an economic system consisting of both State-controlled and privately controlled business organizations. Government Agencies, such as Central Statistical Services, Ministries of Commerce, Industry, Employment etc., all collect information about the various aspects of the activities of business organizations. Much of this information is a direct output of the accounting system, for example, levels of sales activity, profits, investments, stocks, liquidity, dividend levels, proportion of profits absorbed by taxation etc. This information is very important in evolving policies for managing the economy.

Governments, in addition, can compel the disclosure of information which is not otherwise made available to the public, such as future investment plans, expected future profits and so on.

By and large, however, governments tend to expect accounting information to be presented in a uniform manner, so that the rules applying to accounting methods and the preparation of accounting reports for government use are the same as those which govern the nature of accounting information disclosed to investors and shareholders. If governments base policy decisions on accounting information which distorts the true position, it is evident that the ill-effects of such decisions will be widely felt. The failure to adjust for the effect of inflation, for example, not only gives an excessive view of company profits but may lead the government to believe that company profits are running at a sufficiently high level to enable firms to finance investments and provide an adequate return to shareholders. We may say, therefore, that all parties having an interest in business organizations should be concerned with the quality of the accounting information produced, as well as the relevance of that information to their own needs. It is for this reason that we devote Chapter 4 to a thorough examination of the conventions which govern the nature of financial accounting information.

The information needs of creditors

We may define as creditors all those who have provided goods, money or services to business organizations and have accepted a delay in payment or repayment. Creditors may be short-term or long-term lenders. Short-term creditors include suppliers of materials and goods, normally described as trade creditors, credit institutions such as bankers and hire-purchase firms who lend money for interest on a relatively short-term basis, and those who have provided services and are awaiting payment, for example, employees, outside contractors who have made repairs, electricity and gas undertakings who have presented accounts and have not yet been paid. Long-term creditors are those who have lent money for a long period, usually in the form of secured loans.

The main concern of creditors is whether or not the organization is credit-worthy, that is, will it be able to meet its financial obligations? They are interested in the organization's profitability only insofar as it affects its ability to pay its debts. On the other hand, creditors are very concerned with the firm's liquidity, that is, those cash or near-cash resources which may be mobilized to pay them, as well as the willingness of banks and other creditors to act like them in being willing to await payment. Creditors react quickly to changes of opinion about a firm's credit-worthiness, and if there is any doubt that a firm may not be able to pay, they will press for immediate settlement of debts owing and probably drive into bankruptcy a firm whose prospects in the medium and longer term are not necessarily bad.

Creditors are interested, therefore, mainly in financial accounting information which deals with solvency, liquidity and profitability, that is, with obtaining reports which will describe a firm's financial standing. We shall consider these aspects of financial reporting in Part 2, and in particular, we shall examine the adequacy of criteria applied to the analysis of financial statements, such as solvency, liquidity and profitability ratios.

The information needs of other groups

We have dealt so far with the information needs of four major groups which have vested interests in business organizations, and we have discussed the nature of their information requirements. How far and how adequately their information needs are suitably satisfied depends largely upon the pressure which these groups may exert upon the accountant to produce information tailored to these needs. How well they are able to articulate their information needs, how well accountants are able to understand the reasons why the information is needed and how willing and able accountants are to provide that information will be the theme of much of this book. We may say, for example, that the information needs of management are more adequately met than those of employees, shareholders, creditors and also governments. But there are two further groups in society who are interested in the activites of business organizations, and who are pretty well excluded from receiving information: the local community and customers.

(a) *The information needs of the local community*
Local communities are very dependent on local industries, not only because they provide employment, but also because they affect directly the entire socio-economic structure of the environment. Firms provide employment, they create a demand for local services, they cause an expansion in commercial activities, as well as extensions in the provision of welfare services as the

economic well-being of the community improves. Large firms, in particular, are able to exert a dominating influence on the local social framework which often is reflected in the corporate personality of the inhabitants. Miners, steelworkers, shipbuilders and workers in the motor industry do have styles of living and attitudes forged to some extent by the industries in which they work and live.

Local industries have positive and negative influences on the locality. Pollution, despoliation, congestion are all negative aspects of their activities which constitute external direct and indirect social and economic costs, which are borne by the community.

The local community has an interest in the activities of local industries, and evidently requires much more information of social benefits and costs than the public relations-type information which is presently disclosed. The social audit points to a possible remedy for the lack of objectivity in the information presently disclosed.

(b) *The information needs of customers*
Of recent years, Consumers Councils and other bodies have been formed in order to restore in some measure the disproportionate balance of power which has appeared in our society between the large and powerful producers of consumer goods and the voiceless masses of our population who, subjected to subliminal advertising, monopoly practices, and suffering from ignorance, have been at the former's mercy. In a few instances, the Monopolies Commission have acted to protect consumers, but their power to intervene is based upon law.

Customers may well have little influence in markets increasingly dominated by large business organizations, and it is difficult at this stage to see how, even if more information were made available, the balance might be redressed. Certainly, one may suggest that customers are interested in information indicating the fairness of pricing policies, such as the relative proportion of unit price which consists of costs, profits and taxes, as well as the differential costs between one product and another product produced by the same firm at a different price. For example, why should one electric shaver cost £10 more than another, and in what ways is this difference value for money? Clearly, there will be many more social changes in our society before questions of this sort will be loudly heard and answers demanded.

Accounting information and the allocation of resources

The various groups of information users which we have just discussed share a common concern, which is to make decisions about the allocation of scarce resources between competing ends. Students of economics will find such a statement echoes a popular definition of the subject matter of economics. The importance of accounting information is that it makes such an allocation possible in a market economy, where individuals and organizations are largely free to allocate the resources which they control between competing ends. Therefore, the theoretical objective of an accounting information system is to permit information users to make optimal decisions, that is, to make the best allocation of the resources which they control. As we have seen, optimal decision making may only be understood in relation to the objectives of decision makers, so that the various groups of information users whose information needs we have just discussed may be said to have quite different and occasionally competing decision objectives. Optimal decision making also means that the results of decisions should have a certain quality: optimal means that they should be the best possible results which could have been achieved under given circumstances, and implies a standard against which actual results may be compared.

We are stating, therefore, that the objective of accounting information systems is to enable decision makers to attempt to optimize the allocation of the resources which they control, and to assess the actual results of their decisions against the forecast results. A measure of the efficiency of the decision-making process is the extent to which the actual result compares to the optimal result. In this connection, the terms 'efficiency' and 'effectiveness' are used in the literature in a special sense. The term 'efficiency' is usually reserved for the analysis of input-output relationships, so that the 'efficiency' of a factory production process may refer to the degree of technical skill with which inputs of production factors are transformed into finished goods, as well as to the success with which input factors' values in monetary terms are transformed into outputs also valued in monetary terms. By contrast the term 'effectiveness' is reserved for the analysis of the success with which policy objectives are attained. Thus, we may talk of 'organizational effectiveness' in discussing how well management decisions lead to the attainment of organizational objectives.

Consequently, we may say that the 'effectiveness' of an accounting information system is the extent to which it enables its users to make optimal decisions. By examining the different objectives which we assume they have, we are able to judge the 'effectiveness' of accounting information by reference to the relevance of that information to the types of decisions which they wish to make. Management makes decisions about the allocation of men, materials, machines and money in such a way that the firm's objectives may be reached. As we shall see in Part 5, firms have different objectives, and income is one of these objectives. Often, it is thought that the size of the firm's income reflects the 'efficiency' of management in transforming inputs of factors of production into sales of finished goods. It is evident, however, that in our analysis income figures, though important, should not be confused with 'managerial effectiveness'.

Behavioural aspects of decision making

As we saw in Chapter 1, the central purpose of accounting is to produce information which will influence behaviour. Unless accounting reports have the potential to influence decisions and actions, it is difficult to justify the cost of preparing such reports. Traditionally, accounting reports have been addressed to shareholders and investors. In Part 4, the behavioural aspects of investor decision making will be discussed and the role of accounting information in that context will be examined. In particular, the response of the Stock Exchange to the disclosure of accounting information by the reaction of share prices will be seen to be one way in which the influence of accounting reports on investors may be judged. In Part 5, the behavioural aspects of decision making within organizations will be examined and the role of management accounting information as an influence in this respect will be discussed.

Since, from a management point of view, the purpose of accounting information is to enable the organization to attain its goals, it must follow that the effectiveness of accounting information is evidenced in the manner in which it affects behaviour. In this sense, we may say that unless accounting information serves to produce the desired action, it has served no purpose at all. Research has shown, for example, that even when managers have all the information which they need, they do not always make the right decisions. Hence, the human process which leads managers to recognize or fail to recognize the significance of accounting information deserves a better understanding, and accountants need to be aware of the role of accounting information in enabling managers to identify their mistakes and to learn from them. Feedback information, for example, plays an important part in this process.

A systems approach to the study of accounting

The study of the firm as an organization consisting of several systems, for example, an operating system, a financial system, a personnel system and a marketing system, enables one to see the accounting system as one element of an interacting whole. This manner of seeing the nature of the various elements of an organization is known as the systems approach.

The accounting system is the most important element of an organization's information system, for the following reasons:

(1) The accounting information system is the only one which enables management and external information users to get a picture of the whole organization.

(2) The accounting information system links other important information systems such as marketing information, personnel, research and development and production information, in that the information which is produced by these other systems may ultimately be expressed in financial terms in planning strategy to attain organizational goals.

Moreover the systems approach to the study of accounting permits the integration of accounting into a coherent framework in which its role is concerned with the provision of information for decision making.

This kind of approach allows accounting information to be viewed as ultimately affecting all members of society having connections with business organizations, in terms of the welfare theory of accounting which was mentioned in Chapter 1. Furthermore, the systems approach requires that account be taken of all the sources of information available to an individual. For example, as we shall see in Part 4, investors receive information from sources other than financial reports. The Stock Exchange is often able to anticipate the information contained in such reports. Therefore, in considering the changes which ought to be made to the kind of accounting information disclosed to investors, the systems approach requires the informational content of the other sources of information available to investors to be considered.

The systems approach also enables us to integrate modern technological developments into the study of accounting. With the development of the computer, for example, rapid advances have been made in electronic data processing. These advances have affected accounting in a number of ways. Firstly, information systems have been formalized, so that information may be fed directly from the computer to decision makers without the intervention of accountants. Secondly, computers have made possible the merger of accounting and non-accounting information, leading to the centralization of information services and reductions in duplication and hence information costs. Thirdly, there has been an increase in the accuracy of the information provided, resulting directly from the reduction of duplication.

Finally, the systems approach widens the possible applications of information. Thus, one of the developments which has influenced management decision making in recent years is operational research, which is concerned with the study of the behaviour of the various parts or sub-systems of an organization in such a way that all its activities may be analysed as a whole. Operational research uses mathematical techniques for solving business problems, and its growing importance is reflected in the increasing use of management decision models which attempt to predict and compare the predicted outcome of alternative strategies. Traditionally, mathematicians have specialized in the expression and the solution of complex logical problems, and although the techniques which they had evolved had a potential use for decision making in organizations, they were not employed in business situations because of the time-lag which existed in the processing of data. The advent of the computer has closed the technological gap, and has greatly contributed to the increased importance of quantitative methods in management. The information required for operational research studies is often not the type which is handled by traditional accounting systems. The systems approach, therefore, not only coincides with the manner of studying organizations by operational research scientists, but by encouraging the integration of accounting and non-accounting information into integrated information systems, it increases the range of applications of the information produced by such systems.

Summary

We began this chapter with an examination of accounting as an information system consisting of three activities—input, processing and output. The systems characteristic of accounting suggests that the systems approach is the ideal way of studying the subject. It is not sufficient, however, to view accounting purely as an operating system, for its relevance and usefulness may only be judged by the degree with which its output meets the needs of the users of accounting information. By identifying the basic goal of an accounting information system as being the provision of information for decision making, we provide a framework by which to judge the effectiveness of that system.

There are many approaches to the study of decision making—economic, behavioural and quantitative, and the inter-disciplinary nature of decision theory has the inevitable consequence that accounting has also become an inter-disciplinary subject. The systems approach facilitates an inter-disciplinary study of accounting because it requires that it be viewed, not in isolation, but as one element in a broad informational context.

Questions

1. Discuss the nature of accounting as an information system.
2. State the groups of persons having vested interests in a business organization and examine the nature of their information needs.
3. Evaluate the role of accounting information in the allocation of resources.
4. Explain what is meant by the 'systems approach', and examine the reasons for the application of this approach to the study of accounting.

3 The role of accounting theory

Underlying the discussion of accounting as an information system is the important question of the field of knowledge to which accounting information refers. This question raises issues about the nature and significance of accounting theory, the different approaches to developing accounting theory and the relationship between accounting theory and accounting practice.

The purpose of this chapter is to consider these various problems with a view to establishing the role of accounting theory.

The nature of theories

Essentially, theories are generalizations which serve to organize otherwise meaningless masses of data, and which thereby establish significant relationships in respect of such data. The construction of theories requires a process of reasoning about the problems implied in the data under observation, as a means of sorting out the most basic relationships. Thus, theory construction is also a process of simplification, which requires assumptions which permit the representation of reality by a generalization which is easily understood. The close association of theory and data, or facts, is fundamental to the notion of good theory, for the reliability of a theory is dependent not only upon the facts to which it refers, but also upon an interpretation of those facts requiring validation and continuous re-assessment.

Theories are concerned with explanation. Explanation consists of relating a set of observations to a theoretical construction of reality which fit those observations. If no theoretical scheme is available that seems to do this reasonably well, the desire for explanation leads to the creation of a scheme of ideas which provides a definition of the problem observed as well as an understanding of it in the form of explanation. In both cases, relating observations to existing theory, and constructing theory to fit observations have the objective of providing explanation of those observations.

A misunderstanding of the relationship which exists between facts and theories gives rise to a great deal of misconception about the role of theories. Thus, the complaint that 'it's all right in theory but not in practice' implies that the person making the complaint must hold the belief that an alternative theory provides a different explanation of the facts in question.

The word 'theory' itself gives rise to misunderstanding, and may mean different things to different people. This arises because explanations are made at different levels. At one extreme, explanations are purely speculative, resulting in speculative theories, for example that 'outer space probes are affecting the weather'. To the natural scientist, speculative theories are not really theories at all. In his view, explanations have to be conclusive before they are given the status of theories. To this end, their assumptions require verification by the test of experience. Therefore, at another extreme are to be found explanations which are accepted only when they have been verified. Empirical theories are constructed by the process of verifying assumptions, or hypotheses, through the test of experience. This process is known as the 'scientific method', and is illustrated in Fig. 1.3.

World of facts
↓
Recognition of a problem
↓
Collection and organization of data
↓
Formulation of propositions and definitions
↓
Development of hypotheses
↓
Testing hypotheses
↓
Theory verification, modification or rejection
↓
Theory acceptance

Fig. 1.3.

Empirical theories assist in making 'predictions', for while they consist of generalizations which explain the present, future occurrences also replicate the same conditions. It is in providing both explanations and predictions that empirical theories have acquired such an importance for making decisions about the future which are based on assumptions derived from experience.

Accounting theory

The word 'theory' is also used at different levels in the literature of accounting. Thus, references to 'accounting theory' may mean purely speculative interpretations or empirical explanations. These references usually do not indicate the level of theory which is implied.

According to Hendriksen,

'Accounting theory may be defined as logical reasoning in the form of a set of broad principles that (1) provide a general frame of reference by which accounting practice can be evaluated, and (2) guide the development of new practices and procedures. Accounting theory may also be used to explain existing practices to obtain a better understanding of them. But the most important goal of accounting theory should be to provide a coherent set of logical principles that form the general frame of reference for the evaluation and development of sound accounting practices.' (Hendriksen, 1977.)

The relationship between accounting theory and accounting practice is indicated in Fig. 1.4. The influence of policy makers in relating accounting theory and accounting practice is also illustrated in Fig. 1.4.

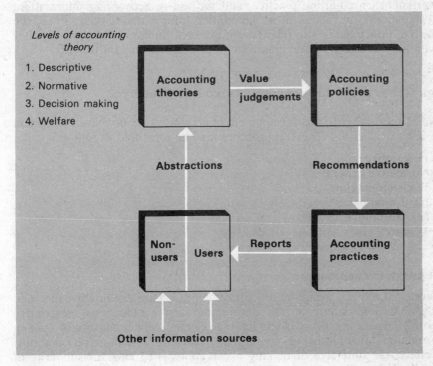

Fig. 1.4.

Figure 1.4 shows that the role played by theory in accounting is very different from that played in the natural sciences, where theories are developed from empirical observations. In effect, the reverse is the case in accounting, since practice may be changed to accommodate theory. According to Ijiri,

'Contrary to the fields of linguistics, meteorology or chemistry, accountants can change their practices relatively easily. Therefore, it becomes an essential problem for accountants to know how accounting practices should be developed in the future. The sanctions by which accounting policies have become implemented are quite essential in understanding the field of accounting, since it is possible to change practices to fit theories!! This is unthinkable for scientists in other fields for whom phenomena are almighty. No matter how beautiful and elegant the theory may be, if it does not fit the empirical phenomena, it is replaced by one which fits better.' (Ijiri, 1971.)

Figure 1.4 also illustrates how the form of accounting information reported to decision makers depends on the practices adopted. These practices are imposed by accounting policy makers who, having knowledge of accounting theories, have the responsibility of responding to the needs of users of accounting information.

It is evident that deficiencies in the four significant areas denoted in Fig. 1.4, namely, accounting theory, policy making (by the profession and the government), accounting practice, and the use of accounting information, will impair the usefulness of an accounting information service. Thus, the failure of policy makers to incorporate research findings in the policies they devise may reduce the potential usefulness of accounting information.

Approaches to the development of accounting theory

Several approaches to the development of accounting theory have emerged in the last two decades. These approaches may be identified as follows:

1 Descriptive
2 Normative general
3 Decision-making
   (i) Empirical
   (ii) Normative specific
4 Welfare

The descriptive approach

Theories developed using the descriptive approach are essentially concerned with what accountants do. In developing such explanations, descriptive theories rely on a process of inductive reasoning, which consists of making observations and of drawing generalized conclusions from those observations. In effect, the objective of making observations is to look for similarity of instances, and to identify a sufficient number of such instances as will induce the required degree of assurance needed to develop a theory about all the instances which belong to the same class of phenomena.

As applied to the construction of accounting theory, the descriptive approach has emphasized the *practice* of accounting as a basis from which to develop theories. This approach has attempted to relate the practices of accountants to a generalized theory about accounting. In this view, accounting theory is to be discovered by observing the practices of accountants because 'accounting theory is primarily a concentrate distilled from experience . . . it is experience intelligently analysed that produces logical explanation . . . and . . . illuminates the practices from which it springs'. (Littleton and Zimmerman, 1962.)

The descriptive approach results in descriptive or positive theories of accounting, which explain what accountants do and enable predictions to be made about behaviour, for example, how a particular matter will be treated. Thus, it is possible to predict that the receipt of cash will be entered in the debit side of the cash book.

In effect, the descriptive approach is concerned with observing the mechanical tasks which accountants have traditionally performed. In 1952, the Institute of Chartered Accountants in England and Wales stated that 'the primary purpose of the annual accounts of a business is to present information to proprietors showing how their funds have been utilized, and the profits derived from such use'. (I.C.A.E.W., 1952.)

Underlying the descriptive approach is the belief that the objective of financial statements is associated with the stewardship concept of the management role, and the necessity of providing the owners of businesses with information relating to the manner in which their assets have been managed. In this view, company directors occupy a position of responsibility and trust in regard to shareholders, and the discharge of these obligations requires the publication of annual financial reports to shareholders. With the growth of very large corporate enterprises, the weakening of the links between ownership and management created a need for a more elementary notion of stewardship, in which the disclosure of financial information was aimed at protecting shareholders from fraudulent management practices. Sterling provides a perceptive comment on the significance of the descriptive approach in the following terms:

> 'Probably the most ancient and pervasive method of accounting theory construction is to observe accountants' actions and rationalize these actions by subsuming them under generalized principles. For example, if the accounting anthropologist has observed that accounting man normally records a conservative figure and general-izes this as the principle of conservatism, then we can test this principle by observing whether or not accounting man does in fact record a conservative figure.' (Sterling, 1970.)

As we shall see in Part 2 and Part 4 when discussing the work of the Accounting Standards Committee in relation to the development of account-ing standards, it is evident that the descriptive approach to theory construc-tion in accounting plays a very influential role in shaping perceptions of the problems of accounting and the manner in which they should be solved. In effect, the Accounting Standards Committee has been concerned with discussing the variety of practices used by accountants and with reaching a consensus on the most feasible basis on which to reduce the diversity of these practices through the process of standardization.

Figure 1.5 overleaf illustrates the framework within which descriptive accounting theory has developed.

Basic concepts
The establishment of concepts is very important to the development of a theoretical framework. Accounting concepts have been given terms which are used to describe the events that comprise the existence of business of every kind. It is for this reason that accounting is often characterized as 'the language of business'. The basic concepts which are listed in Fig. 1.5 provide the essential material of accounting theory.

Assets are things of value which are possessed by a business. In order to be classified as an asset the money measurement convention demands that a thing must have the quality of being measurable in terms of money. The assets of a business comprise not only cash and such property as land, buildings, machinery and merchandise, but also money which is owed by individuals or other enterprises (who are called debtors) to the business.

Liabilities are the debts of the business. Most firms find it convenient to

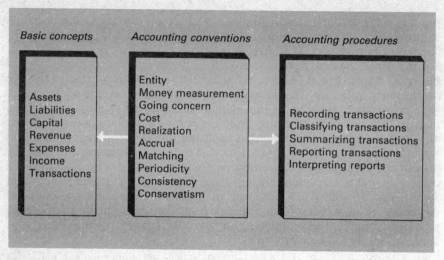

Basic concepts	Accounting conventions	Accounting procedures
Assets Liabilities Capital Revenue Expenses Income Transactions	Entity Money measurement Going concern Cost Realization Accrual Matching Periodicity Consistency Conservatism	Recording transactions Classifying transactions Summarizing transactions Reporting transactions Interpreting reports

Fig. 1.5.

purchase merchandise and other items on credit rather than pay cash at the time of purchase. This gives rise to liabilities in the form of trade creditors. Creditors originate also when a firm borrows money as a means of supplementing the funds invested by the owner. The reason why amounts of money owed to the creditors by a business are known as liabilities is that the business is liable to the creditors for the sums owed.

Capital is the excess of assets over liabilities and represents the owner's claim against the business. If we know the total assets and the total liabilities we can find the capital by subtraction. As we will illustrate in Part 2, the assets of a business must always be equal to the liabilities and the owner's capital. This is the result of double-entry book-keeping, whereby each transaction has a two-fold effect in its accounting treatment.

Revenue is earned by a business when it provides goods and services to customers. Whereas a trading business will derive revenue mainly from the sale of merchandise, a business that renders services, such as a garage, will derive revenue as a result of charging for the service. It is not necessary for a business to receive cash before recognizing that revenue has been earned. As we discuss in Chapter 4 the accrual convention recognizes revenue which arises from the sale of goods or services on credit.

Expenses are incurred in earning revenue. Examples of expenses are the salaries paid to employees and the rent paid to the landlord. When expenses are not paid for at the time they are incurred but are to be paid for at some future time the amount of such expenses is recorded as a liability.

Income results when the total of the revenue of a business for a certain period of time, such as a year, exceeds the total of the expenses for that period. As we will see in Part 2, income accrues to the owner of the business and increases his claim against the business. The increase is reflected in the capital of the business.

Transactions are events which require recognition in the accounting records. They originate when changes in basic concepts are recorded. A transaction is financial in nature and is expressed in terms of money.

Accounting conventions

Accounting conventions determine the rules which are applied to accounting procedures. Accounting conventions are constantly being adapted to meet the changing demands of business, and at any point in time there may be more than one accepted way of treating a particular class of transaction. A thorough knowledge of these conventions is necessary for a complete understanding of the data contained in financial statements. Accounting conventions are discussed in Chapter 4.

Accounting procedures

Recording is the mechanical process by which financial transactions are systematically placed in accounting records. Recording may be made in the form of pen markings by hand, or it may be accomplished by various mechanical or electronic devices. Transactions are analysed so that they can be *classified* according to a predetermined system of accounting. Periodically, this recorded and classified information is summarized by the preparation of financial statements and reports to the managers of an enterprise and to other interested parties. *Interpreting* basically refers to that utilization of the recorded, classified and summarized data which reveals and emphasizes significant changes, trends and potential developments in the affairs of an enterprise.

Financial statements

Conventional accounting procedures are associated with the periodic production of financial statements. Two such statements are the balance sheet, and the income statement. Their contents are illustrated below. Funds flow and cash flow statements are additional financial statements, which explain the flow of financial resources to and from the enterprise. They are dealt with in Chapter 12.

(i) *The balance sheet*, sometimes called the Statement of Financial Position lists the assets and liabilities of the business at the close of the accounting period. At the same time, it provides a measure of the capital invested by the owner(s) in the business. Figure 1.6 (overleaf) is an illustration of a balance sheet drawn up at the close of business on 31 December 19X1 for Ivor Camera who operates as a photographer.

It will be seen that the balance sheet has four main sections—fixed assets, current assets, capital and other liabilities. This classification assists the financial analysis of the business. Fixed assets are deemed to be available for use in the business, and are not intended for resale. They include assets having a long life in use, such as buildings, plant, machinery and vehicles, which are deemed to be available for use in the business, but are not intended to generate profits by their resale. Current assets represent those assets which are transformed during the operating cycle into cash, inventories such as materials, supplies, work-in-process and finished goods, as well as debtors.

Ivor Camera
Balance Sheet as at 31 December 19X1

Owner's capital	£	£	Fixed assets	£	£
Capital 1 Jan.	20,000		Buildings	16,000	
Income for 19X1	10,000		Equipment	7,000	
	30,000				23,000
Drawings	5,000				
		25,000			
Current liabilities			Current assets		
Trade creditors		4,000	Inventory	1,000	
			Trade debtors	4,500	
			Cash	500	
					6,000
		29,000			29,000

Fig. 1.6

Cash balances are always shown as current assets, as such balances are regarded as available for immediate use by the business.

(ii) *The income statement* is used to show the calculation of the profit of the business for the accounting period. Figure 1.7 illustrates the manner in which this calculation is made by the deduction of expenses from the revenues of the period.

Ivor Camera
Income Statement for the period ending 31 December 19X1

	£	£
Revenues		
Fees earned		18,500
Expenses		
Rent	3,000	
Advertising	1,000	
Heating and lighting	500	
Supplies used	2,000	
Travelling	2,000	
		8,500
Net income for the period		10,000

Fig. 1.7

It will be seen that the net income for the period is added to the owner's capital in Fig. 1.6. Until such time as the owner draws upon that income, it remains in the business and is described as 'retained income'. In effect, the net income which is retained adds to the invested capital, and the drawings reduce invested capital.

The normative general approach

The 1950s and 1960s began to witness a much greater concern on the part of academic accountants with the problems of accounting theory. In particular, the search for a 'general theory of accounting' based on a coherent set of logical principles, was an attempt to provide accounting with similar foundations as other sciences, such as mathematics, physics and chemistry. Protagonists of the 'general theory school' argued that

'Accountants do not appear to have any complete system of thought about accounting. There are unquestionably several systems of thought about the practice of accounting: systems which attempt to categorize the kinds of things accountants do in practice. These systems are almost all the subject can boast of in the way of a theory, and for this reason accounting lacks the sharpness, the progressiveness and the vitality of other technology.' (Chambers, 1955.)

The initial stages in the debate on the needs for a coherent theory of accounting was marked by the publication in 1955 of Chambers' 'Blueprint for a Theory of Accounting'. This argued that accounting theory and accounting research should be less concerned with describing current practice, and should be more concerned with the development of better accounting practice. It included an 'exposure list' in the form of four major propositions as building blocks for a theory of accounting. Its particular importance lay in the emphasis which it attached to the construction of a normative general theory of accounting.

The normative approach to theory construction is concerned with establishing 'what should be', and in this context is less influenced by observations of 'what is'. It asserts that it is feasible and desirable to develop theories of accounting which are independent of current practice. The normative approach reflected a degree of disillusionment with the problem of relating accounting practice to economic and social realities. It was concerned with the possibility of developing normative theories which might serve the purpose of imposing theoretical standards on the quality of information and theoretical standards of relevance on the information output of conventional accounting systems. In particular, it reflected a concern with the lack of comparability between financial statements arising from the use of a variety of alternative accounting rules.

Chambers' 'Blueprint for a Theory of Accounting' stated in clear terms the nature and purpose of theory and practice: that

'It is necessary to distinguish between systems of rules relating to the practice of accounting and a theory of accounting. A system of rules is necessary for the consistent practice of any art, and it is useful to attempt to sort out the rules which appear to be followed. Only if the rules are adequately described is it possible to discover inconsistencies in the system. But adequate description does not assist in determining which of two inconsistent rules should be adopted and which should be abandoned. The question must be referred to a more fundamental proposition or set of propositions, to the theory of the subject.' (Chambers, 1955.)

Normative theories are concerned essentially with stating specific objectives which are regarded as imperatives, for example, 'that a theory of business income *should be* addressed to the problem of determining the amount which may be distributed to shareholders during the accounting period whilst ensuring that the capital of the business is not thereby diminished'. Such a statement of objective typifies the sort of hypothesis on which normative theories are based.

Normative theories rely heavily on the process of *deductive* reasoning, which begins with a basic set of propositions about the subject under study, as seen in the example of 'business income' mentioned above. Deductive reasoning is the converse of inductive reasoning which, as we saw in the previous section, is the basis of reasoning used in constructing descriptive or positive theories. Deductive reasoning moves from the making of general statements to the making of particular statements. The construction of a theory based on deductive reasoning is illustrated in Fig. 1.8.

Objectives
↓
Basic assumptions (propositions and postulates)
↓
Deduce principles
↓
Deduce rules and procedures
↓
Produce results (financial reports)

Fig. 1.8.

A major criticism of this approach is that if the assumptions are stated broadly enough to secure general agreement, they may be dismissed as self-evident. Alternatively, if they are stated specifically, they may fail to gain general agreement. A good example of this dilemma was the reception given to two documents issued by the Accounting Principles Board in the U.S.A., namely, 'The Basic Postulates of Accounting' (1961) and 'A Tentative Set of Broad Accounting Principles for Business Enterprises' (1962). The hope was that these two studies would provide the foundation for subsequent studies and for the issue of further statements by the Accounting Principles Board. Postulate A-2 mentioned in the first document stated that 'most of the goods and services that are produced are distributed through exchange, and are not directly consumed by producers'. Clearly, no one would dispute that assertion. On the other hand, the principle mentioned in the second document that 'profit is attributable to the whole process of business activity' and the suggestion that concepts of value should be brought into accounting was viewed by some commentators as an 'accounting revolution'. The Accounting Principles Board summarized the situation as follows: 'The Board believes, however, that while these studies are a valuable contribution to accounting thinking, they are too radically different from present generally accepted accounting principles for acceptance at this time.' (A.I.C.P.A., 1962.)

Decision-making approaches

The expansion of behavioural research into accounting during the 1970s resulted in an interest in decision making theories of accounting. This mood was well captured in the following statement by the American Accounting Association in 1971:

'To state the matter concisely, the principal purpose of accounting reports is to influence action, that is, behaviour. Additionally, it can be hypothesized that the very process of accumulating information, as well as the behaviour of those who do the accounting, will affect the behaviour of others. In short, by its very nature, accounting is a behavioural process.' (A.A.A., 1971.)

Two types of decision-making theories of accounting have resulted from this approach, namely, empirical theories and normative specific theories.

Empirical approaches
The early 1970s witnessed a substantial increase in empirical research. One reason for this development was dissatisfaction with the normative approach, which had failed to produce the desired single and all-encompassing framework for treating the problems of accounting theory.

Indeed, none of the efforts invested in the 1960s in developing a normative theory of accounting gained sufficient acceptance. Many of the studies conducted produced untested conclusions, and often contained untested value judgements about accounting. According to Caplan,

'They have neglected a fundamental aspect of scientific reasoning—they provide no evidence to support their logic except the opinions of authors. Although these theory formulations often contain valuable insights about accounting, in the final analysis they represent only 'armchair' theorizing, which the reader can accept or reject depending on his own perceptions. They simply do not stand by themselves as convincing and compelling works or research. The essential difficulty is, of course, one of methodology.' (Caplan, 1972.)

As a reaction to the period associated with studies in normative accounting theories, the empirical approach sought to make accounting research more rigorous and to improve the reliability of results. Sophisticated statistical techniques became increasingly used for this purpose. Furthermore, the expansion of university courses in accounting increased the number of students with a quantitative background, who could conduct research in this way. The university departments of accounting, desiring to enhance their status within the universities, viewed the possibility of empirical research based on the 'scientific method' as a useful springboard to this end. The implications of the empirical approach to research in accounting were significant for the development of accounting theory. These implications are discussed further in Part 4.

The normative specific approach
Unlike empirical research, which concentrates on how users of accounting

information apply this information in decision making, the normative specific approach to theory construction is concerned with specifying the manner in which decisions ought to be made as a pre-condition to considering the information requirement.

The normative specific approach focuses on the decision models which should be used by decision makers seeking to make rational decisions. This focus is seen as providing insights on the information needs of decision makers, as a basis for developing accounting theory.

The normative specific approach is used in this text as a basis for examining the information needs of investors and employees. This problem is discussed in Part 4.

The welfare approach

The welfare approach is an extension of the decision-making approaches, which considers the effects of decision making on social welfare. Basically, decision-making approaches limit the field of interest to the private use of accounting information. If accounting information had a relevance limited to private interests, the decision-making approaches would provide a sufficient analysis of information needs. It is because of the external social effects of decisions made on the basis of accounting information that there is imputed a social welfare dimension to accounting theory.

The theoretical objective of the welfare approach is the maximization of social welfare, which is defined as the benefits accruing to all members of society from decisions made by individuals about the use of resources under their control. In this respect, a disadvantage of the classical individual decision-making approach which hitherto has been reflected in the debate about accounting policies is that it does not provide a basis for developing accounting policies which would maximize social welfare. In this respect, the Trueblood Report took the view that the appropriate policy for accounting was the provision of information for making economic decisions (A.I.C.P.A., Study Group on Financial Objectives, 1973). Implicit in this view is that accounting should provide information for decision making by individuals, without any consideration of social welfare effects. As May and Sundem pointed out, such a delineation of *what* accounting policy makers should be concerned with precludes the possibility of making comparison among alternative policies having different social welfare effects (May and Sundem, 1976).

The welfare effects which are associated with the use of financial statements may be discussed from various standpoints.

(1) The effects of financial information on the welfare of individual decision makers may be deemed to be one important standpoint. Since investment decisions imply the comparison of alternative investments, external users of financial information require as much consistency and comparability as is practicable between the financial statements of enterprises generally. We shall discuss this point further in Part 4, but it may be mentioned at this stage that it was the lack of comparability between the financial statements of enterprises which lay at the root of much criticism of

the accounting profession in the 1960s, and led to the setting up in the United Kingdom of the Accounting Standards Committee in 1970. The Press took the view that the accounting profession had a duty to increase the quality of reported financial information to give better protection to shareholders and other interested users of company financial reports.

(2) The effects of financial information on social welfare may also be seen from the standpoint of the distortion arising from the possession of superior knowledge by one segment of a particular group of users, which would have consequential changes in the distribution of wealth within the group. For example, if an investor has access to inside information about an enterprise, and this information is not freely available to other investors, he would be able to make decisions which may improve his welfare at the expense of other investors.

(3) The effects of financial information may also be viewed from the standpoint of the allocation of resources in the economy. The importance of accounting information as regards the allocation of scarce resources was discussed earlier in Chapter 2. Financial statements provide the investors with data which assist in establishing the market price of company shares. As we shall see in Part 4, there is research evidence to show that accounting data have an important effect on share prices. Ideally, financial reports should contain data which make it possible for investors to evaluate investment opportunities, if the allocation of resources throughout the economy is to maximize social welfare in accordance with classical economic theory.

(4) The approaches to accounting theory which have been mentioned so far assume that information is a free commodity, and therefore that no costs are incurred in producing information. Clearly, from a social welfare view-point, costs are significant in considering the level of information to be made available, given that resources are scarce and could be employed in other activities. The costs of collecting and processing data and distributing information should be taken into account in considering the level of information provided to users. The difficulty which stands in the way of developing this analysis further lies in the problem of defining and measuring the benefits associated with the use of information, for the optimum level of information output ought also to be seen from the perspective of the payoffs associated with costs. As we shall see below, some attempts have been made to define the payoffs which may be associated with information costs.

(5) The effects of financial information on welfare may be viewed from the standpoint of the vested interests of groups within an organization. The needs of these groups were discussed in Chapter 2. It is evident that the alteration of accounting policies in favour of one group and away from another group will affect the distribution of income and wealth within society. In this respect, the movement towards disclosing information to employees and the concept of social responsibility accounting, which are discussed in Chapters 24 and 25 respectively, are clearly causing such a change.

Staubus lists potential positive and negative payoffs to various groups which result from producing one particular type of information under general headings, as follows:

(A) Potential positive payoffs from an accounting method

1 Direct payoffs to parties associated with the entity, namely, present and prospective owners, creditors, suppliers, customers, employees and government taxing and regulatory bodies, through
   (a) improvements in their own decisions, using information supplied by the entity and produced with the accounting method or information system in question, and
   (b) higher direct compensation from the entity due to its more effective management and greater profitability with the aid of the information in question.
2 Payoffs to competitors through more useful information about the reporting entity's activities.
3 Diffused benefits through the better functioning of the economy, such as through the allocation of resources, reduction in variations in the level of economic activity, and the effects of the division of income as between investment and consumption.

(B) Potential negative payoffs from an accounting method

1 Reduction in the profitability of competitors, and in distributions to their constitutents, through better decisions by the reporting entity.
2 Reduction in the profitability of the reporting entity through better decisions by its competitors and by its creditors, suppliers, customers and employees who bargain with the entity.
3 Reduction in the profitability of the entity due to the effects upon management decisions of reporting to shareholders and others by means of the accounting method under evaluation.
4 The costs of producing information, such as accounting and auditing costs.
5 The costs of analysing and using accounting information.
   (Staubus, 1977.)

Clearly, a major difficulty in developing welfare theories of accounting lies in the complexities involved in any attempt to maximize welfare. Since there are multiple users of financial statements, the costs and the benefits to each user of a particular accounting measure would be impossible to calculate. Arrow's Impossibility Theorem demonstrates the impossibility facing society of making rules on a collective basis which also satisfy the needs of particular individuals (Arrow, 1963).

Nevertheless, these difficulties should not detract from the significance of the welfare approach to developing accounting theories. Whilst it would be unreasonable to demand those responsible for making accounting policies to construct a system of financial reporting which maximizes social welfare, it should be apparent to them that welfare considerations should be of prime importance in policy making.

Accounting policy makers

There are two main groups which determine accounting policy. First, the Government employs the legislative process to ensure that a minimum level of information is disclosed in company reports. It also acts as a spur to prompt the accountancy profession into action, where there is an apparent urgent need. An example of this influence was the establishment of the Sandilands Committee by the Government to consider the problem of accounting under conditions of price-level changes. This problem will be discussed in Chapter 20. Another example was the Employment Protection Act, 1975, which places a general duty on the employer to disclose information requested by trade union representatives at all stages of collective bargaining. This problem is discussed in Chapter 24.

Second, the accountancy profession itself acts as a regulatory body and deals with the problems of accounting standards implied in financial reports. The influence of the accountancy profession in making accounting policy is discussed in Chapter 4.

Summary

This chapter has been concerned with an examination of the role of accounting theory in developing knowledge through the construction of theories. The importance of such theory construction for the improvement of accounting practice has also been discussed. The nature of theory was examined in detail in order to establish precisely the significance of theory to knowledge in general, and to accounting in particular. The several approaches to the development of accounting theory were reviewed. Attention was drawn to the successive stages beginning with descriptive theories, and proceeding to normative and to decision-making theories of accounting. The chapter concluded with an introduction to a movement towards welfare-oriented theories of accounting, and a discussion of the role of those responsible for making accounting policies in using the insights produced by research and incorporated in theories of accounting.

References

1. A.A.A. 'Report of the Committee on the Behavioural Science Content of the Accounting Curriculum', *Accounting Review Supplement*, Vol. 46, 1971.
2. A.I.C.P.A. *Statement by the Accounting Principles Board*, 1962.
3. Arrow, K. J. *Social Choice and Individual Values*, 2nd ed., John Wiley & Sons, 1963.
4. Caplan, E. H. 'Accounting research as an information source for theory construction', *in* Sterling, R. R. *Research Methodology in Accounting*, p. 47, Scholars Book Co., 1972.
5. Chambers, R. J. 'Blueprint for a theory of accounting', *Accounting Research*, January, 1955.
6. Hendriksen, E. S. *Accounting Theory*, 3rd ed., Richard D. Irwin, 1977.

7. Ijiri, Y. 'Logic and sanctions in accounting', *in* Sterling, R. R. & Bentz, W. F. (eds), *Accounting in Perspective*, South Western Publishing Co., 1971.
8. I.C.A.E.W. *Accounting in Relation to Changes in the Purchasing Power of Money*, Recommendation No. 15, (May 1962), paragraph 1.
9. Littleton, A. C. & Zimmerman, V. K. *Accounting Theory: Continuity and Change*, Prentice-Hall, 1962,
10. May, R. J. & Sundem, G. L. 'Research for accounting policy: an overview', *Accounting Review*, October, 1976.
11. Staubus, G. J. *Making Accounting Decisions*, pp. 36–7, Scholars Book Co., 1977.
12. Sterling, R. R. 'Theory construction and verification', *Accounting Review*, July, 1970.

Questions

1. Examine the nature of theories.
2. Analyse the relationship between accounting theory, accounting policy and accounting practice. To what extent does the quality of accounting policy and accounting practice depend on accounting theory?
3. Distinguish 'basic concepts', 'conventions' and 'accounting procedures.'
4. Define the following terms: assets, liabilities, capital, income and expenses.
5. What is a balance sheet? What is an income statement? How are these two statements related?
6. Contrast the descriptive and general normative approaches to theory construction.
7. Compare the specific normative and empirical approaches to theory construction, and discuss the reasons for the popularity of the empirical approach.
8. Explain how the welfare approach to accounting theory differs from other approaches.

Part 2 FINANCIAL ACCOUNTING—THE HISTORICAL COST APPROACH

Introduction

Insofar as business firms are concerned, a distinction is normally made between *financial accounting*, which is the activity of recording and analysing the financial results of transactions as a means of arriving at a measure of the firm's success and financial soundness, and *management accounting*, which is the activity of providing information to enable management to make efficient decisions as regards the use and allocation of the firm's resources. In this part, the traditional practices of financial accounting based on historical cost valuations are examined. The approach used is based on a descriptive analysis of the practices of accountants, and leads to a descriptive theory of financial accounting. Therefore, we shall be concerned with *what* accountants do and the conventions and standards by which their activities are regulated.

As we pointed out in Chapter 3, the financial reports produced on the basis of financial records kept may be analysed also in terms of the relevance of the information provided to users for the purposes of decision making. We suggested that such an analysis should be conducted in terms of a normative theory. In this part, we shall restrict ourselves to the discussion of descriptive theories of financial accounting which focuses on accounting practices only, and we shall address the problem of users' needs in Part 4, using normative theories for that purpose.

The purpose of this part is to examine the nature and the practices of financial accounting which is concerned with the following activities:

(a) recording financial transactions;
(b) summarizing and presenting financial information in reports.

Financial accounting information is used by a variety of interested parties. Managers require financial information so as to evaluate the financial results of past decisions, for the evaluation of past performance is an important part of management decision making. Shareholders and investors need financial information which will enable them to predict both their income from the firm and the value of their investment, and to judge the risks attached thereto. Hence, shareholders and investors require financial accounting information for the purpose of making decisions about their investment in the firm. Besides shareholders and investors, there are other external users of financial information, notably the Inland Revenue, which requires a firm to submit financial accounts for the purpose of assessing its tax liability, and trade unions and employees who have a vested interest in the financial performance of the company.

The nature and methods of financial accounting are determined to a considerable extent by the conventions which exist among accountants for identifying, evaluating and communicating financial information. This is particularly true of the information which is provided for external users such as shareholders and investors. It is evident that unless accountants obey the same rules as regards selecting, measuring and communicating information to external users, the latter will be placed at a great disadvantage in respect of the reliance which may be attached to the information they receive. The usefulness of accounting conventions lies in the uniformity and comparability of information which is made possible thereby. Accounting conventions do secure for external users a much greater degree of comparability in the information emanating from the same firm over a period of years. Accountants do not attempt, however, to meet the specific information needs of external users, and the information which they do provide is dictated by the conventions which they have followed for a very long time, rather than the information needs of external users.

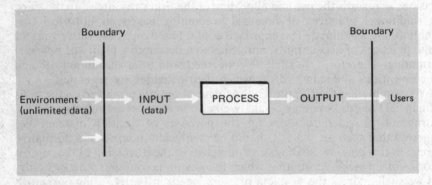

Fig. 2.1

The users of external reports have no control, therefore, over their content. We may contrast Fig. 2.1, which illustrates the boundaries of the financial accounting system for external users, against the user-oriented model shown on page 13 (Fig. 1.2). In this case, there is no control by the user over the final output. Hence, it may be suggested the information system for external decision makers is not user oriented. The output, and therefore also the input into this system is determined by conventions which are embodied in accounting tradition and in law. External users are provided with reports on a take-it-or-leave-it basis, although more useful information could be provided for them without imposing additional costs on the firm. However, in view of the broad objectives and definition of accounting as an information system, which we adopted in Part 1, we would expect to find inherent limitations in current external reporting practices. We shall discuss these limitations in Part 4.

A basic assumption underlying communication theory is that there is a clear separation between the transmitter and the receiver of information. This is acknowledged also in financial reporting as regards the distinction which is drawn between the function of the accountant as the transmitter of information and the external user as the receiver of information. The external user relies upon the accountant to provide him with a significant supply of information for making economic decisions. It is for each user to evaluate and interpret this information in the course of formulating decisions which only he may make. It is not the objective of either the accountant or of financial reports to make such evaluations and draw conclusions for the external user. Consequently, it is not the function of the accountant to value a firm for the external user: on the contrary, it is for the investor to establish the value of the firm as an investment and to bear the risk involved in acting on such a valuation. The function of the accountant in this analysis is to assist the external user in valuing the firm by the provision of such information as is necessary for that purpose.

In line with this reasoning, we consider in this part the problems associated with the production of financial accounting information. We examine how data is selected from the environment, and the manner in which it becomes an input into the financial accounting system. We discuss also the manner in which the output of the financial accounting system is formulated as financial reports. We shall examine in Part 4 the relevance of these reports to the decisions which shareholders and investors wish to make.

We have limited our analysis of financial accounting information to those aspects which we consider important and relevant to the textbook as a whole. We have divided this part into three sections. In Section 1, we examine financial accounting method to gain an understanding of its nature and of the principles underlying its procedures. In Section 2, we analyse the process of periodic measurement, which is one of its main applications. In Section 3, we select for closer analysis the application of financial accounting procedures to the production of financial statements for corporate enterprises.

One important application of financial accounting method relates to the use of accounting records for the day-to-day control of assets and liabilities. These technical aspects of control are treated as a 'background subject' in this text, so as not to detract from the important theoretical and practical aspects of the accountant's role in providing information for decision-making purposes.

Section 1 Financial Accounting Practice

4 Financial accounting conventions

The conventions of financial accounting are particularly significant to the development of accounting theory in two ways. First, they are themselves part of an empirical process for developing rules of financial accounting. In this sense, they may be regarded as belonging to the corpus of accounting theory. Second, they reflect the influence of the institutional forces which shape the philosophy of accounting in a given economic and social environment. Thus, the accounting profession in the United Kingdom and in the United States is a powerful influence in shaping the development of accounting within the context of the problems found in those countries.

The conventions of accounting discussed in this chapter may be seen as related to the general problem of developing viable theories of financial accounting. As we shall see, their origin lies in a historical process of development. The on-going nature of this process is discussed in Chapter 5, where the review of the conventions of financial accounting by the accounting profession is seen to focus on the formulation of standard accounting practices.

We mentioned in the Introduction to this part that the nature of financial accounting information is dictated not by the needs of external users, but rather was determined to a considerable extent by the conventions existing among accountants for identifying, evaluating and communicating financial information.

In this chapter, we analyse the nature and the effects of accounting conventions on the manner in which accountants generate financial information. The need for these conventions is discussed, as well as the problems which they pose. The chapter concludes with a discussion of the need for financial accounting standards to reduce the diversity of accounting practices which are permitted under existing conventions.

In effect, the conventions and standards discussed in this chapter reflect and explain the systems of thought which determine accounting practice, and which form the basic concepts of the descriptive theory of financial accounting to which this part is addressed.

The nature of financial accounting conventions

Textbooks refer variously to accounting principles, accounting postulates, accounting concepts, accounting imperatives and accounting assumptions to describe those basic points of agreement on which financial accounting theory and practice are founded. We prefer to use the term 'accounting conventions' to stress that the ground rules of financial accounting are not the subject of immutable law, but are based on consensus. Conventions define the assumptions on which the financial accounts of a business are prepared. Financial transactions are interpreted in the light of the conventions which govern accounting methods. In effect, the conventions of financial accounting largely determine the interpretations given in financial reports of the events and results which they portray. For example, the conventions relating to the recognition of revenue determine the dimension of the income which will be reported to shareholders and the value of the enterprise as judged from the balance sheet.

If accountants as a group wish to change some of their conventions, they are free to do so. Indeed, accounting bodies in Britain and in the United States are engaged in the review of their conventions and practices, and for this purpose, the Financial Accounting Standards Board was established in the United States in 1973 (replacing the Accounting Principles Board) and in the United Kingdom the Accounting Standards Committee was established in 1970 with similar objectives.

The term 'accounting conventions' serves in another sense to underline the freedom which accountants have enjoyed in determining their own rules. There is no tradition of State interference in the USA and UK, for example, as regards the practice of accounting. Such laws as are to be found are contained in statutes dealing with the activities of corporate bodies, such as the Companies Acts, which specify the nature of the accounting information that must be disclosed to shareholders, and the Income Tax and Corporation Tax Acts, which impose a duty on business firms to submit accounting information for the purpose of assessing the liability to tax. So far, neither Parliament nor the Courts have issued directives to the accounting profession as regards the conventions which they should observe. In France, by contrast, there is a different political tradition, and there is legislation dealing with accounting practices and they are detailed in the *Plan Comptable*, which is an edict issued by the French Government detailing the manner in which accounting statements should be prepared.

Figure 2.2 illustrates the manner in which financial accounting conventions act as filters in selecting data as input into the processing system and as output of information for users.

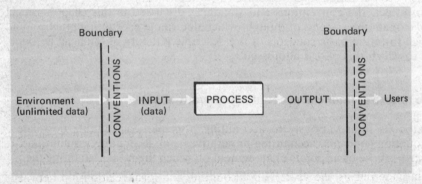

Fig. 2.2.

Types of financial accounting conventions

We may classify accounting conventions into two broad groups—those which may be said to go to the very roots of financial accounting, which we shall call 'fundamental conventions', and those which bear directly on the quality of financial accounting information, which we shall describe as 'procedural conventions'.

In our view, there are only two 'fundamental conventions' which may be said to characterize financial accounting:

(a) the entity convention, which states that financial accounting information relates to the activities of a business entity only, and not to the activities of its owners;

(b) the money measurement convention, which limits the recognition of activities to those which can be expressed in monetary terms.

The alteration of either of these two conventions would change the entire nature of financial accounting.

There are several 'procedural conventions', which though of great importance, affect the manner in which financial accounting information is selected, analysed and communicated. Some of these conventions are the subject of criticism, for example, the realization convention which holds that a gain in value may only result from a transaction. The following conventions are generally regarded as the most important conventions in this group:

(a) the going-concern convention	(e) the matching convention
(b) the cost convention	(f) the convention of periodicity
(c) the realization convention	(g) the convention of consistency
(d) the accrual convention	(h) the convention of conservatism.

Fundamental conventions

(a) *The entity convention*
The practice of distinguishing the affairs of the business from the personal affairs of its owner originated in the early days of double-entry book-keeping some 400 years ago. Accounting has a history which reaches back to the beginning of civilization, and archaeologists have found accounting records which date as far back as 4000 B.C., well before the invention of money. Nevertheless, it was not until the 15th century that the separation of the owner's wealth from the wealth invested in a business venture was recognized as necessary. This arose from the habit of employing managers or stewards to run a business and to require them to render accounts of their stewardship of the funds and assets entrusted to them. Consequently, the 'capital' invested in the business represented at once not only the initial assets of the business but a measure of its indebtedness to the owner. This principle remains enshrined in modern financial accounting, and the owner is shown as entitled to both the 'capital' which he has invested in the business, and also the profits which have been made during the year. The accounting and legal relationship between the business and its owner is shown on the balance sheet, which states the

firm's assets and liabilities and hence indicates its financial position and financial well-being.

Example

J. Soap has recently inherited £30,000 and decides that the moment is opportune for him to realize his life-time ambition and open up a hairdressing salon. Accordingly, he makes all the necessary arrangements to begin on 1 April 19X0, under the name 'J. Soap—Ladies Hairdresser', and commits £10,000 of his money to that business. He will, therefore, open another account at his bank under the name 'J. Soap—Ladies Hairdresser', or he may simply call it the 'No. 2 account'.

As a result, the financial position of the firm on 1 April 19X0, from an accounting point of view will appear as follows:

J. Soap—Ladies Hairdresser
Balance sheet as at 1 April 19X0

Capital account	£10,000	Cash at bank	£10,000

The business is shown as having £10,000 in cash as its asset at that date, and as owing J. Soap £10,000, that is, recognizing its indebtedness to him in respect of the capital he has invested.

The accounting effect of the entity convention is to make a clear distinction between J. Soap's private affairs and his business affairs: what he does with his remaining £20,000 is of no concern to the accountant, but what happens to the £10,000 invested in the business is the subject-matter of accounting.

The interesting aspect of the entity convention is that it establishes a fictional distinction between J. Soap and the business which is not recognized at law: he remains legally liable at law for the debts of the business, and should the business fail, he will have to pay the creditors out of his private funds.

In the case of corporations, there is a legal distinction between the owners, that is, the shareholders and the business, so that the shareholders are not liable for the corporation's debts beyond the capital which they have agreed to invest. The accounting treatment of the relationship between the shareholders and the corporation is no different from that accorded to the sole trader and his business, except of course that the capital of the corporation is divided into a number of shares.

Example

Multiform Toys Ltd is registered on 1 April 19X0 as a public company, the objectives being to manufacture a wide range of children's toys. The promoters of the company need £100,000 to launch the company. They decide to offer for sale 100,000 ordinary shares of £1 each to the public, and the promoters themselves will subscribe for 25,000 of these shares.

If we assume that all the shares have been taken up and paid for on 1 May 19X0, the balance sheet of the company will be as follows:

Multiform Toys Ltd
Balance sheet as at 1 May 19X0

Share capital	£100,000	Cash at bank	£100,000

The promoters have become shareholders, along with the members of the public who have subscribed for the shares. The liability of the company to the shareholders amounts to £100,000, and the company has £100,000 in cash by means of which it may pursue its objectives.

The effect of the entity convention in the case of incorporated business is to recognize the separate identity of the company from that of its shareholders. The shareholders themselves are not liable for the debts of the company, and their total liability is limited to the £100,000 which they have subscribed. We shall discuss full implications of incorporation from an accounting point of view in Chapter 13.

(b) *The money measurement convention*
Both trade and accounting existed before the invention of money, which we know began to circulate in the 6th century B.C. Its role as a common denominator by which the value of assets of different kinds could be compared encouraged the extension of trade. By Roman times, money had become the language of commerce, and accounts were kept in money terms. Hence, there is an accounting tradition which dates back some 2000 years of keeping the records of valuable assets and of transactions in monetary terms. It should not appear surprising, therefore, that accounting information today reflects the time-hallowed practice of dealing only with those facts which are capable of expression in money.

The money measurement convention sets an absolute limit to the type of information which may be selected and measured by accountants, and hence limits the type of information which accountants may communicate about a business enterprise.

Example

The Solidex Engineering Co Ltd is an old-fashioned company which specializes in the production of a single component used in the manufacture of mining gear. The balance sheet of the company as at 31 December 19X0 reveals the following position:

The Solidex Engineering Co Ltd
Balance sheet as at 31 December 19X0

	£		£
Share capital	100,000	Land and buildings	30,000
		Equipment	25,000
		Inventories	30,000
		Cash	15,000
	100,000		100,000

For some time, it has been known that a competitor has developed a better product, and that the company is likely to lose its market. The managing director is ill, the production manager and the accountant are not on speaking terms and the labour force is resentful about the deterioration in working conditions in the factory. The buildings are dilapidated, but the land itself is valuable. The equipment is old and needs a great deal of maintenance, and as a result, there is a considerable wastage of labour hours owing to machinery breakdown.

It is clear from the foregoing example that the most significant information of interest to shareholders is not what is contained in the balance sheet but the information which is left out of it, and which is much more relevant to an understanding of the firm's position. Yet, the accountant is unable to measure and communicate that information to shareholders directly in money terms, although all these facts may explain poor income figures. The reader of a financial accounting report should not expect, therefore, that all or perhaps even the most important facts about the business will be disclosed, and this is why there is such a premium on 'inside' information in order to make correct assessments of the firm's true position. One of the major problems of accounting today is to find means of solving the measurement problem: how to extend the quality and the coverage of information in a way which is meaningful. The advantage of money, of course, is that people are able to grasp the meaning of facts which are stated in money, and it remains the most obvious standard of measurement in accounting.

There are further problems associated with the practice of using money as a standard of measurement in accounting. Money does not have a constant value through time, nor does the value of specific assets remain the same in relation to money. Until recently, accountants turned a blind eye to this problem by assuming that the money standard did have a constant value. The rising rates of inflation in the 1960s and 1970s destroyed this fiction.

Financial accounting records serve two distinct and important purposes. First, they provide evidence of the financial dimensions of rights and obligations resulting from legal contracts. For this purpose these records must be kept in the form of unadjusted money measurements. Second, they are used as a basis for providing financial information for shareholders, investors and a variety of users who need such information for decision making. For this purpose, the money measurements must reflect the economic reality of business transactions and for this reason must be adjusted for changes in price levels. In this part, we shall discuss the first purpose of financial accounting records, and in Parts 3 and 4, we shall discuss the second purpose.

It is clear from our discussion so far that the abandonment of either of the two conventions which we have examined would alter the nature of financial accounting completely. Communicating information about a business entity in money terms is the basis of modern financial accounting theory and practice. The conventions which we shall now discuss relate to the treatment of data.

Procedural conventions

(a) *The going-concern convention*

The valuation of assets used in a business is based on the assumption that the business is a continuing business and not one on the verge of cessation. This convention is important: many assets derive their value from their employment in the firm, and should the firm cease to operate the value which could be obtained for these assets on a closing-down sale would be much less probably than their book value.

Example

The Zimbabwe Gold Mining Company Ltd has been mining gold for many years in Southern Africa. The assets of the company consist of a mineshaft half a mile deep which enables the company to reach the gold reef, small gauge railway tracks and trucks within the mine, lifting gear, conveyor belts, crushing plant and sundry equipment. The balance sheet of the company at 1 April 19X0 shows the following position:

The Zimbabwe Gold Mining Company Ltd
Balance sheet as at 1 April 19X0

	£		£
Share capital	500,000	Mineshaft	500,000
Retained income	300,000	Land and buildings	25,000
		Plant and equipment	200,000
		Tools	15,000
		Gold in transit	50,000
		Cash at bank	10,000
	800,000		800,000

The mineshaft was sunk originally with the money raised by the issue of shares, and the other assets were financed out of loans which were repaid out of income, which was not distributed to shareholders. In terms of the entity convention the total liability of the company to shareholders is, therefore, £800,000—which is the amount which they might expect to receive if the company ceased to operate. For the time being, apart from £60,000 in gold or cash, the balance of their interest is substantially the mineshaft and the plant and equipment amounting to £700,000. If the gold reef ceased to be economically workable and the mine had to be abandoned, the mineshaft, being purely a hole in the ground, would become valueless, and so would much of the plant. Hence, it is unlikely that shareholders would get back even a fraction of their investments.

The going-concern convention indicates the need to relate the value of assets to the future profits which they will make possible. This convention opens the way for the method favoured by economists of finding the present value of an asset by reference to the discounted value of future returns which are expected to be derived from the use of that asset.

(b) *The cost convention*

By convention, however, accountants determine the value of an asset by reference to the cost of its acquisition, and not by reference to value of the returns which are expected to be realized. Hence, the 'value in use' of assets which the going-concern convention maintains is the cost of acquisition. To the accountant, the difference between the value in use and the cost of acquisition of an asset is income:

Value in use − Cost of acquisition = Income

Example

W. E. Audent & Son is a professional firm of chartered accountants with a large auditing practice. Its major asset is the staff of audit clerks. The value in use of the staff may be calculated by reference to the hourly rate at which their services may be charged out to clients; the cost of securing their services to the firm is represented by their salaries; and the annual profit of the firm is in substance the difference less, of course, the administrative expenses of running the firm.

In accounting, cost is used as a measure of the financial 'effort' exerted in gaining access to the resources which will be deployed in earning revenues. Since these resources are secured through financial transactions, the financial effort is measured at the time of acquisition, which coincides, of course, with the legal obligation to pay for those resources in money. The cost convention raises the following problems:

(a) The historic cost of acquisition of assets is not a dependable guide to their current value because it fails to reflect:
  (i) changes in the general purchasing power of money;
  (ii) changes in the specific value of individual assets in relation to money.
(b) The historic cost of acquisition of assets used up in the activity of earning income does not form a dependable basis for calculating income.

Example

John Smith is a dealer in hides. He obtains his yearly supplies from Canada in the autumn, and sells them in the United Kingdom during the ensuing 12 months. In October 19X0 he bought 20,000 hides at an average cost of $20 Canadian, equivalent to, let us say £10, and by September 19X1 had sold them all at an average price of £20, making an overall profit of £20,000. Meanwhile, the posted price of Canadian hides has increased by 50 per cent so that to replace inventory which he has sold during the year he will now have to pay an average of £15 a hide. Hence, the income of £20,000 is overstated by £10,000 because the hides sold have been valued at £10 instead of £15 each—which is their current value in Canada.

(c) The accounting practice of writing off the cost of certain assets as depreciation against income means that it is possible to remove the cost of these assets from the accounts altogether. For a long time, for example, it was the practice of banks to reduce the value of land and buildings to £1 and so create secret reserves.

(d) Since incurring a cost depends upon a financial transaction, there are assets which create income for the firm which can never appear as such in the accounts. Often the major asset of a highly successful firm is the knowledge and the skill created as a result of teamwork and good organization. This asset will not appear in the accounts, since the firm has paid nothing for it, except in terms of salaries which have been written off against yearly profits. Allied to this problem is the failure in making any mention in the balance sheet of the value of the human assets of the firm. Long ago, the economist Alfred Marshall stated that 'the most valuable of all capital is that invested in human beings' (Marshall, 1964, 8th edn), and it is universally recognized that the firm's human assets are its chief source of wealth. Yet, it is only recently that accountants have begun to recognize this fact, and efforts are now being made to find ways in which information on the value of human assets may be most appropriately presented. Other important assets of which no mention is made in financial accounting statements are, for example, the value to the firm of its hold on the market, which may be a very valuable asset if the firm enjoys a monopoly position, and the value of the firm's own information system, which will affect the quality of its decisions.

Many of the most controversial issues in financial accounting theory and practice revolve around the cost convention. External users of financial statements basically wish to have information of the current worth of the firm on the basis of which they may make investment decisions. Accountants argue that there must be an objective basis to the information which they provide, and to them 'objectivity' means being able to verify information from the results of transactions which create legal rights and obligations. The need to report the legal rights and obligations existing in money terms at law, and the desire to express the value of the assets and liabilities in real terms under changing money values has been at the heart of the debate about inflation accounting.

(c) *The realization convention*
The realization convention is also closely related to the cost convention, for as the recorded value of an asset to the firm is determined by the transaction which was necessary to acquire it, so any change in its value may only be recognized at the moment the firm realizes or disposes of that asset. The realization convention reflects totally the historical origin of accounting as a method for recording the results of transactions. To an accountant there is no certainty of income until a sale has been made: hence, increases in value which have not been realized are not recorded.

The realization convention is strongly criticized by economists. They argue that if an asset has increased in value then it is irrelevant that it has not been sold. For economists, it is sufficient that the gain in value could be realized for that gain to be recognized. The realization convention, it is true, may lead to absurd conclusions.

Example
William James and George Lloyd have bought a pair of dilapidated cottages

in Gwynedd for £5000. They spend £2000 on restoring the cottages, so that their total cost amounts to £7000. Both cottages are identical and form part of one unit, that is, they are semi-detached. The cottages were bought as part of a speculative venture to make profit out of the popularity of Welsh cottages as holiday homes. A businessman from Manchester offers to buy both cottages for £10,000 each, but the partners decide to sell only one of the cottages and to retain the other for sale at a higher price in the future.

From an accounting point of view, the cottage which is sold is recognized as being worth £10,000, and the difference of £6500 between the accounting cost and the sale price is the realized income. The second cottage, which could also have been sold for £10,000 to the same man, is recorded as being worth only £3500—being the costs associated with acquiring and restoring it.

Unrealized gains in value are widely recognized by non-accountants. Bankers, who are perhaps the most cautious of men, are prepared to lend money on unrealized values: businessmen reckon as income increases in the value of assets even though they are unsold—yet accountants will not do so unless and until a contract of sale has taken place which creates a legal right to receive the agreed value of the asset sold.

As a result of the realization convention, two classes of gains may be distinguished—'holding gains' which are increases in value resulting from holding an asset, and 'trading or operating gains' which are gains realized as a result of selling assets. 'Holding gains' are not recorded, but 'operating gains' are reported. The realization convention means, in effect, that the reported income of a business is a part only of the total increases in value which accrue to a firm during an accounting period.

The realization convention does not require the accountant to await the receipt of cash before recording a transaction. Indeed, in many cases the delivery of goods and the receipt of cash occur after the legal agreement which determines the timing of the transaction.

Example

On 1 January 19X0, Midlands Motor Engineers receive an order from one of their accredited dealers for five tractor engines each costing £400. The engines are despatched on 10 January, and on 5 February, a cheque for £2000 is received in payment.

From a legal point of view, the acceptance of the order on 1 January marks the timing of the sale, and the creation of the contractual obligation to deliver the engines as well as the contractual right to receive payment. Accounting follows the law in this respect, and it is common practice to write to confirm the receipt of an order and its acceptance, so as to leave no doubt as to the legal and accounting position.

On occasions, however, when a contract is for work which cannot be completed for a long period of time, the contract may stipulate when rights to payment arise. This is particularly the case as regards large civil engineering contracts, shipbuilding contracts and large government contracts. In these situations, accounting practices once more follow the law, and the timing of the right to receive cash is determined by the contract.

Example

Westlands Civil Engineering Co Ltd is awarded a Government contract for the building of a 50-mile section of a motorway. The work is required to be completed in three years. Payments are to be made by the Government on the basis of the work completed in each three-monthly period. It is agreed that an independent firm of quantity surveyors will certify the volume of work completed in each period, and that these certificates will form the basis for calculating the period payments to the company on the 'percentage-of-completion' method.

In accordance with this contract, the timing of the realizations will depend upon the issue of the certificates by the quantity surveyors.

(d) *The accrual convention*

The realization convention which asserts that gains in value may not be recognized until the occurrence of a transaction is reinforced by the accrual convention, which applies equally to revenues and expenses.

The accrual convention makes the distinction between the receipt of cash and the right to receive cash, and the payment of cash and the legal obligation to pay cash, for in accounting practice there is usually no exact coincidence in time between cash movements and the legal obligations to which they relate.

Let us examine, firstly, the manner in which the accrual convention applies to revenues. Revenue may be defined as the right to receive cash, and accountants are concerned with recording these rights. Cash receipts may occur instantaneously and also as follows:

(a) before a right to receive arises;
(b) after the right to receive has been created;
(c) cash may be received in error.

The accrual convention provides a guideline to the accountant as to how to treat these cash receipts and the rights related thereto.

Example

Mrs Smith is an old lady who occupies a flat owned by Mereworth Properties Ltd. The rent is payable monthly in advance on the 1st day of each month, and amounts to £25 a month. She is very forgetful, and rarely does a month pass without some complication in the payment of her rent.

On 1 January she sends her cheque for £25 in respect of the rent due for January. This rent is due and payable to the company, and must be included in its revenue for that month. On 10 January Mrs Smith sends another cheque for £25, thinking that she had not paid her rent for January. This is a cash receipt to which the company is not presently entitled, and it must either be returned to Mrs Smith, or it may be kept on her behalf as a payment in advance of her February rent—but only if she agrees. The accountant returns her cheque saying that she has already paid her rent for January, and she receives this letter on 20 January. She forgets to pay her rent on 1 February. The accountant is obliged to include the rent due in February in the revenue for that month, even though it is only ultimately paid on 15 March. Until Mrs

Smith has paid her rent for February, she will be a debtor of the company for the rent owing.

Similar rules apply to the treatment of expenses incurred by the firm. Expenses may be defined as legal obligations incurred by the firm to pay in money or money's worth for the benefit of goods or services which it has received. Cash payments may occur instantaneously and as follows:

(a) before they are due for payment;
(b) after due date for payment;
(c) cash may be paid in error.

The accrual convention requires the accountant to treat as expenses only those sums which are due and payable. If a payment is made in advance, it must not be treated as an expense, and the recipient is a debtor until his right to receive the cash matures. Cash paid in error is never an expense, and until it is recovered the person to whom it was paid is also a debtor. Where an expense had been incurred, however, and no payment has been made, the expense must be recorded, and the person to whom the payment should have been made is shown as a creditor.

We shall see in Chapter 8 the importance of the accrual convention as regards record-keeping and the presentation of financial accounting statements.

(e) *The matching convention*

One of the important purposes of financial accounting is to calculate income resulting from transactions. This means identifying the gains resulting from transactions and setting off against those gains the expenses which are related to those transactions. The realization convention identifies the timing of gains, and the accrual convention enables the accountant properly to record revenues and expenses; neither, however, helps the accountant to calculate income. The matching convention links revenues with their relevant expenses.

Example

On 1 April Cash and Carry Ltd purchase for resale 2000 tins of beans at a cost of 5p a tin. The selling price is 8p a tin. During the month of April 1000 tins are sold. What is the profit for the month which is attributable to this line of goods?

We know that the expenses are $2000 \times 5p = £100$, and that the revenues are $1000 \times 8p = £80$. On the face of it, therefore, Cash and Carry Ltd have made a loss of £100 less £80, that is, £20. This conclusion is nonsense, because we are setting off against the sale proceeds of 1000 tins the cost of acquiring 2000 tins.

In accordance with the matching convention, the accountant establishes the income for the month of April by calculating the cost of purchasing 1000 tins of beans and setting this expense against the revenue realized from the sale of these tins:

Sales revenue	1000 tins @ 8p = £80
Cost of sales	1000 tins @ 5p = £50
Income from sales	£30

The 1000 tins remaining unsold remain in the accounting records as assets, and when they are eventually sold the income from sales will be calculated by deducting the cost of acquisition against the sales revenue which is realized.

The matching of revenues and expenses is very often a most difficult problem in accounting, and many types of expenses are not easily identifiable with revenues.

Example

Bloxwich Pharmaceutical Co Ltd manufactures and sells pharmaceutical products. Its major activity is the manufacture of antibiotics, which accounts for 80 per cent of its sales revenue. The remaining 20 per cent of its sales is derived from beauty creams. Its expenses for the year 19X0 are as follows:

Manufacturing costs of antibiotics	£500,000
Manufacturing costs of beauty creams	20,000
Administrative costs	100,000
Selling and financial costs	50,000
Research and development costs	150,000
Total expenses for the year	£820,000

In the same year, the total revenue from sales of both antibiotics and beauty creams amounts to £1,000,000. Calculate the income on the antibiotics side of the business.

We can begin to answer this problem as follows:

Sales revenue from antibiotics (80% of total)	£800,000
Manufacturing costs of antibiotics	500,000
	300,000
Other expenses	?
Income in respect of antibiotics	?

Clearly, we should need to have more information in order to allocate the administrative, selling and financial costs as between the antibiotics and the beauty creams. It is unlikely that an exact allocation could be made, and in the end, an estimate would be made.

As regards the research and development costs, which are concerned with developing new antibiotics and beauty creams, there is an even more difficult problem. Strictly speaking, we should not set these costs against the revenues of the year, since the benefits of this expenditure will not occur in this year.

Much of this expenditure, however, may not lead to new products. Therefore, if we ignore this expenditure, the company's reported income will be inflated and unrealistic.

From the foregoing example, it is seen that the exact matching of revenues and expenses is often impossible. Nevertheless, the computation of periodic income requires that expenses be allocated, where necessary, in order that the financial results may be stated in a consistent manner.

(f) *The convention of periodicity*

It may safely be assumed that the custom of making periodic reports to the owner of a business dates from the time when wealthy men employed servants to manage and oversee their affairs. Periodic accounting has its origin in the idea of control, therefore, and company law to this day sees the role of financial accounting reports as being essentially the communication of financial information from the managers of the business, that is the directors, to the owners of the business, that is the shareholders. However much we may disagree with this view of the relationship of directors and shareholders as being unrealistic, we must accept that there is an element of shareholder control over company directors which stems from the legal duty laid on the latter to issue financial reports on their stewardship of the firm's assets.

The convention of periodicity is now established by law as regards certain types of reports such as balance sheets and profit and loss accounts. The Companies Act requires yearly reports to shareholders, and the Income Tax Acts require accounts for all businesses to be submitted yearly. There is no reason, however, to prevent companies from providing financial information at more frequent intervals to investors, if they so wish.

The idea of making yearly reports has grown out of custom, and many would question the wisdom of selecting an arbitrary period of 12 months as a basis for reporting upon the activities of a business. The idea of yearly reporting is strongly entrenched, and even the Government runs its business on a yearly basis and budgets for one year, although many of its activities are continuing ones which cannot be seen correctly in the perspective of 12 months. This is equally true for all large companies, and many smaller businesses.

Example

Universal Chemicals Ltd manufactures a wide range of chemical products and has factories throughout the country. Owing to unusually difficult labour relations, Government control on prices, rising raw material costs and stiffening competition, its reported income for the year ended 31 December 19X0 has decreased by 10 per cent over the previous year. Its borrowings, however, have increased by 20 per cent due to an enlarged capital investment programme which is designed to add substantially to income in about five years' time.

Clearly, in this case the reader of the report for the year 19X0 should consider the report in its proper context, and look to the long-term trend of income and to the better financial position which is expected in the future.

The convention of periodicity as expressed in yearly accounting fails to make the important distinction between the long-term trend and the short-term position. Hence, it places limits on the usefulness of the information communicated to shareholders and investors.

Together with the matching convention, the convention of periodicity seeks to relate all the transactions of one particular year with the expenses attributable to those transactions. From a practical point of view, accountants are compelled to carry forward expenses until they can be identified with the revenues of a particular year, and to carry forward receipts until they can be regarded as the revenues of a particular year in accordance with the realization convention. Since all assets are 'costs' in accounting, the convention of periodicity creates difficulties for accountants as regards the allocation of fixed assets as the expenses of particular years. We shall examine this problem when we come to discuss depreciation in Chapter 9.

So far we have mentioned the effect of the convention of periodicity on the usefulness of the information communicated to external users, but we should say a word about its effect on income measurement. The majority of economists treat accounting income as the 'income' of a business, and hence as a measure of the income which investors and shareholders derive from their investment in the firm. As a result, they impose the economic criteria appropriate to the measurement of economic income to accounting income and are very dissatisfied with shortcomings of accounting income which they see as stemming from accounting conventions for calculating periodic income. Ideally, of course, an accurate measurement of the income or loss of a business can only be made after the business has ceased operating, sold off all its assets and paid off all its liabilities. The net income accruing to investors would then be the difference between the sum total of all their receipts, either as dividends or capital repayments, and their initial investment. It is clear, however, that accounting income is merely the result of completed transactions during a stated period: the convention of periodicity is a statement of this view.

(g) *The convention of consistency*

The usefulness of financial accounting information lies to a considerable extent in the conclusions which may be drawn from the comparison of the financial statements of one year with that of a preceding year, and the financial reports of one company with those of another company. It is in this way that we may deduce some of the most important information for decision making, such as an indication that there has been an improvement in income since last year and that therefore it is worth buying more shares, or the income of Company A is better than that of Company B and given current share prices one should switch from holding shares in Company B and buy those of Company A.

The comparability of financial statements depends largely upon the choice of accounting methods and the consistency with which they are applied. A change in the basis on which a firm values inventory, for example, may result in an income figure different from that which would have been computed had the accountant adhered to a consistent basis of valuation. If firms wish to change their method for treating a particular problem, such as the valuation of inventory or the value attached to a particular asset, they may do so, but they should mention the effect on the reported income of the change in accounting methods.

Comparing the accounts of different companies is altogether more difficult, and unfortunately the accounting methods of individual firms are not the same. There is no uniformity of accounting methods which would provide the consistency of treatment of information necessary for the comparison of the accounts of different companies. Whereas the accounting convention of consistency is generally followed by individual firms, there is no agreement at all that different firms should use the same accounting methods. Hence, the needs of investors for greater comparability of information between companies is frustrated by accounting conventions which insist on the one hand on consistency, but allow on the other hand different methods of measurement and treatment which cannot yield comparable results. The Accounting Standards Committee is charged with the task of trying to secure agreement on appropriate accounting methods which will ensure a higher degree of comparability of accounting information, and we shall examine some of its achievements so far in this part. It is clear that European integration will hasten progress towards uniformity in accounting standards.

(h) *The convention of conservatism*

The convention of conservatism reflects the accountant's view of his social role and his responsibilities towards those for whom he provides information. It is seen at work in some of the conventions which we have examined in this chapter, for example, the realization convention which requires the realization of a gain before it may be recognized, and the cost convention which holds that the value of an asset is the cost of acquisition.

There are two principal rules which stem directly from the convention of conservatism:

(1) the accountant should not anticipate income and should provide for all possible losses;

(2) faced with a choice between two methods of valuing an asset, the accountant should choose the method which leads to the lesser value.

These two rules contravene some of the conventions of accounting, for example, the cost convention, for if the market value of trading inventory has fallen below the cost of acqusition it must be valued at the market value. Equally, the logic which underlies the realization convention as regards gains, that is, that there is no certainty of receiving a gain until there is a sale, does not extend to the treatment of anticipated losses. Thus, accountants are willing to accrue losses in value which are sufficiently foreseeable to make them a present reality, and in the accountant's mind to ignore such losses might mislead the user of accounting information. One of the clearest explanations of the policy of conservatism was made by G. O. May as long ago as 1946, as follows:

'. . . the great majority of ventures fail, and the fact that enterprises nevertheless continue is attributable to the incurable optimism (often dissociated from experience) as well as to the courage of mankind. In my experience, also, losses from unsound accounting have most commonly resulted from the hopes rather than the achievements of management being allowed to influence accounting dispositions. To me, conservatism is still the first virtue of accounting, and I am wholly unable to agree with those who would bar it from the books of accounts and statements prepared therefrom and would relegate it to footnotes'. (May, 1946.)

The caution of the accountant may well be a foil for the optimism of businessmen, but although it may be highly desirable for the accountant to be conservative in the estimates which he makes, the selection of accounting methods for recording and presenting information on the basis that they understate assets or earnings should not be an overriding principle. Investors and shareholders need reliable and useful information: to understate is as bad as to overstate—investment in a business may be discouraged if it appears to be less valuable than it really is. Users of accounting information, as all others who are faced with making decisions, look for guidance on the lowest value, the highest value and the probable value. In restricting accounting information to the statement of the lowest value, the accountant is prevented from fulfilling the social role expected of him as a supplier of comprehensive financial information.

Summary

The conventions of accounting serve as guide-posts, but they do tend to emphasize the reliability of information rather than its usefulness. The conflict between reliability and usefulness has caused controversy in accounting. At one extreme, there are accountants who contend that if a measurement is useful, further justification is unnecessary. At the other extreme, others hold that the reliability of accounting information is the most important criterion, and will ultimately determine the extent to which external users will accept accounting statements for the purpose of making investment decisions.

The effect of accounting conventions on financial reporting may be criticized for three reasons:

(a) They prevent change, for the fact that conventions have to be generally agreed prevents new conventions being adopted.
(b) Generally accepted practice does not necessarily provide the most useful information for decision making.
(c) Accounting conventions do not create uniformity.

The effect of generally accepted accounting conventions on external financial reports is to create a degree of diversity which is at variance with the objective of efficient resource allocation.

References

1. Marshall, Alfred. *Principles of Economics*, 8th ed., Macmillan, London, 1964.
2. May, G. O. *Financial Accounting: A Distillation of Experience*, Macmillan, New York, 1946.

Questions

1. Examine the role of so-called conventions in the analysis of accounting transactions and the preparation of financial statements.
2. Consultat Inc. is a firm of consulting engineers, newly established to advise on a large project taking three years to complete. Their fee for this work is a percentage of the total project costs, payable on completion of the project. In the interim, advances on the final fee are made at six-monthly intervals. The total project costs will not be known until the project is completed. The following advances were received by Consultat Inc. during the three year period:

   year ended 31 December 19X0   £25,000
   year ended 31 December 19X1   £30,000
   year ended 31 December 19X2   £30,000

When the total costs were computed during the year ended 31 December 19X3, it was found that a further sum of £50,000 was due to Consultat Inc.

Required:

(a) Explain how you would show the payments made to Consultat Inc. during the periods covered by the project. Justify your explanation in terms of the conventions of accounting which you consider apply to this situation.

(b) Would you change your reasoning at all in the light of the following information?

(i) the advance payments are not contractual but discretionary on the part of the paying company;

(ii) a clause in the consulting agreement requires Consultat Inc. to undertake— free of charge—extra work to remedy defects appearing within three years of the completion of the project.

Suggest how you would treat these problems by reference to accounting conventions.

3. Bloxwitch Engineers Ltd borrows £100,000 at a fixed interest rate of 10 per cent for a period of five years for the purpose of acquiring a stamping press of advanced design. Suggest how you would treat the accounting aspects of the transactions associated with the acquisition and the financing of the stamping press in the following circumstances:

(i) by the end of the third year of use, the stamping press has been depreciated to £70,000, but due to a new design having appeared, its market value is only £30,000. The stamping press, nevertheless, continues to generate the same level of revenue as it did in the first year of use;

(ii) during the fourth year, the stamping mill generates only £8000 of revenues, and the Managing Director of Bloxwitch Engineers Ltd has written an instruction to the effect that 'since the mill is now making a loss of £2000 when interest is taken into account', it should be sold forthwith. The market value has now fallen to £15,000. The monies realized are to be applied to the acquisition of further plant, and the interest charge remains to be paid during the following and final year of the loan.

Support your discussion of the accounting problems you have identified by reference to the conventions which justify your reasoning.

4. Lewis, Jones and Peers, newly qualified as architects, decide to form a partnership on 1 January 19X0. During their first year of business, a substantial operating loss is realized amounting to £20,000. They had anticipated such a loss and had provided sufficient funds to cover it when they first formed the partnership. 'After all', said

Peers, 'it is well known that the first year of business for architects always produces a loss, since they are really establishing the business. They do, in fact, earn little money as they build up contacts which will earn future revenues'. 'That's right', continued Lewis, as he was explaining to the accountant, who has prepared the income statement showing the loss of £20,000, 'you can't show the £20,000 as a loss, when it is the cost of setting up the business. To be consistent with the facts, you have to show the £20,000 as an asset on the balance sheet'. 'Yes, I agree', concluded Jones, 'that is the most conservative way of looking at the situation. Then, we recognize the creation of an asset we can write off over several years and match against the future revenues which are really the result of this year's efforts'.

How would you deal with the arguments of your clients, if you were the accountant in this situation? Refer the problems you see to such accounting conventions as are applicable to them, and in particular, explain how you would deal with the terms 'consistent' and 'conservative' used by the partners in their discussion with you.

5 Financial accounting standards

The financial accounting conventions discussed in Chapter 4 were seen as core elements in the development of a descriptive theory of financial accounting. The review of the conventions of financial accounting which was conducted by the accounting profession in the 1970s, and which has resulted in the publication of a series of Statements of Standard Accounting Practice, is part of the on-going process of developing accounting practice by seeking a consensus among practitioners.

The conventions of accounting permit a variety of alternative practices to co-exist. As a result, the financial results of different companies cannot be compared and evaluated unless full information is available about the accounting methods which have been used. Not only have the variety of accounting practices permitted by the conventions of financial accounting made it difficult to compare the financial results of different companies, but the application of alternative accounting methods to the preparation of the financial reports of the same company have enabled entirely different results to be reported to shareholders.

The need for the imposition of standards on accounting practice has arisen because of the lack of uniformity existing as regards the manner in which periodic income could be measured and the financial position of the enterprise could be represented. The purpose of this chapter is to examine the significance of the development of accounting standards for a descriptive theory of financial accounting based on conventions and consensus.

The importance of comparability

The information contained in published financial statements is especially important to external users, such as shareholders and investors, for without such information they would have to take decisions about their investments under an extreme degree of uncertainty. A major problem lies in the fact that there are no formal channels for communicating to companies the type and nature of the financial information which external users themselves believe they require, and the manner in which such information ought to be presented. Traditionally, Parliament has assumed the responsibility for specifying by law the type and the minimum level of information which companies should disclose in financial statements, and the accounting profession has assumed the responsibility for ensuring the proper presentation of such information. In this respect, it is evident that the conventions applied to the presentation of financial information should not permit too much discretion to individual accountants, and that the manner in which financial information is treated in financial statements should conform to carefully considered standards.

The function of accounting standards may best be examined by reference to the basic purpose of financial statements, which may be stated as being concerned with the communication of information affecting the allocation of resources. Ideally, such information should make it possible for investors to evaluate the investment opportunities offered by different firms and to allocate and ration scarce resources to the most efficient ones. In theory, this process should result in the optimal distribution of scarce resources within the economy, and should maximize their potential benefit to society.

In this analysis of the purpose of financial statements, it becomes apparent that one of the most important criteria for the presentation of financial information is that which ensures an appropriate standard of comparison between different firms. It requires that the accounting methods used by different firms for presenting information to investors should allow correct comparisons to be made. For example, they should not permit a company to report profits which result simply from a change in accounting methods, rather than from increased efficiency. If companies were free to choose their accounting methods in this way, the consequence might well be that deliberate distortions would be introduced in the pricing of shares on the Stock Exchange, leading eventually to a misallocation of resources in the economy. This would occur as relatively less efficient companies are able to report fictitious profits, and as a result ultimately to divert capital to themselves on very favourable terms and away from the more efficient companies, which have adopted more rigorous accounting methods.

Reasons for concern about standards

In the United Kingdom, the Institute of Chartered Accountants in England and Wales began to make recommendations about accounting practices as early in 1942. Ultimately a series of 29 recommendations on accounting practices were issued with the objective of codifying the best practices which ought to be used in particular circumstances. However, there were several disadvantages to this procedure:

(a) The recommendations were not mandatory, and were issued for the guidance of members of the Institute.
(b) The recommendations did not result from fundamental research into the objectives of accounting, but merely codified existing practices.
(c) The recommendations did not reduce the diversity of accounting methods. For example, Recommendation No. 22, 1960, which was concerned with inventory valuation, recommended five different methods of computing the cost of inventory. Furthermore, four of these methods could be computed differently for partly and fully finished inventories. To complicate matters further, Recommendation 22 stated that cost could be defined in three different ways!

In the late 1960s, there was a spate of public criticism of financial reporting methods, which arose from the publicity accorded to aspects of the financial statements of a number of companies. These included Pergamon Press, General Electric Company and Vehicle and General Company. The manner in which these cases jolted the accounting profession may be judged from the example of the General Electric Company.

In 1967, the General Electric Company (GEC) made a takeover bid for Associated Electric Industries (AEI). AEI produced a profit forecast for that year of £10 million, which was based on ten months' actual profit and two months' budgeted profit. The GEC takeover bid was successful, and afterwards, GEC reported that, in fact, AEI had made a loss of £4.5 million for that year. According to GEC auditors, £9.5 million of the £14.5 million difference between the two calculations of income for 1967 was due to difference in judgement about such matters as the amounts written off inventory and the provision for estimated losses.

The angry reaction of the press to the disclosure of the amended figures for 1967 centred on the possibility that two different accounting firms could justifiably produce such widely differing results for the same year. One observer commented that it appeared that accounting was really an art form, and that it seemed that two firms of accountants looking at the same figures were capable of producing profit figures as far apart as a Rubens is from a Rembrandt.

The Accounting Standards Committee (ASC)

The response of the accounting profession to the criticism which it received at this time was to establish the Accounting Standards Committee. The initiative taken by the Institute of Chartered Accountants in England and Wales in 1969 in establishing the Accounting Standards Committee was almost immediately supported by the Institute of Chartered Accountants of Scotland and the Institute of Chartered Accountants in Ireland. By 1976, the remaining three accounting bodies in the United Kingdom, namely, the Association of Certified Accounts, the Institute Cost and Management Accountants, and the Chartered Institute of Public Finance and Accountancy, had also become associated with the Accounting Standards Committee.

The prime objective of the Accounting Standards Committee has been to narrow the areas of difference and variety in accounting practice. The procedure used for this purpose is initiated by the issue of an 'Exposure Draft' on a specific topic for discussion by accountants and the public at large. Comments made on the Exposure Draft are taken into consideration when drawing up a formal statement of the accounting method to be applied when dealing with that specific topic. This formal statement is known as a Statement of Standard Accounting Practice (SSAP). Once the Statement of Standard Accounting Practice has been adopted by the accounting profession, any material departure by any company from the standard practice to be used in presenting its financial report is to be disclosed in that report.

To date, the following Exposure Drafts and Statements of Standard Accounting Practice have been issued:

Statements of Standard Accounting Practice Issued

SSAP	Explanatory foreword (revised May 1975)	Jan 71
SSAP 1	Accounting for the results of associated companies (amended Aug 1974)	Jan 71
SSAP 2	Disclosure of accounting policies	Nov 71
SSAP 3	Earnings per share (revised Aug 1974)	Feb 72
SSAP 4	The accounting treatment of government grants	Apr 74
SSAP 5	Accounting for value added tax	Apr 74
SSAP 6	Extraordinary items and prior year adjustments (revised April 1975)	May 74
SSAP 8	The treatment of taxation under the imputation system in the accounts of companies (revised Dec 1977)	Aug 74
SSAP 9	Stocks and work in progress	May 75
SSAP 10	Statements of source and application of funds	July 75
SSAP 12	Accounting for depreciation	Dec 77
SSAP 13	Accounting for research and development	Dec 77
SSAP 14	Group accounts	Sept 78
SSAP 15	Accounting for deferred taxation	Oct 78
SSAP 16	Current cost accounting	Mar 80
SSAP 17	Accounting for post balance sheet events	Sept 80
SSAP 18	Accounting for contingencies	Sept 80
SSAP 19	Accounting for investment properties	Nov 81

Exposure Drafts issued

ED 3	Accounting for acquisitions and mergers	Jan 71
ED 26	Accounting for investment property companies	Sept 80
ED 27	Foreign currency translation	Oct 80
ED 28	Accounting for petroleum revenue tax	Mar 81
ED 29	Accounting for leases and hire purchase contracts	Oct 81

The list of topics on which Exposure Drafts and Statements of Standard Accounting Practice have been issued shows that the work of the Accounting Standards Committee is profoundly affecting the development of accounting theory and methods. The discussion of individual Exposure Drafts and Statements of Standard Accounting Practice will be referred to in later chapters, where the topics covered by these documents themselves are analysed.

The earlier discussion in this chapter of the relationship between accounting conventions and accounting methods implies matters of accounting policy. For this reason SSAP 2, which deals with the disclosure of accounting policies, is highly significant to the central issues to which this chapter is directed, and its provisions are examined in detail in the following section.

SSAP 2: Disclosure of Accounting Policies

SSAP 2 is addressed to the relationship between accounting concepts, accounting methods and accounting policies. The relationship is illustrated in Fig. 2.3, where it is seen that accounting concepts provide the foundations to both accounting methods and policies.

The terminology adopted by SSAP 2 differs from the terminology used in

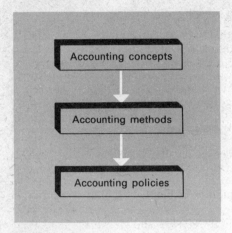

Fig. 2.3

this text. Thus, the term 'concepts' is used in SSAP 2 when referring to 'conventions', and 'bases' is used when referring to 'methods'. The fuller definitions of the terminology of SSAP 2 is as follows:

Fundamental accounting concepts are broad general assumptions which underlie the periodic financial accounts of business enterprises.

Accounting bases are the methods which have been developed for expressing or applying fundamental accounting concepts to financial transactions and items. By their nature, accounting bases are more diverse and numerous than fundamental concepts, since they have evolved in response to the variety and complexity of types of business and business transactions and, for this reason, there may justifiably exist more than one recognized accounting basis for dealing with particular items.

Accounting policies are the specific accounting bases judged by business enterprises to be most appropriate to their circumstances and adopted by them for the purpose of preparing their financial accounts.

SSAP 2 states that there are four fundamental accounting concepts which should be regarded as established standard concepts. They are as follows:

The going-concern concept, which implies that the enterprise will continue in operational existence for the foreseeable future. This means, in particular, that the profit and loss account and balance sheet assume no intention or necessity to liquidate or reduce significantly the scale of operation.

The accruals concept, which requires that revenue and costs are accrued, matched with one another so far as their relationship can be established or justifiably assumed, and dealt with in the profit and loss account of the period to which they relate, provided, generally, that where the accrual concept is inconsistent with the prudence concept (see below), the latter prevails. The accruals concept implies that the profit and loss account reflects changes in the amount of net assets that arise out of the transactions of the relevant period, other than distributions or subscriptions of capital. Revenue and profits dealt with in the profit and loss account are matched with associated costs by including in the same account the costs incurred in earning them, so far as these are material and identifiable.

The consistency concept, which requires that there should be consistency of accounting treatment of like items within each accounting period and from one period to the next.

The concept of prudence, which requires that revenue and profits be not anticipated, but recognized by inclusion in the profit and loss account only when realized in the form either of cash or of assets (usually legally enforceable debts), the ultimate cash realization of which can be assessed with reasonable certainty; provision be made for all known liabilities (expenses and losses) whether the amount of these is known with certainty or is a best estimate in the light of the information available.

SSAP 2 is concerned with ensuring that accounting bases are disclosed in financial reports, whenever significant items are shown which have their significance in value judgements, estimated outcome of future events or uncompleted transactions, rather than ascertained amounts. In the words of SSAP 2,

> 'In circumstances where more than one accounting basis is acceptable in principle, the accounting policy followed can significantly affect a company's reported results and financial position, and the view presented can be properly appreciated only if the principal policies followed are also described. For this reason, adequate disclosure of the accounting policies should be regarded as essential to the fair presentation of financial accounts.'

The need for a financial reporting framework

The work of the Accounting Standards Committee should be judged in the context of its role in the development of accounting theory. We suggested earlier in this chapter that both the conventions of accounting and their review by the Accounting Standards Committee in the guise of accounting standards, should be seen as part of a descriptive theory of accounting. In effect, such a theory is the consequence of the process of looking at the practices adopted by practising accountants, and obtaining a refinement of those practices by a process of consensus.

The Accounting Standards Committee has been criticized on the ground that its programme of work is the formulation of accounting standards without a prior formulation of a sound theoretical base from which to develop such standards. Indeed, in some respects, the programme of the Accounting Standards Committee reflects the spirit of an earlier period during which the accounting profession issued 'recommendations' on what were considered to be 'accounting principles'. In particular, it reflects the same concern with the standardization of accounting methods by simply codifying what is considered to be the best of existing methods, without in any way addressing the fundamental problems which they pose for users of accounting information. Thus, matters such as the relevance of these methods in producing information useful for their needs, are not contemplated in the current programme of standardization.

In effect, the Accounting Standards Committee has addressed itself to what may be described as 'short-term' problems, which by their apparent urgency seem to imply a priority of treatment, whereas many of their underlying features reflect issues of a 'long-term' and fundamental theoretical nature. Many of the controversies with which the Accounting Standards Committee has been concerned have their originating cause in the failure to establish a theoretical framework from which to consider their solution. For example, the controversy over the problem of accounting for changing prices in the United Kingdom would have been less contentious if accountants had been able to agree on definitions of such fundamental concepts as 'income' and 'capital'.

There is a need to invest considerable effort in research into the fundamental objectives of accounting, if the standard of financial reporting practice is to be improved. This problem is discussed more fully in Part 4.

Summary

The conventions of financial accounting and the statements of standard accounting practice issued by the Accounting Standards Committee represent a theory of accounting which has evolved by descriptions of the practices of accountants.

The conventions of accounting have permitted a variety of practices to evolve. Consequently, the lack of uniformity of such practices has made it difficult for users of financial reports to compare the results of different companies. The need for comparability has been judged to be one of the most important criteria for the presentation of financial reports. The reasons for concern about the quality of accounting information based on conventions were discussed, and were seen to relate to the different results which could be drawn from the same set of data.

The purpose of this chapter was to examine and to evaluate the work of the Accounting Standards Committee, and the importance of this work. Whilst this work has been very carefully undertaken, and has resulted in the reduction of variety of accounting practices, the final judgement may be seen to rest in the absence of a financial reporting theory which reflects clearly established objectives of accounting.

Questions

1. Discuss the purpose underlying the issue of an accounting standard.
2. Identify the four 'fundamental accounting concepts' mentioned in SSAP 2 and compare them with the corresponding conventions discussed in Chapter 4.
3. Explain the meaning of an 'accounting base'. State why accounting bases are more diverse than fundamental concepts.
4. Assess the significance of the work of the Accounting Standards Committee with respect to the development of accounting theory.

6 The generation of financial accounting data

In a previous chapter, we examined the nature and the boundaries of the financial accounting system. We noted that the conventions of financial accounting constituted one of the boundaries insofar as they act as a filtering process for the data which is fed into the financial accounting system. We concluded that these conventions played a crucial role in determining the nature of financial accounting information.

The purpose of this chapter is to examine the processes involved in the generation of financial accounting data prior to its transformation into financial accounting information.

An outline of the information generation process

The generation of financial accounting information is the result of a process involving the following stages:

(a) the preparation of source documents;
(b) the entry of basic data into subsidiary records;
(c) the posting of data from the subsidiary records into the ledger, which is the formal record of data.

The production of financial accounting information in the form of financial reports may be illustrated as in Fig. 2.4 on p. 72.

Although the principles underlying the financial accounting system have remained unchanged, its processes have undergone and are still undergoing modification and improvement. In particular, technological change has dramatically affected these processes. The advent of electronic data processing (EDP) has considerably speeded up and streamlined the data recording process, and indeed, as we shall see, has permitted the integration of several stages of this process into one single operation.

In this chapter we shall be concerned with an analysis of the traditional data recording practices relating to source documents and subsidiary books, and we shall examine the impact of recent changes on these practices. We shall examine the process of preparing financial reports in subsequent chapters.

Source documents

As we explained in Chapter 4, financial accounting data originates in financial transactions. Source documents are designed to capture the details of these

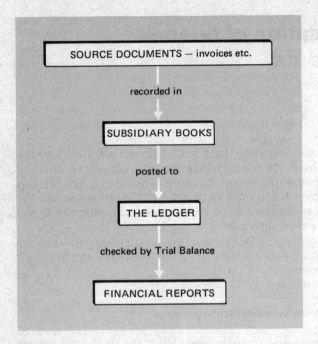

Fig. 2.4.

accounting events. Source documents also have a very important functional purpose as regards the activities of an enterprise.

Data flows generated within a business may be classified according to their sources. (i) Financial accounting data flows are generated from activities conducted between the firm and external groups such as customers and suppliers of materials, goods, services and finance. (ii) Data flows generated for the internal purposes of the business constitute a substantial volume of the total information flows. These flows are generated and channelled through a Management Information System (MIS) whose function it is to meet the information needs of management for the purposes of management planning and control. Since the firm is an open system, it is clear that the initial impetus for any activity stems from some agent in the firm's environment. The relationship between external and internal data flows and the complexity of the documentation involved in facilitating these flows are illustrated in Fig. 2.5. Figure 2.5 shows the focal role played by accounting data in relation to the firm's basic operations as well as the nature of the source documents involved in the generation of financial accounting data.

Source documents related to sales

The function of the sales department is to encourage the sales of the firm's products. Once a salesman has concluded a sale with a customer, he completes a sales order form. The original copy is sent to the customer as an

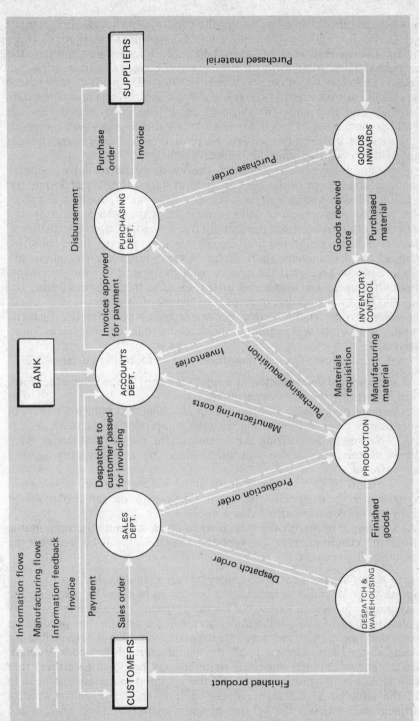

Fig. 2.5 Data sources for the basic business operations of a manufacturing firm. (Adapted from Thierauf, R. F., *Data Processing for Business Management*, John Wiley & Sons, New York, 1973.)

acknowledgement of the order, and in the case of a credit sale, one copy of the sales order form goes to the credit control department for approval. If the goods are already held in stock, the credit control department will pass the authenticated sales order form to the inventory control department so that the release and despatch of the goods may be effected. An advice note is sent to the customer as soon as the goods are despatched advising him of the date of despatch and the mode of transport used. The goods themselves are normally accompanied by a delivery note stating the description of the goods and the quantity involved though not the price. The customer acknowledges receipt of the goods by signing the delivery note.

Once the goods have been released by the inventory control department for despatch, a further copy of the sales order form stating the date of despatch is sent to the invoice section of the accounts department, so that the sales invoice may be prepared. The sales invoice states the nature, quantity and price of the goods ordered and the amount due to the firm from the customer. Customers are normally required to pay within one to three months, depending on the agreed credit terms. Often, however, customers are required to pay on receipt of the invoice, though some firms issue statements each month showing the number of invoices sent to the customer during the month and the total sum due in respect of the month's orders.

The sales invoice is the source document which provides the financial accounting data which will subsequently be recorded in the financial accounting system.

The sales order form is used, therefore, for the following purposes:

(a) As a record and confirmation of a sale. One copy of the sales order form will be kept by the sales department.
(b) As a means of initiating a procedure for checking the credit-worthiness of a customer prior to proceeding with the completion of the order.
(c) As a document authorizing the release of the goods from stocks. One copy of the sales order will be retained by the inventory control department.
(d) As a means of checking and despatching the right goods to the right customer by the despatch department. One copy of the sales order will be kept by this department for this purpose.
(e) As a means of preparing the sales invoice which will state the amount due from the customer. One copy of the sales order will be kept by the accounts department.

Where goods are not kept in inventory but are manufactured to order, the receipt of an order puts the production process in motion. We examine the cost accounting process in Part 5, but for the purposes of this chapter, we may note that a copy of the production order will be sent to the production manager and one copy to the accounts department, which is responsible for collecting all the costs associated with the manufacture of the goods ordered. Figure 2.5 shows that the materials required may be obtained either from existing stocks or by purchase. Where the required materials are held in stock, the issue of a materials requisition form to the inventory control department will procure the release of these materials. One copy of the materials requisition form will be retained by the inventory control department and one copy will be sent to the accounts department for costing purposes. Where the required materials have to be purchased, the production department will issue a purchase requisition form to the purchasing department for the required materials.

Source documents related to purchases

The purchasing department is concerned with procuring the raw materials, equipment and supplies needed by the firm. Each request must be made by means of a requisition form stating the nature and the quantity required and bearing the signature of the manager having authority to requisition purchases. The purchasing department selects a suitable supplier and sends him a purchase order form setting out the description, quantity and required delivery date of the goods, together with instructions as regards despatch and invoicing. The purchase order form will refer to the quoted price of the goods according to the suppliers' catalogue or other statements of the supply price, although quoted prices contained in advertisements for sale are not binding in law on suppliers. In effect, the purchase order form is an offer to purchase and once accepted by the supplier constitutes a legal contract between buyer and seller. Copies of the purchase order are distributed to the several departments which will be concerned with it, that is, the receiving department which will need to know the details and the date of receipt of the order, the inventory control department to advise of the pending arrival of goods and to serve as a check on the receiving department, the accounts department for checking that the price quoted compares with the price list, and the ordering department, to confirm that the order has been placed.

Source documents related to the receipt of goods

Upon delivery of the goods, the receiving department verifies that the goods delivered compare in every detail with its copy of the purchase order. Once the delivery note is agreed, a goods received note is prepared which details the description of the goods received, their quantity, quality and condition. A copy of the goods received note is sent to the department concerned with the audit of the receipt of goods, which is usually the purchasing department. A copy of the goods received note is also sent to the accounts department, and the department responsible for the order. The inventory control department is notified of the receipt of the goods as well, since it is responsible for the storage, distribution and control of inventories. The inventory control department keeps records of inventories, and ensures that adequate inventory levels are maintained.

In due course, the supplier will send an invoice stating the description, quantity and price of the goods ordered, the date of acceptance of the order, which is usually shown as the date of despatch of the goods, and the amount now owing. The invoice is checked by the accounts department against the goods received note, and if there are no queries, the invoice is cleared for payment in due course. Normally, invoices are paid monthly. This permits the workflow in the accounting department to be efficiently organized and allows the payment procedure to be properly supervised.

The entry of basic data in the subsidiary books

The accounting record of the events described in the source documents which we have just examined begins with the issue or receipts of invoices. Although legal obligations are created with the acceptance of an order, either by the firm or its suppliers, for practical reasons, accountants do not record these obligations until they are formally stated. Should there be any dispute, however, about the existence of an order, the appropriate source document would provide legal evidence of that order.

The practice of keeping daily records of accounting events in a diary or roughbook dates from the early history of accounting. The practice of keeping a daily journal was recommended by Paciolo in 1494 for the purpose of enabling the businessman to check daily the records kept by his clerk. Once agreed, they could be entered into the ledger. It became a golden rule in accounting that no entry should appear in the ledger which has not already passed through the journal.

At first, the journal was used to record all commercial transactions. It was entered chronologically and showed the details of these transactions as well as the ledger account to which the entry was ultimately posted, as follows:

Date	Journal description	Folio	(Dr.) £	(Cr.) £
Jan. 5	Goods Dr. To A. Smith Being 100 shirts bought for resale	L5 L7	100	100
Jan. 5	B. Jones Dr. To Cash Being wages due to the week ending 5th January	L10	5	5

The basic data entered in the journal consisted of:

(a) the date of the transaction
(b) the name of the purchaser or the asset purchased
(c) the name of the seller or the asset sold
(d) the sum involved
(e) a short narrative describing the transaction.

Periodically, the entries in the journal were transferred to the main record, described as the ledger, by a procedure known as posting. The folio references in the journal indicated the pages in the ledger to which the postings were made.

As trade expanded and the number of transactions to be entered in the journal multiplied, it became the practice to group the entries to be made in the journal into the following classes:

(a) purchases of trading goods on credit terms
(b) sales of trading goods on credit terms

(c) cash payments and receipts
(d) all other transactions.

This classification not only enabled entries of like nature to be kept together, but facilitated the operation of entering basic data into the books of subsidiary records. It led to the division of the journal into four parts, which were renamed as follows:

(a) the purchases day book, in which were entered credit purchases;
(b) the sales day book, in which were entered credit sales;
(c) the cash book, in which were recorded all cash transactions;
(d) the journal, in which were recorded transactions which could not be recorded in the other subsidiary books. To this day, the journal has retained its particular use as a book of original entry for such transactions.

The day books

Since the greatest bulk of source documents relate to the purchase or sale of goods, the function of the purchases and sales day books is to allow such data to be collected and transferred in a summarized form to the ledger. Hence, their purpose is to keep the ledger relatively free from unnecessary data. An example of a purchases day book is given below:

Purchases day book

Date	Name	Invoice No.	Folio	£
June 1	S. Smith	101	L15	50
2	W. Wright and Co	113	L20	35
2	J. James	148	L10	140
3	T. Tennant	184	L16	20
3	Transferred to purchases account		L50	245

The posting of the purchases day book to the ledger is effected by transferring to the account of each supplier the value of the goods supplied in the period, and transferring the total value of all purchases in the period to the purchases account. The details entered in the day books are obtained from the invoices, which are carefully filed and kept for a period of about six years when they may be destroyed.

The sales day book is entered in the same manner as the purchases day book, except that the source document is the duplicate copy of the invoice sent to the customer.

The cash book

Only cash transactions are entered in the cash book, whose purpose it is to record all payments and receipts of cash. As we shall see later, the cash book has a dual role, for in addition to being a book of original entry, it is also part of the ledger.

As the practice grew of using cheques for the settlement of business debts, so the cash book came to reflect this practice, and to record all payments out and into the firm's bank account.

Unlike the day books, the cash book records receipts and payments side by side, so that concurrent flows in and out are seen together and their impact on the bank balance may be readily seen. At the end of the accounting period, the cash book is reconciled with the bank statement by means of a bank reconciliation statement which explains any difference between the balance recorded in the cash book and that recorded by the bank. This difference is invariably due to the time lag between the posting of a cheque to a creditor and its clearing through the bank, delays in clearing cheques paid in, bank charges and direct payments into and by the bank.

Where transactions take place in cash as well as by cheques, and trade discounts are given and allowed, the cash book is given extra columns, and becomes known as a 'three-column cash book'. The transfer of cash in and out of the bank account is recorded as well as the receipts and payments by cheques, as follows:

Cash book

Date	Details	Folio	Dis-counts all'd £	Cash £	Bank £	Date	Details	Folio	Dis-counts rec'd £	Cash £	Bank £
Jan. 1	Balance	J1		50	800	Jan. 1	B. Brown	L3	7		103
1	Sales	L15		60		1	Purchases	L14		20	
1	W. White	L9	5		95	1	Cash				20
1	Bank			20							

The explanation of some of these entries is as follows:

Jan. 1 B. Brown—this represents the payment of an account owing to Brown amounting to £110 which was settled by the payment of £103, the balance being in the form of a discount which was received.

Jan. 1 W. White—this represents the receipt of a cheque for £95 in settlement of an amount owing of £100, a discount of £5 being allowed.

Jan. 1 Bank—this represents a cash cheque drawn on the bank for £20. The corresponding payment of cash by the bank is shown on the other side of the cash book.

For security reasons, few firms like to keep large sums in cash about their premises and cash takings are banked daily. Moreover, it is sound practice to use cheques for the settlement of debts, so that there is generally no need to keep cash on hand beyond relatively small sums. All firms, therefore, tend to have a petty cash box to meet any immediate need for cash, for example, enabling a secretary or porter to take a taxi to deliver a document, or to buy a small article which is urgently required.

The cashier is usually entrusted with the petty cash box and any payments must be claimed by means of a petty cash voucher signed by an authorized person, who is usually a head of department. The cashier is given a petty cash float which may be say £50 and pays out petty cash only against petty cash vouchers, which he retains. As the petty cash float decreases, so petty cash vouchers of an equivalent value accumulate in the petty cash box. In due course, the vouchers are checked or audited and the petty cash paid out is refunded to the cashier, thereby restoring the petty cash float to its original sum.

The development of data processing systems

Although the system of source documents remains today much as we have described, two important developments have changed the nature of the system of recording financial transactions. The first of these developments is attributable to the mechanization of the record-keeping process, which began gradually with the use of early-generation calculating machines and progressed to the evolution of accounting machines capable of several operations simultaneously, and eventually to increasingly sophisticated electronic data processing systems based on computers. The second of these developments is attributable to the wish to integrate the data generating activities of the various departments of an organization within the scope of formalized management information systems. The availability of computers after the Second World War made such an integration possible, and as a result, encouraged the application of computerized information and control systems to the manifold problems of business organizations.

These twin developments acted jointly to produce a number of significant effects. Firstly, they greatly extended the utility of data by its dispersion through the organization, and at the same time, they reduced the duplication of data generation taking place in different departments. Secondly, the efficiency of the data generation process was increased by a progressive reduction in the stages involved, and the increase in the speed with which their operations could be performed. Thirdly, not only did these developments encourage a greater flexibility in the availability and utility of data, but they led to a massive expansion in the data coverage.

The recent history of data processing systems has emphasized the inter-dependency of all sectors of organizational activity, and the inter-dependency of their information needs. For this reason, the term 'integrated data processing' came into vogue in the 1950s to symbolize the nature of modern data systems.

The 'write-it-once' principle

The first development to which we referred is based, conceptually at least, on the 'write-it-once' principle, that is, the simultaneous production of source documents and the streamlining of the recording process. Hence, although the source documents which we mentioned earlier remain in common usage, they are no longer always prepared in the step-by-step manner which we described, being either prepared simultaneously or duplicated automatically.

The write-it-once principle is evident in the progressive stages in the development of data processing methods. Three examples of these developments are as follows:

(a) The development of multi-copy stationery involving the use of 'sets' of forms which may be separated once completed. An invoicing set would consist of a top copy, which would be the invoice itself, and beneath would be found the other source documents, that is, a copy of the invoice for accounting records, an advice note, a request to inventory control to release the goods for despatch and a packaging label. These 'flimsy' copies may be distinguished by a system of different colours.

(b) The simultaneous posting of data by means of 'writing boards' to which several records may be pegged and posted in one operation. Thus, once the sales invoice has been completed, the details may be posted immediately by pegging on the writing board the customer's monthly statement, his ledger account and the sales day book. These sheets are interleaved with carbon paper. The statement is then returned to the customer's file until further invoices need to be entered, and at the end of the month, it is sent to the customer. The ledger account is returned to the permanent file, and the sales day book may remain pegged so that invoices to other customers may be posted. Several writing boards may be in use at the same time. The advantages of this system are that the chances of posting errors are minimized with the reduction in stages in posting data, and documents such as statements are ready for despatch at the end of each month and do not require further attention, save actual mailing.

(c) The use of 'ledgerless book-keeping' involves the elimination of the traditional posting process mentioned above, thus streamlining the process. Consider for example the sales day book, which is simply an analysis of copy invoices. Its main purpose is to provide a total for posting to the ledger. It is possible to simplify and streamline the posting process simply by dispensing with the sales day book and relying on the copy invoices, which may be filed in specially made cabinets after they have been recorded in the ledger.

The process of ledgerless book-keeping may be extended further to provide for a degree of rationalization in the ledger itself. The debtors' ledger, for example, containing all the individual debtors' accounts may also be dispensed with by placing reliance on the record of transactions contained in copy sales invoices. These copy invoices may be filed in an 'unpaid invoices' cabinet. On receipt of payment, the invoice is removed from the 'unpaid invoices' cabinet, a remittance slip is made out, the payment is recorded directly in the cash book and the remittance slip is attached to the invoice which is subsequently filed in the 'paid invoices' cabinet.

According to Bower *et al.* (1970),

'A ledgerless bookkeeping system is one in which communication media are filed as records rather than being used as source documents from which to post to ledger accounts and other records. . . . Ledgerless bookkeeping applied to accounts receivable requires that at the time a sales invoice is prepared, an adequate number of copies of the invoice are made, including at least one accounts receivable copy. The accounts receivable copy is sent to the accounts receivable section where it is filed by customer name. At any given time, the unpaid invoices in the customer file can be totalled to determine the amount which customers owe to the company. When cash is received, the invoice is withdrawn and stamped paid, after which it is filed in a paid invoice file. . . . There is no more economical system than ledgerless bookkeeping. It is simple and can be effective'.

The mechanization of accounting

Clearly, the write-it-once principle made it possible for the accounting process to be mechanized. The first stage in this process was the evolution of accounting machines. Secondly, there followed punched card data processing systems. Thirdly, electronic data processing was made possible by the development of sophisticated digital computers.

(a) *Accounting machines*
In effect, accounting machines are a combination of a typewriter with an adding machine. Accounting machines were an improvement on the writing boards for instead of being handwritten, postings could be typed.

(b) *Punched card data systems*
Punched card systems rely on the use of cards for recording data. Cards are punched according to a code, and once they have been checked, they may be resorted to almost endlessly for the preparation of records, analyses, reports and statements.

Three basic steps are involved:

(i)   punching the required data on to cards
(ii)   sorting the cards into a desired order
(iii) tabulating the data recorded on the cards onto printed forms as required.

The most important element in punched card data systems is, of course, the punch card itself, of which an example is shown on page 82. The cards may be punched manually by means of a punch. The equipment required consists of a sorter and a tabulator.

As may be seen from Fig. 2.6, it is required to establish a code for the data to be punched on the card. This requires that 'fields' be defined on the card for particular types of data, and that sufficient space be provided for recording the data appropriate to the defined fields. A sales card, for example, may be designed to capture data which relates to dates, despatch points, invoice numbers, product groups, weight, sales value, customer, salesman etc. Such cards may be sorted at any time into groups for the purpose of tabulating specific information, such as sales by regions, sales by salesman, product sales analysis etc.

It is evident that punched card data systems are capable of much greater flexibility than conventional accounting systems, which are limited to recording financial transactions. Nevertheless, all typical accounting records and reports may be prepared from punched cards, as may be noted from Fig. 2.7. As may be seen, the data recorded on a sales invoice may be punched on to cards, which are tabulated so that the data recorded on them may be entered in the sales day book. Similarly, details of payments made by customers in respect of those sales invoices may be punched on other cards and the cash book may be completed on the basis of these cards. Both sets of cards may be merged by tabulation with the opening balances on each customer's account in the ledger, so that monthly statements may be prepared, the ledger

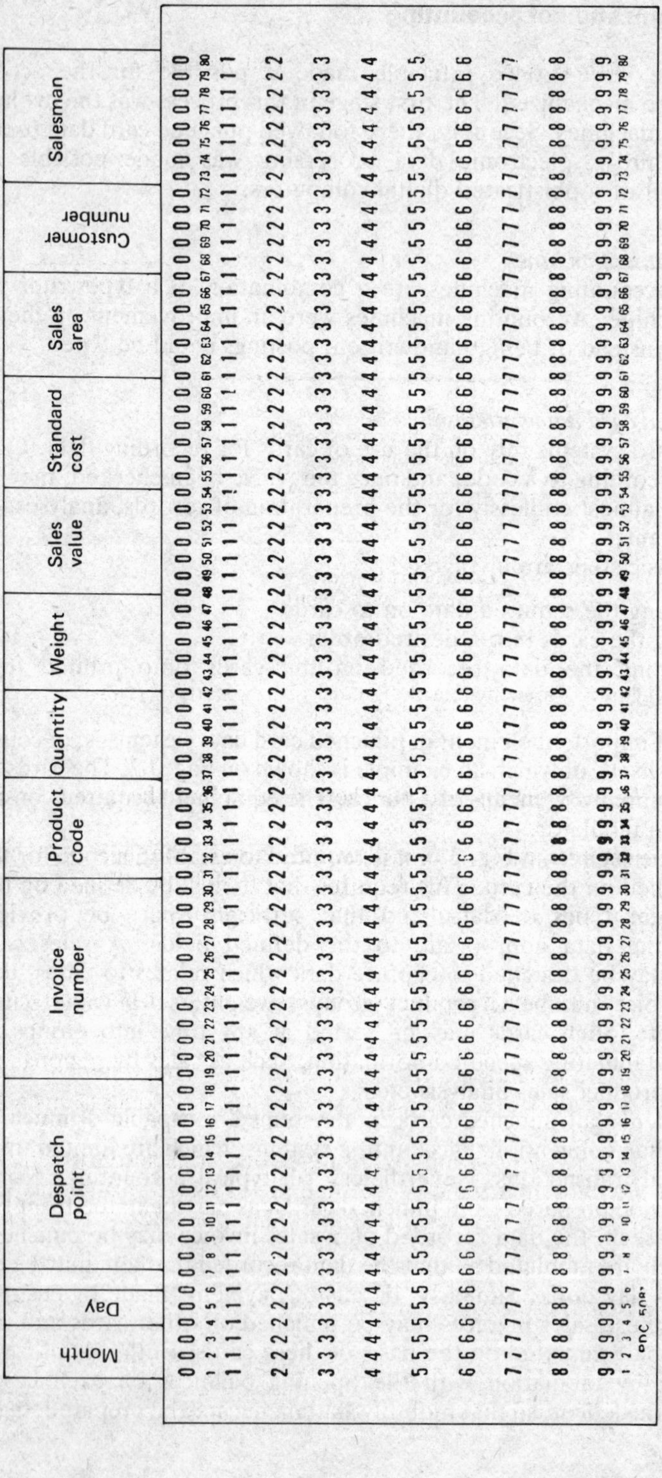
Month
Day
Despatch point
Invoice number
Product code
Quantity
Weight
Sales value
Standard cost
Sales area
Customer number
Salesman

Fig. 2.6.

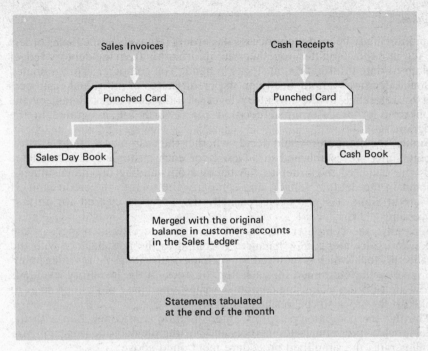

Fig. 2.7 Application of punched card systems to the record of sales.

account may be written up and the new balance on the account may be calculated.

Although punched cards are still widely used, the use of tabulating machines for processing punched cards has declined in popularity because of the advantages in this respect of computer applications.

(c) *Electronic data processing (EDP)*
The main advantages which digital computers enjoy over punched card data systems are as follows:

(i) Computers are much faster than punched card data systems.
(ii) Computers may store data and internalize the operations of data retrieval and analysis.
(iii) Computers may be programmed to make decisions automatically on the basis of the data input, and as we shall see in Part 5 this feature is most important as regards management planning and control.

The steps involved in developing a computer program are as follows:

(a) the problem must be stated in detail with reference to the stages in its solution;
(b) these stages are then stated in the form of a flowchart;
(c) the instruction is coded for the computer in accordance with the flowchart.

Example

Computers may be made to process sales orders relatively easily. Sales orders are fed into the computer, together with information from the debtors' ledger and up-to-date information on stocks in hand. The computer is programmed to make decisions automatically on the credit status of individual customers and by reference to the inventory level of individual stock items, by the application of predetermined decision rules which are integrated in the program.

Firstly, the computer would decide whether the customer is credit-worthy. Credit limits are established in advance for each customer. The computer adds the value of the order to the balance outstanding on the customer's account in the debtors' ledger, and compares the total to the credit limit. If the credit limit has not been reached, the order is cleared for further processing.

Secondly, the computer adjusts the inventory records in respect of the order and calculates a new balance. It compares the new balance with the balance in stock which is required for each particular item. A 're-order point' will have been determined for each item of stock. If the inventory level falls below the re-order point, the computer writes a purchase requisition so as to replenish the stock to the designated level.

Thirdly, the computer performs other operations in connection with the order, such as preparing sales invoices and posting the debtors' ledger. Figure 2.8 illustrates the simplified procedure mentioned above.

Figure 2.9 explains in detail the manner in which a computer may be programmed to determine the credit status of a customer.

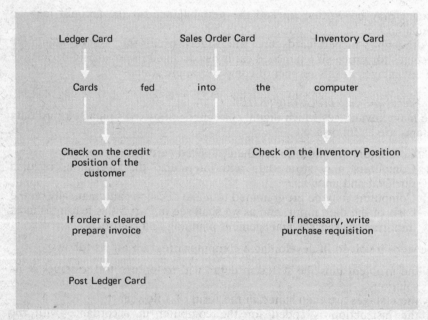

Fig. 2.8.

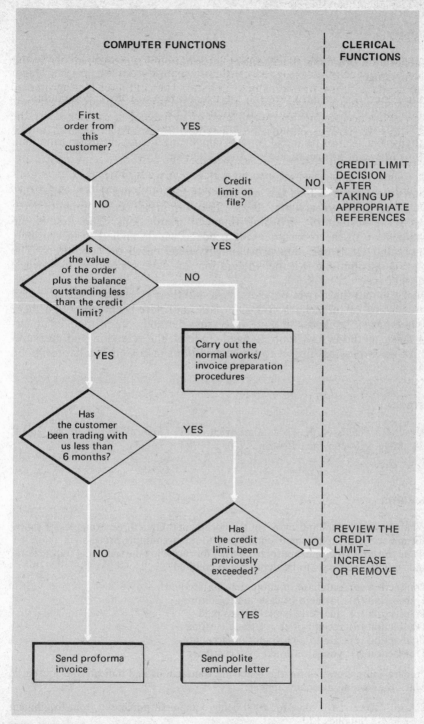

Fig. 2.9 Credit status test. (From Clifton, H. D. & Lucey, T., *Accounting and Computer Systems*, Business Books Ltd, London, 1973).

Summary

The generation of financial accounting information is a process involving the following stages:

(a) the generation of data through the preparation of source documents;
(b) the entry of basic data into subsidiary books;
(c) the posting of data from subsidiary books into the ledger;
(d) the production of financial reports converting financial information data into financial information.

This chapter is concerned principally with stages (a) and (b) above.

Source documents reflect the activities conducted by the firm, so that data flows correspond to activity flows. Two important developments have changed the system of recording financial transactions. The first is the mechanization of the record-keeping process, which has led to increasingly sophisticated electronic data processing systems based on computers. The second is attributable to the integration of data generated by several departments.

We examined these twin developments and their effects on the generation and recording of financial accounting data, and noted that, although there have been great advances in data processing methods, the principles underlying these methods have not changed. Indeed, the selection and measurement of data remains subject to the conventions discussed in Chapter 4.

Reference

Bower, J. B., Schlosser, R. E. & Zlatkovich, C. T. *Financial Information Systems*, p. 374, Allyn & Bacon Inc., Boston, 1970.

Questions

1. What do you understand by a 'source document'? Give three examples of source documents, and explain their importance to the accounting process.
2. Name the book of original entry to be used for recording the following transactions, and state the accounts to be debited and credited:

Transaction (a) purchase of equipment on account
Transaction (b) payment of cash to a creditor
Transaction (c) quarterly bank charges paid
Transaction (d) receipt of cash from a customer
Transaction (e) sale to a customer on account
Transaction (f) goods returned by a customer.

3. Prepare journal entries for the following transactions and indicate the journal in which they would normally appear:

1 April   Received invoice for £400 being equipment purchased from Equipment Supplies Ltd
2 April   Received invoice for £700 for goods supplied by Jones Ltd

4 April   Received cheque for £50 from J. Brown for goods supplied

Sent cheque to S. Supplier for £250 in payment of purchases effected in March

5 April   Received an invoice from Standfast Suppliers Ltd for goods supplied £800

6 April   Invoiced J. Shepherd for goods sold £98

7 April   Received a cheque for £70 from W. Smith in settlement of his account for goods sold

8 April   Received Rates Statement showing rates due £500

9 April   Banked weekly cash takings of £700

4. Show the following entries as they would appear in a three-column cash book:

1 May   Credit balance at bank £700, cash in hand £5

Cash drawn from bank for the till £30

Cheque sent to Brown for £67 in settlement of amount due of £70, discount being received for prompt payment

2 May   Received cheque from Jones for £45 in payment of invoiced amount of £47, less trade discount

3 May   Cash sales for the day £190

4 May   Banked cash sales of previous day £190

5 May   Sent cheque to Blewett £100 being instalment due on loan repayment

6 May   Took £10 out of the till for taxi fares

7 Data processing and double-entry book-keeping

We saw in the preceding chapter that financial accounting data has its source in original records of financial transactions. We noted two very important aspects of data generation in accounting. First, when reporting to external users, accounting information is presented in a form which is only concerned with the monetary aspect of a firm's activities. Hence, it ignores data which deals with the type and quantities of resources which the firm utilizes, the nature and the quantity of its products, and the quality and usefulness of those products to society. Equally, traditional accounting is not concerned with the activities of the firm as a social unit consisting of people whose livelihood and happiness depend on its financial success as well as the manner in which their working lives are organized. Nor, indeed, does accounting concern itself with the role and importance of a particular firm as regards society as a whole. Second, we noted that accounting conventions play a determining role as regards the nature and the quality of the data which accountants process.

The purpose of this chapter is to examine the structure which accounting has evolved for handling financial accounting data.

The accounting equation

Financial accounting is based on a simple notion known as the accounting equation. In effect, the accounting equation depicts the equality which exists between the resources owned by the enterprise and the claims against the enterprise in relation to those resources.

One side of the accounting equation expresses, in monetary terms, the resources held by the enterprise. These resources are known as 'assets'. The acquisition of assets by the enterprise will have been financed by funds provided either by the owner(s) or from borrowings. The funds provided by the owner(s) constitute the 'capital' of the enterprise. The funds borrowed constitute liabilities and are known as such. Therefore, the other side of the accounting equation describes how the acquisition of assets has been financed and the claims which exist against the business as a result.

The accounting equation may be stated as follows:

$$Capital + Liabilities = Assets$$

It will be evident that the concept underlying the accounting equation is that the enterprise itself is merely a vehicle through which assets are held and utilized, and that claims exist against those assets to their full monetary value. Given that liabilities arising from borrowings are stated as legal debts of determined monetary sums, the owners of the enterprise are entitled to the balance of the assets after liabilities have been settled. Accordingly, the accounting equation may be used to express the capital as follows:

$$\text{Capital} = \text{Assets} - \text{Liabilities}$$

It follows from our discussion in Chapter 4 that the balance sheet is founded on the accounting equation, for it is a list of the assets held by the enterprise against which is set a list of the claims existing against the enterprise. Both lists are equal in total.

Transactions and the accounting equation

Given that the balance sheet indicates the financial position of an enterprise at a given point in time, successive transactions would maintain the accounting equation on which the balance sheet rests, though its dimensions and its constituent elements would vary. It is possible to record the effects of successive transactions on the balance sheet equation.

Transaction 1. Returning to the example cited earlier (see page 48), where J. Soap invested £10,000 on 1 April 19X0 in a ladies hairdressing business. On 1 April 19X0, the opening transaction would be shown as follows:

Balance sheet 1

	£		£
Capital	10,000	Assets: Cash at bank	10,000

The manner in which the subsequent transactions affect the balance sheet through the accounting equation may be seen from the following examples:

Transaction 2. J. Soap paid the monthly rent for the business amounting to £500. This is an expense of the month. Its effect on the balance sheet is to reduce cash by £500, and at the same time reduce the capital by the same amount. The balance sheet after this transaction would appear as:

Balance sheet 2

	£		£
Capital	9500	Assets: Cash at bank	9500

Transaction 3. J. Soap purchased equipment for £2000 from Hairdressers' Supplies Ltd on credit. As a result of this transaction, a new asset appears on the balance sheet in the form of the equipment purchased, and a liability of £2000 is created in respect of the amount unpaid. The balance sheet now appears as follows:

Balance sheet 3

	£		£
Capital	9,500	Assets: Equipment	2,000
Liability:			
Account payable	2,000	Cash at bank	9,500
	11,500		11,500

It will be noted that, although the balance sheet totals increase by £2000, there is no change in the capital of the business. Instead, the balance sheet shows that the equipment purchased has been financed by a liability of exactly that amount.

Transaction 4. J. Soap paid salaries amounting to £200 in cash for part-time assistance. This is an expense of the month, and its effect on the balance sheet is to reduce cash by £200 and the capital by the same amount. The balance sheet now appears as follows:

Balance sheet 4

	£		£
Capital	9,300	Assets: Equipment	2,000
Liability:			
Account payable	2,000	Cash at bank	9,300
	11,300		11,300

Transaction 5. J. Soap's revenue from clients for the month of April amounted to £1500, of which £400 was received in cash. Clients who had accounts with him were charged a total of £1100, and at the end a sum of £100 remained outstanding in respect of these credit accounts. The effect of these transactions is to increase the capital by £1500 and to increase cash at bank by £1400. The amount outstanding of £100 requires a new asset account to be opened—Debtors—in the sum of £100. The balance sheet now appears as follows:

Balance sheet 5

	£		£
Capital	10,800	Assets: Equipment	2,000
Liability:		Account receivable	100
Account payable	2,000	Cash at bank	10,700
	12,800		12,800

Transaction 6. J. Soap withdraws cash in the sum of £400 for his own use. The effect of this withdrawal is to reduce capital by £400 and cash by the same amount. The withdrawal of cash from the business is the reverse of the first transaction in which J. Soap invested in the business. Consequently, the capital account is reduced by the amount of the withdrawal. The balance sheet now stands as follows:

Balance sheet 6

	£			£
Capital	10,400	Assets:	Equipment	2,000
Liability:			Account receivable	100
Account payable	2,000		Cash at bank	10,300
	12,400			12,400

Simplifying the recording of transactions

The process of drawing up a new balance sheet after each transaction would be an extremely cumbersome process in practice, given the large number of transactions which an enterprise may conduct daily. In effect, the problems which present themselves are threefold. First, how to calculate the effects of successive transactions in terms of the income they have generated? Such a calculation would explain why there occurred an increase in the capital from an original amount of £10,000 to £10,800, prior to the withdrawal made by J. Soap. Second, how to reflect the interest of the owner, J. Soap, in the business in a convenient manner? Such a calculation would involve summarizing the effects of transactions on the capital account as it stands at the end of the accounting period. Third, how to devise a system of recording transactions which avoids the necessity of drawing up successive balance sheets?

The first problem indicated above is resolved by summarizing all transactions associated with the income earning process during the period in a statement known as the income statement. Unlike the balance sheet, which states the financial position of the enterprise at different points in time, the income statement seeks to establish the success or failure of the enterprise in the result of transactions over a period of time. The preparation of the income statement involves identifying the revenues of the period, and the expenses which may properly be charged against these revenues. In the example of J. Soap above, the successive balance sheets for the month of April, which resulted in the increase in the capital account from £10,000 to £10,800 by balance sheet 5, may be summarized by an income statement for April 19X0 as follows:

J. Soap—Ladies Hairdresser
Income statement for April 19X0

	£	£
Revenue		1500
Expenses:		
Rent	500	
Salaries	200	700
Net income for April		800

The second problem mentioned above, namely portraying the interest of the owner of the business at the close of the accounting period, involves using both the income statement of the period and the balance sheet at the close of the period. In this respect, the income statement and the balance sheet complement each other. The income statement summarizes the operating results between two successive balance sheets, and these results are reflected in the capital shown on the closing balance sheet. The factors which have affected the value of the owner's capital at the date of the closing balance sheet may be summarized in a detailed statement of the capital account. As regards the example of J. Soap given above, the analysis of the capital account would be shown on the closing balance sheet as follows:

J. Soap—Ladies Hairdresser
Capital account as at 30 April 19X0

	£	£
Balance, 1 April 19X0		10,000
Net income for April	800	
Less: Drawings	400	400
Balance, 30 April 19X0		10,400

The third problem mentioned above, that of devising a system of recording transactions which avoids drawing up successive balance sheets, was resolved several centuries ago by the invention of the system of double-entry book-keeping.

The nature of double-entry book-keeping

The collection and recording of data is known as book-keeping. The practice of recording financial data in 'books' dates from a very long time ago. These books were usually 'bound books'— bound so as to prevent the possibility of fraud either by the insertion or the removal of pages. Nowadays, mechanical and electronic data processing have removed the book-keeper as a person concerned with entering the results of financial transactions into the 'books'. Instead, large firms have computerized the keeping of the 'books', and smaller firms use electronic accounting machines which make use of 'cards' which form parts of a 'bank' of cards. The only people nowadays who keep their financial records in bound books or ledgers are those whose businesses are on a very small scale.

The double-entry system of book-keeping remains, however, the basis for record-keeping regardless of whether or not a firm employs advanced electronic data processing (EDP) techniques, mechanical or manual methods. It remains, therefore, the logical method for recording financial information, and as such it is the basis of financial accounting practice.

The term 'double-entry' adds a special meaning to the process of book-keeping. It is a method of recording financial data as transactions involving flows of money or money value between different accounts. It involves a network of integrated accounts, in which an account is designated for each accounting item. The entries recorded on the successive balance sheets of J. Soap for April 19X0 would appear in a double-entry book-keeping system.

Transaction 1. The initial investment of £10,000 cash by J. Soap in the ladies hairdressing business would be shown as a flow of money from the capital account to the cash book, as follows:

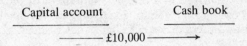

Capital account   Cash book

————— £10,000 —————→

Business transactions are represented in double-entry book-keeping as flows of money or money value as between the various accounts concerned, but clearly any one transaction involves only one flow, as shown above. In order to identify the direction of any one flow, all accounts are divided into two parts. A flow out of the account is recorded on the right-hand side, and a flow into an account is recorded on the left-hand side. Hence, the transaction shown above would appear as follows:

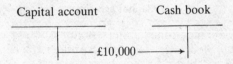

Capital account   Cash book

├——— £10,000 ———→|

Flows-out could conveniently be described by a minus sign, but the accounting convention which dates from the Italian origins of book-keeping utilizes the term *Credit* (Cr.), which means 'to give'. Likewise flows in could be described by a positive sign, but the accounting appellation is *Debit* (Dr.), which means 'to receive'. Hence, this additional information may be inserted in the accounts to identify the direction of the flow, and replacing the arrow which we have used up to now.

Capital account		Cash book	
	Cr. £10,000	Dr. £10,000	

There is now only one additional item of information which is required to identify the transaction flow, and that is, the point of origin and the point of destination. This, too, is made easy in book-keeping by the simple expedient of describing in the *Credited* account where the flow is going, and by inserting in the *Debited* account the source of the flow.

Capital account		Cash book	
	Cr. Cash £10,000	Dr. Capital £10,000	

In practice, accountants know very well that the left-hand side of an account is the debit side, and vice versa for the right-hand side, so that they do not head up the accounts with Dr. or Cr. In the old days, they used to add the word *By* on the narration of *Credit entries*, and *To* on the narration of *Debit entries*—but this too is unnecessary, and many accountants have abandoned this practice. The reader will occasionally find entries recorded as follows:

Capital account

	By cash	£10,000

Cash book

To capital	£10,000	

We shall not, however, use these superfluous terms. Lastly, the date of the transaction must be recorded, and it is done as follows:

Capital account

	19X0		
	1 April	Capital	£10,000

Cash book

19X0			
1 April	Capital	£10,000	

To simplify the exposition of the double-entry book-keeping system in the examples which follow, the dates will be omitted.

In the manner in which transactions are recorded under this method, the reader will have been quick to notice an important feature—the flow has remained constant in value as it has moved from the *credited* account to the *debited* account. As a result, double-entry book-keeping possesses a mathematical foundation which has its logic in the simple proposition that as regards any one transaction the *credit* must be equal to the *debit*. At any time, therefore, the arithmetical precision of the book-keeping process may be checked by adding up all the *debit* entries and all the *credit* entries. If the total *debit* entries do not equal, that is *balance* with the *credit* entries, there has been an error in the recording process. As we shall see on page 102, the *trial balance* is the means whereby accountants check for arithmetical errors in recording transactions. If the *trial balance* shows a difference as little as 1p between the *total debits* and the *total credits*, the error must be found. This is because accountants know that the result of a great many cumulative errors may boil down to a difference of only 1p.

The virtue of double-entry book-keeping is that it is a logical and precise system for recording financial transactions as flows of money or money value. It is easy to operate, and simple to adapt to modern computer methods by using positive and negative electric charges to signal whether an account should be *debited* or *credited*.

Transaction 2. The payment of rent in the sum of £500 by J. Soap is interpreted as a flow of money from the cash book to the rent account. It reduces cash by £500 and appears as an increase in the balance shown in the rent account by £500. The rent account is an 'expense' account which will be transferred later to the income statement for the purposes of calculating the net income for April. The entries will appear as follows:

Cash book				Rent account	
		£			£
	Rent	500	Cash		500

Transaction 3. The purchase of equipment in the sum of £2000 on credit by J. Soap from Hairdressers' Supplies Ltd does not involve the payment of cash, but requires the debt owing to Hairdressers' Supplies Ltd to be shown. This is effected by opening an account in the name of Hairdressers' Supplies Ltd showing a credit balance of £2000, being the sum owing to that company. The entries would be as follows:

Hairdressers' Supplies Ltd account		
		£
	Equipment	2000

Equipment account		
	£	
Hairdressers' Supplies Ltd	2000	

Transaction 4. The payment of £200 as wages for part-time assistance is another example of an expense account. Note that in the case of such expense accounts, the persons receiving payment are not named on the accounts themselves. Separate records would be kept in the form of a wage book, rent book, etc. The entries would be as follows:

Cash book				Wages account	
		£			£
	Wages	200	Cash		200

Transaction 5. The treatment of the revenue generated from the sale of hairdressing services involves two problems. First, the cash sales involving the receipt of cash amounting to £400 are entered directly as follows:

Sales account				Cash book	
		£			£
	Cash	400	Sales		400

The treatment of credit customers is rather more complex. First, the individuals concerned are shown in the debtors' ledger. The total amount of credit sales during the month amounting to £1100 appears in a summary account known as the debtors' account. The entries are as follows:

Sales account			Debtors' account	
	£			£
	Debtors 1100		Sales	1100

The payments effected by the debtors during the month totalled £1000, leaving an amount outstanding of £100 at the end of April and shown as follows:

Debtors' account				Cash book	
	£		£		£
Sales	1100	Cash	1000	Debtors	1000
		Balance	100		
	1100		1100		

In effect, these various entries would appear as follows:

Sales account			Cash book	
	£			£
Cash	400	Sales		400
Debtors	1100	Debtors		1000

Debtors' account			
	£		£
Sales	1100	Cash	1000
		Balance	100
	1100		1100

Transaction 6. J. Soap withdrew £400 for his personal use in cash. This transaction, which reduces his capital account by £400, could be entered directly as follows:

Capital account				Cash book	
	£		£		£
Cash	400	Balance	10,000	Capital	400

The effect of this transaction would be to reduce the capital account by £400 to £9600. This reduction could be shown as follows:

Capital account			
	£		£
Cash	400	Balance b/d	10,000
Balance	9600		
	10,000		10,000

In order to avoid making too many entries in the capital account in respect of regular withdrawals by the owner of a business, the normal practice is to show withdrawals in a separate drawings account. At the end of the accounting period, the drawings account is transferred in total to the capital account, so that there is only one entry made in respect of drawings. Using the drawings account, the withdrawal of £400 would be shown as follows:

Drawings account		Cash book	
	£		£
Cash	400	Drawings	400

Double-entry book-keeping as a 'closed' system

We noted in Part 1 that the term 'system' is commonly used to mean any unit which may be identified as an independent whole, having its own objectives and its own internal functions. An 'open' system is one whose behaviour is affected by external factors. The British economy, for example, is an 'open system' because it is affected by its trading relationships with the rest of the world. A 'closed' system is one in which all the functions are internalized in the system, and are not affected by outside factors. Double-entry book-keeping has the characteristics of a closed system in that all the transactions which are recorded take place within the accounts system. By this we mean that all flows resulting from transactions are depicted as having their origin in an account which is found in the system, and they have their destination in another account which is in the system. It is quite impossible for a flow to originate from an account outside the accounts system. Likewise, it is impossible for a flow of money or of money value to go to an account outside the accounts system.

Example

Let us go back to the example given above. J. Soap opens up a business under the name of 'J. Soap—Ladies Hairdresser'. He invests £10,000 in cash into the business. The effect of the entity convention is to require J. Soap to open and to keep separate books for the business of J. Soap—Ladies Hairdresser, which is regarded in accounting as a separate entity from J. Soap himself. Double-entry book-keeping gives expression to the entity convention since all the accounts of J. Soap—Ladies Hairdresser relate only the financial transactions of that business. To all intents and purposes, J. Soap himself is an external party as far as the business is concerned.

The question is—how can we depict the flow of £10,000 from J. Soap into the business? Now, we have said that no flow may originate from outside the accounts system. Hence, we must have an account within the accounts system whence it has originated. That account is the account of J. Soap himself in his capacity as owner of the business, which we described above as the *capital* account. The source of the flow of £10,000 is therefore found in the *capital* account, and its destination is the *cash* account.

Capital account

		£
	19X0	
	1 April	10,000

Cash book

19X0		£	
1 April	Capital	10,000	

Let us suppose, for a moment, that on 2 April, Joe Soap decides that he has put too much money in the business and wishes to take out £3000. In the accounts system, the transaction could be shown as follows:

Capital account

		£			£
19X0			19X0		
2 April	Cash	3000	1 April	Cash	10,000

Cash book

		£			£
19X0			19X0		
1 April	Capital	10,000	2 April	Capital	3000

The significance of these entries reflects the fact that accounting is not concerned with the destination of the actual sums of money, but simply portraying the full transaction as a *record* of the flow of money. Successive entries are made in accounts which have been opened, and where a transaction involves a new account, then that account is opened. Likewise, if an account is no longer needed, it may be closed.

The implications of these statements as far as book-keeping being a closed system of accounts are:

(1) The book-keeping system of any firm is infinitely elastic in size. As many accounts are opened as are necessary to record in full the transactions which have taken place. It is not surprising, therefore, that large businesses have many thousands of accounts. Prior to the development of accounting machines and computers, these firms needed a very large accounting staff to cope with this work alone. Electronic data processing has had a revolutionary impact on this aspect of the work of the accountant.

(2) All the accounting flows of money or of money value take place between the various accounts found in the system. The accounts system, therefore, consists of a set of 'interlocking accounts'.

(3) The accounts themselves represent 'realities'—whether they are persons or assets involved in transactions.

(4) Firms are continually involved in transactions: this activity is mirrored in the constant flow of money and of money value in the accounts system.

(5) Since all the flows have both their source and their destination in the

accounts to be found in the system, the total *debits* and the total *credits* remain equal at all times.

Accounts as descriptions of transactions

We have already noted that the accounts system is used to describe the direction of a flow of money or of money value, as well as the timing of the flow. Business transactions affect a firm in different ways: some are concerned with the acquisition of assets to be used in earning profits, others concern the supply of capital to the firm, either by the owner or by lenders, others relate to goods purchased or sold to persons so that the exchange of goods expressed as money value creates rights or liabilities in money terms, and others yet relate to revenues and costs.

If a firm is to make any sense of the large number of accounts which are kept, some grouping of accounts is necessary, so that accounts of the same business nature are kept together. The integration of accounts into groupings enables the accountant to extract the information which he needs with much greater ease. For example, to find out how much is owed to persons by the business, the accountant has merely to go to the accounts of the *creditors*. This term means that such persons have been the source of a flow of money, or of money value to the firm, and have not been repaid. Likewise, the *debtors'* accounts are referred to to find out how much is owing to the business by those people who have received money or money value and have not settled their account.

Transactions frequently involve two different classes of accounts, and indeed may affect more than two accounts.

Example

J. Soap supplies hairdressing services to Mrs B. Brown and her two unmarried daughters, to the value of £20 on 1 April 19X0. In the accounts of J. Soap, the transaction will be shown as a flow of money value (goods) from the sales account, which is a nominal account to Mrs B. Brown's account, which is a personal account.

Sales account

	19X0	£
	1 April Mrs B. Brown	20

Mrs B. Brown account

19X0	£	
1 April Sales	20	

Since Mrs Brown has received money value from J. Soap she is a *debtor* to the amount of £20. At the end of the month, J. Soap will send her a statement showing that £20 is now due for payment. Mrs B. Brown sends her cheque for £20, which will be banked on 1 May. This is shown as another transaction, which is the settlement of a debt, as follows:

Mrs B. Brown account

19X0		£	19X0		£
1 April	Sales	20	1 May	Cash	20

Cash book

19X0		£	
1 May	Mrs. B. Brown	20	

Thus, this transaction is one between a *personal* account and a *real* account. At this point, we may make two interesting observations:

(a) A 'credit' transaction is treated as a flow of money value to or from a personal account, and involves the creation of a debt towards the business, or a liability against the business. Hence, the use of the terms *debtor* and *creditor* respectively to denote the nature of such legal rights.

(b) The payment of a debt, or of a liability, involves another accounting transaction which records the flow of money from or to the appropriate personal account to or from the cash book. In this connection, the cash book records all the money flows through the firm's account at its bank.

The mathematical implications of double-entry book-keeping

We have already noted that the arithmetical correctness of the entries made in the accounts may be verified by means of a trial balance which involves comparing the total debit flows with the total credit flows.

During any accounting period, there may have been several entries in an individual account, so that several debits and several credits may be shown. A simple calculation may be made to calculate the net balance, for the purpose of the trial balance itself, and to ascertain the net state of the account.

Example

In the foregoing example several cash transactions took place during the month of April, as follows:

Cash book

	£		£
Capital	10,000	Rent	500
Sales	400	Wages	200
Debtors	1,000	Drawings	400

If we wished to extract the *balance* on the cash book, the procedure for so doing is simply to add up both sides of the account and to calculate the difference. This difference is known as the *balance*.

Cash book

	£		£
Capital	10,000	Rent	500
Sales	400	Wages	200
Debtors	1,000	Drawings	400
		Balance	10,300
	11,400		11,400

This balance represents the excess of the debit entries over the credit entries, and it represents also the fact that there remains £10,300 in cash. In order to show this fact in the account after it has been balanced, the *balance* is brought down as a *debit balance*.

Cash book

	£		£
Capital	10,000	Rent	500
Sales	400	Wages	200
Debtors	1000	Drawings	400
		Balance c/d	10,300
	11,400		11,400
Balance b/d	10,300		

Balancing the accounts is the first stage in preparing the trial balance. Some accounts will have *debit* balances and others will have *credit* balances. When we compare the total balances, they should be equal.

The trial balance

The trial balance is merely a list of the balances extracted from all the accounts arranged in such a way that the debit balances are listed on one side and the credit balances on the other side.

Example

The following trial balance was extracted on 30 April 19X0 from the books of Joe Soap—Ladies Hairdresser:

Trial balance as on 30 April 19X0

	Debit balances	Credit balances
	£	£
Capital account on 1 April 19X0		10,000
Drawings	400	
Cash	10,300	
Rent	500	
Wages	200	
Equipment	2,000	
Sales		1,500
Debtors	100	
Creditors		2,000
	13,500	13,500

The trial balance not only serves to act as a check on the mathematical correctness of the book-keeping process, but it is a summary of the balances of all the accounts, which, as we shall see in the next chapter, serves as a working paper in the course of preparing financial statements. We may note that in the process of summarizing information for the purpose of the trial balance, the personal accounts of the debtors and the creditors have been totalled.

The trial balance will not reveal the following types of errors:

(a) Errors of omission, where a transaction has been completely over-looked.

(b) Errors of principle, where an amount is correctly recorded but it is placed in the wrong class of account—for example, where the purchase of equipment is shown under purchases rather than under equipment.

(c) Errors of commission, where an amount is correctly recorded in the right class of account, but is entered in the wrong account—for example, where a sale of £50 to Mr B. Brown is entered in Mrs B. Brown's account.

(d) Errors of original entry—where the transaction is recorded in the wrong amount—for example, where a sale to Mrs B. Brown of goods to the value of £20 is recorded as £2.

(e) Errors in recording the direction of the flow—where the correct account is recorded but instead of being shown, for example, as a debit to the cash book and a credit to Mrs B. Brown's account it is shown the other way round.

(f) Compensating errors which cancel each other out will not be revealed. Thus, an error in adding up the trade debtors which is cancelled out by a similar error in adding up the trade creditors will not be revealed.

Summary

The evolution of double-entry book-keeping has provided accounting with a method of processing data in a systematic manner, and with a means of checking the accuracy of accounting records which was built into its processes by virtue of the interlocking nature of the accounts system. At the end of an accounting period, it is axiomatic that the total debit entries must be equal to the total credit entries.

With the advent of computerized accounting systems, and the widespread use of accounting machines, the usefulness of the double-entry method as a check on the accuracy of record-keeping has largely disappeared. Nevertheless, double-entry book-keeping remains the basis for recording financial transactions as flows of money, or of money value from one account to another, whether or not the accounts system is computerized.

Far more significant, however, as regards the usefulness of the data recorded in the double-entry system are the effects of accounting conventions, which require in particular that the values recorded should be determined by transactions.

Questions

1. Show the effects of the following transactions on the accounting equation. For this purpose, enter these transactions in columns as under:

Col. 1 Capital	+	*Col. 2* Liabilities	=	*Col. 3* Assets
....		....		....
....		....		....

Transaction (*a*) J. Johnson opens a garage by investing £20,000 in cash in the business

Transaction (*b*) he borrows £5000 from the bank

Transaction (*c*) he purchases petrol for £1000 and pays in cash

Transaction (*d*) he buys equipment to the value of £10,000 and agrees to pay that sum within four weeks

Transaction (*e*) he purchases second-hand cars from Middleton Motors and pays £15,000, being the agreed amount

Transaction (*f*) customers pay £2000 for services rendered

Transaction (*g*) wages paid amount to £1000.

2. Show the accounting effects of the following transactions by reference to the balance sheet and the income statement. (Example: cash sale £200 would add £200 to revenue on the income statement and £200 to the asset cash on the balance sheet.)

Transaction	Accounting effects	
	Balance sheet	*Income statement*
Cash sales £400	....	
Cash purchases £75	....	
Received from trade debtor £35	....	
Equipment purchased on credit terms £345	....	
Invoice received for repairs to machinery £67	....	
Wages paid £78	....	
Payment of rent due last month £90	....	
Equipment sold as scrap £20	....	
Loan received £600	....	
Bank interest charged £49	....	

3. Bill Cashing sets up practice as an architect, investing £10,000 of his own money into the business and effecting a transfer of that sum from his personal account to his business account at the Midland Bank Ltd. The transfer is effected on 1 January 19X0, the date on which he formally commenced. The following transactions took place in the following month:

1 January	Paid office rent for January £200
1 January	Purchased office equipment on account from Equipit Ltd £1000
1 January	Purchased office supplies on account from W. Brown for £150
3 January	Hired a junior out of school
4 January	Surveyed a property for A. Bond and sent out an invoice for £50
7 January	Decided that he should transfer his own car to the business at a value of £2000
10 January	Bought petrol for £10
11 January	Took a client to lunch at a cost of £20, and was asked to prepare plans for a new factory for which work he estimated he would earn £1200
17 January	Conducted another property survey for A. Bond and invoiced him for £60
20 January	Took another prospective client to lunch at a cost of £30, and found that he would not be able to undertake work for that client
30 January	Paid the office junior his monthly wage of £70
30 January	Sent a cheque to Equipit Ltd for £1000
30 January	Sent a cheque to W. Brown for office supplies £150
30 January	Banked a cheque received from A. Bond for £50

Required:

Enter these transactions in Bill Cashing's accounting records, and test the arithmetical accuracy of your work by preparing a trial balance when you have completed the entries needed to be made.

4. As at 31 December 19X0, the accountant of AB Ltd extracted a trial balance from the firm's accounting records and, there being a difference, inserted a balancing figure in a suspense account.

   Later, it was found that:

(i) a payment of £150 for stationery in the cash book had been posted in the ledger as £50;

(ii) a total of £637 in the sales day book had been carried forward as £673;

(iii) an amount of £60 paid to S. Jones on 2 January 19X1 had been included in the purchase ledger balances shown in the trial balance;

(iv) goods which cost £75 had been returned to R. Brown and, whilst a correct entry had been made in the purchases returns book, £175 had been posted to the credit of R. Brown's account in the sales ledger;

(v) at the beginning and end of the accounting period inventory was valued at £1250 and £2250 respectively. In error, the latter figure had been shown in the trial balance;

(vi) discounts allowed amounting to £325 had been credited to the appropriate nominal ledger account;

(vii) £256, being the amount of discounts received, had been debited to the nominal ledger as £265;

(viii) cash at bank was shown in the trial balance as £350. In fact this was the balance shown by the bank passbook which on 31 December 19X0 was £20 in excess of the bank balance correctly recorded in the cash book.

After rectification of the above discrepancies the books balanced.

Required:

Show journal entries necessary to correct the above errors and set out the suspense account as it would finally appear in the books.

Section 2 Periodic measurement

8 Double-entry book-keeping and periodic measurement

In the previous chapter, we examined the double-entry method as a means of recording financial transactions as flows of money or of money value. We said that firms are continually involved in transactions, and that this activity is mirrored in the double-entry book-keeping process by the constant flow through the accounts system of the money or money values involved in those transactions.

The accounts system is merely a repository of financial data about transactions. To be meaningful, this data must be extracted from the accounts system and organized in such a way that it is useful to those who need information for decision making. The convention of periodicity which we mentioned in Chapter 4 represents the view that, although the activities of a firm continue through time so that the decisions taken at one point in time cannot be separated from their effects whenever they materialize, those activities should nevertheless be regularly assessed. In other words, the financial health of a business should be tested at periodic intervals. The convention of periodicity poses problems in adapting the data recorded in the accounts system so that it will correctly reflect the result of the transactions concluded in the selected period, and the financial health of the firm at the end of that period. The two accounting statements which are employed for this purpose are the income statement for the year, and the balance sheet as at the end of the year.

The purpose of this chapter is to examine the preliminary stages in the preparation of these statements.

Problems in periodic measurement

The reader will recall that when we discussed the convention of periodicity in Chapter 4, we noted that not only should the transactions of a period be identified, but also that the expenses attributable to those transactions should be matched with the revenues derived from them in accordance with the matching convention.

The first major problem, therefore, in adapting the information recorded in the accounts system has a two-fold aspect:

(a) to identify the revenues attributable to transactions concluded during the year;
(b) to identify the expenses related to those revenues.

The second major problem concerns other adjustments which must be made in order to arrive at a measure of the surplus or deficit of revenues over expenses. These adjustments involve an element of judgement, for example, how much to write off in respect of depreciation and bad debts, and what adjustments to make in respect of expected losses. We are required to make such adjustments because the end-product is intended to be a statement of the income or loss made in the accounting period. We shall consider these problems in the next chapter.

The idea of periodic measurement which underlies financial reporting presents complex problems, and we have devoted much of Part 3 to the analysis of these problems.

Identifying the revenues and expenses of the period

The data recorded in the accounts system provides the basis for identifying the revenues and expenses of an accounting period. Firstly, we need to extract from the accounts system the data recorded in respect of all the transactions concluded in the period. We saw in Chapter 7 that the summary of all the transactions is obtainable by means of a trial balance drawn up on the last day of the accounting period.

Example

The following trial balance was extracted from the books of John Smith on 31 December 19X0, being the end of the first year of trading.

	£ Dr.	£ Cr.
Capital		25,000
Motor vehicles	10,000	
Furniture and fittings	2,500	
Purchases	31,000	
Cash at bank	6,000	
Sales		70,000
Sundry debtors	18,000	
Sundry creditors		3,500
Rent	4,500	
Salaries	22,800	
Insurances	400	
Motor expenses	2,000	
Light and heat	1,000	
General expenses	300	
	98,500	98,500

The meaning of revenue and expense

The trial balance does not make any distinction between flows of income and flows of capital, neither does it make a distinction between expenditure incurred to earn revenue and expenditure on the acquisition of assets. The first problem is to identify the revenues of the year, and this is a matter of definition. By revenue we mean the flows of funds, that is money or rights to money, which have resulted from the trading activities of the business, as distinct from funds (capital) invested by the owner or loans made by creditors and others. In this case, the only revenue item shown on the trial balance is the revenue from sales amounting to £70,000. The second problem is to identify the expenses. We define expenses as the costs of running the business during the accounting period. By contrast, capital expenses are the costs incurred in acquiring fixed assets or adding to the income-earning structure of the firm. The calculation of periodic income is by means of a formula which deducts expenses from revenues:

Periodic income = Revenues − Expenses

Looking at the trial balance, the expenses of the year, as defined, are as follows:

	£
Purchases	31,000
Rent	4,500
Salaries	22,800
Insurances	400
Motor expenses	2,000
Light and heat	1,000
General expenses	300

An alternative way of defining expenses, which is the definition adopted by accountants, is to treat as expenses all those costs the benefit of which has been exhausted during the year. Looking at the expenses which we have identified in the trial balance, it is clear that the benefit derived by the firm from expenditure on these items is limited to the accounting period. The only exception is the goods purchased which have not been sold by the end of the year, and we shall discuss this problem in Chapter 10.

We have completed, therefore, the first stage in periodic measurement by identifying the revenue and expenses attributable to the 'income-earning' transactions of the firm during the year, which we may list as follows:

	£		£
Purchases	31,000	Sales	70,000
Rent	4,500		
Salaries	22,800		
Insurance	400		
Motor expenses	2,000		
Light and heat	1,000		
General expenses	300		

Periodic measurement and the accrual convention

The next task of the accountant is to verify that the revenues and expenses are attributable to the accounting period. It is the normal practice to record in the expense accounts those amounts actually paid during the period. As a result, at the end of the period, these accounts may be understated or overstated. Likewise, it is possible that there may be some outstanding revenue due to the business, other than sales revenue, which must be brought into the year's income.

The governing principle which affects these adjustments is the accrual convention which we discussed in Chapter 4. The accrual convention, it will be recalled, makes a distinction between the receipt of cash and the right to receive cash, and the payment of cash and the legal obligation to pay cash. As there is often no coincidence in time between the creation of legal rights and obligations and the transfer of cash, it follows that the accountant must scrutinize the revenue and expenses accounts to make sure that amounts due and payable are accrued. Similarly, any payments made in advance must be excluded and carried forward to the next accounting period. The adjustments are effected in the accounts themselves.

The accrual of income

At the end of an accounting period, the total sales income for the year will have been recorded already in the accounts system, and the amounts unpaid by customers in respect of these sales will have been included under sundry debtors. The outstanding income which may not already have been recorded is limited, therefore, to income other than sales, such as rent receivable, commissions receivable etc. The accountant must adjust his end-of-year figures so as to include all the income to which the business is legally entitled, even though it has not been received.

Example

On 1 December 19X0, John Smith had sub-let a portion of his premises, which had never been utilized, for a monthly rent of £60 payable in advance on the 1st of each month. By 31 December 19X0, the date on which the trial balance was extracted, the rent receivable had not yet been received. To accrue the rent receivable, the accountant must enter the amount accrued in the rent receivable account as follows:

Rent receivable account

	19X0	£
	31 Dec. Accrued	60

This amount is taken to the income statement as income for the year 19X0, and at the same time is brought down as a debt due to the business by being shown as a *debit balance*.

Rent receivable account

19X0	£	19X0	£
31 Dec. Income statment	60	31 Dec. Accrued c/d	60
	60		60

19X1
1 Jan. Accrued b/d 60

Students are often puzzled that rent receivable should be a credit flow. The reason is that the rent receivable account is used to denote the source of a flow of funds so that there is a flow out from the rent receivable account into the cash account. Let us assume that on 1 January 19X1, the rent outstanding is paid. The entries would be as follows:

Rent receivable account

19X1	£	19X1	£
1 Jan. Accrued b/d	60	1 Jan. Cash	60

Cash book

19X1	£		
1 Jan. Rent receivable	60		

In adjusting the receipts for the year so that they will correctly show the income of the year, the accountant accrues income not yet received, as we have seen above, but also carries forward to the following year any receipts of the current year which are the income of the following year.

If, however, there had been an omission of income from the accounts of the preceding year, and this income is received in the current year, it would be impossible to go back and adjust the accounts of the previous year. Those accounts will have been closed at the end of that accounting period. The accountant will include last year's income in the current year's income, and indicate that it was an omission from last year, or explain how this income arose. Adjustments of this nature often arise out of the settlement of legal disputes or compensation claims.

The accrual of expenses

The accrual of expenses occurs far more frequently than the accrual of income, for it is the nature of things that businessmen tend to delay the payment of expenses. As a result, nominal accounts such as rent, insurance, wages, light and heat etc., require to be adjusted so as to show the total payments due and payable in respect of the accounting year. Occasionally, however, firms are obliged to pay in advance for services, so that there is a possibility that a portion of the payment relates to the next accounting period.

We may say, therefore, that the accrual of expenses involves two types of adjustments:

(a) an accrual in respect of expenses of the year which have not yet been paid;
(b) an exclusion from the recorded expenses of that part which relates to the next year.

Example

Let us return to the trial balance extracted from John Smith's books. We are informed that:

(a) The yearly rent is £6000 payable quarterly. The quarterly rent of £1500 payable on 1 December had not been paid.

(b) Insurance premiums paid amounting to £400 included a payment of £50 in respect of a new policy taken out on 31 December 19X0.

It is clear, therefore, that the legal obligation in respect of the rent is understated in the rent account by £1500. Equally, the insurance premiums applicable to the year ended 31 December 19X0 amount to £350 and not £400. It is necessary to adjust these accounts as follows:

(a) to increase the rent chargeable as an expense by £1500;

(b) to decrease the insurance chargeable as an expense by £50.

Underpayment of rent
Let us assume that the rent payments were made on due date as follows:

Rent account

19X0		£
1 Feb.	Cash	1500
1 May	Cash	1500
1 Aug.	Cash	1500

The amount which should be charged against the income for the year ended 31 December 19X0 is £6000. The rent unpaid at the 31 December 19X0 may be accrued as follows:

Rent account

19X0		£
1 Feb.	Cash	1500
1 May	Cash	1500
1 Aug.	Cash	1500
31 Dec.	Accrued	1500

Having made this adjustment, the rent account for the year ended 31 December 19X0 may be closed by transferring the rent of £6000 to the income statement for the year ended 31 December 19X0. The rent unpaid is, of course, a liability of the firm on the 31 December 19X0, and this is shown by bringing down the amount accrued as a *credit* balance on the rent account. The adjusted rent account will appear as follows:

Rent account

19X0		£	19X0	£
1 Feb.	Cash	1500	31 Dec. Income statement	6000
1 May	Cash	1500		
1 Aug.	Cash	1500		
31 Dec.	Accrued			
	c/d	1500		
		6000		6000
			19X1	
			1 Jan. Accrued b/d	1500

We note that the rent outstanding at 31 December 19X0 is £1500, and we have brought this amount down to show:

(a) that there is a *credit* balance outstanding at 31 December 19X0;
(b) that on 1 January 19X1 there is an outstanding liability in respect of the previous year, so that the firm will have to pay £7500 during the year ended 31 December 19X1

The trial balance on 31 December 19X0 may now be adjusted as follows:

	£	£
Rent	6000	
Rent accrued		1500

If the firm pays the rent outstanding on 2 January 19X1, and thereafter pays the rent on due date, the rent account for the year 19X1 will appear as follows:

Rent account

19X1		£	19X1	£
2 Jan.	Cash	1500	1 Jan. Accrued b/d	1500
1 Feb.	Cash	1500	31 Dec. Income statement	6000
1 May	Cash	1500		
1 Aug.	Cash	1500		
1 Dec.	Cash	1500		
		7500		7500

Prepayment of insurance
Let us assume that the insurance premiums were paid in advance as follows:

1 January 19X0	£350
31 December 19X0	50
	£400

These transactions will be shown in the insurance account as under:

Insurance account

19X0		£	
1 Jan.	Cash	350	
31 Dec.	Cash	50	

The premium paid on 31 December 19X0 is the *prepayment* of an expense for the year ending 31 December 19X1. Hence, it cannot be shown as an expense for the year ended 31 December 19X0. Thus the purpose of the adjustment is:

(a) to measure the expense applicable to the year ended 31 December 19X0, and to transfer this amount to the income statement for that year;
(b) to carry forward the premium paid in advance to the following year.

The adjusted account will appear as follows:

Insurance account

19X0		£	19X0	£
1 Jan.	Cash	350	31 Dec. Income statement	350
31 Dec.	Cash	50	31 Dec. Prepaid c/d	50
		400		400
19X1				
1 Jan.	Prepaid b/d	50		

We may note that the insurance prepaid at 31 December 19X0 is brought down as a *debit* balance on 1 January 19X1, and as a result:

(a) there is a *debit* balance in favour of the firm on 31 December 19X0;
(b) the firm will not have to pay the premium of £50 in the subsequent year, if the yearly premium is only due and payable on 1 January each year.

The trial balance on 31 December 19X0 may now be adjusted as follows:

	£	£
Insurance	350	
Insurance prepaid	50	

Assuming that the firm pays the insurance premium in the following year on due date, the insurance account for that year will be as follows:

Insurance account

19X1		£	19X1	£
1 Jan.	Prepaid b/d	50	31 Dec. Income statement	400
1 Jan.	Cash	350		
		400		400

The reader will have observed how easily the accounts system permits the adjustments made in respect of the accruals of revenue and expenses to be reconciled with the subsequent receipts and payment of cash. Although we have interfered with the recording process in order to adjust the accounts so as to reflect the true picture at the end of the accounting period, the double-entry system continues to record the accounting flows and is not itself affected by the adjustments which have been made.

The results of the accrual adjustments

The reader will recall that the trial balance is merely a working paper which the accountant uses to extract the information which he requires from the accounts system, and to check its accuracy. We may alter the original details shown on the first trial balance to reflect the adjustments which we have so far made.

Example

The adjusted trial balance for John Smith's business as at 31 December 19X0 may be set out as follows:

	£ Dr.	£ Cr.
Capital		25,000
Motor vehicles	10,000	
Furniture and fittings	2,500	
Purchases	31,000	
Cash at bank	6,000	
Sales		70,000
Sundry debtors	18,000	
Sundry creditors		3,500
Rent	6,000	
Rent accrued		1,500
Insurance	350	
Insurance prepaid	50	
Salaries	22,800	
Motor expenses	2,000	
Light and heat	1,000	
General expenses	300	
Rent receivable		60
Rent receivable	60	
	100,060	100,060

The effect of these adjustments on the revenues and expenses for the year ended 31 December 19X0 may be summarized as follows:

	£		£
Purchases	31,000	Sales	70,000
Rent	6,000	Rent receivable	60
Salaries	22,800		
Insurance	350		
Motor expenses	2,000		
Light and heat	1,000		
General expenses	300		

It will be noted also that the adjustments have given rise to the following balances on the accounts:

			£	£
Rent accrued	—	Credit balance		1,500
Insurance prepaid	—	Debit balance	50	
Rent receivable	—	Debit balance	60	

As these balances represent sums owing by the business and debts due to the business, they will be shown, as we shall see in Chapter 10, as liabilities and assets respectively at the end of the accounting period.

The matching of revenues and expenses

The purpose underlying the accountant's effort to identify and correctly measure the revenues and expenses of an accounting period is to attempt to match them so as to obtain a measure of the 'financial effort' of earning the revenues of that period. The accountant's concern is always with financial efficiency which he equates with income. The matching of expenses and revenues is far more complicated than appears at first sight. So far, we have assumed that by correctly measuring the revenues and expenses attributable to the accounting year they have been correctly matched. In other words, we have made the assumption that the expenses of the accounting period are the expenses related to the revenues of that period. The realization convention permits the accountant to recognize only financial results in the form of sales revenues. It is well known, of course, that there is a time-lag between buying or manufacturing goods for sale and actually selling those goods. At the end of an accounting period, therefore, there will always be goods awaiting sale and raw materials unused. The expenses attributable to unsold goods and unused materials, usually described as inventories, must be excluded from the expenses of the period and carried forward to the next accounting period, when the goods will have been sold and the materials used. The importance of inventory adjustments to the correct measurement of periodic income is crucial.

Inventory adjustments

By definition, the closing inventory at the end of an accounting period is the residue of the purchases of that period which remains unsold or unused.

Example

John Smith's purchases account includes all goods purchased during the year ended 31 December 19X0. At the end of the year, the inventory of materials unused is quantified, and its cost price is valued at £3000. The accounting problems relating to this inventory are as follows:

(a) Since the business has to pay for all goods purchased, it would be illogical to reduce the purchases account by the amount of inventory at the end of the year. Hence, the purchases account must not be adjusted and the total purchases must be charged as expenses.

(b) By charging all purchases against sales, however, the profit for the year would be overstated by £3000. Means must be found, therefore, to take the closing inventory out of the income calculation. This is effected by opening an inventory account on 31 December 19X0 and posting the inventory to it.

Inventory account

19X0	£	
31 Dec.	3000	

As soon as an account is opened for the purpose of recording a flow of value it is necessary to describe the source of the flow and its destination. We know that the purchases account is not the source of the flow of inventories to the inventory account, because we have deliberately refused to adjust the purchases account. We know also that, but for the need to measure income, we would not value inventories at the end of the year. Hence, by a fiction, the accountant states that the inventory adjustment comes from the income statement which is employed to measure income. The full accounting entries are, therefore, as follows:

Income statement for the year
ended 31 December 19X0

	19X0	£
	31 Dec. Inventory	3,000

Inventory account

19X0	£	
31 Dec. Income statement	3000	

The effect of these entries is to solve the problem of income measurement, because the *credit* flow from the income statement is taken into the calculation of income, as follows:

	£		£
Purchases	31,000	Sales	70,000
		Closing inventories	3,000

The debit balance on the inventory account represents an asset which is carried over to the next year's income statement. The inventory account is an interesting account because it exists only to measure income, and since that is done on the last day of the accounting year, the inventory account only exists for one day. In fact, the closing inventory on the last day of the year is the opening inventory on the first day of the next accounting year. Hence, on the first day of the next accounting period, the inventory must be posted to the income statement of the next period, as follows:

Income statement for the year
ended 31 December 19X1

19X1	£	
1 Jan. Inventory	3,000	

Inventory account

19X0	£	19X1	£
31 Dec. Income statement	3,000	1 Jan. Income statement	3,000

The reader will now observe that the inventory account has served its purpose and may be closed. This is done by drawing a double line beneath the entries.

Inventory account

19X0	£	19X1	£
31 Dec. Income statement	3,0000	1 Jan. Income statement	3,000

In practice, the accountant will not reverse the inventory into the income statement of the year 19X1, until 31 December 19X1 when he prepares that account. As a result, the trial balance for the year ended 31 December 19X1 will include a debit balance in respect of the inventory account in the amount of £3000. As the trial balance is always extracted before the inventory adjustment is made, the opening inventory always appears on the trial balance but the closing inventory is never shown.

Summary

In this section of Part 2, we consider the procedural problems involved in periodic measurement. This chapter deals with the problems of adapting the financial accounting data lodged in the data processing system to the objective of measuring periodic income.

The first stages in the measurement of periodic income are:

(a) the identification of the revenues attributable to transactions concluded in the accounting period;
(b) the identification of the expenses related to those revenues.

The accruals convention requires the inclusion of amounts receivable and payable, as well as amounts received and paid, in the measurement of revenues and expenses. We examined the accounting procedures involved in accruing revenue and expenses.

The objective of periodic measurement is the matching of revenues and expenses to establish accounting income. The exclusion of inventories unsold at the end of the accounting period is a further problem in periodic measurement considered in this chapter.

Questions

1. State the conventions which apply to the manner in which periodic revenues and expenses are identified and related. Illustrate your answer.
2. If goods which cost £10,000 were in inventory on 1 January, goods purchased during the year amounted to £40,000 and goods costing £15,000 were in inventory at 31 December, state the cost of the goods which were sold during the year.
3. From the following information construct the combined Rent and Rates Account for the year ended 30 June 19X9 showing the figures that would appear for rent and rates in the income statement and the figures that would appear in the balance sheet as at 30 June 19X9.

   The property of the business was rented at £1600 per annum payable quarterly in arrears on the usual quarter days. The rates were £600 per annum payable half yearly in advance on 1 October and 1 April in each year. The rent was one quarter in arrears on 30 June 19X8 and the rates for the half year to 30 September 19X8 had not been paid.

The following transactions took place during the year to 30 June 19X9:

19X8
July 2   Cash—One quarter's rent to 24 June 19X8
July 2   Cash—Half year's rates to 30 September 19X8
Oct. 10   Cash—Half year's rates to 31 March 19X9
Oct. 10   Cash—One quarter's rent to 29 September 19X8

19X9
Jan. 4   Cash—One quarter's rent to 25 December 19X8
April 6   Cash—Half year's rates to 30 September 19X9
April 6   Cash—One quarter's rent to 25 March 19X9

4. Star Enterprises Ltd is a company formed to manage the affairs of a successful pop group. All the group's revenue and expenses are recorded in the company's books. The group's recording contract with IME Records stipulates a payment of advance royalties of £50,000 on the recording of a record. Actual royalties are 50p per record. Any sales in excess of 100,000 copies will result in additional royalties being paid. If sales are less than 100,000 then any excess advance is recouped from future payments.

During the year ended 31 March 19X8 the company received the following royalties:

	£	£
Advance Record 1.		50,000
Advance Record 2.	50,000	
Less Shortfall on Record 1.	17,000	33,000
Additional royalties Record 2.		44,000
Advance Record 3.		50,000

Record 3 was recorded and released shortly before the year end. No sales figures are yet available.

The company has also incurred advance expenditure of £35,000 on promoting a tour the group will undertake during April, 19X8.

Required:

(a) State the accounting principles which are used in revenue and expense recognition.

(b) Write a report to the management of the company advising on the treatment of royalties and advance expenditure, and showing how these items will be treated in the accounts to 31 March 19X8.

(Question supplied by A. J. Naughton, Leeds Polytechnic)

9 Losses in asset values and periodic measurement

In the previous chapter, we discussed the various adjustments which were needed to the data extracted from the double-entry book-keeping system, so that this data might correctly reflect the revenues and expenses appropriate to the activities conducted during the accounting period in question. The accrual of revenues and expenses involved, as we saw, the exclusion from the data of payments and receipts of other periods.

In this chapter, we shall discuss adjustments which are made in respect of losses in asset values. The first adjustment which we shall examine concerns the depreciation of fixed assets. The second adjustment is the loss in the value of debtors caused by the recognition that a portion of the debtor balances will not be paid and must be recognized as bad debts, and that a further portion may ultimately prove to be bad so that a provision for doubtful debts must also be made.

The treatment of losses in asset values

Unlike gains, losses in asset values do not have to await realization before they may be recognized. The convention of conservatism requires that losses should be recognized as soon as possible, so as to ensure that income and capital values are not overstated in financial accounting reports.

Losses in asset values appear under a variety of guises. Losses of cash and stock by theft, embezzlement or accidental damage are written off immediately against income, insurance recoveries being treated as a separate matter. Losses to fixed assets due to accidental damage, theft or other causes are also written off against income, as are losses arising on the sale of fixed assets which result from a difference between the sale price and the book value of the assets sold. Most fixed assets also diminish in value as their usefulness is exhausted over a period of years. Finally, losses in asset values also result from the exercise of judgement, as in the case of bad debts when accountants have to decide whether a recorded value does exist at all. In this connection, a discretion exists as regards the valuation of such assets as goodwill and organization costs usually described as 'fictitious assets', in that intangible asset values are frequently written off purely as an act of judgement.

Losses in the value of fixed assets

Losses in the value of fixed assets arising through sale, accidental loss or theft present no difficulties from an accounting viewpoint, for such losses are written off immediately against income. By contrast, the diminution in value described as depreciation has been the subject of much controversy. As an accounting concept, depreciation has a complex nature and now occupies an important role in three different areas of the subject. First, it is related to the problem of cost allocation, both as regards the matching of revenues and expenses in the process of income measurement, and as regards product costing in management accounting. Secondly, it is related to the concept of capital maintenance in income theory. Thirdly, as Baxter has shown, it is central to decision making as regards the life and the replacement of fixed assets (Baxter, 1971). The notion of depreciation has varied and multiplied in such a way that its analysis is not an easy matter. In this chapter, we shall take a limited view of depreciation, and we shall concern ourselves purely with its financial accounting implications.

The nature of depreciation

The term 'depreciation' is susceptible to four different meanings (Goldberg, 1962):

(a) a fall in price
(b) physical deterioration
(c) a fall in value
(d) an allocation of fixed asset costs.

Depreciation as a fall in price

A fall in the price of an asset is one aspect of depreciation, but it is not a reliable guide to a valid accounting concept of depreciation. A fall in price may occur independently of any decrease in the usefulness of an asset, for example, the immediate fall in price occurring on the purchase of a new asset.

Depreciation as physical deterioration

Depreciation in this sense is a physical fact. It means impaired utility arising directly through deterioration or indirectly through obsolescence. It is implied in much of the discussion of this concept of depreciation that an asset is 'used up' through use, so that the 'use' of an asset is the extent to which it has been used up. It is evident that these ideas are represented in the rates of depreciation which are attached to depreciable assets. It should be noted, however, that an asset is not necessarily 'used up' through use, for adequate maintenance may prevent deterioration in some cases. Thus, if irrigation ditches are well maintained, they will not deteriorate through use.

The concept of depreciation as deferred maintenance has not been properly investigated, although it may well be a concept of depreciation which may be more relevant than conventional concepts of depreciation as regards certain types of assets.

Depreciation as a fall in value

There are some problems associated with the use of the term 'value' and the relationship of depreciation to the concept of value. Value may mean 'cost value' 'exchange value', 'use value' (utility) or 'esteem value'. Clearly, 'cost value' is not affected by events occurring after acquisition, so that it is not meaningful to relate depreciation to a fall in cost value. 'Exchange value' changes only twice in the experience of the owner of an asset—at the point of purchase and at the point of sale. In this sense, depreciation may mean only a fall in price between two points, and we have already discussed this concept of depreciation. Depreciation as a decrease in utility is also already covered by the concept of physical deterioration, whilst the notion of the esteem value of an asset is entirely subjective and not amenable to an objective concept of measurement.

If one were to attempt to relate the notion of depreciation to economic income, however, one would have the basis of an accounting concept of particular usefulness for decision making. The economic value of an asset may be regarded as the discounted value of expected future cash flows associated with that asset in a particular use. Hence, depreciation may be conceptualized and measured as the progressive decrease in the net cash flows yielded by the asset as its economic utility declines through time, for whatever reason. Normally, of course, its income-earning capacity falls due to increasing inefficiency arising from physical deterioration. As regards certain classes of assets, for example computers, falls in economic value have occurred more rapidly from obsolescence. Baxter discusses this concept of depreciation, but rejects it as an operational one for accounting purposes (Baxter, 1971).

Depreciation as cost allocation

The orthodox view among accountants is that depreciation represents that part of the cost of a fixed asset to its owner which is not recoverable when the asset is finally put out of use by him. Provision against this loss of capital is an integral cost of conducting the business during the effective commercial life of the asset and is not dependent upon the amount of profit earned.

The practice of treating depreciation as an allocation of historic cost is based on two assumptions:

(a) that the expected benefit to be derived from an asset is proportional to an estimated usage rate;
(b) that it is possible to measure the benefit.

Hence, the current practice is part of the procedure of matching periodic revenues with the cost of earning those revenues. The essential difference between fixed assets and current operating expenses is that the former are regarded as costs which yield benefits over a period of years, and hence must be allocated as expenses against the revenues of those years, whereas the latter yield all their benefits in the current year, so that they may be treated as the expenses of that year and matched against the revenues which they have created.

The practice of treating depreciation as an allocation of costs presents a number of serious theoretical problems. The known objective facts about an asset are few, and adequate records are not usually kept of the various incidents in the life in use of an asset apart from its purchase price. Repair and maintenance costs, for example, are charged separately as well as running costs. Other unresolved problems concern the selection of appropriate bases for allocating the cost of depreciable assets, for example, should depreciation be calculated by reference to units of actual use rather than simply time use? Finally, should the residual value of an asset be regarded as a windfall gain or should it be set-off against the replacement cost of the asset rather than used as a point of reference for calculating the proportion of the cost of fixed assets which should be allocated as depreciation?

The accounting concept of depreciation

According to the A.I.C.P.A., depreciation accounting is 'a system of accounting which aims to distribute the cost . . . of tangible capital assets, less salvage (if any), over the estimated useful life of the unit . . . in a systematic and rational manner. It is a process of allocation, not of valuation'. (A.I.C.P.A., 1953.)

From the foregoing definition of depreciation accounting, two important points may be made:

(a) Depreciation accounting is not concerned with attempting to measure the value of an asset at any point of time. One is trying to measure the value of the benefit the asset has provided during a given accounting period, and that benefit is valued as a portion of the cost of the asset. Hence, the balance sheet value of depreciable assets is that portion of the original cost which has not yet been allocated as a periodic expense in the process of income measurement. It does not purport to represent the current value of those assets.

(b) Depreciation accounting does not itself provide funds for the replacement of depreciable assets, but the charging of depreciation ensures the maintenance intact of the original money capital of the entity. Indeed, a provision for depreciation is not identified with cash or any specific asset or assets.

Depreciable and non-depreciable fixed assets

The most common types of fixed assets are:

(a) Land and buildings
(b) Plant and machinery
(c) Furniture and fittings
(d) Motor vehicles
(e) Tools and sundry equipment.

The essential difference in the accounting treatment of fixed assets is to be found in the distinction made between depreciable and non-depreciable assets. Generally, land and buildings are not depreciated: on the contrary, they are sometimes revalued from a historical cost basis. Other fixed assets such as plant and machinery, furniture and fittings, motor vehicles, tools and sundry equipment are depreciated, although, exceptionally, tools and sundry equipment are placed on a revaluation basis or a replacement basis as a means of calculating the amount to be charged as a periodic expense. It may be said, therefore, that the distinction between depreciable and non-depreciable fixed assets rests on the susceptibility of an asset to physical deterioration or obsolescence. Thus, commercial buildings such as shops and offices are not generally depreciated, but industrial buildings normally are.

Factors in the measurement of depreciation

There are four factors which are important in the process of measuring depreciation from an accounting viewpoint, as follows:

(a) identifying the cost of the asset
(b) ascertaining its useful life
(c) determining the expected residual value
(d) selecting an appropriate method of depreciation which must be systematic and rational.

Identifying the cost of the asset

Depreciation is calculated on historical cost values, which include acquisition costs and all incidental costs involved in bringing an asset into use. In the case of buildings, for example, cost includes any commissions, survey, legal and other charges involved in the purchase, together with all the costs incurred in preparing and modifying buildings for a particular use. In the case of plant and machinery, all freight, insurance and installation costs should be capitalized.

Problems occur where firms manufacture assets, for example, an engineering firm may construct a foundry. In such cases, the cost of labour, materials, etc. associated with the activity of construction should be segregated from those associated with the normal income-generating activities, and they should be capitalized. There are costing problems involved in ascertaining such costs. Moreover, improvements effected to existing assets should also be capitalized. The distinction between a repair and an improvement is not always easy to establish. In some circumstances, the intention may be to repair but the cheaper solution is a replacement. An old boiler, for example, may be replaced more cheaply than repaired. The cost of repairs is chargeable as a current expense: the cost of replacement should be capitalized.

Ascertaining the useful life of an asset

The useful life of an asset may be defined as that period of time during which it is expected to be useful in the income earning operations of the firm. In most cases, the useful life is determined by two factors:

(a) the rate of deterioration
(b) obsolescence.

The rate of deterioration is a function of the type of use to which the asset is put, and the extent of that use. A lorry used by civil engineering contractors may have a shorter life expectancy than a lorry employed by cartage contractors, for the former may operate in rough terrain, whereas the latter will be used on roads. It is not unusual to find that the estimated useful life of a lorry in the first case may be two years or even less, whereas the estimated life in the second case may well be four years. Moreover, an asset which is used more intensively will have a shorter life than an asset which is used for shorter periods. In this respect, assets are built to certain specifications which determine to some extent their durability in use. The useful life is determined on the basis of past experience, which is a good indicator of the probable life of a particular asset.

It should be pointed out, however, that the estimated useful life of an asset is also a question of policy and may be determined accordingly. Thus, a car hire firm may decide to renew its fleet each year, and in this case, the useful life of its fleet of cars is one year for the purpose of calculating depreciation.

The problem of taking obsolescence into account in assessing the useful life of an asset is altogether more complex, for obsolescence occurs with the appearance of an asset incorporating the result of technological developments. It is possible to assume in respect of certain assets, such as cars, that each year may see the introduction of an improved model, so that owners of fleets of cars may decide that obsolescence, or assumed obsolescence is a more important factor in the useful life of cars than depreciation. Relying on a pattern of new models or improved versions each year, the owners of fleets of cars may decide to renew the fleet each year. However, it is hard to distinguish the extent to which such decisions are influenced by the need to have the latest product or to avoid excessive repair bills stemming from large mileages. It would seem, therefore, that the problem of obsolescence is one which affects the useful life of existing fixed assets and so accelerates their progress towards the scrapheap. Accordingly, the estimated useful life of an asset should be determined by that length of time which, as a matter of policy, it is wished to employ an asset. That length of time will be a function of a number of factors, but the most important will be the increasing cost of employing that asset due to higher yearly maintenance costs and possible declining revenues.

From a theoretical point of view, there is a point at which the net cash inflows associated with an asset are equal to the costs of operating that asset. Those costs may be expressed as the opportunity costs represented by revenues forgone as a result of using that asset rather than replacing it, or the opportunity costs represented by alternative returns, which may be derived from cash outlays committed to repairs and maintenance. These two measures of opportunity cost need not, of course, necessarily be equivalent. In terms of this analysis, the length of useful life of an asset would be determined as in Fig. 2.10.

Determining the expected residual value

The residual value of an asset must be estimated at the time of acquisition so

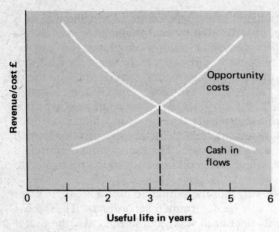

Fig. 2.10

that the net cost may be allocated to the accounting periods during which the asset is usefully employed. The residual value is the expected market value of the asset at the end of its useful life. Hence, the residual value will depend on the manner and on the length of time that the asset is to be used. Where, for example, it is intended to use an asset until it is quite worn out or obsolete, its residual value will be negligible. Where, as in the example of the replacement of fleets of cars, the length of useful life is shortened to one year, the residual value will be high.

Where it is intended to extract the maximum use from an asset, the residual value should be a nominal one: where it is intended to replace the asset when it still has some useful life, its residual value should be estimated on a conservative basis so as to minimize the effects of variations in the price of second-hand assets. The costs to be allocated against the revenues of the accounting periods involved are calculated as follows:

Cost of acquisition (say)	£2000
Residual value (say)	200
Costs to be allocated as depreciation	1800

Selecting the method of depreciation

There are several methods of depreciation but the most common ones are the straight-line method and the decreasing-balance method.

The matching convention requires that 'the choice of the method of allocating the cost of a long-term asset over its effective working life should depend upon the pattern of expected benefits obtainable in each period from its use' (Barton, 1975).

(a) *The straight-line method*
The formula for calculating the annual depreciation under the straight-line method is as follows:

$$\text{Annual depreciation} = \frac{\text{Acquisition cost} - \text{Estimated residual value}}{\text{Expected useful life in years}}$$

Example

A lorry is acquired at a cost of £3000. Its estimated useful life is 3 years, and its residual value is estimated at £600.

$$\text{Annual depreciation} = \frac{£3000 - £600}{3 \text{ years}}$$

$$= £800 \text{ per annum}$$

The straight-line method allocates the net cost equally to each year of the useful life of an asset. It is particularly applicable to assets such as patents and leases where time is the important factor in the effluxion of the benefits to be derived from the use of an asset. Whilst it is often used for other assets as well, it suffers from the following disadvantages:

(a) it does not reflect the fact that the greatest loss in the market value of an asset occurs in the first year of its use;
(b) it does not reflect the unevenness of the loss in the market value of an asset over several years;
(c) it does not reflect the diminishing losses in value which occur in later years, as the asset approaches the end of its useful life.

For these reasons, the straight-line method of depreciation does not provide an accurate measure of the cost of the service potential allocated to the respective accounting periods during which an asset is employed.

(b) *The decreasing-balance method*
To calculate the annual depreciation under this method, a fixed percentage is applied to the balance of the net costs not yet allocated as an expense at the end of the previous accounting period. The balance of the unallocated costs will decrease each year, as a result, and theoretically, the balance of the unallocated costs at the end of the estimated useful life should equal the estimated residual value. The formula which is used to calculate the fixed percentage to be applied to the allocation of net costs as depreciation is as follows:

$$r = 1 - \sqrt[n]{\frac{s}{c}}$$

where n = the expected useful life in years
s = the residual value (this value must be a significant one or the depreciation rate will be nearly one)
c = the acquisition cost
r = the rate of depreciation to be applied.

Example

Calculate the rate of depreciation to be applied to a lorry acquired at a cost of £3000, having an expected useful life of three years and an estimated residual value of £600.

$$r = 1 - \sqrt[3]{\frac{£600}{£3000}}$$

$$= 1 - 0.58$$

$$= 0.42 \quad \text{or} \quad 42\%$$

The depreciation calculation for each of the three years would be as follows:

		£
	Cost	3000
Year 1.	Depreciation at 42% of £3000	1260
	Unallocated costs end of year 1	1740
Year 2.	Depreciation at 42% of £1740	731
	Unallocated costs end of year 2	1009
Year 3.	Depreciation at 42% of £1009	424
	Residual value at end of year 3	585

The small difference between the estimated residual value of £600 and the resulting residual value of £585 arises solely from calculating the percentage depreciation to the nearest two decimal places.

In practice, the percentage rate of depreciation is not calculated so precisely. A rate is selected which approximates the estimated length of useful life, for example an estimated useful life of three years would imply a $33\frac{1}{3}$ rate of depreciation. This practice is reflected in the depreciation rates applied by the taxation authorities for calculating depreciation allowances for tax purposes.

The advantage of the decreasing-balance method is that it approximates reality in respect of certain assets, for example motor vehicles, where the depreciation calculated in the first year is greatest, thereby reflecting the greater loss in market value at this stage of a vehicle's life.

Depreciation and total asset costs

The total costs associated with the benefits derived from fixed assets consist of depreciation and the cost of repairs and maintenance. It follows, therefore, that the proper application of the matching convention to the allocation of total asset costs requires that depreciation and repairs and maintenance be considered jointly as regards the selection of an appropriate method for allocating total asset costs to the accounting periods benefiting from their use.

The depreciation calculated under the two methods which have been examined may be compared in Figs. 2.11 and 2.12.

The cost of repairs and maintenance may be assumed to increase through time, as the asset deteriorates through use. This is reflected in real life by the

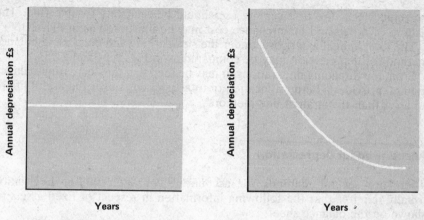

Fig. 2.11 Straight-line method.

Fig. 2.12 Decreasing-balance method.

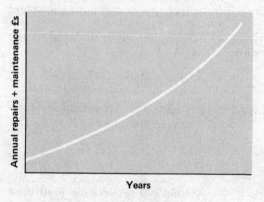

Fig. 2.13 Annual maintenance costs.

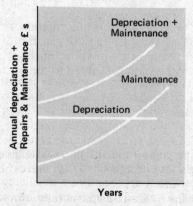

Fig. 2.14 Straight-line method.

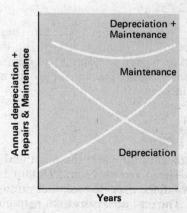

Fig. 2.15 Decreasing-balance method.

expectancy that the first year in use should be relatively trouble free. The pattern of repair and maintenance cost may be illustrated as in Fig. 2.13.

The total annual asset costs under the straight-line and decreasing-balance methods of depreciation may be compared as in Figs 2.14 and 2.15.

From the foregoing illustrations, it may be seen that the decreasing-balance method provides a better allocation of total asset costs over the useful life of an asset than the straight-line method.

Accounting for depreciation

There are several methods for accounting for depreciation. Legislation usually requires that the following information in respect of fixed assets be shown on the balance sheet:

(a) the cost or valuation, as the case may be;
(b) the aggregate amount provided or written off since the date of acquisition or valuation, as the case may be, for depreciation or diminution in value.

The method prescribed for arriving at the amount of fixed assets is the difference between (a) and (b) above.

Example

The historical cost of plant and machinery is £100,000. Accumulated depreciation to date is £60,000 and the book value is, therefore, £40,000. This information is disclosed as follows:

Fixed assets	Cost	Accumulated depreciation	Book value
	£	£	£
Plant and machinery	100,000	60,000	40,000

The accounting procedure required to generate this information is to record the acquisition cost, or valuation as the case may be, in the asset account, and to accumulate depreciation yearly in a provision for depreciation account. The annual provision for depreciation is charged to the income statement.

Example

Let us assume that the plant and machinery shown in the previous example was acquired on 1 Jan. 19X0 for £100,000, that its estimated useful life is five years, the expected residual value is nil, and that depreciation is calculated on a straight-line basis at the rate of £20,000 a year. The appropriate accounts would record the following data by the end of the year 19X2.

Plant and machinery account

19X0		£	19X0		£
1 Jan. Cash		100,000	31 Dec. Balance c/d		100,000
		100,000			100,000
19X1			19X1		
1 Jan. Balance b/d		100,000	31 Dec. Balance c/d		100,000
19X2			19X2		
1 Jan. Balance b/d		100,000	31 Dec. Balance c/d		100,000
19X3					
1 Jan. Balance b/d		100,000			

Provision for depreciation account

19X0	£	19X0	£
31 Dec. Balance c/d	20,000	31 Dec. Income statement	20,000
	20,000		20,000
19X1		19X1	
		1 Jan. Balance b/d	20,000
31 Dec. Balance c/d	40,000	31 Dec. Income statement	20,000
	40,000		40,000
19X2		19X2	
		1 Jan. Balance b/d	40,000
31 Dec. Balance c/d	60,000	31 Dec. Income statement	20,000
	60,000		60,000
		19X3	
		1 Jan. Balance b/d	60,000

Income statement for the y.e. 31 Dec. 19X0
Provision for depreciation £20,000

Income statement for the y.e. 31 Dec. 19X1
Provision for depreciation £20,000

Income statement for the y.e. 31 Dec. 19X2
Provision for depreciation £20,000

Accounting for the sale or disposal of assets

The correct cost of the benefits derived from the use of assets cannot be ascertained until the assets have completed their useful life and have been sold or otherwise disposed of. In the meantime, the annual provision for depreciation is merely an estimate of that actual cost. The practice in accounting for dealing with this problem is to make an adjustment to the income calculated for the year of sale or disposal in respect of any difference between the book value and the realized value of the asset. It is not the practice, therefore, to attempt to re-open previous years to make a correction for the actual depreciation suffered.

The method is to open an asset realization account, and to reverse the existing entries in the asset and the provision for depreciation accounts in respect of the asset sold or disposed of, recording directly in the asset realization account the sale price, if any, obtained.

Example

On 31 Dec. 19X3, plant and machinery acquired at a cost of £100,000 in 19X0 was sold for £30,000. The accumulated depreciation to date was £60,000. The accounting procedure for dealing with this event is as follows:

Plant and machinery account

19X3	£	19X3	£
1 Jan. Balance b/d	100,000	31 Dec. Asset realization	100,000
	100,000		100,000

Provision for depreciation account

19X3	£	19X3	£
31 Dec. Asset realization	60,000	1 Jan. Balance b/d	60,000
	60,000		60,000

Cash book

19X3	£
31 Dec. Asset realization	30,000

Asset realization account

19X3	£	19X3	£
31 Dec. Plant & machinery	100,000	31 Dec. Cash	30,000
		31 Dec. Provision for depreciation	60,000
		31 Dec. Income statement	10,000
	100,000		100,000

Income statement for the y.e. 31 December 19X3

	£
Loss on sale of plant and machinery	10,000

Narrowing accounting differences

In Chapter 5 we discussed the problems created in financial reporting by the existence of a variety of accounting practices permitted by the conventions of accounting. These problems appear in the lack of comparability between the financial reports of different companies, and in the consequent inability of users of financial reports to make informed judgements about different enterprises. It was seen that the Accounting Standards Committee had been established with the purpose of increasing the uniformity of accounting practice by narrowing areas of difference and variety in accounting practice.

Depreciation is one area where substantial differences exist between the range of accounting methods permitted by the conventions of accounting. In common with other topics of controversy in accounting, many of the differences have their source in the means adopted for allocating costs. As it is usually found impossible to devise cost allocation methods which are entirely objective, accountants have to resort to methods which are more or less arbitrary. For example, the straight-line method of depreciation assumes that asset costs should be allocated to successive periods in uniform amounts, whereas the decreasing-percentage method of depreciation assumes that rate of allocation should be constant through time. The assumptions underlying these two alternative methods of depreciation are defensible in the context of the circumstances which they also assume. In effect, 'for each situation in which allocation is contemplated, there is a variety of possible allocation methods, each of which could be defended. The allocation problem arises because there is no conclusive way to choose one method in preference to all others, except arbitrarily'. (Thomas, 1974.)

Although there is no solution to the problems posed by the existence of competing methods of allocating fixed asset costs through depreciation to successive accounting periods, users of financial reports may be assisted in evaluating the financial results reported, and making the adjustments necessary when comparing different companies. It was for this reason that the Accounting Standards Committee issued SSAP 12 Accounting for Depreciation, which came into force in January 1978.

The 1970s witnessed an increasing tendency for companies to account for the effects of inflation upon fixed assets and this led to widely varying treatments of the depreciation figure. The statement is essentially a re-statement of basic principles.

Depreciation is defined in the statement as the 'measure of the wearing out, consumption or other loss of value of a fixed asset, whether arising from use, effluxion of time or obsolescence through technology and market changes.' Depreciation should represent a fair allocation of a fixed asset's value over the useful life of the asset. To determine a fair allocation requires consideration of the cost or valuation of the asset, its nature and expected useful life and its estimated residual value. Cost less residual value should then be allocated over the periods benefiting from the asset's use throughout its expected useful life.

The statement requires that provision for depreciation of fixed assets having a finite useful life be made by allocating the cost or revalued amount less estimated residual values of the assets as fairly as possible to the periods expected to benefit from their use. On a revision of the estimated useful life of an asset, the undepreciated cost should be charged over the revised remaining useful life. Where the method of depreciation is changed, which is only permissible where the new method will give a fairer presentation of the results and financial position, the undepreciated cost should be written off over the remaining useful life on the new basis, commencing with the period in which the change is made, and the effect, if material, disclosed in the year of change. Where assets are revalued, depreciation should be based on the revalued amount and current estimate of remaining useful life with the effect, if material, disclosed in the year of change.

The following should be disclosed in the financial statements for each major class of depreciable asset:

(a) the depreciation methods used;
(b) the useful lives or the depreciation rates used;
(c) total depreciation allocated for the period;
(d) the gross amount of depreciable assets and the related accumulated depreciation.

No specific method of depreciation is laid down in the statement, this being the responsibility of the management of the business, i.e. to select a method most appropriate to the asset in question. Freehold land need not normally be depreciated but buildings with a limited life should be. This latter requirement was a major innovation.

Losses through defaulting debtors

The necessity to give credit to customers for the purposes of expanding sales results in the investment of substantial funds in what are in effect short-term loans to customers. There are three important financial aspects as regards debtors which are of interest both to management and investors. Firstly, there is the problem of working capital management in respect of the balance of claims in favour of and against the firm, and its implications in respect of liquidity and solvency. Secondly, there is the problem of the overall level of debtors in relation to other assets, and the need for the firm to have sufficient funds to invest in the maintenance and expansion of its income-earning structure. This is a problem which has implications for present and future profitability. Thirdly, there is the problem of risk associated with the recovery of amounts due from debtors. This is a problem of credit control and the prevention of financial losses due to default by debtors.

The valuation of amounts due from debtors at the end of an accounting period presents no difficulty as regards determining debtor balances in an objective manner. Providing that accounting records have been kept properly, the objectivity of the valuation of outstanding debtors is founded in the law of contract and in a claim enforceable at law against the debtors. The recoverability of debts, however, is a question to which the accountant must address himself, since the convention of conservatism requires that losses should be recognized as soon as they arise. The recoverability of debts for financial reporting purposes is a question of law in some cases and judgement in others. Thus, where a debtor has been declared insolvent, the recoverability of the debt is subject to the law of bankruptcy, and where no dividend is likely, the loss must be recognized and the amount written off as a bad debt. Where, however, a debtor cannot be traced or is unable to pay due to personal circumstances and the sum involved does not warrant legal expenses on its recovery, the decision to recognize the loss is a question of judgement. By and large, accountants examine their debtor ledgers at the end of the financial year and identify such debts as are likely to be bad debts by reference to the delay in payment and the attempts made to secure payment. Those debts which are considered to be irrecoverable are written off as bad debts, and if they should be recovered subsequently, the debt is restored in the debtor ledger and the payment recorded.

The failure to deal adequately with the problem of defaulting debtors will distort the measurement of income and asset values in the following respects:

(a) The measurement of income for an accounting period will be overstated to the extent that any credit sales taken into income have created debts which are not recoverable.

(b) The measurement of income for the subsequent accounting period will be understated to the extent that debts created in the previous accounting period are recognized belatedly as bad and written off against the income of the subsequent accounting year.

(c) The balance sheet statement of the value of debtors incorporates debts which, though legally enforceable, are not recoverable. It is not possible, for example, to recover debts from bankrupt persons, or persons who cannot be traced.

It is required, therefore, that:

(a) losses arising from bad debts should be recognized as soon as possible and written off the value of total debtors;

(b) the risk of further possible losses should be anticipated in accordance with the convention of conservatism.

Accounting practice is to deal separately with the problem of debts which are recognized as bad, and the problem of anticipating further losses in the future. In effect, three types of debts are distinguished:

(a) good debts
(b) bad debts
(c) doubtful debts.

The treatment of bad debts

Careful supervision of debtor accounts will minimize the level of bad debts. The enforcement of time limits for the settlement of accounts helps in the prevention of the build-up of arrears of debts and in identifying the possibility of bad debts. Once a debt is recognized as bad, it should be written off immediately to the bad debts account, so that the list of debtor accounts represents only good debts, that is, those which are expected to be honoured.

Example

H. Smith Ltd, a firm of building contractors, had been regular customers of Hervey Building Supplies Ltd and enjoyed a credit limit of £1000. On 1 January 19X0, the balance on its account in the books of Hervey totalled £900, and purchases in the month of January 19X0 totalled £150. H. Smith informed Hervey on 5 February of its inability to make payment in respect of its account. Hervey decided to stop granting further credit to H. Smith until the position was clarified. Shortly thereafter, it was discovered that H. Smith were insolvent, and that it was unlikely that any portion of the outstanding debt of £1050 would be paid. On 1 March, it was decided to treat the debt as a bad debt.

The accounting entries in the books of Hervey would be as follows:

H. Smith Ltd account

19X0	£	19X0	£
1 Jan. Balance	900	1 March Bad debt	1050
31 Jan. Sales	150		
	1050		1050

Bad debts account

19X0		
1 March H. Smith Ltd	1050	

At the end of the accounting period, the total on the bad debts account is transferred to the income statement for the year.

Example

Let us assume that the only bad debt incurred by Hervey Building Supplies Ltd was in respect of H. Smith Ltd in the sum of £1050, as above. The bad debts account for the year ended 31 December 19X0 would be closed as follows:

Bad debts account

19X0	£	19X0	£
1 March H. Smith Ltd	1050	31 Dec. Income statement	1050
	1050		1050

Income statement for the y.e. 31 Dec. 19X0

	£
Bad debts	1050

The treatment of doubtful debts

The question of doubtful debts, as distinct from bad debts, is examined only at the end of each accounting period when the accountant addresses himself to the problem of measuring the income for the year. A final scrutiny of the debtors account will have eliminated all those accounts which are considered to be bad and the necessary transfers will have been made to the bad debts account. Of the remaining debtors, some may ultimately prove to be bad but there may be reasonable grounds for hoping that all remaining debtors will settle their accounts. The convention of conservatism requires that the risk should be discounted of further debts proving to be bad. The normal practice is to create a provision for doubtful debts out of the current year's income, without seeking to identify particular debts as being doubtful of recovery. There are several methods of estimating the level of doubtful debts. The most common method is to allow past experience to establish the percentage of debtors which prove to be bad, and to calculate the provision for doubtful debts by applying this percentage to the debtors outstanding at the end of the accounting period. A more accurate method is to classify debtor balances in terms of their age, and to apply to the several groups of debts the loss rates established by experience.

Example

The debtor balances existing in the books of the Bumpa Trading Company at the end of the accounting year are as follows:

Duration of debts	Balance	Loss rate %	Provision
	£		£
Less than 1 month	10,000	1	100
1–2 months	3,000	3	90
2–3 months	1,000	5	50
3–4 months	500	10	50
Over 4 months	100	20	20
	14,600		310

One of the advantages of this method of creating a provision for doubtful debts is that it enables management to understand the relationship between the slow collection of debts and the financial losses caused by defaulting debtors.

The accounting entries would be as follows:

Income statement for the year ended 31 December 19X0

	£
Provision for doubtful debts	310

Provision for doubtful debts account

19X0	£
Income statement y.e. 31 Dec.	310

The provision for doubtful debts is not identified with any individual debtors. It is carried forward as an estimated liability, and is shown on the balance sheet as follows:

Balance sheet as on 31 December 19X0

. . . . . .	£	£
Debtors	14,600	
Less: Provision for doubtful debts	310	
		14,290

In this manner, the objective of presenting a realistic valuation of trade debtors is achieved.

Summary

This chapter examined two important problems in the measurement of periodic income, namely, depreciation and financial losses resulting from bad debts. Both problems are concerned with the manner in which losses in asset values should be recognized. Depreciation is in itself a difficult problem from a theoretical viewpoint, and its treatment in accounting as an allocation of historical costs is a limited view of this problem. Nevertheless, such treatment is compatible with the matching convention for allocation to cost of acquisition of assets to the revenues derived from their use. Not all assets are depreciable, and depreciation should take into account such factors as all the relevant costs of acquisition as well as the useful life of assets.

Two methods of depreciation were examined, and their implications were discussed. The adjustments required on the sale or disposal of assets were also examined.

Losses through defaulting debtors were analysed and their impact on the measurement of periodic income was discussed. Accounting adopts a two-stage approach to this problem, namely the recognition of losses actually incurred by declaring certain debts as *bad*, and the provision against the risk of loss through creating provisions for doubtful debts.

References

1. A.I.C.P.A. Accounting Research Bulletin No. 43, 1953.
2. Barton, A. D. *The Anatomy of Accounting*, University of Queensland Press, 1975.
3. Baxter, W. T. *Depreciation*, Sweet and Maxwell, London, 1971.
4. Goldberg, L. 'Concepts of depreciation', *in* Baxter, W. T. & Davidson, S. (eds), *Studies in Accounting Theory*, Sweet and Maxwell, London, 1962.
5. Thomas, A. L. 'The allocation problem: Part 2', *Studies in Accounting Research*, p. 2, A.A.A., 1974.

Questions

1. Analyse the main factors which should be considered when selecting a policy for depreciating fixed assets.
2. Lodgemoor Company acquired a machine on 1 July 19X1 for £48,000 and immediately spent a further £2000 on its installation. The machine was estimated to have a useful life of eight years and a scrap value of £4000 at the end of this time.

   Required:

   Compute the depreciation for the year ended 30 June 19X2 if the company chooses to use:

   (*a*) The straight-line method
   (*b*) The decreasing-balance method

3. Beale Company purchased a machine on 1 January 19X1, at an invoice price of £142,600. Transportation charges amounted to £2000, and £3400 was spent to install the machine. Costs of removing an old machine to make room for the new

one amounted to £1200, and £200 was received for the scrapped material in the old machine.

Required:

(*a*) State the amount of depreciation that would be recorded on the machine for the first year on a straight-line basis and on a decreasing-balance basis, assuming an estimated life of eight years and no salvage value expected at the end of that time.

(*b*) Compute the depreciation provision for the year ended 31 December 19X3, assuming a revised total life expectancy for the machine of 12 years; assume that depreciation has been recorded through December 31 19X2 on a straight-line basis.

4. From the following information relating to the fixed assets of a business prepare the following accounts as they should appear in the ledger of the business:

(*a*) plant and machinery account;
(*b*) motor vehicles account;
(*c*) plant and machinery provision for depreciation account;
(*d*) motor vehicles provision for depreciation account;
(*e*) asset realization account(s).

The plant and machinery was acquired on 1 January 19X5, at a cost of £7500 and the motor vehicles were acquired on 1 July 19X7, at a cost of £3500.

It has been the practice of the business to depreciate assets using the straight-line method of providing for depreciation and they estimate the life of the plant to be ten years and the motor vehicles to be five years.

The accounts of the business are made up to 31 December in each year and it is usual to calculate depreciation for a full year on the assets in the possession of the business at balance sheet date.

During the year to 31 December 19X9, a new machine costing £1000 was acquired and a machine bought on 1 January 19X5 for £500 was sold for £325; and a car costing £750 on 1 July 19X7, was sold for £400.

5. Explain the main provisions of SSAP 12.
6. The year-end balance on the debtors' account amounted to £100,000. Net sales for the year totalled £1,200,000. Explain how you would deal with the following information.

(1) An analysis of the debtors' ledger indicates that irrecoverable debts amount to £11,400
(2) Past trends suggest that 5 per cent of debts eventually have to be written off as irrecoverable
(3) The existing provision for doubtful debts amounts to £3000

10 Preparing an income statement and a balance sheet

In Chapter 9, we examined the role of the trial balance as a working paper which enables the accountant not only to check the arithmetical accuracy of the entries recorded during an accounting period, but which also serves as a basis for considering adjustments to be made for the purpose of measuring periodic income. The extraction of a trial balance at the close of the accounting period is the first step, therefore, in the preparation of an income statement and a balance sheet.

We examined in Chapter 8 how the trial balance should be adjusted in respect of the accrual into the accounting period of revenues and expenses, and we analysed in Chapter 9 the nature of the losses in asset values which have to be taken into consideration in the measurement of periodic income.

The purpose of this chapter is to summarize the various adjustments which must be made to the trial balance, and the manner in which these adjustments are incorporated into the process of preparing an income statement and a balance sheet.

Preparing an income statement

The preparation of an income statement is a two-stage exercise. The first stage is an informal one and consists of using the trial balance as a worksheet for accumulating all the data which incorporate the various adjustments which we referred to earlier. When the adjusted trial balance has been certified and confirmed, the adjustments are formally entered in the appropriate accounts, and the income statement is formally included in the accounts system. It is important to remember that the income statement is an account to which the revenue and expense accounts for the accounting period are transferred as summarized totals, and which exists solely for the purpose of measuring the accounting income for that period. As we shall see in Part 4, the income statement also forms part of the process of financial reporting, and many problems in this respect arise from the fact that the income statement is an integral element in financial accounting, and is subject to its conventions.

The following example illustrates the nature of the income statement.

Example

Let us return to the trial balance given on page 108, which showed the following list of balances extracted from the books of John Smith on 31 December 19X0, being the end of the first year of trading.

	£ Dr.	£ Cr.
Capital		25,000
Motor vehicles	10,000	
Furniture and fittings	2,500	
Purchases	31,000	
Cash at bank	6,000	
Sales		70,000
Sundry debtors	18,000	
Sundry creditors		3,500
Rent	4,500	
Salaries	22,800	
Insurances	400	
Motor expenses	2,000	
Light and heat	1,000	
General expenses	300	
	98,500	98,500

We noted in Chapter 8 that the following adjustments were required:

(1) Rent unpaid at the end of the year was £1500.
(2) Insurance paid in advance amounted to £50.
(3) Rent receivable, but not recorded in the account, amounted to £60.
(4) Closing inventories at 31 December 19X0 were valued at £3000.

We are now given the following additional information:

(1) Depreciation is to be charged on the undermentioned assets and is to be calculated on the depreciating-balance method. Their estimated residual value is shown in brackets.

Motor vehicles	20%	(£1000)
Furniture and fittings	10%	(£250)

(2) Bad debts to be written off amounted to £180, and a provision for doubtful debts is to be created in the sum of £178.

Adjusting for accruals

We saw in Chapter 8 that the adjustments for accruals resulted in the following revisions of balances in the trial balance:

	Original balance	Adjustment	New balance
	£	£	£
(a) Rent	4500	1500	6000
(b) Insurance	400	50	350
(c) Insurance prepaid	—	50	50
(d) Rent receivable	—	60	60
(e) Rent receivable	—	60	60

We explained in Chapter 4 that items (a), (b) and (d) represented adjustments to the revenues and expenses of the year and affected the income statement. The following resulting balances on the accounts affect the balance sheet and we shall see later in this chapter how they are incorporated in that statement:

	£ Dr.	£ Cr.
Rent accrued		1,500
Insurance prepaid	50	
Rent receivable	60	

The corrected total revenues and expenses may now be listed on a worksheet used in the preparation of the income statement:

Draft income statement for the year ended 31 December 19X0

	£		£
Purchases	31,000	Sales	70,000
Rent	6,000	Rent receivable	60
Salaries	22,800		
Insurance	350		
Motor expenses	2,000		
Light and heat	1,000		
General expenses	300		

Adjusting for inventories

We noted in Chapter 8 that periodic measurement involved valuing the inventory of goods unsold at the end of the accounting period. The closing inventory is valued, as we saw in Chapter 4, in accordance with the cost convention, and represents the residue of the purchases of the year which have not been sold at the year-end, and which will be sold in the next accounting period. Opening inventories are shown, therefore, as a *debit balance* in the trial balance, whereas closing inventories do not appear since they are valued after the close of the accounting period. It is for this reason that the appropriate entries must be made in the inventory account to make possible the measurement of periodic income. In the example in question, there is no opening inventory since we are dealing with the first year of trading.

We saw in Chapter 6 that the adjustment for closing inventory had a two-fold effect. First, it is effected by means of a credit entry in the income statement and a debit entry in the inventory account. Second, it results in a debit balance in the inventory account which must be incorporated in the balance sheet.

The closing inventory adjustment may be entered on the draft income statement as follows.

Draft income statement for the year ended 31 December 19X0

	£		£
Purchases	31,000	Sales	70,000
Rent	6,000	Rent receivable	60
Salaries	22,800	Closing inventory	
Insurance	350	31 December 19X0	3,000
Motor expenses	2,000		
Light and heat	1,000		
General expenses	300		

Adjusting for the loss in asset values

We mentioned in Chapter 9 the most important losses in asset values which the accountant has to recognize in the measurement of periodic income. We do not propose to deal in this text with the variety of gains and losses in asset values which may occur, since we are concerned only with the analysis of the process of periodic measurement and with an examination of the most significant losses in asset values which enter into this process.

In the example, we are required to deal with depreciation, bad and doubtful debts.

(a) *The calculation of depreciation*
The depreciation to be charged against the income for the year is as follows:

	£	£
(i) *Motor vehicles*		
Cost	10,000	
Estimated residual value	1,000	
Net cost for depreciation purposes	9,000	
Depreciation for the year 19X0 at 20%	1,800	1,800
Residual balance for depreciation in following years	7,200	
(ii) *Furniture and fittings*		
Cost	2,500	
Estimated residual value	250	
Net cost for depreciation purposes	2,250	
Depreciation for the year 19X0 at 10%	225	225
Residual balance for depreciation in following years	2,025	
Total depreciation for the year		2,025

It is the usual practice to detail in the income statement the component elements of the provision for depreciation, and as we shall see later fixed assets are also described in their categories on the balance sheet. The provision for depreciation in respect of the different fixed assets may be reconciled, therefore, with the yearly additional provision for depreciation shown on the balance sheet.

(b) *Calculation of the provision for doubtful debts*

Duration of debt	Balance £	Loss rate %	Provision £
Less than 1 month	15,960	$\frac{1}{2}$	80
1–2 months	1800	5	90
2–3 months	40	10	4
over 3 months	20	25	4
	17,820		178

These adjustments may be included in the draft income statement as shown below:

Draft income statement for the year ended 31 December 19X0

	£		£
Purchases	31,000	Sales	70,000
Rent	6000	Rent receivable	60
Salaries	22,800	Closing inventory	
Insurance	350	31 December 19X0	3000
Motor expenses	2000		
Light and heat	1000		
General expenses	300		
Depreciation			
Motor vehicles 1800			
Furniture and fittings 225	2025		
Bad debts	180		
Provision for doubtful debts	178		

Calculating the periodic income

The details shown on the draft income statement above are sufficient to permit the calculation of the income for the year ended 31 December 19X0. The income statement is set out, however, so as to enable significant information to be immediately apparent. In this respect, a distinction is made between *gross income* and *net income*, the former being the income resulting after the deduction from the gross sales revenue of expenses directly connected with the production or purchase of the goods sold, whilst the latter reflects the deduction of overhead expenses from gross income. Although the net income figure is the most important result, dividing the income statement into two parts highlights the burden of overhead expenses, as well as focusing attention on important aspects of business activity.

(a) *Calculating gross income*

In the case of a trading business—as is the case in the example quoted—the gross income from trading may be shown as follows:

	£		£
Purchases	31,000	Sales	70,000
Less: Closing inventory at			
31 December 19X0	3000		
Cost of sales	28,000		
Gross trading income	42,000		
	70,000		70,000

This arrangement shows the following significant points:

(a) Although purchases amounted to £31,000, the cost of goods actually sold amounted to only £28,000. Hence, the gross trading income expressed as a percentage of sales was:

$$\frac{42,000}{70,000} \times 100 = 60\%$$

This percentage is often referred to as the gross profit ratio. Expressed as a percentage of cost of sales, the gross trading income was:

$$\frac{42,000}{28,000} \times 100 = 150\%$$

(b) The level of trading activity may also be judged from the average length of time inventory is held. The rate of inventory turnover may be calculated as follows:

$$\frac{\text{Cost of sales}}{\text{Average inventory}}$$

The average inventory is obtained by the arithmetic mean of the opening and closing inventory. In the example under consideration, the rate of inventory turnover for the year was as follows:

$$\frac{28,000}{3000} = 9.3 \text{ times}$$

so that inventory was held for approximately 39 days (365 days ÷ 9.3).

The segregation of the gross trading income in the process of calculating periodic income provides useful ratios for the analysis of trading performance, and for indicating areas of trading where efficency might be improved.

It is the practice for business to seek to identify the gross income. Thus manufacturing firms show manufacturing gross income, contracting firms show contracting gross income and so on.

The problem of deciding which expenses to include in the calculation of the gross income lies in defining direct as distinct from indirect operating expenses. Direct expenses, such as purchases, freight and other expenses associated with the acquisition of goods for resale, for example, are included in the calculation of gross income.

(b) *Calculating the net income*

The calculation of the net income is affected by charging against the gross income the indirect expenses which have been accumulated in the trial balance, and other expenses such as depreciation, bad debts and provisions for doubtful debts. Using the data given in the example, the net income for the year ended 31 December 19X0 may be calculated as follows.

	£		£
Rent	6000	Gross trading income	42,000
Salaries	22,800	Rent receivable	60
Insurance	350		
Motor expenses	2000		
Light and heat	1000		
General expenses	300		
Depreciation			
Motor vehicles 1800			
Furniture and fittings 225			
	2025		
Bad debts	180		
Provision for doubtful debts	178		
	34,833		
Net income	7227		
	42,060		42,060

Miscellaneous income, such as interest, rents and dividends, which form a minor element in the business income are usually shown in the calculation of the net income rather than in the calculation of the gross income.

The segregation of the net income calculation also affords a clearer view of significant ratios. The net income is itself the most significant performance result, and its dimensions may be assessed not only in relation to the gross trading income, but also to gross revenue. The net income as a percentage of sales indicates the level of activity required to produce £1 of net income, and may be calculated as follows:

$$\frac{\text{Net income before interest and tax}}{\text{Sales}}$$

Thus, whereas the percentage of gross income to sales was 60 per cent the percentage of net income to sales was only 13 per cent, indicating thereby not only the relative burden of direct and indirect expenses but also the relative efficiency of the business.

The formal presentation of the income statement

Although the income statement is part of the accounts system, and may be shown in an account form, its formal presentation has been influenced by its use as a financial reporting statement. This influence has encouraged the further classification of indirect expenses into selling, administrative and financial expenses, and the presentation of the income statement in a vertical form as follows:

John Smith Esq. trading as general dealer
Income statement for the year ended 31 December 19X0

	£	£	£
Sales			70,000
Cost of sales			
Purchases		31,000	
Less: Closing inventory		3,000	
			28,000
Gross trading income			42,000
Other income			
Rent			60
Total income			42,060
Selling and distribution expenses			
Salesmen's salaries	12,000		
Motor expenses	2,000		
Depreciation—Motor vehicles	1,800	15,800	
Administrative expenses			
Rent	6,000		
Office salaries	10,800		
Insurance	350		
Light and heat	1,000		
General expenses	300		
Depreciation—Furniture			
and fittings	225		
		18,675	
Financial expenses			
Bad debts	180		
Provision for doubtful debts	178	358	
Total overhead expenses			34,833
Net income			7,227

Preparing a balance sheet

The preparation of a balance sheet is a two-stage exercise, and in this sense, it follows the same pattern as the preparation of an income statement, that is, an informal stage based on a worksheet, and a formal stage represented by the balance sheet presented as a financial report. There are, however, a number of important differences between an income statement and a balance sheet. First, from a procedural point of view, the income statement is part of the accounts system and as we explained earlier, it is itself an account. By contrast, the balance sheet is not an account, but a list showing the balances of the accounts following the preparation of the income statement. Second, the income statement is the effective instrument of periodic measurement in accounting, whereas the balance sheet does not set out to do other than state residual balances. Third, residual debit balances are shown on the balance sheet as *assets*, and there are problems stemming from this description which we discuss in Chapter 11. Fourth, by attaching accounting measurements to debit and credit balances described as assets and liabilities respectively, the balance sheet is often interpreted as indicating the net worth of the business. This is a misconception, and in the case of corporations has led to much controversy. We explore these problems further in Part 3.

Collecting and classifying balances

The preparation of the balance sheet need not await the entry of all the adjustments into the individual accounts following the preparation of the income statement. It may be prepared in draft form from the trial balance and the finalized draft of the income statement.

In accounting, debit balances are either assets or expenses. The preparation of the income statement involves the removal from the trial balance of all expenses in respect of the year, so that any debit balances remaining are treated as assets. These assets, as defined, are classified as follows:

(i) Long-term assets representing an enduring benefit to the enterprise. Long-term assets described as fixed assets, for example, plant and machinery, are subject to depreciation. Other long-term assets, such as land and intangible assets may or may not be subject to depreciation or other changes in their book value. We examine these problems in Chapter 11.

(ii) Short-term assets, described as current assets, are the following:

 (a) Closing inventories at the end of the accounting period;
 (b) Trade debtors;
 (c) Pre-payments on expense accounts, for example, insurance paid in advance;
 (d) Cash at bank and cash in hand.

The measurement of closing inventories presents particular problems, which we discuss in Chapter 11. We have already examined the accounting problems relating to trade debtors which arise from the writing-off of bad debts and the making of provisions for doubtful debts. We shall deal presently with the verification of cash at the bank.

By contrast, credit balances on the trial balance are either liabilities, revenues or investments in the firm in the form of capital and long-term loans. The removal of periodic revenues from the trial balance means that the remaining credit balances are either liabilities or investments. The provision for depreciation is one of a number of exceptions to this rule. These exceptions, as in the case of prepayments shown as debit balances, arise from accounting procedures. Credit balances are collected and classified as follows:

(i) Capital account, representing the owner's original investment in the firm and accumulated profits;

(ii) Long-term borrowings;

(iii) Short-term liabilities, described as current liabilities, which include such credit balances as sundry creditors, accrued expenses, payment received in advance, provisions for taxation and bank overdrafts.

Verifying balances

Accounts are usually subjected to yearly audits, that is, they are checked in detail by a firm of professional auditors, who are themselves accountants. The purpose of the audit is not only to check on the accuracy of the records, but also to ensure that the statements contained in those records are correct.

Thus, the existence of assets evidenced in the assets accounts is verified, as well as the existence of liabilities evidenced in various creditors' accounts. In the case of corporations, audits are obligatory and auditors are appointed by shareholders to act as watchdogs over their interests. In this connection, they are required to certify that both the income statement and the balance sheet reflect a true and fair view of the information they are legally required to convey.

Bank reconciliation statement

It is unlikely that on the stated day, the balance at the bank as shown in the cash book will correspond with the statement of the balance at the bank produced by the bank itself. This is due not only to the normal delays occurring in the process of clearing cheques, but also to delays in lodging and presenting cheques for payment. Moreover, payments and receipts may be effected directly through the bank and by-pass the accountant. For example, dividends and interest receivable may be payable on instruction directly into the bank account, and routine payments may be effected by stop-orders and direct debit procedures. The bank also charges commission, fees and interest directly to the account, and the bank statement is used to convey these details to the client.

The bank reconciliation statement is an accounting procedure for reconciling the balance at the bank as per the bank statement with the balance at the bank as per the cash book, whenever a bank statement is received.

When preparing a balance sheet, the balance at the bank as shown in the cash book must be supported by a bank statement stating the balance on the last day of the accounting period, and the bank reconciliation statement explains any differences which have not been already adjusted in the cash book. Thus, any charges such as bank commission and interest will be entered in the cash book and will be shown as expenses in the income statement. In effect, therefore, the bank reconciliation statement explains the nature of the unadjusted differences between the cash book and the bank statement.

Example

The balance at the bank according to the cash book was £6000 on 31 December 19X0. According to the bank statement the balance was £6500. The difference is explained as follows:

(i) Cheques received from debtors on 31 December 19X0 which were not banked until 2 January 19X1 amounted to £250.
(ii) Cheques sent to creditors on 31 December 19X0 and not presented for payment until after 1 January 19X1 amounted to £750.

Bank reconciliation statement as on 31 December 19X0

	£
Balance at bank as per bank statement	6500
Add: Cheques received but not lodged	250
	6750
Less: Cheques issued but not presented	750
Balance at bank as per cash book	6000

The formal presentation of the balance sheet

In the case of corporations, legislation usually provides rules for the presentation of both the income statement and the balance sheet. As we shall see in Chapter 12, these rules apply to published financial reports. The rules reflect the recommendation of the accounting profession, and are designed not only to secure sufficient disclosure, but to permit salient features to be quickly recognized. It is usual, therefore, to classify assets and liabilities in groupings as we mentioned earlier, and also to rank them according to liquidity. Thus, asset groupings are shown from the most fixed to the most liquid, and liabilities from the long-term to the most current.

The importance of the balance sheet, together with the income statement, for the purpose of financial reporting and investment decision making, has focused attention on the arrangement of particular groupings to assist the interpretation and the analysis of results. We shall deal with this analysis in Chapter 13, but we may mention at this stage that the relationship between long-term finance and long-term investment needs of the firm (long-term capital as defined in finance) and short-term finance and short-term financial needs (working capital) is important to financial analysts. Other areas of interest are, of course, the return on capital employed which is the ratio of net income to equity capital (owner's investment in the firm), liquidity and solvency.

The vertical form of presentation of the balance sheet is as on page 151.

Summary

This chapter has been concerned with the accounting procedures for preparing and presenting the two main financial reports, namely, the income statement and the balance sheet.

The extraction of the trial balance at the close of the accounting period marks the first stage in the preparation of these reports. Earlier chapters have examined the adjustments required for the purposes of periodic measurement. These include accurals, depreciation and adjustments in respect of bad and doubtful debts. All these adjustments are effected informally on working sheets, and once they have been verified and confirmed, the final accounts may be drawn up.

The importance of the income statement lies not only in the fact that it is the main vehicle of periodic measurement and provides the measurement of periodic income, but also in the fact that it is itself part of the accounts system. The objective purpose underlying the preparation of the income statement is the measurement of net income, which is used as a basis for measuring business efficiency. The distinction between gross income and net income facilitates the analysis of the financial results, as does the classification of expenses under various categories.

By contrast, the balance sheet is a list of residual balances following the preparation of the income statement. It forms no part of the accounts system. The balance sheet is used in conjunction with the income statement in the analysis of the financial performance of the business, and the treatment

John Smith Esq. trading as general dealer
Balance sheet as on 31 December 19X0

	£	£	£	£
Capital employed				
Capital account			25,000	
Net income for the year			7,227	
				32,227
Represented by				

Fixed assets	Cost	*Provision for deprecia-tion*	*Net*	
	£	£	£	
Motor vehicles	10,000	1,800	8,200	
Furniture and fittings	2,500	225	2,275	
	12,500	2,025	10,475	10,475
Current assets				
Inventories at cost			3,000	
Debtors		17,820		
Less: Provision for doubtful debts		178	17,642	
Accruals and prepayments			110	
Cash at bank			6,000	
			26,752	
Less Current liabilities				
Creditors		3,500		
Accruals		1,500	5,000	
Net working capital			21,752	
				32,227

and classification of assets and liabilities is important to this analysis. Consequently, particular attention is paid to the manner in which important financial aspects of the business are highlighted in the presentation of the balance sheet.

Questions

1. Jack Daw has prepared the following balance sheet as at 30 June 19X8 (see p. 152).
   Daw asks you to audit his accounts and in the course of your examination you find:

   (1) a dividend of £100 has been paid direct to the bank and no entry has been made in the books

	£		£	£
Capital account		Plant at cost	8,000	
Balance, 1 July 19X7	10,000	less depreciation	2,000	6,000
Income for the year	2,050	Vehicles at cost	1,000	
	12,050	less depreciation	3,000	
				2,000
Creditors and				
provisions	5,000	Inventory		7,000
Bank overdraft	1,000	Debtors	3,200	
		Less provision		
		for doubtful debts	200	3,000
		Petty cash	—	50
	18,050			18,050

(2) a bad debt of £100 should be written off and you agree with Daw that the provision for doubtful debts should be fixed at 10 per cent of the remaining debtors

(3) an additional item of plant, costing £500, has been charged to repairs. It was agreed that this should be depreciated by 10 per cent on cost

(4) the inventory on 30 June 19X8 was overvalued by £250

(5) on counting the petty cash you find there is only £10 in the box. It seems likely that the balance has been stolen by an employee who is missing.

Required:

(a) A statement showing the necessary adjustments to the income for the year to 30 June 19X8.

(b) The amended balance sheet as on 30 June 19X8.

2. The balances in the books of account for John Reeve at 31 March 19X7 are given below:

	£
Sales	50,000
Purchases	30,000
Inventory, 1 April 19X6	35,000
Administration expenses	5,000
Selling expenses	5,000
Trade creditors	27,000
Bank overdraft	32,000
Trade debtors	55,000
Debentures	50,000
Plant and machinery, at cost	80,000
Plant and machinery, depreciation provision, 1 April 19X6	30,000
Fixtures and equipment, at cost	40,000
Fixtures and equipment, depreciation provision, 1 April 19X6	10,000
Capital account, 1 April 19X6	51,000

You are also given the following information:

(a) On 31 March 19X7, the inventory was valued at £40,000.

(b) Depreciation of plant and machinery and fixtures and fittings is to be calculated at the rate of 20 per cent of cost.

Required:

Using the vertical form of presentation, prepare the income statement for the year ended 31 March 19X7 and a balance sheet as at that date.

3. The following trial balance was extracted from the books of T. Bone as at 31 December 19X6:

	£	£
Capital account		20,500
Purchases	46,500	
Sales		60,900
Repairs	848	
Motor car (cost)	950	
Car expenses	318	
Freehold land and buildings	10,000	
Balance at bank	540	
Furniture and fittings (cost)	1,460	
Wages and salaries	8,606	
Discounts allowed	1,061	
Discounts received		814
Drawings	2,400	
Rates and insurances	248	
Bad debts	359	
Provision for bad debts 1 Jan. 19X6		140
Trade debtors	5,213	
Trader creditors		4,035
General expenses	1,586	
Inventory 1 Jan. 19X6	6,300	
	86,389	86,389

The following matters are to be taken into account:

(1) inventory at 31 December 19X6 was £8800
(2) wages and salaries outstanding at 31 December 19X6 were £318
(3) rates and insurances paid in advance at 31 December 19X6 amounted to £45
(4) during the year, Bone took goods ex stock valued at £200 for his own use. No entry had been made in the books in this respect
(5) depreciation is to be provided at the rate of 20 per cent on the motor car and at 10 per cent on furniture and fittings
(6) the provision for bad debts is to be reduced to £100.

Required:

Prepare an income statement for the year ended 31 December 19X6, and a balance sheet as at that date.

4. On 30 June 19X9 the bank column of John Smith's cash book showed a debit balance of £12,600. On examination of the cash book and bank statement it was revealed that:

(1) cheques amounting to £935 which were issued to creditors and entered in the cash book before 30 June were not presented for payment until after that date
(2) cheques amounting to £230 had been recorded in the cash book as having been paid into the bank on 30 June, but were entered on the bank statement on 1 July
(3) a cheque for £70 had been dishonoured prior to 30 June, but no record of this fact appeared in the cash book

(4) a dividend of £340 paid direct to the bank had not been recorded in the cash book
(5) bank interest and charges of £60 had been charged in the bank statement but not entered in the cash book
(6) no entry had been made in the cash book for a trade subscription of £15 paid by banker's order in January 19X9.

Required:

(*a*) To make appropriate adjustments in the cash book bringing down the correct balance.
(*b*) To prepare a statement reconciling the adjusted balance in the cash book with the balance shown in the bank statement.

11 Reporting recorded assets and liabilities

The purpose of this chapter is to examine further the logic and the methodology which underlie the traditional manner in which assets and liabilities are recorded and depicted on the balance sheet. First, we discuss the conventional historical cost valuation of assets and the implications of this method of valuation for balance sheet purposes. Second, we discuss the adjustments to historical cost values which are made at the stage of preparing the balance sheet. Third, we review the implications of the variety of different results obtained from traditional accounting practices. In this chapter, therefore, the concern is with historical cost valuation. The discussion of current cost accounting is deferred to Part 3.

The financial accounting conventions which we examined in Chapter 4 may be said to have their origin in the concept of stewardship accounting. A number of these conventions have a determining influence on valuation for financial reporting purposes, and reflect the stewardship concept of financial reporting as regards the manner in which boards of directors should communicate information to shareholders about the way in which their funds have been handled. For example, when a transaction occurs, it is said that both parties to the transaction are agreed as to the exchange value of the asset involved: that value may be verified at that point, that is, it is an objective measure of value for accounting purposes. It follows, therefore, that the cost of acquiring assets has traditionally been thought to provide the best method of valuing assets for financial reporting purposes on the assumption that the objective of financial reporting is to explain to shareholders how their funds have been handled.

Since the stewardship concept of financial reporting has its roots also in the prevention of frauds, it is interesting to note that one of the major arguments in favour of historical cost valuation is the prevention of fraud. Accountants feel that to depart from this basis of valuation would open the way to fraudulent practices since other measures of value are essentially in the nature of opinions.

We shall note that the convention of conservatism leads to a modification of the cost convention in certain cases, and to reporting to shareholders the lowest likely value. If the realizable value of stocks, for example, is lower than its historical cost value, the convention of conservatism requires that the realizable value be adopted.

The convention of consistency requires that once a basis of valuation has been adopted, it should not be changed except for valid reasons.

Finally, it should be noted that Company Law stipulates the manner in which values should be reported. In the United Kingdom, the law generally reflects the conventions of accounting, and in this respect, we may say that in developing legal rules for financial reporting, the law has followed its tradition of codifying conventions existing among practitioners.

The valuation of assets

The key to an understanding of the manner in which the accountant approaches the problem of valuation is to be found in the classification of assets. Fixed assets are long-term assets whose usefulness in the operations of the firm is likely to extend beyond one accounting period. They are not intended for resale, so that their value depends upon the future cash flows which they are intended to generate. By contrast, current assets are those assets which are intended to be exhausted in the income-earning operations of the next accounting period, and this includes their availability for meeting current liabilities.

There are three general rules for valuing fixed assets:

(a) The enterprise should be considered as a going concern, unless the facts indicate to the contrary. This means that the valuation of fixed assets should reflect the continued expectation of their usefulness to the enterprise. For this reason, their realizable value is inappropriate, and their historical cost is regarded as the most objective measure of value. Historical cost includes the original purchase price and, in addition, all other costs incurred in rendering the asset ready for use. In Part 3 we shall see that it may be argued that historical cost does not value a firm as a going concern.

(b) Changes in the market value of fixed assets are traditionally ignored in the valuation process.

(c) Depreciation in value attributable to wear and tear should always be recognized.

The valuation of fixed assets

The valuation of land

Land is valued at cost despite rises or falls in market value. Cost includes broker's commission, surveying and legal fees and insurance charges. In addition, draining, levelling and landscaping costs and other improvements such as fencing, sewerage and water mains should be included, though it is quite common in the case of farm accounts for these improvements to be shown separately because of the different tax allowances which they occasionally enjoy. Land is not generally regarded as susceptible to depreciation as understood in accounting.

The definition of assets in accounting reflects its orientation towards the law. In this connection, only assets in the ownership of the business may be classed as assets for accounting purposes. This definition poses a particular problem in the case of land. Strictly speaking, only freehold land lies in the ownership of the business for accounting purposes. Leasehold land enjoyed subject to the payment of rent is not classified as an asset, and the rent-charge appears as an expense in the income statement. By contrast, a long lease acquired by the payment of a capital sum is shown as an asset, and the capital payment is usually allocated as expenses over the period of the lease. Leasehold rights extending to 99 and 999 years, for example, are virtually undistinguishable from freehold rights for accounting purposes. Ground rents are chargeable as yearly expenses.

The valuation of buildings

As in the case of land, buildings are valued on a historical cost basis—whether they have been acquired or constructed. Construction costs include such incidental expenses as architect's fees, inspection fees and insurance costs applicable to a construction project. Where an existing building has been purchased, the costs of rendering the building suitable for its intended purpose should be added to the purchase price in arriving at its historic cost value.

The valuation process for buildings differs from that of land in two ways:

(a) A cost of maintenance is involved in the repairs which have to be made from time to time in the upkeep of the building. Such asset maintenance expenses are charged as they are incurred to the income statement. Additions and improvements to the building, which are distinguished from repairs, must be capitalized and added to the value of the building on the balance sheet.

(b) Buildings depreciate in the course of use and as they become dated. Whereas this may not always be true of residential property, it is invariably true as regards industrial and farm buildings. In such cases, the account value should be shown at cost less the accumulated depreciation to date of the balance sheet.

The valuation of plant and machinery and other fixed assets

Plant and machinery, furniture and fittings, motor vehicles, tools and sundry equipment are usually valued at historic cost with proper allowance for depreciation. Cost includes purchase price, freight charges, insurance in transit and all installation costs. As we saw in Chapter 9, the purpose of depreciation in accounting is to allocate the cost of fixed assets to the several years of their useful life to the firm.

The valuation of natural resources

Natural resources, such as oil, gas, coal and other minerals as well as forests and other plantations are valued at cost—whether they are developed or acquired. Development costs which must be capitalized include the costs of exploration, such as drilling for oil.

The revaluation of fixed assets

During the 1960s the practice of historical cost accounting for fixed assets was modified in an attempt to deal with the problems created by changing prices. Increasingly, companies began to adopt the practice of revaluing fixed assets, and entering the revalued figures in the balance sheet.

The practice of revaluing assets was recognized by legislation in the United Kingdom in 1948, when the Companies Act of that year stipulated that fixed assets should be shown at cost, or, if it stands in the company's books at a valuation, the amount of the valuation. No guidance was given, however, by the Act as to when a valuation should be made, except in the case of property where a 'substantial difference' between book and market value should be indicated in the balance sheet. Surveys carried out by the Institute of Chartered Accountants and by the Sandilands Committee, established by the British government to consider the problem of inflation accounting, revealed that many companies were departing from the historical cost principle in their financial reports, though revaluations of property were much more common than revaluations of other fixed assets, whilst most companies were retaining the historical cost method of calculating depreciation. The Sandilands Report (1975) concluded that

> 'The piecemeal way in which revaluations have been carried out has created considerable confusion and difficulty. Few companies have revalued all their assets, few revalue their assets on a regular annual basis, and few disclose the exact basis of the revaluation. The result is that present-day balance sheets in this country consist of a mixture of entries at historic cost and valuations prepared on different bases'.

The valuation of current assets

Current assets consist of cash and other assets, such as debtors and inventories, which are expected to be converted into cash or to be used in the operations of the enterprise within one year. The most complex problems lie in the valuation of the different types of inventories existing at the end of an accounting period. In Part 5, we shall see that closing inventories consist of three types—raw materials, work-in-progress and finished goods. The production process may be viewed as a process of adding value to successive categories of inventories, that is, from raw material to finished goods. Inventories' values, therefore, affect the income statement as well as the balance sheet. Since they are an important constituent of the expenses chargeable against sales revenue, they occupy a key position in the determination of periodic income.

The valuation of inventories

Inventories are traditionally stated at historical cost. SSAP 9 'Stocks and Work in Progress' requires that the cost of inventory 'should comprise that expenditure which has been incurred in the normal course of business in bringing the product or service to its present location and condition'. With respect to the acquisition costs reflected in inventory values, they should be added to the cost of purchasing, the cost of packaging and transport. Where applicable, trade discounts should be deducted from the purchase price.

There are, however, many different methods for determining the cost value of inventories, and these methods produce valuations which differ markedly from each other. A simple example serves to illustrate how three different valuation methods lead to divergent values.

Example

A firm has an opening inventory of 100 items valued at £1.00 each. During the accounting period, 100 units were purchased for £1.20 each and a further 100 units were purchased for £1.30 each. There remained 100 units in inventory at the end of the accounting period, that is, after 200 units had been sold for £300.

The firm is considering the effects of the undermentioned three methods of inventory valuation:

(a) FIFO (first-in-first-out)
(b) LIFO (last-in-first-out)
(c) Weighted average cost.

The effects of these alternative methods may be seen from the tabulation of inventory data below:

	Unit	Unit cost (£)	Value (£)
Opening inventory	100	1.00	100
First purchase	100	1.20	120
Second purchase	100	1.30	130

(a) The FIFO method assumes that the oldest items in inventory are used first, so that the items in inventory are assumed to be the remnants of more recent purchases. The result of the application of FIFO to the given data is that the cost of goods sold during the year is taken to be £220, and the value of the closing inventory is £130.

Advocates of the FIFO method argue that its underlying assumption is in accordance with conventional practice that goods purchased first are sold first, and that this method eliminates the opportunities for management to manipulate income results and inventory values by selecting out of the existing inventory the values which serve their purposes best. Under conditions of rising prices, FIFO requires that the inventory of the earliest date and prices be deemed sold first, with the effect that the income statement reflects a higher level of income than would have been the case if current replacement costs had been used. Closing inventory values are shown at the more recent acquisition prices and approximate current replacement costs.

(b) The LIFO method assumes that the most recently purchased inventories are used first, so that the items remaining in inventory at the end of the year are assumed to be the remnants of earlier purchases. Under this method, the cost of goods sold during the year is taken to be £250, and the value of the closing inventory is £100. The LIFO method has the reverse effect, therefore, to FIFO on the measurement of income and the valuation of closing inventories.

Though LIFO approximates the replacement cost basis of valuation as regards the input of resources to the income earning process, it does not necessarily correspond with replacement cost valuation. LIFO reflects the latest cost price of the specific commodity, which may or may not be the actual replacement cost. In the case of seasonal buying, for example, the cost of the last purchase may not be equivalent to the current replacement cost. As a result, LIFO eliminates only an indeterminate part of the effects of specific price changes. Indeed, when sales exceed purchases, that is, when inventories are being depleted, the gap between replacement cost and LIFO may become very great. A classic example of this situation arose in the United States during the Korean War, which resulted in inventory reduction on such a scale that Congressional approval was given for Next-In-First-Out inventory valuation as a relief for taxpayers who were on the LIFO basis! (Fremgen, 1962.)

A further disadvantage of the LIFO method of inventory valuation is that it leads to distortions in balance sheet valuations. This is defended on the grounds that the income statement is the more important document since income measurement is the major point of interest among shareholders. According to Moonitz (1953), however, 'this leaves unanswered the important query as to how it is possible to have reasonably accurate statements of income accompanied by admittedly inaccurate balance sheets. Where is the difference buried and what is its significance?'

(c) The weighted average cost method requires the calculation of the unit cost of closing inventory by means of a formula which divides the total cost of all inventory available for sale during the accounting period by the physical units of inventory available for sale.

The weighted average cost of the 300 units available for sale may be calculated as follows:

$$\frac{\text{Total cost of annual inventory}}{\text{Total annual units of inventory}} = \frac{£350}{300} = £1.167 \text{ per unit}$$

Hence, the cost of goods sold during the year is £233, whilst the value of the closing inventory is £117. The weighted average cost method is a compromise, therefore, between the extreme points established by FIFO and LIFO respectively.

The effects of different methods of inventory valuation on the calculation of income may be seen in the example given below. For simplicity, it is assumed that the business is considering a change in the method of inventory valuation which gave an opening inventory value of £100.

	FIFO	LIFO	Weighted Average
	£	£	£
Purchases	250	250	250
Add: Opening inventory	100	100	100
	350	350	350
Less: Closing inventory	130	100	117
Cost of goods sold	220	250	233
Sales	300	300	300
Net income	80	50	67

This simple example shows that the closing inventory may be valued at £130, £100 or £117 depending on the assumptions made about the flow of costs. Three different income figures result from using different inventory valuation methods, namely £80, £50 and £67. It should be remembered that the closing inventory for one year becomes the opening inventory of the following year. Therefore, in the long-term, there will be no difference in the calculation of the net income of the business. It is in the short-term that different inventory valuation methods give different results. This fact emphasizes the significance of any changes in the inventory valuation method used.

LIFO is a method of inventory valuation which is commonly used in the United States but its use in the United Kingdom is prohibited by the Inland Revenue authorities.

The 'lower of cost or market' (LCM) rule

The valuation of inventories at cost or market value, whichever is lower, is a rule which has long and widely been observed in financial accounting. The rule was originally justified in terms of the convention of conservatism, which as applied to the valuation of inventories meant that there should be no anticipation of profit and that all foreseeable losses should be provided for in the value reported to shareholders. Thus, if the cost value of an inventory item was £1.20 and the market value was £1.00, the end of year inventory valuation should be based on the lower value, and the difference written off against income.

The relation of the LCM rule to the other rules governing cost allocation and income determination in accounting may be questioned. If, for example, periodic income is to be measured by a rigorous process of matching revenues with their related product costs, it would seem inappropriate to charge against current revenues the cost of products which have not yet been sold, thereby relieving the revenues of a future period of a portion of their proper burden. Hence, the rule violates the matching convention, resulting in a distortion of current and future income measurements, thereby affecting their reliability as indicators of business performance. For this reason, some have argued that the rule is 'starkly illogical' and have suggested that it should be abandoned save in the case of obsolete or damaged inventories (van Pelt III, 1962). Others however, have reconciled the rule with the matching convention on the grounds that only 'useful' costs should be carried forward to the next accounting period (May, 1947). Costs which are not useful are those which exceed the market value of the inventory in question. The measure of the loss represented by the difference between cost and market value of such inventories may validly be treated as a cost of conducting business during the currency of the accounting period. According to this interpretation of the LCM rule, the lower of these two values represents the residual useful stock.

Different meanings of 'market value'

Whilst most accountants would agree with the LCM rule, there seems to be little unanimity as to which market value is the most useful. According to one author, the net realizable value interpretation of market value is most commonly accepted in the United Kingdom and Australia; in the United States, market value means replacement or reproduction cost; in Canada and most European countries, net realizable value is used for the valuation of finished goods and replacement cost is applied to the valuation of raw material inventories (Mueller, 1964).

The net realizable value concept is based on the theory that the usefulness of a measurement of inventory value is to be found in its function as an indicator of the recoverable value of the inventory concerned. So long as the expected net realizable value is equal to the costs which have been incurred, there is no possibility of an accounting loss occurring.

The replacement cost concept of market value is based on the idea of the 'utility' of inventory. According to the American Institute of Certified Public Accountants (1953), 'as a general guide, utility is indicated primarily by the current cost of replacement of the goods as they would be obtained by purchase or reproduction'. Hence, the notion of utility in this context is related to the ability to generate income, for at the time of acquisition, each unit of inventory is regarded as incorporating a gross income potential which is to be realized at the time of sale. The measure of the retained usefulness of inventory held at the end of the accounting period is to be found, therefore, in an assessment of the expenditure which would have to be incurred to produce or to purchase inventory having an equivalent gross profit potential. Where inventory may be replaced at a cost which is lower than the acquisition cost of currently held inventory, the fall in the replacement cost is regarded as indicating that the expected gross income potential of current inventory has decreased. For this reason, the lower of the cost of current inventories and their replacement cost is used in the United States to measure the residual income potential of inventories on hand, and to determine the amount of their acquisition cost which appropriately should be written off as having lost their usefulness for producing future income. As a result, subsequent revenues are not charged with the cost of acquiring inventories which is higher than current costs, and distortions are not introduced into the measurement of income.

The replacement cost concept of market value assumes that a decrease in the replacement cost will be accompanied by a corresponding decrease in the net realizable value of currently held inventories. Where there is no evidence to suggest that a fall in selling prices will take place, there is no likelihood of a failure to recover the cost of acquisition of existing inventories. Consequently, no loss of gross income potential is incurred. For this reason, A.I.C.P.A. Research Bulletin No. 43 recommended an upper and a lower limit for replacement cost as a definition of 'market' in the LCM rule. Therefore, no loss should be recognized if the fall in replacement cost does not reflect a similar fall in expected selling price, because a loss should not be recognized in the current accounting period, if it will result in the recognition of abnormal income in a later period.

General criticism of the LCM rule

The LCM rule has long been criticized primarily on the basis of its inherent inconsistency. Thus, if current replacement cost is objective, definite, verifiable and more useful when it is lower than acquisition cost it also possesses these attributes when it is higher than acquisition cost (Sprouse and Moonitz, 1962). The conservatism reflected in the LCM rule for asset valuations in one period results in an over-statement of income in the subsequent period. The consequence of recognizing decreases in value but not increases in value occurring prior to sale is reflected in a shifting effect in periodic income measurement.

The valuation of debtors

The problems associated with the valuation of debtors were discussed in Chapter 9.

The valuation of other assets

Investments

In financial accounting, investments are defined as shares and other legal rights acquired by a firm through the investment of its funds. Investments may be long-term or short-term, depending upon the intention of the firm at the time of acquisition. Where investments are intended to be held for a period of more than one year, they are in the nature of fixed assets: where they are held for a shorter period, they are in the nature of current assets. Shares in subsidiary and associated companies are usually not held for resale, and hence would be classified as being of the nature of fixed assets. Short-dated Government stocks, for example, may provide a convenient vehicle for the investment of excess funds not immediately needed. Such short-term holdings would be classified as current assets in the balance sheet. It is the practice, however, to show investments separately in the balance sheet and not to include them under the heading of 'fixed assets'.

Investments are recorded at their cost of acquisition, and whilst substantial decreases in value may be written off against current income, appreciations in value are not recognized until realized.

Legislation in the United Kingdom requires that a note be appended to the balance sheet in respect of both long- and short-term investments, where there is a difference between the book value and the market value. In the case of long-term investments, there is the further requirement of distinguishing investments which are quoted on a stock exchange from unquoted investments as follows:

	£	£
Investments		
Quoted securities (market value £57,000)	80,000	
Unquoted securities (Director's valuation £7000)	15,000	
		95,000
Current assets		
Marketable securities (market value £25,000)	20,000	
		20,000

Intangible assets

Intangible assets are non-physical assets in the form of legal rights, privileges and competitive advantages which are relatively long lived. They are not intended for sale, but are intended to be used by the firm. The following are examples of intangible assets:

(a) *Patents*

A patent represents a temporary monopoly which is granted to an inventor and which is protected by law during its duration. It gives the inventor the exclusive right to sell or to use his invention for a fixed period of years. Whilst the cost of registering a patent at the Patent Office is relatively small, firms often pay large sums to inventors for the purchase of patents. The cost of development and registration, or the cost of acquisition, whichever is appropriate, is shown as an asset on the balance sheet for it represents a valuable right.

(b) *Trade-marks*

Firms often market their products under a trade-mark, which is a distinguishing mark for their products. 'St. Michael', for example, has become a world-wide trade-mark for the products of Marks and Spencers. Trade-marks are a form of guarantee that the product is a genuine product of the firm in question. The firm's reputation for quality is associated in the public mind with its trade-marks. Trade-marks are registered and may not be used by another firm. The costs associated with registering trade-marks are shown as assets on the balance sheet.

(c) *Copyrights*

Copyrights are similar to patents and trade-marks, but apply to literary and artistic works. Authors, artists and designers enjoy the exclusive right to use, sell or license their work for a fixed period of years.

Where rights such as patents or copyrights are licensed in favour of another, a royalty is paid to the owner of the right. The export of knowledge in the form of licensing patent and copyrights has become a way of trading, where owing to circumstances a firm has been unable or unwilling to establish a manufacturing base in a foreign country. In such cases, the foreign company manufactures the product under licence, and pays a royalty on an agreed basis. Industrial and chemical products and processes are often produced or employed under licence.

(d) *Franchises*

A franchise is a monopoly right to trade in a particular area or as regards a particular activity. Franchises are common in the motor trade, for example, where distribution networks are based on accredited dealers who are sole selling agents for particular makes. Another typical franchise is the monopoly right granted by a government to a corporation to operate a public transport system. The costs of negotiating and acquiring the franchise should be capitalized.

(e) *Organization costs*
The costs involved in setting up a business entity are regarded as constituting intangible assets. They comprise all preliminary expenses such as the legal costs associated with company formation and registration, and other legal, underwriting and accounting fees. It is the practice to write them off as soon as possible.

(f) *Research and development costs*
Accounting procedures with regard to the treatment of research and development costs pose an issue which is common to all intangible assets—to what extent should theoretical concepts of intangible assets be tempered by practical considerations? SSAP 13 'Accounting for Research and Development' illustrates these problems in its attempt to produce a prescription for the treatment of research and development expenditures in accordance with the four concepts on which SSAP 2 is based namely, going concern, accruals, consistency and prudence, as discussed in Chapter 5.

SSAP 13 defines research and development under three main headings: pure research (being work directed primarily towards the advancement of knowledge), applied research (being work directed primarily towards exploiting pure research other than work defined as development expenditure) and development (being work directed towards the introduction or improvement of specific products or processes). As regards expenditure falling within these first two categories, which may be regarded as part of a continuing operation required to maintain a company's business and its competitive position, this should be written off against revenue in the year in which expenditure is incurred. This excludes the cost of fixed assets acquired or constructed for research and development activities over a period of time which should be capitalized and written off over the useful life of the assets. Expenditure on development should be written off in the year of expenditure except in the following circumstances, where it may be deferred to future periods:

(a) there is a clearly defined project;
(b) the related expenditure is separately identifiable;
(c) the outcome of such a project has been assessed with reasonable certainty as to its technical feasibility, and its ultimate commercial viability;
(d) if further development costs are to be incurred on the same project, the aggregate of such costs together with related production, selling and administration costs are reasonably expected to be more than covered by related future revenues; and
(e) adequate resources exist, or are reasonably expected to be available, to enable the project to be completed and to provide any consequential increases in working capital.

In the circumstances defined above, development expenditure may be deferred to subsequent years, and shown on the balance sheet as an asset to the extent that its recovery can be regarded as reasonably assured. Deferred development expenditure should be reviewed at the end of each accounting period and where the circumstances which have justified the deferral of the expenditure no longer apply, the expenditure, to the extent considered irrecoverable, should be written off immediately.

It is interesting to compare SSAP 13 with the United States standard, FASB Statement No. 2, which prescribes that all expenditure on research and development should be written off in the year incurred rather than capitalized as intangible assets. The American approach is inconsistent with the accruals and matching convention and, therefore, cannot be justified in accordance with descriptive accounting theory. However, the standard has greatly simplified accounting practice in this area and has eliminated the manipulation of research and development expenditure for the purpose of adjusting reported income.

(g) *Advertising expenditure*

It is the practice to write off advertising expenditure as it is incurred, on the grounds that it supports the current level of sales. Where it is clear, however, that such expenditure is incurred in order to generate future sales, it should be treated as an asset and carried forward until such time as it may be matched with those sales.

(h) *Goodwill*

Goodwill may be described as the sum of those intangible attributes of a business which contribute to its success, such as a favourable location, a good reputation, the ability and skill of its employees and management, its long-standing relationships with creditors, suppliers and customers. The valuation of goodwill is a controversial topic in accounting because of its vague nature and the difficulty of arriving at a valuation which is verifiable. Hence, in view of its lack of accounting objectivity, it is generally excluded from the balance sheet. Goodwill only enters the accounting system in connection with a valuation ascribed to it in the acquisition price of a business. In such a case, that portion of the purchase price which exceeds the total value of the assets taken over less the liabilities taken over, represents the amount paid for goodwill. At this point, therefore, there is no objective measure of the value of goodwill.

There are two viewpoints regarding the manner in which goodwill should be treated in financial reports. One viewpoint is that goodwill should be eliminated from the balance sheet by being deducted from the shareholders' equity by an adjustment to the reserves, as soon as goodwill arises by the acquisition of any business. According to this view, goodwill is a payment made by shareholders for the expected future earnings of the business acquired. Hence, the goodwill is associated directly with the interests of the shareholders in the company.

The other viewpoint is that goodwill should be shown as an asset, and be treated as other fixed assets. Therefore, goodwill should be capitalized and written off over a period of years. This treatment of goodwill is commonly found in the United States. Proponents of this view argue that an expense has been incurred in acquiring the benefit of future earnings. As the benefit associated with goodwill is exploited, and the enhanced earnings actually materialize, they should be matched with the costs associated with the goodwill which gave rise to them. If costs are not matched in this way, there is an overstatement of income.

In practice, many companies in the United Kingdom do not write off goodwill immediately on acquisition, but show it as a deduction from reserves.

The valuation of intangible assets creates problems, for although they are often the most important assets, financial accounting conventions inhibit their recognition. The cost and money measurement conventions, for example, inhibit a proper valuation of such assets: the former because the cost of acquisition may be small in comparison with fixed assets, or completely hidden as in the case of goodwill, the latter because of the difficulty of obtaining objective measurements. The convention of conservatism causes such items as research and development and advertising expenditure to be treated as periodic expenses in situations where they should be capitalized. Indeed, it is thought that the presence of large intangible asset values in a balance sheet might be interpreted as a sign of financial weakness.

The exclusion of substantial intangible asset values from the balance sheet is another aspect of the segregation of the role of the accountant and the role of the investor as regards financial accounting information. The role of the accountant is defined by the framework of conventions which we discussed in Chapter 4. The role of the investor is to evaluate the information prepared by the accountant and to form his own judgement about the valuations attached to balance sheet assets. In this respect, the investor has to form his own judgement about the value of intangible as well as tangible assets in arriving at a valuation of the business as an investment.

The valuation of liabilities

Liabilities may be defined as currently existing obligations which the firm intends to meet at some time in the future. Such obligations arise from legal or managerial considerations and impose restrictions on the use of assets by the firm for its own purposes.

To be recognized as a liability in accounting, the following tests must be satisfied:

(a) the liability must exist at the present time;
(b) it must involve expenditure in the future;
(c) it must be ascertained with reasonable accuracy;
(d) it must be quantifiable;
(e) its maturity date must be known at least approximately (Barton, 1975).

The capital invested by the owner or shareholders in an enterprise is not regarded as a liability in accounting. We shall deal with the accounting treatment of the owner's or shareholders' equity presently, but we should mention at this stage that shareholders have a right at law to the payment of a dividend once it has been declared. As a result, unpaid or unclaimed dividends are shown as current liabilities. It is the practice to show proposed dividends as current liabilities also, since such proposed dividends are usually final dividends for the year which must be approved at the annual general meeting before which the accounts for the year must be laid.

The valuation problem

The valuation of liabilities is part of the process of measuring both capital and income, and is important to such problems as capital maintenance and the ascertainment of a firm's financial position. Hence, 'the requirements for an accurate measure of the financial position and financial structure should determine the basis for liability valuation. Their valuation should be consistent with the valuation of assets and expenses' (Barton 1975). The need for consistency arises from the objectives of liability valuation, which are similar to those of asset valuation. Probably the most important of these objectives is the desire to record expenses and financial losses in the process of measuring income. However, the valuation of liabilities should also assist investors and creditors in understanding the financial position of the firm.

In accordance with the manner of valuing assets in economics, liabilities may be valued at their discounted net values; in accordance with accounting conventions, they may be recorded at their historic value, that is, the valuation attached to the contractual basis by which they were created.

Example

A firm acquired a piece of land for £20,000 on 1 January 19X0, £10,000 being payable immediately and £10,000 on 1 January 19X1. No interest is payable on the outstanding balance. The two different valuations of the outstanding liability at 1 January 19X0 are as follows:

(a) Discounted net value of £10,000 assuming that the current rate of interest is 10%:

$$£10,000 \times \frac{100\%}{100\% + 10\%}$$

i.e. £10,000 × 0.9091 = £9091.

(b) Historical value of £10,000 by reference to the contract to pay £10,000 on 1 January 19X1 is, of course, £10,000.

There is no gap between the two methods of valuation as regards liabilities which are payable immediately, and it is only as the maturity date of liabilities lengthens that the gap appears. Whilst accounting conventions dictate that the valuation of liabilities should be based on the sum which is payable, it is accounting practice to make a distinction between current and long-term liabilities. As regards current liabilities, there is little difference between the discounted net value and the contractual value of liabilities. In this connection, current liabilities are defined as those which will mature during the course of the accounting period. The gap between the two methods of valuation is significant as regards long-term liabilities. Long-term liabilities are valued on the basis of their historical value, that is, by reference to the contract from which they originated, and hence, during periods of inflation or where the interest payable is less than the current market rate of interest, the accounting valuation will certainly be overstated by comparison with the discounted net value. Here again, a true perspective on this problem may be obtained by reference to the separate role of the accountant and the investor which we stated in the introduction to this part. The accountant records the liability as the sum which will be payable: it is for the investor to value the real cost of that future burden.

Contingent liabilities

Contingent liabilities are those which will arise in the future only on the occurrence of a specified event. Although they are based on past contractual obligations, they are conditional rather than certain liabilities. Thus, guarantees given by the firm are contingent liabilities rather than current liabilities. If a holding company has guaranteed the overdraft of one of its subsidiary companies, the guarantee is payable only in the event of the subsidiary company being unable to repay the overdraft.

Contingent liabilities are not formally recorded in the accounts system, but appear as footnotes to the balance sheet.

Deferred liabilities

The two major types of deferred liabilities are:

(a) Deferred performance liabilities
(b) Deferred tax liabilities.

Deferred performance liabilities exist under a number of forms, the most common being pre-payments which cannot be taken into the income of the current year and are carried forward to the following year. We examined the adjustments required to deal with pre-payments in Chapter 8. Other deferred performance liabilities are created under contracts of sales which provide for post-sale services. Thus, sales of many consumer appliances provide for labour-free servicing of appliances under guarantee. Whilst the realization convention requires the accrual of revenue in the year of sale, provision should be made for the deferred performance liability in the form of an estimate of the after-sale servicing costs. This may be obtained by reference to past experience and expressed as a percentage of total sales for the purpose of calculating the amount which should be shown as a liability.

Deferred tax liabilities arise from the fact that tax is assessed in relation to 'taxable income' and not to 'accounting income'. Hence, whilst the taxation authorities use the information contained in the annual accounts for the purposes of computing the taxable income, the tax payable in respect of that income is not finally assessed until the subsequent year or years. For this reason, the accountant will create a provision for the tax likely to be payable and will show it as a deferred tax liability.

The valuation of shareholders' equity

A consideration of the problem of valuing shareholders' equity is beyond the scope of this book and properly belongs to the theory of finance. Nevertheless, the shareholders' equity is a significant section of the balance sheet for two reasons:

(a) it completes the accounting equation as follows:

$$\text{Assets} - \text{Liabilities} = \text{Shareholders' equity}$$

(b) it links the balance sheet and the income statement since the retained profits are absorbed in the shareholders' equity.

The accounting valuation of the shareholders' equity is made up of a number of items:

(a) the cash received from shareholders in respect of the shares issued to them;
(b) the premiums, if any, paid by shareholders over and above the nominal value of issued shares;
(c) the accumulated capital and revenue reserves created out of past profits;
(d) undistributed retained profit carried forward for distribution in a subsequent year, in the form of dividend equalization accounts or otherwise.

The accounting valuation of the shareholders' equity has virtually no significance in relation to the market value of the equity, which may be determined, in the case of quoted companies, by reference to the share price determined by the Stock Exchange. The economic valuation of the shareholders' equity may be derived from the present value of discounted future net cash flows expected to be earned by the firm.

As regards the valuation of the shareholders' equity, the accountant is concerned only with recording the historical values associated with its several constituent elements in accordance with accounting conventions. He leaves the problem of valuation to the investor.

Summary

It is necessary to understand the logic and methodology which underlie the recorded values of assets and liabilities in order to appreciate the nature of financial accounting information. A number of conventions surround the problem of valuation of assets and liabilities shown on income statements and balance sheets.

This chapter examines the accounting approach to the valuation of fixed and current assets, and considers the effects of inflation in modifying the historical cost convention for fixed asset valuation. This chapter also illustrates the effects of traditional accounting practices in creating variety in the accounting treatment of different items. The valuation of liabilities is also discussed, although it presents a less difficult problem from an accounting viewpoint. Nevertheless, accounting makes virtually no contribution to the valuation of the shareholders' equity, although this is a central problem for shareholders and investors.

References

1. A.I.C.P.A. Accounting Research Bulletin No. 43, 1963.
2. Barton, A. D. *The Anatomy of Accounting*, University of Queensland Press, 1975.
3. Fremgen, J. M. 'Involuntary liquidation of LIFO inventories', *Journal of Accountancy*, December, 1962.
4. May, G. O. 'Inventory pricing and contingent reserves', *Journal of Accountancy*, November, 1947.
5. Moonitz, M. 'The case against LIFO', *Journal of Accountancy*, June, 1952.
6. Mueller, G. G. 'Valuing inventories at other than historical cost—some international aspects', *Journal of Accounting Research*, Autumn, 1964.
7. van Pelt III, J. V. 'Inventory valuation lacks accounting standards', *NAA Bulletin*, March, 1962.
8. Sprouse, R. T. & Moonitz, M. 'A tentative set of broad accounting principles for business enterprises', *Accounting Research Study* No. 3, A.I.C.P.A., 1962.
9. The Sandilands Report. *Report of the Inflation Accounting Committee*, p. 100, HMSO Cmd 6225, 1975.

Questions

1. You are the Chief Accountant of a retailing company which operates from a number of departmental stores throughout the country. You are approached early in 19X2 by a member of your staff who is preparing the annual accounts for the Barnsley store for the year ended 31 December 19X1. He seeks your advice on the following matters:

   (a) how to treat the goodwill arising on the acquisition of a local bakery during 19X1. The Barnsley store acquired the bakery for the purpose of securing its own supply of bread. The cost was £85,000 including goodwill of £20,000;
   (b) whether to depreciate the cost of the freehold of the furniture department's warehouse which was purchased during the year. The cost was £44,000 split between land £10,000 and buildings £34,000. Legal fees of £800 were also incurred;
   (c) how to value two items of stock which he is unsure of. These are:

   (i) a large stock of over-ordered Christmas cards costing £780
   (ii) a stock of skateboards purchased in 19X0 for £1000;

   (d) whether to treat an advertising campaign as an expense in 19X1 or to carry it forward to 19X2. The campaign costing £1700 involved a series of advertisements in the Barnsley Sun newspaper in December 19X1 informing readers of the January sale. The sale was not as popular as it has been in recent years.

   Required:

   Draft a memorandum to your member of staff setting out the accounting principles to be followed in each of the above cases and give advice on the most appropriate treatment in the circumstances given.

                    (Question supplied by A. J. Naughton, Leeds Polytechnic)
2. A fire completely destroyed Arthur's Timberyard and all his accounting records, during the night of 31 December 19X6.

From copy bank statements and circularization of his debtors and creditors, Arthur was able to ascertain the following figures.

	£
Debtors, 1 January 19X6	5130
Creditors, 1 January 19X6	1790
Cash paid to creditors during the year	22,220
Cash received from debtors during the year	30,080
Creditors, 31 December 19X6	1870
Debtors, 31 December 19X6	6050

Arthur's trading accounts for the two years ended 31 December 19X5 were as follows:

	Year ended Dec. 19X4	Year ended Dec. 19X5		Year ended Dec. 19X4	Year ended Dec. 19X5
Opening inventory	1235	1700	Sales	18,850	25,740
Purchases	13,660	17,718			
	14,895	19,418			
Less closing inventory	1700	1400			
	13,195	18,018			
Gross income	5655	7722			
	£18,850	25,740		£18,850	25,740

Assuming that the ratio of gross income to sales remained the same in 19X6 as in previous years, calculate the value of the inventory destroyed by fire. Submit your workings.

3. Viva Ltd does not keep records of stock movements. A physical stocktaking is made at the end of each quarter and priced at cost. This figure is used for compiling quarterly accounts. Draft accounts have been prepared for the year ended 31 March 1980, but have not been completed as the details of the stock count on 31 March 1980 have been mislaid and cannot be found. The company operates on a gross profit mark-up of $33\frac{1}{3}$ per cent of cost.

You have ascertained the following facts:

(a) the total of sales invoiced to customers during January, February and March 19X1 was £53,764. This figure includes £4028 relating to goods despatched on or before 31 December 19X0. The total of the goods despatched to customers before 31 March 19X1 but invoiced in the following month was £5512;

(b) the total of purchase invoices entered in the purchase day book during January, February and March 19X1 was £40,580 and this figure includes £2940 in respect of goods received on or before 31 December 19X0. Invoices relating to goods received in March 19X1 but which were not entered in the purchase day book until April 19X1 totalled £3880;

(c) the value of the stock at cost on 31 December 19X0 was £42,640;

(d) in the stock sheets at that date:

(i) the total of one page was over-cast by £85
(ii) 120 items, the cost of which was £2 each, had been priced at 40p each
(iii) the total of the stock in one section, which was £5260, had been included in the summary as £5620

Required:

Show how you would arrive at the figure for the stock at cost as on 31 March 19X1.
(Question supplied by A. J. Naughton, Leeds Polytechnic)

4. Purchases and sales data for the first three years of a firm's operation were as follows (purchases are listed in order of acquisition):

	19X1	19X2	19X3
	£	£	£
Sales	12,000 units @ 50	15,000 units @ 60	18,000 units @ 65
Purchases	4000 units @ 22	5500 units @ 32	7000 units @ 40
	6000 units @ 25	6000 units @ 34	4500 units @ 43
	5000 units @ 30	4000 units @ 37	5000 units @ 45

Required:

(a) Prepare a schedule showing the number of units on hand at the end of each year.
(b) Compute the year-end inventories for each of the three years using (a) FIFO (b) LIFO.
(c) Prepare income statements for each of the three years based on (a) FIFO (b) LIFO and (c) weighted average.
(d) Which method of inventory valuation do you consider the most logical? Why?

5. Examine the problems of accounting for research and development expenditure, and explain the requirements of SSAP 13.

12 Funds flow and cash flow statements

The two financial statements so far discussed constitute the traditional format by which information is conveyed about the financial performance and the financial status of the enterprise. The income statement contains details of the financial performance resulting in a figure of net income; the balance sheet provides details of the financial status of the enterprise in the form of a listing of assets and liabilities as at the close of the accounting period.

The purpose of the funds flow statement and the cash flow statement is to provide additional information of interest to users of financial reports. In this respect, the funds flow statement provides a reconciliation between the opening and the closing balance sheets relating to the accounting period by explaining the changes which have occurred and the means by which these changes have been effected. It provides an analysis of the sources of additional funds available to the enterprise during the accounting period, and an analysis of the manner in which they have been utilized. The funds flow statement integrates the additional funds generated by the enterprise through its income-generating operations as well as external funds supplied during the year. In effect, the funds flow statement explains how changes in the *dimensions* of the financial status of the enterprise have occurred. By contrast, the cash flow statement has the stricter purpose of explaining the changes in the cash situation of the enterprise during the accounting period. In this respect, the cash flow statement is more closely associated with the problem of liquidity, and the cash available to the enterprise. For this reason, the cash flow statement is particularly meaningful to users of financial information.

The funds flow statement

According to Jaedicke and Sprouse (1965), accounting flows may be classified into three distinct types—income flows, funds flows and cash flows. There are different interpretations given to the term 'funds', which range from a narrow definition identifying 'funds' with 'cash' to an enlarged definition which links 'funds' to the 'working capital' of the enterprise. Such a definition of funds is directed to the working capital available to the enterprise to finance its operations, since working capital is defined as the excess of current assets over current liabilities. The definition of 'funds' adopted in this text is that based on working capital.

Form and content of funds flow statements

The funds flow statement is concerned with the problems of financial management. It is used as a supplementary statement to the income state-ment and the balance sheet to explain what the firm has done with the additional funds which it has obtained from all sources during the accounting year. The funds flow statement will show, for example, if the firm has applied its income to increasing its holdings of cash or reducing its liabilities, or a mixture of both.

The main sources of funds are as follows:

(1) new capital introduced by the owner
(2) loans to the business
(3) operating income, after adjustment for non-cash expenses
(4) sale of assets or investments.

The main applications of funds are as follows:

(1) withdrawals by the owner
(2) repayments of loans
(3) operating losses, should they occur
(4) purchase of assets or investments
(5) taxation.

In considering funds flow statements, care must be taken to avoid confusion between two fundamental ways in which changes may be mea-sured. One method is based on identifying the flows of the variables involved, and the second on the inventory of those variables. The mathematical principle is simply that a change may be quantified either: (i) by identifying the sum total of all increases and decreases in funds; or (ii) by measuring the difference between the two total inventories connected by this change. Figure 2.16 illustrates the principle involved. The area $t_0 \times t_1$ represents the change

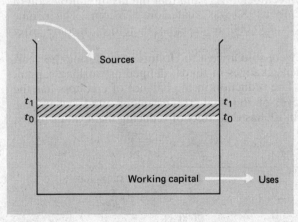

Fig. 2.16.

in the inventory of working capital in the time period covered by the funds flow statement. It may be explained either by: (i) the excess of sources of funds over the uses of funds; or (ii) itemizing the component changes in current assets − current liabilities (CA − CL), that is, as follows:

$$(CA - CL)_{t_1} - (CA - CL)_{t_0}$$

Accordingly, the funds flow statement may be presented as follows:

Funds flow statement
For the period from . . . . . to . . . . .

Funds at the beginning of period . . .			xxxxxx
Funds changes during the period	*Sources*	*Applications*	
(1) Net funds from operations	xxx		
(2) Funds transactions with owner			
Capital introduced	xxx	xxx	
Withdrawals			
(3) Funds transactions with long-term creditors			
Loans obtained	xxx		
Loans repaid		xxx	
(4) Funds transactions involving plant, and other non-current assets			
Acquisitions		xxx	
Disposals	xxx		
Totals			
Net increase (decrease) in funds			xxxxxxx
Funds at the end of the period. . . .			xxxxxxx

Example

The following balance sheets relate to Extoll Imports, which is an importing firm owned by Alfred Holfort.

It may be noted that the tax liability existing at 31 December 19X0 was paid during the year ended 31 December 19X1, and that the taxation provision of £10,000 existing at 31 December 19X1 was created out of income. The income for the year amounting to £30,000 represents, therefore, income after provision for taxation.

Note also that premises were sold at cost to Holfort's son during the year.

The analysis of component changes in funds, defined as working capital, is as shown below. (*Note:* The reduction in the balance of creditors has the effect of increasing the level of funds at 31 December 19X1, where the increase in the taxation liability has the effect of reducing the level of funds, as defined.)

	Increase £	Decrease £
Inventories		4000
Debtors	2000	
Cash		7000
Creditors	7000	
Taxation		2000
	9000	13,000
		9000
Net change		4000

Balance sheets as on 31 December

Capital employed	19X0 £	£	19X1 £	£
Capital (1 January)	50,000		60,000	
Income for the year	25,000		30,000	
	75,000		90,000	
Withdrawals	15,000		20,000	
	60,000		70,000	
Long-term loan	20,000		—	
		80,000		70,000

Represented by

Fixed assets	Cost £	Dep. £	Net £		Cost £	Dep. £	Net £
Premises	30,000	—	30,000		20,000	—	20,000
Equipment	10,000	2000	8000		15,000	3000	12,000
	20,000	2000		38,000	35,000	3000	32,000

Current assets			
Inventories at cost	50,000		46,000
Debtors	15,000		17,000
Cash	15,000		8000
	80,000		71,000

Less Current liabilities				
Creditors	30,000		23,000	
Taxation	8000		10,000	
		38,000		33,000
Net working capital		42,000		38,000
		80,000		70,000

Funds flow statement for the year ended 31 December 19X1

	£	£	£
Funds at 1 January 19X1 (working capital)			42,000
Net funds from operations			
Income for the year	30,000		
Add: Non-cash expenses			
Depreciation	1000		
	31,000		
Funds transactions with owner			
Withdrawals		20,000	
Funds transactions with long-term creditors			
Loan repayment		20,000	
Funds transactions involving assets			
Sale of premises	10,000		
Purchase of equipment		5000	
	41,000	45,000	
Net decrease in funds			4000
Funds at 31 December 19X1			38,000

A comprehensive illustration

Table 2.1 shows the balance sheets for P. Crookes Ltd as at 31 December 19X0 and 19X1 together with an abridged income statement for the year ended 31 December 19X1. Table 2.2 sets out the working involved in using the information contained in Table 2.1 for the purpose of preparing the funds flow statement. Table 2.2 contains four stages which are discussed below.

Stage 1 Balance sheet changes are calculated and are expressed in the middle columns as changes in debit and credit balances. For example, share capital account has been credited with £50,000, and this increase is shown as a credit in the 'Changes' column. Fixed assets have increased from £225,000 to £270,000 during the year, an additional debit of £45,000, which is shown as

Table 2.1
The balance sheets for P. Crookes Ltd as at 31 December 19X0 and 19X1 were as follows:

	31 December	
	19X0	*19X1*
	£	£
Share capital	150	200
Share premium account	25	30
General reserve	40	40
Retained income	10	—
Shareholders' funds employed	225	270
12% Debentures	80	100
Total funds employed	305	370
Represented by:		
Fixed assets, at cost less depreciation	225	270
Inventory	50	60
Debtors	50	60
Cash	55	62
	155	182
Creditors	30	30
Provision for taxation	20	22
Dividends proposed	25	30
	75	82
Net working capital	80	100
	305	370

Abridged income statement for the year ended 31 December 19X1

Trading income	57
Less: Depreciation	15
Net income for the year before tax	42
Retained income brought forward from 19X0	10
	52
Less:	
Provision for taxation	22
Dividends proposed	30 52
Retained income carried forward	Nil

such in the 'Changes' column. Since the balance sheet is always an exact equation between assets and liabilities + capital, it follows that the net changes between assets and liabilities + capital must also always be exactly equal.

Stage 2 Details of the changes which were calculated in Step 1 are transferred to the top half of the 'Adjustments' columns. These are then transferred to the lower half of the 'Adjustments' columns by means of the double-entry principle. These transfers are discussed below:

(1)   50,000 £1 shares were issued at a total value of £55,000 during 19X1. This explains the increase in share capital and share premium. In the 'Adjustments' columns £55,000 is transferred to the bottom half of these columns as follows:

Share capital	Dr.	£50,000	
Share premium	Dr.	£5000	
Issued share capital	Cr.		£55,000

(2)   Retained income is analysed into the factors which have caused the change of £10,000. First, the trading income of £57,000 for 19X1 is shown as being transferred from the top half of the 'Adjustments' column to the bottom half:

Retained income	Dr.	£57,000	
Income from operations	Cr.		£57,000

Secondly, retained income is credited with £67,000 which has arisen from three factors:

	£
Depreciation	15,000
Taxation	22,000
Proposed dividend	30,000
	67,000

Although depreciation reduces net income, it has no immediate impact on the working capital provided by normal operations. Fixed assets, taxation provision and proposed dividends are debited with £15,000, £22,000 and £30,000 respectively.

(3)   Depreciation for the year is added to the change in fixed assets in order to calculate the purchases of fixed assets during the year:

	£
Balance of fixed assets at 31 December 19X1	270,000
Depreciation for the year	15,000
	185,000
Balance at 31 December 19X0	225,000
Purchase of fixed assets in 19X1	60,000

(4)   Debentures have increased by £20,000, and this is transferred from the top half of the 'Adjustments' column to the bottom half.

Table 2.2

			Changes		Adjustments		Working capital	
31 December	19X0	19X1	Dr.	Cr.	Dr.	Cr.	Appn.	Source
	£000	£000	£000	£000	£000	£000	£000	£000
Share capital	150	200			50	50		
Share premium	25	30			5	5		
General reserve	40	40						
Retained income	10	—		10		57	67	
	225	270						
12% Debenture	80	100			20	20		
	305	370						
Represented by:								
Fixed assets net	225	270	45			15	60	
Inventory	50	60						
Debtors	50	60						
Cash	55	62						
	155	182						
Creditors	30	30						
Provision for taxation	20	22						
Dividends proposed	25	30						
	75	82						
Working capital	80	100	20			20		
	305	370	75	75				
Arising from operations						57		57
Dividends proposed					30		30	
Issue of shares						55		55
Issue of debentures						20		20
Taxation provision					22		22	
Purchase of fixed assets					60		60	
Net increase in working capital					20		20	
					279	279	132	132

Stage 3 The entries in the bottom half of the 'Adjustments' column are shown as applications and sources in the two right hand columns of Table 2.2.
Stage 4 The funds flow statement is prepared in Table 2.3 from the information set out in Table 2.2.

SSAP 10: Statements of Source and Application of Funds

The Accounting Standards Committee recognized the importance of the funds flow statement in SSAP 10 'Statements of Source and Application of Funds' published in January 1976. According to SSAP 10,

'A Funds Statement should show the sources from which funds have flowed into the company and the way in which they have been used. It should show clearly the funds generated or absorbed by the operations of the business and the manner in which any resulting surplus of liquid assets has been applied or any deficit of such assets has been financed, distinguishing the long-term from the short-term. The statement should distinguish the use of funds for the purchase of new fixed assets from the funds used in increasing the working capital of the company.'

SSAP 10 applies to all enterprises with a turnover or gross income of more than £25,000 per annum. Appendix 1 of SSAP 10 suggests that the format of the funds flow statement for a company without subsidiaries should take the form adopted in Table 2.3.

An important way in which our funds flow statement differs from that proposed in SSAP 10 is in the treatment of dividends and taxation. According to the standard these two items should be disclosed as being paid in the period. This is different from our treatment where the application of funds was based on dividends declared for the period and on taxation which is currently provided. Unfortunately, the standard is not very clear in observing the principles involved in changes to the final accounts. These changes can be explained in two ways: (i) by demonstrating the *flow* of variables involved and (ii) by demonstrating the changes in the *stocks* of those variables. Viewed from this standpoint it may be seen that SSAP 10 confuses these two aspects without identifying the figure that is really under analysis—the change in working capital. This makes these statements unnecessarily complicated and what should be an aid to the understanding of the results of an enterprise's activities, adds to confusion. Table 2.4 on p. 182 is based on the concept of funds which is adopted by SSAP 10.

Table 2.3

P. Crookes Ltd
Funds flow statement for the year ended 31 December 19X1

Source of funds	£000	£000
Income before tax	42	
Adjustment for items not involving the movement of funds:		
Depreciation	15	
Total funds generated from operations		57
Funds from other sources		
Issue of shares for cash	55	
Issue of 12% debentures	20	75
		132
Application of funds		
Dividends proposed	30	
Taxation payable	22	
Purchase of fixed assets	60	112
		20
Increase in working capital		
Increase in inventories		10
Increase in debtors		10
Increase in proposed dividends		(5)
Increase in provision for taxation		(2)
Movement in net liquid funds:		
Increase in cash balance		7
		20

Table 2.4 *P. Crookes Ltd*
Funds flow statement for the year ended 31 December 19X1

	£ 000	£ 000
Source of funds		
Income before tax	42	
Adjustment for items not		
involving the movement of funds:		
Depreciation	15	
Total funds generated from operations		57
Funds from other sources		
Issue of shares for cash	55	
Issue of 12% debentures	20	75
		132
Appreciation of funds		
Dividends paid	25	
Taxation paid	20	
Purchase of fixed assets	60	105
		27
Increase in working capital		
Increase in inventory	10	
Increase in debtors	10	
(Increase) in creditors excluding		
taxation and proposed dividends	0	
Movement in net liquid funds:		
Increase in cash balance	7	27

The cash flow statement

The cash flow statement summarizes the flow of cash in and out of the firm over a period of time. In this sense, it is really an analysis of the cash account. The cash flow statement is important for a number of reasons. First, by focusing on cash flows, it explains the nature of the financial events which have affected the cash inventory. Thus, if a firm had a balance of £x at the beginning of the accounting period and £y at the end of the accounting period, the cash flow statement will explain the reason for the difference. Second, the cash flow statement is important for financial planning purposes. As we shall see in Part 5, budgeted cash flow statements are a crucial element in the process of budgetary planning, indicating cash surpluses and shortfalls resulting from budget plans. These surpluses and shortfalls are expressed sequentially over the planning period and require management to deal with the forecasted cash surplus or deficit, the former involving a short-term investment of surplus cash, the latter a short-term borrowing arrangement. Third, the cash flow statement brings into sharp contrast the enterprise's earning capacity with its spending activity. Accounting conventions restrict the income statement to matching periodic revenues with the cost of earning those revenues. The cash flow statement is not restricted in this way: hence, it provides an extended view of the financial inflows and outflows by including both capital and revenue flows. Thus, borrowings and capital injections, as well as proceeds from the realization of assets are incorporated with the cash generated from sales to give a more complete picture of financial inflows: repayments of loans, capital expenditure, dividends and taxation are incorporated with revenue expenses to give a more complete picture of financial outflows.

Our purpose in this chapter is to deal with the historical analysis of cash flows. Planned or budgeted cash flows will be examined in Part 5.

Form and content of the cash flow statement

The objective of a cash flow statement is to reconcile the opening balance with the closing balance of cash at the end of an accounting period. Hence, it begins with the balance at the beginning of the year.

An important distinction between an income statement and a cash flow statement is that the former includes adjustments in respect of expenses accrued in the calculation of periodic income, whereas the latter excludes such adjustments. The largest item of difference between them is the allocation of fixed asset costs as depreciation, and it is normal to adjust accounting income in this respect to arrive at a cash flow statement of operating revenues. Other differences between the income statement and cash flow statement procedures are reflected in changes in balance sheet items. These would include changes in balances of trade debtors and trade creditors stemming from credit as distinct from cash trading.

The form and content of a cash flow statement, and its purpose may be seen from the following example:

Example

The income statement for the year ended 31 December 19X0 showed that Highstreet Stores made a profit of £18,000. Nevertheless, the bank balance had fallen from £10,000 at the beginning of the year to £3000 at the 31 December 19X0. Worried by this adverse trend in the cash position in the

	£	£
Cash receipts		
Cash receipts from sales and debtors		145,000
Loan raised to extend premises		20,000
		165,000
Cash disbursements		
Purchases of goods and payments to creditors	109,000	
Payments of wages and salaries	10,000	
Payment of interest and bank charges	1000	
Expenditure on extension of premises	30,000	
Payments in respect of new fittings	5000	
Cash withdrawn by owner	10,000	
Payment of miscellaneous expenses	7000	
		172,000
Excess of cash disbursements over cash receipts during the year		(7000)

face of a good profit result, the owner of the business asked his accountant for a full explanation of the fall in the cash balance.

An analysis of the cash receipts and disbursements during the year produced the summary of cash movements shown on p. 183.

From this information, a cash flow statement for the year may be prepared which will explain the change in the net cash balances at the beginning and end of the accounting period. However, in order to produce a cash flow statement which will provide some insight into the cash position, the analysis of cash receipts and cash disbursements must be re-arranged and classified to show the causes of the cash receipts and the purposes for which cash was expended. It is advisable, therefore, to segregate cash flows associated with current operations from cash flows connected with capital items as shown below.

Cash flow statement for the year ended 31 December 19X0	£	£	£
Bank balance at 1 January 19X0			10,000
Net cash flows from current operations			
Cash receipts from sales and debtors		145,000	
Less			
Purchase of goods and payments to creditors	109,000		
Payments of wages and salaries	10,000		
Payment of interest and bank charges	1000		
Payment of miscellaneous expenses	7000		
		127,000	
		18,000	
Less			
Payments from profits to owner		10,000	
Cash flow from current operations available for capital purposes		8000	
Net cash flows on capital items			
Cash obtained by loan		20,000	
		28,000	
Less			
Expenditure on extension to premises	30,000		
Payments in respect of new fittings	5000		
		35,000	
Excess of cash payments over cash receipts during the year			7000
Bank balance at 31 December 19X0			3000

The explanation of the fall in the bank balance from £10,000 to £3000, despite a profit result of £18,000, is to be found in the extent of the capital expenditure during the year. Total capital expenditure amounting to £35,000 was financed to the extent of £20,000 by loan, and £8000 from the cash flow generated by current operations. The difference of £7000 had to be found from cash available in the bank account.

Cash flows and financial management

The usefulness of cash flow statements extends beyond a simple analysis of cash receipts and cash payments. First, as Fig. 2.17 shows, it provides an insight into the critical areas of financial management by identifying two important classes of cash flows, namely operating cash flows and financing cash flows. This distinction draws attention to the net cash flows from operations and the net financing cash flows. The net operating cash flows classify the capability of the firm to support dividend payments to shareholders. It is these net cash flows which are of critical importance to investors and shareholders, as we shall see in Part 4. The financing cash flows explain the relationship between the firm and those who finance its operations.

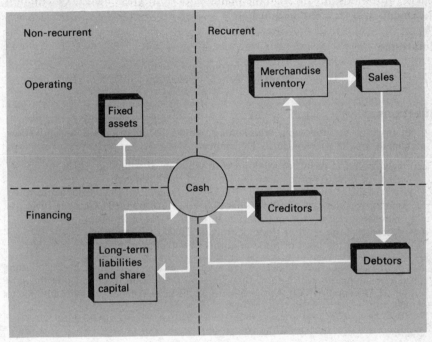

Fig. 2.17.

Summary

The income statement and the balance sheet are important statements because they are used as means of conveying information about the earnings and the financial position of the enterprise. By contrast cash flow and funds flow statements are addressed to highlighting the financial management aspect. The cash flow statement analyses cash inflows and outflows with a view to explaining the difference between cash balances at the beginning and close of the accounting period. The funds flow statement is addressed to detailing the sources and uses of funds during the accounting period and working capital.

Cash flow and funds flow statements may be used to provide supplementary information to that contained in the income statement and balance sheet. Funds flow statements are being increasingly adopted by companies for financial reporting purposes. As we shall see in Part 4, one aspect of the controversy in financial reporting concerns cash flow accounting as an alternative to income accounting. The argument for cash flow statements in that context is that since a firm's success depends on its ability to maximize its cash flows through time, cash flow statements would be more meaningful than conventional income statements and balance sheets.

Cash flow and funds flow statements are important for financial planning purposes. In this context, they are associated with budget forecasts. The particular importance of the cash flow budget is to highlight the financial consequence of budget plans and project the cash surpluses and deficits which will occur periodically through the planning period. This function of cash flow statements will be examined in Part 5.

Reference

Jaedicke, R. K. & Sprouse, R. T. *Accounting Flows: Income, Funds and Cash*, Prentice-Hall Foundations of Finance Series, Englewood Cliffs, N.J., 1965.

Questions

1. Explain how the following transactions would be reported on a funds flow statement for the year ended 31 December 19X4:

   (a) new capital introduced: £1000 in cash, equipment valued at £2000 previously used for private purposes by the owner of the business;
   (b) sale of plant purchased for £1500 on 30 December 19X0 and depreciated annually at the rate of 10 per cent and sold for £400 on 31 October 19X4;
   (c) increase investment in inventories during the year of £5400;
   (d) decrease in the level of trade debtors of £3000 over the year;
   (e) decrease in the level of trade creditors of £4000 over the year.

2. Simpson is a wholesale dealer. After a year's successful trading, his accountant produces statements which show that Simpson made a profit of £8000 in the year ended 31 December 19X1. At the same time his bank balance fell from £10,000 to £3000.

   Required:

   Given the information below prepare a statement explaining the fall in Simpson's bank balance.

Balance sheet as at 31 December 19X0

	£	£		Cost £		Depreciation £	£
Capital account			Premises	20,000		—	20,000
balance 1 Jan.			Equipment	2,000		500	1,500
19X0	37,700		Vehicles	2,000		700	1,300
income 19X0	5,000			24,000		1,200	22,800
	42,700						
drawings	2,000		Inventory	20,000			
		40,700	Debtors	5,000			
			Cash at bank	10,000			
							35,000
Trade creditors		17,100					
		57,800					57,800

Balance sheet as at 31 December 19X1

	£	£		Cost £	Depreciation £	£
Capital account			Premises	20,000	—	20,000
balance 1 Jan.			Equipment	2,000	700	1,300
19X1	40,700		Vehicles	3,000	1,000	2,000
income 19X1	8,000			25,000	1,700	23,300
	48,700					
drawings	4,700		Inventory	24,000		
		44,000	Debtors	4,000		
Trade creditors		10,300	Cash at bank	3,000		
						31,000
		54,300				54,300

3. James Johnstone Ltd has the following balance sheets of the year end for two consecutive years 19X5 and 19X6:

	19X5 £		19X6 £
Capital	12,000		10,500
Long-term loan	8,000		10,000
	20,000		20,500
Represented by			
Fixtures	2,000		1,500
Plant	12,000		14,000
Inventory	8,000		9,000
Debtors	5,000		7,000
Cash	3,000		—
	30,000		31,500
Creditors	9,000	7,000	
Accruals	1,000	2,000	
Bank overdraft		2,000	
	10,000		11,000
	20,000		20,500

The following details are also provided:

			£
Plant account	—	Balance at 31 12 X5	12,000
		Acquisitions 19X5/X6	4,000
			16,000
		Depreciation for year	2,000
		Balance at 31 12 X6	£14,000
Fixtures account	—	£500 depreciation has been written off for 19X5/X6	
Capital account	—	Balance 31 12 X5	£12,000
		Net profits 19X5/X6	4,000
		Capital introduced	1,000
			17,000
		Drawings	6,500
		Balance 31 12 X6	10,500

Required:

(a) A funds flow statement for the year ended 31 December 19X6 carefully set out in an informative style.

(b) A short financial commentary on the funds flow statement you have prepared.

Section 3 The Application of Financial Accounting Method to Corporate Enterprises

13 Financial accounting information for corporate enterprises

We mentioned in the Introduction to this part (p. 41) that the selection for closer analysis of the application of financial accounting procedures to the generation of financial accounting information for corporate enterprises was justified on two grounds:

(a) The industrial and commercial expansion which has occurred in the Western industrialized countries over the last 100 years has been affected to a considerable extent by the activities organized by companies. Probably the most important factor in this expansion has been the facility afforded by the corporate structure for the mobilization of large supplies of financial capital lodged in the private sector of the economy. Consequently, the study of corporate activity constitutes the most important area of interest to students of accounting and the management sciences generally, many of whom will make their careers as company executives. Applying the criterion of relevance to the selection of teaching material has led us to focus attention on corporate financial accounting as the major application of financial accounting method of interest to students. Therefore we have excluded large areas of conventional material found, for example, in the application of financial accounting method to partnership activities and to such problems as the accounting treatment of royalties and returnable containers.

(b) We have devoted Part 4 to the analysis of financial reporting, which is concerned with the supply of financial accounting information to shareholders and investors. Many financial reporting problems stem directly from the application of financial accounting procedures to the generation of the information content of financial reports. Hence, this section serves also as a necessary introduction to Part 4. The efficiency of the corporate sector of the economy depends, in the first instance, upon a sufficient flow of investment funds to that sector, and an efficient allocation of available funds among individual companies. The quality of the investment decision-making process depends to a large extent upon the quality and adequacy of financial information available to investors. Herein lies the social importance of the information content of financial reports.

The purpose of this chapter is to examine the financial accounting implications of incorporation, and the procedures applied to the financial accounting problems peculiar to public as distinct from private companies. We define public companies as those private sector companies in which the public at large may become shareholders, and private companies as those private sector companies which have a restricted and selected number of individuals as shareholders.

The nature of corporate enterprises

Companies are created and regulated by law. By a legal fiction, the legal personality of a business enterprise established as a company is different from the legal personality of the various individuals having an interest therein, whether as owners, managers or employees. This means, for example, that although a company has no physical life, it may nevertheless own property, enter into contracts, sue and be sued in a court of law and undertake any activity consistent with the objectives envisaged at the time of its creation. It acts through its employees, whether as managers or subordinates, with whom it enters into contracts of employment.

The proprietors of a company are recognized in law as being those persons owning its capital. The capital is divided into shares or stock, and by acquiring shares, investors become *shareholders*. As evidence of their legal title to the shares they own, shareholders are issued with *share certificates*. Shares are transferable property rights, and may be negotiated either privately or through a Stock Exchange. Stock Exchanges have rules for granting permission for the shares of individual companies to be traded on the Stock Exchange, or to be 'quoted on the Stock Exchange', which is the term given to such permission.

Companies are usually established by the formal registration of documents with a Public Registrar charged with enforcing statutory provisions in respect of enterprises operating as companies. In the United Kingdom, for example, individuals wishing to incorporate themselves for the purpose of carrying on trade are called *promoters*, and it is their responsibility to arrange for the process of incorporation. This involves lodging a number of documents with the *Registrar of Companies* and paying the required fees. The two most important documents are the *Memorandum of Association*, which defines the powers and objectives of the companies and the *Articles of Association* which contains the rules for its internal regulation. The name, objectives and the capital clauses are found in the Memorandum of Association. For our purposes, the capital clause is the most important for it states the number, classes and value of the shares which the company has power to issue for the purpose of raising capital. The *authorized capital* is stated in the capital clause, and it is the maximum capital which the company may raise. The capital clause may be altered, however, by a formal process.

A company obtains capital by the issue of shares. Investors are invited to apply for shares. They usually have to pay a portion of the purchase price on application and the balance when the shares have been formally allotted to them. The capital clause states the value of each share as a nominal figure. Thus, the authorized capital may be stated to consist of 1 million shares of £1 each, giving the company an authorized capital of £1 million. When a company offers shares for sale, however, it may set a price which is higher than the *nominal value*, and it need not offer for sale all the shares which it is authorized to sell. That portion of the authorized capital which is sold is called the *issued capital*.

Once shares have been issued, they become the property of the individual investors who have acquired them, and these investors are free to sell their shares to anyone. The sale price is negotiated between buyer and seller, and the deal may be effected through a Stock Exchange if the shares are quoted shares. The seller transfers his shares formally to the buyer by notice to the company, and the buyer is registered in the *register of shareholders* as the new shareholder. Shares which are transferred in this way are known as *registered shares*. An alternative type of shareholding, which is restricted by law in some countries, is known as a *bearer share*. A bearer share is more easily transferred than a registered share since the share certificate does not detail the name of the shareholder, and he is not registered in the register of shareholders. Consequently, bearer shares are transferable by hand.

A company receives only the issue price of a share. The legal effect of shareholding is to grant ownership rights in respect of the fraction of capital represented by the share, and a right to receive the appropriate portion of corporate net income distributed in the form of a *dividend*. Companies usually retain a portion of net income for re-investment, and distribute the balance as dividends. We shall consider shortly the accounting consequences of the distinction made between *retained income* and *distributable income*.

The distinction between ownership and management is one of the most distinctive features of corporate activity. As owners, shareholders may be considered as having ultimate control over the activities of the company through their right to appoint *directors*. The rights of shareholders to exercise control over the affairs of companies are usually defined by legislation. Once appointed, directors exercise day-to-day control of the company's affairs, and although they are accountable to shareholders, the diffusion of shares among many shareholders usually places directors in a very strong position vis-à-vis shareholders. Although they are treated as stewards of corporate assets on behalf of shareholders, the effective power to make decisions of major importance in respect of those assets lies almost entirely in their hands. We discuss in Part 5 problems of corporate planning and control in terms of managerial responsibility.

Social change is affecting the traditional method of regulating corporate enterprises in a number of ways. First, the recognition of the right of employees to share managerial responsibility is an important feature of the democratization of corporate control. Some European countries have already legislated for two-tier boards of directors, and this feature has been included in the *Societas Europea SE*, the European Company which is formed by registration in the European Commercial Register kept by the Court of the European Communities in Luxembourg. Employee participation in the management of companies is an explicit admission that the interests of employees are as important as those of shareholders. Second, the concept of social responsibility, which we discuss in Part 4, further broadens the classical notion of stewardship as a definition of the function of directors to include a responsibility to all sections of society having an interest in the activities of corporate enterprises. Thus, consumers, as well as the local community, are included in the group of those having a vested interest in the nature of corporate activity.

Financial accounting implications of corporate status

Corporate status, as distinct from the simple one-man type of business which we examined in Section 2, implies a distinctive treatment of the Capital Structure and of the allocation of the net income as between dividends and retained income.

The normal procedure for dealing with the financial accounting implications of corporate status is to establish a separation of functions between the accountant and the company secretary. The former is usually concerned with the normal financial accounting procedures directed at recording normal business transactions: the latter usually maintains the register of shareholders, including such details as the record of shareholders' names and addresses, class and number of shares held, instructions regarding correspondence and payment of dividends. Much of the routine work of the secretary's department in this respect involves recording the transfer of shares and the payment of yearly dividends to shareholders. The specialized nature of share transfer work, as well as its sheer volume in some corporations, often requires a separate department under a share transfer registrar. In such cases, the share transfer registrar is a senior official of the company.

The financial accounting aspects of the share capital with which the accountant is concerned consist of the ledger records associated with shareholders, that is, the share capital account, the dividend account, and those accounts retaining income in the form of capital or current reserves. We shall deal with the nature of these accounts shortly. All these accounts are concerned with aggregate figures.

Example

Excel Corporation Limited is a public company having a share capital of one million £1 shares held in different proportions by 20,000 individual shareholders. The detailed records of individual shareholding are kept by the share transfer registrar, and the accountant will keep the following ledger record:

Share capital account

	£
Sundry shareholders	1,000,000

The capital structure

The capital structure may consist of both share capital and loan capital, and represents the long-term capital available to the company, as distinct from the short-term capital represented by the credit facilities offered by trade creditors and bank overdrafts. Shareholders are regarded at law as owners. The share capital is at risk, and in the event of business failure shareholders may lose all the capital invested since they rank last as claimants on the residual assets of the corporation. By contrast, loan capital is made available by creditors on a long-term basis. Thus, a company may invite the public to supply loan capital for a period of say 5 years at a rate of interest of say 10 per cent. Individuals may offer varying sums, and receive from the company a certificate of indebtedness which is known as a *debenture certificate*. Debentures frequently involve the mortgage of specific corporate assets to the body of debenture-holders represented by a *trustee for debenture-holders*, and in the event of the company defaulting in any way on the conditions of the debenture instrument, the specified assets may be seized and sold on behalf of the debenture-holders. The charge on the corporate assets may be fixed, as we have mentioned, or floating, that is, not be specific as regards any particular assets but applying to all corporate assets. Debenture-holders are guaranteed, therefore, both repayment of loan capital and interest as specified in the conditions of issue. It is the duty of the trustee for the debenture-holders to act before any loss threatens debenture-holders. Very large and financially strong companies may be able to raise long-term loans without mortgaging their assets to lenders. They issue certificates of indebtness described as *unsecured notes*, which also carry an obligation to pay interest and to redeem at the end of the stated period. Holders of unsecured notes rank as ordinary creditors in an insolvency.

Shares, debentures and unsecured notes may all be quoted on a Stock Exchange and transacted between buyers and sellers. Appropriate registers of debenture-holders and holders of unsecured notes must be kept by the company.

The share capital may consist of different classes of shares, but the two most common classes of shares are preference shares and ordinary shares.

Preference shares give preferential rights as regards dividends, and often as regards the repayment of capital on winding-up. Preference shares may be issued as redeemable preference shares, that is, they may be redeemed and cancelled by the company. In general, however, the rule is that a company may not acquire its own shares, and a reduction of capital usually has to be approved by the court. Preference shares may also be issued as cumulative preference shares, which means that if the net income of any particular year is insufficient to pay a dividend to preference shareholders of this class, the right to receive a dividend for that year is carried forward to the following year, and so on, until such time as the accumulated dividend entitlement may be declared and paid out of income. Preference shareholders are usually entitled to a fixed dividend expressed as a percentage of the nominal value of the share. Thus, a holder of 100 preference shares of £1 each carrying a fixed dividend rate of 8 per cent will be entitled to a total yearly dividend of £8. However, preference shares may also be issued as participating preference shares meaning that in addition to the fixed dividend rate entitlement, they participate in the remainder of the net income with ordinary shareholders. It is common for conditions to be imposed limiting the participating rights of such shares to allow for a minimum level of dividend for ordinary shareholders. Thus, a participating preference share may carry a right to a fixed dividend of 8 per cent and a right to participate in the remaining net income after the ordinary shareholders have received a dividend of 20 per cent.

Ordinary shares provide the bulk of the share capital. In return for bearing the risk involved in financing corporate activities, ordinary shareholders enjoy the right to the whole of the net income—either as dividends or, if retained, as the increased value of net corporate assets— subject to the rights of preference shareholders. Some companies do not issue preference shares, and obtain the whole of the share capital in the form of ordinary shares. The reason for issuing a variety of shares—preference shares of different classes and ordinary shares—is to tap the funds held by investors with differing investment needs. A young man with money to invest will be looking for growth in the value of his capital and will be attracted to buying ordinary shares in a company having good prospects of expansion. A retired person will be looking for a safe investment providing a steady income, and will doubtless wish to hold some preference shares. Institutional buyers, such as pension funds and insurance companies, also have a wish to hold shares of different classes. Where a company has issued preference shares, the ordinary shares may be described as deferred shares. On occasion, however, deferred shares may be a separate class of shares to both preference and ordinary shares, and may be issued in restricted numbers to managers of the company. In such a case, deferred shares carry an entitlement to dividend only after the ordinary shareholders have received a specified dividend rate.

Gearing and the capital structure

The nature of the capital structure has important implications for financial management purposes, and in this respect, the gearing is an important consideration.

The gearing expresses the relationship between the proportion of fixed interest (loan capital) and fixed dividend (preference shares capital) to ordinary shares. A company with a large proportion of fixed interest and fixed dividend bearing capital to ordinary capital is said to be highly geared.

Example

Companies Alpha, Beta and Gamma have the same total capital which is issued as follows:

	Alpha £	Beta £	Gamma £
Share capital			
8% Preference shares of £1 each	40,000	10,000	—
Ordinary shares of £1 each	20,000	80,000	100,000
Loan capital			
7% Debentures of £1 each	40,000	10,000	—
	100,000	100,000	100,000

The gearing of these three companies may be calculated as follows:

(a) Alpha   (40,000+40,000): 20,000 or   4:1
(b) Beta   (10,000+10,000): 80,000 or 0.25:1
(c) Gamma   :100,000 or   ∞

Alpha is, therefore, the most highly geared company.

The importance of the gearing is that fluctuations in net income may have disproportionate effects upon the return accruing to ordinary shareholders in the case of a highly geared company, and hence on the pricing of ordinary shares on the Stock Exchange. Directors looking for stability in the price of the company's ordinary shares will be swayed by this consideration when faced with raising further capital. For taxation reasons, the net cost of debenture interest may be lower than the net cost in dividends of further issues of ordinary shares. Similarly, fixed dividend preference shares may also cost less than issuing ordinary shares. The following example shows the effects of fluctuating net income levels on the return to ordinary shareholders, assuming that the available net income is wholly distributed.

Example

The consequence of fluctuations in net income on ordinary shareholders in Alpha Company, Beta Company and Gamma Company geared in the ratios established in the example above may be judged as follows:

		Alpha	*Beta*	*Gamma*
		£	£	£
Assuming net income of £15,000				
Net income		15,000	15,000	15,000
8% Preference shares	3200		800	—
7% Debentures	2800		700	— —
		6000	1500	
Available for ordinary shares		9000	13,500	15,000
Maximum dividend for ordinary shareholders		$\dfrac{9000}{20,000}= 45\%$	$\dfrac{13,500}{80,000}=16.875\%$	$\dfrac{15,000}{100,000}= 15\%$

		Alpha	*Beta*	*Gamma*
		£	£	£
Assuming net income of £10,000				
Net income		10,000	10,000	10,000
8% Preference shares	3200		800	—
7% Debentures	2800		700	—
		6000	1500	
Available for ordinary shares		4000	8500	10,000
Maximum dividend for ordinary shareholders		$\dfrac{4000}{20,000}= 20\%$	$\dfrac{8500}{80,000}=10.625\%$	$\dfrac{10,000}{100,000}= 10\%$

Hence in a highly geared company such as Alpha, a fall of $33\frac{1}{3}$ per cent in net income has produced a fall of 56 per cent in the maximum dividend payable to ordinary shareholders.

Accounting procedures applied to the capital structure

The share capital

We mentioned earlier that a distinction exists between the authorized capital and the issued capital. The former is the maximum limit in the total value of shares of different classes which a company is permitted to issue under the conditions of its registration; the latter is the actual value of shares of different classes which have been issued. The reason why companies do not establish the value of the authorized capital greatly in excess of their anticipated requirement lies in the taxes imposed on the value of the authorized capital, which deter promoters from incurring unnecessary expenses.

The financial accounting procedures applied to the treatment of the share capital may be said to have two main objectives:

(a) recording the issue of shares and the consideration received in respect of such shares;

(b) providing information about the share capital in a balance sheet.

We do not propose to deal with the procedures applied to the redemption of redeemable preference shares, or those applied to the issue of bonus shares, since these procedures are not essential to the thesis of this book. It may be mentioned, however, that bonus shares are commonly issued free of cost to existing shareholders in proportion to their shareholdings by way of distribution of accumulated income.

(a) *Recording the issue of shares*

It has become the practice for companies seeking to make an issue of shares to the public to employ the services of merchant bankers not only to act as advisers but also to deal with the details of the issue, such as issuing the prospectus advertising the offer of the shares for sale, recording the applications from investors and the monies received with the applications, the allotment of shares to individual shareholders where an offer has been over-subscribed, and arranging for the shares under-subscribed to be taken up by the underwriters who have acted as insurers in respect of the issue of the shares in return for a commission. The detailed accounting procedures for dealing with the issue of shares need not detain us, for they have become part and parcel of a rather specialized aspect of work.

The central financial problems relating to the issue of shares concern the nature of the shares to be issued, that is, whether to issue preference or ordinary, how many to issue and the price to be attached to such shares. All these are problems in respect of which a company will seek expert advice. The financial accounting procedures which we shall consider reflect merely the outcome of the decisions taken.

We mentioned earlier that shares may be described in the capital clause of the memorandum of association as having a nominal value. This practice applies in the United Kingdom, although in the United States, for example, it is the practice for shares not to have a nominal value, and they are issued as 'shares of no par value'. This means that the recorded issue value of the share capital reflects the price determined at the time of issue.

In the United Kingdom, the practice of attaching a nominal value to shares makes it theoretically possible for the following terms to be attached to the issue of shares:

(i) Shares may be issued at par, that is, a share having a nominal value of £1 is issued at a price of £1.
(ii) Shares may be issued at a premium, that is, a share having a nominal value of £1 is issued at a price higher than £1.
(iii) Shares may be issued at a discount, that is, a share having a nominal value of £1 may be issued at a price which is less than £1. In practice, legislation attaches very strict conditions to the issue of shares at a discount.

A number of considerations affect the issue of shares, not the least of which is that the issue should be a financial success. This means that the corporation should receive a realistic price for the shares offered and that the issue should be wholly subscribed by the market.

The following examples show the accounting procedures applied to the issue of ordinary shares at par and at a premium.

The issue of ordinary shares at par
The Omega Co Ltd has issued 2 million ordinary shares of £1 each at par. The purchase price has been paid on application and allotment and the corporation's bank account has been credited with the amount received. The entries in the company's accounts are as follows:

Ordinary share capital account

	£
Sundry ordinary shareholders	2,000,000

Sundry ordinary shareholders

	£		£
Ordinary share capital	2,000,000	Cash	2,000,000

Cash account

	£
Sundry ordinary shareholders	2,000,000

We have already noted that the detailed list of individual shareholdings does not form part of the financial accounting system, but rather of the register of shareholders. Hence, the sundry ordinary shareholders account does not exist as such: it is represented by the register of shareholders. From a financial accounting viewpoint, only the ordinary share capital account and the cash book are significant.

The issue of ordinary shares at a premium
The Onedin Co Ltd has issued 2 million ordinary shares of £1 each at a

premium of 50 per cent, that is, at a price of £1.50 a share. The purchase price has been paid on application and allotment and the company's bank account has been appropriately credited. The practice in the United Kingdom is to separate the par value of the shares from the share premium. Legislation allows a greater flexibility in the application of the share premium account, for example in redeeming preference shares at a premium.

The accounting entries are as follows:

Ordinary share capital account

		£
	Sundry ordinary shareholders	2,000,000

Share premium account

		£
	Sundry ordinary shareholders	1,000,000

Sundry ordinary shareholders

	£		£
Ordinary share capital	2,000,000	Cash	3,000,000
Share premium	1,000,000		
	3,000,000		3,000,000

Cash Account

Sundry ordinary shareholders	3,000,000

As we explained earlier, the sundry ordinary shareholders do not exist as a formal account, but are found in the register of shareholders. Consequently, the only accounts of significance are the ordinary share capital account, the share premium account and the cash book.

In the United States and Canada, the practice for the last 50 years has been to issue shares of no par value. These simplify the accounting process, for there is no need to have a share premium account and the share capital account shows the amount actually received from the sale of shares. The case against shares of fixed nominal value is that they bear no relation to any realistic value of the issued shares, and hence the nominal value is virtually meaningless.

The procedures which have been outlined above apply equally to the treatment of other classes of shares, such as preference shares.

(b) *Providing information about the share capital*
Details of the share capital are shown on the balance sheet, and in this way information is communicated to shareholders and investors about the manner in which the corporation is capitalized. The information which should be disclosed is generally the subject of legislation, and the debate about the nature and extent of information disclosure forms the subject matter of Part 4.

The information which is usually required to be disclosed about the share capital is as follows:

(i) The authorized share capital showing in respect of each class of shares the number and the value of the shares authorized to be issued.

(ii) The issued share capital showing in respect of each class of shares the number of the shares issued and the proportion of the share price paid-up. Although it is usual for companies to ask for the whole purchase price to be paid at the time of issue, some ask for the purchase price to be paid upon call. Thus, a portion is payable on application and allotment and the balance remains uncalled until needed. The uncalled capital represents a valuable source of funds to the corporation for once shareholders have agreed to take up shares they are debtors in respect of the agreed purchase price.

(iii) Any calls unpaid on the issued capital are also usually required to be shown.

(iv) Where redeemable preference shares are issued, the earliest date of redemption must also be shown.

(v) The share premium account, where applicable, must also be shown.

Example

The following information about the share capital appears on the balance sheet of the Odin Firework Co Ltd:

Share capital			£
Authorized:	100,000 8% Redeemable preference shares		
	of £1 each (*see* note 1)		100,000
	500,000 Ordinary shares of £1 each		500,000
			600,000
Issued:	100,000 8% Redeemable preference shares		
	of £1 each fully paid		100,000
	400,000 Ordinary shares of £1 each		
	50 pence paid	200,000	
	Less: calls unpaid	500	
			199,500
			299,500
Share premium account			5,000
	Shareholders' equity		304,500

Note 1:

8% Redeemable preference shares. These shares must be redeemed between 1 January 1990 and 31 December 1992.

Note the following points:

(a) The authorized and the issued capital are both shown, but the authorized capital is ruled off so that it is not included in the calculation of the total shareholders' interest, known as the shareholders' equity.

(b) Calls unpaid are deducted from the issued capital.

(c) Notes are usually attached to the balance sheet for the purpose of explanation.

(d) In the example, the share premium account represents a premium of 5 per cent on the issue of the preference shares.

Loan capital

There is very little difference in the accounting treatment of loan and share capital. Registers of debenture-holders and of holders of unsecured notes are kept, and the method of issue is identical to that of shares insofar as the issuing process tends to be conducted on behalf of the company by merchant bankers. Debentures may be issued at par, at a premium or at a discount. Premiums received on the issue of debentures are regarded as capital profits, and are usually transferred to a capital reserve account. Discounts allowed on the issue of debentures are treated as capital losses, and legislation in the United Kingdom requires such discounts to be shown separately on the balance sheet until they are written off.

Example

Hightrust Investment Company offers for sale 10,000 9 per cent debentures in units of £100 at a premium of 5 per cent. The debentures are repayable on 31 December 1990. The accounting entries are as follows:

9% Debentures 1990 account

		£
	Sundry debenture-holders	100,000
Capital reserve account		
	Sundry debenture-holders	5000
Cash book		

£
Sundry debenture-holders   105,000

As in the case of the issue of shares, details of individual debenture-holders would be found in the register of debenture-holders. There is no such account as a sundry debenture-holders account.

The presentation of the loan capital on the balance sheet is usually as follows:

Loan capital

	£
10,000 9% Debentures of £100 each	100,000
(*see* note 5)	

Note 5: These debentures are redeemable at par on 31 December 1990. Note the following points:

(a) the loan capital appears below the share capital on the balance sheet;

(b) the capital reserve account represents a capital profit belonging to the shareholders. It would appear, therefore, below the share premium account and be incorporated in the calculation of the shareholders' equity.

Accounting procedures applied to periodic income

The important difference between a company and an un-incorporated business such as a sole trader lies in the manner in which periodic income is appropriated. In the case of the un-incorporated business, the net income belongs to the owner and is transferred to the capital account at the end of the accounting period. By contrast, once the net income of a company has been ascertained, the board of directors have to decide the proportion which should be paid out to shareholders as dividends and the proportion which should be retained.

In considering the manner in which the net income should be appropriated, the following factors are important:

(a) Adequate provision should be made in respect of corporation tax payable on the net income for the year. In this connection, under- or over-provisions in respect of previous years have to be taken into account.
(b) Adequate provision should be made for anticipated expenditure on the replacement of fixed assets. During periods of inflation, in particular, the cost of replacing fixed assets exceeds amounts provided for in the provision for depreciation.
(c) Adequate provision should be made for capital expenditure which is planned to be financed out of earnings.
(d) Where a company wishes to provide a degree of stability in the level of yearly dividends by means of a dividend equalization account, care should be taken that sufficient reserves are accumulated in that account.
(e) The level of retention of income should also be dictated by working capital requirements, and for this purpose, transfer of net income to a general reserve may be made.

It is quite common for companies to distribute only about half their after-tax income to shareholders. Usually an interim dividend is declared during the accounting period in anticipation of a final dividend, which is declared after the final results for the year have been ascertained.

Example

Delta Expandite Co made a net income of £5 million for the year ended 31 December 19X0. Estimated corporation tax payable on those profits was calculated at £2 million. The directors recommended the following appropriations of the distributable net income in the accounts laid before shareholders at the annual general meeting:

(a) the fixed assets replacement reserve should be increased by £200,000;
(b) the capital expenditure reserve should be increased by £500,000;
(c) the dividend equalization reserve should be increased by £300,000;

(d) the general reserve should be increased by £750,000;

(e) an interim dividend of £200,000 having been declared during the year, the directors proposed a final dividend of £1 million to be paid to ordinary shareholders registered at the close of business on 28 February 19X1. (Note: there was no other class of share in issue.)

The income statement laid before shareholders for their approval would show the following appropriations:

		£
Net income for the year before tax		5,000,000
Less: Provision for corporation tax on the income for the year		2,000,000
Distributable income		3,000,000
Transfers to reserves:		
Fixed assets replacement reserve	200,000	
Capital expenditure reserve	500,000	
Dividend equalization reserve	300,000	
General reserve	750,000	
		1,750,000
Available for distribution		1,250,000
Interim dividend for the year	200,000	
Proposed final dividend for the year	1,000,000	
		1,200,000
Undistributed income carried forward		50,000

Note that it is customary to close the register of shareholders for a brief period after the close of the accounting period for the purpose of determining the names of shareholders entitled to the dividend. The reason for this is that share dealings on the Stock Exchange continue, and daily the company is faced with share transfer forms to process as shareholders sell their shares and are replaced by new shareholders. Freezing the register of shareholders allows a list of shareholders to be drawn up to whom dividends are paid. If they have already sold their shares, and the buyers have not yet registered the transfer, the conditions of sale apply to the dividend entitlement. Usually, shares are traded on the Stock Exchange *cum dividend* (with dividend) until the formal dividend declaration, when they go *ex dividend*, that is, they are sold without the dividend declared.

Accounting procedures for the payment of dividends

The rule is that shareholders are not entitled to a dividend unless and until a dividend has been declared. Usually, articles of association allow directors to declare an interim dividend, but the declaration of a final dividend is subject to the approval of the body of shareholders convened at the annual general meeting, which is held once a year to deal with the business reserved to shareholders. Thus, directors are not entitled to declare a final dividend, but they propose a final dividend and ask shareholders to approve the proposal. The consequences of these rules are as follows:

(a) the income statement laid before shareholders shows the final dividend as a proposed dividend:
(b) although no liability exists to shareholders for the payment of a final dividend until it is approved by shareholders at the annual general meeting, the proposed final dividend is shown on the balance sheet as a current liability as follows:

	£
Current liabilities	
Sundry creditors	. . . . . .
Provision for taxation	. . . . . .
Proposed dividend	. . . . . .

The responsibility for drawing up the *dividend list* lies with the share transfer registrar who keeps the register of shareholders. The dividend list contains the name, addresses and number of shares held by each individual shareholder. The individual's dividend entitlement is easily calculated, and payment is made either by cheque or direct to a bank account, according to instructions given by the shareholders.

The accountant merely opens a dividend account to which the dividend payable is transferred. The exact amount payable in respect of the dividend is transferred to a special dividend account at the bank, so that the dividend warrants issued should tally in total with the credit established at the bank.

Example

The accounting entries in respect of the final dividend of £1 million (dividend No. 12) proposed by the directors of the Delta Co would be as follows:

Income statement for the year ended
31 December 19X0

	£
Dividend No. 12	1,000,000

Dividend No. 12

	£
Income statement for the year ended 31 December 19X0	1,000,000

Note that it is usual to number the dividends for ease of reference, and to keep the dividend list for each dividend in company records.

Published financial accounting statements

One of the areas of great controversy in accounting is the extent to which financial information should be disclosed to shareholders. As we shall see in

Part 4, it is usual for legislation to be used as a means of compelling companies to disclose information. The central issue revolves around the minimum level of disclosure compatible with the information requirements of shareholders and the protection of business interests.

Until recently, there was little public discussion of the information requirements of shareholders, and it was assumed that their needs were met through the traditional income statement and balance sheet. In this respect, the information content of these statements is an abridged version of the full financial accounts laid before the board of directors. In considering these accounts, the board of directors has additional information in the form of detailed cash flow statements, budget forecasts and analysis of results and may ask for any further information required to enable them to assess the company's financial performance and position much more accurately than is possible from the limited contents of the published financial statements released to shareholders. We consider in Chapter 14 the manner in which a limited analysis of published financial statements may be made and interpreted by shareholders.

The statutory requirements relating to the disclosure of financial information is currently governed by the Companies Acts 1948, 1967 and 1976. Many of the statutory requirements contained in these Acts have been enlarged as the result of the issue of subsequent Statements of Standard Accounting Practice, which are binding upon the accounting profession. For all practical purposes, the information disclosed in financial reports may be regarded as determined by statute and the standards imposed upon the accounting profession by its own professional organization.

The statutory requirements relating to the information which should be disclosed to shareholders affect three documents prepared by companies. These documents are:

(1) The directors' report
(2) The income statement
(3) The balance sheet

As we saw in Chapter 12, SSAP 10 requires the publication of an annual flow of funds statement.

The directors' report

The details required by statute to be disclosed in the directors' report include statements on the following:

1. The state of the company's affairs.
2. Recommended dividend.
3. Proposed transfers to reserves.
4. Principal activities of the company and its subsidiaries.
5. Market value of land shown on the balance sheet, if the market value differs substantially from the balance sheet value.
6. Significant changes in fixed assets.
7. Proportions of turnover and contribution to net income of the principal activities.

8. Turnover of exports from the United Kingdom, where exports exceed £250,000.
9. Average number of employees on the payroll throughout the year, where they exceed 100, and their aggregate remuneration.
10. Political or charitable contributions, where they total more than £50.
11. Shares or debentures issued during the year, with details.
12. Names of directors who served during the year.
13. Directors' ownership of shares and debentures in the company.

The income statement

The details required by statute to be disclosed in the income statement or in notes attached to the income statement include the following:

1. Turnover for the financial year, where it exceeds £250,000.
2. Income from quoted investments and income from unquoted investments, both being shown separately.
3. Total remuneration paid to directors, and an analysis of such remuneration.
4. Number of employees, other than directors, with remuneration in excess of £10,000, divided in brackets of £2500.
5. Provisions for depreciation.
6. Debenture interest and interest on other loans.
7. Hire of plant and machinery, if material.
8. Auditor's remuneration.
9. Charge of corporate taxation.
10. Amounts provided for any redemption of share capital or debentures.
11. Dividends paid or proposed.
12. Transfers to and from reserves.
13. Material profits or losses from activities not usually undertaken by the company.
14. Any material effect caused by circumstances of an exceptional or non-recurrent nature.
15. Any material effect of a change in the basis of accounting.
16. Comparative figures for the preceding year.
17. SSAP 3 requires that earnings per share should be calculated on a standard basis and that it should be disclosed in a prominent position in the company's accounts.

The balance sheet

The details required by statute to be disclosed in the balance sheet or in notes attached to the balance sheet include the following:

1. Authorized share capital.
2. Issued share capital.
3. Share premium account.
4. Aggregate reserves and provisions.
5. Loans, distinguished as between bank loans and overdraft, loans repayable within five years, loans not fully repayable within five years.

6. Fixed assets, showing the undermentioned details:
   (a) the total of fixed assets must be stated separately;
   (b) it must be stated whether they are stated at cost or valuation, and the aggregated depreciation to date must be given;
   (c) if any fixed assets are shown at valuation, the year of valuation must be made known, and for a current valuation the company must give particulars of the valuer and the basis of valuation;
   (d) the aggregate amount of fixed assets acquired and disposed of during the year must be shown;
   (e) land must be subdivided as between freeholds, long leases defined as leases over 50 years, and short leases;
   (f) capital expenditure authorized by the directors, if material, as well as that contracted for.
7. Total of current assets must be shown separately.
8. Quoted investments must be shown separately from unquoted investments, and the value for quoted investments must be shown as a note.
9. The following must be shown separately:
   (a) preliminary expenses;
   (b) issue and commission expenses in respect of shares and debentures;
   (c) discount on debentures;
   (d) discount on shares.
10. Contingent liabilities not provided for.

The Anglesee and Far-West Corporation			(1)
Income statement for the year ended 31 December 19X5			
		19X5 £	19X4 £
Turnover for year—Net sales		90,000	75,000
Income before taxation		8,000	6,000
	19X5 £	19X4 £	
after charging:			
Depreciation of fixed assets (note 1)	1,400	1,200	
Directors' remuneration as managers	12,000	9,000	
Interest on bank and short-term loans			
repayable within 5 years	200	150	
Interest on other loans	450	450	
Cost of hiring plant and machinery	200	250	
Auditors' remuneration	150	150	
and after crediting			
Interest received	70	120	
Taxation (note 3)		3,300	2,000
Income after taxation for the year		4,700	4,000
Retained earnings at beginning of year		7,300	5,000
		12,000	9,000
Proposed dividend		4,000	2,000
Retained earnings at end of year		8,000	7,000
Earnings per share (note 5)		58.75p	66.7p

The nature of the information conveyed to shareholders in published reports is depicted in the example given, which conforms with the legal requirements in the United Kingdom, both as to content and as to the additional information which is given in the notes to the accounts.

As may be seen, the corporation is not required to disclose the details of its operating costs, save those listed in the income statement (p. 206). Note 1 explains the accounting policies adopted for treating accounting items in accordance with SSAP 2. Note 4 reveals the distribution of directors' emoluments.

The balance sheet emphasizes the make-up of net assets employed in earning income, and the manner in which the corporation is financed. Notes 1, 2, 3, 6 and 7 provide appropriate explanations of items appearing on the balance sheet.

The Anglesee and Far-West Corporation Balance sheet as at 31 December 19X5	(2)	
	19X5	19X4
Share capital	£	£
Ordinary shares of £1 each—authorized	12,500	6,000
Issued and fully paid	12,500	6,000
Retained earnings	8,000	7,000
	20,500	13,000
Deferred taxation (note 1)	900	1,000
Debenture stock secured on the assets of the company:		
£4500 10% Debentures 1985/1987	4,500	4,500
	25,900	18,500
Represented by		
Fixed assets		
Land, buildings and equipment (note 2)	15,000	14,000
Current assets		
Inventories (notes 1 and 6)	16,000	10,000
Accounts receivable and prepaid expenses	13,000	7,000
Short-term deposits	1,000	2,000
Cash and bank balance	200	300
Total current assets	30,200	19,300
Current liabilities		
Bank loan and overdraft	2,000	1,500
Accounts payable and accruals	10,000	8,800
Corporation tax (note 3)	3,300	2,500
Proposed dividend	4,000	2,000
Total current liabilities	19,300	14,800
Net current assets	10,900	4,500
Net assets employed	25,900	18,500

T. E. Bear, Managing Director
S. N. O. White, Director

The Anglesee and Far-West Corporation   (3)
Notes on the accounts for the year ended 31 December 19X5

1. Statement of accounting policies:

No depreciation is provided on freehold land. Depreciation of fixed assets has been calculated using the decreasing-balance method to write off the cost of these assets over their estimated useful lives using the following rates per annum:

Buildings 5%
Plant and machinery 15%

Research and development costs are written off in the year in which they are incurred.

Inventories are stated at the lower of average cost, and net realizable value. Deferred taxation is computed on the deferral method and arises from timing differences in the recognition of depreciation for accounting and taxation purposes.

2. Land, buildings and equipment comprise:

	Freehold land and buildings £	*Plant & equipment* £	*Total* £
Cost at beginning of year	10,000	12,000	22,000
Additions during year	—	4000	4000
Disposals during year	—	(2000)	(2000)
Cost at end of year	10,000	14,000	24,000
Accumulated depreciation	4000	5000	9000
Net book value at end of year	6000	9000	15,000

Government grants have been deducted in arriving at cost.

3. The charge for taxation on the profits for the year under review is computed as follows:

Corporation tax	3400
Deferred taxation—adjustment	100
	3300
Retained earnings brought forward	7000
Tax overprovided in previous years	300
	7300

4. The number of directors in each range of emoluments (excluding pensions contributions) for the year ended 31 December 19X5 was as follows:

£2501–£5000	1
£5001–£7500 (Highest paid director: £7500)	1

Auditors' report to the members of
The Anglesee and Far-West Corporation

5. Earnings per share are calculated on earnings of £5000 (19X4, £4000) and on the average number of shares in issue during the year, 8000 (19X4, 6000).

6. Inventories:

	19X5 £	19X4 £
Materials	10,000	6000
Work in progress	3000	2000
Finished goods	3000	2000
	16,000	10,000

7. Bank loan. The bank loan of £10,000 is repayable within five years.

In our view, the accounts set out on pages — to — give a true and fair view of the state of the company's affairs at 31 December 19X5 and of the income for the year ended on that date and comply with the Companies Acts 1948 to 1976.

W. E. Audent & Co.
Anglesee 31 January 19X6.

Taxation in company accounts

Before April 1973, company income was liable for corporation tax and any distribution made from company income to shareholders liable to income tax in the hands of shareholders. Clearly, this system attempted to encourage companies to retain their earnings and increase investment.

The imputation system

A new system of corporation tax was introduced known as the imputation system. It had two basic objectives: (i) to eliminate the built-in discrimination which applied under the previous scheme against the distribution of income; (ii) to harmonize with systems already in force, or soon to be adopted, within the EEC.

The rules of the imputation system are as follows:

(a) A company pays corporation tax at a single rate on all its income whether distributed or not.

(b) A company distributing income in the form of dividends is in addition required to make to the Inland Revenue an advance payment of corporation tax (ACT). This rate is limited to the basic rate of income tax, presently 30 per cent, and is deemed to have been borne by ('imputed to') the shareholders.

Example

A company with a taxable income of £100,000 declares a net dividend of £21,000. The rate of corporation tax is assumed to be 52 per cent.

	£
Income before tax	100,000
Corporation tax at 52%	52,000
	48,000
Net dividend	21,000
Retained earnings	27,000

The advance corporation tax in respect of the dividend of £21,000 is calculated by assuming that the net dividend is a sum paid after advanced corporation tax at the rate of 30 per cent as follows:

	£
Net dividend	21,000
ACT at 30%	
$£21,000 \times \dfrac{100}{70}$	9,000
Gross dividend	30,000

(i) It is, as the name implies, advance corporation tax, which is paid in advance of the 'mainstream' corporation tax of £43,000 (£52,000 − £9000).
(ii) It is imputed to the individual shareholder in the form of a tax credit which covers his liability to basic income tax at 30 per cent.

Where a shareholder's marginal rate is higher than 30 per cent, he will pay the difference between the basic and his actual rate.

Two methods of showing corporation tax in the income statement are:

	£	A £	B £
Taxable income		100,000	100,000
Corporation tax	52,000		52,000
Less ACT	9000		
Mainstream corporation tax		43,000	
		57,000	48,000
Dividends paid net	21,000		21,000
Add ACT	9000	30,000	
Retained income		27,000	27,000

Both presentations give the same retained income, but differ in their treatment of ACT. In method A, ACT is treated as part of the cost of the dividend, whereas method B treats it as part of the tax on the company's income. SSAP 8, The Treatment of Taxation Under the Imputation System in the Accounts of Companies, recommends method B.

'The fact that the dividend will carry a tax credit is a matter affecting the receipt rather than the company's method of accounting for the dividend. Accordingly it is considered appropriate that dividends should be shown in the Income Statement at the amount paid or payable to the shareholders . . . It follows that the charge in the Income Statement should embrace the full amount of corporation tax and not merely the mainstream liability.'

The above presentations illustrate a point of principle which is fundamental to the present system of corporation tax. The payment of dividends and consequently ACT to the Inland Revenue does not affect the total corporation tax which is paid by the company. It merely alters the timing of the payment. ACT is payable under a regular quarterly accounting system which ensures that payments of ACT outstanding are settled within three months of dividends being paid. The mainstream corporation tax liability is normally settled 9 months after the end of the accounting period.

Computing taxable income

Financial accounting, which is governed by a 'true and fair' presentation of financial position and the results of operations, does not share in all respects the principles which govern the computation of taxable income. Differences between 'book' and tax accounting originate from the following:

(i) Some items which appear in the income statement are not allowed for tax purposes. These include entertaining expenses of home-country customers and certain types of donations and subscriptions.

(ii) Dividends received from other companies which are resident in the UK, which is known as franked investment income, does not incur corporation tax, because the company making this payment will already have paid ACT on this dividend.

(iii) Timing differences. The first two categories give rise to permanent differences where, because of special legislation, particular revenues or expenses are omitted from the computation of taxable income. A timing difference, on the other hand, arises when an item is includable or deductible in income for tax purposes in one period, but in income for general reporting purposes in another. The different treatment of fixed assets creates timing differences because depreciation is not an allowable deduction for tax purposes, capital allowances being granted instead.

Example
A company has an accounting income of £150,000, depreciation of £50,000, entertaining expenses and donations of £10,000, dividend received of £10,000 and capital allowances of £100,000. Taxable income is calculated as follows:

	£	£
Accounting income		150,000
Add depreciation		50,000
Add entertaining etc.		10,000
		210,000
Less capital allowances	100,000	
Less dividend received	10,000	110,000
Taxable income		100,000

Deferred taxation

The provision for deferred taxation originates from the timing differences which we discussed above. SSAP 15, Accounting for Deferred Taxation, is intended to bring a greater degree of uniformity to the accounting treatment of taxation where there are differences of timing between accounting and taxation recognition of income or expenditure. According to this statement

'The effect of timing differences on taxation liability in relation to reported income would be of little significance if taxation was not regarded as relevant to the performance of the business for the period, and the only accepted indication was the income before taxation. The view is widely held, however, that the income after taxation is an important indication of performance being the fund of earnings which supports (or perhaps does not support) the distribution of income by way of dividend. So far as the Balance Sheet is concerned, the relationship between funds provided by shareholders and other sources of finance may be distorted if provision is made for deferred taxation which can be demonstrated with reasonable probability not to be needed'.

SSAP 15 identifies five categories of timing differences:

(a) short-term timing differences from the use of the receipts and payments basis for taxation purposes and the accruals basis in financial statements: these differences normally reverse in the next accounting period;
(b) availability of capital allowances in taxation computations which are in excess of the related depreciation charges in financial statements;
(c) availability of stock appreciation relief in taxation computations for which there is no equivalent charge in financial statements;
(d) revaluation surpluses on fixed assets for which a taxation charge does not arise until the gain is realized on disposal;
(e) surpluses on disposals of fixed assets which are subject to rollover relief.

The accounting procedure is to debit the income statement for any year with the tax on accounting income. The difference between this debit and the Corporation Tax due for the year is transferred to a deferred taxation account, which must be shown separately in the balance sheet.

Example

A company buys a machine for £50,000 which it intends to use for five years. By using the straight-line depreciation method £10,000 would be written off each year. However, given the present system of capital allowances (100 per cent of the cost of the equipment) for tax purposes, the entire cost of the machine may be written off in the first year. We assume accounting income is £200,000. Deferred taxation for the year is calculated as follows:

	£
Accounting income	200,000
Add depreciation	10,000
	210,000
Less capital allowances	50,000
Taxable income	160,000
Tax on accounting income (52% of £200,000)	104,000
Tax on taxable income (52% of £160,000)	83,200
Deferred taxation	20,800

The income statement would be debited with the full amount of tax of £104,000 described as follows:

Corporation tax (including £20,800 credited to deferred taxation account)   £104,000

The deferred taxation account balance of £20,800 would be shown as a separate item in the balance sheet.

Summary of SSAP 15, Accounting for Deferred Taxation

The potential amount of deferred tax for all timing differences should be disclosed by way of note, distinguishing between the various principal categories of deferred tax and showing for each category the amount that has been provided within the accounts.

Deferred taxation dealt with in the income statement should be shown separately as a component of the total tax charge or credit in the income statement or by way of note to the financial statements. The income statement or a note thereto should indicate the extent to which the taxation charge for the period has been reduced by accelerated capital allowances, stock appreciation relief and other timing differences.

Deferred taxation account balances should be shown separately in the balance sheet and described as 'deferred taxation'. They should not be shown as part of shareholders' funds.

Summary of SSAP 8, The Treatment of Taxation Under the Imputation System

Dividends received must be shown with the related tax credit, the tax then being included in the taxation charge in the income statement.

Dividends paid or proposed must be shown without the related tax credit or ACT.

ACT on proposed dividends should be included as a current tax liability in the balance sheet, the proposed dividend being shown in current liabilities without the addition of the related ACT. The charge for corporation tax in the income statement should show the total liability and not merely the mainstream liability.

EEC legislation and company reports

The EEC company law harmonization faced the problem of uniting two fundamentally different approaches to company regulation and accountability existing in Europe. On the one hand, the French approach, based on the Code Napoléon, and the German approach, made central government responsible for laying down the detailed rules of company accountability and could be seen as a legalistic and prescriptive approach. In contrast, the British and Dutch accountancy professions have a long tradition of self-regulation and central government has limited the extent of detailed legislation to a minimum.

The principal change to company law which arises from the Fourth Directive on company law, which was adopted by the EEC in July 1978, is the introduction of three classifications of companies based on size:

Top tier:	All companies which exceed the following criteria: — turnover £5,750,000 — balance sheet total £2.5 million — average number of employees 250.
Middle tier:	All public companies which do not fall within either the top tier or the bottom tier.
Bottom tier:	Small private companies which do not exceed the following criteria: — turnover £1,400,000 — balance sheet total £700,000 — average number of employees 50.

Additionally, for the purpose of the accounting requirements a subsidiary of a public company may not be treated as a small private company.

The purpose of making this distinction is to reduce the burden on small companies of preparing what many would say are excessively detailed financial statements. The Fourth Directive distinguishes, in the case of both small and medium companies, between accounts which are drawn up by a company for circulation to shareholders and the information to be included in the accounts which are to be published. This distinction is new to the UK.

The concessions permitted by the Fourth Directive given to medium and small sized companies in respect of the disclosures they must make are summarized on p. 215.

Large and listed companies are required by the Fourth Directive to disclose more information in their annual accounts than has hitherto been required— in particular, net turnover must be analysed by geographical market; the cost of sales and gross income must be disclosed; average numbers of employees as per category must be disclosed, together with the total wages bill; social security payments and pensions must also be disclosed; and the company must make a statement of the events that have occurred after the financial year end and reveal future developments. Unlike medium-sized and small companies no conditions on disclosures are allowed.

Under the Fourth Directive companies will be required to conform with one of the prescribed formats. Balance sheets may be either vertical or horizontal, but the order in which items appear will be fixed. For example, intangible assets, however small, will have to be shown above tangible assets, and the retained income for the year will have to be shown separately. Four possible income statements are specified, two vertical and two horizontal. Once a company has chosen particular formats for its accounts, these can only be changed in exceptional circumstances. Examples of formats based on the Companies Act 1981 are given on pp. 215–18.

In conclusion, the legislation of accounting methods and presentation has very significant implications for the accountancy profession. Up to now the development of accounting standards and practice in Britain has been largely the prerogative of the profession itself. Now that the EEC has become the crucible for future developments, the accountancy profession has to switch its role to one of lobbying and making its views felt at the various stages of the law-making process in Europe.

Medium sized companies	**Drawing up and circulating to shareholders**	**Publishing***
Balance sheet	No concession	Some aggregation of items allowed
Income statement	The omission of certain information regarding turnover and trading margins	No further concession beyond that allowed on drawing up
Notes to accounts	The omission of net turnover broken down by categories of activity and geographical markets	Some further concession
Directors' report	No concession	No concession
Small companies		
Balance sheet	Extensive abridgement	Extensive abridgement
Income statement	The omission of certain information regarding turnover and trading margins	Not required (as long as profit or loss shown in balance sheet)
Notes to accounts	The omission of several items of supplementary information including the omission of the analysis of net turnover	No further concession
Directors' report	No concession	Not required

*The concessions on publication take into account the concessions allowed on drawing up.

Profit and loss account format
1. Turnover
2. Cost of sales
3. Gross profit or loss
4. Distribution costs
5. Administrative expenses
6. Other operating income
7. Income from shares in group companies
8. Income from shares in related companies
9. Income from other fixed asset investments
10. Other interest receivable and similar income
11. Amounts written off investments
12. Interest payable and similar charges
13. Tax on profit or loss on ordinary activites
14. Profit or loss on ordinary activities after taxation
15. Extraordinary income
16. Extraordinary charges
17. Extraordinary profit or loss
18. Tax on extraordinary profit or loss
19. Other taxes not shown under the above items
20. Profit or loss for the financial year

Balance sheet format

A. Called up share capital not paid

B. Fixed assets

   I Intangible assets
1. Development costs
2. Concessions, patents, licences, trade marks and similar rights and assets
3. Goodwill
4. Payments on account

   II Tangible assets
1. Land and buildings
2. Plant and machinery
3. Fixtures, fittings, tools and equipment
4. Payments on account and assets in course of construction

   III Investments
1. Shares in group companies
2. Loans to group companies
3. Shares in related companies
4. Loans to related companies
5. Other investments other than loans
6. Other loans
7. Own shares

C. Current assets

   I Stocks
1. Raw materials and consumables
2. Work in progress
3. Finished goods and goods for resale
4. Payments on account

   II Debtors
1. Trade debtors
2. Amounts owed by group companies
3. Amounts owed by related companies
4. Other debtors
5. Called up share capital not paid
6. Prepayments and accrued income

   III Investments
1. Shares in group companies
2. Own shares
3. Other investments

   IV Cash at bank and in hand

D. Prepayments and accrued income

E. Creditors: amounts falling due within one year

1. Debenture loans
2. Bank loans and overdrafts
3. Payments received on account
4. Trade creditors
5. Bills of exchange payable
6. Amounts owed to group companies
7. Amounts owed to related companies
8. Other creditors including taxation and social security
9. Accruals and deferred income

F. Net current assets (liabilities)

G. Total assets less current liabilities

H. Creditors: amounts falling due after more than one year

1. Debenture loans
2. Bank loans and overdrafts
3. Payments received on account
4. Trade creditors
5. Bills of exchange payable
6. Amounts owed to group companies
7. Amounts owed to related companies
8. Other creditors including taxation and social security
9. Accruals and deferred income

I. Provisions for liabilities and charges

1. Pensions and similar obligations
2. Taxation, including deferred taxation
3. Other provisions

J. Accruals and deferred income

K. Capital and reserves

I Called up share capital

II Share premium account

III Revaluation reserve

IV Other reserves
1. Capital redemption reserve fund
2. Reserve for own shares
3. Reserves provided for by the articles of association
4. Other reserves

V Profit and loss account.

Summary

In this chapter, we have examined the nature of corporate enterprise and the financial accounting implications of incorporation. These implications stem from the manner in which they are capitalized and from the manner in which the net income is appropriated. We discussed particular financial problems such as gearing.

The accounting procedures relating to the share capital are concerned principally with recording the issue of share capital, and with providing information about the share capital in financial accounting reports. There is little difference between the accounting treatment of share capital and loan capital.

The accounting procedures application to the periodic income are concerned with the manner in which the income is appropriated to various purposes. The size of the dividend is a problem of financial policy which directors have to consider in relation to capital requirements, its effect on the share price and the availability of other sources of finance.

We considered also the procedures relating to the payment of dividends, and in this way maintained the focus of the chapter on the financial accounting problems arising directly from corporate status.

We discussed the extent to which financial accounting information is disclosed to shareholders. We noted the limited extent of this disclosure, and indicated that this is an important controversy in accounting which would be discussed in Part 4.

We examined the nature of taxation in company accounts and the importance of accounting standards. Finally we considered the future of company reporting in the light of the Fourth Directive, as adjusted by the Companies Act 1981.

Questions

1. The partnership of Black, White and Grey are considering forming a Limited Company to obtain the benefits of limited liability. However, they are uncertain as to whether the capital of the company should be in shares or debentures and are also unsure of the method of appropriating profit.

   At 31 December 19X0 the Capital accounts of the partners were:

Black	£11,000
White	9000
Grey	12,000

   Interest of 10 per cent per annum is allowed on the capital accounts.

Black is effectively the managing partner and receives a partnership salary of £5000 p.a. White works part-time in the business but does not receive a salary. Grey no longer takes any active part in the business. The balance of profits are shared equally.

The budgeted profit for 19X1 is £65,000 before any appropriation to the partners.

Required

(a) Advise the partners on the difference between debentures and ordinary shares and suggest the most appropriate capital structure for the new company.
(b) Advise the partners on a suitable method of rewarding themselves when the company is formed. Prepare a Profit and Loss Appropriation account for year ended 31 December 19X1 on the assumption that the company is formed on 1 January 19X1, and your recommendations are accepted. Assume a Corporation Tax rate of 50 per cent.

(Question supplied by A.J. Naughton, Leeds Polytechnic)

2. Scheid and Sons Ltd are considering expanding their operations. Several alternative strategies are being discussed for financing this expansion. The latest balance sheet of the company as at 31 December 19X9 is as follows:

Scheid and Sons Ltd
Balance Sheet as at 31 December 19X3

	£		£
Authorized and issued			
share capital		*Fixed assets*	
8% cumulative preference			
shares of £1 each	30,000	Land and buildings	40,000
Ordinary shares of		Plant and equipment	90,000
£1 each	50,000		
Retained earnings	30,000		
Shareholders equity	110,000		
Long-term debt			
12% loan repayable 19X9	90,000		
Current liabilities		*Current assets*	
Trade creditors	25,000	Inventories	50,000
		Debtors	40,000
		Cash	5000
	225,000		225,000

The Board of Directors of the company has identified the following possible alternative ways of obtaining the additional £50,000 required during the following year.

(a) Issue additional ordinary shares
(b) Issue additional 8 per cent preference shares
(c) Raise an additional long-term loan at 12 per cent

Discuss the company's existing capital structure in terms of its gearing, and examine the advantages and disadvantages of each alternative method of financing the expansion plan.

3. The Moonshine Exploratory and Mining Co Ltd has an authorized capital of 50,000 ordinary shares of £1 each, of which 40,000 have been issued and are fully paid. The following trial balance was prepared as at 31 December 19X2, after the preparation of the trading account for the year.

	Dr. £	Cr. £
Ordinary share capital account		40,000
Share premium account		10,000
General reserve		4000
Fixed assets replacement reserve		6000
Land and buildings (at valuation)	35,000	
Plant and machinery (at cost)	80,000	
7% Debentures, 19X9		21,000
Stock as at 31 December 19X2	14,300	
Trade creditors and accrued expenses		17,200
Trade debtors and prepayments	12,400	
Provision for depreciation at 1 January 19X2		
Land and buildings		8500
Plant and machinery		35,600
Investments at cost		
Quoted (market value at 31 December 19X2: £4500)	4000	
Unquoted (directors' valuation at 31 December		
19X2: £10,000)	8000	
Bank balance	19,200	
Gross income for the year		31,700
Administrative and selling expenses	6400	
Interest on debentures	1470	
Income from investments		
Quoted		470
Unquoted		800
Directors' fees	3500	
Retained income, 1 January 19X2		9000
	£184,270	£184,270

Required:

Prepare final accounts for publication using the data given above, after making adjustments for the following matters:

(i) depreciation at the rate of 2 per cent per annum on the valuation figure for land, and 10 per cent per annum on the cost of plant and machinery is to be provided.
(ii) a dividend of 10 per cent on the ordinary shares is proposed.

4. Fireglow Limited has an authorized capital of 100,000 ordinary shares of £1 each, of which 75,000 have been issued and are fully paid. The following trial balance was extracted from the books as at 31 December 19X2 after the preparation of the trading account for the year:

	Dr. £	Cr. £
Share capital account		75,000
Share premium account		7500
Fixed asset replacement reserve		5000
General reserve		14,000
Land and buildings at cost	27,900	
Fixtures and fittings at cost	52,000	
Depreciation to 31 December 19X1		11,520
Vehicles at cost	5700	
Depreciation to 31 December 19X1		1280
9% Debentures 19X9		6000
Stock at 31 December 19X2	29,560	
Trade creditors		11,200
Trade debtors	23,180	
Quoted investments at cost (market value £5000)	2000	
Cash in hand	130	
Cash at bank	12,370	
Debenture interest (paid 30 June 19X2)	270	
Investment income		870
Gross income for the year		34,900
Administrative expenses	7620	
Selling expenses	4260	
Directors' fees	3000	
Auditors' fees	540	
Retained income at 31 December 19X1		1260
	£168,530	£168,530

The following adjustments are to be made:

(a) the fixed assets replacement reserve is to be increased by £1000 and the general reserve to be increased by £2000;

(b) it is proposed to declare a dividend of 5 per cent on the ordinary share capital;

(c) depreciation is to be provided for the year ended 31 December 19X2 at the following rates on cost value:
fixtures and fittings 10 per cent
vehicles   20 per cent

(d) it is estimated that United Kingdom corporation tax at the rate of 45 per cent will amount to £6000 and a provision is to be made for this amount.

Required:

Prepare a financial report for the year ended 31 December 19X2 for publication in accordance with the Companies Acts.

14 Interpreting and comparing financial reports

Financial reports are combinations of facts and personal judgements both of which are influenced in the manner of presentation to users by accounting conventions. In attempting to interpret the meaning of the information disclosed, it is necessary to be aware of the limitations imposed by accounting conventions and methods of valuation, which, as we have noted in previous chapters may seriously distort the basic underlying events of importance to investors.

Ratio analysis is the most widely used technique for interpreting and comparing financial reports. Ratios are useful because they can be used to summarize briefly relationships and results which are significant to an appreciation of critical business indicators of performance, for example, the ratio of net income to assets employed. Moreover, ratios are particularly useful for the purpose of comparing performance from year to year, and the performance of different companies, given that aggregate figures are always of differing orders of magnitude.

The collection of ratios on a systematic basis allows trends to emerge, and throws into relief the significance of changes indicated by the analysis of current events. Since the future is uncertain, the analyst has to rely substantially on past behaviour for predicting future changes. In this respect, the trends indicated by systematic ratios are very useful for making predictions. For example, it is not known which soccer team will win the championship next season. Hence, in making any predictions in this respect, one has to rely on the performance of all the clubs in previous seasons.

The function of ratio analysis, therefore, is to allow comparisons to be made which assist in predicting the future. In this connection, it should be stressed that the knowledge that the Alpha Co has a ratio of net income to assets employed of 10 per cent in the year 19X0 is meaningless by itself. To be meaningful, that ratio must be compared with the ratios obtained from the results of previous years, and may be made even more meaningful by comparing it with those of its competitors. In this respect, inter-firm comparisons were facilitated in the United Kingdom when the Centre for Inter-Firm Comparisons Ltd, a non-profit-making organization, was established in 1959 by the British Institute of Management in association with the British Productivity Council. This organization obtains confidentially from subscribers a large amount of management accounting information, computes therefrom a battery of ratios, and reports these ratios to the subscribers, together with the 'best' and 'worst' and the 'average' of all subscribers within a given industrial class. By contrast, the external analyst is confined to the information disclosed in published financial reports, and he tends to rely on such other information as he is able to obtain from other sources in assessing the performance and prospects of individual firms.

The nature of ratio analysis

Numerous ratios may be computed from financial reports and from other sources, notably Stock Exchange share prices. In this chapter, we shall limit our discussion to a number of important ratios which focus on two critical areas, namely, the ability of the firm to survive and grow, and the efficiency of its financial performance.

From the investor's viewpoint, these particular ratios are related directly to the two central issues, which we postulated in Chapter 1 to be the focal points of a normative theory of financial reporting. We argued that the maintenance and increase of the value of the capital invested was the first consideration, and that the second consideration was the level of income which investors expected to derive from the invested capital. Clearly, both these considerations are inter-related and inter-dependent.

The maintenance of the value of the capital invested depends in the last analysis on the ability of the firm to survive, for shareholders, and particularly ordinary shareholders, bear the burden of risk if the company should fail. Solvency is the most important criterion of the firm's ability to survive. Solvency is the ability of the firm to meet its debts as they come due for payment, and it is a question of both fact and law. If a creditor presses his claim for payment of the sum which is due to him, and the firm is unable to pay, its inability so to do is a question of fact. The firm may have substantial assets which may not be realizable. Its future prospects may not be necessarily bad—what is crucial, however, is that it has insufficient liquid resources, that is, cash or near cash, to meet an individual claim, and, moreover, has no further credit facilities available. Solvency becomes a question of law by the formal process in which the creditor seeks the recovery of a debt through a court of law, and upon a direction by the judge that the firm has defaulted upon a payment of a debt ordered by the court, the firm is declared insolvent. The legal procedure for the firm's liquidation by winding-up ensues under a liquidator appointed by the court. Solvency is related, therefore, to the problem of liquidity in relation to the size of current obligations in favour of creditors, and to available credit facilities.

The level of income which investors expect to derive from their investment is related in the first instance to the firm's current financial performance, and in the next instance to its future growth prospects. The income of shareholders may be seen as consisting of a stream of dividend flows. Dividends tend to be related to the level of current earnings, that is, realized income, and this in turn is reflected in the market value of the shares. Ratio analysis enables views to be formulated about the efficiency of current financial performance by relating net income to such indicators as net assets or share prices, and as far as the investor is concerned by relating dividends to corporate net income and to share prices. In the case of quoted shares, current financial performance does influence share price, and in this sense affects the value of the investor's capital. Ratios of financial performance, therefore, affect economic income, which we argue, is the best criterion of income for decision making by investors.

The analysis of solvency

We mentioned earlier that solvency was a question of fact in the first instance. Given the nature of financial reports, it follows that ratio analysis may make only a limited contribution to assessing solvency for the following reasons:

(a) The balance sheet statement of the firm's total current liabilities and total current assets at the end of the last accounting period may indicate that its financial stability is precarious, but solvency happens in the present and not in the past. In this respect, a firm may be perfectly solvent on the last day of the accounting period, and may now be insolvent by reason of the sudden withdrawal of a large credit facility upon which it relied.

(b) The balance sheet does not reveal sources of credit which the firm may tap, nor the willingness of current creditors and investors to see the firm through a difficult period.

Given these limitations, we may say that the usefulness of ratios of solvency lies as indicators for predicting insolvency (Beaver, 1966; Altman, 1968; Glautier, 1971). The financial stability of an enterprise in the short-term is the central concern in the analysis of solvency. Nevertheless, investors are also interested in the analysis of longer-term implications of the current financial position. For this reason, we propose to discuss both short-term and long-term solvency.

Short-term solvency

Although shareholders bear the ultimate risk of losing their capital in the event of insolvency, unsecured creditors likewise run the risk of financial losses. In the face of a deteriorating financial situation, long-term creditors, such as debenture-holders, may either attempt to realize their security by selling specific assets mortgaged under the debenture instrument, or they may be willing to hold their hand if a viable rescue operation is mounted. Short-term creditors such as trade creditors are generally not willing to allow credit to a firm which is running into financial difficulties, and action from creditors is usually the precipitating cause of an act of insolvency.

Small firms in difficulties perish quickly: large firms, however, bring losses to many around them, not only to short-term creditors but to financial institutions which have supported capital expenditure programmes and granted credits. Indicators of short-term financial stability are particularly important, therefore, in respect of larger firms whose shares are publicly quoted, for if action is needed to prevent losses early signs are required to enable such action to be taken. There are two classes of ratios which are useful in this respect:

(a) Ratios which relate current assets to current liabilities, and indicate an imbalance between the burden of immediate debts in relation to the firm's ability to meet such debts.

(b) Ratios which indicate the rate at which short-term assets are liquidated, thereby affording a measure of the elasticity with which they are transformed into cash.

(a) *Ratios of current assets to current liabilities*

Two ratios in common use are:

(i) the current ratio;
(ii) the acid-test (or quick) ratio.

The current ratio is the ratio of current assets to current liabilities expressed as follows:

$$\frac{\text{Current assets}}{\text{Current liabilities}}$$

For example, if a firm has current assets valued at £4000 and current liabilities amounting to £2000, the current ratio is 2:1. It will be recalled that the surplus of current assets over current liabilities also measured working capital, that is, the funds conventionally regarded as being available to finance current operations.

A number of problems stem from the use of the current ratio as a predictor of financial stability. First, since current assets include inventories, trade debtors as well as cash, an element of subjectivity is introduced into this ratio by methods of valuing inventories and by the assessment of the likelihood of bad debts. Second, an efficient business may be able to reduce inventories and debtor levels without affecting its financial stability, which is secured by a high rate of funds flowing from current operations. Hence, its current ratio may conceivably be less than 2:1, for example, and it will still be a viable concern. By contrast, a firm with a high current ratio represented by high levels of inventories, debtors and cash may be a very inefficient firm, and the current ratio may conceal a poor rate of funds generation, and hence a very unstable situation. For this reason, Glautier (1971) has argued that the current ratio is not a useful indicator of solvency from a theoretical viewpoint. Nevertheless, it should be said that what is a normal current ratio is peculiar to given industries, and financial analysts tend to look for current ratios falling within acceptable limits.

The acid-test ratio applies where the inclusion of inventories in the current ratio means that as a measure of solvency it includes current assets which are not immediately realizable, such as inventories, debtors and prepayments. Thus, a firm could have a current ratio, which on the face of it is healthy by conventional standards, which may include a preponderance of inventories of raw materials and finished goods, which in the light of prevailing economic conditions may be difficult to realize in cash. The acid-test ratio excludes inventories and gives a sharper focus on the assets which are more readily convertible into cash. It is calculated as follows:

$$\frac{\text{Current assets} - \text{Inventories}}{\text{Current liabilities}}$$

For example, if current assets are valued at £4000 including inventories valued at £2000 and current liabilities amount to £2000, the acid test ratio would be 1:1, thereby indicating a coverage of current liabilities by cash or near cash current assets.

Whilst the acid-test ratio is a stricter indicator of solvency, it suffers from the same disadvantages which affect the current ratio, that is, it ignores the importance of cash-flows from current operations and by emphasizing cash and debtor balances tends to put the less efficient firm in a more favourable light.

(b) *Ratios of the cash elasticity of current assets* (*i.e. activity ratios*)
Given that current assets normally consist of cash, debtors and inventories, the firm's ability to meet current liabilities depends upon the rate at which cash flows into the firm from current operations. Since sales is the critical event in this respect, the rate at which inventories are sold is clearly crucial. Where a substantial proportion of sales are on credit terms, the rate at which debtors settle their accounts is also crucial. For these reasons, the following ratios are good indicators of the cash elasticity of current assets:

(i) average inventory turnover
(ii) collection period of trade debts.

(i) The average inventory turnover is calculated by the following formula:

$$\frac{\text{Cost of goods sold during the period}}{\text{Average inventory held}}$$

Example
If the firm's gross sales at cost during the accounting period amounted to £900,000 and the opening and closing inventories are £110,000 and £90,000 respectively, the average inventory turnover is as follows:

$$\frac{£900,000}{(110,000 + 90,000)/2}$$

i.e., $\dfrac{900,000}{100,000}$

= 9 times.

This ratio means that the average length of time that inventory is held before being sold is 365 days/9, that is, 41 days.

The average inventory turnover ratio is only a crude measure of the rate at which inventories are sold for the purpose of comparing the cash elasticity of inventories of different enterprises. Different marketing situations face different industries and trades. A butchery will clearly have a much higher inventory turnover rate than a firm selling luxury goods. Methods of inventory valuation will also distort the significance of inter-firm comparisons.

Nevertheless, the average inventory turnover may give a useful indication of trading difficulties facing a particular firm by comparing it with the average inventory turnover for previous periods. A fall in the average inventory turnover may indicate stiffening competition, adverse marketing circumstances or a degree of obsolescence in the firm's products. At the same time, firms operating in similar markets may be expected to have roughly similar average inventory turnover ratios, so that even as a crude ratio of comparability, it may be a useful indicator for investors. In fact, since cost of sales are not disclosed, analysts use sales figures as the numerator in this ratio.

(ii) An important measure of the cash elasticity of debtor balances may be obtained from the average collection period of trade debtors. The first stage is to establish the average amount of credit sales per day, which may be obtained by the following formula:

$$\text{Average credit sales per day} = \frac{\text{Total annual credit sales}}{365}$$

The average collection period may be determined as follows:

$$\text{Average collection period} = \frac{\text{Trade debtors as per balance sheet}}{\text{Average credit sales per day}}$$

$$\text{or} \quad \frac{\text{Trade debtors as per balance sheet} \times 365}{\text{Total credit sales}}$$

Example

Given that total annual credit sales in the year 19X0 amounted to £1,460,000 and that total trade debtors at 31 December 19X0 were £160,000, the collection period for debtors may be calculated as follows:

Average credit sales
$$\frac{£1,460,000}{365}$$
$$= £4000$$

Average collection period
$$\frac{£160,000}{£4000}$$
$$= 40 \text{ days}$$

These calculations show that 40 days is the approximate time required to collect trade debtors outstanding at 31 December 19X0. By applying this ratio, analysts establish if the average collection period for debtors is too slow. A rough rule of thumb which is sometimes used by credit agencies is that the average age of trade debts should not exceed $1\frac{1}{3}$ times the net credit period. If a firm gives 30 days' credit for the settlement of debtor accounts, the average collection period should not exceed approximately 40 days.

(c) *Other factors affecting short-term solvency*

In addition to the ratios mentioned above, other factors which should be taken into account when evaluating short-term solvency include:

(i) The size of operating costs. Neither the income statement nor the balance sheet reveal the cash required to meet current operating costs such as payroll, rent and other expenses, except where these are shown as outstanding on the balance sheet. Where a firm has very little current debt in its favour on the balance sheet, and it is faced, for example with large payroll obligations, it may be extremely short of cash.

(ii) Bank credit. A firm which has sufficient credit facility at the bank may, as we mentioned earlier, have lower current and acid test ratios.

(iii) Seasonal patterns of trade. Where firms normally expect seasonal patterns of trade, there will be distortions in the solvency ratios arising from seasonal build-up of inventories, trade debtors and cash depletions during the time interval across the peak season. Where such seasonal patterns of trade exist, they should be taken into account when making inter-firm comparisons.

Long-term solvency

We defined solvency as the ability to meet current liabilities as they fall due for payment. The long-term financial stability of the firm may be considered as dependent upon its ability to meet all liabilities, including those not currently payable.

Two ratios which are considered important in this respect are:

(a) External claims against total assets expressed as a percentage (non-equity)

$$\frac{\text{Long-term debt} + \text{Current liabilites}}{\text{Fixed assets} + \text{Current assets}} \times 100$$

(b) the interest coverage ratio.

(a) *The shareholders' equity ratio*
This ratio is considered by many analysts to be equal in importance to the current ratio as an indicator of financial stability. It is computed as follows:

$$\text{Shareholders' equity ratio} = \frac{\text{Shareholders' equity}}{\text{Total assets}}$$

It is generally felt that the larger the proportion of the shareholders' equity, the stronger is the financial position of the firm. This is related to the notion of 'gearing' which we discussed in Chapter 13. By increasing long-term borrowing, the firm may increase its current assets thereby creating a more favourable current ratio. At the same time, however, it reduces the shareholders' equity, signalling a possible over-dependence on outside sources for long-term financial needs. This creates problems associated with high levels of gearing, namely, where net income tends to fluctuate, the burden of fixed interest payments will greatly distort the dividend payable to shareholders and will, by that fact, affect the share price.

Although no explicit rules of thumb exist regarding desirable shareholders' equity ratios, financial analysts may have a general idea of the appropriate financial structure of a particular company by considering the stability of its income. The nearer a company comes to having a stable and assured income, the more it may safely use long-term credit.

(b) *Interest coverage ratio*
The ability of a firm to meet its debt service costs out of current earnings is a rough indicator of its long-term solvency. Long-term loans which are usually in the form of debentures carry interest charges which must be paid regularly. The inability to meet such interest charges places the firm's solvency into jeopardy. The interest coverage ratio is calculated as follows:

$$\text{Interest coverage ratio} = \frac{\text{Income before interest and tax}}{\text{Periodic interest charges}}$$

Generally speaking, a firm which can cover its debt service costs several times over by its operating income even in a poor year would be regarded as a satisfactory risk by long-term creditors.

The analysis of financial performance

There are two aspects of a company's financial performance of interest to investors. First, its financial performance may be assessed by reference to its ability to generate income. Ratios of financial efficiency in this respect focus on the relationship between income and sales and income and assets employed. Second, its financial performance may be assessed in terms of the value of its shares to investors. In this sense, ratios of financial performance focus on earnings per share, dividend yield and price-earnings ratios.

The analysis of efficiency as earning power

The overall measure of earnings performance for purposes of comparison is the ratio of return on capital employed. This ratio is made up of several components, two of the most important of which are the asset-turnover ratio and the return-on-sales ratio.

The ratio of return on capital employed
There are several ways of expressing this ratio, and care must be taken in making inter-firm comparisons that the basis used is the same. The ratio of return on capital employed may be expressed as follows:

(1) Net income/Shareholders' equity (i.e., Share capital + Reserves)
(2) Net income + Interest/Equity capital + Long-term liabilities
(3) Net income/Gross tangible assets

The main problem with this ratio lies in the diversity of generally accepted principles applying to the measurement of net income and values. In selecting the appropriate denominator, for example, there is also a choice as indicated above. When considering the firm's efficiency in generating income, it is more appropriate to use total assets, that is net fixed assets plus current assets, as the denominator. Investors, on the other hand, would be more interested in relating net income to the value of the shareholders' equity. In this section, we shall assume that we are seeking a measure of the firm's internal efficiency in the generation of income, and use the ratio of net income to total assets.

The factors which affect the ratio of return on capital employed may be broken down into the following ratios:

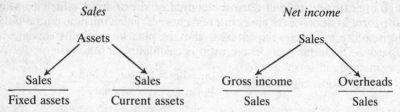

These ratios may be further subdivided, for example, by a closer analysis of the components of current assets, that is inventories and debtors, and the elements of direct and overhead expenses.

The ratio of return on capital employed is generally expressed as follows:

$$\text{ROCE} = \frac{\text{Sales}}{\text{Capital employed}} \times \frac{\text{Net income}}{\text{Sales}} \times 100$$

(i) *The asset turnover ratio*

The first component of the formula for calculating the ROCE is an asset utilization ratio. It is intended to reflect the intensity with which assets are employed. Thus, if the firm has a low ratio of sales to assets, it is implied that some substantial under-utilization of assets is occurring, or alternatively that assets are not being efficiently employed. This ratio focuses, therefore, on the use of assets made by management. Because it is a measure of past managerial efficiency in this respect, it is thought to provide a reasonable basis for forecasting management's future efficiency. It is considered to be a prime determinant of the level of future income flows.

(ii) *The ratio of net margin on sales*

This is the second component of the formula for calculating the ROCE. It seeks to assess the profitability of sales, that is, the efficiency of sales as a critical event in generating income.

The ratio of net margin on sales varies widely from industry to industry, so that it should be used solely for comparing similar companies in the same industry, or in comparing the performance of the same company over a period of time. Some companies may operate in an industry which is characterized by low profit margins and high levels of turnover, for example, manufacturers and distributors of foodstuffs.

In considering the relevance of ratios of performance, conventional accounting measurements introduce limitations. Current value accounting removes at least two basic difficulties. First, the effect of the timing differences in the acquisition of assets, which results in the aggregation of assets of differing money value is removed, and similar values are added together. Second, the use of historic cost measurements results in arbitrary allocations, e.g., LIFO and FIFO allocations of inventories to the cost of sales. Replacement cost accounting increases the usefulness of ratio analysis by providing uniformity in cost allocations, since all costs are allocated at their replacement price.

The analysis of the efficiency of investment decisions

In buying the shares of a particular company, the investor is seeking to make the best allocation of his investment funds. Although the earnings efficiency of that company is very important to him, it has to be related to its shares. For this reason, several ratios are used by investors to appraise the performance of companies in terms of share prices and yields.

(i) *Ratio of earnings per share*
SSAP 3 requires the results for the year to be expressed as earnings per share. The usefulness of this information is related to the pricing of shares on the Stock Exchange. For ordinary shares the ratio is calculated as follows:

$$\text{EPS.} = \frac{\text{Net income after tax} - \text{Preference dividend requirement}}{\text{No. of ordinary shares}}$$

This ratio is significant only for ordinary shareholders in the majority of cases, since preference shareholders usually have the right only to a fixed dividend.

It is generally acknowledged that the market value of ordinary shares is closely related to the earnings per share. Hence, this ratio is used as a basis for predicting the future value of ordinary shares, and may assist also in formulating forecasts of future dividends. The problems of income measurement which we discussed in earlier chapters are not eliminated by the expedient of translating accounting income into earnings per share. This ratio does not, therefore, provide a reliable tool for comparing the financial performance of firms.

(ii) *Dividend yield*
The dividend yield focuses closely on the value of the declared dividends to an investor. It is calculated as follows:

$$\text{Dividend yield} = \frac{\text{Ordinary dividend per share}}{\text{Market price per ordinary share}} \times 100$$

$$\text{or alternatively} = \frac{\text{Nominal dividend rate} \times \text{Nominal value of share}}{\text{Market price per share}}$$

Investors interested in seeking high-yielding shares are able to compare the dividend yield of alternative share investments, and select for purchase those shares with the highest yield.

(iii) *Dividend-coverage ratio (or pay-out ratio)*
The ability of a company to continue to pay current dividend levels in the future may be forecasted by the dividend-coverage ratio, which may be calculated as follows:

$$\text{Dividend coverage} = \frac{\text{After tax earnings}}{\text{Total gross dividend}}$$

Where the dividend-coverage ratio is, for example, three times the current gross dividend to ordinary dividend, it may be taken as a good indication that the present dividend level will be maintained in the future since the company has an ample margin of earnings to make its current dividend declaration.

(iv) *Earnings yield*
The earnings yield expresses the dividend yield in relation to the market price of the share. It is calculated as follows:

Earnings yield = Dividend coverage ratio × Dividend

$$\text{or alternatively} = \frac{\text{After-tax earnings per share}}{\text{Market value of the share}} \times 100$$

(v) *Price-earnings ratio*
This ratio seeks to relate earnings per share to the current market price of the share. It is the reciprocal of the earnings yield. It allows an investor considering the purchase of ordinary shares to obtain a more accurate view of the return on investment implied by current earnings. In effect, it is a capitalization factor. The price-earnings ratio is calculated as follows:

$$\text{PE ratio} = \frac{\text{Market price per share}}{\text{Earnings per share}}$$

Example

If the earnings per share in the Zebrox Co is £10 and the Stock Exchange share price on the date of publication of this result is £25 per share, the price-earnings ratio is 2.5. This ratio may be used to compare several share purchase alternatives in making a decision to invest.

Ratios as predictors of business failure: Empirical studies

Empirical studies have been undertaken to determine the extent to which financial ratios may be used to predict business failure. The ability to predict company failure is particularly important from both the private investor's viewpoint and the social viewpoint as it is an obvious indication of resource misallocation. An early warning signal of probable failure would enable both management and investors to take preventative measures.

In a study using more powerful statistical techniques than used by his predecessors, Beaver (1966) found that financial ratios proved to be useful in the prediction of bankruptcy, in that such bankruptcy could be predicted at least five years before the event. He concluded that ratios could be used to distinguish correctly firms that would fail from those that would not, with much more success than would be possible by random prediction. One of his significant conclusions was that the most effective predictor of bankruptcy was the ratio of both short-term and long-term cash flow to total debt. The next best ratio was the ratio of net income to total assets. One of Beaver's most surprising findings was that the current ratio was among the worst predictors of bankruptcy. Turnover ratios were found to be at the bottom of the list of effective predictors. Generally, Beaver found that 'mixed ratios', which had income or cash flows compared to assets or liabilities, outper-formed short-term solvency ratios which had been believed traditionally to be the best predictors of bankruptcy.

In a later study, Beaver (1968) suggested that business failure tends to be determined by permanent factors. He argued that if the basic financial position of a company was sound and profit prospects were good, it would recover from a temporary shortage of liquid assets, but that if the long-term prospects in these regards were not good, business failure could not be prevented by a good liquid position.

Altman (1968) extended Beaver's univariate (single variable) analysis to allow for multiple predictors of business failure. He used a multiple discrimi-nant analysis for the purpose of developing a linear function of a number of explanatory variables to predict bankruptcy. Altman used 22 financial ratios based on data obtained one year before bankruptcy, and selected five financial ratios for the purposes of establishing his final discriminant function. These five financial ratios were:

(a) working capital/total assets as an indicator of liquidity;
(b) retained earnings/total assets as an indicator of the age of the firm and its cumulative profitability;
(c) earnings before interest and tax/total assets as an indicator of profitability;
(d) market value of the equity/book value of debt as an indicator of financial structure;
(e) sales/total assets as an indicator of capital turnover.

Altman's five-variable model correctly identified 95 per cent of the total sample of companies tested for bankruptcy. This percentage rate of success in predicting bankruptcy fell to 72 per cent when the data used was obtained two years prior to bankruptcy. As earlier data was used in testing the model, so its predictive ability became more unreliable.

Taffler and Tisshaw (1977) applied Altman's multiple discriminant analysis to companies in the United Kingdom. They tested the predictive value of 80 different ratios in a variety of combinations. The best results were found when four ratios were combined in accordance with weighting which reflected their significance to the analysis of business failure.

The ratios used by Taffler and Tisshaw and the weightings which they were given were as follows:

(a) Profit before tax/current liabilities (53 per cent), which according to them 'is a profitability measure indicating the ability of an enterprise to cover its current liabilities through its earning power. If it has a low or negative value, its downside risk is clearly greater than that for the average company'.

(b) Current assets/total liabilities (13 per cent), which according to them 'is related to the conventional current ratio, and is a measure of the working capital position of the firm. The greater the ratio, the sounder the enterprise'.

(c) Current liabilities/total assets (18 per cent), which according to them 'measures the company's current liabilities position and is a financial leverage ratio. The greater its magnitude, the more serious the problems the company has to face in financing the cost of its debt and the acquisition of new debt'.

(d) Immediate assets − current liabilities/operating costs − depreciation (16 per cent), which according to them 'calculates the time for which the company can finance its continuing operations from its immediate assets, if all other sources of short-time finance are cut-off, and is a ratio relatively new to the accounting literature . . . and is akin to the acid test'.

All these empirical studies present evidence to support the conclusion that firms which avoided bankruptcy had stronger ratios in areas of significant analysis than firms which went bankrupt.

Argenti (1977) has drawn attention to three limitations of financial ratio analysis which restrict the usefulness of financial ratios for predicting business failure, in the following terms:

(a) While ratios may show that there is something wrong and while a sequence of them over time may show that it is getting worse, it is doubtful whether one could predict collapse on the evidence of these ratios alone. The ability of ratios alone to predict corporate collapse has not been conclusively proved.

(b) Their value has been eroded by inflation. Figures that appear to show an improvement may conceal a deterioration in real terms.

(c) Managers start 'creative accounting' when they know things are wrong, thus hiding the tell-tale symptoms. Creative accounting involves making the company's results look better than they are, for example, by cutting expenditure on routine maintenance. This phenomenon explains why so many people do not appreciate the serious difficulties of suspect companies until the day on which insolvency is announced.

Summary

Ratio analysis provides the most commonly used indicators to assess and compare the financial performance of companies, both over time and as between different companies. However, unless ratios are collected in a systematic and uniform manner, comparisons may be very misleading. For this reason, they are most useful when collected and developed by such organizations as the Centre for Inter-firm Comparisons.

It is very important that external users of financial reports should understand the limitations of ratios based on conventional accounting measurements, otherwise their analyses will not be sound nor their interpretations valid. The conclusion which may be drawn from our examination of ratio analysis is that its general usefulness and relevance to investors would be enhanced by increasing the uniformity of financial reporting practices and adopting current value accounting.

Considerable interest exists in the possibility of using financial ratios as predictors of business failure. Several studies have been conducted that show that there exist ratios and combinations of ratios which are significant in this regard. Nevertheless, caution is required in accepting the conclusions suggested by financial ratios as regards business failure.

References

1. Altman, E. I. 'Financial ratios, discriminant analysis and the prediction of corporate bankruptcy', *Journal of Finance*, 1968.
2. Argenti, J. *Corporate Collapse: the Causes and Symptoms*, Nelson, 1977.
3. Beaver, W. H. 'Financial ratios as predictors of failure', *Journal of Accounting Research*, No. 4, 1966.
4. Beaver, W. H. 'Alternative accounting measures as predictors of failure', *The Accounting Review*, January, 1968.
5. Dev, S. 'Ratio analysis and the prediction of company failure', *in* Edey, H. & Yamey, B. S. (eds), *Debits, Credits, Finance and Profit*, Sweet and Maxwell, 1974.
6. Glautier, M. W. E. 'Towards a reformulation of the theory of working capital', *Journal of Business Finance*, Spring, 1971.
7. Taffler, R. J. and Tisshaw, H. 'Going, going, gone—four factors which predict', *Accountancy*, March, 1977.

Questions

1. The following information relates to the operations of the East Lancashire Trading Company for the three year period ended 31 December 19X3:

Income statement

	19X3 £	19X2 £	19X1 £
Net sales	1,000,000	900,000	800,000
Cost of goods sold	600,000	550,000	545,000
Gross margin	400,000	350,000	255,000
Selling and administrative expenses	300,000	275,000	220,000
Net income before tax	100,000	75,000	35,000
Tax at 50%	50,000	37,500	22,500
Net income after tax	50,000	37,500	12,500
Dividends	30,000	25,000	10,000
Net increase in retained earnings	20,000	12,500	2500

Balance sheet

	19X3 £	19X2 £	19X1 £
Assets			
Land and buildings	500,000	450,000	425,000
Plant and equipment (net)	450,000	500,000	410,000
Inventory (at cost)	635,000	600,000	520,000
Trade debtors	425,000	410,000	440,000
Cash	40,000	55,000	63,000
	2,050,000	2,015,000	1,858,000
Shareholders' equity and liabilities			
Ordinary share capital £1 shares fully paid	600,000	600,000	600,000
Share premium account	125,000	125,000	125,000
Retained earnings	532,500	512,500	500,000
12% debentures 19X9	200,000	200,000	200,000
Trade creditors	495,500	492,500	390,000
Accrued expenses	15,000	17,000	9000
Taxation	52,000	43,000	24,000
Provision for dividends	30,000	25,000	10,000
	2,050,000	2,015,000	1,858,000

Required:

From the foregoing information, calculate the following ratios for the years 19X2 and 19X3 (assume that all sales are on a credit basis and the year is 360 days):

(i)   The current ratio
(ii)   The acid-test ratio
(iii)   The average inventory turnover
(iv)   The average collection period for debtors
(v)   The shareholders' equity ratio
(vi)   The return on capital employed
(vii)   The earnings per share.

Evaluate the liquidity position of the company at the end of 19X3 as compared to 19X2.

2. Evaluate the usefulness of financial ratio analysis as a method of assessing the financial state of an enterprise. Use the case below to illustrate your answer.

Case
A summary of the results of Sandygate Enterprises Limited for the last three years:

	Year ended 31 December		
	19X4	*19X5*	*19X6*
	£	£	£
Sales	480,000	560,000	690,000
Income before tax	63,000	70,000	74,000
Tax	23,000	25,000	28,000
Income after tax	40,000	45,000	46,000
Dividends	30,000	30,000	36,000
Retained income for year	10,000	15,000	10,000
Share capital (600,000 £0.25 shares)	150,000	150,000	150,000
Retained income	85,000	100,000	110,000
Shareholders' funds	235,000	250,000	260,000
10% debentures	65,000	150,000	150,000
Capital employed	300,000	400,000	410,000
Market price per share at 31 December	£1	£1.50	£1.25
Debt interest	£6,500	£15,000	£15,000

15 Financial accounting for groups of companies

A major financial feature of the years just before the Second World War and certainly over the last 25 years has been the emergence of large corporate groups, made up of a family of related companies brought together by processes of merger and acquisition. Although a company may not acquire or hold its own shares, it may acquire and hold the shares of another company. Thus, it may become a shareholder of the other company, and by obtaining an effective majority of the shares in issue, it may obtain the control of that company by the power which it acquires with its shareholding to elect and control the board of directors. As a result, although both companies are distinct legal entities, the fact that one controls the other links them closely together in the identity of their financial and trading policies.

It is difficult to give one single reason why a group may consist of 100 companies rather than being just one very large company, but probably the main reason is the degree of specialization permitted by the group structure. Frequently, different subsidiaries, as the members of the group are known, have different product lines or functions within the group and enjoy a measure of autonomy, whilst retaining the benefits of management expertise and finance provided within the group.

The parent-subsidiary relationship was originally defensive. If a company had a risky venture in mind, it could form and finance an entirely separate and distinct company, so that if the venture failed, it would insulate itself from the financial repercussion of the failure and only the subsidiary company would be wound up. Nowadays, it is thought unlikely that any major group would put into liquidation a subsidiary which had got into difficulties, but financial crises have occurred in the United Kingdom which have demonstrated the unwillingness of major financial groups to provide more than the minimum financial assistance to their subsidiaries.

The group structure has essentially been used for the purpose of financing and structuring business expansion—either by absorbing competitors or opening up new territories—whilst ensuring the retention of control in the hands of the group. As a result, financiers and entrepreneurs have succeeded in building up empires with the assistance of funds raised from the public, and they have acquired in this process very great economic and political power. In this respect, the emergence of the multi-national companies presents the spectacle of large and powerful groups having, in some cases, a larger annual budget than some of the countries in which they operate.

The purpose of this chapter is to consider the nature of the financial accounting information provided to shareholders and investors about groups of companies.

Legal obligation to disclose financial accounting information

The potential which groups have to misuse shareholders' funds and the assets of subsidiary companies appears immense. However, whilst major failures, scandals and frauds have involved complicated and confusing corporate structures, there is very little evidence of groups being deliberately managed in a dishonest manner.

Disclosure of financial accounting information has always been one of the cardinal principles of Company Law, and the view has developed that a group should report as an economic entity and not as a collection of separate legal entities. In this connection, this view is now firmly established in the United Kingdom, and is likely to be accepted generally in other countries. For this reason, we shall consider the problem of consolidated accounting information in terms of the United Kingdom practice.

At the outset, it should be mentioned that consolidation does not imply that individual companies need not prepare income statements and balance sheets of their own. Indeed, each individual company in a group still has to publish its own annual accounts to its shareholders, which, in the case of a wholly owned subsidiary, will be the parent corporation. These accounts are available for public inspection through the Registrar of Companies. The financial statements of the parent or holding company and those of individual subsidiaries cannot reveal the overall group financial position, and it is for this reason that group or consolidated accounts are required to provide an overall view of the group.

Although it was left to the Companies Act 1948 to make the major strides in the development of the law applicable to consolidated accounts in the United Kingdom, many companies adopted the group reporting format well in advance of legislation. The previous Companies Act of 1929 had paid scant attention to the problem of consolidation, for the abuses which were subsequently to be perpetrated were not foreseen. The Act of 1929 required the disclosure in the balance sheet of the parent company of holdings of shares in subsidiaries, and also a statement showing how the aggregate income had been dealt with, without requiring the disclosure of the aggregate income involved. Thus, prior to the Companies Act 1948, the disclosure of information was left to the discretion of directors in effect. The present position is that companies with subsidiaries must present group accounts in the form of a consolidated income statement and a consolidated balance sheet. SSAP 14 'Group Accounts', which had the effect of summarizing accounting practice as regards the consolidation of accounts, and which at the same time reflected the legal requirements of the Companies Acts, became mandatory on 1 January 1979.

The definition of a subsidiary company

Consolidated accounts are not required unless a parent–subsidiary relationship exists, as defined in Section 154 of the Companies Act 1948. A company becomes the subsidiary of another company in any one of the following circumstances:

(1) One company must be a member of the other and control the composition of its board of directors. This is the most common situation and is basically linked with voting power. If a company holds more than half the voting power of a company, usually by becoming the owner of more than half the vote-carrying equity shares, the latter company is a subsidiary of the first company. It is quite possible to hold much less than half the total share capital but still have a majority of the voting power, by means of non-voting and restricted voting shares. The Act does not mention voting power because this is only one way, albeit the most common one, of controlling the composition of the board. The definition chosen was purposely left wide so that other means of controlling the composition of the board, such as the right to appoint or prevent the appointment of a director might constitute control over the composition of the board.

(2) One company must hold more than half in nominal value of the equity share capital of the other. Equity capital is defined under this section as 'issued share capital excluding any part thereof which, neither as respects dividends nor as respects capital, carries any right to participate beyond a specified amount in a distribution'. Equity capital thus includes the non-voting ordinary share. Under this section a company may become a subsidiary through the medium of another company. If Company A holds 30 per cent of the equity capital of Company C and Company B holds 21 per cent of C's equity capital, then should B become the wholly owned subsidiary of Company A, this results in C also becoming a subsidiary of Company A.

(3) Where the company is the subsidiary of the holding company's subsidiary. If Company A becomes the parent company of Company B then A automatically takes over as parent any existing subsidiary of Company B.

The Jenkins Committee (1962) proposed the repeal of definition (2) above but it remained unchanged in the 1967 Companies Act. It was pointed out that the present definition may result in a company being considered as a subsidiary of two other companies. For example, through owning most of the non-voting shares, a company could hold more than half the equity shares capital, but another company through holding a majority of the voting shares could control the appointment and removal of directors. Jenkins considered that the entire test of a subsidiary should be based on membership and control of the board, by whatever means this is achieved.

The obligation to disclose information concerning subsidiaries

Following the recommendations of the Jenkins Committee that companies should disclose more information about their subsidiaries, S.3 of the Companies Act 1967 provides that certain information be given in respect of each subsidiary, namely its name, country of incorporation if different from that of the holding company and the identity and proportion of issued shares held of each class of the subsidiary's shares. There is a provision that if there are a large number of subsidiaries, only those whose results principally affect the amount of income need be listed. Schedule 2 of the 1967 Act requires any holding company to disclose separately in its balance sheet the aggregate amounts of:

(a) assets consisting of shares in its subsidiaries;
(b) indebtedness from subsidiaries; and
(c) indebtedness to subsidiaries.

The accounting requirements of groups are mainly set out in the Companies Act 1948, Sections 150–154 and in the second schedule to the 1967 Act. The legislation is tortuous in places, being designed to anticipate every situation, but essentially the legislation states that group accounts are accounts or statements dealing with the state of affairs and the income of the company and its subsidiaries (S. 150) and that group accounts shall give a true and fair view of the company and the subsidiaries (S. 152), and further, that group accounts shall comprise a consolidated balance sheet and a consolidated profit and loss account (S. 151). Group accounts are required in each case where the company has a subsidiary at the end of its financial year and is not itself the wholly owned subsidiary of another company incorporated in Great Britain (S. 150). Alternative accounting forms to consolidated accounts are permissible, so long as they give the same or equivalent information and may take the following forms:

(a) consolidated accounts dealing respectively with the company and one group of subsidiaries and other groups of subsidiaries;
(b) separate accounts dealing with each of the subsidiaries;
(c) statements expanding the information about the subsidiaries in the company's own accounts;
(d) any combination of the above (S. 151).

SSAP 14 requires that uniform group accounting policies be followed by holding companies when preparing consolidated financial reports.

Consolidated accounts

The purpose of consolidated accounts is to show in two statements, the consolidated income statement and the consolidated balance sheet, a composite picture of the income and financial position of the several companies which make up the group. It should be emphasized that each company remains a separate legal entity and a separate accounting entity and that the group is an economic and reporting entity.

Group accounts are prepared for the use of shareholders of the holding company. They are entitled to receive only the financial statements of the holding company, and do not receive copies of the financial statements of its subsidiary companies. Without a view of the totality of the activities of the holding company and its subsidiaries, it is evident that shareholders of the holding company would be given only limited information in the financial statements of the holding company. The purpose of group accounts, therefore, is to provide information to shareholders of the holding company and its subsidiaries as one economic entity.

Group accounts have two major disadvantages. First, they may be taken to imply that companies within the group are financially interdependent, and that they will assist each other to the extent of meeting each other's debts. Shareholders would be misled if they assumed such to be the situation. In fact, a holding or parent company may watch the creditors of an insolvent subsidiary company go unpaid without having to step in and pay them on behalf of the subsidiary. Second, where companies within a group differ with respect to profitability, growth potential and business risk, aggregating the results of such companies will conceal important information from shareholders, for example, where the solvency of one company in the group hides the insolvency of another company in the group. In such cases, segment reporting rather than group reporting may be more useful to shareholders. We discuss segment reporting in Part 4.

The simplest position is that of a parent company with just one subsidiary, and initially this structure will be used to examine the principles behind the construction of consolidated accounts. The number of subsidiaries and sub-subsidiaries, and the further complications that can be thought up in practice, can quickly border on the mind bending, but the majority of these, whilst complicating the arithmetic, add nothing to the principles.

In illustrations throughout this chapter the parent company will be called P Ltd, the subsidiary company S Ltd, and the combined group G Ltd, rather than 'the consolidated accounts of P Ltd and its subsidiary S Ltd'. This helps to emphasize an important point—G Ltd does not exist except as an abstract figment of the legislator's imagination. G Ltd is not a real company, it has no books and accounts of its own; it is merely a vehicle for combining the accounts of real underlying companies which, by virtue of holding shares in one another, are required to report as one economic unit. Thus it is an important first step to realize that although the parent company has a full set of double-entry accounting records and so do its various subsidiaries and any other connected companies, G Ltd, not being a legal entity, has no books of its own and its final accounts, being the combination of the final accounts of several companies, are not prepared from underlying double-entry records. In practice consolidated accounts are prepared by a series of schedules, rather than as the natural end product of a logical accounting system. A moment's thought will show that consolidated accounts are not just the simple combination of the accounting figures of the underlying companies.

Example 1

P Ltd acquired all the share capital of S Ltd at 1 January after which the two balance sheets show the following position.

	P Ltd £m.	S Ltd £m.		P Ltd £m.	S Ltd £m.
Share capital	100	40	Assets *less* liabilities	60	40
			Investment—shares in S	40	
	100	40		100	40

The combined balance sheet, G Ltd, is not just £100 m. + £40 m. = £140 m., because one of the main assets of P Ltd is an investment in S Ltd amounting to the entire net assets of S Ltd. The share capital of S Ltd £40 m. must be set against the investment in S Ltd £40 m. in the books of P Ltd. Although there is nothing at all wrong with either the accounts of P Ltd or S Ltd, the group position requires that the real position be revealed and that in reality the investment in the books of P Ltd is the various assets less liabilities of S Ltd. The group balance sheet is as follows:

G Ltd

	£m.		£m.
Share capital	100	Assets *less* liabilities	100

To treat the position otherwise would be to count the same item twice—once as an asset and once as a liability—and it is vital that accounts reveal the reality of the situation.

It is evident from the foregoing example that the main work in the preparation of consolidated accounts consists of cancelling out investments in the shares in subsidiaries held by a parent company against the share capital and reserves of the various subsidiaries, so that the group accounts reflect the reality of its economic situation.

Problems in the consolidation of group accounts

Two major problems arise on the consolidation of group accounts which we avoided in Example 1:

(a) P Ltd bought the investment in S Ltd for exactly the same amount as the net assets involved, £40 m. This is hardly realistic and in most cases the shareholders of S Ltd would demand a premium over the book valuation of the assets before relinquishing control and accepting shares in P Ltd to replace the shares they held in S Ltd. In other words P Ltd would have to pay a premium to persuade them to change management.

(b) Example 1 shows the position immediately after takeover but both companies will still continue to trade independently and make profits. The income of a subsidiary will increase the net assets of that subsidiary and also increase the value of the investment of the parent company in the subsidiary. From the group point of view, income will increase the net assets of the group.

Consolidating subsidiaries acquired at a premium

Example 2

Let us assume that P Ltd makes an offer to the shareholders of S Ltd to buy their shares for £2 each.

The balance sheet of P Ltd at 1 January is as follows:

	£m.
Ordinary share capital—shares of £1 each	140
Share premium account	110
General reserve	30
Retained income	20
	300
Fixed and current assets *less* liabilities	300

The balance sheet of S Ltd before the takeover on 1 January is as under:

	£m.
Ordinary share capital—shares of £1 each	50
General reserve	20
Retained income	10
	80
Fixed and current assets *less* liabilities	80

Assuming that the takeover is a complete success, the balance sheet of P Ltd will be as follows:

	£m.
Ordinary share capital—shares of £1 each	140
Share premium account	110
General reserve	30
Retained income	20
	300
Fixed and current assets *less* liabilities	200
Investment—shares in S Ltd at cost	100
	300

The balance sheet of S Ltd immediately after the takeover bid has gone through will be unchanged. All that has happened from the point of view of S Ltd is that the shares formerly held by various shareholders are now held by one shareholder, P Ltd. The former shareholders in S Ltd have sold their shares to P Ltd for what they have accepted as the market price.

To obtain control, P Ltd has had to pay a premium to ensure that the shareholders in S Ltd would accept the offer. To get control P Ltd has paid £20 m. for an intangible asset usually termed goodwill. Neither of the above balance sheets shows anything for goodwill. P Ltd can legitimately argue that it has bought an investment in shares which cost £100 m. But from the point of view of the group, the reality is that the acquisition of S Ltd has added net assets of £80 m. and goodwill of £20 m., calculated thus:

	£m.	£m.
P Ltd has paid		100
for net assets of S Ltd.		
Share capital	50	
General reserve	20	
Retained income	<u>10</u>	<u>80</u>
		<u>20</u>

but more usually shown in accounting form as:

Cost of control account (G Ltd)

	£m.		£m.
Investment—in S Ltd	100	Share capital (S Ltd)	50
		General reserve (S Ltd)	20
		Retained income (S Ltd)	10
		Balance = Group goodwill	20
	<u>100</u>		<u>100</u>
Goodwill b/d	20		

and the group balance sheet immediately after acquisition:

	£m.
Ordinary share capital—shares of £1 each	140
Share premium account	110
General reserve	30
Retained income	<u>20</u>
	<u>300</u>
Fixed and current assets *less* liabilities	
(200 + 80)	280
Cost of control/Goodwill	<u>20</u>
	<u>300</u>

It should now be seen that the investment account in the books of P Ltd has been cancelled against the share capital and reserves of S Ltd so that in the consolidated balance sheet above the underlying assets of S Ltd are brought in. The apparent maintenance of the double entry principle in the construction of the cost of control account above is illusory. It should be seen for what it is, namely an adjusting schedule where an item in the accounts of P Ltd is cancelled against items in the accounts of S Ltd.

An extension of a principle first brought out in Example 1 can now be examined. In Example 1 the share capital of S Ltd was offset against the investment in the balance sheet of P Ltd, so that neither account appeared in the consolidated account. In Example 2, not only the share capital of S Ltd but also the reserves at the date of acquisition have been offset against the investment account in the balance sheet of P Ltd. These reserves are regarded from the group point of view as capitalized at the date of takeover and are not now available for distribution. If the reserves of S Ltd at the date of acquisition were merely added to the reserves of its parent, it might appear that they are available for distribution, and it is a principle that pre-acquisition reserves are treated as capitalized on the date of takeover. The logic of this practice has been challenged in recent years and there has been some relaxation of this principle and this has led to the pooling of profits as from the date of takeover.

At this stage a definition of cost of control, which also appears in published accounts under the name of just 'goodwill' or 'goodwill arising on consolidation' may be attempted. The cost of control arising on consolidation is the excess of the purchase price over the book value of the net assets (being capital plus reserves) acquired at the date of acquisition. It will be recalled that the problems posed by the existence of goodwill as regards the preparation of financial reports, was discussed in Chapter 11.

At the end of the year, 31 December, the balance sheets of the two companies are as follows:

	P Ltd £m.	S Ltd £m.
Ordinary share capital—shares of £1	140	50
Share premium account	110	—
General reserve	30	20
Income statement, 1 January	20	10
Income for the year	12	15
	312	95
Fixed & current assets *less* liabilities	212	95
Investment—shares in S Ltd at cost	100	—
	312	95

(b) *Consolidating group income*

At the end of the year the income of both companies results in a corresponding increase in their net assets. The income of a subsidiary made after acquisition is regarded as distributable from the group point of view and is combined with the income of the parent to show the group income on the consolidated balance sheet.

Consolidated income statement (G Ltd)

	£m.			£m.
		Balance b/f at 1 Jan.	(P Ltd)	20
Group income c/d	47	Income for year	(P Ltd)	12
		Income for year	(S Ltd)	15
	47			47
		Balance b/d		47

and the balance at 31 December is as follows:

Consolidated balance sheet—31 December (G Ltd)	
	£m.
Ordinary share capital—shares of £1 each	140
Share premium account	110
General reserve	30
Retained income	47
	327
Fixed & current assets *less* liabilities	307
Cost of control of subsidiary	20
	327

The income of the subsidiary in future years will also be added along with the income of the parent company and the balance brought forward on the income statement, so that a total figure for group income is carried forward at the end of each year.

The treatment of dividends

Dividends may be paid either by the parent company, or the subsidiary, or by both companies. (The following examples ignore all questions of taxation.)

Dividend paid by Parent Ltd

A dividend declared by P Ltd will be paid to the shareholders of P Ltd, and the payment of the dividend will reduce the reserves and the cash resources of P Ltd and of the group, since the funds will be paid outside the group. If a dividend of £14 m. is declared the effect on the group balance sheet will be to reduce the balance on the income statement to £33 m. (47 m. − 14 m.) and the group net assets to £293 m. (307 m. − 14 m.). The entries required are those normally required for recording the declaration and payment of a dividend. If the dividend is proposed but will not be paid until after balance sheet date, it will appear as a current liability in the group balance sheet.

Dividend paid by Subsidiary Ltd

If S Ltd declares a dividend it will be paid to its sole shareholder—P Ltd. Although S Ltd will pay the dividend and P Ltd will receive it, no funds will pass outside the group and although it will mean that the income statement of S Ltd will be decreased and the income statement of P Ltd will be increased by the same amount, there will be no change in the overall group income statement.

Example 3

S Ltd pays a dividend of £10 m. to P Ltd. The journal entries are as follows:

		Dr. £m.	Cr. £m.
In the books of S Ltd	Income statement	10	
	Cash or proposed dividend account		10
In the books of P Ltd	Cash or dividend receivable account	10	
	Income statement		10

From the point of view of the group, the total on the income statement is still the same, although the distribution between the companies is different:

<table>
<tr><td colspan="4" align="center">Consolidated income statement (G Ltd)</td></tr>
<tr><td></td><td>£m.</td><td></td><td>£m.</td></tr>
<tr><td></td><td></td><td>Balance b/f at 1 Jan. (P Ltd)</td><td>20</td></tr>
<tr><td></td><td></td><td>Income for year (P Ltd 12 + 10)</td><td>22</td></tr>
<tr><td>Group income c/d</td><td>47</td><td>Income for year (S Ltd 15 − 10)</td><td>5</td></tr>
<tr><td></td><td>47</td><td></td><td>47</td></tr>
<tr><td>Proposed dividend (P Ltd)</td><td>14</td><td>Balance b/d</td><td>47</td></tr>
<tr><td>Balance</td><td>33</td><td></td><td></td></tr>
</table>

Thus an inter-company dividend although altering the distribution of income and funds within a group, does not alter the total income. Only in the case of a dividend which passes outside the group are the group income and net assets reduced. Parent companies frequently require subsidiaries to declare and pay dividends to them so that the parent has control over group financial policy, and may require a profitable subsidiary to make over funds to the parent which the parent itself uses or it may loan the cash to another not so profitable subsidiary. In the above example S Ltd pays a dividend of £10 m. to P Ltd, so that when P Ltd pays a dividend of £14 m. the drain on its cash resources is only a net £4 m. The above covered the situation in which the dividend paid by the subsidiary is declared and paid out of income arising after the date of the acquisition. The dividend received by the parent is regarded as distributable to the shareholders of P Ltd.

Dividends paid out of pre-acquisition income

A dividend paid by a subsidiary to its parent and agreed to be paid out of income existing at the time of takeover (pre-acquisition income) is treated quite differently. Such a dividend is said to be paid out of reserves which have been capitalized for group accounting purposes and such a dividend amounts to a capital return on the purchase price paid by the parent for the shares it bought in the subsidiary. In effect it amounts to a refund of part of the purchase price and is so treated in the accounts. In practice, it is rare for a dividend to be paid from pre-acquisition income, but where a dividend is paid which is larger than post-acquisition income, a LIFO rule is applied, that is, the most recent income is deemed to have been paid out, and only the excess is assumed to have been paid out of capitalized pre-acquisition income.

Example 4

The balance sheets of P Ltd and S Ltd immediately after takeover on 1 January are as follows.

	P Ltd £m.	S Ltd £m.
Ordinary share capital—shares of £1 each	140	50
Share premium account	110	—
General reserve	30	20
Retained income	20	10
	300	80
Fixed & current assets *less* liabilities	200	80
Investment—shares in S Ltd at cost	100	—
	300	80

On 2 January, just after the acquisition, S Ltd declares and pays a dividend amounting to £8 m. out of its income statement which from the group point of view is out of pre-acquisition income which has been capitalized.

		Dr. £m.	Cr. £m.
In the books of S Ltd	Income statement	8	
	Cash		8
In the books of P Ltd	Cash	8	
	Investment—shares in S Ltd		8

P Ltd cannot credit the dividend received direct to its income statement and the dividend is not regarded as being distributable to the shareholders of P Ltd. From the group point of view little has changed. The balance on the cost of control account has not changed, and although the detailed figures have changed, the make-up of the goodwill figure is still the same, as shown below:

Cost of control account (G Ltd)

Investment—cost of shares in S (P Ltd)	£m.	£m.	Share capital (S Ltd)	£m.	£m.
	100		General reserve (S Ltd)		50
less dividend from S	8				20
		92	Retained income *less* dividend to P Ltd	10	
				8	2
			Balance being group goodwill		20
		92			92
Balance b/d		20			

The balance sheets just after the payment of the dividend would be as follows:

	P Ltd £m.	S Ltd £m.	G Ltd £m.
Ordinary share capital—shares of £1	140	50	140
Share premium account	110		110
General reserve	30	20	30
Retained income	20	2	20
	300	72	300
Fixed and current assets *less* liabilities	208	72	280
Investment—shares in S Ltd at cost	92		
Cost of control/Goodwill			20
	300	72	300

The consolidated balance sheet is the same as that in Example 2. An intercompany dividend out of pre-acquisition income does transfer cash from the subsidiary to the parent but otherwise has no real effect.

The treatment of minority shareholders

The above examples have assumed that the parent company is able to persuade all the shareholders of the proposed subsidiary to transfer their shares to it, and that the subsidiary becomes a wholly owned subsidiary. It is not always the case that all the shareholders accept the offer, and a substantial minority may turn down the offer and remain as shareholders in S Ltd. The City Code on Takeovers and Mergers does not allow bids for only part of the share capital of a company, and a takeover bid has to be made for 100 per cent of the shares not already held by the parent. The bidding company in offering to buy 100 per cent of the capital of the proposed subsidiary commonly makes its offer conditional on acceptance by 90 per cent of the outside shareholders, so that it can take advantage of S 209 and compulsorily purchase a small minority of shareholders up to 10 per cent of the outstanding capital. If the bidding company obtains control of more than 50 per cent of the voting share capital, but clearly has no chance of obtaining a 90 per cent acceptance level, because a sizeable minority of shareholders are opposed to the bid, it still may decide to go ahead with the bid and allow a minority of shareholders to retain their shares in what will become a subsidiary company. Most subsidiaries are 100 per cent owned, often having been set up by the parent company itself, but it is not uncommon to find a subsidiary in which a minority of shareholders hold up to 25 per cent of the voting capital. There may well be good reasons for this. Most takeovers are amicably agreed between the parties and are small in size and are often for private companies in family businesses and the former shareholders may wish to retain some small interest in what was their own company, and the parent may be willing to keep the family connection with a view to retaining the goodwill of customers and the management expertise of the former owners.

Such minority shareholders still retain an interest in their original company and are not members of the group. Their interest, called a minority interest, may theoretically extend up to 50 per cent of the net assets but is commonly less than 25 per cent. A minority interest clearly needs to be excluded from the capital and reserves of the group, because the minority has no claim on the group. It would be possible to consolidate just (say) the three-quarters of the net assets of the subsidiary company which have been acquired by the group, but this approach is not adopted. All the assets and liabilities of the subsidiary are included in the group accounts and the minority interest is shown as a deduction proportional to the interest of the minority sharehol-ders. This is quite proper because although the group does not own all the net assets of the subsidiary it does have effective control of all of them, including those in which the minority have an interest. A parent company only needs bare voting control which is just a little more than 50 per cent to be in a position to control 100 per cent of the assets. The treatment may be shown diagrammatically:

S Ltd

Interest of group 75%	Fixed and current assets *less* liabilities 100%	included in group accounts 100%
Minority interest 25%		

Thus the minority are entitled to their share of the share capital and reserves at the date that the parent company acquires its controlling interest and their share of income made after acquisition. If a subsidiary company which has a minority passes outside the group, and reduces the total interest of the minority the proportion paid to the minority passes outside the group, and reduces the total interest of the minority by the amount of the dividend as shown in the group balance sheet. SSAP 14 provides that minority interests in the share capital and reserves of a group should be disclosed separately in the consolidated balance sheet. Similarly, the profits and losses attributable to minority interests should be shown separately in the consolidated income statement.

Acquisitions and the creation of minority interests

An example will be worked through in detail to further illustrate the principles and calculations involved.

Example 5

P Ltd acquired a 75 per cent interest in the share capital of S Ltd on 1 April. The draft summarized accounts of the two companies at 31 March next are as follows:

	P Ltd	S Ltd
	£	£
Ordinary shares of £1 each	100,000	40,000
General reserve	30,000	—
Retained income	11,000	5000
Current liabilities	12,000	8000
Proposed final dividend	5000	6000
Corporation tax	17,000	9000
	175,000	68,000
Freehold property at cost	112,000	30,000
Plant & machinery at book value	28,000	12,000
Inventory	17,000	10,000
Debtors	14,000	9000
Cash and bank balances	4000	7000
	175,000	68,000

Income statements

		P Ltd		S Ltd
Income for year		34,000		18,000
less taxation		17,000		9000
		17,000		9000
Balance b/f at 1 April		8000		6000
		25,000		15,000
Dividend paid	9000		4000	
Dividend proposed	5000		6000	
		14,000		10,000
Balance c/f at 31 March		11,000		5000

A consolidated balance sheet of the group is to be prepared at 31 March taking into account that no entries have been made in the books of P Ltd in respect of the purchase of the shares in S Ltd. These shares were acquired on the basis that five new shares in P Ltd were issued for every six shares in S Ltd, and that each share in S Ltd was agreed to be worth £1.50. The dividend paid by S Ltd was paid shortly after acquisition and is out of pre-acquisition income.

(a) *Calculating the purchase price*
The first task is to calculate the price P Ltd paid for its 75 per cent interest in S Ltd and to record the transactions in the books of P Ltd which so far have remained unentered. P Ltd buys 75 per cent of the share capital of S Ltd, i.e., 30,000 shares and since each share in S Ltd is agreed to be worth £1.50, the total purchase price is £45,000. The terms of issue are that six shares in S Ltd are to be exchanged for five shares in P Ltd. Thus P Ltd will issue $\frac{5}{6} \times 30,000$ = 25,000 shares and since it is agreed that the total purchase price is £45,000, the 25,000 ordinary shares of £1 each are issued at a premium of £20,000. The

entries in the books of P Ltd to record the acquisition of the majority interest in S Ltd are:

Journal of P Ltd	Dr.	Cr.
Investment account—shares in S Ltd	£m.	£m.
at cost	45,000	
Ordinary share capital account		25,000
Share premium account		20,000

Being purchase of a 75% shareholding
in S Ltd at 1 April at agreed value.

(b) Calculating the cost of control

P Ltd has paid £45,000 to gain a three-quarters holding in S Ltd. The calculation of the cost of control is slightly complicated in that shortly after acquisition S Ltd pays a dividend of £4000, agreed to be out of pre-acquisition income and also because a minority of 25 per cent in S Ltd retain their shares in S Ltd.

Cost of control account at 1 April (G Ltd)

Investment—shares in S			Share capital		
(P's books)		45,000	(S's books)		30,000
less dividend from S			Income statement		
(P's books)		3000	(S's books)		
		42,000	$\frac{3}{4} \times 6000$	4500	
			less dividend		
			paid	3000	1500
			Balance = Goodwill		10,500
		42,000			42,000
Balance b/d		10,500			

Note that P Ltd acquires three-quarters of the share capital and three-quarters of the income statement balance at 1 April. This is three-quarters of the net assets at the date of takeover. The dividend paid by S Ltd will go £3000 to the parent and £1000 to the minority. P Ltd will receive this dividend, debiting cash and crediting the investment account for the shares in S Ltd. Since no entries for the acquisition have been made in the books of P Ltd (but they have been recorded for S Ltd) the bank account of P Ltd will be increased by £3000 to £7000.

Journal of P Ltd	Dr.	Cr.
Cash	3000	
Investment a/c—shares in S Ltd		3000
(Receipt of dividend from S Ltd)		

The consolidated income statement is calculated as:

Consolidated income statement (G Ltd)			
Cost of control	£m.	Balance b/f 1 April	£m.
$\frac{3}{4}$ × pre-acquisition		(P Ltd)	8000
income (S Ltd)	4500	Balance b/f 1 April	
Minority interest		(S Ltd)	6000
$\frac{1}{4}$ × pre-acquisition			
income (S Ltd)	1500		
		Income for year after	
		tax (P Ltd)	17,000
Minority interest		Income for year after	
$\frac{1}{4}$ × year's income		tax (S Ltd)	9000
(of £9000)	2250		
Dividend paid (P Ltd)	9000		
Dividend proposed (P Ltd)	5000		
Balance = Consolidated			
income	17,750		
	40,000		40,000
		Balance b/d	17,750

The pre-acquisition income is split between the cost of control and the minority interest. Of the year's income after tax of the subsidiary, one-quarter is allocated to the minority, and the dividends of P Ltd, which go to the shareholders of the group, are deducted in the group income statement. The proposed dividend between the subsidiary and parent does not affect the group income. When paid it will affect the two companies but not the group position.

(c) *Recording the minority interest*

Minority interest account (G Ltd)			
Dividend paid (S Ltd)		Share capital	
$\frac{1}{4}$ × £4000	1000	(S Ltd)	10,000
Dividend proposed		Income statement	
$\frac{1}{4}$ × £6000	1500	(S Ltd) at 1 April	1500
(current liability)		Income for the year	2250
Balance = Minority			
interest	11,250		
	13,750		13,750
		Balance b/d	11,250

The interest of the minority is made up of their share of the capital and reserves at the date of acquisition plus their share of income made since acquisition, less their share of dividends paid and proposed. Clearly their interest is in their one-quarter share of net assets at the balance sheet date, and the minority can be easily cross-checked in this case as:

S Ltd

Ordinary shares	£40,000	at 31 March
Income statement	5000	
	45,000	
$\frac{1}{4} =$	11,250	

It is usual to show a proposed dividend due to a minority as part of the group current liabilities, rather than as part of the minority interest because it will be paid shortly after the balance sheet date and also is part of the liabilities of the group, being an amount due to persons external to the group.

The consolidated balance sheet is as under. The balance sheets of P Ltd and S Ltd are also given.

	P Ltd	S Ltd	G Ltd
Ordinary shares of £1 each	125,000	40,000	125,000
Share premium account	20,000	—	20,000
General reserve	30,000	—	30,000
Retained income	11,000	5000	17,750
Minority interest			11,250
Current liabilities	12,000	8000	20,000
Proposed final dividend	5000	6000	6500
Corporation tax	17,000	9000	26,000
	220,000	68,000	256,500
Cost of control			10,500
Freehold property	112,000	30,000	142,000
Plant & machinery at book value	28,000	12,000	40,000
Inventory	17,000	10,000	27,000
Debtors	14,000	9000	23,000
Cash and bank balances	7000	7000	14,000
Investment—shares in S Ltd at cost	42,000		
	220,000	68,000	256,500

Summary

It has been explained that group accounts are not the accounts prepared from a set of books kept by a group, but are an amalgamation of the accounts of the companies making up the group. Neither are they the straight addition of like items in different balance sheets, but a total view of the group. The accounts of the parent company usually have the biggest influence on the group accounts and the accounts of the subsidiaries are merged with those of the parent so that the group reports on the entire income, assets and liabilities under its control. The important adjustments, called primary adjustments, are to bring out the group figures for cost of control, income and where applicable the minority interest.

The cost of control (goodwill) has earlier been defined as the excess of the purchase price over the proportion of net assets acquired in the subsidiary as at the date of acquisition. The income figure for the group represents the total of the income of the parent plus its share of the profits of the subsidiary made since acquisition, less the dividends of the parent company. Pre-acquisition income is regarded as capitalized and non-distributable. The minority interest is entitled to its share of net assets of a subsidiary at the date of takeover, plus its share of profits made since acquisition, less its share of any dividends paid or proposed.

Reference

The Jenkins Committee Report, HMSO, 1962.

Questions

1. The following are the summarized balance sheets of a holding company and its subsidiaries at 31 March 19X8. The holdings in the subsidiary companies were acquired on 1 April 19X7.

	Pip Ltd £	Squeak Ltd £	Wilfred Ltd £		Pip Ltd £	Squeak Ltd £	Wilfred Ltd £
Share capital:				*Fixed assets:*			
Ordinary shares of £1	500,000	100,000	80,000	At cost less depreciation	315,000	120,000	77,000
10% preference shares of £1	—	10,000	—	*Shares in subsidiaries at cost:*			
Reserves:				80,000 ordinary shares in Squeak Ltd	110,000		
General reserve	—	10,000	—	50,000 ordinary shares in Wilfred Ltd	45,000		
Retained earnings	75,000	19,000	8000				
Debentures	—	20,000	—	Debentures in Squeak Ltd	5000		
Current liabilities:				Current assets	250,000	70,000	41,000
Trade creditors	100,000	20,000	30,000				
Proposed dividends:							
Ordinary	50,000	10,000	—				
Preference	—	1000	—				
	725,000	190,000	118,000		725,000	190,000	118,000

Income statements for the year ended 31 March 19X8 were:

	Pip Ltd	Squeak Ltd	Wilfred Ltd
Balance 31.3.X7	50,000 (Cr.)	10,000 (Cr.)	(2400) (Dr.)
Dividend received from Squeak Ltd 1.4.X7	2000	—	—
Net profit for year	73,000	30,000	10,400
	125,000	40,000	8000
Transfer to general reserve		10,000	—
Dividends proposed:			
Ordinary	50,000	10,000	—
Preference	— 50,000	1000 21,000	— —
Balance 31.3.X8	75,000	19,000	8000

Prepare a consolidated balance sheet as at 31 March 19X8 for Pip Ltd and its subsidiaries. Ignore taxation.

16 Problems in the preparation of consolidated financial statements

In Chapter 15, we examined the general principles associated with the practice of consolidating the financial statements of groups of companies. The examples which were chosen for this purpose were simplified to avoid many of the complications which arise in practice. This chapter is addressed to an analysis of the financial accounting implications of the most common problems which arise when consolidating financial statements. The list of problems considered in this chapter is not exhaustive; while they add to the volume of data to be processed and increase the arithmetical complexity of consolidation, they do very little to extend the principles which we have already examined. Hence, this chapter serves to test the logic of those principles.

Consolidating the financial statements of multiple subsidiaries

In the examples we examined in Chapter 15, it was assumed that the parent company has but one subsidiary. This assumption is unrealistic, as most public companies have several subsidiaries and often a public group will consist of over a hundred companies. Where there is more than one subsidiary company, then in each case the cost of control, group income statement, and minority interest if applicable, will need to be calculated. The resulting figures will be put together so that in the group balance sheet one total figure will be given for each of the primary adjustments.

The acquisition of a subsidiary at less than book value

Occasionally a subsidiary may be acquired for less than the apparent or given value of its net assets, in which case goodwill will appear as a negative figure. For example, P Ltd acquires for £100,000 a 60 per cent interest in S Ltd, whose balance sheet at the date of acquisition shows:

	£
Ordinary shares of £1 each	120,000
Share premium account	60,000
Reserves including retained profits	20,000
	200,000

then the cost of control will be:

Cost of control account (G Ltd)

	£m.		£m.
		Share capital (S Ltd) 60%	72,000
Investment—S Ltd		Share premium (S Ltd) 60%	36,000
(P Ltd)	100,000	Reserves (S Ltd) 60%	12,000
Balance c/d	20,000		
	120,000		120,000

The credit balance on the cost of control account is usually shown separately as a capital reserve in the balance sheet, under a heading such as 'Surplus arising on acquisition of subsidiary'. Less commonly it may be deducted from any goodwill in the balance sheet, so that a figure for the net cost of control is shown in the group accounts.

The treatment of losses made by subsidiaries

Subsidiaries do not always yield income, but may sustain a loss. A parent will have to bear its share of losses made by its subsidiary and a minority interest will also have to bear its proportionate share of any loss.

Example 6

P Ltd acquires 80 per cent of the ordinary share capital of S Ltd for £70,000, whose balance sheet at the date of acquisition shows:

	£
Ordinary share capital	100,000
Income statement (Dr)	(30,000)

During the first year after acquisition S Ltd makes a further loss of £10,000. Then:

Cost of control account (G Ltd)

Income statement (S Ltd)		Share capital (S Ltd)	
80%	24,000	80%	80,000
Investment in S (P Ltd)	70,000	Balance = Goodwill	14,000
	94,000		94,000
Balance b/d	14,000		

Minority interest in S Ltd (G Ltd)

	£		£
Income statement (S Ltd)		Share capital (S Ltd)	
20%	6000	80%	20,000
Loss for year 20%	2000		
Balance c/d	12,000		
	20,000		20,000
		Balance b/d	12,000

The parent's share of the loss for the year, £8000, will be set against the income of the parent in the group income statement.

Consolidating subsidiaries having complex capital structures

A subsidiary company may have a more complex share capital structure than so far envisaged. Commonly it may be found to have some form of fixed interest share capital, usually preference shares, with a fixed share of the income and no voting rights. If no offer is made for such shares during the takeover, the preference shareholders become a minority of the group and are included in the calculation of the minority interest of that subsidiary.

Example 7

P Ltd acquires 75 per cent of the ordinary share capital of S Ltd, but none of the preference shares, at a time when the net assets of S Ltd are:

		£
Ordinary share capital		50,000
10% Preference shares		30,000
Reserves including retained income		40,000
		120,000
The minority interest will consist of		
Ordinary share capital	25%	12,500
10% Preference shares	100%	30,000
Reserves including retained income	25%	10,000
		52,500

Further, in calculating the proportion of the income of S Ltd due to P Ltd, the dividends paid or due to the minority preference shareholders must be deducted before calculating the interests of the ordinary shareholders i.e., P Ltd and the minority holders of ordinary shares in S Ltd. Suppose that the income is £19,000. It will be apportioned as under:

	£	£
Preference shareholders		
(fixed dividend)		3000
P Ltd 75%	12,000	
Ordinary minority in S Ltd	4000	16,000
25%		19,000

A preference dividend due but not paid will not be included with the minority interest, but will be shown as a proposed dividend under the current liabilities, in just the same way as a dividend due to the ordinary minority shareholders. Debenture holders are not shareholders and do not form part of a minority interest. They are debt creditors and their position will be considered later.

Subsidiaries acquired during an accounting period

It will be rare in practice for a subsidiary to be taken over on the same day as the first day of the financial year of the parent company so that the two accounting periods coincide. It is a requirement that the financial year-ends coincide after takeover. In the usual case of a subsidiary taken over during its financial year either proper final accounts can be specially prepared at the date of acquisition so that pre- and post-acquisition income can be distinguished or an apportionment can be made on a time or some other rational basis to determine the division of pre- and post-acquisition income. A consolidation may include a subsidiary which is taken over mid-way during the parent's financial year and the income of the subsidiary in that year may have to be split as to 50 per cent prior to acquisition and 50 per cent after acquisition. In fact much of the secret of dealing with problems of consolidating accounts lies in an appreciation of the significance of the various dates involved. The date of acquisition is important for calculating the goodwill and considering whether any dividends are being paid out of pre-acquisition income, and the date of the final accounts is important for determining the income made since acquisition and the total of the minority interest.

Consolidation and inter-group transactions

As well as primary adjustments there arise several secondary adjustments which are commonly needed in consolidated accounts. These arise mainly because of inter-company trading between a parent and its various subsidiary companies, which if not eliminated during the consolidation process may lead to 'double counting'. For example, P Ltd may make a loan of (say) £2000 to its subsidiary. P Ltd will include S Ltd in its debtors as a debtor for £2000, and S Ltd will include P Ltd among its creditors for £2000. Just to cross add the debtors and creditors of both companies would lead to an overstatement of the figures for current assets and current liabilities in the group balance sheet. True enough, S does owe P £2000, but the group position is that the £2000 is an internal or inter-company loan and is neither an external asset nor liability of the group. It must therefore be eliminated by reducing the debtors of P Ltd and also the creditors of S Ltd, viz.:

Debtors of P Ltd	£2000	Creditors of S Ltd	£2000

Just the same rules apply for loans made between the various subsidiaries and each other if they are members of the same group. The same procedure applies for cancelling out in the group accounts any inter-company current accounts. Where a parent has regular transactions with its subsidiary, probably in the nature of inter-company purchases and sales, each company will maintain a record of its transactions with the other company. At the end of a financial period these two current accounts will be reconciled if they are not in agreement, using the same procedures as for branch accounts.

Example 8

At 31 December the current account of P Ltd with its subsidiary shows a debit balance of £6000 and the current account with P Ltd in the books of S Ltd shows a credit balance of £4500. The difference is due to cash in transit from the subsidiary to its parent which is not received by P Ltd until after the end of the financial year.

Books of P Ltd

Current account with S Ltd

	£		£
Balance b/d	6000	Cash in transit a/c	1500
		Balance c/d	4500
	6000		6000
Balance b/d	4500		

Cash in transit account

Current account—S	1500	

Books of S Ltd

Current account with P Ltd

	Balance b/d	4500

In the consolidated balance sheet the cash in transit account will appear as one of the assets and the two current accounts will cancel each other out. Cross holdings of loan capital or debentures between related companies are also cancelled out in the group accounts. The loan interest paid by one company on loan stock held by another member of the group must also be cancelled out against the loan interest received by that company.

Where there are mutual dealings—sales and purchases—between the companies in the group, transfers of goods between the companies may take place at a transfer value which is higher than cost. The point of this is to split the income earned on the completed transaction between the supplying company and the company which eventually sells the product outside the group. In preparing a consolidated income statement it will be necessary to eliminate such inter-company dealings from the total of group sales and purchases, so that no double counting occurs. A problem arises where one of the companies is at the financial year-end holding goods in inventory supplied by another company in the group at a price in excess of original cost. Such inventory will be included in the holder's books and inventory sheets at cost price to the buying company, which is cost price plus a profit margin from the group viewpoint, and in compiling group accounts it will be necessary to deal with the unrealized income. If the inventory of S Ltd includes goods received from P Ltd, at a cost of £2200 but the cost to P Ltd was £2000, from the group point of view, the inventory of S Ltd carries an unrealized income of £200. This would be adjusted on consolidation:

	Dr.	Cr.
	£	£
Consolidated income statement	200	
Consolidated inventory		200

i.e., both the group income and the group inventory is reduced by £200. Where the subsidiary is wholly owned by its parent, it is clear that it is proper to remove from the group accounts the full amount of the unrealized income. If a minority is involved the position is a little more complicated. Where the inventory is held by a partly owned subsidiary the usual practice is to provide for the whole of the unrealized income, as above, so that inventory appears at its cost price in the consolidated balance sheet. Where the subsidiary is the supplying company and there is a minority shareholding in the subsidiary, the inter-company income has been earned from the point of view of the minority, and the view may be advanced that the minority should not be debited with its proportion of the unrealized income i.e., the minority should be entitled to its proportion of the income for the year before adjustment. But from a group point of view the income is not yet made and it can be argued that the adjustment should be made in proportion to the shares in the income of the subsidiary company e.g.:

	Dr. £	Cr. £
Consolidated income statement	150	
Minority interest	50	
Consolidated inventory		200

Other treatments are also possible, but in most cases the amounts involved are not material and some variety in practice is permissible.

Much the same sort of situation arises in dealing with inter-group income arising on a sale or transfer of fixed assets between companies in the same group. Assume that P Ltd sells an item of plant which stood in its own books at £7000 to its wholly owned subsidiary for £8000 and that group policy is for each company to provide depreciation on this type of asset at a rate of 20 per cent per annum. Then the adjusting entries are:

	Dr. £	Cr. £
Consolidated income statement	1000	
Consolidated plant account		1000
Being elimination of unrealized income in plant transferred within group		
Consolidated provision for depreciation	200	
Consolidated income statement		200
Being excess depreciation (1600 − 1400) written back		

Consolidated income statements

The disclosure requirements of the Companies Acts ensure that a group publishes a consolidated income statement as part of group accounts. The parent company has to publish its own balance sheet as well as a consolidated balance sheet but the situation with regard to the income statement is rather different. Under the provisions of S.149(5) the income statement of the parent need not be published if the consolidated income statement 'shows how much of the consolidated income for the financial year is dealt with in the accounts of the (parent) company'. The information required by this subsection is usually given as the second part of the consolidated income statement, and the parent's income statement is dispensed with.

The major part of the consolidated income statement is constructed by merging the figures given in the separate income statements of the separate companies. The full income of each subsidiary is included and the total of the minority interest for the year is shown as a deduction. This is consistent with showing the group position as a whole, and then deducting external claims. Dividends paid between companies will cancel each other out and secondary adjustments for such things as unrealized income in respect of inventory and inter-company loan interest are excluded by the techniques outlined above. The final part consists of a section analysing in which companies' income arises and is to comply with S.149. The method of approach will be illustrated in the following example.

Example 9

On 1 July P Ltd, which has held 80 per cent of the ordinary share capital of Si Ltd for several years, acquired 90 per cent of the issued ordinary share capital of Sii Ltd. It may be assumed that income occurs evenly over the year. The share capital and reserves position of the three companies as at 1 January previously were as follows:

	P Ltd		Si Ltd		Sii Ltd
	£	£	£	£	£
Ordinary shares of £1 each		10,000	4000		2000
Income statement at					
1 January	5000		Dr., 1000	10,000	
less dividends					
(paid in March)	2500	2500		6000	4000

The income statements of the three companies for the year to 31 December following were as follows:

	P Ltd		Si Ltd		Sii Ltd	
	£	£	£	£	£	£
Sales		70,000		40,000		20,000
Cost of sales		40,000		20,000		17,000
Gross income		30,000		20,000		3000
Investment income		1000		400		500
Dividend receivable						
from Si		4000				
		35,000		20,400		3500
Depreciation	3000		2000		1500	
Directors'						
remuneration	7000		3000		500	
Loan interest paid	500		500		—	
Audit fees	500		50		30	
General						
expenditure	1900	12,900	850	6400	2770	4800
		22,100		14,000		(1300)
Corporation tax		9100		7000		
		13,000		7000		(1300)
Dividends						
proposed		6000		5000		—
Net income for the						
year retained		7000		2000	Dr.	(1300)

Notes:

(a) During the year P Ltd sold goods totalling £15,000 to Si Ltd, at a price based on cost plus 25 per cent. One-third of these goods were still held in inventory by Si Ltd at 31 December.

(b) The loan interest paid by Si Ltd is on a loan stock, half of which is owned by P Ltd.

Working schedule for consolidated income statement.

	£	£
Sales (130,000 *less* inter-co. 15,000)		115,000
Cost of sales (77,000−15,000)		62,000
		53,000
Investment income (1900 *less* inter-co. 250)		1650
		54,650
Less unrealized income in inventories	1000	
Depreciation	6500	
Directors' remuneration	10,500	
Loan interest paid (1000−250)	750	
Audit fees	580	
General expenses	5520	24,850
		29,800

Adjustments for consolidating income

Calculation of minority interest
Si 20% × after tax income of £7000	1400	
Sii 10% × loss for year	(130)	1270

Calculation of pre-acquisition loss
Sii 90% × ½ × loss of £1300	585

Calculation of balance on group income statement brought forward
P Balance	2500	
Si 80% × loss brought forward of £1000	(800)	1700

Calculation of analysis of income between companies
P Profit 7000 + Balance b/f 2500 *less*		
inventory provision 1000		8500
Si 80% × (income 2000 *less*		
loss b/f 1000)	800	
Sii 90% × half a year's income 650	(585)	215
Group retained income		8715

Group income statement for the year ended 31 December

	£	£
Group turnover		115,000
Group trading income		29,800
after taking into account		
Depreciation	6500	
Directors' remuneration	10,500	
Loan interest	750	
Audit fees	580	
and Investment income	1650	
Taxation		16,100
		13,700
Add pre-acquisition loss of subsidiary		
acquired during the year		585
Less minority interest		(1270)
		13,015
Add Balance brought forward		1700
		14,715
Proposed dividend		(6000)
Group retained income		8715
Dealt with by the parent company		8500
Dealt with by subsidiaries		215
Group retained income		8715

The sub-subsidiary relationship

A subsidiary company may itself have a subsidiary company which then becomes a sub-subsidiary (Ss Ltd) of the parent company. The principles of consolidation already discussed do not change, but the arithmetic becomes more involved.

Example 10

At the start of year 1, P Ltd acquired a 90 per cent shareholding in S Ltd at a cost of £113 m., when its reserves stood at £10 m.: at the start of year 2 S Ltd acquired a 75 per cent shareholding in Ss Ltd for £65 m. when its reserves amounted to £16 m. At the end of year 2 the separate balance sheets of the three companies making up the group were as follows.

	P Ltd £m.	S Ltd £m.	Ss Ltd £m.
Ordinary shares of £1 each	300	100	60
Revenue reserves (at end of year 1)	40	20	16
Income for year 2	15	14	12
	355	134	88
Fixed & current assets *less* liabilities	242	69	88
Investment—shares in S Ltd at cost	113		
Investment—shares in Ss Ltd at cost		65	
	355	134	88

The cost of control in each company is found as under:

Cost of control account (G Ltd)

	£m.		£m.
Investment—shares in S Ltd at cost	113	Share capital—S Ltd (90%)	90
		Revenue reserves (90% × £10 m.)	9
		Balance = cost of control	14
Investment—shares in Ss Ltd	65	Share capital—Ss Ltd (75%)	45
		Revenue reserves—(75% × £16m.)	12
		Balance = Cost of control	8
	178		178

There are now three claimants to the income of Ss Ltd:

(a) the minority shareholders in Ss Ltd as to 25 per cent of the net income of their company;

(b) the minority shareholders in S Ltd who have a claim to a 10 per cent share in the three-quarters of the income of Ss due to S Ltd; and

(c) the shareholders of P Ltd who have a 90 per cent interest in the three-quarters of the income of Ss Ltd which is due to S Ltd.

Thus the post-acquisition income of Ss Ltd is allocated as follows:

	£m.	£m.
Ss Ltd—Income for year 2		12
(a) minority in Ss—one-quarter		3
due to S Ltd—three-quarters		9
(b) minority in S Ltd—10%	.9	
(c) due to P Ltd—90%	8.1	9

The calculation of the consolidated income is:

Consolidated income statement (G Ltd)

			P Ltd		
			Balance brought forward		40
			Income for year 2		15
			S Ltd		
			Income for year 1 (90%)		9
Balance = Consolidated			Income for year 2 (90%)		12.6
income		84.7	Ss Ltd		
			Income for year 2		
			(as above)		8.1
		84.7			84.7
			Balance b/d		84.7

The minority interest is calculated in the usual way.

Minority interest account (G Ltd)

			S Ltd	
			Share capital (10%)	10
			Revenue reserve (10%)	2
			Income for year (10%)	1.4
			Share of income of Ss Ltd	.9
				14.3
Balance = Minority interest		36.3	Ss Ltd	
			Share capital (25%)	15
			Revenue reserves (25%)	4
			Income for year (25%)	3
				22
		36.3		36.3
			Balance b/d	36.3

To prove the accuracy of the minority interest in the group, it is necessary to remember that there is an implicit consolidation of Ss Ltd with S Ltd. This notional consolidation would produce the following balance sheet:

S Ltd 'group' balance sheet		
	£m.	£m.
Share capital		100
Revenue reserve		20
Retained income S Ltd	14	
Ss Ltd	9	23
		143
Minority interest in Ss Ltd (25% × 88)		22
		165
Fixed and current assets		
less Liabilities		157
Cost of control		8
		165

It can now be seen that the one-tenth minority shareholders in S Ltd claim £14.3 m. (i.e., $\frac{1}{10}$ × £143 m.), and this plus the £22 m. minority interest in Ss Ltd amounts to £36.3 m., which appears in the final consolidated balance sheet.

Consolidated balance sheet—end of year 2	
	£m.
Share capital—shares of £1 each	300
Consolidated income account	84.7
Minority interest	36.3
	421.0
Cost of control	22
Fixed & current assets *less* liabilities	399
	421

Merger or acquisition?

In the examples given in Chapter 15 the reserves of a newly acquired subsidiary company were treated as capitalized as at the date of acquisition, and it was mentioned at the time that the logic of capitalizing reserves at the point of the takeover which has the effect that such reserves cannot be distributed in the future to shareholders, has been challenged in recent years. Basically it is being suggested that reserves of the parent and those of the subsidiary both before and after acquisition should just be added together and regarded as jointly available for distribution.

It is argued that there are really two types of takeover—the acquisition and the merger—and the difference between the two is really a question of size. (American literature tends to use the terms *purchase* and *pooling* in place of *acquisition* and *merger*.) The takeover of a small company by a large parent company which has the effect that the small company is subsumed as part of a large group is termed a purchase or acquisition. A merger takes place between companies of similar size, and where both businesses are continued side by side. In early 1971 the ASC issued an Exposure Draft (ED 3) entitled 'Accounting for Acquisitions and Mergers' which recognized these two types of takeovers and that a different accounting treatment for each type could be justified. The main difference between the two methods of accounting is in the treatment of pre-acquisition income, the cost of control and the share premium. The acquisition method has been used in Chapter 15 and because the concept underlying it is that of a business purchase, the acquiring company will record the shares acquired at cost price, cost price being the value of the consideration given.

The main concept underlying a merger is that of continuity of the merging businesses. No assets are to be distributed to shareholders and no new capital is being subscribed. The only change that takes place is in the separate ownerships which are considered to have been pooled into one common ownership and re-allocated among the individual owners. It is essential that there should be no gross disparity in size between the amalgamating businesses, otherwise the owners of the smaller business would not have much of a say in the affairs of the combined enterprise. Under the merger method the accumulated profits at the date of the merger are not regarded as pre-acquisition profits and are treated as remaining available for distribution.

Clearly it is not enough to say that in a merger the companies must be of 'roughly similar size' and ED 3 defined the characteristics of a merger under four working rules, all of which must be met:

(a) The substance of the main businesses of the constituent companies continues in the amalgamated undertaking. Thus the takeover of a subsidiary company following which most of the fixed assets were sold off or where the nature of the business was changed would not be a merger.

(b) The equity voting rights of the amalgamated undertaking to be held by the shareholders of any one of the constituent companies is not more than three times the equity voting rights to be held by the shareholders of any of the other constituent companies. Thus if three companies A, B and C Ltd, agree to merge and the former shareholders of A Ltd receive 50 per cent of the shares in the combined undertaking, 30 per cent of the shares going to the former shareholders of B Ltd, and 20 per cent to C Ltd, the combination could be classed as a merger as the largest constituent company A Ltd (with 50 per cent of the shares) is not more than three times the size of the smallest company, C Ltd (with 20 per cent of the shares). But if the figures were A Ltd 50 per cent, B Ltd 35 per cent, and C Ltd 15 per cent, company C would not be regarded as a party to the merger since the former shareholders of A Ltd would receive more than three times the number of shares allotted to the former shareholders of C Ltd. B Ltd could be regarded as a merger with A Ltd, but C is an acquisition.

(c) At least 90 per cent in value of the offer is in equity voting capital identical to the original equity capital.

(d) The offer is accepted by shareholders representing at least 90 per cent of the total equity capital (voting and non-voting).

If all the four conditions are met it is considered that the companies have in effect become partners and there is a genuine pooling of profits. The suggested three to one rule in (b) above is arbitrary, but offers a working guide as to whether an individual company is being merged or purchased. The 90 per cent criteria in rules (c) and (d) are also arbitrary but intended to demonstrate that the ownership has continued much as before.

The ASC recommended the following accounting method for mergers. The shares transferred to the holding company as part of a merger should be recorded in the books of the holding company at the nominal value of the shares issued in exchange. No share premium is recognized or necessary on the new shares issued by the holding company. As a consequence of using the nominal value the only difference to be dealt with on consolidation will be the difference between the nominal value of the shares issued as consideration by the holding company and the nominal value of the shares transferred by the shareholders of the new subsidiary company to the holding company. Where the nominal value of the shares issued is less than that of the shares transferred the difference should be treated as a reserve (non-distributable) arising on consolidation. If the nominal value of the shares issued is greater than that of the shares received in exchange, the difference is the extent to which the reserves of the subsidiary have in effect been capitalized consequent on the merger, and this difference should therefore be treated on consolidation primarily as a reduction of the existing reserves; it should be applied firstly against any unrealized surplus and secondly against revenue income or realized surpluses. Essentially this indicates that to the extent that reserves are regarded as capitalized, non-distributable reserves are capitalized before distributable reserves.

Where there is some additional consideration in some form other than equity shares, for example cash or loan stock, the value of such additional consideration should be included by adding it to the nominal value of the shares issued by the holding company, so as to arrive at the total consideration paid for the shares in the merged subsidiary, and this total of the consideration would be debited to the investment in the subsidiary account. By following these procedures the reserves in the consolidated accounts will thus be either:

(a) the total of the reserves of the constituent companies increased by any reserve arising on consolidation; or

(b) the total of the reserves of the constituent companies reduced by any part of the reserves of subsidiaries which have been in effect capitalized as a result of the merger.

Example 11

In this example the reserves of the constituent companies are increased by a reserve arising on consolidation.

P Ltd has just increased its share capital by issuing 70,000 ordinary shares of £1 each plus a cash payment of £10,000 to gain 90 per cent control of the issued share capital of S Ltd. The separate balance sheets of the two companies immediately after the merger are as follows:

	P Ltd £	S Ltd £
Ordinary shares of £1 each	270,000	100,000
Capital reserves		20,000
Revenue reserves	50,000	30,000
	320,000	150,000
Fixed & current assets *less* liabilities	240,000	150,000
Investment—shares in S Ltd	80,000	
	320,000	150,000

Note that the cost of the shares in S Ltd is recorded in the books of P Ltd at the nominal value of the shares issued in exchange (£70,000) plus the value of any additional consideration (£10,000 in cash). The 70,000 ordinary shares of £1 each will have been issued at a premium (they must have been to comply with condition (c) above that 90 per cent in *value* of the offer is in equity voting capital) but such premium is not recognized when using the merger- or pooling-of-interest method. In preparing the consolidated balance sheet the investment account in P's books is set against the nominal value of the shares purchased in S Ltd, thus,

		£
Nominal value of shares in S Ltd pooled by P Ltd		90,000
Cost of investment in S Ltd:		
Shares at nominal value	70,000	
Cash	10,000	
		80,000
Capital reserve arising on consolidation		10,000

and the full consolidated balance sheet appears as under:

Consolidated balance sheet after merger—G Ltd

	£
Ordinary shares of £1 each	270,000
Capital reserve arising on consolidation	10,000
Capital reserves (90% × 20,000)	18,000
Revenue reserves (50,000 + 90% × 30,000)	77,000
Minority interest (90% × 150,000)	15,000
	390,000
Fixed & current assets *less* liabilities	390,000

The minority interest is calculated in the same manner in a merger as in an acquisition.

Example 12

In this example the nominal value of the shares issued by P Ltd exceeds the nominal value of the shares purchased in S Ltd, and the excess is treated as a capitalization of reserves of the subsidiary. The facts are as in the previous example but P Ltd issues 110,000 £1 ordinary shares plus cash of £10,000 to gain control of a 90 per cent shareholding in S Ltd. In this case the separate balance sheets of the two companies immediately after the merger are as follows:

	P Ltd £	S Ltd £
Ordinary shares of £1 each	310,000	100,000
Capital reserve		20,000
Revenue reserves	50,000	30,000
	360,000	150,000
Fixed & current assets *less* liabilities	240,000	150,000
Investment—shares in S Ltd	120,000	
	360,000	150,000

The cost of the shares in S Ltd as recorded in the books of P Ltd is 110,000 shares of £1 each plus £10,000 in cash, a total of £100,000. Offset against this is the proportion of share capital and reserves acquired in S Ltd up to a total of £120,000, viz.,

	£	£
Cost of investment in S Ltd		120,000
Share capital of S Ltd (90% × 100,000)	90,000	
Capital reserve (90% × 20,000)	18,000	
Revenue reserves (90% × 30,000 is 27,000 but only 12,000 needs to be capitalized, the remainder can be pooled)	12,000	120,000

The consolidated balance sheet will be as follows:

Consolidated balance sheet after merger—G Ltd

	£
Ordinary shares of £1 each	310,000
(Capital reserves—nil)	
Revenue reserves (50,000 + 27,000 − 12,000)	65,000
Minority interest	15,000
	390,000
Fixed & current assets *less* liabilities	390,000

The main difference between the merger method and the more commonly used acquisition method lies in the treatment of the reserves of the subsidiary at the date of acquisition. The acquisition (purchase) approach regards these as capitalized at the date of the takeover against the purchase price. The purchase price is based on a realistic assessment of the current values of the shares issued by the parent company. So where the purchase price exceeds the value placed on the proportion of the net assets acquired in the subsidiary, a difference or figure for goodwill will arise. The merger or pooling method regards the situation as being one where previously independent companies have merged as voluntary partners and that consolidation should be the mere amalgamation of balance sheets. Taking the valuation of the shares exchanged at face or par value is a mere book-keeping device to cancel out the shares issued by P Ltd against those of S Ltd on consolidation, with any resulting difference being treated as an increase in reserves (Example 11 above) or as a capitalization of existing reserves (Example 12 above).

On acquisition the assets of the newly purchased subsidiary are usually revalued so that a realistic figure may be attached to goodwill. In a merger of companies, a revaluation may not take place, so that similar assets but with very different book values may be added together because, for instance, different depreciation policies have been followed in the two companies. This has become one of the objections to the merger method but a revaluation of net assets at the time of merger with consequent adjustment to reserves would remove these objections. Generally there has been little enthusiasm for adoption of the merger method, and although Exposure Draft 3 was issued in early 1971, it has not appeared as an accounting standard.

Summary

This chapter has examined some of the complications in consolidating accounts. Some of the complications discussed have been of minor signifi-cance but the sections on consolidated income statements and the merger system of accounting are of great importance. The reader will now be aware of some of the conceptual difficulties which arise when consolidating the accounts of a group of companies, and of some of the practical solutions put forward to deal with these difficulties. The standards of reporting for groups of companies has advanced considerably since 1948 but it still remains one of the more difficult areas in which to attempt to standardize financial account-ing.

Questions

1. Set out below are the balance sheets for Macro Ltd and Micro Ltd as at 31 December 19X8.

	Macro Ltd £000		Micro Ltd £000	
Ordinary share capital				
Shares of £1 each fully paid	1800		600	
Reserves—retained earnings	4050		702	
Profit and loss account year ended				
31 December 19X3	652		144	
12% debentures	750		—	
	7252		1446	
Represented by:				
Fixed assets—net of depreciation	5121		1230	
Shares in Micro Ltd at cost				
400,000 ordinary shares	962		—	
Current assets				
Inventory	1244		514	
Debtors	2105		390	
Bank	960	4309	46	950
Less current liabilities				
Corporation tax	315		60	
Trade creditors	2825	3140	674	734
Net current assets		1169		216
		7252		1446

Macro Ltd bought its holding in Micro Ltd on 1 January 19X5 when the latter's reserves stood at £312,000. During the year ended 31 December 19X8 Macro Ltd has consistently sold some of its product to Micro Ltd and at the close of the year, Micro Ltd has goods in the inventory at cost of £208,000 which were supplied by

Macro Ltd. Macro Ltd's policy has been to sell its product at 33⅓ per cent on cost.
  In the debtors' figure of Macro Ltd is the current account of Micro Ltd standing
at £57,000 whilst in the creditors of Micro Ltd, the account of Macro Ltd stands at
£40,000. The difference is due to the fact that Micro Ltd had mailed a cheque for
£17,000 to Macro Ltd on 31 December 19X8 which was not received until 5 January
19X9.

Required:
(*a*) Prepare a consolidated balance sheet for the group as at 31 December 19X8.
(*b*) What alternative treatments are available for any of the items involved in the
    procedure of consolidation?

2. The balance sheets of Expanding Ltd, and its two subsidiary companies Growing
Ltd and Declining Ltd, as at 31 March 19X0 were as follows:

	Expanding Ltd	*Growing Ltd*	*Declining Ltd*
	£	£	£
Fixed assets	525,000	210,000	60,000
Investments:			
in Growing Ltd (100,000 shares)	140,000	—	—
in Declining Ltd (40,000 shares)	32,000	—	—
Inventory	63,000	83,000	28,000
Trade debtors	60,000	36,000	15,000
Growing Ltd	24,000	—	—
Declining Ltd	16,000	9000	—
Bank	10,000	7000	2000
Income account	—	—	15,000
	870,000	345,000	120,000
Ordinary shares of £1 each	400,000	150,000	50,000
General reserve	200,000	45,000	—
Income account	150,000	60,000	—
Trade creditors	120,000	68,000	46,000
Expanding Ltd	—	22,000	16,000
Growing Ltd	—	—	8000
	870,000	345,000	120,000

Notes
(1) At 31 March 19X0 goods transferred at cost £2000 were in transit between
    Expanding Ltd and Growing Ltd, and a cheque for £1000 was in transit
    between Declining Ltd and Growing Ltd.
(2) The closing inventory of Expanding Ltd included goods supplied by Growing
    Ltd, at an invoice value of £3600. Growing Ltd had priced these at cost, plus
    20 per cent.
(3) At the date of acquisition, Growing Ltd had a credit balance on income
    account of £21,000, and a general reserve of £15,000. Since becoming a
    subsidiary dividends of £30,000 have been paid, of which £12,000 has been paid
    out of pre-acquisition profits. Expanding Ltd has credited all dividends
    received to its income account.
      Declining Ltd had a debit balance of £5000 on income account when it
    became a subsidiary.

Prepare a consolidated balance sheet for the group as at 31 March 19X0.

Part 3 FINANCIAL REPORTING— ALTERNATIVE VALUATION APPROACHES

Introduction

We mentioned in Part 1 that the provision of information to meet the needs of users of accounting information should determine the objectives of an accounting information system. Therefore, the criterion by which the effectiveness of an accounting information system should be judged is the usefulness of its information output for the various purposes to which it is applied. Hence, if we were able to identify the nature of the decision-problems facing the several groups of persons with vested interests in organizations, we should be able to develop normative theories of accounting which would enable us to construct models for communicating information to these groups.

The reader will recall that in Part 1, we identified the following groups as having vested interests in business organizations, namely, management, shareholders and investors, employees, government, creditors, the local community and customers. In Part 2, we examined the methods used in accounting for selecting, processing and presenting information through the medium of four principal statements, that is, the income statement, the balance sheet, the funds flow statement and the cash flow statement. These statements and their underlying financial accounting procedures interpret all events in monetary terms, in accordance with the basic accounting convention which limits the recognition of events to those which can be expressed in monetary terms.

In effect, the four principal financial accounting statements have meaning insofar as money itself is meaningful in the context in which information is communicated in these statements. For example, the income statement is concerned with establishing the net income resulting from the transactions of the period under review, and the balance sheet is concerned with representing the financial position of the business as at the date of the balance sheet. It is clear that, whatever is implied by these two statements, much of their meaning depends upon the significance of the money values attached to the various items on which information is given. For example, if an asset is shown at a valuation of £1000 on the balance sheet, does this mean that it could be sold for £1000? Or, does it mean that it originally cost £1000?

In effect, the process of attaching money measurements to accounting events and items is essentially a process of valuation. Valuation enters into accounting measurements in two senses. First, the money standard of measurement is itself unstable through time. One pound today does not have the same value as one pound yesterday, or one pound tomorrow, since the purchasing power of money over other goods and services changes. Second, the use of money measurements in accounting implies a choice between one of several different valuation bases. It is possible to represent the original cost of acquisition of an asset by the enterprise as a representation of a past financial effort. Equally, it is possible to represent the value of an asset to the enterprise in terms of the future net benefits it represents.

Accounting for changes in the value of money is a subject which has long occupied the attention of accounting researchers. It was not until 1975, however, and the publication of the Sandilands Report, that the subject received attention from accountants generally. The ensuing lively debate illustrated the problem of producing a consensus regarding the best method of dealing with price level changes. One reason for the controversy which characterized the inflation accounting debate was due to the failure of accountants to reach agreement on the objectives of financial reports.

In Part 1, various approaches to financial reporting practices were discussed. The stewardship concept of financial reporting is identified with historical cost accounting. This concept focuses on safeguarding assets rather than on presenting measurements useful for decision making. Clearly, financial reports should provide some safeguards against the misuse of assets by management, but they should also provide measurements to shareholders indicative of the efficiency with which assets have been employed. The latter type of measurement is relevant for decision making by shareholders and investors.

This part is concerned with the problems of providing measurements relevant for decision making, rather than dealing with the problems implied in stewardship accounting narrowly defined. The analysis of the problems involved in the provision of measurements relevant for decision making requires a prior agreement on the criteria for judging the acceptability of alternative measurements. Conventionally, financial reports have relied on historic cost measurement. It has become apparent, however, that applying the criterion of relevance to users' information needs, historic cost measurements fail to satisfy these needs. The implications of the criterion of relevance are more fully discussed in Part 4.

In this part, we also examine a second criterion which is implied in the selection of appropriate accounting measurements, namely the criterion of feasibility which embraces such aspects of the measurement problem as objectivity, ease of understanding as well as considerations of costs of implementation. It is these issues which are involved in the examination of alternative accounting valuation systems.

Unfortunately, the selection of accounting measurements on the basis of the two criteria of relevance and feasibility does not rely on a simple set of accept/reject decision rules. To some extent each measurement currently available meets both criteria, but meets them at different levels of quality. For example, an accounting method which utilizes a measurement which scores highly for relevance, may not score well for feasibility.

The importance of understanding the interaction and interdependence between valuation and measurement is apparent in such important areas of accounting as income determination and asset valuation. In this sense, the notions of capital and income are largely dependent on valuation concepts.

In this part, six valuation concepts are discussed. They are as follows:

(a) *Historical cost*, which as we saw in Part 2, is the conventional valuation concept used in accounting. Resources are valued in accordance with their cost of acquisition by the enterprise. The historical cost valuation concept poses many difficulties under price-level changes.

(b) *Present value*, which is a concept which relates the value of an asset to the decision to hold it and to derive its utility from using it in the production of income. The present value is defined as the sum of the future expected net cash flows associated with the use of the asset, discounted to its present value.

(c) *Current purchasing power*, which is basically an adjusted historical cost concept, in which adjustments are made to recorded historical cost values for changes in the purchasing power of money by means of a consumer price index.

(d) *Current replacement cost*, in which the value of an asset is determined by the current cost of replacing it, and using the replacement to maintain the same service to the enterprise. It requires current market price data as a basis for preparing financial reports.

(e) *Net realizable value*, which estimates the value of an asset to the enterprise as the amount which would be realized from its sale, after adjusting for selling expenses.

(f) *Current cost accounting* which is a valuation concept which combines the concept of current replacement cost and net realizable value in determining whether selling (exit) or buying (entry) prices should be used for the purposes of establishing the value of an asset to the business.

This part consists of five chapters, as follows:

Chapter 17, Capital, Value, Income, which deals with the conceptual problems involved in the valuation of the enterprise and the measurement of income.

Chapter 18, Accounting and Economic Concepts of Income and Value, which considers two different approaches to income measurement and valuation.

Chapter 19, Current Purchasing Power Accounting, which examines a proposed method for dealing with the instability of the accounting standard of measurement by indexing its purchasing power as a means of making adjustments for maintaining a constant value.

Chapter 20, Current Value Accounting, which examines a proposed method for dealing with the instability of the accounting standard of measurement in terms of representing asset values at their current value to the enterprise. This method was recommended for adoption in the United Kingdom.

Chapter 21, Current Cost Accounting, which discusses the system adopted by the accounting profession in the United Kingdom for dealing with the problems implied in the changing value of money in financial reports.

17 Capital, value, income

We stated in Chapter 2 that the objectives of financial reporting to investors should be found in the decisions which investors have to make about their investment in companies. Hence, we argued, financial reporting should be concerned with the provision of such information as is required for making those decisions. We assumed, also, that investors were principally concerned with the worth of their investments in two senses. Firstly, they are concerned with maintaining and increasing the value of their capital. Secondly, they are concerned with maintaining and increasing the income which is derived from that capital. Financial reporting ought to be concerned, therefore, with the valuation of shareholders' capital and income. In accordance with the stewardship concept of financial reporting, feedback information is required in order that investors may ascertain the present value of share capital and income. The decision-making concept of financial reporting asserts that financial reports should contain information which is useful in assisting investors to predict future changes in capital and income.

Three concepts are involved in financial reporting—capital, value and income. Together they provide the focus for this part. The purpose of this chapter is to introduce and explain the nature of these three concepts.

Capital

To the economist, the term 'capital' relates to those assets which are used in the production of goods and services. The capital of the firm is represented by the firm's inventory of assets, and investment by the firm occurs when the inventory is increased. From the point of view of society, the term 'capital' is restricted similarly to those assets which produce goods and services. Capital includes, therefore, physical assets in the form of buildings, plant and machinery, housing, hospitals, schools as well as intangible assets such as technology, human skills (human capital) etc.

In accounting theory, a person's capital is increased by that portion of his periodic income which he has not consumed. Financial accounting procedure effects this transfer by crediting the net income to the capital account, and if his level of consumption, or drawings, is less than that income, the capital is increased by the difference. In the case of companies, dividends are analogous to drawings, and retained income is added to the total of the shareholders' equity. One of the important implications of income measurement in the case of companies lies in calculating what may safely be distributed as dividends.

Early writers on book-keeping recommended, as a first step in the record-keeping process, the preparation of an inventory or statement of capital showing all the personal and real property, as well as debts due and owing on the first day of business. Paciolo in 1494 advised the businessman to prepare his inventory in the following way:

'First of all, he must write on a sheet of paper or in a separate book all his worldly belongings, that is, his personal or real property. He should always begin with the things that are more valuable and easier to lose . . . He must then record all other things in proper order in the Inventory.' (Gene Brown and Johnston, 1963.)

It is evident that at this stage of development, accounting made no distinction between personal capital and business capital. In the course of subsequent developments, however, a distinction emerged between total wealth and wealth committed to business activities. Whereas in Paciolo's time, capital was taken to mean the entire amount of what was owned, the capital account became ultimately a device which described and quantified that portion of private wealth invested in a business enterprise.

The development of the entity theory of accounting, as distinct from the proprietory theory, which culminated in the appearance of the joint stock company, gave expression to two important notions. First, as we saw in Part 2, an enterprise could be separated from its owner by a legal fiction and used by him as a vehicle for conducting business. Second, the fictional life granted to the enterprise by accounting practice, and additionally in the case of corporations by law was to serve limited purposes. The capital account was to remain the umbilical cord linking the enterprise to its owner or owners. In line with this view, the enterprise continued to be regarded as an asset and this view has important implications for the valuation of capital and income.

From the foregoing, it is evident that there are some fundamental differences between economists and accountants in the manner in which the notion of capital is conceptualized. As Littleton (1961) points out, the balance sheet presentation of 'capital' emphasizes its legal rather than its economic aspect, for capital is shown as a liability, whereas in economics, capital refers to assets. The assets held by a business and actively employed by it are usually greater in value than the so-called 'capital'. In the light of modern interests, we may say that the terminology of financial reports in this respect is misleading. However, supposing that the total assets employed by an enterprise were to be re-defined as its 'capital', there remains a number of problems:

(a) the valuation of business capital;
(b) the valuation of investors' financial interests, that is, personal capital;
(c) the methods selected for these valuations;
(d) the manner in which these valuations are to be communicated.

From our previous discussion of the objectives of financial reporting, we may say that investors are interested primarily in the valuation of their shareholding and this valuation is dependent on the valuation of business capital.

Capital maintenance

We stated earlier in this chapter that investors are concerned with maintaining the value of their capital. The concept of capital maintenance is central to discussions regarding price-level adjustments. There is general agreement that income is a residue available for distribution once provision has been made for maintaining the value of capital intact. Difficulties begin to emerge when discussion turns to the consideration of the meaning of 'capital maintenance'. Several alternative interpretations of this concept have been offered and are illustrated in Fig. 3.1. It will be noted from Fig. 3.1 that five concepts of capital maintenance are listed, as well as six valuation systems. The combinations of capital maintenance concepts and valuation systems indicated in Fig. 3.1 are discussed in this chapter.

(a) The money capital concept

According to this concept, the measurement of periodic income should ensure that the monetary value of the shareholders' equity is maintained intact. In effect, the income of the period amounts to the increase in monetary terms in the shareholders' equity measured between the beginning and the end of the period. It is this amount which may be distributed as income to ensure that the money capital is maintained intact. The money capital maintenance concept is reflected in historical cost accounting.

(b) The investment purchasing power concept

This concept defines the assets of the enterprise in terms of their potential earning power expressed as the present value of all cash flows to be generated in the future. It gives rise to economic income, which may be stated as the change in the earning power of the enterprise in respect of any period plus distributions made to shareholders during such period. This concept of capital maintenance accords with the classical definition of economic income as being the difference between the opening and closing value of shareholders' equity based on such a valuation of assets.

(c) The consumer purchasing power concept

The objective of this concept is to maintain the purchasing power of the shareholders' equity by constantly updating the historical cost of assets for changes in the value of money. The translation of historical asset cost is effected by a retail price index, and results in the representation of asset values in common units of purchasing power. This concept of capital maintenance purports to show to shareholders that their company kept pace with general inflationary pressures during the accounting period, by measuring income in such a way as to take into account changes in the price-levels. In effect, it intends to maintain the shareholders' capital in terms of monetary units of constant purchasing power. The use of a retail price index based on

Accounting valuation concepts

Capital maintenance concepts	1 Historical cost	2 Present value	3 Current purchasing power	4 Replacement cost	5 Net realizable value	6 Current cost accounting
A Money capital	Conventional accounting					
B Investment purchasing power		Economic income and value				
C Consumer purchasing power			SSAP 7			
D Operating capacity				Edwards Bell		Sandilands SSAP 16
E Disposable wealth					Chambers Sterling	

Fig. 3.1

the range of goods and services restricts adjustments for changes in the purchasing power of money to those changes which would be experienced by consumers.

(d) The operating capital concept

The consumer purchasing power concept of capital maintenance views the capital of the enterprise from the standpoint of the shareholders as owners. Hence, it reflects the proprietorship concept of the enterprise as regards both income and capital, and seeks valuation systems which fit this view. By contrast, the operating capacity concept of capital maintenance views the problem of capital maintenance from the perspective of the enterprise itself, thereby reflecting the entity concept of the enterprise.

The operating concept states that the productive (operating) capacity of the enterprise should be maintained as a prime objective in the course of income measurement. The operating capacity concept of capital maintenance asserts that income is a residue after provision has been made for replacing the resources exhausted in the course of operations. In this view, 'there can be no recognition of income for a period unless the capital employed in the business at the beginning of the period has been maintained . . . The starting point will be the various items making up the capital.' (Goudeket, 1960.) The criteria imposed on income measurement by the operating concept are met by the system of replacement cost accounting, in which assets are valued at their replacement cost to the firm. Replacement cost accounting takes into account changes in the prices of commodities specific to the enterprise, either directly or by using specific price indices to measure changes in the prices of similar commodities.

(e) The disposable wealth concept

Whereas all previous concepts of capital maintenance envisage the enterprise as a going concern, the disposable wealth concept suggests that the maintenance of capital should be viewed from the perspective of the realizable value of the assets of the enterprise. Accordingly, the measurement of periodic income is required to take into account changes in the realizable value of net assets attributable to the shareholders' equity. At the beginning of the accounting period, the shareholders' equity, defined as the capital of the enterprise, is valued by reference to the realizable value of assets, after deducting realization expenses. A similar valuation of the net amount which would accrue to shareholders from the realization of assets is made at the end of the accounting period.

The disposable wealth concept of capital maintenance is based on the proprietorship theory of the enterprise. However, it interprets this theory in terms of the 'exit' rather than the 'entry' values of enterprise assets.

Income

The concepts of capital and income are closely related. Irving Fisher (1919) expressed their relationship as follows: 'A stock of wealth existing at a given instant of time is called capital; a flow of benefit from wealth through a given period of time is called income'.

An analogy may be found in the relationship between a tree and its fruit—it is the tree which produces the fruit, and it is the fruit which may be consumed. Destroy the tree, and there will be no more fruit: tender the tree with care and feed its roots and it will yield more fruit in the future.

Once the concept of value is introduced into the relationship between capital and income, however, the exact nature of this relationship becomes clearer. According to Irving Fisher (1969):

'It would seem . . . that income must be derived from capital; and, in a sense, this is true. Income is derived from capital goods, but the value of the income is not derived from the value of capital goods. On the contrary, the value of the capital is derived from the value of the income . . . Not until we know how much income an item will probably bring us can we set any valuation on that capital at all. It is true that the wheat crop depends on the land which yields it. But the value of the crop does not depend on the land. On the contrary, the value of the land depends on its crop.'

Economic and accounting theory are both concerned with the relationship between capital and income and in the implications of this relationship. There is agreement between accountants and economists on a number of aspects of the relationship and considerable disagreement as regards the valuation of capital and income. There is agreement, for example, that only income should be available for consumption, and that in arriving at a measure of income, it is necessary to maintain the value of capital intact. Since the ultimate aim of economic activity is the satisfaction of wants, it follows that income is identified as a surplus which is available for consumption. The valuation of income in this analysis is subject to a fairly conservative criterion which Hicks expressed as follows: 'The purpose of income calculations in practical affairs is to give people an indication of the amount which they can consume without impoverishing themselves.' (Hicks, 1946.)

Income plays a central role in many business and personal decisions since it is based essentially on the notion of spending capacity. As Hicks pointed out, income should be an operational concept providing guidelines to spending. As applied to business corporations, Hicks's definition of income has been interpreted to define the income of a corporation in any one year as the 'amount the corporation can distribute to the owners of the equity in the corporation and be as well off at the end of the year as at the beginning' (Alexander, 1962). It is evident, however, that income is used for other purposes as well. For this reason, we should examine the objectives of income measurements before proceeding to the analysis and selection of appropriate concepts.

The objectives of income measurement

Income as a measure of efficiency

Income is used as a measure of efficiency in two senses. First, the overall efficiency of a business is assessed in terms of the income generated. Hence, income tends to provide the basic standard by which success is measured. There are clearly problems in focusing upon financial efficiency to the detriment of other concepts of business efficiency—such as its effectiveness as a social unit and its efficiency in developing and using new ideas and processes. Nevertheless, those who support the use of income as a measure of business efficiency argue that in the last analysis, all other aspects of efficiency converge on income. Second, shareholders assess the efficiency of their investments by reference to reported income. Hence, the allocation of investment funds, the selection of portfolios and the operations of the financial system depend upon income as a standard by which decisions are taken.

Income as a guide to future investment

As we shall see in Part 5, the selection of investment projects is made on the basis of estimates of future cash flows. These estimates are self-fulfilling to the extent that risk and uncertainty have been sufficiently discounted in the decision-making process. In a more general way, however, current income acts to influence expectations about the future. This is particularly so as regards investors who have to rely on financial reports and whose willingness to hold and to subscribe for further shares will be affected by reported income.

Income as an indicator of managerial effectiveness

Management is particulary sensitive about the income which is reported to shareholders since its effectiveness both as decision makers and as stewards of resources is judged by reference to reported income. It is in this respect that auditors play a key role in ensuring that the statements placed before shareholders reflect a 'true and fair' view of the financial results. What is 'true and fair' may be a contentious problem amoung accountants. Nevertheless, what is evidently neither true nor fair rarely avoids comment.

Income as a tax base

The tendency of most governments to require a substantial share of corporate income in the form of taxation means that the manner in which corporate tax is assessed is critically important to shareholders and management. Although taxation legislation does not define 'income', it does specify what is taxable and what is deductible in arriving at a measure of taxable income. Much litigation in this area has revolved around the meaning of words, but the taxation authorities accept accounting income as the base from which to work out taxable income.

Income as a guide to creditworthiness

A firm's ability to obtain credit finance depends on its financial status and its current and future income prospects. For this reason, credit institutions and banks require assurances of a firm's ability to repay loans out of future income and look upon current income levels as a guide in this respect.

Income as a guide to socio-economic decisions

A wide range of decisions take into account the levels of corporate income. Thus, price increases tend increasingly to be justified in terms of income levels and wage bargaining procedures usually involve appeals by both sides to their effects on corporate income. Government economic policies are guided by levels of corporate income as one of the key social indicators.

Income as a guide to dividend policy

The distinction between capital and income is central to the problem of deciding how much may be distributed to shareholders as dividends. A series of important cases have been concerned with the concept of capital mainte-nance, and rules have been established for the measurement of distributable income with a view to protecting the interests of creditors. Thus, there is a rule which provides that losses in the value of current assets should be made good, whereas in arriving at the measure of distributable income, there is no need to make good losses in the value of fixed assets.

Nowadays, however, dividend policy is much more directed towards establishing the proportion of current income which should be retained and the proportion which should be distributed. This is because companies expect to finance their investment needs from retained income.

Income concepts for financial reporting

The application of different accounting valuation concepts to asset valuation and income measurement offers a variety of alternative bases for drawing up financial reports. In this part, we shall examine the implications of reporting to shareholders on the basis of the following six alternative accounting valuation concepts listed in the Introduction to this part, namely, historical cost, present value, current purchasing power, replacement cost, net realiz-able value and current cost.

As stated in the introduction to this part, the evaluation and selection of alternative accounting valuation systems depends on the manner in which they satisfy criteria of acceptability. We noted in particular, that the criteria of relevance and feasibility were highly significant in this regard. One problem in evaluating alternative valuation systems for financial reporting purposes is that each alternative satisfies these criteria in different ways. For example, historical cost has a high degree of feasibility but little relevance, whereas present value has a high degree of relevance but little feasibility.

A second problem which will be examined in this part stems from alternative definitions of capital maintenance. Thus, there is some controversy about the manner in which concepts of capital maintenance may be made operational for financial reporting purposes. For example, the debate which followed the Sandilands Report illustrates that the operating capacity concept of capital maintenance does not immediately suggest agreement about the choice of an accounting valuation system which would satisfy the objectives of such a concept of capital maintenance.

Summary

The purpose of this chapter was to examine the implications for financial reporting of three concepts—capital, value and income. Two meanings may be attached to the concept of capital. First, capital may be seen as the totality of enterprise assets which give rise to income. Second, capital may be seen as the investment made by shareholders in the equity of the enterprise and from which they expect to derive income in the form of dividends. Investors are concerned not only with the interdependence of the value of their shareholdings and the value of enterprise assets, but also with maintaining the value of that capital. The value of capital and the measurement of income are also interdependent in the sense that income is the difference between the value of capital at two points in time. Therefore, a central issue in the measurement of periodic income is the notion of capital maintenance. Difficulties arise in reporting income due to the different concepts of capital maintenance discussed in this chapter.

Further problems arise in financial reporting from the application of different valuation concepts to asset valuations. The combination of different capital maintenance and asset valuation concepts lies at the heart of much of the controversy in financial reporting. The problem of selecting a financial reporting framework requires the evaluation of alternative accounting valuation systems in terms of criteria of relevance and feasibility.

References

1. Alexander, S. S., revised by Solomons, D. 'Income measurement in a dynamic economy', *in* Baxter, W. T. & Davidson, S. (eds), *Studies in Accounting Theory*, p. 139, Sweet and Maxwell, London, 1962
2. Fisher, I. *Elementary Principles of Economics*, p. 38, 1919.
3. Fisher, I. 'Income and capital', *in* Parker, R. H. & Harcourt, G. C. (eds), *Readings in the Concept and Measurement of Income*, p. 40, Cambridge University Press, 1969.
4. Gene Brown, R. & Johnston, K. S. *Paciolo on Accounting*, p. 27, McGraw-Hill, 1963.
5. Goudeket, A. 'An application of replacement value theory', *Journal of Accountancy*, July, 1960.
6. Hicks, J. R. *Value and Capital*, 2nd ed., p. 172, Oxford University Press, 1946.
7. Littleton, A. C. *Essays on Accounting*, p. 244, University of Illinois Press, 1961.

Questions

1. How do accountants define capital?
2. Distinguish between the following concepts of capital maintenance, money capital, investment purchasing power, consumer purchasing power, operating capital and disposable wealth.
3. How are the concepts of income and wealth related?
4. State the objectives of income measurement. Do we require different concepts of income in order to fulfill these objectives?
5. Define various income concepts listed in this chapter.

18 Accounting and economic concepts of income and value

Accounting concepts

Accounting concepts of income and value have been influenced mainly by two conventions—the cost and the realization convention. These conventions have received much criticism in recent years because they restrict the usefulness of financial accounting reports for decision-making purposes.

The effects of the cost convention

The basis of valuation in financial accounting is historical cost. This convention clearly conflicts with the going-concern convention of valuation when the value of money itself is changing. In effect, historical cost income is based on a venture rather than a going-concern view of the firm.

Under the venture concept, each asset purchased is regarded as a separate venture, so that income is determined for each venture. Thus, net income is measured by setting off against revenues the cost of the assets ventured in earning those revenues. The replacement of those assets is treated as a distinct second venture, for which funds should be raised independently.

By contrast, the going-concern concept which is supported by most businessmen and economists holds that the business enterprise should be considered as a unified continuing concern rather than a series of separate individual ventures.

The historical cost method of valuation seriously distorts the measurement of income, when the value of money is changing. This distortion results from the difference between the historical cost and the current cost which, as we shall see later, is a function of the time gap between the acquisition and the utilization of assets committed to earning periodic revenues. For items such as wages and other current expenses, this difference may be very small, but for such assets as inventories and fixed assets, there may be a substantial difference between the acquisition cost and the current cost when those assets are charged against revenue under the matching rule. Under conditions of rising prices, the historical cost may bear no resemblance to the current cost of assets, with the result that income is overstated. Conservative asset values on the balance sheet are contrasted by over-optimistic income measurements in the income statement.

The historical cost method of valuation creates a particular problem in periods of inflation when money units of different values are brought together in the accounting process as though they were money units of the same value. Such arithmetic is quite incorrect, for it involves adding together amounts expressed in different measurement scales. Accordingly historical cost values are not additive during periods of changing money values.

Example

A firm constructed a building at a cost of £100,000. Ten years later, a similar building was constructed at a cost of £200,000. In accordance with the conventions of historical cost accounting, these two items were added together in the balance sheet to show a total historical cost of £300,000. Clearly, the two buildings are not comparable in the sense that the second building is a building which is either twice as large as the first or more costly to build. In effect, no such conclusions could be drawn. Adding together pounds which represent units of different purchasing power is similar in nature to adding together pints, quarts and gallons without converting them to a common denominator. Consider what would be the effect of such arithmetic on the depreciation provision for the buildings. If we assume that the buildings are in fact identical, an annual rate of depreciation of 5 per cent would provide depreciation at the rate of £5000 for the first building, and £10,000 for the second building. Therefore, it may be concluded that the entire arithmetic underlying the balance sheet representation of asset values would be incorrect under inflation, when asset values purchased at different times are added together in asset totals.

The main advantage which is claimed for historical cost valuation is that it is verifiable. The stewardship approach to financial reporting theory is the major factor which supports this method of valuation. It may be argued, however, that if it is objectivity which the accountant is seeking, he should restrict himself purely to counting cash, since this asset is virtually the only one in respect of which complete objectivity is possible. As soon as the accountant moves away from cash, he is dealing with subjective factors. For example, there are many alternative measures available for valuing inventories, calculating depreciation, allocating overheads and providing for bad debts. Consequently, a 'true' measure of objectivity under historical cost valuation is not possible.

The effects of the realization convention

In accordance with the realization convention, the accountant does not recognize changes in value until they have crystallized following a transaction. Until a right enforceable at law comes into existence, gains in book values are ignored for the purpose of income measurement.

It has been suggested that there are two principal reasons which favour the practice of measuring income on realization rather than on accrual. The first is that a sale affords an objective measure of a change in value, and the second is that 'the sale is generally considered to be the most decisive and significant event in the chain of transactions and conditions making up the stream of business activity' (Paton, 1962).

By focusing on realized gains and ignoring unrealized gains, the realization convention can lead to absurd results.

Example

Two investors each have £1000 to invest. They both invest £1000 in the shares of Texton Ltd. The shares of Texton Ltd double in value by the end of the accounting period. On the last day of the accounting period, the first investor sells his shares for £2000 and places this sum in the Homestead Building Society. Hence, one investor has £2000 in the building society and the other holds shares in Texton valued at £2000. They are both equally well-off, yet under the realization convention, the investor who has sold his shares is seen as having realized income of £1000, whereas the investor who has held on to his shares is shown as having no income from this source.

Economic concepts

The process of valuation is central to all aspects of decision making. As we shall see in Part 5, capital budgeting decisions require forecasts to be made about the present value of streams of future net cash receipts associated with investment projects. Similarly, investors may also be regarded as exchanging current assets, namely cash or cash equivalents, for a stream of future dividends in the form of cash dividends or increments in the value of their shares.

In this analysis, capital is valued on the basis of discounted future net receipts. Therefore, it is directly relevant to the information needs of shareholders and investors. The value of the firm to the shareholder is computed in such a way as to facilitate the investment decision, which is to seek that investment which will yield the highest value.

In economics, the value of capital is derived from the value of income. The economic concept of income relies on Hicks's definition of income as 'the amount which a man can consume during a period and still remain as well off at the end of the period as he was at the beginning' (Hicks, 1946). This concept of income was adopted by Alexander to define the income of a company as the amount the company can distribute to shareholders and be as well off at the end of the year as it was at the beginning (Alexander, 1962).

In contrast with accounting valuations based on money values, economic income is measured in real terms, that is, by eliminating the influence of variations in the value of money. Moreover, it results from changes in the value of assets rather than from the matching of revenues and expenses. It is, therefore, what Hendriksen (1972) has termed a 'capital maintenance concept of income', since 'well-offness' may be interpreted as maintaining capital intact. It is measured by comparing the value of the company at two points in time in terms of the present value of expected future net receipts at each of those two points.

The economic concept of income treats assets of all kinds as representing future receipts expected to flow from them to the firm. The main measurement problem lies in comparing the capitalized value of these future net receipts expected both at the beginning and at the end of the accounting period, for the difference represents income, that is, what may be consumed under the Hicksian criterion. Hicks himself recognized the problems of measurement involved in his criterion in the following terms:

> 'At the beginning of the week the individual possesses a stock of consumption goods, and expects a stream of receipts which will enable him to acquire in the future other consumption goods . . . Call this Prospect I. At the end of the week he knows that one week out of that prospect will have disappeared; the new prospect which he expects to emerge will have a new first week which is the old second week . . . Call this prospect II. Now if Prospect I were available on the first Monday, we may assume that the individual would know whether he preferred I to II at that date: similarly, if Prospect I were available on the second Monday, he would know if he preferred I to II then. But to enquire whether I on the first Monday is preferred to II on the second Monday is a nonsense question; the choice between them could never be actual at all; the terms of comparison are not in pari materia.' (Hicks, 1946.)

Hicks was making a very crucial point regarding the measurement problem of his criterion, for comparative states of well-offness at Prospect I and Prospect II must be established in order to know how much may be spent. Neither points or prospects are comparable in reality for they exist at different times.

The economic concept of income based on Hicks's criterion is an estimate, since in deciding how much may be spent, Prospect II must be estimated from the standpoint of Prospect I. In view of this problem two concepts of economic income have evolved. The first concept is called ex-ante income, and compares Prospect II to Prospect I from the time perspective of Prospect I. The second concept is called ex-post income, and compares Prospect II to Prospect I from the time perspective of Prospect II. Neither concept overcomes the fundamental difficulty which Hicks pointed out, that is, that one cannot compare alternatives which are not available together at the same time in making decisions requiring a concept of income. Despite this difficulty, income ex-ante and income ex-post have become established as central concepts in the theory of economic income.

It is important always to remember that both income ex-ante and income ex-post are based on estimates of future expected net receipts both at Prospect I and Prospect II. The valuation of income is inseparable, therefore, from the valuation of assets, since assets are valued in terms of the present value of the sum of future expected net receipts associated with the use by the firm. The valuation of income and capital in economics is based, therefore, on predictions.

Estimation of ex-ante income

The nature of ex-ante income may be seen from the following example.

Example

Seeking to maximize the return on its funds, Excel Ltd plans to invest those funds in the purchase of assets, which at 1 January 19X0 are expected to produce the following future net receipts:

Year	Amount
	£
19X0	10,000
19X1	10,000
19X2	10,000
19X3	10,000

This stream of expected future net receipts represents a return on investment of 10 per cent, which may be assumed to be the best return obtainable by Excel Ltd. Accordingly, the present value of those future net receipts discounted at 10 per cent may be calculated as follows:

Year	Expected net receipts at end of year	Present value on 1 January 19X0
	£	£
19X0	10,000	$10,000/1.10 = 9091$
19X1	10,000	$10,000/(1.10)^2 = 8264$
19X2	10,000	$10,000/(1.10)^3 = 7513$
19X3	10,000	$10,000/(1.10)^4 = 6831$

Present value of expected future net receipts at
1 January 19X0   31,699

Since the present value of expected future net receipts associated with the purchase of those assets is £31,699, Excel Ltd would be unwilling to pay more than this sum for those assets. Hence, we may say that economic value of those assets is £31,699 at 1 January 19X0.

The present value of the expected future net receipts on 1 January 19X1 may be calculated as follows:

	£
Cash received at end of year 19X0	10,000
Present value of future new receipts	
end of year 19X1	9091
end of year 19X2	8264
end of year 19X3	7513
Present value of the assets in terms of actual and future expected net receipts on 1 January 19X1	34,868

The two valuations of the present value of the assets enable us to calculate ex-ante income as follows:

	£
Present value of assets at 1 January 19X1	34,868
19X0	31,699
Ex-ante income for the year 19X0	3169

Note that since the income of £3169 represents the expected increase in the value of the assets during the year, given an expected rate of return on investment of 10 per cent, it also represents 10 per cent of the initial value of those assets estimated at £31,699 on 1 January 19X0.

Estimation of ex-post income

In the foregoing example, the income for the year 19X0 has been calculated on the basis that the expected future net receipts at the end of the year 19X0 remained the same as those at the beginning of the year. Under such conditions, ex-ante and ex-post income would be the same.

If, however, the present value of expected future net receipts at the end of the year 19X0 are different from the present value of those expected receipts at the beginning of the year, we may say that the ex-post income is different from the ex-ante income. The ex-ante income refers, therefore, to the estimated income derived from the time perspective of the beginning of the year, and the ex-post income refers to the estimated income derived from the time perspective at the end of the year.

Example

Let it be assumed that the revised estimates of the present value of future net receipts on 1 January 19X1 are as follows (the estimates at 1 January 19X0 are in brackets):

Year	Expected net receipts at end of year as at 1 January 19X1		Present value of expected receipts as at 1 January 19X1		
	£	£	£	£	£
19X0	10,000	(10,000)	10,000		(9091)
19X1	9000	(10,000)	8182 (9000/1.10)		(8264)
19X2	9000	(10,000)	7438 $(9000/(1.10)^2$		(7513)
19X3	9000	(10,000)	6762 $(9000/(1.10)^3$		(6831)
Present value of expected future net receipts on 1 January 19X1			32,382		(31,699)

Ex-post income for the year 19X0, based on the revised estimates established on 1 January 19X1 is as follows:

	£
Estimated present value on 1 January 19X1	32,382
19X0	31,699
Ex-post income for 19X0	683

The ex-post income for the year 19X0 is made up of the following components:

	£
Ex-ante income	3169
Ex-post adjustment	2486
Ex-post income	683

The subjective nature of economic income

The net present value method of valuation presents measurement problems in a number of ways. Accuracy of measurement depends upon the degree of certainty under which the forecasts of expected future cash flows are made. Ideally, the size of the net future cash flows should be estimated with reasonable accuracy as should the time-profile of these future cash flows. This is because a sum of money in two years' time is worth more than the same sum of money in three years'. We shall discuss the problems further in Chapter 29 when we examine capital budgeting decisions.

The net present value concept also requires that the discount rate selected for reducing the future cash flows to their present value should reflect accurately the time-value of money. If interest rates are going to fluctuate during the time period considered for using the asset, it follows that the correct present value of the asset will be distorted simply because the correct discount rate has not been applied.

Because the future cash flows and discount rate cannot be determined with certainty, Edwards and Bell (1961) call economic income 'subjective income', and dismiss the concept on the grounds that it cannot be satisfactorily applied on an operational basis. They echo, therefore, Hicks's own dissatisfaction with the concept, which we mentioned earlier in this chapter.

We mentioned in Part 2 that because of uncertainty surrounding the valuation of a firm, it is not the accountant's function to value the firm for the shareholder or investor. On the contrary, it is for the investor to establish the firm's value as an investment and to bear the risk implied in such a valuation. The role of the accountant is to furnish information which is useful for this purpose. The usefulness and relevance of the information provided in financial reports lies in the effectiveness with which it allows the investor to formulate valuations with some degree of accuracy. In the face of uncertainty, accuracy can never be guaranteed, but information about past and current performance may be used as a basis of developing projection and estimates of likely future trends. The adequacy of the accountant's presentation of information for this purpose, the clarity and sufficiency of disclosure are the central problem, therefore, facing the accounting profession in this area. The investor should use the information provided to make his own estimates of future net receipts, and taking into account his assessment of the degree of uncertainty involved in those estimates, he should discount those estimated net receipts by an appropriate discount rate to arrive at his valuation of the firm. This valuation will retain a high degree of subjectivity, for the discount rate will vary from individual to individual depending upon their respective risk preferences. Therefore, the concept of well-offness is really a matter of an individual's personal preferences. For all these reasons, the concept of economic income has little applicability to the problem of financial reporting.

Summary

Conventional accounting concepts of income and value possess a limited usefulness for decision making, because of the limitations inherent in the conventions of historical cost and realization which govern the measurement of accounting income. Under conditions of inflation, conservative asset values on the balance sheet contrast with over-optimistic income measurement in the income statement. Changes in value are not reported as they occur. Changing money values also undermine the stability of the unit of measurement in accounting.

Under conditions of certainty, economic income provides an ideal concept for financial reporting purposes. The value of the firm's future net receipts may be capitalized, thereby providing the investor with a basis for decision making.

The presence of uncertainty, which is the general rule, precludes the use of economic income because of its essentially subjective nature. Future cashflows and discount rates cannot be estimated with certainty. For this reason, the accountant does not attempt to value the firm. Instead, financial reports are concerned with past performance, and the investor is required to make his own valuations from the information made available to him.

Despite these practical limitations, the importance of economic concepts of income and value lies in the emphasis they place on the importance of value and value changes rather than on historic costs. Moreover, they stress the limitations of accounting conventions such as the realization convention for financial reporting purposes, and emphasize the importance of the concept of capital maintenance to income measurement.

References

1. Alexander, S. S., Income Measurement in a Dynamic Economy, in *Studies in Accounting Theory*, Baxter, W. T. & Davidson, S. (eds), Sweet and Maxwell, London, 1962.
2. Hendriksen E. S., *Accounting Theory*, Richard Irwin, Homewood, Illinois, 1972.
2a. Edwards, E. O. & Bell, P. W., *The Theory and Measurement of Business Income*, University of California Press, 1961.
3. Paton, W. A., *Accountants Handbook* 3rd edn quoted in Alexander, S. S. Income Measurement in a Dynamic Economy in *Studies in Accounting Theory* Baxter, W. T. & Davidson S. (eds), Sweet and Maxwell, London, 1962.
4. Hicks, J. R., *Value and Capital*, 2nd edn, p. 172, OUP, 1946.

Questions

1. How does the historical cost concept of income conflict with the going-concern concept?
2. What is the importance of 'well-offness' in Hicks's definition of income?
3. How is economic income calculated on (a) an *ex-ante* basis (b) an *ex-post* basis?
4. Explain the limitations which may be found when measuring economic income.

19 Current purchasing power accounting

Accounting measurements are based on a monetary standard which hitherto has been assumed to be stable. However, experience of recent history has proved this assumption to be unrealistic with the result that the measurement of corporate income during periods of changing price levels has become a controversial issue.

Price changes may be seen as having general and specific effects. General price changes reflect increases or decreases in the value of the monetary unit. In this case, all individual prices are assumed to change in the same direction, so that the value of a currency in relation to goods and services is different through time. For example, if £15 can only buy today what £10 would have bought on an earlier date, we may say that the price level has increased, the purchasing power of money has fallen and the economy is in a period of inflation.

By contrast, specific price changes occur for several reasons. Changes in consumer tastes, technological improvements, speculation by buyers are all reasons found at the root of specific price changes. Thus, increased demand for houses in the face of a limited supply will force up the price of houses, even if the general price level is constant. It is common, however, for people to hedge against inflation by investing in property and this factor may also influence property prices. Hence, we may say that whilst specific price changes may occur independently of changes in the general price level, changes in the price level may induce disproportionate changes in the price level of specific goods.

Adjusting for the effects of price changes may take the following forms:

(a) general adjustments,
(b) specific adjustments based on current costs (see Chapter 20).

Adjustments for general price level changes

In 1974, the professional accounting bodies in the United Kingdom recommended that a supplementary statement should be attached to the financial reports of companies showing the conversion of the figures in the financial reports in terms of their current purchasing power (CPP) at the closing day of the accounting period. They recommended that the Retail Price Index (RPI) should be used to effect the conversion of historic cost values into current purchasing power equivalents (SSAP 7, 1974, withdrawn 1978).

CPP adjustments are limited to dealing with changes in the general purchasing power of money which occur during periods of inflation or deflation. Accordingly, the view is taken that the purpose of price level adjustments is to express each item in the financial report in terms of a common monetary unit, that is, in terms of £s of the same purchasing power. The RPI is assumed to reflect the general movement in price of all goods and services. Thus, the doubling of the RPI from 100 to 200 between two points in time would mean that the purchasing power of money had fallen by half during that time interval.

Historical cost accounting is based essentially on the money capital maintenance concept. Such a concept asserts that all funds available to the firm in excess of the original contribution of funds by shareholders make the firm better off. High levels of inflation experienced in recent years have undermined the validity of this assertion. CPP accounting attempts to deal with this problem by adjusting historical cost measurements for the effects of inflation. As a result, the purchasing power held by the firm is maintained. The income which results from CPP adjustments may be defined as those gains arising during the accounting period which may be distributed to shareholders so that the purchasing power of the shareholders' interest in the company is the same at the end of the year as it was at the beginning. However, as we shall see in this chapter, the adjustment of historic cost for the effects of inflation of itself cannot ensure the maintenance of the productive capacity of the assets held by the company. The price level correction alone ignores the fact that capital may be dispersed through changes in individual prices if those relevant to the individual firm rise at a rate slower than the rate of change in the price level. Also the real capital will increase if the relationship is reversed.

Monetary and non-monetary items

For the purpose of CPP accounting it is necessary to distinguish two classes of items—monetary and non-monetary items.

Monetary items may be defined as those fixed by contract or by their nature and are expressed in £s regardless of changes in the price level. They include monetary assets such as cash, debtors and loans, and exist as money or as claims to specified sums of money. Holders of monetary assets suffer a loss in the general purchasing power of their assets during periods of inflation. Thus, if one holds money in the form of a bank deposit and the yearly rate of inflation is 25 per cent, the loss in the purchasing power of that money by the end of the period will be 25 per cent.

Monetary items include monetary liabilities such as creditors, bank over-drafts and long-term loans. As the value of money falls during a period of inflation, it follows that the value of such liabilities in current £s will fall similarly, and this fall represents a purchasing power gain to the debtor. Consequently, those who incur monetary liabilities gain at the expense of creditors during periods of inflation, since they will settle these liabilities with £s possessing less purchasing power than those they have previously received—directly or indirectly at the time the liabilities were incurred.

Non-monetary items are assets and liabilities such as fixed assets, inventories and shareholders' equity which are assumed neither to gain nor to lose in value by reason of inflation (and vice versa in the case of deflation). This is because price changes for these items will tend to compensate for changes in the value of money. For example, if one had inventories on hand at the beginning of the year which remained unsold at the end of the year, there would be no purchasing power loss since one may assume that when sold, the sale price would be adjusted upwards to take account of the fall in the value of money.

For example, assume that £100,000 were spent on the purchase of land on a date when the RPI stood at 100, and that the Index now stands at 150. The assumption underlying this movement in prices is that £150,000 in today's £s have the same purchasing power as £100,000 when the RPI stood at 100. Hence, to report on the purchasing power invested in the land, its acquisition cost should be stated as £150,000. This value does not say anything about the present market value of that particular piece of land. Property values may have increased more or less than the general movement in prices indicated by the RPI. The particular piece of land mentioned in this example may now be worth £300,000 or only £90,000. Hence, the figure of £150,000 represents only the historic cost of acquisition adjusted for the decrease in the general value of the £.

Nevertheless, the acceptance of the need to adjust accounting measurements for inflation is a recognition of a fundamental proposition in income theory, namely, that provision should be made for maintaining the value of capital intact. Hence, there can be no recognition of income for a period unless it has been established that the purchasing power of the capital employed in a firm is the same at the end of the accounting period as it was in the beginning.

A simple example serves to explain the nature of adjustments which are required to financial reports based on historical cost measurements in order to remove the effects of general price level changes.

Example

Bangored Supplies Ltd was formed on 1 January 19X0, with a share capital of £75,000 which was fully subscribed in cash on that date. On the same day, equipment was purchased for £45,000, of which £20,000 was paid immediately, the balance of £25,000 being payable 2 years hence. The price level index was 100 on 1 January 19X0.

Goods were purchased in two instalments prior to actually commencing business as follows:

1st purchase in the sum of £44,000, when the price level index was 110;
2nd purchase in the sum of £45,000, when the price level index was 120.

All sales were made when the price level index was 130, and expenses of £16,000 were also incurred at the same index level. Inventories were valued on the FIFO methods and the closing inventory was valued at £29,000. The price level index at 31 December 19X0 was 130.

The income statement and balance sheet in respect of this year, prepared on a historical cost basis, were as follows:

```
Balance sheet as at 31 December 19X0
                                        £          £
Share capital                                    75,000
Retained income                                  19,500
Long-term loan                                   25,000
                                                119,500

Represented by
  Fixed assets                                   45,000
    Less: Accumulated depreciation                4500
                                                 40,500

Current assets
  Inventories                        29,000
  Debtors                            19,000
  Cash                               39,500
                                     87,500
Less:
  Current liabilities                 8500
    Net working capital                          79,000
                                                119,500
```

```
Income statement for the year ended
           31 December 19X0
                                        £          £
Sales                                           100,000
Cost of goods sold                               60,000
Gross operating income                           40,000
Expenses                             16,000
Depreciation (10% of £45,000)         4500
                                                 20,500
Net operating income                             19,500
```

We are required:

(a) To calculate the purchasing power gain or loss on the monetary items.
(b) To prepare an inflation adjusted income statement for the year ended 31 December 19X0.
(c) To prepare an inflation adjusted balance sheet as at 31 December 19X0 when the price level index was 130.

(a) *Calculation of purchasing power gain or loss on monetary items during the year ended 31 December 19X0*

	Unadjusted monetary items	Conversion factor	Adjusted monetary items
	£		£
Net current monetary items on			
1 January 19X0 (cash invested)	75,000	130/100	97,500
Add: Sales	100,000	130/130	100,000
	175,000		197,500
Less:			
Purchases of equipment	20,000	130/100	26,000
Purchase of goods			
(i) index at 110	44,000	130/110	52,000
(ii) index at 120	45,000	130/120	48,750
Expenses	16,000	130/130	16,000
	125,000		142,750
Net current monetary items on			
31 December 19X0	50,000		54,750
Unadjusted net current monetary items on			
31 December 19X0			50,000
Purchasing power loss for the year ended			
31 December 19X0			4750

(b) *Preparation of inflation adjusted income statement for the year ended 31 December 19X0*

	Unadjusted	Conversion factor	Adjusted
	£		£
Sales	100,000	130/130	100,000
Cost of goods sold			
At index 110	44,000	130/110	52,000
At index 120	16,000	130/120	17,333
Expenses	16,000	130/130	16,000
Depreciation	4500	130/100	5850
	80,500		91,183
Net income	19,500		8817

(c) *Preparation of inflation adjusted balance sheet as at 31 December 19X0*

	Unadjusted £	Conversion factor	Adjusted £
Share capital	75,000	130/100	97,500
Retained income	19,500	—	8817
Accumulated purchasing power gain			2750
	94,500		109,067
Represented by			
Fixed assets	45,000	130/100	58,500
Less: Accumulated depreciation	4500	130/100	5850
	40,500		52,650
Current assets			
Inventories	29,000	130/120	31,417
Debtors	19,000	130/130	19,000
Cash	39,500	130/130	39,500
	87,500		89,917
Less: Current liabilities	33,500	130/130	33,500
Net working capital	54,000		56,417
Total assets	94,500		109,067

Calculation of accumulated purchasing power gain
Gain on unpaid balance of purchase price of
equipment

Adjusted balance (£25,000 × 130/100)	32,500
Unadjusted balance	25,000
	7500
Less: Loss as computed on monetary items	4750
Net accumulated purchasing power gain	2750

An appraisal of CPP accounting

CPP accounting restates historical cost in terms of current purchasing power. It is an attempt to remove the major objection to historical cost valuations, which we discussed in the previous chapter, namely that the unit of measurement changes when price levels change. The intention is that this objection should be removed by an adjustment which results in units of the 'same purchasing power' being added together in the measurement process.

Common £ accounting can be applied with a high degree of objectivity, required of accounting valuation, as it does not depart in principle from historical cost based measurement. Price level adjustments are verifiable by reference to the index used to measure changes in the purchasing power of money, and result in alterations to historical cost measurements which are themselves objective. Therefore, both criteria of objectivity and verifiability are satisfied in CPP accounting.

As we stated earlier, SSAP 7 recommended that companies should continue to publish accounts on a historical cost basis, but that in addition, a supplementary statement should be presented showing the effect of converting conventional accounts into £s of current purchasing power. The Sandilands Report ruled out CPP accounting because it did not like the idea of two sets of accounts, nor the use of different measurement units. According to the Sandilands Report, users of financial reports would be confused. This view was expressed as follows:

> 'Our description of the application of the CPP method . . . shows that it is complicated, and we believe that many users of accounts are likely to misunderstand the information presented in CPP statements unless it is carefully interpreted by the company. We consider that CPP accounting is conceptually the most difficult method of inflation accounting suggested to us in evidence. The main reason for this is the use of a unit of measurement other than the monetary unit on which to base the published accounts of companies. We believe that it is not widely understood that CPP supplementary statements are drawn up in different units of measurement from the basic accounts to which they relate.' (Sandilands Report, 1975, p. 121.)

Another objection to CPP accounting is raised by some authorities who believe that there is no such thing as generalized purchasing power (Gynther, 1974). Organizations and people do not see themselves as holding general purchasing power when they hold money; rather, they see themselves as holding specific purchasing power in respect of those relatively few items which they wish to purchase. Hence, the purchasing power of money should be related to those items on which money is intended to be spent. A unit of measurement which relies for its validity on the purchasing power of money assessed by reference to a set of goods and services will not be equally useful to all individuals and entities.

Moreover, the concept of income on which these adjustments are based is not one which maintains the service potential of capital. A general price index, particularly a consumer's price index, is a weighted average of the price change occurring in a wide variety of goods and services available in the economy. Therefore, adjusting financial data for the effects of inflation is not the same as reporting current values. Price-adjusted data still represents costs, or funds, committed to non-monetary items: these costs are merely translated into the equivalent costs in terms of today's £s.

General price indices assume that the movements in the price of all goods correspond with each other. However, only by coincidence will a change in the general price index correspond with the change in the price of any particular good or service during the same period. Indeed, there is no reason why they may not move in opposite directions. For example, the price of colour television sets was falling in the 1960s in the UK at a time when the general price index was rising. Hence, if the general price index has increased, many specific price changes will be running at a lower level than the general index, whilst many others will be running at a higher level, and there may be some specific price decreases. Furthermore, the discrepancies between specific price and general price changes are likely to be even more pronounced when the general price index is based on consumer goods, and the specific price index relates to producer goods, such as those represented by the assets of a typical business enterprise. Thus, a general price index will not be relevant to any business entity which needs to make adjustments to asset valuations in order to maintain the value of its capital in the long term.

Controversy surrounds the treatment of gains and losses arising on monetary items. General price level accounting includes such gains and losses in the periodic income. Hence, a company's pre-tax income will be dramatically different, according to the nature of its financial structure, before and after these adjustments have been made. Property companies, whose largest balance sheet item is often their liabilities to banks, finance houses and other credit institutions, find their adjusted income statement showing exceptionally good results. But the 'gains' resulting from these adjustments do not increase sums available for distribution as dividends to shareholders, since they are purely accounting adjustments. They could only be distributed by drawing on existing cash resources or by borrowing. Hence, if the net 'gains' on monetary items are regarded as available for distribution, the users of adjusted financial reports could be seriously misled.

The Sandilands Committee summarized its view of CCP accounting as follows:

'In summary, we do not think the concept of profit adopted by CPP supplementary statements, when appended to historic cost accounts, is useful to shareholders. It fails to show the company's 'operating profit', it is potentially misleading in including net gains on monetary items which exist only in terms of current purchasing power units and not in terms of monetary units, and it shows how far the 'purchasing power' of a shareholder's investment has been maintained in a sense which is not useful to him for any practical purpose. If CPP does not provide useful information for shareholders, from whose point of view it is conceived, it is unlikely to provide useful information for other users of accounts.' (Sandilands Report, 1975 pp. 131–2.)

Summary

If the value of money is changing, it is clear that the money standard of measurement ceases to be efficient. Financial reports should be adjusted, therefore, for the effects of changes in the value of money for the following reasons:

(a) to provide a more accurate basis for assessing the value of a shareholder's investment in a company;
(b) to enable more meaningful comparisons to be made between the reported results of successive years;
(c) to enable more meaningful inter-company comparisons to be effected.

The unsatisfactory nature of historical cost as a basis for financial reporting is reflected in the fact that companies have been increasingly incorporating partial adjustments for inflation in their reported values. The revaluation of fixed assets by firms in the United Kingdom, and the adoption of LIFO by companies in the United States are examples of this phenomenon.

CPP accounting allows adjusted historical costs to be matched against current revenues. It computes losses arising through holding monetary items during periods of inflation.

CPP accounting has serious limitations. It may be argued, for example, that the concept of generalized purchasing power does not exist; that individuals hold specific purchasing power for the assets they wish to buy. Price level accounting, moreover, does not necessarily maintain the productive capital of the firm: it merely maintains the general purchasing power of the firm. Also, the distribution of monetary 'gains' could seriously affect the firm's liquidity.

References

1. Gynther, R. S., Why use general purchasing power?, *Accounting and Business Research*, Spring 1974.
2. Moonitz, M., The Case against LIFO, *Journal of Accountancy*, June, 1953.
3. *Report of the Inflation Accounting Committee*, p. 100, HMSO Cmd paper 6225, 1975, The Sandilands Report.
4. SSAP No. 7, *Accounting for Changes in the Purchasing Power of Money*, London, 1974, withdrawn 1978.

Questions

1. The directors of Minerva Ltd are extremely pleased with the progress of the firm. After comparing the 19X2 and 19X6 accounts they find that total assets have increased by more than 30 per cent and in addition the net profits have doubled over the period.

	(£000's)	
Income statements	*19X2*	*19X6*
	£	£
Sales	1200	2000
Cost of goods sold	880	1350
Gross margin	320	650
Operating expenses (including depreciation)	140	290
Income before taxation	180	360
Less taxation	60	120
Income after taxation	120	240
Balance sheets		
Ordinary share capital	300	300
Retained earnings	180	332
	480	632

Represented by:	£	£	£	£	£	£
Fixed assets						
Machinery at cost		300			500	
Less depreciation to date		30	270		214	286
Current assets						
Inventory	140			300		
Debtors	110			140		
Bank	60	310		46	486	
Less:						
Current liabilities						
Creditors		100	210		140	346
			480			632

You are given the following information:

1 Over the 5 years the general price level index which was stable in the two years before 19X2 has risen as follows: 19X2 = 100, 19X3 = 120, 19X4 = 125, 19X5 = 135, 19X6 = 150.
The price index given each year is the average for that year as well as the index for the end of the year.

2 Twenty per cent of the cost of goods sold in 19X6 were purchased when the price index was at 135, and eighty per cent of the goods purchased when the price index was at 150.

3 The cost of machinery in use, and the depreciation charged, all stated in thousands of pounds, each year was as follows:

	19X2	19X3	19X4	19X5	19X6	
Machinery in use at cost	300					
Additions		80	100	—	20	
Depreciation provisions						Total each year
19X2	30					=30
19X3	30	8				=38
19X4	30	8	10			=48
19X5	30	8	10			=48
19X6	30	8	10		2	=50

Required:

Convert the statements for 19X2 and 19X6 so that they will be stated in uniform pounds at the 150 price index.
(Compute to the nearest thousand pounds)
Assume that the taxation system has not altered during this period.

2. Enterprises A & B commenced business on 1 January 19X4, when they purchased their respective fixed assets. The balance sheets of A & B at 31 December 19X4 were as follows:

		A £		B £
Capital contributed		4000		4000
Profit		900		900
Long-term loan		—		3000
		4900		7900

		A £		B £
Represented by				
Fixed assets				
Plant and machinery		4000		2000
Less: Depreciation (10%)		400		200
		3600		1800
Building		—		5000
		3600		6800

Current assets					
Inventory	500			400	
Debtors	1000			1000	
Cash	800			900	
	2300			2300	
Less: Current liabilities					
Creditors	1000	1300		1200	1100
		4900			7900

Other information available:

1 Replacement cost of assets:

	A	B
Plant and machinery	5000	2600
(These refer to the *new* assets not the partly used ones)		
Building		7000
Inventory	650	500

2 The general price index has increased by 20 per cent during the year on a base index of 100 at 1.1.X4.

3 Inventories, debtors and creditors accrued evenly throughout the year.

Required:

Using as much information from that above as you consider appropriate answer the question: which enterprise has the better financial performance? Explain and justify your answer.

20 Current value accounting

The debate concerning the appropriateness of adjustments for price level changes has highlighted the problems associated with historic cost measures. Neither partial nor general adjustments to historic cost measures deals satisfactorily with the problem of price level changes.

Current value accounting is a radical alternative to the proposals we discussed in Chapter 19. It represents an attempt to combine desirable aspects of economic theory with the conventional accounting method based on historic costs. Current value income models use current market prices which are incorporated in the traditional accounting format.

For reporting purposes, concepts of income are required which satisfy the criteria of relevance and feasibility. We noted in Chapter 17 that concepts of income which were relevant were not necessarily feasible and vice versa. Whereas economic income is more relevant to decision making than accounting income, it does not satisfy the criteria of feasibility. By contrast, accounting income fails to satisfy the criteria of relevance, though it does meet the criteria of feasibility.

Current value accounting attempts to bridge the gap between accounting and economic income by providing measurements which are both relevant and feasible. Current values are applied to the measurement of income and capital for the purpose of financial reporting, thereby providing more relevant information to investors than the information based on historical cost records found in the financial accounting system. Objectivity is maintained in an accounting sense by retaining the realization convention for timing value changes.

The result is that the financial accounting system recording historical cost data retains its usefulness for establishing the legal rights and obligations created as a result of transactions, whereas the financial reports which are directed at investors contain information concerning the value of income and capital based on the current value of the items appearing in those reports.

Current value accounting takes three forms:

(a) Replacement cost accounting—which is based on the current acquisition value of assets, so that in effect, they are valued at their current entry price.
(b) Realizable value accounting—which is based on the current realizable value of assets, that is, at their current exit price.
(c) Current cost accounting—which is concerned with the value to the business of assets, and which combines replacement cost and realizable value accounting.

Replacement cost accounting

The basic concept underlying replacement cost accounting is that the firm is a going concern, which is continuously replacing its assets. Therefore, the cost of consuming such assets in the income generation process should be equivalent to the cost of their replacement. Replacement cost accounting differs from current purchasing power accounting in that it is concerned with the manner in which price changes affect the individual firm. It focuses on the specific commodities and assets employed by the firm by taking into account changes in the price of such commodities and assets reflected in specific price indices or price indices of groups of similar commodities and assets.

Replacement cost accounting is addressed to the concept of capital maintenance interpreted as maintaining the operating capacity of the firm, and involves:

(a) calculating current operating income by matching current revenues with the current cost of resources exhausted in earning those revenues;
(b) calculating holding gains and losses;
(c) presenting the balance sheet in current value terms.

Components of replacement cost income (RCI)

The treatment of the two components of replacement cost income (RCI), namely current operating income and holding gains and losses, is a controversial matter in the literature of accounting.

Current operating income results from operating activities and is calculated by matching revenues with the current cost of resources exhausted in these activities. Holding gains and losses result from holding rather than operating activities.

According to the method of replacement cost accounting suggested by Edwards and Bell (1961), holding gains and losses should be reported together with current operating income in the measurement of RCI.

The importance of the distinction between operating and holding gains has received considerable attention from many quarters. One committee of the American Accounting Association stated that:

> 'Typically revenue may be related to at least two efforts of management. One of these is the effort to operate effectively in carrying out the production and/or service functions of the business. The other is the effort to occupy an advantageous position in the market . . . This would help interested parties to evaluate the effectiveness of management insofar as its buying efforts were concerned; but more importantly, it would remove from the data pertaining directly to operations those amounts realised simply as a result of market fluctuations.' (A.A.A. Committee, 1965.)

In contrast to accounting income, RCI recognizes holding gains as well as operating gains. In identifying holding gains as they arise, thereby distinguishing these gains from gains occurring on realization, the pattern of income recognition differs under replacement cost accounting from that associated with conventional accounting income, as may be seen from the following example:

Example

During the year ended 31 December 19X0, an asset was acquired at a cost of £40. By 31 December 19X0 its replacement cost had risen to £60. It was sold during the year ended 31 December 19X1 for £100, and at the time of sale, its replacement cost was £65.

For the purpose of measuring accounting income, the income arising from the sale of the asset (assuming no depreciation) would accrue in the year ended 31 December 19X1 and would be calculated as follows:

$$\text{Accounting income} = \text{Revenue} - \text{historical cost}$$
$$= £100 - £40$$
$$= £60$$

For the purpose of measuring RCI, three distinct gains are recognized which occur as follows:

(i)   A holding gain in the year ended 31 December 19X0 measured as the difference between the replacement cost at 31 December 19X0 and the acquisition cost during the year, that is, £60 − £40 = £20.
(ii) A holding gain in the year ended 31 December 19X1 measured as the difference between the replacement cost at 31 December 19X0 and the replacement cost on the date of sale, that is, £65 − £60 = £5.
(iii) An operating gain resulting directly from the activity of selling measured as the difference between the realized sale price and the replacement cost at the date of sale, that is, £100 − £65 = £35.

These differing timings of income recognition may be compared as follows:

Year ended 31 December	19X0	19X1
	£	£
Accounting income	—	60
Replacement cost income		
Holding gains	20	5
Current operating gain	—	35

It is clear from this example that the RCI concept provides more detailed information than the accounting income concept for the purpose of evaluating the results of activities. Moreover, RCI indicates whether the sales proceeds are sufficient to cover the cost of the resources sold, that is, whether the activity of selling itself is efficient. Where the goods sold are manufactured by the firm, current operating income indicates whether the manufacturing process is profitable, for the input factors of production are valued at their current replacement cost. Hence, from a long-term point of view, it affords a means of evaluating the firm as a going concern.

Income measurement by historic cost and replacement cost compared

The extent of the differences between these two concepts of income are revealed by a more comprehensive example.

Example

The financial position of Preifat Ltd, as revealed by the balance sheet as at 31 December 19X0 using historical cost measurements, is as follows:

	£		£
Share capital	1400	Fixed asset	1000
		Inventory	400
	1400		1400

The fixed asset shown on the balance sheet was acquired on 31 December 19X0 and has an estimated life of 5 years, with no scrap value.

Data recorded in respect of the year ended 31 December 19X1 is as follows:

	£
Sales	2000
Purchases at historical cost	700
Closing inventory at historical cost	200
at replacement cost	250
Cost of goods sold at replacement cost	1000

It was also estimated that the replacement cost of the fixed asset had risen to £1200 by 31 December 19X1.

On the basis of this information, the accounting income for the year 19X1 may be computed as follows:

Accounting income for the year ended 31 December 19X1

	£	£
Sales		2000
Cost of goods sold:		
Opening inventory	400	
Purchases	700	
	1100	
Closing inventory	200	
		900
		1100
Depreciation (£1000 ÷ 5)		200
Accounting income		900

By contrast, the calculation of the components of replacement cost income gives a more comprehensive analysis of the nature of operating and holding gains, as follows:

Replacement cost income for the year ended 31 December 19X1

	£	£
Sales		2000
Cost of goods sold (at replacement cost)		1000
		1000
Depreciation (£1200 ÷ 5)		240
(i) *Current operating income*		760
(ii) *Holding gains*		
(a) Realized through use during the year:		
Fixed assets	40	
Inventory	100	
		140
(b) Unrealized at the end of the year		
Fixed assets	160	
Inventory	50	
		210
Total holding gains		350
Current operating income plus holding gains		1110

Note:

(a) Depreciation is calculated on the replacement cost of the fixed assets (£1200) rather than on the historical acquisition cost (£1000). By this means, the depreciation provision is more realistic in relation to the current cost of resource utilization.

(b) Inventories are charged against sales at their current replacement cost at the time of sale.

(c) Holding gains are of two kinds:

(i) Realized holding gains which result from the application of replacement cost values to the input of resources to the income generation process. In the example, depreciation charged under replacement cost accounting is £40 greater than that charged under historic cost accounting. Similarly, the cost of goods sold under replacement cost is £100 greater than that charged under historic cost accounting. Both amounts represent holding gains realized by reason of the use or the sale of assets.

(ii) Unrealized holding gains which result from the increased value of assets held by the firm and remaining unused or unsold at the end of the accounting period. In the example, the unrealized holding gains are calculated as follows:

(a) Fixed assets: unallocated value at the end of the accounting period:

under replacement cost:	£1200−240 = £960
under historic cost:	£1000−200 = 800
unrealized holding gain	160

(b) Inventories: inventories unsold at the end of the accounting period:

under replacement cost:	£250
under historic cost:	200
unrealized holding gain	50

Historic cost and replacement cost balance sheets compared

The effect of applying historic and replacement cost valuations to balance sheets is seen in the following balance sheet drawn from data given in the example.

As may be observed, the application of replacement cost values attempts to reflect economic reality by maintaining the value of asset balances in line with changes in the value of money and changes in the specific value of the assets concerned.

Balance sheet as at 31 December 19X1
(assuming that all sales and purchases were paid in cash)

	Historic cost £	Replacement cost £
Share capital	1400	1400
Retained income		
Accounting income	900	
Current operating income		760
Revaluation reserve		350
	2300	2510
Represented by:		
Fixed assets	1000	1200
Less: Accumulated depreciation	200	240
	800	960
Current assets		
Inventories	200	250
Cash	1300	1300
	2300	2510

Notes. Cash balance is calculated as follows:

Sales £2000 − Purchases £700 = £1300 Cash balance

The treatment of holding gains

One of the controversial issues in the debate about replacement cost accounting is whether holding gains constitute income. There is little doubt that current operating income satisfies the accounting convention relating to realization, and at the same time is directed to the maintenance of capital, which is a basic principle in the measurement of economic income.

From a theoretical viewpoint, there is strong support for the argument that holding gains should not be treated as income, that is, they should not be regarded as available for distribution. Assuming that the firm is a going concern, the holding gain resulting from the increase in the current replacement cost of specific assets should be retained for the purpose of replacing those assets, for one of the objectives of replacement cost accounting is to ensure the maintenance of capital through the replacement of the values exhausted in earning income. The distinction between realized and unrealized holding gains, which is important in this respect may be preserved in the appropriate account, which is the asset revaluation reserve account.

An evaluation of replacement cost accounting

As a method of financial reporting, the objective of replacement cost accounting is to provide a concept of income which will satisfy the criteria of relevance and feasibility which were discussed earlier.

Replacement cost income is more relevant to investors than accounting income for the purpose of decision making. First, it provides for the maintenance of the service potential of capital by charging against revenue the cost of replacing the assets exhausted in earning revenue. Second, an important distinction is made between operating income and holding gains, thereby allowing investors to appraise the firm as a going-concern. Third, it recognizes changes in the value of assets, since they are related to current market prices. For these reasons, investors are provided with information which is more relevant than accounting income for evaluating the business, and they are placed in a better position to predict the future. By providing more accurate valuations of assets in use, replacement cost accounting is likely to lead to a more efficient allocation of financial resources than that afforded by conventional accounting methods. A further argument in favour of replacement cost accounting lies in the diversity of values found in conventional accounting due to the employment of a variety of valuation methods, such as LIFO, FIFO or average cost. With replacement cost accounting, however, values are uniformly derived from the current replacement cost of specific assets, so that comparisons are much more meaningful.

As regards the criterion of feasibility, Dickerson (1965) has shown that replacement cost accounting is not too time consuming and costly for practical implementation. Applying himself to the problem of converting data from historical cost to replacement cost for a small producer of moulded plastic articles, he reported that 95 hours of work were involved in that translation, of which 40 hours were spent on familiarizing himself with the data.

Criticisms are sometimes advanced against replacement cost accounting on the ground that the measurements involved are subjective. There exist, however, Government Indices which relate to fixed assets of various kinds which may be employed for the purpose of calculating the replacement cost of specific fixed assets. The Sandilands Committee recommended that the Government Statistical Service should publish as soon as possible a new series of price indices specific to particular industries for capital expenditure on plant and machinery. Such a series of indices should be designed to provide a 'standard reference basis' for making reasonable approximations of current replacement costs. The derivation of replacement costs for inventories could present problems. However, when the various different methods of valuing inventories at the present time are considered, it appears that replacement cost provides a more objective measure. Another criticism made by Sterling (1970) is that replacement cost measurements imply the substitution of specific asset values for money measurements, thereby abandoning a common unit of measurement.

A major problem arises, however, during periods of rapid technological change. Most authorities argue that since a measure of the profitability of existing operations is required, current replacement costs should be measured in terms of the market prices prevailing for the actual fixed assets which are exhausted in producing income. Some authorities are opposed to this view since it seemingly ignores the effect of technological change. They argue that the replacement cost of new generation assets should be used, because 'the primary interest is in the long-run prospects of the firm, and there seems to be no particular reason why these long-run prospects would be indicated by the prospects of the present mode of production, when becoming obsolete'. Accordingly, if the firm is using a second generation computer made obsolete by the development of third generation computers, they argue that the current replacement cost should be based on the current market price of third generation rather than second generation computers.

Realizable value accounting

Both historical cost and replacement cost accounting employ entry values, that is, they are based on the acquisition cost of assets. By contrast, realizable value accounting employs exit values, that is, it is based on the realizable price of assets.

The distinction between entry and exit values leads to two different concepts of income—realized and realizable income. Realized income arises only upon sale, so that unsold assets are valued at cost. By contrast, realizable income is based on the current selling price of the assets, thereby indicating the revenue which could be obtained should the assets be sold. As a result, unsold assets are valued not at cost, but at realizable value.

The case for realizable value accounting

The realizable value model is based on the concept of opportunity cost, that is, value is expressed in terms of the benefit lost in holding assets in their present form rather than in the next best alternative form. For example, as regards closing inventories, the next best alternative to holding inventories is selling them, so that on an opportunity cost basis, the value of closing inventories is what they would realize if sold.

Chambers and Sterling have argued in favour of realizable value accounting. According to Chambers, for example, the most important characteristic of the firm is its capacity to adapt to a changing environment, and in this way, to ensure its survival. The survival of the firm depends, therefore, on its ability to acquire goods and services, which is related to the realizable value of its existing assets. Chambers coined the term 'current cash equivalent' to indicate the realizable value of the firm's currently held assets, that is, the cash represented by those assets and available, if sold, for investing in market alternatives and consequently redeploying its resources.

By contrast, replacement cost accounting reflects a relatively static situation, and does not inform investors about the economic sacrifice made in holding resources in their current form.

Another argument in favour of realizable value accounting is that realizable value income is an acceptable surrogate for economic income, for it indicates future cash flows which may result from the realization of currently held assets. As we argued in Chapter 4, the present value of future cash flows associated with the holding of assets is the most relevant concept of value from the point of view of investors. Backward looking concepts, such as historical cost and replacement cost values, are poor surrogates as predictors of future cash flows.

Finally, a further argument in favour of realizable value lies in its relevance to the needs of creditors for information about the market value of the assets held by a company to which they have extended credit facilities, particularly if the security for loans and other forms of credit is represented by liens or mortgages over such assets.

Components of realizable income

Realizable income reflects the periodic change in the value of enterprise capital measured in terms of resale price. It consists of two components:

(a) Realized gains resulting from the sale of assets during the accounting period, which are measured as the difference between the actual realized revenue from sale and the realizable value estimated at the beginning of the period.
(b) Unrealized gains resulting from changes in the realizable value of assets which have remained unsold at the end of the accounting period.

Example

During the year ended 31 December 19X0 an asset was acquired for £40. At 31 December 19X0, its estimated realizable value was £85, and it was sold during the year ended 31 December 19X1 for £100. The realizable income for the years ended 31 December 19X0 and 19X1 is as follows:

	19X0	*19X1*
Realizable income		
Unrealized gain	£85 − 40 = £45	
Realized gain		£100 − 85 = £15

We noted in our earlier discussion of holding gains arising under replacement cost accounting that such gains could not be treated as part of replacement income. The reason for this view is to be found in the capital maintenance criterion to which replacement cost income is directed. By contrast, the realizable value concept of income is directed towards measuring the firm's ability to adapt to a changing environment, and for this purpose, income is required to measure changes in the firm's command over goods and services. This may be measured by reference to both realized gains, and unrealized gains which result, as we mentioned earlier, from changes in the realizable value of assets during the year. Hence, under realizable value income, no distinction is maintained between current operating income and holding gains. Assets are shown on the balance sheet at their realizable value.

Limitations of exit values

Exit values imply a short-run approach to the analysis of business operations because they entail disposition and liquidation values being shown on the balance sheet. Hence, business operations resulting in realizable income only indicate that it is worth staying in business in the short run, not that it is worth replacing assets and staying in business in the long term. Realizable value accounting values all assets at exit prices even though many assets are not held for resale.

It has been argued that the crucial test of the usefulness of exit values in financial reports lies in the treatment of highly specific assets, which may have very little value for anyone except the present owner for whom they were constructed (Solomons, 1971). The most extreme example of such assets are mineshafts—which being large holes in the ground have no exit value. Such assets may be presumed to have been worth as much to the firm as their acquisition or construction costs. Otherwise, it is clear that they would not have been acquired or constructed. The question is—what would be the sense of writing such assets down to their current realizable value?

Another limitation of exit values lies in their anticipation of operating income, before the critical event giving rise to revenue has occurred. It has been argued, for example, that

'If profit is to be recognized at a moment of time, we must select that moment. The economist gives a clue in the formulation of entrepreneurship as the function of directing a business, bearing the risks and reaping the rewards of the business. This suggests that profit is earned at the moment of making the most crucial decision or of performing the most difficult task in the cycle of a complete transaction.' (Myers, 1973.)

Where production is the critical event and sale presents no problem, the valuation of inventory at net realizable value gives a better indication of managerial performance than does replacement cost. Where selling is the main difficulty, the sale is the critical event which must occur before managerial performance may be correctly evaluated, for without a contract of sale or an active quoted market for the product, the accountant has little evidence of managerial accomplishment. The accountant must assume, in these circumstances, that the product will be sold for at least the break-even price, so that replacement cost is the most suitable measurement of value in these circumstances.

'Value to the business' as a criterion

The concept of 'value to the business' should determine whether exit or entry values should be used in the valuation process. One way of determining 'value to the business' is to reverse the opportunity cost concept, and to define opportunity value as the least costly sacrifice avoided by owning the asset. This approach to the valuation of an asset to the business has been adopted by a number of economists. Bonbright (1937), for example, defined opportunity value in the following terms: 'The value of a property to its owner is identical in amount with the adverse value of the entire loss, direct and indirect, that the owner might expect to suffer if he were deprived of the property.'

In no sense may historical cost be measured as the value of an asset to the business because it is not related to the amount which would have to be paid for the asset, the amount that might be gained from disposing of it or the amount to be gained by holding it. It remains to consider therefore, the other three bases of valuation which were listed in the Introduction:

(a) the current purchase price (replacement cost) of the asset (RC);
(b) the net realizable value of the asset (NRV);
(c) the present value of expected future earnings from the asset (PV).

It has been argued (Parker and Harcourt, 1969) that six hypothetical relationships exist between these three values:

		Correct valuation basis
(1)	NRV>PV>RC	RC
(2)	NRV>RC>PV	RC
(3)	PV>RC>NRV	RC
(4)	PV>NRV>RC	RC
(5)	RC>PV>NRV	PV
(6)	RC>NRV>PV	NRV

In (1) and (2) above, NRV is greater than PV. Hence, the firm would be better off selling rather than using the asset. The sale of the asset necessitates its replacement, if the NRV is to be restored. We may say, therefore, that the maximum loss which the firm would suffer by being deprived of the asset is RC.

In (3) and (4) above, PV is greater than NRV, so that the firm would be better off using the asset rather than selling it. The firm must replace the asset in order to maintain PV, so that the maximum loss which the firm would suffer by being deprived of the asset is again RC.

The general statement which may be made, therefore, in respect of the first four cases (1) to (4) is that, where either NRV or PV, or both, are higher than RC, RC is the appropriate value of the asset to the business. As regards a current asset, such as inventories, RC will be the current purchase price (entry value). In the case of a fixed asset, RC will be the written down current purchase price (replacement cost), since the value of such an asset will be the cost of replacing it in its existing condition, having regard to wear and tear.

As regards cases (5) and (6), RC does not represent the value of the asset to the business, for if the firm were to be deprived of the asset, the loss incurred would be less than RC. Case (5) is most likely to arise in industries where assets are highly specific, where NRV tends to zero and where RC is greater than PV, so that it would not be worth replacing the asset if it were destroyed, but it is worth using it rather than attempting to dispose of it. The conclusion which may be reached as regards fixed assets, is that except in the rare occurrence of case (5), fixed assets which are held for use should be valued at RC if such assets are to represent their value to the business.

Case (6) applies to assets held for resale, that is, where NRV must be greater than PV. If RC should prove to be greater than NRV, such assets would not be replaced. Hence, it implies that they should be valued at NRV or RC, whichever is the lower. This recommendation, despite its superficial resemblance to the lower of cost or market value which we argued to be illogical in Part 2, is not a concession to the convention of conservatism, but represents an attempt to measure the value of assets to the business. If RC exceeds NRV, inventories will not be replaced so that NRV represents their value to the firm. Conversely, where NRV exceeds RC, inventories are worth replacing, so that their value to the firm is determined by RC.

Current cost accounting v CPP accounting

The 'value to the business' criterion was supported by the Sandilands Committee which recommended that an accounting system known as *current cost accounting* (CCA) should become the basis of financial reporting. The principal features of CCA are:

(a) Financial reports should continue to be drawn up in terms of monetary units.
(b) Financial reports should show the 'value to the business' of the company's assets at the balance sheet date.
(c) Income for the year should consist of the company's operating gains and should exclude all holding gains. Extraordinary gains may be shown as income, but they should be distinguished from operating gains.
(d) Financial reports drawn up in this way should become the basic published financial reports of companies. In addition the net book value of assets, and depreciation for the year on a historic cost basis should be shown in note to the financial report.

The Sandilands Committee did not recommend that CPP statements should be attached to CCA reports for the reason that 'little useful additional information would be presented to a user of accounts by such a procedure and the effect would be to confuse him and to make the annual statements too complex'. (Sandilands Report, 1975, p. 165.)

As we mentioned in Chapter 19 the Sandilands Report rejected the profession's proposals for CPP accounting. This action was bound to provoke heated discussion about the relative merits of the two systems. The Consultative Committee of the Accountancy Bodies in the United Kingdom and Ireland (CCAB) found the Sandilands Report unacceptable on the grounds that CCA did not take account of all aspects of inflation. Therefore, they did not agree with the statement made in the Sandilands Report that 'CCA is a fully comprehensive method of accounting for inflation.' (Sandilands Report, 1975, p. 4.) In a memorandum the CCAB put its case in the following terms:

'The aspects of inflation which the CCA system does not deal with at all, or does not deal with adequately are:

(a) the decrease in value of monetary assets;
(b) the decrease in value of obligations represented by monetary liabilities;
(c) the whole effect of inflation on the value of the proprietor's interest in the company or other organization concerned, irrespective of whether that interest is represented by non-monetary or monetary assets;
(d) the description of the incremental difference between an asset's original cost and its value to the business as a 'holding gain' is potentially misleading as the whole or part of the 'gain' will be the result not of a real gain in wealth, but of a decrease in the value of money;
(e) the problems of making valid comparisons over a period of time when the unit of measurement (the £ sterling) is unstable.'

(*Accountant's Weekly*, 7 November 1975, 'What the CCAB has finally told the Government.')

Monetary items

In the CCAB memorandum a simple example was given of the problems which would be created by the Sandilands Report proposal in the case of monetary items.

Example

A company has £100 in the bank at the beginning of the year. During that year, no transactions were conducted and the closing balance at the bank at the end of the year remains £100.

The application of the proposals of the Sandilands Report would result in the firm showing neither a profit nor a loss. Given that the rate of inflation is 20 per cent a year, however, it is true of course that the £100 at the bank is worth less at the end of the year than it was at the beginning. As a result, the business has lost 20 per cent of the value of its asset and the proprietors have lost 20 per cent of the value of their investment.

The decrease in the value of obligations represented by monetary liabilities is the converse. Thus, if a business has an overdraft of £100 at the beginning of the year, conducted no transactions and had an overdraft of £100 at the end of the year, inflation at the rate of 20 per cent per annum would be reflected in a corresponding decrease of the real burden of the obligation of the business, even though the monetary obligation to the bank remains at £100.

The question is—how should such gains and losses be treated? Where a monetary loss has been sustained, as in the case of bank balances, it is suggested that a debit entry should be made in the income statement, thereby reducing the income for the year, and that a corresponding credit entry should be made in a 'diminished purchasing power of money reserve'. As regards monetary gains, as in the case of bank overdrafts, the converse accounting entries could be made.

However, the problem with such treatment of monetary gains and losses is that it implies that the greater the borrowings the greater are the monetary gains. Property companies are a particular case in point. The largest monetary items on their balance sheet are liabilities to banks, finance houses and other credit institutions. Since inflation makes a virtue of indebtedness, the income statements of such companies would be painted in glowing terms.

A study conducted by London stockbrokers Phillips and Drew (see *Accountants' Weekly*, 31 October 1975, 'CCA could badly hit company profits') illustrated the massive size of monetary gains involved in reported corporate income under conditions of inflation, and the effects of alternative accounting methods.

Phillips and Drew took as their figures total United Kingdom corporate income for 1974—excluding banks and oil companies—and worked out the following figures:

(a) under historical cost accounting, total corporate income in 1974 amounted to £3.9 billion;
(b) under CCA, total corporate income in 1974 would have been £1.6 billion, that is, 60 per cent less than under historical cost accounting;
(c) under CCA plus the recognition of gains on monetary items as discussed above, which would have amounted to £1.7 billion, total corporate income in 1974 would have been £3.3 billion, that is, 15 per cent less than under historical cost accounting.

The implications for companies, shareholders, investors and the government of these figures need hardly be explained. They affect the size of reported income as regards retained income and dividends and the real burden of corporate taxation. Hence, because of the dangers of making accounting entries in respect of gains or losses on monetary items, there is a case for showing them separately in a supplementary statement rather than adding them to operating gains.

Non-monetary items

The proposals put forward by the Sandilands Committee show the change in the value of proprietorship interest in a company, but fail to show how that change in value is to be compared to the general rate of inflation. The CCAB illustrated this point in its memorandum by the following example.

Example

At 1 January 19X0, the capital invested in a business was £200, represented by non-monetary (fixed assets) valued at £100 and monetary assets (cash at bank) amounting to £100.

At 31 December 19X0, the business held the same fixed assets, but on the basis of CCA these had been revalued at £115. The business still held £100 at the bank.

The general price level increased by 25 per cent during the year 19X0.

Ignoring the results of trading operations and the effect of taxation, the effect of CCA would be as follows:

(a) there would be a holding gain of £15 on non-monetary assets calculated by reference either to the Index of Asset Values proposed by Sandilands or their realizable value;
(b) there would be no gain or loss in respect of monetary assets;
(c) there would be an increase in the value of capital invested from £200 to £215.

However, given that the general price level increased by 25 per cent during the year, the value of the capital invested should have risen to £250 in order that its value be maintained at the end of the year to its level at the beginning of the year. In fact, under CCA, it is only £215, which is £35 less than its value under CPP. This difference of £35 consists of:

		£
(a)	a loss on monetary assets (reflecting the whole of the fall in the value of money)	25
(b)	a loss on non-monetary assets (because the money value of these assets has not increased at the same rate as the general increase in the price level)	10
		35

This example highlights that the holding gain of £15 measured under CCA does not reflect the decrease in the purchasing power of the capital invested in the business (£50). Accordingly, the CCAB argued that 'the full extent of the fall in the purchasing power of the capital invested should be recognized in accounts which purport to show the effects of inflation'.

The foregoing example does not discredit CCA in those cases where the replacement cost of non-monetary assets is higher than its value under CPP. In such a case, CPP accounting will not maintain the firm's operating structure. As we have mentioned in the previous chapter, the concept of capital maintenance is more relevant to the operations of a business enterprise than the general purchasing power concept. Therefore, if a choice has to be made between CCA and CPP, CCA should be adopted. If the proprietors wish to know the impact of general inflation on the company's assets and income, it is better that such information be disclosed in supplementary statements than be incorporated in the basic financial reports.

Summary

Current value accounting combines the best characteristics of economic and accounting income, by associating values and changes in values with transactions. Current value accounting takes two forms: replacement cost accounting and realizable value accounting.

Replacement cost accounting involves:

(a) calculating current operating income by matching current revenues with the current cost of resources exhausted in earning those revenues;

(b) calculating holding gains and losses;
(c) presenting the balance sheet in current value terms.

It provides a long-run income concept, which is associated with existing production processes, thereby maintaining the service potential of capital employed. It provides more useful and more detailed information for decision making than traditional accounting concepts, while not impairing their 'objectivity'.

Realizable value accounting is a short-run concept of income, because it implies liquidation values. Hence, it is not a feasible method of accounting for general use.

The concept of 'value to the business' should be applied to the selection of 'entry' or 'exit' values. The value to the business of an asset is the maximum loss which the firm would suffer if it were deprived of that asset. In the vast majority of cases, the maximum loss is the replacement cost of the asset.

The Sandilands Report supported the 'value to the business' criterion in its recommendation regarding CCA. The professional accounting bodies criticized the Sandilands Report on the grounds that it did little to recognize the effect of inflation on monetary assets and liabilities. They suggested a compromise which would combine CCA and CPP. This problem was dealt with in the statement on current cost accounting which is discussed in the next chapter.

References

1. A.A.A. Committee on the Matching Concept, *Accounting Review*, April, 1965.
2. Bonbright, J. C. *The Valuation of Property*, p. 71, McGraw-Hill, 1937.
3. Dickerson, P. J. *Business Income—A Critical Analysis*, Institute of Business and Economic Research, Berkeley, University of California Press, 1965.
4. Edwards, E. O. & Bell, P. W. *The Theory and Measurement of Business Income*, Berkeley, University of California Press, 1961.
5. Lemke, K. W. 'Asset valuation and income measurement', *The Accounting Review*, January, 1966.
6. Myers, J. H. 'The critical event and recognition of net profit', *in* Zeff, S. A. & Keller, T. F. (eds) *Financial Accounting Theory*, p. 159, McGraw-Hill, 1973.
7. Parker, R. H. & Harcourt, G. C. *Readings in the Concept and Measurement of Income*, p. 17, Cambridge University Press, 1969.
8. Solomons, D. 'Asset valuation and income determination: appraising the alternatives', *in* Sterling, R. R. (ed) *Asset Valuation and Income Determination*, p. 110, Scholars Book Co, New York, 1971.
9. Sterling, R. R. *Theory and Measurement of Enterprise Income*, University of Kansas Press, 1970.
10. Chambers, R. J. *Accounting, Evaluation and Economic Behaviour*, Prentice Hall, Englewood Cliffs, New Jersey, 1966.
11. Report of the Inflation Accounting Committee, HMSO Cmd paper 6225, the Sandilands Report, 1975.

Questions

1. ABC Ltd has traded for several years. Its accounts are kept on a conventional historic cost basis.

Balance sheet

	31/12/X3	31/12/X4		31/12/X3	31/12/X4
Capital	38,100	38,100	Plant	100,800	100,800
Retained profit	8490	19,260	Less Depn.	37,800	44,800
	46,590	57,360		63,000	56,000
Loan	27,000	27,000	Inventories	4290	7560
Creditors	3600	8600	Debtors	9000	24,000
			Cash	900	5400
	77,190	92,960		77,190	92,960

Indices	General	Stock	Plant
Date capital acquired	50		
Date plant acquired	80		70
Date opening inventories acquired	85.8	110	
1 January 19X4	90	120	100
30 June 19X4	100	130	115
30 Sept. 19X4	105	135	122
31 Dec. 19X4	110	140	130

No purchases or sales of plant took place during the year. No dividends have been paid or proposed. Ignore taxation.

Closing inventory was valued at 30 September prices.

Required:
Prepare a balance sheet as at 31 December 19X4 on a CPP basis and on an RC basis.

2. T. A. Lee Ltd carries on business as an electrical appliance wholesaler. The following information prepared on a historical cost basis relates to the year ended 31 January 19X5.

Sales			395,810
less	Opening inventory	31,070	
	Purchases	243,222	
	Closing inventory	(46,088)	228,204
	Gross profit		167,606
less	Wages and salaries	65,010	
	Selling and administrative expenses	19,668	
	Depreciation	20,128	104,806
	Net trading profit		62,800

The opening inventory was purchased on average on 31 December 19X3, and the closing purchased on average on 31 December 19X4. The electrical appliance price index contains the following figures:

31/12/X3	104
31/1/X4	106
31/7/X4	112
31/12/X4	117
31/1/X5	118

The depreciation charge relates to warehouse equipment which was purchased on the following dates:

30/6/X2	22,800
31/12/X2	36,750
31/3/X3	41,090
Total	100,640

Depreciation is charged at 20 per cent straight line.

The price index for such equipment contains the following figures:

30/6/X2	94
31/12/X2	99
31/3/X3	102
31/1/X4	111
31/7/X4	116
31/1/X5	121

Required:
(a) From the information available restate the trading results utilizing replacement costs.
(b) Discuss the purpose of adjusting the historical cost profit to reflect replacement costs. Briefly discuss the relevance of the replacement cost profit as a guide to dividend policy.
(Question supplied by A. J. Naughton, Leeds Polytechnic.)

3. Keaton Ltd started business 1 January Year 1. Set out below is the balance sheet on a historic cost basis as at 31 December:

		Year 1		Year 2
		(£ 000)		(£ 000)
Land		110		110
Plant cost	40		40	
depreciation	4	36	8	32
Inventories		90		120
Debtors		30		50
Bank		60		50
		326		362
Creditors		50		80
		276		282
Share capital		250		250
Retained earnings		26		32
		276		282

The realizable value of the assets is as follows:

Land	150	160
Plant	25	22
Inventories	130	170

The income statement for Year 2 on a historic cost basis is:

Sales	130
Cost of sales	90
	40
Depreciation	4
	36
Dividend	30
Retained earnings	6

Required:

Prepare balance sheets at the end of Years 1 and 2 on the basis of realizable value accounting.

(Question supplied by A. J. Naughton, Leeds Polytechnic.)

21 Current cost accounting

The analysis of the features of the problem of accounting for inflation which was conducted by the Sandilands Committee, and was published in its report in 1975, established the importance of the concept of maintaining the operating capital of the enterprise during inflation. As we noted in Chapter 20, current cost accounting is concerned with the value of net assets to the business, and combines replacement cost and realizable value measurements in considering the values which should be attached to such assets.

The debate which followed the publication of the Sandilands Report in 1975 led to subsequent reviews of its proposals. In this respect, the Sandilands Report had proposed merely a skeleton framework, and it was left to the Morpeth Committee, appointed by the Accounting Standards Committee, to provide specific rules for making current cost accounting operational. The Morpeth Committee published its report in the form of Exposure Draft 18 in 1976. Up to this stage, both the Sandilands and Morpeth Reports were committed to the view that it was theoretically inconsistent to dilute the application of current cost accounting, defined on the basis of current replacement values, with purchasing power adjustments to monetary assets. Yet, it was evident that inflation affected both monetary assets and monetary liabilities, as well as the current cost of replacement of physical assets. Financial companies, in particular, claimed to have had their interests ignored in the recommendations made by the two committees. Eventually, the Accounting Standards Committee appointed Mr William Hyde of Oxford University to produce a set of interim inflation accounting standards, which were published in November 1977 and became known as the Hyde Guidelines. The Hyde Guidelines won quick acceptance, and led to the publication of ED 24 in 1979, which developed further the recommendations made by Hyde and allowed for an additional adjustment to the monetary value of working capital under inflationary conditions.

As a result, there was published in 1980 SSAP 16, Current Cost Accounting, which now blends both replacement cost and realizable value principles in adjusting historic cost measurements for inflation.

The purpose of this chapter is to discuss the principles underlying the current cost accounting method of dealing with inflation, which has been adopted in the United Kingdom.

Main features of current cost accounting

SSAP 16 adopts the precise definition of large companies used in the EEC Fourth Directive which reduces the number of companies subject to its application. According to SSAP 16 the basic objective of current cost accounting is to provide more useful information than that available from historical cost accounting alone, for the guidance of the management of the business, the shareholders and others on such matters as the financial viability of the business, return on investment, pricing policy, cost control and distribution decisions, and gearing.

Current cost accounting is described as a modification to historical cost profit to arrive at 'the surplus after allowing for the impact of price changes on the funds needed to continue the existing business and to maintain its operating capability, whether financed by share capital or borrowings'. The operating capability is assumed to be represented by net operating assets, which include not only physical assets such as fixed assets and inventories, but also the net monetary working capital.

The main features of SSAP 16, Current Cost Accounting, are as follows:

(1) Current cost information should be published in addition to historical cost information as part of the annual financial reports.

(2) The current cost accounts should consist of an income statement and a balance sheet with explanatory notes. The Appendix at the end of this chapter illustrates the nature of such documents under current cost accounting.

(3) The current cost income statement should show the current cost operating profit or loss. This is derived by making three adjustments to historical cost profit before interest and taxation in respect of depreciation, cost of sales and monetary working capital. The nature of these adjustments are discussed later in this chapter.

(4) The current cost income statement should also include a figure which is attributable to shareholders. This is derived by making a gearing adjustment to the current cost operating profit.

(5) Current cost earnings per share based on the current cost profit attributable to shareholders should be disclosed.

(6) The current cost balance sheet should include fixed assets and inventories at their value to the business. The balance sheet may be shown in summary form and should include a separate current cost reserve showing the effects of three elements:

(i) revaluation surpluses or deficits arising from price changes in respect of fixed assets and inventories;
(ii) the monetary working capital adjustment;
(iii) the gearing adjustment.

The depreciation adjustment

The depreciation adjustment reflects the difference between the depreciation calculated on the current cost of fixed assets and the depreciation charged in computing the historical cost income. The accounting policy adopted for the purpose of calculating the historical cost profit should be followed when calculating the depreciation on the current cost of fixed assets. Hence, once an enterprise has established the current cost of an asset, the determination of the depreciation adjustment is a simple matter. The current cost depreciation charge may be computed by revising the depreciation charge in accordance with the change in the appropriate index level between the year of the purchase of the asset and the current year. This calculation is illustrated below:

Asset Y	Historical cost £	Index factor	Current cost £
Cost in year 1	1200	$\times \dfrac{200}{150}$	1600
Depreciation at 10% per annum	720		960
	480		640

Index for Asset Y

Year	Index
Mid 1	150
End 6	200

Depreciation adjustment

	£
Current cost depreciation per annum	10% of £1600 = 160
Historical cost depreciation per annum	10% of £1200 = 120
Depreciation adjustment	40

The adjustment to the current cost reserve

The net increase in the value of Asset Y to be credited to the current cost reserve is arrived at by deducting the net historical cost of Asset Y from its net current cost at the end of year 6, both sums being calculated before taking depreciation into account, as follows:

	Net book value end of year 6 £	+	Depreciation for year 6 £	=	Net book value before depreciation £
Current cost	640	+	160	=	800
Historical cost	480	+	120	=	600
Net credit to the current cost reserve					200

Where the movement in the cost of a major asset is known to have been significantly different from the movement in the relevant index, the current replacement cost of the asset should be obtained from the supplier's price lists or by a valuation performed by external valuers who are experts in the valuation of plant and machinery.

Where an asset has been rendered obsolete in design and technology, reference should be made to its replacement by a modern equivalent asset.

The value to the business of the existing asset is then the cost of purchasing that proportion of the modern asset that would give the same output at the same unit cost of production as the existing asset.

The cost of sales adjustment (COSA)

The cost of sales adjustment refers to the difference between the current cost of inventories at the date of sale and the amount charged as the cost of goods sold in computing the historical cost profit. As we shall see in Part 5, business enterprises use standard costing systems for the purpose of obtaining timely information about the cost of inventories. These standard costing systems are designed to identify and to reflect, inter alia, changes in the current cost of purchased inventories. Where a standard costing system is in use, it is possible to derive an analysis of the variances which are differences between historical and standard costs, and to use this analysis to identify the extent to which current costs differ from standard costs. This information may be used to adjust the standard cost of goods sold to their current costs.

Where standard costing systems are not used, it is possible to average out the changes in the cost of sales. This method involves valuing the opening and closing inventories at the average cost for the year. The cost of sales is established as the purchases of the year, which are already stated at their average price for the year, adjusted by the revised values of the opening and closing inventories.

Example

Historical cost data

	£000
Opening inventory	350
Add: Purchases	2300
	2650
Deduct: Closing inventory	540
Cost of sales at historical cost	2110

Index for the cost of inventory

At the beginning of the year	100
At the end of the year	120
Average for the year	110

(i) *Revise opening and closing inventories to average cost for the year*

$$\text{Opening inventory} \quad 350 \times \frac{110}{100} \quad = £385$$

$$\text{Closing inventory} \quad 540 \times \frac{110}{100} \quad = 495$$

(ii) *Compute the current cost of sales using the revised amounts for the opening and closing inventories*

	£
Opening inventory	385
Add: Purchases	2300
	2685
Less: Closing inventory	495
Cost of sales on current cost basis	2190

(iii) *Calculate the cost of sales adjustment*

	£
Cost of sales on current cost basis	2190
Less: Cost of sales on historical cost basis	2110
Cost of sales adjustment	80

The monetary working capital adjustment (MWCA)

The purpose of this adjustment is to apply the concept of current value to monetary assets, to achieve the same effect as do the depreciation and the cost of sales adjustments in respect of fixed assets and inventories. Monetary working capital consists of trade debtors plus inventory not subjected to the cost of sales adjustment less trade creditors. Provided that it can be shown that it would be misleading to exclude them from monetary working capital, part of the bank balances and bank overdrafts, where applicable, may also be included in monetary working capital.

The objective of the monetary working capital adjustment and the cost of sales adjustments is to take account of the effects of changing prices on the financing requirements necessary to maintain the working capital applied to the day-to-day operations of the business. The relationship between the MWCA made in respect of trade debtors and trade creditors and the COSA is as follows:

(a) when sales are made on credit the business has to finance the changes in its input prices until the sales result in a receipt of cash. The part of the MWCA related to trade debtors, in effect, extends the COSA to allow for this; and

(b) conversely, when materials and services are purchased from suppliers who offer trade credit, price changes are financed by the supplier during the credit period. To this extent extra funds do not have to be found by the business and this reduces the need for a COSA and in some cases for a MWCA on debtors. The part of the MWCA related to trade creditors reflects this reduction.

SSAP 16 points out that there can be difficulties in practice in identifying, on an objective basis, those monetary assets and liabilities which are part of the net operating assets of the business. Nevertheless, a practical way of doing this has to be accepted if the operating profit is to be identified. Reasonable accuracy and objectivity may usually be achieved by including only trade debtors and trade creditors within monetary working capital, with an extension in the case of financial institutions. However, fluctuations in the volume of stock, debtors and creditors may lead to contrary fluctuations in cash or overdraft. It is necessary to include this element of cash or overdraft within monetary working capital if to do so has a material effect on current cost operating profit. Monetary working capital may also include cash floats required to support the business operations. The treatment adopted should be applied consistently.

Evidently, the method used to compute the monetary working capital adjustment should be compatible with that used to compute the cost of sales adjustment. For example, the sales of finished goods give rise to trade debtors. Hence, all things being equal, changes in the amount of finance required to support the increased level of trade debtors associated with price inflation will tend to be proportional to changes in the cost of goods finished. Consequently, the change in the index of finished goods prices is used to calculate that part of the monetary working capital which relates to supporting trade debtors. Equally, since the purchase of raw materials in the case of a manufacturing company gives rise to trade creditors, the change in the index of raw material prices is used to calculate that part of the monetary working capital which relates to trade creditors.

Example

		End Year 1 £	End Year 2 £
Historical cost balance sheets			
Trade debtors		60,000	80,000
Trade creditors		50,000	65,000

		Finished goods	Raw materials
Index numbers			
End year 1		100	105
Average year 2		110	114
End year 2		118	120

			£
Trade debtors adjustment			
Increase in trade debtors	£80,000	$-$ £60,000	= 20,000
Less:			
Index adjustment	£80,000 $\times \dfrac{110}{118}$	$-$ £60,000 $\times \dfrac{110}{100}$	= 8576
			11,424

			£
Trade creditors adjustment			
Increase in trade creditors	£65,000	$-$ £50,000	= 15,000
Less:			
Index adjustment	£65,000 $\times \dfrac{114}{120}$	$-$ £50,000 $\times \dfrac{114}{105}$	= 7464
			7536
Monetary working capital adjustment			3888

It should be noted that most of the problems associated with the calculation of the monetary working capital adjustment arise from the needs to identify monetary assets and liabilities associated with the net borrowing requirement. This net borrowing requirement affects the gearing adjustment which has to be made under current cost accounting.

The gearing adjustment

We noted in Chapter 13 that the capital structure of a company has important implications for financial management purposes. In particular, the gearing is important, since it expresses the relationship between fixed interest (loan capital) and fixed dividend (preference shares) to ordinary shares. A company that has a large proportion of fixed interest and fixed dividend bearing capital to ordinary capital is said to be highly geared.

The purpose of the gearing adjustment is to allocate equitably the current cost adjustments in order that the full burden should not fall on ordinary shareholders, where they themselves have not financed the entire assets in respect of which the adjustments are made. This adjustment, subject to interest on borrowing, indicates the benefit or cost to shareholders which is realized in the period, measured by the extent to which a proportion of the net operating assets are financed by borrowing. The current cost profit attributable to shareholders is the surplus after making allowance for the impact of price changes on the shareholders' interest in the net operating assets, having provided for the maintenance of lenders' capital in accordance with their repayment rights.

SSAP 16 requires a gearing adjustment to be made where a proportion of the assets of the business is financed by borrowing. Net borrowing is defined as the amount by which liabilities (defined in (1) below) exceed assets (defined in (2) below):

(1) the aggregate of all liabilities and provisions (including convertible debentures and deferred tax but excluding dividends) other than those included within monetary working capital;
(2) the aggregate of all current assets other than those that are subject to a cost of sales adjustment and those that are included within monetary working capital.

The gearing adjustment itself results from the application of the gearing ratio to the net adjustments made in converting the historical cost income to current cost income. The gearing ratio is found in the relationship between net borrowing (L) and the average ordinary shareholders' interest obtained from the opening and closing balance sheets (S), as follows:

Gearing ratio $= \dfrac{L}{L + S}$

Example

Shareholders' interest	Opening balance sheet £	Closing balance sheet £	Average £
Share capital	100	100	100
Reserves (including the current cost reserve)	50	60	55
	150	160	155
Net borrowing	100	110	105
	250	270	260

Current cost adjustments	£
Cost of sales	20
Monetary working capital	10
	30
Depreciation	15
Current cost adjustments	45

Gearing adjustment

Gearing ratio $\dfrac{105}{105 + 155} = 40.48\%$

Gearing adjustment $45 \times 40.48\% = £18$

The gearing adjustment has been the subject of considerable controversy. Everyone would agree that during inflation shareholders benefit from long-term loans, as their repayment is ultimately made in monetary units of smaller purchasing power. Whilst the gearing adjustment appears to be more acceptable than a current purchasing power adjustment, it is less clear why the gearing ratio should be applied to the current cost adjustments rather than to the entire increase in net asset values. SSAP 16 recognizes this controversy and states that:

'There are a number of possible methods for calculating a gearing adjustment. For the reasons set out it is believed that the method defined in the Standard is the most appropriate and, on the grounds of the need for comparability between company accounts, it has been made definitive. This does not prevent those who wish to show in addition the effect of a different method of calculating a gearing adjustment from doing so by way of a note to the accounts. It would help users if those adopting this course explained their reasons for so doing.'

Distributable profit: interpretation and limitations

SSAP 16 considers the relationship between current cost accounting and distribution policy as follows:

'The amounts that can prudently be distributed depend not only on profitability, but also on the availability of funds. This is so with all systems of accounting. When determining distribution policy, consideration must be given to factors not reflected in profit, such as capital expenditure plans, changes in the volume of working capital, the effect on funding requirements of changes in production methods and efficiency, liquidity, and new financing arrangements. The current cost profit attributable to shareholders should not be assumed to measure the amount that can prudently be distributed. Although the impact of price changes on the shareholders' interest in the net operating assets has been allowed for, the other factors still need to be considered. Even if the effect of such factors is neutral, a full distribution of the current cost profit attributable to shareholders may make it necessary to arrange additional finance (equal to the gearing adjustment) to avoid an erosion of the operating capability of the business. However, an increase in the value to the business of the assets may provide increased cover for such financing.'

With regard to interpretation and limitations SSAP 16 states:

'Current cost accounts allow for the impact of specific price changes on the net operating assets, and thus the operating capability, of the business. The same tools of analysis as those applied to historical cost accounts are generally appropriate. The ratios derived from current cost accounts for such items as gearing, asset cover, dividend cover and return on capital employed will often differ substantially from those revealed in historical cost accounts but should be more realistic indicators when assessing an entity or making comparisons between entities.

As with historical cost accounting, CCA is not a substitute for forecasting when such matters as a change in the size or nature of the business are under consideration. It assists cash flow forecasts, but does not replace them. It does not measure the effect of changes in the general value of money or translate the figures into currency of purchasing power at a specific date. Because of this it is not a system of accounting for general inflation. Further, it does not show changes in the value of the business as a whole or the market value of the equity.'

The current cost reserve

The current cost balance sheet includes a reserve in addition to those included in historical cost accounts. The additional reserve may be referred to as the current cost reserve. The total reserves will include, where appropriate:

(a) unrealized revaluation surpluses on fixed assets, inventories and investments; and
(b) realized amounts equal to the cumulative net total of the current cost adjustments, that is:
   (i) the depreciation adjustment (and any adjustments on the disposal of fixed assets);
   (ii) the two working capital adjustments; and
   (iii) the gearing adjustment.

Example of presentation

The appendix reproduces the example of presentation of cost accounts which is included in SSAP 16.

Appendix

This Appendix does not form part of the Statement of Standard Accounting Practice. The methods of presentation used are illustrative of the accounts of a manufacturing company. They are in no way prescriptive and other methods of presentation may equally comply with the Standard. The example assumes that historical cost accounts are published as the statutory accounts.

EXAMPLE OF PRESENTATION OF CURRENT COST ACCOUNTS

Y Limited and Subsidiaries

**Group current cost profit and loss account
for the year ended 31st December 1980**

1979 £000		1980 £000
18,000	Turnover	20,000
2420	Profit before interest and taxation on the historical cost basis	2900
1320	Less: Current cost operating adjustments (note 2)	1510
1100	*Current cost operating profit*	1390
(170)	Gearing adjustment	(166)
180	Interest payable less receivable	200
10		34
1090	Current cost profit before taxation	1356
610	Taxation	730
480	*Current cost profit attributable to shareholders*	626
400	Dividends	430
80	Retained current cost profit of the year	196

| 16.0p | Current cost earnings per share | 20.9p |
| 5.2% | Operating profit return on the average of the net operating assets | 6.0% |

£000	**Statement of retained profits/reserves**	£000
80	Retained current cost profit of the year	196
1850	Movements on current cost reserve (Note 4)	2054
NIL	Movements on other reserves	NIL
1930		2250
14,150	Retained profits/reserves at the beginning of the year	16,080
16,080	Retained profits/reserves at the end of the year	18,330

Where applicable, minority interests and extraordinary items should be presented in a manner consistent with the historical cost accounts.

EXAMPLE OF ALTERNATIVE PRESENTATION OF CURRENT COST PROFIT AND LOSS ACCOUNT

Y Limited and Subsidiaries

**Group current cost profit and loss account
for the year ended 31st December 1980**

1979		1980
£000		£000
18,000	Turnover	20,000
2420	Profit before interest and taxation on the historical cost basis	2900
1320	Less: Current cost operating adjustments (Note 2)	1510
1100	*Current cost operating profit*	1390
180	Interest payable less receivable	200
920		1190
610	Taxation	730
310	Current cost profit after interest and taxation	460
170	Gearing adjustment	166
480	*Current cost profit attributable to shareholders*	626
400	Dividends	430
80	Retained current cost profit of the year	196
16.0p	Current cost earnings per share	20.9p
5.2%	Operating profit return on the average of the net operating assets	6.0%

Statement of retained profits/reserves

£000		£000
80	Retained current cost profit of the year	196
1850	Movements on current cost reserve (Note 4)	2054
NIL	Movements on other reserves	NIL
1930		2250
14,150	Retained profits/reserves at the beginning of the year	16,080
16,080	Retained profits/reserves at the end of the year	18,330

Y Limited and Subsidiaries
Summarised group current cost balance sheet as at 31st December 1980

1979			1980	
£000	£000		£000	£000
		Assets employed:		
	18,130	Fixed assets (Note 3)		19,530
		Net current assets:		
3200		Stock	4000	
700		Monetary working capital	800	
3900		Total working capital	4800	
(400)		Proposed dividends	(430)	
(600)		Other current liabilities (Net)	(570)	
	2900			3800
	21,030			23,330
		Financed by:		
		Share capital and reserves:		
3000		Share capital	3000	
12,350		Current cost reserve (Note 4)	14,404	
3730		Other reserves and retained profit	3926	
	19,080			21,330
	1950	Loan capital		2000
	21,030			23,330

Y Limited and Subsidiaries
Notes to the current cost accounts for the year ended 31st December 1980

1. *Explanatory notes*
(*See paragraph 58 of the Standard and the example in the Guidance Notes*)

2. *Adjustments made in deriving cost operating profit*

1979		1980
£000		£000
400	Cost of sales	460
70	Monetary working capital	100
470	*Working capital*	560
850	Depreciation	950
1320	*Current cost operating adjustments*	1510

3. *Fixed assets*

	31st December 1980			1979
	Gross	Depreciation	Net	Net
	£000	£000	£000	£000
Land and buildings	3780	680	3100	3070
Plant and machinery	25,780	9350	16,430	15,060
	29,560	10,030	19,530	18,130

4. *Current cost reserve*

	£000	£000	£000
Balance at 1st January 1980			12,350
Revaluation surpluses reflecting price changes:			
Land and buildings	200		
Plant and machinery	1430		
Stocks and work in progress	490		
		2120	
Monetary working capital adjustment		100	
Gearing adjustment		(166)	
			2054
Balance at 31st December 1980			14,404
of which: realised (*see (iii) below*)			2494
unrealised			11,910
			14,404

(i) *Where applicable, surpluses or deficits arising on the following should be shown as movements on reserves:*
   (a) *the revaluation of investments (other than those included in current assets);*
   (b) *the restatement of investments in associated companies; and*
   (c) *consolidation differences arising on foreign currency translations.*
(ii) *Where relevant, movements should be shown net of minority interests.*
(iii) *The realised element represents the net cumulative total of the current cost adjustments which have been passed through the profit and loss account, including the gearing adjustment.*

5. *Financing of net operating assets*
   The following is the value to the business (normally current replacement cost net of depreciation on fixed assets) of the net operating assets at the balance sheet date, together with the method by which they were financed:

1979 £000		1980 £000
18,130	Fixed assets	19,530
3900	Working capital	4800
22,030	*Net operating assets*	24,330
19,080	Share capital and reserves	21,330
400	Proposed dividends	430
19,480	*Total shareholders' interest*	21,760
1950	Loan capital	2000
600	Other current liabilities	570
2550	*Net borrowing*	2570
22,030		24,330

Summary

The purpose of this chapter has been to examine the system of current cost accounting recommended for use in the United Kingdom by the Accounting Standards Committee under SSAP 16 Current Cost Accounting. This system is the result of a series of compromises resulting from a debate initiated by the report of the Sandilands Committee in 1975. Current cost accounting is concerned with maintaining the operating capability of the capital of the business and focuses on the value of its net assets, defined as comprising both physical and net monetary assets. Current cost accounting utilizes replacement cost and realizable values in arriving at the adjustments to be made in converting historical cost income to current cost income.

The main features of the required adjustments were examined. They were seen to consist of several items, in particular, a depreciation adjustment which applied to fixed assets, a cost of sales adjustment which deals with changes in inventory costs, and the monetary working capital adjustment which deals with the impact of inflation on trade debtors and trade creditors, and in certain cases, bank balances and overdrafts.

The gearing adjustment reflects the effect of financing assets by borrowing on the current cost profit attributable to shareholders. The current cost reserve shows the effects of these adjustments.

References

1. Report of the Inflation Accounting Committee, 1975, the Sandilands Report.
2. Accounting Standards Committee, ED 18, Current Cost Accounting, 1976.
3. Accounting Standards Committee, Inflation Accounting—an interim recommendation (the Hyde Guidelines), 1977.
4. Accounting Standards Committee, SSAP 16, Current Cost Accounting, 1980.

Questions

1. Barncliffe Ltd prepared historical cost accounts for the year ended 31 December 19X8 as follows:

Profit statement

	£	
Sales		460,000
Opening inventory	40,000	
Purchases	380,000	
	420,000	
Closing inventory	50,000	370,000
Gross income		90,000
Depreciation	5000	
Expenses	25,000	30,000
Net income		60,000

Balance sheet	31 December 19X7	31 December 19X8
Issued share capital	300,000	300,000
10% Debentures	100,000	100,000
Retained earnings	70,000	130,000
	470,000	530,000
Fixed assets		
Buildings at cost	500,000	500,000
Less: Aggregate depreciation	105,000	110,000
	395,000	390,000
Current assets		
Inventory	40,000	50,000
Debtors	20,000	80,000
Cash	40,000	50,000
	100,000	180,000
Creditors	25,000	40,000
Working capital	75,000	140,000
Net assets	470,000	530,000

Indices of price levels

	Buildings	Inventory	R.P.I.
At time of raising long-term capital	100	100	100
At time of purchasing building	100	100	100
31 December 19X7	110	110	120
31 December 19X8	60	120	140
Average for 19X8	85	115	130
At time of purchasing opening inventory	110	110	115
At time of purchasing closing inventory	60	118	135

Required:

1. Prepare (a) CPP balance sheets and income statements corresponding to the foregoing historical cost statements,

      (b) CCA balance sheets and income statements corresponding to the foregoing historical cost statements.

2. Discuss the financial results of Barncliffe Ltd in the light of the alternative measurements calculated from the CPP and CCA statements you have prepared.

2. Set out below are the summarized balance sheets of P.I. Ltd for the years 19X2 and 19X1, prepared on a historic cost basis.

	31 March 19X2 £	31 March 19X1 £
Fixed assets at cost	100,000	100,000
Less: Aggregate depreciation	30,000	20,000
	70,000	80,000
Inventories	17,200	14,500
Debtors	28,000	16,000
Cash	4800	2000
	120,000	112,500
Less: Creditors	13,000	12,500
	107,000	100,000
	£	£
Issued share capital	50,000	50,000
Retained earnings	27,000	20,000
Loan capital	30,000	30,000
	107,000	100,000

The opening inventories were purchased on 28 February 19X1 and the closing inventories were purchased on 29 February 19X2.

Required:

Using the following indices where appropriate:

(i) Prepare a schedule of the current cost adjustments to the income for the year ended 31 March 19X2, as recommended by SSAP 16.
(ii) Prepare a summarized current cost balance sheet as at 31 March 19X2, including an analysis of the reserves.

Indices	Fixed assets	Inventories
Date fixed assets purchased	50	—
28.2.19X1	—	145
31.3.19X1	100	150
30.9.19X1	110	170
29.2.19X2	—	186
31.3.19X2	120	190

Note:

(i) It is acceptable to use the inventory price index for the calculation of the monetary working capital adjustment.
(ii) The current cost value of the equity capital at 31 March 19X1 was £150,500.

      (Question supplied by A. J. Naughton, Leeds Polytechnic)

PART 4 FINANCIAL REPORTING—EXTENDING THE DISCLOSURE OF INFORMATION

Introduction

The scope of accounting was defined in Chapter 1 as being 'to provide information which is potentially useful for making economic decisions and which, if provided, will enhance social welfare'. This definition of the scope of accounting was followed in Chapter 3 by a discussion of the development of accounting theory, where several approaches to accounting theory were discussed. It was seen, in particular, that the current state of accounting knowledge depended substantially on a descriptive approach to accounting theory. This emphasized observations of the practices of accountants as a major source of accounting knowledge. It was for this reason that Part 2 was devoted to an analysis of the knowledge provided by a descriptive approach to accounting theory. Part 3 was seen as necessary in the context of the adjustments considered necessary to historical cost accounting by reason of the instability of the monetary standard of measurement. This instability affects not only the measurement of periodic income but the valuations which are significant in financial reports.

The problem which must be posed, of necessity, is the relevance of accounting information in the context of the needs of users for decision making. This problem, which was posed in the definition of accounting given in Chapter 1, was only dealt with partly in Part 3. In this part, we return to the implications of the definition of accounting as concerned with information useful for making economic decisions having welfare implications. In this sense, we shall return to the problems instanced in Chapter 3 in the discussion of different approaches to accounting theory. This provides an opportunity for examining the manner in which normative and welfare approaches to theory construction in accounting have a role to play in the development of accounting knowledge.

The provision of information intended for economic decisions has implicit welfare effects. These effects were briefly mentioned in Chapter 1, and relate not only to the manner in which the welfare of those receiving and using accounting information is susceptible of improvement, but implies some judgemental aspects as regards the balance of influence which different groups can exert on the enterprise in obtaining advantages for themselves.

It is significant that the disclosure of information to external users has been restricted by the influence which management has been able to exert whenever the need for more extensive disclosure to external users has been at issue. The historical reasons why management has a considerable influence within the accounting profession lies in the manner in which the accounting profession developed in the 19th century. In effect, the directors of large companies were patrons of the accounting profession, and in many areas of accounting responsibility were able to specify the services which they required, and which became a major source of revenue to accountants. The relationship which developed from this connection has been described as follows:

'Despite the growing need for shareholder protection as reflected in company legislation, accountants would be expected to react slowly and to the minimum extent if such calls for more disclosure were not consistent with their patron's wishes . . . It is manifestly unreasonable to expect individual accountants to make a strong stand for independence when they have not the power to do so. This implication does, in fact, highlight dilemmas facing the profession at the moment. How should it go on supporting disclosure of information to shareholders or any other parties when it is not in the interests of the patron to do so?' (Tomkins, 1978.)

Once it is admitted that the process of social change calls for equity in the disclosure of information to external users, and once the needs of external users are admitted to be important, two important problems appear. First, there is the problem of defining these needs. As we shall see in this part, this problem may be approached in different ways. It is possible simply to conduct empirical research to discover these needs in the statement of what users consider necessary for their purposes. It is also possible to try to understand the decisions with which they are faced and to suggest what information they should require. These two approaches reflect contrasting theories of accounting: the first being descriptive, and the second being normative in character. Second, there is the problem of creating some symmetry of treatment in the manner in which their needs are met. In this problem lie the complex welfare issues suggested in Part 1. This problem involves a breach in the power of management to influence the development of accounting knowledge towards their specific needs. It implies that 'the form and standards of disclosure and the definitions of measurement should be determined by third parties such as the Stock Exchange Commission, the accounting profession, the Courts, and professional investors to meet the requirements of users'. (Norby and Stone, 1972.) It also implies that the needs of other users such as employees and trade unions should be satisfied.

This part contains four chapters, as follows:

Chapter 22, which considers the implications of research into current practices for future developments in accounting,

Chapter 23, which examines the needs of investors, and suggests the nature of their information needs,

Chapter 24, which discusses the needs of employees for accounting information; and examines the implications of the Employment Protection Act, 1975 in this respect,

Chapter 25, which considers the problem of corporate social responsibility, and the nature of information which is relevant to this area of accounting responsibility.

References

1. Norby, W. C. & Stone, F. G. 'Objectives of financial accounting and reporting from the viewpoint of the financial analyst', *Financial Analysts Journal*, July-August, 1972.
2. Tomkins, C. *The Development of Accounting*. Discussion paper presented to the Workshop on Accounting in a Changing Social and Political Environment. London, June, 1978.

22 Evaluation of current financial reporting practice

Part 2 examined the nature of current financial reporting practice and the efforts which have been made in recent years towards its improvement. We noted that financial reporting practice was made the subject of much criticism during the 1960s on the following grounds:

1 the lack of uniformity in accounting practice made difficult the comparison of the financial reports of different companies;
2 the multiplicity of accounting practices made it possible for management to select alternative presentations of the financial results which allowed earnings to be manipulated and made it possible to conceal economic realities;
3 changes in the value of money added to the difficulty of comparing the financial statements of different companies in a meaningful manner, and added a new dimension to the problem of financial reporting.

The accountancy profession responded to public criticism by establishing the Accounting Standards Committee, charged with the task of producing standards of accounting practice aimed at remedying the problems of financial reporting. However, since accounting is a social science which is rooted in the value system of the society in which it operates, it was to be expected that the programme of the Accounting Standards Committee (ASC) should itself have been the subject of criticism.

In 1978 the ASC published the Watts Report (ASC, 1978) 'to review the process of setting accounting standards in the light of experience gained since the formation of the ASC in 1969 and to consider what improvements in that process could be effected'. This report highlighted the criticisms which the standard setting process had attracted. For example, the degree of uniformity which should be created by accounting standards has been the subject of controversy. Some believe that standards should seek uniformity, others that they should be more flexible and specify alternatives. Conflicting criticism of this type is a product of the inherent nature of accounting practice, much of which is so firmly rooted in matters of experience, individual circumstances and subjective judgement that it becomes extremely difficult to advocate a blanket standardization of all problem areas. Consequently a certain amount of flexibility in accounting practice is inevitable. This was acknowledged in SSAP 2, which requires, as we saw in Chapter 5, the disclosure of the accounting policies followed in preparing financial statements. However, it should be noted that the financial effects which result from the use of alternative accounting bases need not be disclosed, although such effects are of considerable importance to external users.

An essential feature of any standards system ought to be enforcement. In the U.K. the principal sanction against business enterprises which break SSAPs has been a qualified audit report. Experience suggests that this has not been a successful deterrent. Following the Watts Report, the ASC has been trying to secure the assistance of the Stock Exchange and the Council for the Securities Industry in enforcing standards.

Another controversial area has been the failure of the standard-setting process to recognize user needs. The membership of the ASC, which is composed essentially of accountants, has attracted criticism. Since, as we saw in the Introduction, management exerts considerable influence within the accounting profession, the ASC is open to the charge of having a bias towards industry. It has been argued that a greater recognition of user needs could be achieved by giving equal representation on the ASC to users.

The need for a conceptual framework

The main criticism which may be levelled against the programme adopted by the ASC is that it has failed to establish objectives for financial reports. This results from the failure to develop the accounting standards programme within a framework which would have allowed that programme to proceed in a coherent manner. The Watts Report stated that the ASC was 'frequently criticised for failing to develop an agreed conceptual framework on which a logical series of SSAPs can be based'. The accounting standards programme has to a large extent been prepared within the terms of the four accounting concepts: going concern, prudence, matching and consistency, explicitly recognized in SSAP 2, which stated that it was not the purpose of that standard to establish a theory of accounting, for 'an exhaustive theoretical approach would take an entirely different form and would include, for instance, many more propositions than the four fundamental concepts referred to here'.

However, recognition of only these four concepts has led to contradiction among and between SSAPs. For example, there is an inherent conflict between prudence and matching. Whereas the first draft of ED 14, 'Accounting for Research and Development', was based purely on prudence, SSAP 9 'Stocks and Work in Progress', which is discussed in Chapter 32, is based essentially on the matching convention. Therefore, the lack of definition and the absence of a more comprehensive framework than that allowed by consideration of the four concepts explicitly recognized in SSAP 2 has led to contradictions and inconsistencies in the accounting standards programme.

The principal intention of the accounting standards programme has been to secure greater uniformity in the preparation of financial reports in order that there should be more comparability between different companies in this respect. This presupposes that, in their present general format, financial reports provide useful information to external users. The problem lies in the conventions of accounting and the four fundamental concepts proposed by SSAP 2, which do not themselves necessarily offer the best starting point for developing or improving current accounting practice. It may be argued that a more logical method of proceeding would have been to begin with a consideration of the theoretical problems implied in these conventions, to have discussed the implications of research findings, and to examine the problems of financial reporting in this context.

In Part 1, we took the view that the main objectives of accounting theory should be to provide means for evaluating existing practices, and to provide guidelines for developing new practices. Adopting an information systems approach, we also took the view that as the external users of financial reports have no control over the content of these reports, such reports were not user-oriented. Indeed, the inputs, and therefore, the outputs of the accounting system are determined by conventions which are embodied in accounting traditions and in law. They are not determined by the needs of external users for making decisions.

The failure to establish a conceptual framework for financial reporting purposes lies precisely in the failure to orient financial reporting practices towards the needs of external users. External users are provided with financial information on a 'take-it-or-leave-it' basis. The information provided is limited in nature, although it could be expanded at little additional cost to the firm. Furthermore, the information is historical in character, and as such has little relevance to external users concerned with making decisions on the basis of future expectations. Finally, financial reports are issued only periodically, whereas many external users, particularly investors, are making decisions continually.

The development of a conceptual framework

The following steps would be included in developing a conceptual framework for financial reporting:

(i)   Identify the users of financial reports.
(ii) Identify the decisions these user groups have to take.
(iii) Identify the information which can be provided to assist with these decisions.
(iv) Compare the benefits and costs of providing this information. In deciding between alternative types of information choose the alternative which has the greatest benefit in excess of cost.

The initial problem in constructing a conceptual framework arises from the diverse information needs of different user groups. The recognition of these groups and their diverse objectives is a daunting task, but the Corporate Report provides a useful starting point for the development of a conceptual framework. This report states that 'The fundamental objective of corporate reports is to communicate economic measurements of and information about the resources and performance of the reporting entity useful to those having reasonable rights to such information'. It identifies the groups as having a reasonable right to information and whose information needs should be recognized by corporate reports as follows:

Equity investor group. Investors require information to assist in reaching share trading decisions, in deciding whether or not to subscribe to new issues and in reaching voting decisions at general meetings.

Loan creditor group including existing and potential holders of debentures and loanstock, and providers of short-term loans and finance.

Employee group. Employees and prospective employees require information in assessing the security and prospects of employment and information for the purpose of collective bargaining.

Analyst–adviser group including financial analysts and journalists, economists, statisticians, researchers, trade unions, stockbrokers and other providers of advisory services such as credit rating agencies.

Business contact group including customers, trade creditors and suppliers and in a different sense competitors, business rivals and those interested in mergers, amalgamations and takeovers.

Government including tax authorities, departments and agencies concerned with the supervision of commerce and industry, and local authorities.

The *public* including taxpayers, ratepayers, consumers and other community and special interest groups such as political parties, consumer and environmental protection societies and regional pressure groups.

As we discussed in Part 1, accounting policy makers are concerned essentially with welfare concepts. This raises great problems in attempting to consider all the effects of all the alternative reporting policies on all the parties concerned.

Furthermore, we saw how conflicts can arise between users about the distribution of the rewards of business enterprises which can be affected by the disclosure of information to various parties. We argued that a political judgement is needed as to whose interests are to be served and what trade offs are to be made between the interests of different groups.

The FASB conceptual framework

In recent years accountants within the United States have been examining the fundamental assumptions and philosophy underlying the financial reporting process. The Trueblood Report, published in New York in 1973, represented a dramatic departure from conventional wisdom at that time, and the findings of this report were finally endorsed by the Financial Accounting Standards Board (FASB), the accounting standards setting body in the U.S., in a document published in 1978, 'Statement of Financial Accounting Concepts No. 1—Objectives of Financial Reporting by Business Enterprises'. These important developments are considered in turn.

Trueblood Report—'Objectives of financial statements'

The Trueblood Report addressed itself to the problem of determining the objectives of financial statements, and took the view that their justification could be found only in how well accounting information serves those who use it. The Trueblood Report stated that it 'agrees with the conclusions drawn by many others that:

(1) 'The basic objective of financial statements is to provide information useful for making economic decisions.'

This the report sees as the prime objective and then goes on to list the following additional objectives (pp. 61–66).

(2) '. . . to serve primarily those users who have limited authority, ability, or resources to obtain information and who rely on financial statements as their principal source of information about an enterprise's economic activities.

(3) '. . . to provide information useful to investors and creditors for predicting, comparing and evaluating potential cash flows to them in terms of amount, timing, and related uncertainty.

(4) '. . . to provide users with information for predicting, comparing, and evaluating enterprise earning power.

(5) '. . . to supply information useful in judging management's ability to utilize enterprise resources effectively in achieving the primary enterprise goal.

(6) '. . . to provide factual and interpretive information about transactions and other events which is useful for predicting, comparing and evaluating enterprise earning power. Basic underlying assumptions with respect to matters subject to interpretation, evaluation, prediction, or estimation should be disclosed.

(7) '. . . to provide a statement of financial position useful for predicting, comparing and evaluating enterprise earning power. This statement should provide information concerning enterprise transactions and other events that are part of incomplete earning cycles. Current values should also be reported when they differ significantly from historical cost. Assets and liabilities should be grouped or segregated by the relative uncertainty of the amount and timing of prospective realisation or liquidation.

(8) '. . . to provide a statement of periodic earnings useful for predicting, comparing and evaluating enterprise earning power. The net result of completed earnings cycles and enterprise activities resulting in recognisable progress toward completion of incomplete cycles should be reported. Changes in the values reflected in successive statements of financial position should also be reported, but separately, since they differ in terms of their certainty of realisation.

(9) '. . . to provide a statement of financial activities useful for predicting, comparing, and evaluating enterprise earning power. This statement should report mainly on factual aspects of enterprise transactions having or expected to have significant cash consequences. This statement should report data that requires minimal judgement and interpretation by the preparer.

(10) '. . . to provide information useful for the predictive process. Financial forecasts should be provided when they will enhance the reliability of users' predictions.

(11) '. . . for governmental and not-for-profit organisations an objective is to provide information useful for evaluating the effectiveness of the management of resources in achieving the organisation's goals. Performance measures should be quantified in terms of identified goals.

(12) '. . . to report on those activities of the enterprise affecting society which can be determined and described or measured and which are important to the role of the enterprise in its social environment.'

The objectives adopted by the Trueblood Report, which involved focusing on the decision-making processes of users of financial reports, represented a fundamental change in a tradition, which had been based on the notion of stewardship.

Another innovation was the new emphasis given to reporting cash flows, for previously many writers on accounting theory had been concerned primarily with the problem of the periodic valuation of assets and with interpreting income as resulting from periodic increases in asset values.

The study group was concerned primarily with the needs of investors and creditors. Objectives 11 and 12 above were not pursued subsequently. The information needs of investors and creditors were considered to be 'essentially the same. Both groups are concerned with the enterprise's ability to generate cash flows to them and with their own ability to predict, compare and evaluate the amount, timing and related uncertainty of these future cash flows.' Figure 4.1 illustrates the relationship between the various objectives proposed by the Trueblood Report. It will be noted that these objectives are grouped into five tiers, in accordance with the scheme proposed by Sorter and Gans (1974).

Objectives 5 and 2 listed in the Trueblood Report may be criticized as being unrealistic. Thus, objective 5 depends on the assumption that the principal goal of a commercial enterprise is to maximize cash returns to shareholders. In effect, this assumption determines the standard by which management performance is to be judged. The first difficulty is that it is not possible to provide a satisfactory measure of this standard of managerial performance. In Chapter 23, the usefulness of cash flows in this context is discussed. The second difficulty is that it is doubtful that most organizations seek to maximize cash returns to owners. The third difficulty lies in interpreting organizational objectives in the context of the current social and economic environment.

Objective 2 states that an objective of financial reports is to 'serve primarily those users who have limited authority, ability or resources . . .' The Trueblood Report appeared to take the view that financial reports should produce something for everybody. Accordingly, sophisticated users should be assisted by being provided with details of the complex events which underlie the economic processes to which financial reporting is addressed. For this reason, the Trueblood Report introduced the concept of the earnings cycle. The earnings cycle is intended to indicate the expected duration of the earnings-generating ability of a segment of the enterprise. For example, given that an enterprise has a portfolio of important products, it would be relevant for investors to be provided with information concerning the life-expectancy of these products as regards their ability to contribute to earnings. The earnings cycle reflects the changing profiles of cash receipts and disbursements which are assumed to be associated with such products over time. It assumes that the life of a product reaches a degree of maturity expressed in the level of earnings which it generates, and that eventually it will require replacement by another product if the profitability of the enterprise is to be maintained.

If information concerning earnings cycles were made available to investors, it is evident that sophisticated users would be able to formulate clearer views of the cash-generating ability of enterprises. The Trueblood Report con-

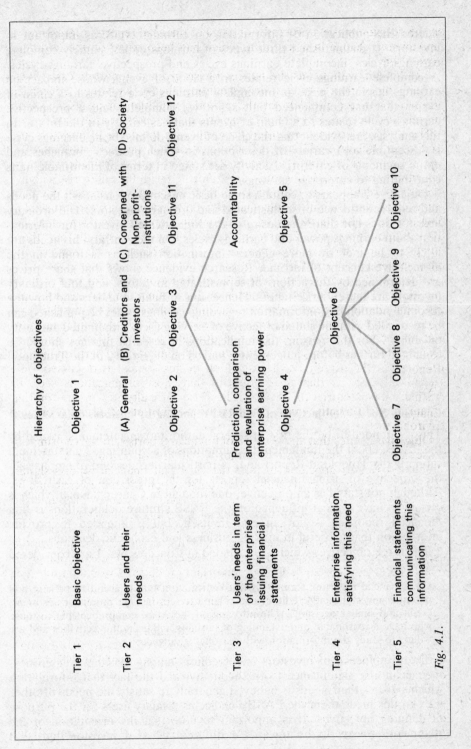

Hierarchy of objectives

Tier 1   Basic objective   Objective 1

Tier 2   Users and their   (A) General   (B) Creditors and   (C) Concerned with   (D) Society
          needs   investors   Non-profit-
                                                               institutions

Tier 3   Users' needs in term   Objective 2   Objective 3   Objective 11   Objective 12
          of the enterprise
          issuing financial
          statements

          Prediction, comparison   Accountability
          and evaluation of
          enterprise earning power

Tier 4   Enterprise information   Objective 4   Objective 5   Objective 6
          satisfying this need

Tier 5   Financial statements   Objective 7   Objective 8   Objective 9   Objective 10
          communicating this
          information

Fig. 4.1.

sidered the publication of information on earnings cycles as important to investors. It distinguished three types of earnings cycles, namely complete earnings cycles, incomplete earnings cycles and prospective earnings cycles. A complete earnings cycle relates to a chain of events whose impact on earnings lies in the past, an incomplete earnings cycle relates to a chain of events that has commenced but is not yet complete, and a prospective earnings cycle relates to a chain of events that lies entirely in the future. In this analysis, it is evident that the chain of events defined by an earnings cycle is susceptible to a variety of descriptions in which products, branches and entire segments of enterprise activity are stated in terms of identifiable units contributing to enterprise earnings.

Objective 2 appears to contain some basic misconceptions about the needs and relative influence of sophisticated and ordinary investors. The ordinary investor does not share the desire of the sophisticated investor for information about earnings power and earnings cycles. On the contrary, his needs are likely to be met by more general information such as is found in the all-inclusive concept of income. Research evidence shows that share prices are determined by the actions of sophisticated investors, and that ordinary investors are merely price takers. Hence, it is difficult to understand how the recommendation that information regarding earnings cycles be published can be reconciled with the stated objective of 'serving users with limited authority or ability'. For this reason, the implications of research findings should be examined further before judgement is passed on objective 2 of the Trueblood Report.

Concepts No. 1—'Objectives of financial reporting by business enterprises'

This is intended to be the first of several authoritative statements, issued by the FASB, about the fundamental assumptions of accounting. This statement supports the Trueblood Report and, in particular, echoes and re-emphasizes the objective of using financial reports for the prediction of cash flows. Although not stated as an objective, one thought in Concepts No. 1 which is certain to have a great influence on the FASB's future deliberations is that 'financial reporting is not an end in itself, but is intended to provide information that is useful in making business and economic decisions'.

The three objectives which are included in Concepts No. 1 are considered below:

(1) 'Financial reporting should provide information that is useful to present and potential investors and creditors and other users in making rational investment, credit and similar decisions. The information should be comprehensible to those who have a reasonable understanding of business and economic activities and are willing to study the information with reasonable diligence'.

The prominence of investors and creditors among existing user groups, their economic significance to the economy, and the fact that information which satisfies their needs is believed generally to satisfy the needs of other user groups made them the FASB's choice as primary users for the purpose of defining objectives. It is important to note that the orientation of the statement appears to be towards a different class of investor than that envisaged in Trueblood's objective 2. Doubtless the findings of efficient market research, which we discuss later in this chapter, has been the prime factor in this difference.

(2) 'Financial reporting should provide information to help present and potential investors and creditors and other users in assessing the amounts, timing, and uncertainty of prospective cash receipts from dividends or interest and the proceeds from the sale, redemption, or maturity of securities or loans. Since investors' and creditors' cash flows are related to enterprise cash flows, financial reporting should provide information to help investors, creditors, and others, assess the amounts, timing, and uncertainty of prospective net cash inflows to the related enterprise'.

In Chapter 23 we consider the practical implications of this objective. There we consider the problems of developing a method of financial reporting which is in tune with the investors' normative decision model which is concerned primarily with estimating the dividends and the risks associated with an investment. In Chapter 23 we examine, also, the advantages of cash flows as compared with income reporting. In Part 3 of this book, we examined the many different definitions of income, and it is apparent that the notion of income means different things to different people. The cash flow concept is unambiguous and less abstract and, therefore, the problem of definition is avoided. Stating objectives in terms of the prediction and evaluation of cash flows provides a vehicle for assessing and evaluating all accounting information. This argument is reflected in objective 3.

Although none of the three objectives of Concepts No. 1 mentions enterprise earning power, earnings are shown to retain their importance in financial reporting, for 'the primary focus of financial reporting is information about earning and its components'. Concepts No. 1 makes it clear that earnings calculations are important not for their own sake but rather because they are thought to provide an indication of an enterprise's cash flow.

(3) 'Financial reporting should provide information about the economic resources of an enterprise, the claims to those resources (obligations of the enterprise to transfer resources to other entities and owners' equity), and the effects of transactions, events, and circumstances that change its resources and claims to those resources'.

Elsewhere, and apparently by way of emphasizing this objective's cash flow implications, Concepts No. 1 states that 'information about resources, obligations and owners' equity also provides a basis for investors, creditors and others to evaluate information about the enterprise's performance during a period . . . Moreover, it provides direct indications of the cash flow potentials of some resources and of the cash needed to satisfy many, if not most, obligations'.

Other research findings

At the beginning of this chapter we stated that the implications of research findings are important for considering the future development of financial reporting. In this section we examine recent research which has a bearing on this problem.

The efficient market hypothesis

In a perfectly competitive market, it is an axiom of economic theory that the equilibrium price of any commodity or service is established at that point where the available demand is matched with the available supply. The equilibrium price reflects the consensus of those trading in the market about the true worth of a good or service, which is based on all publicly available information. If new information becomes available, it is analysed and interpreted by the market. The market for shares formed by the Stock Exchange appears to have the characteristics of a free and competitive market.

Financial theorists have developed two hypotheses about the way the Stock Exchange operates. The first hypothesis assumes that the market is naive, and the second hypothesis assumes that the market is efficient.

The naive market hypothesis assumes that the market reacts in a naive way to the information contained in financial reports. Thus, it assumes that investors are naive and unable to detect subtleties in financial reporting procedures. Hence, the market as a whole reacts naively to information. As the market is composed substantially of investors who are relatively unsophisticated in the analysis and interpretation of financial reports, it assumes that they determine the behaviour of the market as a whole to information contained in these reports. The difficulty with the naive market hypothesis is that research has shown that financial reports are used thoroughly by a minority of shareholders (Dyckman et al., 1975).

The efficient market hypothesis assumes that:

(1) Investors react to new information in such a way as to cause the price of shares traded on the Stock Exchange to change instantaneously. Therefore, an item of information which is disclosed in a footnote to the financial report will be impounded in the share price just as surely as if it had been included in the main body of the report.

(2) The price of shares traded on the Stock Exchange fully reflects all publicly available information.

(3) Abnormal returns cannot be earned by investors, that is, no investor can expect to use published information in such a way as to increase the benefits accruing to him as against those accruing to other investors. Each investor can expect to earn the return on a security commensurate to its risk class.

The assumptions of the efficient market hypothesis have received considerable support from research findings. These findings show that accounting information does have economic significance in that share prices react to new accounting information. Moreover, research indicates that the Stock Exchange reacts almost immediately to the public release of information. Research also shows that sharp price changes occur on the announcement of new information, but no discernible price movements thereafter, since the adjustment made at that time removes the possibility of future abnormal returns to individual investors. This observed behaviour is consistent with the behaviour of an efficient market (Ball and Brown, 1968).

A further condition required of an efficient market is that is should be able to interpret accounting information correctly. A number of research studies have examined the share price reaction to reported earnings reflecting a change in accounting policy. An interesting example of the market's ability to understand changes in accounting policy is illustrated by Sunder's (1975) research into share price reactions to switches in the basis of inventory valuation from FIFO to LIFO and from LIFO to FIFO. The expected results on earnings of these changes were discussed in Chapter 11, and it will be recalled that firms switching from FIFO to LIFO will report lower earnings which will coincide with an improvement in economic earnings resulting from a reduced tax bill. Conversely, firms switching from LIFO to FIFO will report higher earnings as a result of that change and will hope that the market will respond positively to this information, thereby compensating for the negative impact of the increased tax bill that would result from the change. Whilst such changes are not permitted in the United Kingdom, they are allowed in the United States and the American research experience of the impact of changes in accounting policy reflected in inventory valuation changes is illuminating. In effect, research evidence shows that firms switching from FIFO to LIFO did not encounter any adverse price reactions from the market. On the contrary, average share prices rose by an average of 5 per cent more than would have been expected, taking account of market movements during the year when the change in accounting policy occurred. Sunder's research also indicated no market reaction to switches from LIFO to FIFO. In effect, it appeared that such an attempt to improve share prices was both fruitless and expensive in the context of the increased tax bill resulting from the change.

Indeed, many other studies have shown results similar to those produced by Sunder, and it may be concluded from these studies that the market does not respond to earnings increases that result from cosmetic changes in accounting policies.

Finally, it does appear that there has been no major readjustment of share prices in the United Kingdom since companies began to publish inflation-adjusted accounts in varying forms several years ago (Morris, 1975). These findings are consistent with the view that the market made its own assessment of the effects of inflation on company profits, and had already made the necessary adjustments for these effects.

The importance of risk

An investor is interested not only in the return which he expects to receive from his investment but also in the risk attached to the investment. This risk may be defined as the probability that he may sustain a financial loss by investing in a particular company. To minimize the risk associated with investing in one company only, the sensible investor will seek to spread his investment over several companies. In effect, the investor will consider the purchase of one particular security in the context of a portfolio of securities.

It is a basic tenet of portfolio theory that rational investors will prefer to hold portfolios of securities which maximize the expected return for a given degree of risk, or which minimize the degree of risk for a given expected rate of return. The individual investor is required to decide for himself the risk he is willing to bear in exchange for the prospect of larger returns, for evidently the larger the returns, the greater the degree of risk usually associated with such returns. In effect, the decision which he makes reflects his personal risk preferences. The portfolio of securities which an individual will choose will reflect his relative risk preference, and will require predicting the risk associated with the individual securities comprised in the portfolio. It is evident that the analysis of the financial reports of companies should assist individual investors in selecting portfolios of securities.

The development of portfolio theory has been extended beyond the analysis of risk and the selection of securities by means of studies in capital asset pricing. Capital asset pricing models seek to explain the manner in which asset prices are determined in relation to the risk attached to the returns involved. Whilst a more extensive review of the significance of portfolio theory is beyond the scope of this text, research in this area shows the significance of risk to the investor, and the manner in which the returns which he expects are associated with risk categories.

The significance of forecasted earnings

The objective common to most investors might be defined as the maximization of long-run returns consistent with an acceptable degree of risk. The returns themselves comprise interest and dividend income and capital appreciation in the market value of securities. Given that capital appreciation is closely related to the earnings prospects, information useful for forecasting earnings would be highly relevant to investors in regard to the broad spectrum of expected returns.

The prediction of earnings plays a major role in investment analysis. Foster (1978) quoted an interview survey conducted in 1973 in which 534 investment analysts were asked which factors were considered important in appraising companies. The factor most often cited was—'an estimate of future earnings'. According to Backer (1970), 'security valuation models employed by analysts indicate that future earnings is by far the most important determinant of the value of a share of common stock. This explains why a major portion of the security analyst's effort is focused on forecasting company earnings.'

Investors may attempt to use the series of past reported profits or earnings per share, as a guide to future profitability, and the company's future dividend-paying capability. Several empirical studies have taken as their point of reference the behaviour of accounting profits over time, and used earnings per share information based on historical cost calculations. The conclusions of these studies are that past profit trends are not usually repeated in the future. Although sophisticated statistical techniques were used in these studies, it seems that the process of extrapolating from past profit trends is unlikely to prove useful in forecasting future profitability.

The research conducted by Backer showed that the procedure employed by security analysts for forecasting profits closely parallels that used internally by companies. Initially, this procedure requires a projection of sales. After making a sales forecast, profit margins are examined, and other significant operating ratios are compiled from published income statements. These ratios are adjusted for anticipated changes in sales volume, prices and costs, and are then applied to the sales forecasts to obtain profit forecasts.

The significance of non-accounting information

The preceding sections illustrate that factors concerned with expectations are relatively more important than information contained in financial reports for the purpose of decision making by investors. The critical factor which affects future earnings is the level of sales. Research by Baker and Haslem (1973) supports this conclusion by ranking the three most significant factors considered by investors when making investment decisions, as follows:

1   The future earnings prospects facing the company.
2   The quality of management.
3   The future economic prospects of the industry in which the company is located.

It follows that financial reports provide only one source of information to investors. The existence of other sources of information may explain why share prices do not necessarily react to the publication of financial reports to the extent that might be expected. Much of the informational content of financial reports is known by the time these reports are published. As one analyst stated, 'much of this data is available in newspapers. For example, the dominant source of General Motors' earnings is passenger cars. General Motors' passenger car production figures are published weekly'. (Backer, op. cit.)

It follows that year-end financial reports are used mainly to confirm information otherwise obtained during the year. Hence, financial reports may provide a useful check on data gathered from non-accounting sources.

It may be argued that the significance of financial reports to external users depends on the degree of their dependence on such reports for information on which to base decisions. Obviously, if financial reports contained the sum total of information available to external users, and there were no other competing and alternative information sources, the quality of the information contained in financial reports would be of critical importance to efficient decision making. The availability of competing and alternative sources of information reduces the significance of financial reports.

Hagerman et al. (1973) carried out research into the influence of financial reports on the manner in which investment decisions were made. Under laboratory conditions, investors presented with financial reports based on alternative accounting methods, and having access to no other information, were unable to distinguish between the different accounting interpretations of the same economic event. Under real-life conditions, the possession of information about the events underlying the financial reports enabled investors to adjust the decisions which they would have made otherwise, and these adjustments compensated for the effects of differences in accounting policies.

The conclusion of these research studies indicated that, given that investors have alternative sources of information available to them, for example, reports in the financial press and security analyses, which provide a clear understanding of the events underlying financial reports, the search for the best financial reporting procedure is unnecessary. Hopwood (1974) appears to have reached the same conclusion by the process of distinguishing two alternative information contexts. First, in the absence of competing sources of information, or where there are difficulties in using sources of information other than published financial reports—a situation described by Hopwood as a 'monopolistic information context'—, the accounting interpretation of events is not subject to validation by alternative information sources and constitutes the major part of the relevant information available. Second, in a 'competitive information context', not only is it possible to validate the accounting interpretation of events, but financial reports become less significant. The availability of many competing or often more timely sources of information enables the investor to gauge more readily the accuracy or the bias of financial reports, and to ignore their conclusions wherever appropriate.

Implications of research findings

The following inferences may be drawn from research conducted in the area of financial reporting.

(1) Where there is controversy over which of two alternative measurements should be reported to external users, and no additional costs are involved in reporting both measurements, the solution to the controversy lies in reporting both measurements. Use could be made of footnotes to the financial report for this purpose, and the market may be left to interpret the importance of such additional information.

(2) As there is evidence of a direct relationship between the price of a share and its risk, concern for the ordinary investor is ill-founded. The naive investor is a price-taker, and any additional disclosure will be to his advantage. Increased disclosure to the sophisticated investor will improve the predictions which he, the sophisticated investor, is able to make, and thereby reduce the speculative and destabilizing influences which are associated with the uncertainties of stock market behaviour. As the ordinary investor is likely to be a naive investor, and is a price-taker, he has an interest in share prices behaving in an orderly manner.

The call for simplified financial reports may be naive. It is often suggested that published accounting information should be simplified to the level of the understanding of the average investor. Yet, reflecting the increasing complexities of business organizations, accounting information is becoming more complex.

(3) Accountants are not the only suppliers of information. Therefore, one of the functions which should be undertaken by the Accounting Standards Committee is to try to minimize the total cost of providing information to investors. This implies that the Accounting Standards Committee should consider the totality of information used by investors in determining the nature of the information content of financial reports.

(4) Investors are concerned with assessing risk as well as assessing ex-

pected returns. Accordingly, any additional financial information which can be made available will be of benefit.

(5) In their present form, financial reports are of limited usefulness to investors. Generally accepted accounting principles act to reduce the potential usefulness of reported financial information. There is a need to produce financial reports which are more relevant to users.

(6) Accounting research alone cannot determine the financial reporting process. As we discussed in Chapter 3, research serves merely as an input into the policy-making process. Efficient market research, for example, does not consider the total costs and benefits which are associated with alternative accounting reporting methods. These imply welfare judgements which have to be made by accounting policy makers.

Summary

The purpose of this chapter has been to evaluate current financial reporting practice, and the problems associated with the content of these reports. It was seen that the reasons which caused dissatisfaction with the status of financial reporting practice require solutions which are able to stand the test of relevance to users' information needs. The failure of the Accounting Standards Committee's programme of reform was argued to lie in the failure to establish a conceptual framework for financial reports. We examined the work of the FASB in this connection.

An important part of the chapter was devoted to examining the usefulness of financial reports in the context of how stock markets react to information contained in these reports. Two hypotheses directed to explanations of behaviour in these markets were discussed. Whereas some investors may be described as naive in their perceptions of information, the presence of sophisticated investors renders the stock market efficient in its interpretation of information in the process of setting share prices. The ability of the stock market to interpret information produced by alternative accounting policies was reviewed.

The chapter contained a discussion of the importance of risk and of information related to future earnings in the context of the information needs of investors. The role of non-accounting information was examined. Implicit in this discussion is the need to improve the extent and the relevance of the accounting information disclosed in financial reports, if the latter are to be useful for decision making by external users.

References

1. The Accounting Standards Committee, *Setting Accountancy Standards*, 1978.
2. A.I.C.P.A. 'Report of the Study Group on Objectives of Financial Statements', *The Trueblood Report*, New York, 1973.
3. Backer, M. 'Financial reporting for security investment and credit decisions', N.A.A., 1970.
4. Baker, H. K. & Haslem, J. A. 'Information needs of individual investors', *Journal of Accountancy*, November, 1973.

5. Ball, R. & Brown, P. 'An evaluation of accounting income numbers', *Journal of Accounting Research*, Autumn, 1960.
6. Beaver, W. H. 'What should be the FASBs objectives?', *Journal of Accountancy*, August, 1973.
7. Dyckman, T. R., Downes, D. H. & Magee, R. P. *Efficient Capital Markets and Accounting: A Critical Analysis*, Prentice-Hall, 1975.
8. Foster, G. *Financial Statement Analysis*, p. 80, Prentice-Hall, 1978.
9. Hagerman, R. L., Keller, T. F. & Petersen, R. S. 'Accounting research and accounting principles', *Journal of Accountancy*, March, 1973.
10. Hopwood, A. *Accounting and Human Behaviour*, Accountancy Age Books, London, 1974.
11. Morris, R. C. 'Evidence of the impact of inflation on share prices', *Accounting and Business Research*, Spring, 1975.
12. Sorter, G. H. & Gans, M. A. 'Opportunities and implications of the Report on Objectives of Financial Statements', *Journal of Acounting Research*, Supplement to Vol. 12, 1974.
13. Sunder, S. 'Accounting changes in inventory valuation', *The Accounting Review*, April, 1975.

Questions

1. Why did financial reporting attract criticism in the 1960s?
2. How do the objectives of the Trueblood Report differ from those of traditional accounting practice?
3. To what extent has the FASB Conceptual Framework followed the direction of the Trueblood Report?
4. What do the findings of efficient market research show?
5. What are the implications of the research findings discussed in this chapter for the development of financial reporting?

23 Reporting to investors

The central problem of financial reporting has been stated as resting in the need to define its objectives as a pre-condition to resolving the difficulties which have arisen in the last two decades. In the previous chapter, it was noted that the failure of the Accounting Standards Committee lies in its failure to define clearly the objectives of its programme of reform and standardization. It was argued, also, that these objectives should be defined in terms of the information needs of users concerned with making decisions. Therefore, the investigation of this problem ought properly to begin with identifying these needs.

The purpose of this chapter is to consider the problems implied in identifying the information needs of investors.

Problems in identifying investors' needs

At a superficial level, the identification of the information needs of users appears deceptively simple. It seems that it would be sufficient to question users of financial reports and to observe the way in which they make decisions as a means of identifying the decision models used and the information requirement of such models. Accordingly, repeated questionnaires and interviews would isolate the information requirements of users of financial reports. Yet such a method has not proved satisfactory, although it appears ideally suited to the research problem implied.

In effect, the reason why the straightforward questionnaire method has not met with success lies in part in the problems discussed in the previous chapter. Evidently, being accustomed to using financial reports containing information specified largely by accounting conventions, users are unable to make a clear distinction between the type of information they are using and the type of information they should be using. For example, if a naive investor were asked for his views on how the information content of these reports might be improved, he may well reply, 'by reporting a bigger and better balance sheet'.

A further difficulty lies in the making of correct observations of the decision models used by investors. Such observations can reveal only the information currently used. Clearly, investors will be obliged to use what information is available, even though it may be deficient in some respects.

For these reasons, it is clear that empirical research into the decision models employed by users cannot produce satisfactory conclusions about investors' information needs. It follows that the rejection of empirical research compels the consideration of alternative methods of constructing a theory about the information needs of investors. It is suggested, therefore, that progress could be made by adopting a normative approach to the construction of such a theory which is based on a formulation of the decision models which investors ought to be using when making decisions.

Basis for a normative theory of reporting to investors

A starting point in discussing the case for a normative theory of reporting to investors is to examine the implicitly normative characteristics of the process of reporting to users. In this respect, the Corporate Report (1975) stated that reports should be (a) relevant, (b) understandable, (c) reliable, (d) complete, (e) objective, (f) timely, (g) comparable. These characteristics were clearly set out:

(a) 'Relevance is the characteristic which embodies the fundamental notion that corporate reports should seek to satisfy, as far as possible, users' information needs.'

(b) 'Understandability does not necessarily mean simplicity, or that information must be presented in elementary terms, for that may not be consistent with the proper description of complex economic activities. It does mean that judgement needs to be applied in holding the balance between the need to ensure that all material matters are disclosed and the need to avoid confusing users by the provision of too much detail.'

(c) 'The information presented should be reliable in that users should be able to assess what degree of confidence may be reposed in it. The credibility of the information in corporate reports is enhanced if it is independently verified, although in certain circumstances it may be useful for an entity to supply information which is not verifiable in this way.'

(d) 'The information presented should be complete in that it provides users, as far as possible, with a rounded picture of the economic activities of the reporting entity. Since this is likely to be complex, it follows that corporate reports as we define them are likely to be complex rather than simple documents.'

(e) 'The information presented should be objective or unbiased in that it should meet all proper user needs and neutral in that the perception of the measurer should not be biased towards the interest of any one user group. This implies the need for reporting standards which are themselves neutral as between competing interests.'

(f) 'The information presented should be timely in the sense that the date of its publication should be reasonably soon after the end of the period to which it relates.'

(g) 'The information should be expressed in terms which enable the user to compare the entity's results over time and with other similar entities.'

The characteristic of relevance is agreed generally to be the most important, for 'relevance is the primary standard and requires that the information must bear upon or be usually associated with actions it is designed to facilitate or results desired to be produced. Known or assumed information needs of potential users are of paramount importance . . .' (A.A.A., 1966.)

Normative definition of investors' information needs

The problem of defining normatively the information needs of investors may usefully begin by a review of the economics of decision making. In this analysis, it is axiomatic that decision makers are interested in determining the extent of the sacrifices which must be made for the benefits which are expected to follow from the decision. Economic decisions are considered as having three important dimensions, namely, the amount involved, the timing and the uncertainty associated with the amount and the timing of benefits or sacrifices.

Interpreted in terms of the interests of investors, benefits or sacrifices are expressed in terms of the cash flows between themselves and the enterprise. Accordingly, 'investors are concerned with the enterprise's ability to generate cash flows to them and with their own ability to predict, compare and evaluate the amount, timing and related uncertainty of these future cash flows'. (Trueblood Report, 1973.)

It follows that the decisions which investors make require information enabling them to judge the acceptability of cash flows expected to arise from a given investment. The reasoning associated with investors' decision models is that they are assumed to invest in order to be better off as a result than if they had not invested. In effect, this assumes that they are prepared to forgo the benefit of present consumption for the expectation of the higher future consumption made possible by future higher income.

Investors are assumed to invest when the current cost of the investment (and of the consumption forgone) is less than their own valuation of the investment. Conversely, they will disinvest when the current cost of the investment (and the consumption forgone) is greater than their own valuation of the investment. In effect, investors and potential investors are assumed to be constantly comparing the alternative of having cash available for present consumption against the alternative of having cash available in the future for future consumption.

These assumptions may be summarized in an investors' cash flow model and expressed symbolically as follows (A.A.A., 1969; Revsine, 1973):

$$V_0 = \sum_{i=1}^{n} \frac{D_i \alpha i}{(1 + B)^i} + \frac{I_n \alpha n}{(1 + B)^n} - I_0$$

where

V_0 is the net subjective value of the gain or loss to be obtained by an investor for a specific investment at time 0, that is, the investor's estimate of the current value of the investment minus the maximum price he would be willing to pay for the investment. He will increase his investment when V_0 is greater than the market value of his current holdings, he will realize part of his investment when V_0 falls below the market value, and he will maintain his investment at its current level when V_0 equals the market value.

D_i is the dividend per share expected during the period i.

$\alpha\, i$ is a certainty equivalent factor which adjusts the expected cash flows to a value such that a given investor is indifferent between D_i and a cash flow which is certain to be paid. This factor is determined by each investor's attitude to risk. If he is risk averse, $\alpha\, i$ will assume a value between 0 and 1. If the investor is a speculator and a risk-taker, $\alpha\, i$ will be greater than 1.

B is the opportunity rate for a risk-free investment and represents the minimum required return during period i.

I_n is the expected market price at the end of the holding period n.

I_0 is the price of the investment at time 0, when the investment decision is made.

The investor's cash flow model depicted above implies that the investor is concerned primarily with estimating the dividends and the risks associated with an investment. This decision model provides a basis for formulating a normative definition of his information needs, which would include the following (Arnold and Hope, 1975):

(a) forecasts of the cash flows expected by the enterprise in the future;

(b) forecasts of the cash flows expected for all segments of the enterprise in the future;

(c) statements of actual cash flows with explanations of the differences arising between the forecasted and the actual cash flows. This information would have the purpose of providing evidence of the reliability of forecasts made by the enterprise. Clearly, forecasts of future cash flows will be given more credibility and will be considered more reliable to the extent to which it is shown that deviations between forecasts made in the past and subsequent results are small;

(d) statements of changes in expectations of future cash flows with explanations of such changes;

(e) statement of the dividend policy which the enterprise intends to pursue in the future;

(f) forecasts of the realizable value of assets.

Content of cash flow statements

The foregoing normative definition of the information needs of investors emphasizes the significance of the cash flow statement in developing a normative theory of financial reporting to investors. According to this definition, the objective of the cash flow statement should be both to inform investors of the cash flows which they may expect to receive from the enterprise, and to provide evidence of the reliability of cash flow forecasts made in cash flow statements. It may be argued that a cash flow statement should show for at least each of the last three reporting periods the actual cash flows of the enterprise and the latest forecasted cash flows which were made in respect of these three periods. Moreover, the cash flow statement should also show for at least the next three reporting periods the latest forecasts of the cash flows expected by the enterprise as well as the last previous forecasts made by the enterprise in respect of these three periods. It may be argued that a cash flow statement presented in such a form would satisfy the need for information relating to expected future cash flows in the foreseeable period ahead, as well as evidence of the reliability of the previous forecasts made by the enterprise.

Macdonald et al. have suggested that published cash flow statements should distinguish the following elements:

(i) Recurrent cash flows which are associated with transactions expected to recur in the normal course of business at least once in each accounting period. Specifically included are trading flows, taxation outflows associated with other recurrent cash flows, and distributions to investors other than realization of their investment (that is, including divided and interest payments but excluding repayment of loans and share capital).

(ii) Non-recurrent cash flows which are those associated with transactions expected to occur and possibly recur in the normal course of business, but not regularly in each accounting period. Specifically included are flows which are associated with the realization, acquisition and provision of capital resources; finance provided by investors; and the realization of the investments of investors.

(iii) Extraordinary cash flows which are those associated with transactions not expected in the normal course of business. Specifically included are payments or receipts for damages and tax repayments resulting from losses.

Tables 4.1 and 4.2 are examples given by Macdonald et al. Table 4.2 classifies trading flows by principal activities. Within each such classification fixed outflows are shown separately from net variable flows. Where fixed outflows are not attributable to a particular class of activity they should be shown separately. Fixed outflows are those relating to transactions, the volume of which does not vary with the volume of trading.

In Tables 4.1 and 4.2 'F' stands for forecasted cash flows; 'P' stands for previous forecasted cash flows; 'A' stands for actual cash flows; '+' stands for cash inflows; '−' stands for cash outflows. In these statements, the cash flow forecasts for the years 19X0, 19X1 and 19X2 are compared with the actual cash flows in those years, and any significant variance should be explained to investors. The reliability of forecasts would be accessible by reference to the size of any individual variances and the explanations given by management to investors. For the years 19X3 and 19X4 forecasts of cash flows are compared with previous forecasts. Here again, the reasons for variances should be explained.

It was noted earlier in this chapter that reliability is one of the important characteristics of financial reports mentioned by the Corporate Report. The recommendations noted above are clearly addressed to this normative requirement, in addition to being addressed to the provision of relevant information in the form of cash flow forecasts.

Advantages of publishing company forecasts

Financial reports tend not to disclose many specific details which reflect the

Table 4.1 Cash flow statement for a company with three principal trading activities

	19X0		19X1		19X2		19X3		19X4		19X5	
	F	A	F	A	F	A	P	F	P	F	F	F
Recurrent cash flows												
Net trading inflow before tax (see Table 4.2)	±	+	±	+	±	+	±	+	±	+	±	+
Non-trading inflow (by source)	+		+		+		+		+		+	
Non-trading outflow	−		−		−		−		−		−	
Taxation	−		−		−		−		−		−	
(sub-total 1)	‖		‖		‖		‖		‖		‖	
Non-recurrent cash flows												
Realization of capital resources	+		+		+		+		+		+	
Investment by investors	+		+		+		+		+		+	
Acquisition and provision of capital resources	−		−		−		−		−		−	
(sub-total 2)	‖		‖		‖		‖		‖		‖	
Extraordinary												
(sub-total 3)												
Total cash flows for the period (1 + 2 + 3)	±	±	±	±	±	±	±	±	±	±	±	±
Cash retained b/f	+		+		+		+		+		+	
Cash available	±		±		±		±		±		±	
Distributions by investors												
Recurrent (by class)	−		−		−		−		−		−	
Non-recurrent (by class)	−		−		−		−		−		−	
Cash retained c/f	±		±		±		±		±		±	‖

Table 4.2 Cash flow statement for a company with three principal trading activities

	19X0		19X1		19X2		19X3		19X4		19X5	
	F	A	F	A	F	A	P	F	P	F	F	
Division A												
Net variable trading inflow	±	±	±	±	±	±	±	±	±	±	±	±
Less: Fixed trading outflow	−	−	−	−	−	−	−	−	−	−	−	−
(sub-total 1)												
Division B												
Net variable trading inflow	±	±	±	±	±	±	±	±	±	±	±	±
Less: Fixed trading outflow	−	−	−	−	−	−	−	−	−	−	−	−
(sub-total 2)												
Division C												
Net variable trading inflow	±	±	±	±	±	±	±	±	±	±	±	±
Less: Fixed trading outflow	−	−	−	−	−	−	−	−	−	−	−	−
(sub-total 3)												
Net trading inflow before tax and fixed outflows common to all trading (1 + 2 + 3)	±	±	±	±	±	±	±	±	±	±	±	±
Less: Fixed outflows common to all trading	−	−	−	−	−	−	−	−	−	−	−	−
Net trading inflow before tax	±	±	±	±	±	±	±	±	±	±	±	±

management's view of the company's future prospects, their plans for the future and related matters. It has been argued that the disclosure of company forecasts of future profits or cash flows would be very advantageous to investors. The advantages which are perceived as attached to the disclosure of company forecasts are as follows:

(a) Since investment decisions by management are made in the context of the expectations which they hold of the profitability of future operations, the disclosure of their forecasts would represent the essential information needed by investors.

(b) The disclosure of company forecasts would provide investors with the benefit of management's knowledge of company operations, and its views of the future outlook for such operations. Market efficiency does not imply clairvoyance. Therefore, since much information concerning a company's future prospects and plans is not made public, it may be assumed not to be impounded already in share prices. Therefore, it may be argued that the publication of company forecasts would result in more efficient share prices. Such share prices would reflect more correctly the future prospects of the company, and the value of the company's shares. Patell (1976) examined the reaction of share prices to the voluntary disclosure of forecasts of annual earnings per share by 336 companies, and found that, on average, there was a significant share price reaction in the week when forecasts were disclosed.

(c) The public disclosure of information relevant to investors' needs might help prevent abnormal returns accruing to privileged individuals having access to inside information.

(d) The disclosure of corporate plans would provide investors with a better basis for evaluating managerial performance.

Disadvantages of publishing company forecasts

Numerous objections have been made to the proposition that forecasts should be published to investors. The four major objections are as follows:

(a) forecasts are uncertain and may mislead investors;
(b) forecasts may be manipulated by unscrupulous managers;
(c) forecasts are difficult to audit;
(d) forecasts made known to competitors may be harmful to the interests of the enterprise, and therefore to those of its investors.

(a) It is true, of course, that forecasts are uncertain. This uncertainty stems from the variety of elements incorporated in forecasts which are themselves uncertain. However, this does not render forecasts valueless. Thus, budgetary control implies the necessity of forecasting, as do management decisions regarding production levels, manning levels, product development and many other factors relating to business life. Clearly, forecasts made and used within the firm by management are of critical importance to the quality of decision making. Such forecasts will be regarded as reliable in this use to the extent that they are carefully prepared. Their quality will be higher than those which are attempted by outsiders. Indeed, it is for this reason that the publication of profit projections has been practiced for more than a decade in prospectuses and in circulars issued during the course of mergers and takeovers. It follows that the real question at issue is not whether forecasts are sufficiently reliable in an absolute sense, but whether users of financial reports are likely to find such reports more useful if accompanied by forecasts. As the Trueblood Report stated, 'the important consideration is not the accuracy of management forecasts themselves, but rather the relative accuracy of users' predictions with and without forecasts in financial statements.'

(b) It is also true that forecasts may be manipulated by unscrupulous management. However, if management were made accountable by the publication of the results obtained with the forecasts which had been published previously, the need to explain subsequently any material difference between forecasts and results would restrain any tendency to making wild forecasts.

(c) It may also be true that forecasts are more difficult to audit than actual results. Auditors have been reluctant to get involved in the audit of forecasts, and the position of auditors as regards forecasts is confused, particularly in the U.S.A. where the danger of legal action against auditors is considerably greater than in the United Kingdom. The resistance of the accounting profession on reporting forecasts has diminished since the publication of the City Code and the Institute of Chartered Accountants' statement on the matter.

> 'The requirement to report publicly was initially accepted with reluctance at the insistence of the Panel. However, when asked if they would report publicly, if it were not for the Panel, an overwhelming number of accountants said 'yes', they would report publicly. Many pointed out that they had been reporting privately on profit forecasts for some time and they felt that public reporting was not that different.' (Adelburg, 1976.)

The problem of verifying audits is a very controversial subject. It could be argued that although the accountant should have knowledge of forecasting techniques, it does not follow that he should be an expert in this field. Moreover, forecasting is not simply a matter of handling techniques: it requires an expert knowledge of the industry and the markets in which the firm is located. Tomkins (1969) has suggested that a solution to this difficulty lies in the accountant obtaining a second opinion on forecasts from individuals other than the company's officials. Experts in the field of business forecasting outside the firm could be employed to provide such second opinions. Consequently, the auditor would not be legally liable for the forecasts and would be responsible merely for verifying the opinions of the experts concerned.

The problem of verification becomes more complex when forecasts covering several years are involved. Forecasts for the year immediately ahead merely provide an extended view of current achievements. Ideally, investors would need to be provided with forecasts covering a longer period. There would seem to be no reason why five-year rolling forecasts should not be adopted as a framework for disclosure, thereby enabling investors to appraise current performance and plans in relation to the firm's attainment of long-term goals. It would be difficult, however, to propose standard procedures which would ensure the required objectivity for audit purposes, for in the face of an increasing time-span, there could be a very wide divergence of opinion between management and expert forecasters of the forecasts formulated for disclosure purposes. For this reason, some writers have argued that there is little point in verifying these forecasts (Briston and Fawthrop, 1971).

(d) The argument that the disclosure of forecasts to competitors would be harmful to the interests of the enterprise and its shareholders is the same argument which has been advanced for years against the increased disclosure requirements of the Companies Acts, the Stock Exchange and the Statements of Standard Accounting Practice. Forecasts of profits are currently made public during the course of a takeover or merger or issue of shares, when they are thought presumably to do more good than harm. If forecasts were mandatory for all comparable companies, it is difficult to see how an unfair advantage could be gained by a competitor. The only user likely to gain from having such information is the one who is better able to compare and evaluate the prospects of different firms.

The Sandilands Committee considered the case for cash flow forecasting and concluded:

'We doubt whether such a proposal is practicable, at least in the foreseeable future. Many companies by the nature of their business would find it difficult to forecast their cash requirements with sufficient accuracy. Moreover, the proposal would require companies to disclose forecasts of their future position which could be damaging to their prospects. In general, we do not think it reasonable or practicable to require predictions about future events to be disclosed as part of a company's published accounts . . . We doubt whether such a fundamental change would be acceptable to British companies at the present time.'

In making this statement, the Sandilands Committee revealed the attachment to sentiment which afflicts the question of financial reporting. Each sentence in the above paragraph is a denial of fundamental points which we have examined in this part. To assert that firms are unable to make sufficiently accurate forecasts of their cash requirements is to deny the usefulness and, indeed, existence of cash budgeting as a central tool of management. To proceed to assert, by implication, that firms do make cash forecasts but their disclosure would be damaging to their interest exposes the weakness of the first assertion, and is a plea for secrecy and for discrimination in information supply. The third assertion, that it would not be reasonable or practicable to require predictions to be disclosed, is a rejection of our basic premise—that the relevance of financial reports is to be found in information which allows predictions to be made about future events.

Cash flow versus income reporting

Cash flow statements have many advantages over traditional financial reports based on income statements and balance sheets.

(a) Cash is more objective than income, since its measurement is free of subjective valuations. It is also more easily verified than historical cost or current value accounting measurements for receipts and disbursements are evidenced by means of source documents.

(b) The problem associated with distinctions between capital, revenue, income and expenditure, or of allocations of costs between a series of arbitrary time periods, do not arise under cash flow accounting. Hence, although forecasts of either cash flows or of income flows are subject to uncertainty, cash flow forecasts are more objective than forecasts of income flows.

(c) Comparability between firms is enhanced since a common measure is applied, that is, cash, to all the elements of the financial report. The problem of uniformity which we discussed in Chapter 8, therefore, disappears.

(d) Cash is crucial to the survival and progress of an enterprise. The problem of solvency is necessarily tied to the availability of cash to meet current liabilities, whereas conventional accounting treats the problem of solvency as of secondary importance by focusing primarily on income measurement. Many enterprises have shown book profits up to the day when a liquidator has been appointed, and equally, many enterprises have survived despite accounting losses owing to the availability of cash.

Despite the advantages of cash flow over income measures the cash flow statement is usually viewed as a complementary statement rather than a replacement for the income statement. Although income determination is fraught with limitations, income is still accepted to be the primary measure of enterprise performance. At the present time a great deal of evidence points to the fact the management, auditors and users are essentially income oriented (Sprouse, 1978). For this reason the FASB's Concepts No. 1 states that users' 'interest in an enterprise's future cash flows and its ability to generate favourable cash flows leads primarily to an interest in information about its earnings'. Given this orientation towards income we advocate more comprehensive disclosures that would permit individual users of financial statements to make their own measure of income. This kind of approach is supported by the empirical research discussed in the previous chapter which illustrates the usefulness of additional disclosures to the sophisticated investors.

Segment reporting

The ideal method of reporting discussed earlier on page 366 suggested that cash flow forecasts for all the segments of the enterprise should be made available to external users. Advocates of segment reporting argue that the separate segments of an enterprise are usually subject to different economic conditions, different degrees of risk and exhibit different growth rates. A single, all-inclusive report tends to average out these differences, thereby obscuring them. Accordingly, they argue that segment reporting would enable users of financial reports to make better decisions.

Progress towards segment reporting has already occurred in the United Kingdom, where the Companies Act, 1967 requires the disclosure of:

(a) the principal activities of the company and its subsidiaries and any significant changes in such activities during the year; and
(b) with certain exceptions, an analysis of the turnover and profit or loss

before taxation of the company or group between what are, in the opinion of the directors, substantially different classes of business.

There has been a wide variation in the manner in which these disclosure requirements have been interpreted. A significant number of companies do not appear to have complied with the statutory requirements mentioned above.

The ideal method of reporting discussed earlier (p. 366), which was suggested to be a basis for formulating a normative definition of the investor's information needs, does require segmental cash flow forecasts. Such a requirement becomes increasingly relevant when, as a result of diversification, many companies have major products and markets which differ with respect to profitability, growth potential and risk. These segments are likely to be affected differently by changes in general economic conditions, as well as changes in the conditions affecting industry sectors or regions. Consequently, the consolidation of the operating results of diversified segments undermines the reliability of consolidated financial reports for forecasting future income.

The main argument against segment reporting is that a diversified enterprise is, in effect, one business as far as the investor is concerned. Since the investor cannot differentiate one segment of the business from another in respect of the investment he makes in the company's shares, financial reporting should be restricted to providing him with a view of the enterprise as one unit. However, according to Mautz (1968), 'he (the investor) cannot foresee the future of a company if he has no information respecting significant parts which may be moving in directions opposite to that of the total company.'

In the United States, FSAB Statement No. 14 'Financial Reporting for Segments of a Business Enterprise' issued in 1976 required the disclosure of information about enterprise operations in different industries, foreign operations and export sales and major customers. The purpose of such disclosures was an intention to 'assist financial statement users in analysing and understanding the enterprise's financial statements by permitting better assessments of the enterprise's past performance and future prospects.'

Other aspects of the disclosure problem

Interim financial reporting

Interim financial reports provide financial information for a period of less than one year. In the United Kingdom quoted companies have to deliver a six-monthly report of profitability and financial position to their shareholders. In the United States the disclosure requirement is on a quarterly basis. Interim reports are not audited.

One normative characteristic of the process of reporting to users discussed previously in this chapter was that of timeliness. The aim of interim reports is to provide users with more timely information about companies so as to alleviate the disadvantages of the significant time lag between annual reports. Research findings indicate that interim financial reports play an important role in security investment decisions. Changes in share prices, following the disclosure of quarterly earnings are greater than average share price changes during the year (Foster, 1977).

The limitations which circumstances impose on the level of precision attainable in assigning the results of a company's operations to annual periods are severe. The limitations are even more severe when we undertake to assign results to shorter accounting periods. However, American experience indicates that a more extensive use of interim reports in the United Kingdom would enhance the predictability of company reports. Whether interim financial reports should be audited is a very controversial subject. At the present time it is doubtful that the benefits to investors would justify the cost to the reporting companies.

Reporting cost details

As we shall see in Part 5, operating costs fall into categories which behave quite differently under changing volumes of business. Variable costs tend to vary in direct proportion to production levels; programmed costs are budgeted annually in corporate plans, for example advertising and research and development costs; long-run fixed costs change little in total with changes in output.

Some knowledge of a company's cost structure is needed by the investor if reliable forecasts are to be made which take account of the impact of changing output levels on profits. The ability of investors to make such forecasts is impeded by the omission in financial reports of information about a company's cost structure. This problem will be examined further in Part 5, where the effects of SSAP 9 'Stocks and Work in Progress' on investment decisions will be discussed.

Reporting realizable values

The ideal method of reporting mentioned earlier also suggested that estimates of the realizable values of assets should be disclosed. According to the Trueblood Report, 'of primary importance for predicting the risk associated with the firm's cash flows (but also for assessing returns) is the degree of flexibility and manoeuvrability that the management possesses in employing its resources.'

One alternative way of using a firm's resources is to dispose of them. This alternative may be quantified by using market exit values. Clearly, the more convertible into cash are the firm's resources and the greater the realizable value of these resources, the greater is the degree of flexibility and manoeuvrability that management has over the employment of resources. If the market exit values are small, the alternative uses of resources appears to be more restricted. Consequently, the utilization of resources inside the firm will be highly dependent on the marketability of the specific assets of the enterprise.

Reporting the value added

There has been much discussion in the United Kingdom and elsewhere in Europe of the desirability of interpreting enterprise results not in terms of profits but in terms of the value added by the enterprise itself to the resources acquired in transforming those resources into the final product. Value added financial reporting was discussed in the Corporate Report (1975), which suggested that such reports should include a value-added statement.

The concept of 'value added' is relatively easy to understand. It defines the income accruing to the enterprise after payments to external parties for goods and services supplied have been taken into account. It represents the value added to goods and services acquired by the enterprise, which results from the efforts of its own management and employees. In effect, the value added defines the income accruing to the enterprise which will be distributed among those who are involved in its activities as employees and shareholders. An example of a value-added statement given in the Corporate Report showed the following details:

Statement of added value

	£m.	19X0 £m.	£m.	19X1 £m.
Revenue		90.0		100.0
Materials and services acquired		55.0		60.0
Value added		35.0		40.0
Applied as follows:				
To employees		27.0		30.0
To pay suppliers of capital interest on loans	0.9		1.0	
Dividends to shareholders	0.8	1.7	1.0	2.0
To pay Government		3.3		4.0
To provide for maintenance and expansion of assets				
Depreciation	0.9		1.0	
Retained profits	2.1	3.0	3.0	4.0
Value added		35.0		40.0

The value-added statement represents a move in a new and different direction for financial accounting. Over the past decade accountants have given much attention to the question, 'How should we measure income?' The value-added statement asks a different question: 'Whose income should we measure?' Instead of restricting ourselves to reporting the shareholders' income we are reporting the income which has been earned for the whole team of co-operating groups which contribute to the company's performance. The value-added statement is directly relevant to the information needs of all parties with an interest in the company. They are all interested in the wealth the company creates, in how the wealth is shared and in productivity (Morley, 1979). The role of value added in pay bargaining is discussed in Chapter 24.

The importance of educating users of financial reports

From the foregoing discussion of the problem of defining users' needs as a pre-condition to developing a normative theory of financial reporting, it is clearly important that a successful resolution of this problem lies in part in educating users of financial reports. This need is urgent in two respects. First, sophisticated decision makers know the nature of the information which is required. This perception is necessary to the definition of the information input to the decision models used. Second, educated users of financial reports know how to use the information which they contain. According to Sterling (1970), 'the accounting profession ought to devote some of its efforts and resources to the education of the receivers. The profession ought to tell the receivers which decision theories are correct and then supply the data specified by those theories.'

Summary

The purpose of this chapter has been to examine the problems implicit in providing investors with financial reports relevant to their needs. The difficulty in defining these needs by empirical research methods was revealed, and it was suggested that an alternative approach to this problem lay in formulating a normative theory of reporting to investors which could be based on the economics of decision making. A discussion of this suggestion revealed the importance of cash flows to investors, and the need to provide them with financial reports containing details of cash flows. Evidently, the most relevant information is that which is addressed to the future, and in this sense, the publication of cash flow forecasts would seem to meet investors' needs.

Various aspects of the problem of disclosing information to investors were considered, in particular the disclosure of company forecasts, segment reporting, and the disclosure of cost details and realizable values of assets.

References

1. Accounting Standards Committee. *The Corporate Report*, pp. 28–9, London, 1975.
2. Adelburg, A. H. 'Forecasting and the US dilemma', *Accountancy*, October, 1976.
3. A.A.A. *A Statement of Basic Accounting Theory*, 1966.
4. A.A.A. 'An evaluation of external reporting practices—a report of the 1966–1968 Committee on External Reporting', *The Accounting Review*, Supplement to Vol. 44, 1969.
5. A.I.C.P.A. 'Report of the Study Group on Objectives of Financial Reporting', *The Trueblood Report*, New York, 1973.
6. Arnold, J. & Hope, A. 'Reporting business performance', *Accounting and Business Research*, Spring, 1975.
7. Briston, R. J. & Fawthrop, R. A. 'Accounting principles and investor protection', *Journal of Business Finance*, Summer, 1971.
8. Foster, G. 'Quarterly Accounting Data: Time-series properties and predictive ability results', *The Accounting Review*, January, 1977.

9. Lee, T. A. 'A case for cash-flow reporting', *Journal of Business Finance*, Summer, 1972.
10. Macdonald, G., Bird, P. & Climo, T. Statements of Objectives and Standard Practice in Financial Reporting, Accountancy Age.
11. Mautz, R. K. *Financial Reporting by Diversified Companies*, p. 95, Financial Executives Research Foundation, New York, 1968.
12. Morley, M. F. 'The value added statement in Britain', *The Accounting Review*, July, 1979.
13. Patell, J. M. 'Corporate forecasts of earnings per share and stock price behaviour: empirical tests', *Journal of Accounting Research*, Autumn, 1976.
14. Revsine, L. *Replacement Cost Accounting*, pp. 33, 34, Prentice-Hall, 1973.
15. The Sandilands Report. *Report of the Inflation Accounting Committee*, p. 62, HMSO Cmd 6225, 1975.
16. Sprouse, R. T. 'The importance of earnings in the conceptual framework', *Journal of Accountancy*, January, 1978.
17. Sterling, R. R. 'Theory construction and verification', *The Accounting Review*, July, 1970.
18. Tomkins, C. 'The development of relevant published accounting reports', *Accountancy*, November, 1969.

Questions

1. What normative characteristics for financial reporting have been suggested?
2. What information should be provided in order to meet the needs of the investor's normative model?
3. What are the advantages and disadvantages of publishing company forecasts?
4. How does cash flow reporting compare with income reporting?
5. What are the advantages which accrue from value-added statements?

24 Reporting to employees

Traditionally, the focal point of the literature of both accounting and economics has been the needs and the viewpoints of investors. Indeed, the concept of financial management and the theories with which it is associated is founded on the premise that the 'maximization of shareholders' wealth is an appropriate guide for how the firm should act' (van Horne, 1977). Equally accounting research which has attempted to assess the importance and relevance of financial reports to decision makers has been confined largely to the decisions of investors and creditors.

The changing social environment has been concerned with the social imbalance between those having wealth and controlling society through the influence of wealth, and those whose political influence in numerical terms has secured the return of governments committed to reforms and the gradual redistribution of wealth.

In effect, this imbalance is reflected in the significance attached to the interests of investors in the literature of accounting and a major part of research in this field. The indications are that the process of redressing this imbalance has been engaged. Developments in reporting to employees in recent years is evidence of progress in recognizing the importance of employees in the activities of business enterprises. These developments have occurred as a result both of changes in social attitudes and changes in the law.

The purpose of this chapter is to analyse the development of financial reporting to employees in the context of their special interests as users of financial information.

Investor and employee reporting compared

Having already discussed the information needs of investors as users of financial reports, it is interesting to begin the analysis of the information needs of employees by establishing the extent to which they require similar information. The following comparison between the needs of investors and employees may be made:

(1) In both cases, it is necessary to focus upon their needs as users rather than upon their wants. In this respect, the construction of a normative theory of financial reporting to employees is required to overcome the problems of theory construction mentioned earlier in Chapter 23.

(2) The information needs of employees are more complex than those of investors, because employees require additional information on matters of special interest, for example matters of safety. At the same time, the

information deemed in Chapter 23 to be relevant to investors is also relevant to employees. In this sense, both employees and investors are interested in cash flow forecasts.

(3) In both cases, the disclosure of information has been regulated by law. The Companies Acts of 1948 and 1976 prescribe the minimum level of information which should be disclosed to shareholders. The Employment Protection Act (1975) places an obligation on employers to disclose information to trade unions for the purpose of collective bargaining.

(4) In both cases, traditional financial reports in the form of income statements, balance sheets and funds flow statements have limited usefulness. If anything, the timing, presentation and content of corporate financial reports are less relevant to the needs of employees than they are to investors. Thus, these reports do not deal with matters of importance to employees, such as explanations of reductions in the amount of overtime pay and the effects of streamlining the product range.

(5) The impact of management decisions falls more obviously and directly on employees than on investors. A shareholder who dislikes current management policy has the opportunity to sell his shares. An employee does not have such a simple choice, for he may find it difficult to transfer his labour elsewhere.

(6) The role of the auditor has been traditionally to protect the interests of shareholders by ensuring that the financial reports present a true and fair view. The presentation of information to employees does not require auditing in the same sense. Reports to employees are devised and presented by management, and consequently may be discredited. Norkett (1977) noted that 'one problem which recently arose with employee accounts was when an accountant genuinely tried to simplify the presentation and omitted some figures shown in the accounts. The difference was noticed by an employee representative, and the employee accounts were subsequently dismissed as a management con-trick.'

(7) One important difference between investors and employees in the area of financial reporting lies in the historical background to the different treatment accorded to these two groups. Financial reporting to investors originated in the 19th century, whereas there was very little interest in reporting to employees before 1970.

Financial reporting to employees

The accountant has been involved in the process of reporting to employees in two distinct ways:

(1) direct reporting to employees in the form of employee accounts;
(2) reporting as part of the process of collective bargaining.

Direct reporting

Section 57 of the Industrial Relations Act, 1971 imposed a statutory obligation on firms employing more than 350 persons to report directly to employees by means of an annual written statement. When the Industrial Relations Act, 1971 was repealed, and the Trade Union and Labour Relations Act, 1974 was enacted, neither that Act nor the Trade Union and Labour Relations Amendment Act, 1976 re-enacted the obligation to report to employees. At the moment, therefore, there exists no legal obligation of firms to report to employees directly. Nevertheless, the interest in some form of reporting to employees remains very much alive, and the Department of Trade issued in 1976 a preliminary consultative document 'The Aims and Scope of Company Reports', which suggested re-inforcing and extending the 'corporate report' proposals for employee reports.

Scope of employee reports

The purpose of employee reports is to inform employees in the context of a general communicative and consultative philosophy of the corporate environment in which they work. For example, there is a need to inform employees and correct any misunderstanding about the necessity for company profits and for explanations of the manner in which they are applied. Many companies have embarked upon the practice of informing employees about matters of which management believes they should be aware (Hilton, 1978).

The emphasis in employee reports is on making information visually attractive and comprehensible. A general problem is the low level of interest of employees in company affairs, and to overcome apathy, colours, diagrams and cartoons are used. Financial information is shown in the form of bar charts, cakes or other diagrams which are easily understood. In view of the employee's interest in the performance of his own unit, there is a strong need for segment reporting.

Employee reports are not suitable for the purpose of wage negotiations. It is unlikely, for example, that wage negotiations will occur near the release of year-end financial information.

Advantages of employee reports

The main aim of reporting directly to employees is to promote goal congruence by explaining how the interests and efforts of employees relate to those of the firm. The intention is to improve communications and the employees' understanding of the manner in which the firm is being managed in the interests of all participants. For example, employees are more likely to accept technological change if direct reporting can create a climate of opinion in which the interests of employees are identified with those of management.

Another aim of reporting directly to employees is to improve public relations. Management realizes that employee reports have effects which extend beyond the firm. Employee reports are read by persons outside the firm, by members of the employee's family, and friends. They not only have public relations implications, but also may be helpful in the recruitment of personnel.

Disadvantages of employee reports

Two major disadvantages affect employee reports. First, as they are prepared by management for employees, they may be perceived by employees as being slanted towards giving employees only what the management wishes them to know. For this reason, employee reports may not be seen by employees as providing them with information directly relevant to their needs. Second, the desire to simplify employee reports so as to make them readily understandable may lead to misleading generalizations.

Reporting for collective bargaining

In the past, the release of information for collective bargaining purposes has depended on the strengths and abilities of the parties involved in the collective bargaining process. The Employment Protection Act, 1975 altered this situation radically by placing a general duty on employers to disclose information for collective bargaining purposes that is both:

(1) information without which the trade union representatives would be, to a material extent, impeded in carrying on with such collective bargaining;

(2) information which would be in accordance with good industrial relations practice for the employers to disclose to trade union representatives for the purpose of collective bargaining.

Three views on disclosure for collective bargaining

The Employment Protection Act, 1975 did not specify the information which should be disclosed to trade unions. It was left to the Advisory Conciliation and Arbitration Service to give guidelines on this matter.

The first view on disclosure may be found in the Advisory Conciliation and Arbitration Service's Code of Practice (1977) which, whilst not more specific than others who had tried to specify guidelines for information disclosure, did state that the information disclosed should be relevant to matters under negotiation. The Code of Practice provides a list of 'information relating to the undertaking which could be relevant in certain collective bargaining situations'. The main heads of information listed were: pay and benefits, conditions of service, manpower, performance and financial. The Code of Practice stated that 'these examples are not intended to represent a checklist of information that should be provided for all negotiations. Nor are they meant to be an exhaustive list of the types of information, as other items may be relevant in particular negotiations.' The Code of Practice explained restrictions on the general duty to disclose information. These restrictions recognized the sensitive nature of some information, such as cost information on individual products, details of investment plans and details of pricing and marketing. Nevertheless, according to the Code of Practice, it is for the employer to prove that 'substantial injury' to the employer will occur if certain information is disclosed. Furthermore, the cost of providing information should not be disproportionately high in relation to its importance, and the disclosure of information should not be against the national interest. The Code of Practice suggested that a joint arrangement for the disclosure of information for collective bargaining be negotiated, as a means of pre-empting the necessity for employers to prove that disclosure might be substantially injurious.

The second view on disclosure for collective bargaining may be found in a booklet issued by the Confederation of British Industries in 1975 entitled 'The Provision of Information to Employees'. This booklet stressed the need for companies to provide employees with 'as much information as is relevant to their needs and wishes and which will assist them to identify with their company, paying due regard to constraints arising out of competitive requirements and confidentiality'. The booklet listed the type of information which could be provided under a number of headings called 'checklists', for example, information about the company as a whole, the organization of the company, finance, competitive situation and productivity, plans and prospects, and information relevant to employment.

The third view on disclosure is to be found in a number of recommended guidelines issued by the Trade Union Congress in a document in 1974 entitled 'Industrial Democracy'. This document identified information relating to collective bargaining as including manpower, earnings, costs, sources of revenue, directors' renumeration, performance indicators and the worth of the company.

The main limitations of these three sets of views on information disclosure is that they are in the form of checklists or guidelines giving lists of headings randomly brought together. They do not reflect a well-thought-out analysis of the information needs of users based on the normative approach to the construction of a theory of reporting to trade unions and employees, the applicability and merits of which were discussed earlier in Chapter 23. These three views reflect no considered analysis of the normative decision models which those engaged in collective bargaining should use. On the contrary, they reflect very generalized views of beliefs about the information which such users wish to have available.

A normative theory of pay-bargaining information

The construction of a normative theory of financial reporting relevant to pay-bargaining between employers and employees and their representatives ought to be based on the criteria suggested in Chapter 23. It will be recalled that these criteria, based on the Corporate Report, required information to be relevant, understandable, reliable, complete, objective, timely and comparable. The discussion of these criteria in Chapter 23 identified relevance as the most important criterion, and on the basis of that assumption proceeded to identify cash flows to investors as the most relevant information for the decisions which investors ought to make. Using the same type of analogy, the information which may be assumed to be most relevant to pay-bargaining is related to two factors:

(1) the minimum acceptable settlement which is based on considerations of equity, and is made up of a combination of factors including the cost of living, comparability with other industries and value-added;

(2) the ability to pay, which determines whether the firm is in a position to afford to meet a pay claim without endangering profitability (Foley and Maunders, 1977).

The minimum acceptable settlement

The elements making up the minimum acceptable settlement may be analysed in more detail.

(1) *The cost of living.* The need to take account of expected inflation rather than experienced inflation in assessing changes in the cost of living for pay-bargaining purposes has been recognized in recent times when accelerating price rises occurred. Trade union negotiators have been conscious of the need to maintain living standards, and for this reason have attached significance to the maintenance of living standards in real terms. To this end, cost of living data has been used in pay-bargaining to show that money wages and earnings have failed to keep up with the real cost of living, and that added compensation is required to regain lost ground.

(2) *Comparability.* Trade union negotiators make use of two classes of information when engaged in pay-bargaining—external and internal wage data. When negotiations are being conducted at a national level, that is, for all the divisions and plant of the same company or industry, external wage data relating to pay conditions existing in other companies or industries is important in establishing pay comparability. When negotiations are being conducted at a plant level, wage data relating to the wage policy of the entire company or industry is important in establishing pay comparability at the plant level. It follows that the process of pay-bargaining might be improved considerably if more data on the relative earnings of workers were available, particularly on a company basis.

(3) *Value added.* Given the sensitivity attaching to the term 'profit', the Corporate Report (1975) suggested that 'the simplest and most immediate way of putting profit into proper perspective vis-à-vis the whole enterprise as a collective effort by capital, management and employees is by the presentation of a statement of value added'.

Many companies are introducing value-added concepts into wage incentive schemes in order to improve productivity. The first step is to agree a target for the ratio of wages to value added. If performance exceeds this percentage a bonus will be payable, but if performance falls short of the target there will be no bonus and the deficit will be carried forward to reduce any future bonuses. The process of agreeing on the appropriate percentage which ought to accrue to employees is an important aspect of pay bargaining.

The ability to pay

The ability of the firm to meet a pay claim is defined as the distributable operating cash flows less the minimum required by those who have provided the capital. It has been argued that 'all terms and conditions established by collective bargaining are limited by the employer's ability to pay. That capacity is the controlling fact on all the firm's contracts including its union agreements. The union executive needs this basic information as a guide to all proposals.' (Brubaker et al., 1949.)

In the context of the firm's ability to pay, the reliability of future cash flow projections becomes very important. For this reason, cash flow statements containing comparisons of actual cash flows with forecasted cash flows and explanations of deviations between these sets of figures would be as relevant to pay-bargaining as they were seen in Chapter 23 to be relevant to the needs of investors.

Productivity data is also an important aspect of the definition of the firm's ability to pay. Management may be amenable to arguments that link pay increases to increases in productivity, for pay increases may be absorbed by increased productivity without affecting the firm's pricing policy. The government also tends to favour pay agreements based on productivity increases, for they are more likely to result in non-inflationary pay settlements. One crucial problem revolves around measuring productivity changes. For example, there are classes of employees in respect of whose activity the notion of productivity is difficult to express in numbers. This is true of personnel in research and development departments.

The cost structure of the firm is another factor which affects the firm's ability to pay. If a plant operates at a relatively low breakeven point, its ability to pay more will be greater at levels of output which exceed the breakeven point. The plant which has a relatively high breakeven point will have its ability to pay more restricted by the much longer range of output. The importance of the cost structure is discussed in detail in Part 5.

Advantage of disclosure in collective bargaining

The main advantage of disclosing information of the type listed above in the collective bargaining process is that it makes that process more rational. According to the Report of the Commission on Industrial Relations 1974, 'Trade Unions claim that certain advantages might result from improved disclosure of information—a speeding of the bargaining process because information is readily available, a greater likelihood of longer term wage deals, and an increased chance of the employer obtaining greater co-operation from his employees.'

Disadvantages of disclosure in collective bargaining

It is argued that trade union negotiators, particularly shop stewards, lack the necessary level of competence in financial accounting to understand the implications of financial reports used in pay-bargaining. According to Lyall (1975), 'unless negotiators are in a position to be able to understand fully the implications of any information which may be given, it is unlikely that a policy of greater disclosure on information will have the desired effect on improving industrial bargaining'. However, it may also be suggested that, in itself, this is not an argument against disclosure, but an argument for improving the financial knowledge of trade union negotiators.

A second argument against disclosure is that it may increase the bargaining strength of trade unions to the detriment of the long-term interests of the firm. However, trade unionists are only able to take a long-sighted view in wage negotiations if they are presented with all the relevant information.

A further argument against disclosure is that important information may be revealed during collective bargaining which could be harmful to the firm's negotiating position if leaked outside the firm. It seems, however, that the high level of disclosure which has existed in West Germany for many years in this context has not been associated with a problem of breaches in confidentiality.

Disclosure in collective bargaining and management style

Many of the arguments which revolve around the issue of the disclosure of information in pay-bargaining are really issues about management style. It is evident that the successful communication of information during pay-bargaining hinges to some extent on management–union relationships. According to the White Paper on Industrial Democracy (1978),

'People in industry have different interests, and differ about objectives and how they should be achieved. But part of the conflict is due to poor communication, lack of information and lack of trust. One way to change this is to create a framework for employees and their representatives to join in those corporate decisions which affect them and so encourage them to do so. Where decisions are mutually agreed both sides of industry must then share responsibility for them.'

Summary

The purpose of this chapter has been to address the problem of reporting to employees as users of financial reports. Traditionally, the interests of investors have been recognized as paramount both in terms of Company Law and in terms of accounting theory. Changes in the social environment and in political attitudes have begun to emphasize the importance of employees. This process may be seen in the context of the movement towards participation in decision making which has featured largely in the literature of management science, and in the discussion of the concept of industrial democracy which has excited the imagination of progressive elements in Western European countries.

The comparison between investors and employees as users of financial reports indicates a similarity of needs for information for decision making. Financial reporting to employees currently occurs at two levels. First, direct reporting by management to employees as part of the process of good staff/employees relations. Second, information disclosure in the course of pay-bargaining.

It was seen that there exists a need for a normative theory of pay-bargaining information, similar in its construction to that required for investors as users, which would be directed to establishing the information which those engaged in pay-bargaining negotiations require to make efficient decisions.

References

1. Accounting Standards Committee. *The Corporate Report*, London, 1975.
2. Advisory Conciliation and Arbitration Service. *Disclosure of Information to Trade Unions for Collective Bargaining Purposes,* 1977.
3. Brubaker, O. *et al.* 'What kind of information do unions want in financial statements?' *Journal of Accountancy*, May, 1949.
4. Confederation of British Industries. *Guidelines for Action—The Provision of Information to Employees*, 1975.
5. Foley, B. J. & Maunders, K. T. *Accounting Information Disclosure and Collective Bargaining*, Macmillan, 1977.
6. Hilton, H. *Employee Reports—How to Communicate Financial Information*, Woodhead Faulkner, 1978.
7. HMSO. *Industrial Democracy*, White Paper, May, 1978.
8. Lyall, D. 'Opening the books to the workers', *Accountancy*, February, 1975.
9. Norkett, P. 'Stepping into a dangerous minefield', *Accountants Weekly*, 22 July, 1977.
10. *Report of the Committee of Inquiry on Industrial Democracy* (Bullock Report), HMSO Cmd 6706, 1977.
11. *The Future of Company Reports*, HMSO Cmd 6888, 1977.
12. Van Horne, J. C. *Financial Management and Policy*, 4th ed., Prentice-Hall, 1977.

Questions

1. How do the needs of employees for financial information compare with those of investors?
2. What are the advantages and disadvantages of direct reporting to employees?
3. What elements make up the minimum acceptable settlement?
4. What are the problems in estimating ability to pay?
5. What are the advantages and disadvantages of collective bargaining?

25 Social responsibility accounting

We considered in Chapter 2 the several groups having vested interests in business organizations, with a view to determining the scope of the accounting problem, defined as the provision of information for making economic decisions having welfare implications. The review of the role of theory in accounting, conducted in Chapter 3, provided justification for approaching the definition of users' information needs by means of a normative specific approach to constructing theories about such users' needs. Accordingly, we were able to discuss the provision of information for shareholders, investors and employees in Chapters 23 and 24 by attempting to stipulate the information which such groups ought to be using in making economic decisions. In effect, we suggested that the needs of investors emphasized cash-flow expectations in line with the hypothesis that investors were primarily concerned with maximizing their own welfare. Equally, we examined the information needs of employees in the same context, and came to the conclusion that such information as they should require related to matters affecting their welfare as a specific group of individuals.

The concept of social responsibility accounting raises initial problems of defining not only the users of such information, but their objectives in receiving such information. In effect, the concept of corporate social responsibility, which underlies the debate about social responsibility accounting, assumes that there exists a theory about the social role of business firms in modern society. Clearly, such a theory not only explains the public interest in the role of business in society, but would seek to monitor and influence the behaviour of forms in accordance with the value judgements on which such a theory might be considered to be founded.

In a very precise sense, the law exists as an institution having the objective of embodying and expressing those value judgements by which behaviour is to be regulated. In accordance with many Acts of Parliament and legal precedents, the accountability of business firms for matters affecting the social good is strictly laid down and enforced. For example, firms are liable at law for various offences in relation to harmful acts, such as allowing the escape of dangerous substances, failing to provide adequate safety precautions for employees etc. Equally, the law provides very clear rules for the manner in which the accountability of business firms to investors and employees is to be met.

The concept of corporate social responsibility extends beyond notions embodied in current law. Essentialy, it represents an emerging debate having its source in political and social theory. In its present state of evolution, there is very real controversy in the following critical areas:

(a) the nature of corporate social responsibility

(b) the scope of corporate social responsibility;
(c) the objectives to which accounting information might be directed;
(d) the manner in which information is to be reported.

In this chapter, we examine the problems stipulated above and review the development of social responsibility accounting. As we shall see, whilst there appears to be a great deal of uncertainty about the problems which we have indicated, business firms and governments have already committed them-selves to this enlarged concept of business accountability.

The nature of corporate social responsibility

When considering the information needs of investors and employees in Chapters 23 and 24 respectively, the assumptions underlying the normative decision models of those users were based on notions of economic efficiency expressed in terms of cash flows. The concept of social responsibility introduces new dimensions and new problems.

First, there is as yet no generally accepted concept of the social responsi-bility of business enterprises. Almost everyone agrees that they should be socially responsible, though it may be argued that such a view is merely an extension of the universally accepted doctrine that individuals, either single or in groups, should weigh the impact of their actions on others.

Three approaches to the concept of corporate social responsibility may be distinguished:

(a) The first approach originates in classical economic theory as expressed in the hypothesis that the firm has one and only one objective, which is to maximize income. By extension, the objective of a corporation should be to maximize shareholders' wealth. It is asserted that in striving to attain this objective within the constraint of the existing legal and ethical framework, business corporations are acting in the best interests of society at large. This classical interpretation of the concept of corporate social responsibility has been advocated by Milton Friedman (1962) in the following terms:

'. . . there is one and only one social responsibility of business—to use its resources and engage in activities designed to increase its profit, as long as it stays within the rules of the game, which is to say, engages in open and free competition, without deception or fraud . . . Few trends could so thoroughly undermine the very foundations of our free society as the acceptance by corporate officials of a social responsibility other than to make as much money for their shareholders as possible'.

(b) The second approach developed in the 1970s, and recognizes the significance of social objectives in relation to the maximization of income. In this view, corporate managers should make decisions which maintain an equitable balance between the claims of shareholders, employees, customers, suppliers and the general public. The corporation represents therefore, a coalition of interests, and the proper consideration of the various interests of this coalition is the only way to ensure that the corporation will attain its long-term income maximization objective.

(c) The third view regards income as a means to an end, and not as an end in itself. In this view, 'the chief executive of a large corporation has the problem of reconciling the demands of employees for more wages and improved benefit plans, customers for lower prices and greater values, shareholders for higher dividends and greater capital appreciation—all within a framework that will be constructive and acceptable to society'. (Committee for Economic Development, 1971.) Accordingly, organizational decisions should be concerned with the selection of socially responsible alternatives. Instead of seeking to maximize income generally, the end result should be a satisfactory level of income which is compatible with the attainment of a range of social goals.

The change from the second to the third approach to social responsibility is characterized as a move from a concept of the business corporation based on shareholders' interests to one which extends the definition of 'stakeholder'. The former concept views the business enterprise as being concerned with making profits for its shareholders, and treats the claims of other interested groups, such as customers, employees and the community, as constraints on this objective. The latter concept acknowledges that the business enterprise has a responsibility to all stakeholders, that is, those who stand to gain or lose as a result of the firm's activities.

Second, the acceptance of the third view expressed above that 'organizational decisions should be concerned with the selection of socially responsible alternatives' requires clarification of the meaning of 'socially responsible alternatives'. It is evident that unless firms are able to develop clear views of society's preferences and priorities, they will be unable to plan activities which will make a social impact, and much less report in a meaningful way on their social performance. Therefore, without a precise knowledge of such preferences and priorities, much of the discussion of what is socially desirable must pass for subjective judgements, or at worst pure guesswork.

Third, it has been argued that both from a theoretical standpoint and from the standpoint of welfare economics, it is impossible to make public decisions about the social good. According to Arrow's General Impossibility Theorem, 'if we exclude the possibility of inter-personal comparisons of utility, then the only methods of passing from individual tastes to social preferences which will be satisfactory and which will be defined for a wide range of sets of individual orderings are either imposed or dictated'. (Arrow, 1963.)

Fourth, at the operational level, there is the problem of the ever-changing nature of the ordering of social preferences, were such ordering ever possible. Social costs, as well as social benefits, are a function of social perception of what is bad and good about business activity. As a result, the nature of corporate social responsibility is not a static concept. Rather, it is concerned with moving targets many of which are the subject of government action. Such action may take three forms:

(a) Legislation which outlaws undesirable social activities. Many examples exist of public concern with undesirable features of business activity, and of legislation to suppress such activities. One early example in the United Kingdom was the legislation relating to child labour in the 19th century which was made illegal.

(b) Licensing systems may be employed to limit the extent of activities which are useful to society, but present a potential social problem. The licensing of lorries, for example, has been made the subject of certificates of road-worthiness, and attention is now paid to the control of exhaust emission. Thus, licensing may be qualitative as well as quantitative.

(c) It has been argued that taxation is a convenient manner of internalizing external social costs of activities having negative effects on society. The objective is to impose taxes on the firm equal in magnitude to the damage sustained by society from the firm's activities. The obvious purpose of such taxes would be to encourage firms to abate the effects of such activities, or alternatively to finance public programmes for controlling these effects. According to some advocates of the taxation approach to dealing with social costs, business firms would be free to choose between abating the social nuisance and avoiding the tax, or continuing as before and paying the tax. According to other advocates of this approach, there should be a tariff of taxes designed to encourage firms to locate in areas where their methods of production do least harm to the environment. Many environmentalists would probably argue, however, that such by-products as pollution do harm wherever they occur, and that suppression through legislation is the only appropriate course of action for society to take.

From the foregoing discussion of the nature of externalities and the role of government in solving social problems, it is apparent that corporate social responsibility is difficult to define. The question may be asked—to what extent should business enterprises be responsible for dealing with all social problems left unsolved by government? Should they concentrate on solving some of these problems? Or should firms merely operate within a strict interpretation of the letter of the law, and if so, would this adherence to the letter of the law frustrate any claim that their behaviour towards externalities could be anti-social?

In the absence of a clear definition of corporate social responsibility by legislation, individual firms must decide for themselves the nature of their social responsibility as a management concept and constraint. The only guidelines available to a firm in this respect is legislation on the one hand and public opinion and pressure on the other. Subject to these constraints, it is evident that corporate social responsibility may be broadly or narrowly defined, and that individual firms have a fair margin of choice as to the standard of corporate social responsibility which they may be willing to accept.

The scope of corporate social responsibility

Brummet (1973) has identified five possible areas in which corporate social objectives may be found:

(1) Net income contribution
(2) Human resource contribution
(3) Public contribution
(4) Environmental contribution
(5) Product or service contribution.

The term 'contribution' includes both benefits and costs associated with an organization's activities.

Implicit in this definition of the scope of corporate social responsibility are a variety of users having different purposes in using accounting information.

Net income contribution

The growing attention which other social objectives are receiving does not reduce the importance of the income objective. A business organization cannot survive without an adequate financial surplus; and as we shall see in Part 5, long-range planning includes calculating the minimum return to shareholders. The recognition of the importance of other social objectives does not diminish the importance of the income objectives. On the contrary, it adds meaning to the significance of corporate net income by drawing attention to the circumstances under which it has been produced. In this sense, there is a clear correlation between income and other social objectives. The failure to recognize a social problem may well affect the organization's income performance either in the short-term or the long-term. Thus, excessive hours of work under bad working conditions may damage the ability of workers to maintain the level of output. The failure to pay adequate attention to the quality of the product and customer's reactions to poor product quality may ultimately affect sales and income.

Indeed, the failure to plan and attain social objectives will be reflected in the failure ultimately to attain the income target. For this reason, many would argue that the income objective is the complete test of business efficiency, both as regards financial and social goals.

Human resource contribution

This contribution reflects the impact of organizational activities on the people who constitute the human resources of the organization. These activities include:

Recruiting practices	Congruence of employee and organizational goals
Training programmes	
Experience building—job rotation	Mutual trust and confidence
Job enrichment	Job security, stability of work force, lay off and recall practices
Wage and salary levels	
Fringe benefit plans	Transfer and promotion policies
Management-union relations	Occupational health
Employee skills	Freedom from undue stress
Employee knowledge	On the job physical environment
Employee attitudes	On the job safety
Employee self-actualization	

The behavioural implications of managerial decisions will be considered in Part 5. As yet, the development of a human resource accounting method which can cope successfully with measuring the impact of organizational decision on human asset values is experimental.

Public contribution

This area considers the impact of organizational activities on individuals or groups of individuals generally outside the corporation *per se*, for example:

General philanthropy—contributions to educational, cultural, or charitable organizations.

Financial or manpower support for—public transportation, health services, urban housing, day care centres, minority business, community problem solving, minority group programmes and general volunteer community activities.

Equal opportunity employment practices.

Training and employment of handicapped persons.

Taxes paid.

The contribution which corporate enterprises make towards the public good tends to be overlooked in the debate about what they ought to do. It ought to be stated, for example, that the creation of jobs and the provision of employment are important public contributions, as well as the development of local services which often accompanies corporate expansion into a community. The training and employment of the handicapped is an important corporate social contribution.

Environmental contribution

This area involves the environmental aspects of production, covering the use of resources, the production process and the product itself, including recycling and other positive environmental activities. Attention has been drawn in recent years to the negative aspects of organizational activities, such as the pollution of air and water, noise, and the despoliation of the environment. Moreover, industrial activities lead to a net use of irreplaceable resources and a net production of solid wastes.

Corporate social objectives are to be found in the abatement of these negative external social effects of industrial production, and in adopting more efficient technologies to minimize the use of irreplaceable resources and the production of waste.

Product or service contribution

This area concerns the qualitative aspects of the organization's product or service, for example, product utility, product life-durability, product safety, serviceability as well as the welfare role of the product or service. Moreover, it includes customer satisfaction, truthfulness in advertising, completeness and clarity of labelling and packaging. Many of these considerations are important already from a marketing point of view. It is clear, however, that the social responsibility aspect of the product contribution extends beyond what is advantageous from a marketing angle.

The objectives of users of social accounting information

The Corporate Report identified seven groups of users as having a reasonable right to receive information from companies. It did not specify, however, the decision models of these several groups of users, nor did it consider it to be practicable to publish information of a social accounting nature. Clearly, much of the information described above is of a qualitative rather than of a financial nature, and as such would be subjected to use by groups concerned with making value judgements about the firm's social contributions. In effect, identifying such groups of users as having distinctly different objectives from those already considered in the Corporate Report, namely, equity investors, loan creditors, employees, analysts, business contacts, government and public, poses complex problems of identifying what objectives such further groups might have in using social accounting information. For example, it might be considered by one group to be undesirable to conduct trade with another country having a political system with which that group is not in sympathy. Consequently, it might wish to have detailed information about trading activities and customers of the company for the purposes of conducting a political campaign to dissuade the company from conducting such trade. At the same time, of course, the group likely to be affected is already a customer and might consider it as inequitable that it should be penalized for activities beyond its own control as a customer group. Moreover, the objectors might conceivably be a caucus within a group, whose purposes are not identical with those of the majority of the group. The problem is that it becomes extremely difficult not only to identify the objectives for which social accounting information might be required, but also to establish stable patterns of value judgements about the activities reported upon, and stability in the 'opinions' of the individuals forming a group of users. If the objective is to maximize some form of public utility based upon sets of value judgements, it may be impossible to achieve that objective. Thus, Arrow (1963) has indicated the impossibility of establishing public preferences on the basis of the preferences of individuals.

These theoretical problems are implicitly recognized in the debate about corporate social accountability. The need to find a way forward has prompted some authors to state the objectives toward which social accounting information might be directed. For example, Ramanathan (1976) suggests the following three objectives for social accounting information:

(1) to identify and measure the periodic net social contribution of an individual firm, which includes not only the social costs and benefits internalized to the firm, but also those arising from externalities affecting different social segments;
(2) to help determine whether an individual firm's strategy and practices which directly affect the relative resource and power status of individuals, communities, social segments and generations are consistent with widely shared social priorities on the one hand and individuals' legitimate aspirations on the other; and
(3) to make available in an optimal manner to all social constituents relevant

information on a firm's goals, policies, programmes, performance and contribution to social goals.

The first two objectives may be viewed as measurement objectives for social accounting. It is necessary to attain these measurement objectives if the third objective, which is a reporting objective, is to be realized. The development of measurement objectives encounters the problems which were discussed at the beginning of this chapter in that there is an apparent inability at this stage in time to develop measurements of performance which everyone will accept. In this sense, the uncertainty as to the meaning and extent of corporate social responsibility may be seen as impeding agreement on dimensions of the measurement problem as a first stage in the search for appropriate measurements. Second, there is an apparent inability to make creditable cost-benefit and cost-effectiveness analyses to guide decision makers. This problem may be seen as related to the two previous problems, for if the objective of measurement is unclear, measurement standards cannot be developed and analyses cannot be conducted.

Planning for social objectives

Once a firm has determined the extent of its commitment to social objectives, plans may be considered for attaining these objectives. The integration of social and economic goals in the planning process provides the best basis for understanding the interdependence of social and economic goals. In particular, such an integration allows the social implication of economic goals to be more adequately considered in the fusion of these goals in coherent long-range and annual operating plans. Admittedly, the integrated analysis of social and economic goals implies a reform of the planning process.

Bauer and Fenn (1972) recommend a four-stage approach for planning social programmes:

(1) making an inventory of all corporate activities having a social impact;
(2) analysing the circumstances necessitating these activities;
(3) evaluating as best possible the type of social programmes which would be most relevant to the firm's activities;
(4) assessing the manner in which these social programmes match the corporation's own objectives and those of society at large.

The social audit

The social audit consists of an inventory of all activities undertaken by the company which are concerned with its relationship with society. The inventory is established by survey questionnaires in which questions are asked, such as 'what are the company's strengths, weaknesses, opportunities, and threats?' in relation to a range of social problems associated with internal and external circumstances. Commenting on the process of conducting a social inventory for General Mills, Hunt (1974) wrote: 'In developing items to be inventoried, it was decided to pinpoint, "What does society expect of General

Mills?"' Two possible examples would be high quality products and good taste in advertising. Areas where General Mills could have a significant impact were placed high on the list. These included charitable giving, equal employment opportunities, employee safety, product quality and food research. Conversely, areas where General Mills had lesser skills or potential, such as public transportation were de-emphasized. Finally, current topics which consumer advocates tend to emphasize were also covered. These areas included hiring of minorities and women, open dating, packaging and labelling and children's advertising.

The following are some of the things that were eventually included on the list of items to be inventoried. They were divided into three major sectors covering most of the Company's responsibilities. They included: (1) the public, (2) consumers of their products and (3) employees. Included in the public sector were charitable giving, recruiting of women and minorities and ecology. In the consumer sector, items such as advertising and consumer complaints were listed. Also, adequate attention was given to product safety, packaging and labelling. Finally pay and fringe benefits were part of the employee sector, but also included were employee safety and responding to the employee voice (i.e. for job enrichment).

The analysis of the social audit

The analysis of these activities in relation to such internal and external circumstances sheds further light on the nature of the social problems to which the corporate social policy should be directed. This analysis is a pre-condition to considering the type of social programmes which may be required.

Evaluating and selecting social programmes

The selection of social programmes will be influenced by the firm's current performance and views about that performance. One approach to this problem is to carry out 'attitude surveys' (Worcester, 1973). This allows the firm to monitor, and possibly to forecast changes in attitudes among employees, customers, shareholders, government officials and public bodies about the firm's current social programmes. This technique has been used, for example, by General Electric for the purpose of analysing social priorities (Wilson, 1974). First, the major demands of various pressure groups were listed. Next, these demands were ranked in accordance with their intensity, that is, the emphasis which they were given by each pressure group. This method of developing a long-range social policy has led one writer to define social responsibility in terms of 'social responsiveness, that is, the ability of the company to respond constructively and opportunely to changing societal needs and expectations' (Wilson, 1974).

Integrating social and business programmes

The final stage in the evolution of a long-range social policy is to translate plans into social action programmes. These programmes provide a means of allocating corporate resources to the attainment of particular social goals, and through control procedures to ensure that such goals are achieved efficiently. The use of such techniques as budgetary control enables social and business programmes to be jointly implemented.

Although we have expressed the view that the planning process, and implicitly the control process, should be reformed to allow social and economic goals to be considered in an integrated analysis, it is not possible at the present stage of the development of social responsibility accounting to effect such an integration. Hence, the proposals put forward by Bauer and Fenn must be seen as providing a theoretical blueprint for future research in developing tools of analysis in this field. In particular, their suggestion that there should be a matching of corporate social objectives with those of society at large poses very complex problems. At best, corporate managers will be able to place their own interpretation on the objectives of society at large. These objectives are not all known and often appear as part of a shift in public opinion; they are multiple, they often conflict and frequently overlap.

The manner in which information is to be reported

As we noted in Chapter 22, the Trueblood Report considered social accounting to be one of the objectives of financial reporting. The National Association of Accountants (USA) subsequently carried out a survey in 1974 among 695 of its members, which revealed that 71 per cent of respondents agreed that a system of accounting for corporate social performance was needed. In addition, 90 per cent of respondents identified a need for descriptive and numerical, that is non-monetary and monetary, measurements of social performance. Such evidence indicated that accountants were beginning to reflect the views which management in the USA were already adopting with regard to the importance of corporate social activities.

A survey of the approaches adopted by firms to the problem of social reporting has revealed that three basic approaches are employed (Epstein *et al.*, 1976; Parker, 1977).

(1) The descriptive approach appears to be the most prevalent form of corporate social reporting. Descriptive social reports merely list all corporate social activities, and are the simplest and least informative format for social reporting. Descriptive reports have ranged from short sections in the Annual Report to Shareholders to quite separate publications dealing with corporate social responsibility. Many companies which have used the descriptive approach to social reporting have done so in the belief that useful measurement of corporate social performance cannot be developed.

(2) The cost of outlay approach lists corporate expenditure on each social activity undertaken, and offers a contrast to the descriptive reports in the sense that the descriptions of activities are quantified in money terms. One advantage of the cost of outlay approach to social reporting lies in the comparability achieved between successive years in the level of financial commitments to social activities. The main disadvantage of this approach is that no mention of the resulting benefits is made. In this respect, the size of

the financial outlay is not necessarily related to the benefits yielded. Thus, large expenditure may be incurred on training programmes that are ineffective.

(3) The cost-benefit approach discloses both costs and benefits associated with corporate social activities. This approach is the most informative, but suffers from the difficulties which exist in the measurement of the benefits. Critics of this approach assert that output measures in money terms are contrived and are not meaningful, because the benefits are mainly of a qualitative nature for they are concerned with the quality of life.

Summary

The concept of corporate social responsibility emerged in the 1960s when changing social values and expectations gave rise to a debate about the role of business in society. This debate focused on the nature of corporate social responsibility, and gave rise to the possibility that this responsibility could be discharged through a method of social responsibility accounting. It was argued that such a method of accounting would indicate the nature and the manner of the firm's social contributions or outputs. A number of areas of enterprise activity give rise to social contributions, namely the contribution to income, to people, to the public, to the environment and by way of the product or service provided by the enterprise. The manner in which the enterprise could deliberately integrate social objectives in its planning system was examined. Whilst there is evidence that many companies began to publish corporate social reports, there are different approaches used ranging from the descriptive to the cost-benefit approach. A number of problems exist in the area of social responsibility accounting which account for the relative lack of success which has attended the development of operational corporate social accounting systems.

References

1. Accounting Standards Committee. *The Corporate Report*, London, 1975.
2. Arrow, K. J. *Social Choice and Individual Values*, p. 59, Yale University Press, 1963.
3. Bauer, R. A. & Fenn, D. H., Jnr. *The Corporate Social Audit*, The Russell Sage Foundation, 1972.
4. Brummet, L. R. 'Total performance measurement', *Management Accounting N.A.A.*, November, 1973.
5. Committee for Economic Development. *Social Responsibilities of Business Corporations*, p. 22, New York, 1971.
6. Epstein, M., Flamholtz, E. & McDonough, J. J. 'Corporate social auditing in the USA: state of the art and future prospects', *Accounting Organizations and Society*, Vol. 1, No. 1, 1976.
7. Friedman, M. *Capitalism and Freedom*, p. 133, University of Chicago Press, 1962.
8. Hunt, S. M. 'Conducting a social inventory', *Management Accounting N.A.A.*, October, 1974.

9. Parker, L. D. 'Accounting for corporate social responsibility', *The Chartered Accountant in Australia*, October, 1977.
10. Ramanathan, K. V. 'Towards a theory of corporate social accounting', *The Accounting Review*, July, 1976.
11. Worcester, R. 'Monitoring and forecasting public opinion about business', *Journal of General Management*, Vol. 1, No. 1, Autumn, 1973.
12. Wilson, I. H. 'Reforming the strategic planning process: integration of social responsibility and business needs', *Long-Range Planning*, October, 1974.

Questions

1. 'There is as yet no generally accepted concept of the social responsibility of business enterprises.' Discuss.
2. What five areas in which corporate social objectives may be found were identified by Brummet?
3. What problems does a firm face in planning to attain social objectives?
4. How may social information be reported?

Part 5 PLANNING AND CONTROL

Introduction

The significance of the role which the management accountant fulfils today lies in his contribution to the overall management of business operations rather than in the set of procedures for which he is responsible and which relate purely to the financial aspects of management control. Accordingly, an appreciation of management accounting as a field of knowledge is more appropriately developed through the systems approach, which we noted in Chapter 2 is really a way of viewing accounting in the context of the organization as a whole.

The objective of this part is to provide our readers with a coherent and intelligible management framework in which the importance of accounting information may be understood.

One difficulty which arises in this respect is that there is a great deal of controversy about management theory itself. For example, writing in the early 1960s Harold Koontz described management theory as a jungle in which he could identify six different schools of thought. Today, the position remains just as confused and there does not exist a coherent theory of management in which the role of accounting could be unambiguously analysed.

Another difficulty arises from conflicts with regard to the theory of the firm itself. For example, classical economic theory assumed that the firm had the sole objective of profit maximization. This theory provided a purpose for management decision making which was clearly defined, and a need for a type of management accounting information which was unambiguously stated. The subsequent erosion of the supremacy of the classical theory of the firm by the appearance of either modified assumptions about profit maximization or different assumptions about the objectives of the enterprise have destroyed the basis for a coherent view of the objectives for which accounting information might be required by decision makers within the enterprise. Thus, neo-classicists assume that profit maximization cannot be achieved and that the objective of management ought to be to 'satisfice' a profit requirement. Behavioural theories of the firm assume that the firm seeks to expand through the maximization of sales, or alternatively that the objectives of the firm can only be defined from the objectives of the dominant personalities in the enterprise. Finally, there are now radical theories which re-define the role of the business enterprise within society in terms of socially oriented objectives, which may either be assumed to be free enterprise in the process of adjustment to social change or to be imposed by political dictat.

It follows that the absence of coherent theories of the firm and coherent theories of management prohibits the formulation of a normative theory of users' needs for accounting information which would define the information objectives to which accounting might be addressed in the context of decision making within the firm. Consequently, in this part the analysis of accounting information in the context of management decision making is constrained and suffers from the immaturity of extant theories.

There remains, however, the need for some kind of framework in which the contribution of accounting to the management process could be examined. Many would agree that the following factors are important in this regard:

(1) The best way to understand the complexities of enterprise decision making is to recognize that each separate situation requires its own organized solution. Accordingly, companies should be managed in the context of their own peculiar circumstances. Moreover, different companies are, in effect, trying to accomplish different things. They are so diverse in such respects as markets, production methods, ownership and size, that they inevitably have a diversity of objectives.

(2) Regardless of the variety of theories about the firm or about management, it is generally accepted that management has a set of specific functions to perform such as planning, organizing, controlling, communicating and motivating people.

(3) The decision-making process integrates all the management processes, for all managerial functions involve decision making. Hence, the key to understanding management behaviour is the decision-making process. In Part 4, we examined investors' and employees' decisions and developed criteria for information relevant to their decisions. These criteria, which were discussed in Chapter 23 and which emphasized—among others—relevance and understandability, are applicable to management decisions. Accordingly, these criteria suggest that our concern should be with such questions as:

What decisions do management make?
What information is relevant to particular decisions?

(4) Managers of business enterprises are faced with constant changes in the environment within and outside the firm. To survive, business enterprises must themselves be susceptible to change. The ability to evaluate past decisions, to react to current situations and to predict future events should be regarded as critical success factors. Management accountants may be seen to be concerned with the process of change by the analysis of past decisions, the provision of information that appreciates current trends, and participating in the decisions that will affect the future of the enterprise by ensuring that the information that is needed will have relevance to those decisions.

Given this definition of the problems of accounting for management decision making, our scheme of work in the subsequent chapters is as follows:

Section 1: A framework for planning and control

In this section, we examine the concepts of planning and control as they are applied to business organizations. We shall see that central to this analysis is the selection of the goals towards which the activities of such organizations are to be directed. These goals, therefore, provide the focus to the decision-making process.

We examine the management process in some detail so as to establish the role of information in this context. Costs play an important role in the planning and control process. The problems of ascertaining unit product costs are examined in this section.

Section 2: Planning

This section is concerned with a relatively detailed analysis of the planning process. It begins with a discussion of long-range planning as a means of attaining the organization's long-term goals. We proceed with an examination of the stages by which these goals may be realized. This involves, on the one hand, providing the assets which will enable the firm to operate and involves capital expenditure, and on the other hand, realizing long-range plans in annual stages by means of the activities envisaged in the annual budget.

Planning decisions are made in the face of uncertainty. We devote a chapter, therefore, to the analysis of risk and the means by which this problem may be reduced to some extent.

Our discussion of the nature and importance of the annual budget leads us to such problems as the relationship between costs, volume of output and profit, and pricing. Lastly, we examine those types of decisions which tend to be made on a 'once-and-for-all' basis and do not form part of the long-range planning process, for example, such decisions as the acceptance of special offers, dropping product lines and making or buying decisions.

Section 3: Control

We begin this section by relating control to planning by establishing that the purpose of control is to ensure that the firm's activities conform with its plans. We relate the concept of control also to an organizational framework which is aimed at securing the performance of the tasks involved in implementing plans. This enables us to introduce the idea of responsibility accounting.

The importance attached in accounting to the control of costs, which we mentioned earlier, and the use of costs in the control of performance is considered in a chapter on standard costing and associated techniques such as flexible budgeting. Throughout this section, we stress the importance of information feedback as a means of ensuring that actual performance conforms with planned and required performance. We devote a chapter to performance appraisal, in which it will be noted that we recognize the importance of the behavioural factors associated with the human element in organizations. We argue also that the accountant should play a larger role in the design of management information systems.

Section 1 A framework for planning and control

26 The meaning of planning and control

There are two conflicting schools of thought regarding the extent to which the firm is in charge of its own destiny. Market theory postulates that the firm is solely at the whim of prevailing economic and social forces, so that successful management depends upon the ability to 'read' the environment. By contrast, planning and control theory asserts that management has control over the firm's future and believes that the firm's destiny may be manipulated and hence planned and controlled. In this view, the quality of managerial planning and control decisions is the key factor for success.

In reality, business organizations normally operate somewhere in between these two extreme views: many elements, such as raw material prices, are completely outside their control; on the other hand some elements, such as the selling price of its product, are determined by the organization itself. One may make a distinction, therefore, between controllable and non-controllable items. It is the function of management to manipulate the controllable items to the firm's best advantage, and to ensure that it is prepared to meet changes in the non-controllable ones, so as to take full advantage of favourable changes and minimize the impact of unfavourable ones. Planning is essential for all the factors which affect the organization, irrespective of whether or not they are controllable or non-controllable. We may infer from this fact that to the degree that a firm's management reflects the views of control theorists the greater are its chances of success.

The processes of management

Although there are different schools of thought as to what may be understood by the term 'management' and how it should be practised, it is generally accepted that management has five main functions: planning, organizing, controlling, communicating and motivating.

Planning

Planning is the most basic of all management functions, and the skill with which this function is performed determines the success of all operations. Planning may be defined as the thinking process that precedes action and is directed towards making decisions now with the future in mind. Theoretically, the function of planning is to improve the quality of decision making by a careful consideration of all the relevant factors before a decision is made, and ensuring that decisions conform with a rational strategy by which the firm's future is to be shaped. Planning may be seen as consisting of five stages:

(a) Setting organizational objectives.
(b) Assessing the environment in which the organization will be operating, by reference to the external factors which are likely to affect its operations. For this purpose, forecasts have to be made which attempt to predict what will happen in the future, with and without policy changes on the part of the planning organization.
(c) Assessing existing resources, for management is concerned with making the most efficient use of those scarce resources, often called the four M's: men, machines, materials and money. This aspect of the planning function involves both making an estimate of external resources which are accessible, and resources already held which are either idle or which might be more efficiently utilized.
(d) Determining the strategy for achieving stated objectives by means of an overall plan which specifies strategic goals. Strategic decisions are concerned with establishing the relationship between the firm and its environment.
(e) Designing a programme of action to achieve selected strategic goals by means of both long-range programmes and short-range programmes, the latter covering a period of a year or less and containing sets of instructions of the type found in annual budgets.

Thus, decisions are essential at every stage of the planning process, and the key areas may be stated as deciding 'what should be done, when it should be done, how it should be done and who should do it'.

The importance of environmental factors to the planning process is obvious; and it is equally clear that environmental information should not be subjected to a less disciplined treatment than the internal or analytical information, which an organization itself provides. There may sometimes be important areas in which one may criticize the quality of analytical information as being inadequate for the purpose of efficient decision making. Deficiencies in the nature and quality of analytical information will be examined in much greater detail elsewhere in this book. However, there is a need for a continuous flow of information on the environment, for the most important determinant of a firm's potential for growth and improved efficiency is the ability of its management to learn about this aspect. Information systems are now moving away from a heavy emphasis on internal or analytical information and incorporating much more environmental data. As surveys in the United States have shown, the scan of environmental data in which management is interested ranges from market potential of new and existing product lines, to new processes and technology, the actions of competitors, sales regulations, resources and supplies available to government actions and policies.

We may distinguish three kinds of planning activities:

1 Strategic planning which is concerned with a period from three to ten years ahead and which is usually called long-range planning. This forms the subject of Chapter 28.
2 Project planning is an activity which follows the long-range plan, and involves developing plans for the capital expenditures necessary to meet long-term objectives. This forms the subject of Chapter 29.

3   Budgetary planning which converts the firm's long-range plan to the needs of the immediate future. This is usually described as budgeting, and is generally carried out on a one-year basis. The annual budget is then broken down into months, and in some cases into weeks, to chart the path the firm should take in the immediate future. This forms the basis of Chapter 30.

Organizing

Organizing involves setting up the administrative structure for implementing strategic decisions. The administrative design area is therefore concerned with establishing the structure and the shape of the firm or organization, and defining responsibilities and lines of authority. It involves a definition of the tasks necessary to achieve strategic goals, determining who is to perform these tasks and assigning responsibility for their performance. The function of organizing is to co-ordinate these tasks in such a way that the organization is able to work efficiently in fulfilling its objectives. The process of organizing is achieved through departmentalization, by which different specialisms are hived off into separate departments. These departments are linked in a

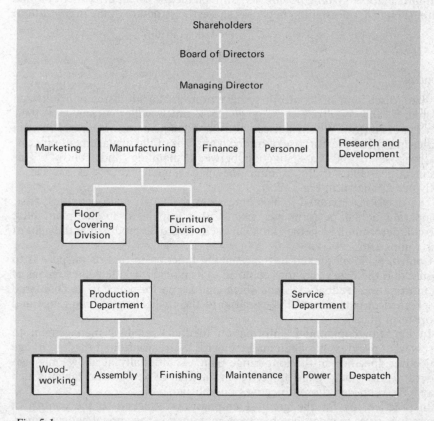

Fig. 5.1.

hierarchy, a formal communication structure that enables instructions to be passed downwards and information to be passed upwards to senior management. Figure 5.1 shows a partial organization structure for a firm which is concerned with two main activities—furniture and floor covering.

A manager may be allotted the task of managing the activities in each of these boxes, which then represent executive positions; the lines represent the formal channels of communication between them. The top five boxes represent the five major functions of this firm—marketing, manufacturing, finance, personnel and research and development. For administrative purposes, the firm is organized according to its product categories; therefore, two divisions—furniture and floor covering—are established.

At the bottom of the pyramid in the figure are the basic organizational units, known as departments; this illustrates the six departments belonging to the Furniture Division. Departments form an occupational classification—in this case they are divided into Production and Service Departments.

A major purpose of any organizational structure is to facilitate the flow of information to and from decision makers. Since management may be said to be the process of converting information into action, organizations should be designed around information flows. Each decision point in this process is a sub-information system having its own elements as input, processor and output. Hence, information networks shape the structure of the organization.

Control

In their discussion of 'control', some writers make no distinction between 'planning' and 'control', thereby giving a much wider meaning to their concept of control. We shall discuss the extended meaning of 'control' later in this chapter. For the purpose of our own analysis of the management process, we propose to make a distinction between 'planning' and 'control'. This distinction enables us to examine the management process as a cycle of activities as shown in Fig. 5.2.

The decisions involved in this area stem from two main activities, first, comparing actual performance against that stipulated in the plan, and, second, determining whether the plan itself should be modified in the light of this comparison.

Control is closely linked to the planning function in that its purpose is to ensure that the firm's activities conform to its plans. It is effected by means of an information feedback system which enables performance to be compared to planned targets. Control is essential to the realization of long-range and short-term plans.

In long-range planning, information feedback enables management to assess what progress has been made towards the realization of the long-range objectives specified in the long-range plan. Additionally, it allows management to review long-range objectives in the light of new circumstances which may have rendered those objectives unrealistic.

In practice, by far the greatest emphasis is attached to the control of operations so as to meet the objectives contained in the annual budget which,

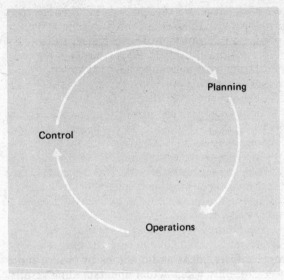

Fig. 5.2.

as we noted earlier, should be seen as part of the long-range plan. Information feedback is an integral part of budgetary control procedures which are intended to be highly sensitive to operational variations on a day-to-day basis. Their aim is to highlight deviations from the budget plan as soon as possible so that remedial action may be taken immediately.

A pre-requisite to the successful performance of the control function is an efficient information system which will reveal the need for corrective action at an appropriate time, enabling managers to judge whether their targets are still appropriate as the environment changes month by month and year by year. The control function is closely linked to the planning function by means of a feedback system which provides information on the results of past decisions. Such a system is necessary to the assessment of the quality of the decision-making process and to its improvement, and is illustrated in Fig. 5.3.

The feedback system provides the great bulk of analytical information used in the planning process. It provides a means also of evaluating planned objectives. Should, for example, the economic climate change, the efficiency of the organization's operations will depend on the swiftness of its reaction to this change by way of alterations to the planned objectives. The feedback system is also instrumental to the making of control decisions for it provides a means of continuously assessing current performance against the strategic plan. Decision making in this sense thus involves making day-to-day adjustments to changing conditions in order to map out the most appropriate course of action needed to implement strategic decisions. Thus, information is the life-blood of any system, and the responsibility for the design of adequate information systems is of paramount concern to management.

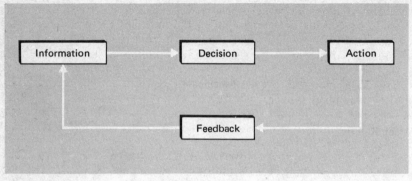

Fig. 5.3.

Communication

Communication is an exchange of facts, ideas and opinions by two or more persons. The exchange is successful only when actual understanding results. Merely saying is not enough; a receiver of information must understand the message which the sender is trying to communicate. Communication occurs when the former understands what the latter means to convey.

Communication involves linking all the management functions by transmitting information and instructions within the organization. Additionally, the communication process relates the organization to its environment by linking it to suppliers of resources, and to the consumers for whom its products are intended.

In any organization, the specialization of tasks and the consequent division of labour creates a situation in which an unrestricted flow of ideas and facts is necessary if it is to function efficiently. A high degree of communication binds the various members of the organization together, uniting them in the pursuit of organizational goals. Hence, an organization may be viewed not only as a decision-making system, but also as a communication system.

The major components in the communication system are the sender, the message and the receiver. The *sender* may be an individual or a computer or other device which is capable of sending a message. The *message* is the information transmitted to the receiver. The medium used for transmitting a message may be written, oral, visual or other forms of communicating meaning. A red light on operating equipment, for example, is often used to indicate a breakdown or a danger. From a management viewpoint, written communication has special advantages in that information may be planned and incorporated into formal procedures, forms, reports, etc., by which means communication is effected. Essentially, procedures which are designed to communicate information should focus on what is important, so as to maximize the possibility of effective communication occurring. This requires a limitation on the number of messages communicated so that the really important information is perceived. The principle of communicating only 'exceptional' information, that is, information about a variance from a predetermined plan which requires immediate attention is a feature of successful communication systems. Moreover, the frequency of communication should be considered in the light of the needs of the receiver, having regard to the effective action which may result from the communication.

Occasionally, the context or situation surrounding communication may affect its transmission or reception. This occurs when interference, such as static on a radio message, prevents the message from being transmitted or distorts the manner in which it is received. The 'gap'/'noise' is the result of factors causing distortions or loss of meaning, and one of the tasks of the designers of information systems is to minimize 'noise' and prevent 'noise' from being accepted as true information.

Lastly, the *receiver* must recognize the context in which the message is sent and received in order that he may interpret the message correctly. The last stage in the communication process involves a human factor, in that the reception of information should produce the correct response. Behavioural factors which impede the required response may render the entire process of communication futile.

The way in which information is communicated and related to planning and control may be illustrated as in Fig. 5.4.

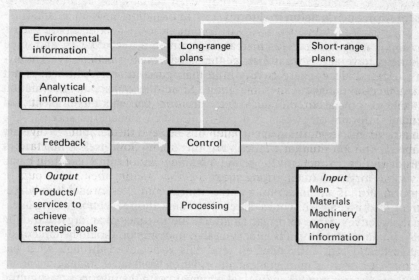

Fig. 5.4.

Figure 5.4 shows how environmental and analytical information is combined in the plans which are designed to meet the organization's objectives. These plans are implemented as resources become inputs which are converted into products and services. The feedback and control systems should function so as to ensure the effectiveness of the plans.

Motivation

This involves getting all the members of the organization to pull their full weight, and finding ways in which individual performance may be improved. When we study motivation, we are studying the influences on a human being and what affects his behaviour. For example, when we ask someone to perform a certain task which we know to be within his capability and experience and it is not done satisfactorily, this failure may well be the result of poor motivation rather than lack of ability.

Some motivating factors are basically biological or physiological and may be looked upon as natural or inherent such as the need for air, water, food, sleep, clothing and housing. Some motivating factors are learned, for example, the combination of needs associated with the individual's ego and a correct evaluation of himself.

Other motivating factors are related to social needs, and these are influenced by the organization of the work situation. Many studies have examined the effects of these needs, and they illustrate how the size, cohesiveness and motives of the group act as controls on the members' own motives. Hence, the organization should create a situation in which group and individual goals coincide to as great a degree as possible.

Information and decision making

Decision making has received increasing attention in recent years, and some authorities have argued that management and decision making are synonymous terms. Indeed, there is very little managerial activity which does not involve decision making in some form. Since the quality of information available is crucial to the quality of decision making, an efficient and adequate information system is a pre-requisite to managerial success. The hallmark of efficient management may thus be seen in the ability to specify accurately the information needed, and this ability is in itself a function of clear definition of objectives, sound planning and control capability and satisfactory organizational arrangements.

Information is an integrating force which combines organizational resources into a cohesive whole directed towards the realization of organizational objectives. Since information affects the fortunes of an organization in such a fundamental way, it is important that information should be effectively organized and efficiently handled, and this is achieved through what has become known as a management information system. A management information system provides individual managers with the information required for making decisions within their own particular areas of responsibility. It may be likened to the central nervous system of an organization in that it consists of a network of information flows to which each decision may be related.

Within this information network decision points may be identified at three levels—strategic planning, management control and operational control (Anthony, 1965).

Strategic planning involves the determination of corporate objectives and goals, as well as the development of broad policies and strategies by which they may be achieved. This activity relies heavily on information about the environment, and has an irregular pattern. Management control is a lower level activity which is concerned with the implementation of the strategic plan and assures that the necessary resources have been obtained, and assures additionally that they are being used effectively and efficiently. This activity is rhythmic, and follows a weekly, monthly or quarterly pattern. Operational control is the process of ensuring that specific tasks are being carried out effectively and efficiently. It is an activity which focuses on individuals' jobs and transactions, and its tempo is 'real time' (that is, data reported as events occur). Operational control is thus exercised over operating systems, and these include stock records, personnel records, data handling and maintenance records. Examples of the relationship between these levels of activity are illustrated as follows:

Strategic planning	Management control	Operational control
Setting marketing policies	Formulating advertising programmes	Controlling the placement of advertisements
Setting personnel policies	Planning staff levels	Hiring and controlling staff

The relationship between these three levels of activities and the information flows is shown in Fig. 5.5.

Strategic planning decisions are based upon data derived both from outside and within the system in the form of environmental and analytical

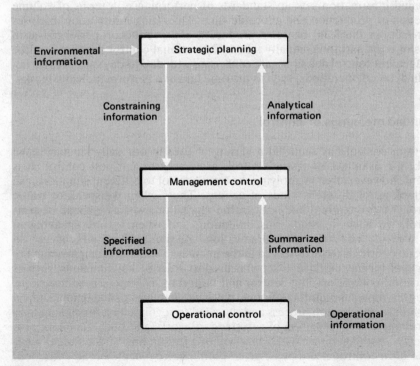

Fig. 5.5.

information; the latter identifies the organization's strengths and weaknesses, and the former enables it to formulate its strategy.

The constraints imposed upon management control decisions emanate from the strategic decisions incorporated in the strategic plan, and for the purposes of management control decisions these constraints are contained in long- and short-term plans. These plans themselves are broken down into detailed programmes for the various operational sub-systems, and into specified information for the purposes of operational control. Hence, management control decisions are based on summarized information which compares the actual performance of cost and profit centres against their planned performance. In order that management should not be inundated with irrelevant information, reports to management should be in the form of statements of variances from the budget plan, and the reasons why these variances have occurred. Management control which is exercised in this way is known as management by exception. Management control decisions are thus concerned with investigating variances, and issuing instructions to operating managers on how to deal with them. Alternatively, management may recognize that the variances are inevitable and uncontrollable, and therefore recommend that the strategic plan should be altered to take account of this fact. In such a case, the decision will take the form of a recommendation of an adjustment to the strategic plan.

Operational control decisions are made at the meeting point between specified and operating information associated with the various sub-systems. Specified information sets up standards of performance in terms of volume and costs of production and allocated time. Operating information discloses the results in the form of items produced, and production performance in terms of costs and time actually taken. Operational control decisions, unlike management control decisions, are concerned with day-to-day variances occurring in detailed operations, such as the time taken to perform individual tasks.

Extended meanings of 'control'

The term control has acquired a variety of uses in our daily language. We speak, for example, of traffic control, arms control and pest control. It is evident, however, that in applying the term control to different situations, we are thinking of different kinds of actions. Thus, when we speak of traffic control, we are really thinking of traffic regulation; when we speak of arms control, we have in mind arms limitation; and when we are speaking of pest control, we mean pest eradication. A similar flexibility of use in the term control is to be observed in the manner in which it is employed in the context of business affairs. Control is used to describe key functions, such as production control, quality control and budgetary control. These functions, however, represent quite different types of activities; production control refers to the production process and the need to regulate that process; quality control implies the rejection of sub-standard work; and budgetary control is concerned with keeping expenditure within a firm in line with a budget plan.

The term control also may be given both a narrow and a broad definition. A narrow definition of control is associated often with the maintenance of standards and the imposition of penalties. The broad concept of control which is to be found in the literature of management science treats the term control as synonymous with management itself. In this sense, control embraces the various processes by which management determines its objectives, draws up plans to attain those objectives, organizes and supervises the operations necessary for the implementation of plans and appraises performance. Control also implies the investigation of deviations from planned objectives, so that performance levels may be brought into line with planned levels. Where necessary, plans and objectives may be changed to meet new circumstances.

One may subject the concept of control to a more complex theoretical analysis which suggests that both normative and descriptive theories of control may be developed. In either context, the crux of control is in measurement. Measurements are required in setting objectives as targets for plans, and since plans are directed towards the future, such measurements are based upon predictions. Prediction is an integral part of control, which in this sense contemplates a future course of action. A normative theory of control recognizes that numerous possible courses of action may exist, each requiring its own control procedure if a system is not to get out of control. Control theory in this sense is based upon what is known as the *law of requisite variety* which states that there must be at least as many variations in the controls to be applied as there are ways for a system to fall out of control. The following example illustrates this principle.

Example

A firm is experiencing a decline in sales and hence has cut back its level of production. Stocks of raw materials, however, are increasing because the purchasing function uses decision rules which are appropriate only for normal conditions, and is not scaling down its levels of purchases. Hence, the control system operating within the firm may be said not to be flexible enough to take into account abnormal circumstances, that is, it has not enough variety to cope with the range of situations with which the system is faced. To remedy this defect, two alternative steps are open to management; either new decision rules must be formulated for the purchasing function which take into account abnormal situations, or the purchasing function must be free to generate its own response to changing circumstances.

The law of requisite variety has important implications for the design of information systems. It implies that decision rules should be devised for making routine decisions. As we saw in Part 1, such decisions may be programmed, and as a result, they may be automated. On the other hand, where decisions involve judgement and experience, the law of requisite variety requires that enough information be provided so that the decision maker himself may generate appropriate responses.

Summary

Planning occurs at all management levels, and the success of other management functions depends upon the quality of planning.

Planning is concerned with both controllable and uncontrollable factors which affect the organization. Controllable factors should be manipulated to the organization's advantage, and the effects of uncontrollable factors should be minimized.

Management is also concerned with such functions as organization, control, communication and motivation. Since decision making is a key characteristic of all management functions, decision making has become synonymous with management.

Information is necessary for decision making, and the quality of information will affect the quality of decisions. Hence, an adequate and efficient information system is a pre-requisite for managerial success.

Decision making may be classified according to the following areas:

(a) strategic planning—which involves the determination of corporate objectives and goals as well as the broad policies and strategies by which they may be achieved;
(b) management control—which is concerned with implementing the strategic plans;
(c) operational control—which is the process of ensuring that specific tasks are carried out effectively and efficiently.

In this part, we shall consider the role of accounting as the most important element of a management information system, and we shall also examine the manner in which accounting information assists management in its various functions.

Reference

Anthony, R. N. *Planning and Control Systems: A Framework for Analysis*, p. 24, Harvard Business School, Boston, 1965.

Questions

1. Distinguish between market theory and planning and control theory.
2. What are the five stages of planning?
3. How is control linked to the planning function?
4. What are the major components of a communication system?
5. Distinguish between strategic planning, management control and operational control.

27 The cost accounting framework

Costs are essentially money measurements of the sacrifices which an organization has to make in order to achieve its objectives. Consequently, costs play a very important role in management decision making, and it is not surprising that accountants are very involved with the collection and the analysis of cost information.

Different costs are used for different purposes. A cost provided by the accountant is useful only if it relates to the problem on hand. Hence, a precise knowledge of the purpose for which the cost measurement is required is a prerequisite to the provision of relevant cost information. For this reason, various cost terms are used, for example, opportunity costs, sunk costs, fixed costs, variable costs, differential costs etc., which are known to have a special meaning in given decision situations. These terms will be examined in this and the subsequent chapters. At this stage, we may say that costs are collected for four major purposes:

(1) To assist in planning decisions, such as the determination of which products to manufacture, the quantities which should be produced and the selling prices. Since planning is addressed to the future, we are interested in future costs for this purpose. Historical costs are useful only insofar as they are reliable indicators of future costs.

(2) To assist in the control of operations by maintaining and improving the efficiency with which resources are employed. Control involves comparing the actual costs of current operations against their planned costs. It follows that since actual costs are monetary surrogates of the resources which have been exhausted in current operations, we should be interested in replacing those resources. Hence, for this purpose, we require replacement costs. The control process assists in keeping current costs in line with planned costs by highlighting inefficiencies. It may also lead to a revision of planned costs.

(3) To assist in the measurement of reported profits, that is, income measurement as understood in accounting. As we explained in Part 2, profit calculations based upon historical costs fulfil a legal rather than a decision-making role. Moreover, for the purpose of performance evaluation and for profit forecasts, adjustments should also be made for changes in the value of money.

(4) To assist in the collective bargaining processes discussed in Chapter 24.

Costs are accumulated in two forms: in terms of their relationship to a person (responsibility accounting) and in terms of product. Responsibility accounting, which uses costs accumulated in the first form, is directed at the control of costs by associating them with individuals in the management hierarchy. This form of accounting plays a central role in the control of operations and we shall deal with it in Chapter 38.

Here we deal with the accumulation of costs in order to calculate full product costs, that is, all the manufacturing costs incurred in bringing the product to a marketable state. One application of full product costs is computing inventory values. Sometimes, non-manufacturing costs such as administrative and marketing costs are added to the full product costs for the purpose of determining the profitability of products and for establishing pricing policies. These product costs are also used in government contracts which seek to establish a 'fair price' by basing the price on total costs.

The elements of cost

The costs of transforming raw materials into finished products are classified into two major categories—manufacturing and non-manufacturing costs.

Manufacturing costs

These costs comprise three elements:

(1) direct material costs
(2) direct labour costs
(3) factory overhead costs.

The term 'direct' cost is applied only to those costs which can be readily identified with the product. Therefore, direct material costs include only those costs which can be directly associated with the finished product. Similarly, if an employee performs a task connected with the making of the product, his wage is considered as a direct labour cost. Direct material and direct labour costs are referred to as 'prime costs'.

In deciding which costs to treat as direct costs, the accountant has to take into consideration the materiality of the item. The expense of determining that some item is a direct cost rather than regarding it as a factory overhead cost may outweigh any benefit attached to such information. Thus, the expense of recording as direct costs such small items as washers, nuts and bolts far outweighs any benefit which may be derived from this exercise.

Factory overhead costs include all the remaining production costs, after direct costs have been determined. They include indirect material costs such as lubricants, and supplies of materials for repairs and maintenance. They also include indirect labour costs such as the salaries and wages of inspectors, timekeepers and workmen who do not work on specific products. Factory overhead costs also include other indirect costs such as heat, light, power and the depreciation of factory buildings, plant and equipment.

The manufacturing cost is the total of all direct and indirect costs. It is the cost of manufacture which is recorded as the stock value of the finished product while it is awaiting sale. Upon sale, the manufacturing cost forms part of the cost of sale for the purpose of calculating the trading profit.

Non-manufacturing costs

These costs are not included in the cost of manufacturing the product, and they are not included, therefore, in the cost of sales. Hence, they are assumed not to attach to the product costs for income measurement purposes. Non-manufacturing costs are 'period' rather than 'product' costs, and they are associated with accounting periods rather than with output. Non-manufacturing costs include administrative and marketing costs. Administrative costs are defined as the costs incurred on executive salaries, head office staff expenses including all clerical and secretarial staff, legal expenses and depreciation on office equipment, furniture, etc. Marketing costs include the activities associated with obtaining orders, such as advertising and selling costs, and activities concerned with fulfilling orders, such as warehousing, packing and delivery.

Total product costs

The elements of cost involved in the calculation of total product costs for a unit of a product may be summarized by the following ascertained unit costs:

	£
Direct material costs	4
Direct labour costs	6
Direct cost per unit	10
Factory overhead costs	8
Manufacturing cost per unit	
Total product cost	18

In calculating total product costs, the accounting problem is to find means of attributing to units of products their appropriate costs for the various decisions which management has to make. The task of calculating the direct material and direct labour costs attributable to individual products is relatively easy. The direct material costs are calculated by ascertaining the quantities of materials used in the product, making due allowance for normal waste, and multiplying the quantity by the raw material purchase price. Similarly, the direct labour costs are obtained by specifying the operations involved in production and the time taken, and multiplying the time factor so derived by the appropriate labour rates. It is in the calculation of total overhead costs per unit that the major accounting problem of cost determination lies.

The problem of overhead costs

The problem of ascertaining the overhead costs applicable to a unit of a product is first and foremost a function of the number of different products which the firm manufactures. Where the firm manufactures only one product, the problem is relatively simple. If, for example, the firm produces 1000 units of the product, and the overhead costs total £2000, the total overhead costs per unit is £2.

Where the firm manufactures more than one product, however, many problems arise in computing unit overhead costs of production. We shall discuss these problems in terms of the undermentioned stages in the ascertainment of full-product costs:

(1) The allotment of factory overhead costs to production cost centres.
(2) The allotment in turn of the costs of production cost centres to individual products.
(3) The selection of an appropriate level of activity for calculating unit product costs. This is necessary because unit costs vary with activity levels, and a choice has to be made as to the activity level which is applicable to future output.
(4) The allotment of non-manufacturing costs to the products.

The allotment of factory overhead costs to production cost centres

Cost centres are locations with which costs may conveniently be associated for the purpose of product costing.

Basically, there are two types of cost centres for which costs are accumulated—production and service cost centres. Production cost centres are those actually involved in production, such as machining and assembling departments. Service cost centres are those which exist to facilitate production, for example, maintenance, stores and canteen.

The first stage in the allotment of factory overhead costs to production cost centres is to collect and classify factory overhead costs as between indirect material, indirect labour or other identifiable cost headings. The next stage is to allocate these costs, where possible, to production and service cost centres. The term 'cost allocation' has a special meaning, being used to refer to the allotment of whole items of cost to cost centres. For example, the salaries of foremen in charge of individual cost centres may be allocated to those cost centres. Items of costs which cannot be allocated to cost centres must be apportioned. The term 'cost apportionment' means the allotment of proportions only of items of cost to cost centres. For example, the cost of rates cannot be alloted to any particular cost centre and must be apportioned between cost centres.

The third stage is to apportion the costs of the service cost centres to the production cost centres. If we assume that a firm has three service cost centres and two production cost centres, as in Fig. 5.6, the apportionment of the service cost centre costs involves selecting appropriate methods for apportioning these costs to the production cost centres.

When the apportionment is completed, the major production cost centres will have accumulated both prime costs and factory overhead costs.

Example

The production process of Simplex Ltd is based on a machining department and an assembly department, which are supported by one service department which is a maintenance department. Consider the following cost information.

Departmental cost data

Direct (or allocated overheads)	Total £	Machining £	Assembly £	Maintenance £
Indirect materials	15,000	8000	5000	2000
Indirect labour	6000	4000	1000	1000
Depreciation of machinery	7000	2500	4500	—
Total direct overhead costs	28,000	14,500	10,500	3000
Indirect (or unallocated overheads)				
Supervisory salaries	6000			
Rates	10,000			
Total overhead factory costs	44,000			

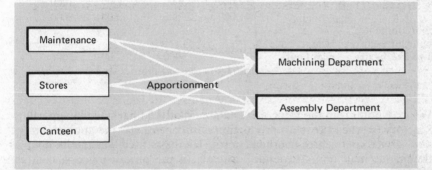

Fig. 5.6.

From this information, we may observe that the first stage in the treatment of overhead factory costs has been completed, since those factory overhead costs which may be directly associated with cost centres have already been allotted. In this connection, it should be mentioned that the direct overhead factory costs are said to be direct to the cost centres concerned, but they remain indirect to the units of the product.

The next stage, therefore, is to apportion the indirect overhead factory costs as between the three cost centres. It will be recalled that indirect factory overhead costs are those which cannot be directly associated with any particular cost centres, but are attached to the factory as a whole. Bases are needed, therefore, to apportion them to the three cost centres in question. These bases should reflect the benefits received by the three departments from these costs. For example, since rates are related to the area occupied by the factory, the area occupied by each cost centre may serve as a basis for apportioning rate charges.

Simplex Ltd has adopted the undermentioned bases for the apportionment of indirect factory overhead costs:

Basis of apportionment	Total	Machining	Assembly	Maintenance
Number of employees	60	30	20	10
Square feet of floor space	100,000	50,000	40,000	10,000
Maintenance man hours	2500	1500	1000	—
Direct labour man hours	10,000	5000	5000	—

Applying these bases to the apportionment of indirect factory overhead costs to the three cost centres, the following distributions are obtained:

Apportionment of factory overhead costs

Overhead costs	Basis	Total £	Machining £	Assembly £	Maintenance £
Indirect materials	Direct	15,000	8000	5000	2000
Indirect labour	Direct	6000	4000	1000	1000
Depreciation of machinery	Direct	7000	2500	4500	—
Supervisory salaries	No. of employees	6000	3000	2000	1000
Rates	Floor space	10,000	5000	4000	1000
		44,000	22,500	16,500	5000
Apportionment of maintenance cost centre overheads	Maintenance man hours	—	3000	2000	(5000)
		44,000	25,500	18,500	—

We may note from the foregoing example that the final stage in apportioning factory overhead costs to production cost centres was the apportionment of the service cost centre overhead costs. The basis used was the number of maintenance man hours expended in each of the production cost centres. Among other methods commonly used in respect of other service cost centres are the following examples:

Service cost centres	Basis of apportionment
Purchasing	Cost of materials purchased or number of orders placed
Stores	Cost of materials used, or the number of stores requisitions
Personnel ⎱ Canteen ⎰	Number of employees
Building maintenance	Space occupied

The allotment of production cost centre costs to products

This stage is the second major step in the ascertainment of full-product costs. As we mentioned earlier, difficulties arise where production cost centres produce more than one product, which is usually the case. It is necessary in such cases to establish a method for attributing to each product an equitable proportion of the production cost centre's overhead costs. The method to 'recover' or 'absorb' these costs relies on the calculation of an 'overhead rate', which is usually linked to one of three factors:

(1) direct labour costs
(2) direct labour hours
(3) machine hours.

A pre-requisite for the calculation of an 'overhead rate' is the selection of an appropriate base for this purpose.

Example

Having completed the apportionment of factory overhead costs to the two production cost centres—machining and assembly—the next problem facing Simplex Ltd is to select an appropriate overhead base for apportioning overhead costs to the products manufactured in these two centres. The following information relates to the machining cost centre:

	£
Direct labour costs	5,000
Direct labour hours	10,000
Machine hours	15,000

On the basis of this information, we are able to calculate three different 'overhead rates' for absorbing overhead costs into the full-product costs of each unit of the different products manufactured by Simplex Ltd. The calculations are as follows:

(a) Overhead rate based on direct labour costs

$$\frac{\text{Cost centre overhead costs}}{\text{Cost centre direct labour costs}} \times 100$$

$$\frac{£25,500}{£5000} \times 100$$

$$= \underline{510\%}$$

Thus, for each £1 of direct labour cost which each unit of a product has incurred in the machining cost centre, that unit will also attract £5.1 of the cost centre's overhead costs. Given that the prime costs incurred by Product A in the machining cost centre are:

	£
Direct labour costs per unit	1.00
Direct material costs per unit	2.00

The full-product costs per unit of Product A at the end of processing through the machining department would be:

	£
Direct costs as above	3.00
Factory overhead costs	5.10
	8.10

(b) Overhead rate based on direct labour hours

$$\frac{\text{Cost centre overhead costs}}{\text{Cost centre direct labour hours}}$$

$$\frac{\text{£25,500}}{10,000}$$

$$= \text{£2.55 per direct labour hour}$$

Thus, for every hour of direct labour spent on making a unit of a particular product in the machining department, that unit will attract £2.55 of that cost centre's overhead costs. Hence, if Product A needs 2½ direct labour hours, the overhead costs apportioned would be £6.375 per unit.

(c) Overhead rate based on machine hours

$$\frac{\text{Cost centre overhead costs}}{\text{Cost centre machine hours}}$$

$$\frac{\text{£25,000}}{15,000}$$

$$= \text{£1.70 per machine hour}$$

Thus, for every hour which is spent on machining a unit of a product in the machining department, that unit will attract £1.70 of that cost centre's overhead costs. Hence, if product A needs 3½ hours of machining, the overhead costs apportioned would be £5.95 per unit.

The choice of one particular overhead rate as against the others may substantially affect the amount of overhead costs apportioned to a unit of product. Consequently, variations in full-product costs may result simply from the manner in which the overhead rate is selected. The 'best' rate to use depends on the particular circumstances facing the firm. The 'direct labour cost' base is easy to use since the necessary information is usually readily available. There may be no relationship, however, between direct labour costs and overhead costs: indeed, most factory overhead costs are incurred on a time basis and are not related to the labour payroll. A further problem resulting from the use of this overhead base is that there will be distortions in the absorption of overhead cost by different products if the rate of pay for similar work is not comparable. The 'direct labour hour' base is usually found to be a better method because most factory overhead costs are more related to time than any other factor. Where, however, there is a greater reliance on machinery rather than on labour, the 'machine hour' base may be the most suitable overhead base for absorbing overhead costs into full-product costs.

Plant-wide versus department overhead rates of recovery

In our discussion so far, we have examined methods of calculating overhead rates which were related to departmental overhead bases. We took the information for the machining department, for example, as a means of calculating overhead rates for the absorption of its own factory overhead costs into the costs of various products processed in that department. It may be felt that an easier and less extravagant method would be to select an overhead base for use by every department, rather than having different overhead bases used by different departments. The argument in favour of departmental overhead rates is that different departments do not incur the same amount of factory overhead costs, as we have already seen, and do not necessarily use the same number of labour or machine hours, nor do they have the same labour costs. It follows, therefore, that the use of a plant-wide overhead rate will not produce an accurate measure of the departmental costs associated with each unit of product. Departmental overhead rates, by contrast, lead to more accurate measurement, as may be seen from the following example.

Example

Eastlands Carburettors Ltd manufactures two types of carburettors, Type X and Type Y, both of which are processed in two departments—Department A and Department B. The following cost information is available:

	Type X £	Type Y £
Direct factory costs per unit	8	8
Direct labour hours		
Department A	4 hours	1 hour
Department B	1 hour	4 hours
Total hours	5 hours	5 hours

Overhead rates based on direct labour hours are given as follows:

Overhead rates	*Per direct labour hour* £
Department basis	
Department A	6
Department B	1
Plant-wide basis	
Department A	3
Department B	3

This information enables us to compare the costs per unit which would result from the use of a plant-wide overhead rate as against departmental overhead rates.

Unit costs using a plant-wide overhead rate

	Type X £	Type Y £
Direct factory costs per unit	8	8
Add: Overhead charge per unit		
(5 hours at £3.00)	15	15
Manufacturing costs per unit	23	23

Unit costs using departmental overhead rates

	Type X £	Type Y £
Direct factory costs per unit	8	8
Add: Overhead charge per unit		
Department A (at £6 per hour)	24	6
Department B (at £1 per hour)	1	4
Manufacturing costs per unit	33	18

It is noteworthy that:

(a) Product X, which spends more processing time in Department A which has the higher overhead rate, is undercosted by £10 when a plant-wide overhead rate is used.

(b) Product Y, however, which spends more processing time in Department B, which has the lower overhead rate, is overcosted by £5 when a plant-wide overhead rate is used.

These wide differences highlight the dangers of using cost measurements which do not lead to accurate statements of unit costs. The absorption of factory overhead costs by means of departmental overhead rates rather than a plant-wide overhead rate yields a more accurate measurement of the costs incurred in manufacturing products. Management decisions which require accurate cost measurements for such purposes as pricing policies and production-mix decisions would be made incorrectly where a plant-wide rather than departmental rate is employed.

The selection of an appropriate level of activity

So far we have classified costs into two categories—direct costs and overhead costs. This classification is helpful in understanding how costs are related to products for the purposes of measuring unit costs of production. We mentioned earlier in this chapter that different cost concepts perform different functions. In order to understand the manner in which costs are affected by different levels of activity, we use another classification. This classification requires that costs be categorized into fixed and variable costs, and its purpose is to define how particular items of costs are affected by changes in activity levels.

Fixed costs are those costs which do not vary with changing levels of activity, for example, factory rent, insurance and rates. Variable costs are those costs which do change directly with changes in the level of activity, for example, raw material costs and direct labour costs. There are costs, however, which are partly fixed and partly variable, for example, maintenance and repairs of machinery and plant equipment, heat, light and power. These are called mixed costs.

The level of activity, therefore, is an economic factor which affects the calculation of the unit cost of output produced. Since fixed costs remain constant as output fluctuates, the greater the output, the lower will be the fixed cost per unit. For example, if fixed costs for the period are £10,000, the fixed cost per unit will depend upon the total number of units produced. If 10,000 units are produced, the fixed cost per unit will be £1; if 5000 units are produced the fixed cost per unit will be £2. This problem does not affect the variable costs, for as we have already noted, variable costs per unit of output remain constant at all levels of activity, assuming always that prices remain stable. For management decision making based on full unit costs, however, the level of activity is an important ingredient which must be taken into account when providing relevant information for such decisions.

The table below illustrates the behaviour of costs as volume changes.

Units produced	Total fixed costs	Total variable costs	Total costs	Average fixed cost per unit	Average variable cost per unit	Average total cost per unit
	£	£	£	£	£	£
1	300	100	400	300	100	400
2	300	200	500	150	100	250
3	300	300	600	100	100	200
4	300	400	700	75	100	175
5	300	500	800	60	100	160

From the foregoing discussion, we must examine the usefulness of the actual—that is current—volume of output as a level of activity upon which to base calculations of full unit costs. Current unit costs will fluctuate according to the actual level of activity; here costs are of little use for decisions regarding the future. Thus, pricing decisions require a more stable view of full costs than that provided as a result of fluctuating levels of output. Moreover, cost control implies that full unit costs incurred in one period are compared with those of other periods. Comparisons based on actual levels of output are unreliable because fixed costs per unit will be different where the output levels are different. Even for inventory valuation purposes, which, as we mentioned, was central to profit measurement, calculations based on actual volume will introduce distortions. Finally, since the calculation of unit costs based on actual volume can only be effected at the end of an accounting period, such unit costs are not relevant to its decision problems, which are more concerned with future than with past costs.

Since actual volume is not a satisfactory basis for calculating a fixed overhead rate which will be useful for the purposes which we have mentioned, the following alternative bases may be considered:

(a) theoretical capacity, which is the capacity of a particular department to maintain output at a 100 per cent level without interruption;
(b) practical capacity, which is the result of making allowances against the theoretical capacity in respect of unavoidable interruptions to output such as time lost for repairs and holidays;
(c) expected capacity as a short-run view of capacity, which is determined by immediate expectations of output levels;
(d) normal capacity, which is an estimate of output capacity based on a period of time long enough to level out peaks and troughs of cyclical fluctuations.

Normal capacity, as defined above, is the most useful level of activity for the purpose of determining a fixed overhead rate which will be relatively stable over a number of years. It will be appreciated that there is an element of subjectivity in the assessment of normal capacity, and it will lead invariably to some under- or over-absorption of fixed factory overhead costs depending on whether the actual level of activity is under or over the normal level. We shall deal with this problem in Chapter 37. Normal capacity often does provide, however, the most reliable and stable basis for calculating full-product costs for decision-making purposes.

Limitations of total cost calculations

It is clear from the foregoing examination of the problems associated with overhead costs that full-product costs cannot be measured with complete accuracy. To some extent, all methods used for apportioning overhead costs are arbitrary, and are based upon assumptions which are subjective to a degree. We stated that the 'benefit received' should be the main criterion for apportioning factory overhead costs to cost centres. It is difficult, however, to find bases which are suitable for this purpose. For example, the cost of the factory personnel department may be apportioned to cost centres on the basis of the relative number of their employees, but this base assumes that all employees will benefit equally from the services of this department. This example is, of course, a gross simplification of the general problem of apportioning overhead costs. Labour turnover and the difference in skills between different classes of employees will influence the time and the effort expended by the personnel department.

We have referred already to the element of subjectivity which enters into the selection of the methods of apportioning overhead costs. This is exacerbated by the degree of subjectivity which may be attached to the selection of the level of activity selected from recovering overhead costs. Indeed, two equally competent accountants may arrive at very different product costs simply because their view of what constitutes a 'normal level' of activity may differ. This problem applies similarly to the allotment of administrative costs. The bases for allotting these costs which we mentioned may be rationalized but may not be defended as being adequate cost accounting procedures. The cost of operating the purchasing department cannot be related, for example to any of the bases which we mentioned.

It is apparent that the main difficulty in computing full and total product costs stems from the presence of fixed overhead costs. The allotment of these costs to product costs on bases which are arbitrary renders the end result of doubtful accuracy. As we shall see elsewhere in this book, incorrect decisions may arise from the inclusion of fixed costs in product costs. For the purpose of external financial reporting, for example, we argue in Chapter 33 that more useful information may be provided if fixed overhead costs are not absorbed in output, but are treated as period costs. Moreover, their inclusion in product costs may give a misleading view of profit results. It is often claimed that for the purpose of long-range planning, product cost information should reflect total costs. However, as we shall see in Chapter 34, there is a case for directing attention away from a narrowly conceived view of price determination based on mark-up percentages on costs to the broader implications of cost-volume-profit relationships. As we shall also see, because of the behaviour of fixed and variable costs over different volumes of output, product cost information based on full costs is irrelevant to the problem of control. A distinction has to be made, therefore, between fixed and variable cost information for control purposes.

It follows that the limitations inherent in full-cost computations should be appreciated by all those using such information for decision making. From an accountant's point of view, specific instruction from management should be awaited for the calculation of product costs inclusive of fixed costs. Even then, a clear distinction should be made between fixed and variable cost components.

Actual and planned costs

At the beginning of this chapter, we stated that cost information is required for the undermentioned four major purposes:

(1) to assist in planning decisions;
(2) to assist in the control of operations;
(3) to assist in the measurement of reported profits;
(4) to report to employees.

The measurement of reported profit requires information of the actual or current costs of production during the accounting period. For the purposes of planning and control decisions, however, information is required not only about historical and current costs, but also about future costs. Since decisions are concerned with future events, the costs which are relevant for decision making are future costs. Past events are useful in this respect only if they influence judgements about future events. As we noted in Part 4, the risk attendant upon decisions stems from the uncertainty affecting future events. Management makes plans on the basis of current knowledge and management judgement about the future. One significant factor which has increased the risk attached to business decisions is inflation. Prior to the occurrence of rapid inflation in the early 1970s, for example, sales forecasting tended to be the major element of uncertainty in profit planning. Cost forecasts were relatively reliable, and appropriate pricing decisions could be made. With high levels of inflation, profit planning is much more uncertain in view of the greater difficulty of forecasting costs and making suitable pricing decisions.

Planning and control decisions are often made on the basis of special types of unit costs which are called standard costs. A standard cost is a pre-determined cost which is established in relation to specific operating conditions, and takes into consideration all the factors and circumstances which are likely to influence production costs. They are applied to both prime and overhead costs, and their objective is to establish standards both for the rate of usage of resources and their input price.

Standard costs are used both for planning and for control purposes. Thus, they are used for the purposes of drawing up plans and budgets, and they are used also for maintaining control over operations.

Actual costs serve two very useful roles for planning and control purposes. As regards planning decisions, they act as feedback information which either validates those decisions, or assists in improving the planning process by examining the reasons for previous errors. For control purposes, actual costs are compared with planned costs as a means of checking that actual performance is conforming with planned performance. Variance analysis, as we shall see in Chapter 37 is a central aspect of the control process.

Standard costs are also used in the measurement of reported profit, as they form the basis on which costs are calculated. If the standards used reflect current conditions, they are current costs, and may be used in a current cost accounting system, as described in Chapter 21. A company that uses a standard cost system will be able to calculate the cost of sales adjustment from the variances associated with purchases.

Summary

Cost information is required for four main purposes:

(1) for planning decisions;
(2) for control decisions;
(3) for the measurement of reported income;
(4) for reporting to employees.

The type of cost information required may be different in each of these cases. We shall analyse the nature and the use of various cost measurements in this part.

This chapter has been concerned with the accounting problems involved in the measurement of unit costs of production. The major difficulty in the measurement of total product costs lies in the calculation and assignment of factory overhead costs. The process of assigning factory overhead costs to units of product occurs in the following stages:

(a) allotting factory overhead costs to production cost centres and finding appropriate levels of activity for this purpose;
(b) allotting the costs of production cost centres to units of product and finding appropriate methods for this purpose.

The use of cost information for planning and control decisions implies that such cost information should reflect the future rather than the past. For this reason, standard costs—which are pre-determined costs—are used. They not only reflect expectations about the costs which will be current in the period ahead, but are intended to deal with the uncertainties implicit in decision making.

Questions

1. As the accountant of the Northumberland Engineering Co. operating in a very competitive industry by means of special jobs to each customer's requirements, you are required to:

   (a) Calculate the (estimated) cost of job enquiry number 876, for which details are given below.
   (b) On the basis of your cost figures, indicate the price you feel should be charged to the customer for job 876; or, if you feel unable to do this, indicate what further information you would need in order to arrive at a price.
   All calculations should be clearly shown and figures justified.

Job Enquiry Number 876
 (i) Estimated direct material cost: £1000
 (ii) Estimated direct labour input:

	Hours	Rate per hour £
Plating Department	81	4.00
Welding Department	14	3.00
Assembly Department	10	2.00

(iii) Indirect departmental costs:

	Plating	Welding	Assembly
Total indirect costs:			
Last year's actual	£20,000	£8000	£4000
This year's budget	£22,000	£9000	£5000

(iv) Activity levels (labour hours):

Last year's actual	£10,000	£8000	£4000
This year's budget	£9000	£10,000	£4000

2. Byfokal Product Ltd uses a pre-determined overhead rate for the purpose of job-order costing. This rate is based on machine-hours with regards to the Machining Department and on direct labour cost with respect to the Assembly and Finishing Department.

   The following forecasts have been used to calculate the predetermined overhead rate for these two departments:

	Machining Department	Assembly and Finishing Department
Machine hours	100,000	30,000
Direct labour hours	60,000	150,000
Direct labour cost	£500,000	£1,250,000
Factory overhead costs	£2,500,000	£2,000,000

The job-order cost sheet for Job Number 35 showed the following information:

	Machining Department	Assembly and Finishing Department
Direct materials used	£3500	£1000
Direct labour cost	£20,000	£28,000
Direct labour hours	2400	3360
Machine hours	4000	672

Required:

1. What is the pre-determined overhead rate for each department?
2. Calculate the total overhead cost for Job 35.
3. The managing director of Marco Fabrication is concerned about the reliability and relevance of the product unit costs which have been used to date for general purposes. Shortly after your appointment as the firm's accountant you are required to write him a report explaining your general approach to the use of cost accounts and in particular the problems of overhead costing. You derive the following information for this purpose:

   The company has two producing departments, Machining and Assembly, and one service department, Canteen. Direct departmental overhead for the coming year is estimated as Machining £50,000, Assembly £40,000 and Canteen £10,000. Details of estimated indirect overhead are as follows:

Rates	£1000
Depreciation	£9300
Light and power	£600

Departmental data

	Kilowatt hours	No. of employees	Cost of equipment	Square feet
Machining	600	20	£10,000	600
Assembly	1100	10	£20,000	1200
Canteen	300	5	£1000	200

	Estimated direct labour cost	Estimated direct labour hours	Estimated machine hours
Machining	£10,000	18,000	8000
Assembly	£15,000	12,000	20,000

The above activity levels are based on what could be attained if production was at full capacity. Expected activity for the coming year is estimated to be 70 per cent full capacity, and normal activity at 80 per cent.

Section 2 Planning

28 Long-range planning

Long-range planning is not a single technique, nor is it just one area of management responsibility. It is a systematic attempt to plan the entire behaviour of the organization in the long-run, and in the case of profit-making organizations, it attempts to increase the rate of profitable growth (Perrin, 1968). In this chapter, we shall examine the stages involved in long-range planning, and we shall discuss the accountant's role in that process.

Long-range planning is concerned with:

1 the determination of long-range objectives;
2 the preparation of the position audit;
3 the formulation of strategy;
4 the preparation and implementation of the plan;
5 the continuous review and up-dating of the plan.

The determination of long-range objectives

The importance of cash flows

In the final analysis, cash flows into and out of a business enterprise are the most fundamental events upon which accounting measurements are based. Management and investors, in particular, are very concerned with the cash flows generated by corporate assets. These cash flows are not only central to the problem of corporate survival, but they are essential to the attainment of corporate objectives. In this part, we are concerned with the management of corporate assets with the view to generating cash flows. The size, timing and risks inherent in estimating future cash flows are critical aspects of this analysis. In Part 4, we argued that the purpose of income measurement is to enable shareholders and investors to predict future cash flows, and noted that cash flow reports were more useful in this respect than conventional income statements.

The recognition of the importance of future cash flows has led many writers to define *the* objective of business corporations in terms of maximizing corporate wealth, defined as the present value of the future stream of net cash flows to be earned by corporate assets. This objective is also expressed as the maximization of shareholders' wealth, since they are deemed in law to be the owners of the enterprise.

In Part 1, we explained that the distinctive feature of the modern business corporation as an 'entrepreneurial unit' is the separation of ownership from management. The power of shareholders to control management is limited to a number of issues, which is the business reserved by law to the Annual General Meeting of Shareholders. This business includes the election of directors, the appointment of auditors, the approval of annual financial reports and of dividend recommendations. In the process of adjusting to social pressures both external and internal to the firm, management has tended to utilize its relative freedom from ownership control to re-define the concept of managerial responsibility. Responsibilities to employees, consumers and to society at large may conflict with responsibilities to shareholders. Nevertheless, profit remains the most widely understood index of business success. Accordingly, profit making, which is regarded as the ability to generate cash flows, remains the basic objective of management.

Objectives and goals

We may identify two basic types of organizational objectives:

1 Broad corporate objectives which are general statements of policy which represent the ideals of the organization.
2 Goals which are derived from these objectives and which establish specific targets for the organization. They include also lesser goals such as targets for sub-units, such as departments, and performance standards for managers and employees.

It follows, therefore, that there exists a hierarchy of goals applicable to every level of the organization, which are subordinated to the main goals and which interpret those goals. The management problem is not simply setting goals, but securing the attainment of those goals. We shall examine the behavioural aspects of the latter problem in Chapter 39 where we discuss the manner in which the style of management known as 'management by objectives' attempts to create a high degree of goal congruence between the personal objectives and organizational goals. For the moment, we shall concern ourselves with the analysis of organizational objectives and organizational goals.

Organizational objectives

These objectives serve as guidelines for establishing goals.

Example

Hygrade Cutlery Ltd has the following objectives:

(1) Profit objective—to achieve a profit level sufficient to reward shareholders adequately and to protect the interests of creditors.
(2) Financial objectives—to secure adequate financial resources and to report to management on the utilization of these resources.
(3) Market objective—to build public confidence and to create goodwill for products bearing the company's name, thereby increasing customers' preference for the company's goods.
(4) Production objective—to increase the efficiency of production of high-quality products.

(5) Employee objective—to provide good jobs, wages and working conditions, work satisfaction, stability of employment and opportunity for advancement, in return for loyalty, skills, initiative, effort and teamwork.

(6) Innovation objective—to develop new and better products.

Organizational goals

Goals are objectives which have been quantified and set as targets. Whereas objectives may sound rather vague or obvious, goals are targets which are intended to apply to the time-span of the planning period.

Example

The goals established by Hygrade Cutlery Ltd for the next five years are as follows:

(1) Profit goals—to attain a profit level of 20 per cent before tax on the market value of the shareholders' equity by the end of the fifth year; to attain a profit level of 16 per cent on total assets by the end of the fifth year; to achieve a profit before tax/sales ratio of 12 per cent for each year; to increase after tax earnings per share by at least 10 per cent per year.

(2) Financial goals—to improve the present cash position; to reduce debtors by 5 per cent; to secure a return of 14 per cent after tax on new capital expenditure.

(3) Market goals—to increase total sales of stainless steel cutlery over the period by 30 per cent; to increase marketing facilities abroad so that the number of customers served by the company will be 20 per cent higher in five years' time.

(4) Production goal—to increase output per employee by 15 per cent over the next five years.

(5) Employee goals—to reduce labour turnover by 15 per cent; to improve the current management development scheme; to introduce management by objectives within two years.

(6) Innovation goal—to introduce a new range of stainless steel family-size teasets within one year.

The position audit

In estimating future cash flows, which are intended to result from a planned course of action, managers are able to draw on a great deal of inside information which is at their disposal. Top managers are placed in a unique position to assess a wide range of opportunities open to the firm, and to relate its present or potential technological, production and financial resources to these opportunities in the process of selecting the best strategy for attaining corporate objectives. This process of assessment is conducted by means of a position audit, which has an external and an internal aspect.

The external audit

The external audit is concerned with the environment in which the firm exists. It is also concerned with identifying opportunities and dangers facing the organization, and in particular in assessing changes in the economic, political, social, technological and industrial environment. If management is able to forecast significant changes in these various aspects of the firm's environment, it will be in a better position to deal with the opportunities and the problems which these changes present.

Forecasting plays a crucial role in the external audit. Two techniques are useful in this respect—economic forecasting and technological forecasting. Economic forecasting is concerned with predicting economic conditions which may have important implications for the firm. Technological forecasting is concerned with predicting changes in technology, so as to anticipate the nature of technological innovation to the advantage of the firm.

The usefulness of forecasts is realized only when they influence decisions, that is, when predictions are assumed to be part of the firm's environment in formulating objectives and goals, and preparing a strategy for attaining them.

The internal audit

The internal audit is focused on the organization's own strengths and weaknesses. It involves an appraisal of every aspect of the organization, including management, labour, products, markets, distribution channels, finance, assets and research and development. The purpose of this appraisal is to discover the reasons for present successes and failures, and to identify key success factors for the future. In conducting the internal audit, management will have much to learn from the experience of its competitors, and in identifying key success factors it will seek to compare its own strengths and weaknesses with those of its competitors.

The main purpose of both external and internal audits is to relate the organization's prospects with the prospects of the industry in which it is operating. The outlook for the industry affects the demand for the products or services of the industry; the supply of products or services is affected not only by productive capacity in the industry, but by labour and material costs peculiar to the industry. The firm's prospects within the industry are a function of its own position in the industry, the degree of competition existing in the industry and the firm's own cost structure. The position audit is, therefore, a learning exercise for the firm.

The formulation of strategy

The position audit outlines the array of factors which should be considered when formulating a strategy for attaining organizational objectives and goals. The role of strategy, therefore, is to select the best way of getting from the present position to the goals which have been derived from the organization's objectives. The first stage in the formulation of a strategy is an analysis of the gap between the present position and the desired position, which takes into account the forecasts which will have been made. Gap analysis involves the following questions:

1   What will happen if nothing is done?
2   What will happen if we pursue present policies?
3   What should be done to attain organizational goals?

Gap analysis and the profit goal

The effects of alternative policies on profits is a very good example of gap analysis. Once the profit goal has been determined, it may be compared with the level of earnings for the business as it is presently operated. If no changes were made, present earnings would probably begin to decline after a period of time. This is because, as technology changes, as market demand and tastes change, as competitors improve performance etc., existing products are likely to become less profitable.

Previous long-range planning exercises, however, will have built into the operations of the firm tactics to counter the fall-off in performance which would have occurred due to the causes mentioned. The difference between these two forecasts may be called the 'improvement gap'. It illustrates the value to the firm of former plans. The difference between the profit improvement figure and the profit goal is called the strategic gap. This represents the profit which the firm is required to make to meet the shortfall in its profit goal, and may be illustrated as in Fig. 5.7.

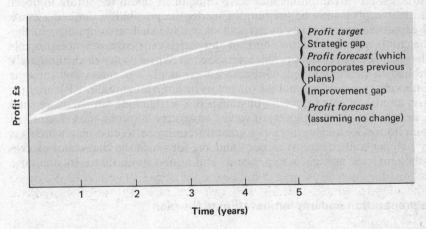

Fig. 5.7.

Long-range planning and gap analysis

The essence of long-range planning is really one of gap analysis. The problem involved in this analysis is the evaluation of alternative strategies for closing the strategic gap and selecting that strategy which is seen as the best one. Future cash flows, and consequently profits, are highly constrained by past and present capital expenditure decisions. Therefore, a pre-requisite to gap analysis is a *search* process to discover suitable projects in which the firm should invest. Throughout the search process, the firm is concerned typically with the following questions:

Can present operations be extended to meet organizational goals? If so, what does this mean in terms of greater penetration of existing markets, the exploration of new markets, the need for finance, assets, manpower etc.?

If present operations cannot be extended, how should the firm proceed? Should less profitable activities be abandoned and resources redeployed in new activities?

The search process is costly and time consuming. An influential factor in determining the scope of search is the affinity between search areas and the present activities of the organization. Areas of search should be chosen which will complement current areas of activity, thereby providing synergistic opportunities. Synergy arises when two activities or actions performed jointly produce a greater total effect than if they had been performed separately. For example, the addition of a restaurant to the activities of a departmental store produces a synergistic effect in that the restaurant makes the store a more convenient place in which to shop, and the store provides a ready clientele for the restaurant. Hence, the total volume of business enjoyed by both the store and the restaurant is greater than if they had been established and maintained as separate businesses in different locations. The synergistic effect is often called the '2 + 2 = 5 effect' for this reason (Ansoff, 1969).

At this stage, assumptions may have to be made about the future in order that realistic plans may be prepared. Clearly, the possibility of making grave and expensive errors exists as a result of making such assumptions. In this connection, one has only to think of the many expensive defence projects undertaken by governments since the Second World War which ultimately have had to be abandoned. Unlike a government, a business enterprise is much more exposed to penalties for errors of large magnitude. Risk analysis has an important role to play in planning. It is a technique which, as we shall see in a subsequent chapter, involves assigning a 'probability factor' to assumptions. Obviously, there is a great difference between a plan which has only a 50 per cent chance of success, and one for which the chances of success are thought to be as high as 95 per cent. This notion is central to risk analysis.

The preparation and implementation of the plan

The selected strategy for the long-run will concentrate on the key factors for success and on the major decisions required. In particular, it will be concerned with basic issues such as the selection of the kinds of products or services which should be produced, their markets, the production process and its location, and the asset structure required.

Once the strategy has been selected, it has to be expressed in more detailed plans which then become the basis for action. Responsibility for implementing the plan will fall upon the management personnel in the various divisions and departments of the organization. In this chapter, we shall examine briefly a small aspect of the planning process, namely financial planning. The reader should bear in mind that long-range planning covers every spectrum of the firm's activities, and detailed plans for all these activities will be drafted.

The continuous review and updating of the plan

Corporate planning is a continuous process which responds to feedback information. Updating may occur both on a continuous and on an annual basis. Corporate planning departments will be continually accumulating information and interpreting the significance of that information to the plan. The time-period envisaged by different firms for long-range planning purposes does vary, but it is quite normal to review the plan at the end of each year, and to incorporate those changes which are deemed to be necessary. This allows changes of every kind to be recognized and so introduces a degree of flexibility into the corporate planning process. At the end of each year, the plan must be extended for a further year so that the roll-over maintains a view of a constant time-period associated with long-range planning. The relationship between the long-range plan and the annual budget plan is very significant, and we shall consider this problem in Chapter 30.

The importance of the long-range profit goal

We stated at the beginning of this chapter that the firm's success depends on its ability to generate a sufficiency of cash flows, symbolized by profit. The selection of a profit target for long-range planning purposes is not just a matter of fixing an arbitrary figure such as £5 million. A profit target of itself has little meaning: its significance appears when it is related to some other measurement, such as total assets employed, when it becomes a meaningful measure of performance. Thus, the return on capital employed (ROCE) which relates profits to assets employed provides an assessment of the significance of a profit target by means of the following formula:

$$\text{ROCE} = \frac{\text{Planned net profit}}{\text{Planned total assets}}$$

There is general agreement that the ROCE is the most important performance measurement for long-range planning and for setting long-range profit targets. It is a common practice to compute the ROCE for each year covered by the long-range plan in order to show whether planned increases in annual profits will keep pace with annual increases in assets. This analysis also indicates the effectiveness with which management will be required to use corporate assets.

In recent years, the usefulness of ROCE measures has been questioned. We shall discuss the controversies involved in the use of ROCE in Chapter 36 of this part. Further difficulties are caused by the manner in which profits and assets might be defined and measured. These difficulties were considered in Part 4.

According to Drucker (1963), there are eight areas of activity to which the firm should direct its attention when formulating its objectives—market standing, innovation, productivity, physical and financial resources, profitability, manager performance and development, worker performance and attitude, and public responsibility. It is in these areas of activity that the several parties having a stake in the firm—shareholders, management, employees, government, customers and suppliers, and the local community—have vested interests. Of the eight areas listed above, profitability is the most important because it provides a means of achieving objectives in the other seven areas. Unless a firm achieves a satisfactory profit goal, it may not survive in the long-term.

The accountant's task is not to attempt the impossible by deciding what should be the maximum possible long-range profit on the basis of assumed long-range resources for planning purposes: his job is to quantify the size of the profit which is required as the profit objective. The required profit as a planning goal is never a theoretical ideal, such as 'the maximum long-term profit' or 'the maximum long-term return to shareholders', but represents rather the outcome of discussion as to what is a possible and desirable target for the time-span considered.

The longer the time-span envisaged as a planning period, the less reliable is the profit target selected as a planning objective. It is for this very important reason that we suggested earlier that the 'maximum long-term profit' is never a planning goal, for it falls beyond a planner's vision. Instead a firm aims to earn a 'satisfactory' profit over the planning period.

As a guide to selecting the profit target, one of the most influential factors is the minimum rate of return expected by investors and creditors. A satisfactory profit ensures that debt and dividend payments may be made, thereby reducing the risks attached to investing in the firm.

If the profit target is set too low to provide a fair dividend for shareholders and sufficient retained profit to finance future expansion, the Stock Exchange's dissatisfaction with performance will be reflected in the company's share price, which in turn will impede the firm's ability to raise fresh capital and undermine its financial standing with creditors. It is, therefore, desirable that the share price should reflect a satisfactory profit target, for the value of a company is represented by the market price of its shares. It is through capital gains, as these shares appreciate in value, that shareholders receive much of their return. The amount of takeover activity in recent years has drawn attention to the fact that management should be aware of the importance of the behaviour of share prices.

Another important factor in long-range profit planning arises from the need of firms to generate capital to finance expansion. Capital generated in this way represents a substantial portion of the capital required by established companies, and profit retentions for this purpose often amount to 50 per cent of net profit.

The firm is faced, therefore, with the unavoidable problem of selecting a long-range profit target which will be satisfactory as regards the various points which we have just discussed. This is a minimum requirement, and unless an attempt is made to attain this profit objective in the long-range plan, the plan itself cannot be regarded as satisfactory.

Before we can calculate a target return on capital employed we must first estimate the returns which shareholders are likely to expect over the planning period. The following factors will affect these returns:

(1) The rate of return which shareholders have had in recent years.

(2) The rate of return which they could earn elsewhere. If a better rate of return is obtainable from similar companies, there will be pressure from management to increase the profit target.

(3) The impact of inflation on the rate of return. The rate of return may have to be increased to compensate shareholders for the falling value of money.

(4) The effects of changes in government policy with regard to taxation. For example, the introduction of capital gains tax, and the restrictions which governments have imposed on dividends in recent years have had serious repercussions on shareholders.

(5) The effects of changes in gearing. It may be possible to increase the return on shareholders' funds by altering the capital structure.

(6) The character of the firm's dividend policy. There are two methods by which the risk borne by ordinary shareholders may be rewarded. The first method emphasizes a high annual rate of dividend, and the second stresses the capital gain which accrues as a result of the increased value of the shares where a company retains and re-invests a high proportion of its profit. There are some who argue that the interests of investors and of the community would best be served by the total distribution of profit as dividends, and that individual companies should go to the market for any capital which is needed for expansion. In practice many companies attempt to strike a balance, distributing approximately half their profits as dividends and retaining and re-investing the balance in their capital expansion plans. As a result, most ordinary shareholders receive a return which is a mixture of annual dividend and capital gain.

Setting profit targets

Once having agreed the returns to shareholders, the next step is to incorporate the results of these calculations in a return on capital employed. This takes into account the amount to be retained in the business and the tax liability.

Consider the position of a firm for which it is calculated that a necessary return to shareholders of £30,000 has been calculated; whilst it is estimated that £20,000 should be retained in the business.

From the figures listed below it is apparent that an earnings figure of £100,000 is required in order to provide for these estimates.

	£
Returns to shareholders	30,000
Retained in business	20,000
Tax (50%)	50,000
Earnings required	100,000

If the firm's total assets are forecasted at £500,000, then a return of 20 per cent on capital employed is required, viz:

$$\frac{\text{Earnings required}}{\text{Total assets}} = \frac{£100,000}{£500,000} \times 100 = \underline{\underline{20\%}}$$

Divisional profit targets

Once the company's overall long-range profit target has been agreed, the next task is to apportion it across the separate parts of the enterprise, whether these be divisions or subsidiary companies. It is not necessary, nor indeed desirable that the overall profit target be evenly spread across the enterprise, for different growth rates and different profit targets are perfectly compatible with sound strategic planning. Thus, it is possible to select a distribution showing an expected rate of return on investments of 30 per cent in respect of one division as against a 10 per cent rate for another division. The reasons for a diversity among planned divisional profit targets may lie in the type of market in which the divisions operate: fast growing markets may offer higher return prospects than mature and established markets. Equally, varying rates of return may reflect the different degrees of risks attached to the different types of activities in which the several divisions may be engaged.

In the discussions leading to the formulation of the overall profit target, the various divisions will have submitted their estimates of the possible profit targets. If there should have existed a gap between the aggregated divisional profit recommendations and the overall target which top management sought to attain, it may have been necessary to revise the corporate strategy and re-examine both the company and divisional profit targets.

Financial planning

We have seen how the main objectives of the firm are expressed in financial form. Detailed financial analysis is necessary to support these financial targets. Since this type of analysis is dealt with throughout this book, this chapter is not detailed in this respect. Indeed, the purpose of this chapter is to emphasize the necessity of setting long-run objectives and of relating short-term decisions to these objectives.

In the field of long-range planning, the accountant's role is to contribute to the management team. The importance of this role should be apparent from our discussions earlier in this chapter of the way profit targets are set.

The accountant's role in this regard has been defined as embracing the following activities:

(1) Providing background information which serves as a prelude to planning. A valuable contribution which the accountant may make in this respect is the preparation of preliminary studies in the form of reviews of past performance, product-mix studies, surveys of physical facilities, and estimates of capital expenditure requirements. Moreover, he has special skills in the analyses of cost-volume profit relationships, profit margins by product lines, cash flows and so on.

(2) Assisting in the evaluation of alternative courses of action which are being considered, and assessing the financial feasibility of the proposed course of action. This requires the accountant to decide what data is relevant, prior to its analysis and expression in financial terms, so that the data base of the long-range plan shall be reliable.

(3) Assembling, integrating and co-ordinating detailed plans into a corporate master plan. In this respect, the accountant has a traditional skill in aggregating data which is particularly relevant.

(4) Translating plans into overall schedules of costs, profit and financial conditions. These schedules may subsequently be used to prepare detailed operating budgets.

(5) Presenting the anticipated results of future operations in financial terms.

(6) Assisting in the critical appraisal and, where necessary, the revision of long-range plans to ensure that they do constitute a realistic basis for directing and controlling future operations.

(7) Establishing and administering the network of operational controls that are necessary to the attainment of the planned objectives. This vital phase of the planning process requires the integration of long- and short-run profit plans, the monitoring of current performance against that planned for the long-term and reporting to management on the realization of the long-term plan.

The long-range financial plan

Long-range financial planning is concerned with ensuring the continuing soundness of the financial structure of the firm, maintaining adequate working capital, and providing additional capital for expansion from earnings, borrowings or by the issue of new shares.

The essential components of the long-range financial plan are a projected income statement, a projected cash flow statement, a capital expenditure forecast, a financing plan and a projection of the capital structure. We shall briefly examine each of these components of the financial plan.

(a) *The projected income statement*
The projected income forecast for the long-range planning period will be set out in the traditional manner, as follows:

Projected income statement

		Years		
	1	2	3	4	5
Sales					
Cost of goods sold					
Selling and administrative expenses					
Depreciation					
Interest charges					
Income before tax					
Tax					
Income after tax					

(b) *The projected cash flow*
The accountant will be particularly concerned with ensuring that the company remains solvent, that it has no liquidity problems and that financial resources for growth are provided. He will be required to estimate the financial needs of the long-range plan and advise on the financing arrangements which may be made to meet these needs.

An estimate of the cash flow pattern broken down over the long-range plan will show when shortages and surpluses of cash are likely to occur, and hence will enable plans to be drawn up to arrange the firm's finances to best advantage.

Long-range cash flow

			Years		
	1	2	3	4	5
Source					
Net cash inflow from operations					
Other receipts					
Total cash available					
Use					
Taxation					
Dividends					
Loan repayment					
Capital expenditure					
Investments					
Total requirement					
Surplus/Shortfall					
Financed by					
New share issues					
Debentures					
Bank balances					

As may be seen from the example on the previous page, the long-range cash flow profile is a very useful tool of analysis in a number of ways. Firstly, it indicates whether or not fresh injections of cash will be necessary to finance the long-range plan, or whether future capital expenditure and the planned expansion of operations can be financed from retained income after taking into account anticipated tax liabilities and dividend payments. Secondly, the long-range cash flow will point out when deficits and surpluses will occur, and so assist in the formulation of a financial strategy over time. Thirdly, the cash flow plan will establish the relative duration of deficits and surpluses, and this information will likewise be most useful from a financing point of view.

(c) *The capital expenditure forecast*
We devote Chapter 29 to an examination of the problem of planning capital expenditure. The capital expenditure forecast will be simply the annual financial requirement to support this expenditure.

(d) *The financing plan*
The financing plan is concerned with ensuring that the necessary finance will

be available to support the long-range plan. If, as a result of the planned activities for the period, a deficit is forecast and it is likely to be of short duration, it may be financed from a number of different sources, for example, by means of a bank overdraft or a temporary run-down of stocks. If, however, the deficit is likely to exist for a longer period, it may be necessary to raise new capital. The financing plan considers the manner in which a financial deficit is to be covered. This may be formulated as follows:

Financing plan

	Years				
	1	2	3	4	5
Finance required					
Financed by:					
New share issue					
Debenture issue					
Short-term borrowing					
Total finance provided					

(e) *The capital structure projection*

It is clear from the foregoing that the financial plan which is devised to support the long-range plan may have important implications for the capital structure of the firm in a number of ways.

First, the company will have to form a view as to the merits or otherwise of altering the gearing of the company. As we saw in Part 2, the gearing represents the ratio of fixed interest stock as against equity capital, and the reader will recall that if a company is highly geared and profit fluctuates over time, the rate of return payable to ordinary shareholders will fluctuate to a proportionately greater extent with consequential effects on the value of the ordinary shares on the market.

Secondly, the management of working capital will be a critical success factor, particularly should the economic climate change during the period, with adverse effects on liquidity and credit facilities. Working capital is defined as the excess of current assets over current liabilities, and is regarded as being available for supporting current operations as distinct from the financing of capital expenditure.

Thirdly, a decision to finance capital expenditure by means of new share or debenture issues will also affect share prices unless dividend rates can be maintained through increased profits. The outcome, in any event, will largely depend upon management's previous record and the firm's standing in the market. The capital structure projection may be formulated as follows:

Year-end capital structure projection

	Years				
	1	2	3	4	5
Shareholders' equity					
Long-term debt					
Total capital					
Debt ratio					

Long-range profit planning and other long-range objectives

In this chapter, we have discussed long-range planning almost exclusively in terms of long-range profit planning and its financial implications. This is because it is one of the most important company objectives, and one of special interest to accountants. It should not be forgotten, however, that long-range planning requires that careful attention should similarly be given to the attainment of other objectives of great importance to the company, for example, those relating to employees, consumers and the local community. Unless a firm gives attention to developing realistic objectives in these other areas the firm will find its ability to make profits very restricted.

It is evident from the nature of the accountant's skills, and the range of activities in which he may be involved, that he has a central role to play in long-range planning. The result of his involvement in long-range planning is to bring him into contact with functions beyond his direct control such as marketing, research and development and production to a much greater extent than is possible in short-term planning.

Summary

The purpose of this chapter has been to emphasize the necessity of setting long-run objectives and of relating short-term decisions to these objectives. Long-range planning has received increasing attention in recent years due to rapidly changing business conditions, which have persuaded management to take a longer view of the firm's activities than has hitherto been thought necessary. It is becoming widely recognized that effective long-range planning should result in a firm being always in the best position with products, resources and processes deployed in such a way as to take advantage of all the opportunities which present themselves. Long-range planning is seen as providing a systematic way of running a company so that not only can it anticipate change, but may actually profit from change. The absence of long-range planning may be detrimental to a firm in a number of ways: for example, current profitability may induce so much complacency that danger signals may be ignored, and in due course, valuable opportunities may not be seized. Equally, an excessive concern with short-term planning may encourage actions in the short-term which are detrimental to the long-term interests of the firm.

A long-range plan may be damaging, however, if it is badly implemented. Thus, a rigid long-range plan may turn out to be inappropriate for new circumstances. It is necessary, therefore, that long-range planning should have a degree of flexibility, so as to allow for adjustments to changing circumstances. Long-range planning should include a continuous scanning process aimed at discovering opportunities, defining constraints and assessing risks.

The accountant has an important role to play in long-range planning, particularly in long-range financial planning.

References

1. Ansoff, H. I. 'Towards a strategic theory of the firm', *reprinted in* Ansoff, H. I. (ed.), *Business Strategy*, pp. 21, 22, Penguin Books, 1969.
2. Drucker, P. F. *The Practice of Management*, p. 52, Heinemann, London, 1963.
3. N.A.A. Research Report No. 42. *Long-Range Profit Planning*, 1964.
4. Perrin, R. 'Long-range planning; the concept and the need', *Long-Range Planning*, September, 1968.

Questions

1. Why are cash flows so important to an enterprise?
2. Distinguish between objectives and goals.
3. Name six typical areas in which a firm may set objectives and goals.
4. What is a position audit?
5. How is strategy formulated?
6. What factors does management take into account in calculating the returns which shareholders are likely to expect over the planning period?
7. What is the role of the accountant in long-range financial planning?
8. What are the main components of a long-range financial plan?

29 Planning capital expenditure

The level of a firm's profits depends upon the success with which it is able to employ all its assets—human and non-human. The firm's future profitability depends on two factors, firstly, maintaining and enlarging its asset structure, and secondly, devising a successful strategy for that asset structure. The previous chapter drew attention to the fact that preparing the capital expenditure plan is part of the long-range planning process. The activity of investing in new assets, often termed *capital budgeting*, involves planning capital expenditure and arranging the financing of this expenditure. It is an area of management decision making which has attracted a great deal of interest among accountants and economists in recent years, and much research has been devoted towards evolving methods for improving the quality of these decisions.

In this chapter, we can only hope to touch upon the main issues. We shall deal mainly with capital expenditure decisions, and we shall examine the relevant factors and the methods which are currently employed for making capital investment decisions. Financing capital expenditure, which is the other aspect of capital budgeting, belongs to a sophisticated area of study known as the Theory of Finance. We shall make only brief reference to this aspect of capital budgeting, and must refer the reader to the literature of the Theory of Finance for a proper treatment of this subject.

Capital investment decisions

Probably the most significant factors affecting the level of profitability in a business is the quality of managerial decisions affecting the commitment of the firm's resources to new investments within the firm. The reasons which render such strategic decisions so important may be listed as follows:

(a) they involve the commitment of substantial sums of money;
(b) this commitment is made for a long period of time, and the element of uncertainty is therefore much greater than in the case of decisions whose effects are limited to a short period of time;
(c) once made, capital investment decisions are almost impossible to reverse should they appear subsequently to have been wrongly made;
(d) occasionally, the success or the failure of a firm may depend upon a single decision. In all cases, the future profitability of the firm will be affected by the decision;
(e) not only is capital expenditure policy of major importance to a firm, but it is of great significance to an industry as well as to the national economy.

Types of capital investment decisions

A capital investment may be defined as an investment which yields returns during several future time periods, and may be contrasted with other types of investments which yield all their return in the current time period. Capital investment decisions may concern the following:

(a) the acquisition or replacement of long-lived assets, such as buildings and plant;
(b) the investment of funds into another firm from which revenues will flow;
(c) a special project which will affect the firm's future earning capacity, such as a research project or an advertising campaign;
(d) the extension of the range of activities of the firm involving a capital outlay, such as a new production line or indeed a new product.

Capital investment decisions encompass two aspects of long-range profitability: first, estimating the future net increases in cash inflows or net savings in cash outlays which will result from the investment; and second, calculating the total cash outlays required to effect the investment.

The analysis of capital investment proposals

In the analysis of capital investment proposals, many of the important facts are uncertain, so that the first problem is to reduce the area of uncertainty before a decision is made. As we shall see in Chapter 31, risk analysis offers methods for handling the problem of uncertainty. The second problem is to ensure that all known facts are correctly assessed and quantified. Both known and uncertain facts are estimated in cash terms, and the methods of capital investment appraisal focus on cash flows.

The selection of investment projects is always a question of considering which of several competing alternatives is the best from the firm's point of view. By quantifying the cash inflows and the cash outlays which are involved in the various alternatives, a decision may be made by selecting that alternative which is preferred by the firm.

Example

Wall Street Finance Ltd is offered the opportunity of selecting two investments, each of which will yield £500,000 yearly. Investment A requires a total cash outlay of £5,000,000—hence it promises a rate of return of 10 per cent. Investment B requires a total cash outlay of £50,000,000—and therefore offers a rate of return of 1 per cent per annum. The firm would prefer investment A. However, if the firm has a minimum acceptable rate of return of 15 per cent, neither project would be acceptable.

We may conclude, therefore, that there are three major factors affecting capital investment decisions:

(a) The net amount of the investment required, expressed as the total cash outlay needed to support the project during its entire life.

(b) The net returns on the investment, expressed as the future expected net cash inflows. These may be actual cash flows, or cash savings.

(c) The rate of return on investment, expressed as a percentage. The determination of the lowest acceptable rate of return on investment will be influenced by a number of factors, among which are the firm's rate of return on its other investment opportunities and the cost of capital to the firm.

The relevant cash flows

Before we proceed to examining the methods of selecting investment projects, let us briefly define the meaning of the terms which we shall be employing.

(a) *Net investment outlays*
These consist of initial investment outlays required to establish the project, and the subsequent investment outlays which are envisaged at the outset, and are distinguishable from operating cash outlays. Thus, initial investment outlays may comprise expenditure on equipment, installation costs, manpower training, working capital etc. Subsequent investment outlays may include 'second stage' developments, plant extensions etc. The analysis of a capital project is in terms of net cash costs to the firm, so that where tax credits are allowable, these credits must be deducted from the total cash costs to obtain the relevant cash outlay.

(b) *Net cash inflows*
These are the operating cash flows associated with the investment over the period of its useful life. They are calculated after deducting operating cash expenditure and taxation. Since there may be year-to-year variation in the profile of these net cash flows, and since their periodic pattern is largely guesswork, they are the most difficult cash flows to quantify.

All cash-flow calculations are made on the basis of the estimated useful life of the investment, which is defined as the time interval that is expected to elapse between the time of acquisition or commencement and the time at which the combined forces of obsolescence and deterioration will justify the retirement of the asset or project. The useful life of the investment may be shortened by market changes which will diminish its earnings.

Methods of appraising capital investments

The more commonly used methods of evaluating capital investment proposals are:

(a) the pay-back period;
(b) the accounting rate of return;
(c) the discounted cash flow techniques, of which there are two main forms:
　(i) the net present value method (NPV)
　(ii) the internal rate of return (IRR).

The pay-back period

This method attempts to forecast how long it will take for the expected net cash inflows to *pay back* the net investment outlays. The pay-back period is calculated as follows:

$$\text{Pay-back period (years)} = \frac{\text{Net investment outlays}}{\text{Average net cash inflows}}$$

Example

Northend Engineering Co Ltd is considering the acquisition of machinery which will considerably reduce labour costs. The following are the relevant facts:

Net investment outlays	£200,000
Estimated annual cash savings (after tax)	60,000
Estimated useful life	5 years
Salvage value	Nil

The pay-back period is as follows:

$$\frac{£200,000}{60,000} \text{ i.e. } 3\tfrac{1}{3} \text{ years}$$

The pay-back method has the advantage of simplicity. By advocating the selection of projects by reference only to the speed with which investment outlays are recovered, it recommends the acceptance of only the safest projects. It is a method which emphasizes liquidity rather than profitability, and its limitations may be stated to be:

(a) It lays stress on the pay-back period rather than the useful life of the investment, and ignores the cash flows beyond the pay-back period. Hence, it focuses on breakeven rather than on profitability.

(b) It ignores the time profile of the net cash inflows, and any time pattern in the net investment outlays. Any salvage value would also be ignored. This method, therefore, treats all cash flows through time as having the same value, so that in the example given, the value of £200,000 invested now is equated with £200,000 of net cash inflows over $3\tfrac{1}{3}$ years.

These problems may be illustrated as follows.

Example

Multiplexed Ltd is considering four different investment projects each costing £20,000. The undermentioned information relates to these projects.

Project No.	1	2	3	4
	£	£	£	£
Initial investment outlay	20,000	20,000	20,000	20,000
Cash inflows				
Year 1	9000	11,000	3000	10,000
Year 2	11,000	9000	6000	6000
Year 3	—	—	8000	4000
Year 4	—	—	10,000	4000
Year 5	—	—	10,000	3000
Pay-back period (years)	2	2	$3\tfrac{1}{3}$	3

A crude application of the pay-back method would select projects 1 or 2 but would be unable to decide between these two projects.

The accounting rate of return

The accounting rate of return method seeks to express the average estimated yearly net inflows as a percentage of the net investment outlays. As, however, it is possible to recover depreciation from the yearly net inflows, the formula is expressed as follows:

$$R = \frac{C - D}{I}$$

where R = the accounting rate of return
$\quad\quad C$ = average yearly net inflows
$\quad\quad D$ = depreciation
$\quad\quad I$ = net investment outlays

Substituting the figures given in our example on p. 453, the accounting rate of return would be calculated as follows:

$$R = \frac{£60,000 - £40,000}{£200,000} \times 100\%$$

$$= 10\%$$

It may be argued, however, that the recovery of depreciation over the useful life of the investment reduces the value of the net investment outlays through time. Assuming an average recovery through depreciation at the rate of £40,000 per year, the average net investment over the estimated useful life of 5 years is £100,000, calculated by using the arithmetic mean method as follows:

$$\text{Average lifetime investment} = \frac{£200,000}{2}$$

$$= £100,000$$

The average lifetime investment may be calculated graphically in Fig. 5.8.

In the light of this argument, the accounting rate of return on investment should express the annual net cash inflows as a percentage of the average annual net investment outlays, so that, substituting the values given in our example, the average return on investment is:

$$R = \frac{£60,000 - £40,000}{£100,000} \times 100\%$$

$$= 20\%$$

This method of evaluating investment projects overcomes the disadvantage of the pay-back method in that it attempts to calculate the profitability of the various projects under study. Its main disadvantage is that it fails to consider

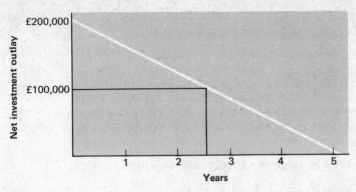

Fig. 5.8.

the changing value of money through time, and treats the value of £1 in the future as equal to £1 invested today. Moreover, it ignores also the differences which may occur through time in the rate of net cash inflows. In both these senses, it suffers from the same defects as the pay-back method.

Discounted cash flows

The methods of investment appraisal which we have just examined are generally regarded as producing misleading results. Discounted cash flow has gained widespread acceptance for it recognizes that the value of money is subject to a time-preference, that is, that £1 today is preferred to £1 in the future unless the delay in receiving £1 in the future is compensated by an interest factor. This interest factor is expressed as a discount rate.

In simple terms, the DCF method attempts to evaluate an investment proposal by comparing the net cash flows accruing over the life of the investment at their present-day value with the value of funds presently to be invested. Thus, by comparing like with like it is possible to calculate the rate of return on the investment in a realistic manner.

To find the present equivalent value of £1 receivable one year hence, one applies the rate of interest to discount that £1 to its present day value. This is the same thing as asking 'what sum of money invested today at the rate of interest would increase in value to £1 a year hence?'

Example

Given that the rate of interest is 10 per cent per annum the following calculations may be made:

£1 invested now at 10 per cent will amount to £1.10 in a year. Conversely, the value of £1.10 a year's hence is worth £1 now if the rate of interest is 10 per cent.

Using this principle, discount tables may be constructed for the value of £1 over several time periods ahead by compounding the interest rate through time, i.e., £1.00 invested for 1 year at 10 per cent will be worth £1.10 at the year end, £1.10 then reinvested for another year at 10 per cent will be worth £1.10 + 0.11 = £1.21 at the end of the second year.

Example

The value of £1 at the end of 1 year at 10% is £1 + .10 = £1.1

£1	2 years	$(£1.1)^2 = £1.21$
£1	3	$(£1.1)^3 = £1.331$
£1	4	$(£1.1)^4 = £1.464$
£1	5	$(£1.1)^5 = £1.611$

Conversely, the present value of £1 receivable at a future date is:

£1 receivable in 1 year's time is $\dfrac{£1}{1.1} = £0.9091$

£1	2	$\dfrac{£1}{1.21} = £0.8264$
£1	3	$\dfrac{£1}{1.331} = £0.7513$
£1	4	$\dfrac{£1}{1.464} = £0.6831$
£1	5	$\dfrac{£1}{1.611} = £0.6208$

The value of money is, therefore, directly affected by time and the rate of interest is the method which is used to express the time value of money. Compound interest tables and discount tables are available which show the value of money at different interest rates over a number of years, so that in actual practice, it is a simple matter to apply the DCF method to the evaluation of an investment.

(i) The net present value

This method is based on an assumed minimum rate of return. Ideally, this rate should be the average cost of capital to the firm (see p. 461) and it is this rate which would be used to discount the net cash inflows to their present value. The net investment outlays are subtracted from the present value of the net cash inflows leaving a residual figure, which is the net present value. A decision is made in favour of a project if the NPV is a positive amount. This method may likewise be applied to the comparison of one project with another when considering mutually exclusive investments.

The rule may be stated as follows:

Accept the project if:

$$\frac{a_1}{(1 + i)^1} + \frac{a_2}{(1 + i)^2} + \ldots + \frac{a_n}{(1 + i)^n} > A$$

where A is the initial project cost

a are the net annual cash inflows

Example
Corween Ltd is considering a project which has a life of 5 years and which will produce an annual inflow of £1000. The investment outlay is £3000 and the required rate of return is 10 per cent.

Year	Inflow	Discount factor (at 10%)	Present value of inflow
1	£1000	0.9091	£909.1
2	£1000	0.8264	£826.4
3	£1000	0.7513	£751.3
4	£1000	0.6831	£683.1
5	£1000	0.6208	£620.8
Present value of net inflows			£3790.7
Cost of investment outlay			£3000.0
Net present value of the project			£790.7

Since the net present value of the cash inflows (a) is greater than the present value of the cash outlay (A), the project should be accepted.

(ii) The internal rate of return
This method requires us to calculate that rate of interest which used in discounting will reduce the net present value of a project to zero. This enables us to compare the internal rate of return (IRR) with the required rate.

The rule may be stated as follows:

Accept the project if:

$$A = \frac{a_1}{(1 + r)} + \frac{a_2}{(1 + r)^2} + \ldots + \frac{a_n}{(1 + r)^n}$$

and $r > i$

where A is the initial project cost r is the solution discount rate
       a are the net annual cash inflows i is the required rate of return

Example
Let us return to the example given above and assume that Corween Ltd applies the internal rate of return analysis to the project under consideration. The analysis would be as follows.

Year	Inflow	Discount factor at 19%	Present value at 19%	Discount factor at 20%	Present value at 20%
	£		£		£
1	1000	0.8403	840.3	0.8333	833.3
2	1000	0.7062	706.2	0.6944	694.4
3	1000	0.5934	593.4	0.5787	578.7
4	1000	0.4987	498.7	0.4823	482.3
5	1000	0.4190	419.0	0.4019	401.9
Present value of net inflow			3057.6		2990.6
Cost of investment outlay			3000.0		3000.0
Net present value of the project			+57.6		−9.4

We can see that the IRR is almost 20 per cent. (It is often possible to approximate the true rate more closely by assuming a linear relationship and interpolating between the two nearest points.) The ascertainment of the IRR at 20 per cent enables us to compare the IRR with the required rate of return on investment by the company.

Net present value and internal rate of return compared

When dealing with simple investment appraisal projects, that is, those involving a once and for all investment outlay followed by a stream of cash inflows, both the NPV and the IRR methods produce the same YES or NO decisions.

But the advantage of the NPV method is the simplicity with which the results are stated. Our example shows that with the NPV method, the expected results are expressed in terms of £s which directly reflect the increased wealth position. The internal rate of return, on the other hand, produces a result which is shown as a percentage, and this result has to be compared with a minimum required rate of return before a decision may be made.

Example

Norwell Industries Ltd is studying two projects, each of which requires a net investment outlay of £3000. Both have a useful life of 5 years, and the estimated profile of the net cash inflows are:

End of year	Project A £	Project B £
1	500	2000
2	1000	1500
3	1500	1500
4	2000	1000
5	2000	500
	£7000	£6500

The desired minimum rate of return is 10 per cent.

Analysis—Net present value

The present value of the two projects may be calculated by using the desired minimum rate of return as a discount factor.

End of year	Discount factor 10%	Project A £	Present value £	Project B £	Present value £
1	0.9091	500	454.6	2000	1818.2
2	0.8264	1000	826.4	1500	1239.6
3	0.7153	1500	1073.0	1500	1073.0
4	0.6831	2000	1366.2	1000	683.1
5	0.6208	2000	1241.6	500	310.4
Present value of total cash inflows			£4961.8		£5124.3
Less: net investment outlay			£3000.0		£3000.0
Net present value			£1961.8		£2124.3

Both projects are acceptable to the firm, and if a choice has to be made between them, Project B would be selected since it produces the highest net present value of the two. The time profile of the net cash inflows is seen to be a determining influence on the result, for although the total cash inflows before discounting are higher with Project A, the cash flows associated with Project B are concentrated in the earlier years and, when discounted, have a higher net present value than A's.

Analysis—The internal rate of return

Taking the net cash inflows estimated for Project A, the rate which will discount the net cash inflows to £3000 is found once again by trial and error. Using discount tables, we establish in this way that the discount rate is between 28 per cent and 29 per cent, as follows:

Cash inflows	Discount factor at 29%	Present value at 29%	Discount factor at 28%	Present value at 28%
£		£		£
500	0.7752	387.7	0.7813	390.7
1000	0.6009	600.9	0.6104	610.4
1500	0.4658	698.7	0.4768	715.2
2000	0.3611	722.2	0.3725	745.0
2000	0.2799	559.8	0.2910	582.0
		£2969.3		£3043.3
Original investment outlay		£3000.0		£3000.0
		−30.7		+43.3

Using the same approach, the IRR from Project B may be calculated as 39 per cent.

The crucial test upon which the final acceptance of a project depends is whether or not the IRR compares favourably with the required rate of return. If the required rate of return is 20 per cent both projects qualify.

One of the problems of comparing rates of return on projects is that direct comparisons between two percentages are meaningless unless referred to the initial outlays, so that their true dimensions may be perceived. This problem should never be lost sight of when using IRR percentages.

With more complicated investment problems, for example, those which require that cash surpluses be set aside to meet an obligation arising at the end of the project's life, both methods assume that those cash surpluses are re-invested at the appropriate rate of return. Thus, where a loan has been raised to finance the project*, the IRR method envisages that the cash surpluses will be re-invested at the IRR discounting rate, whereas the NPV method envisages that they will be re-invested at the minimum acceptable rate of return used in that method. Thus, the advantage of the NPV method is that it makes more realistic assumptions about re-investment opportunities.

---

* The simplifying assumption which we are making for the purpose of illustrating the point is that the firm's finances are linked to specific investment projects, which in reality is not perhaps the case.

More complex problems arise when applying the IRR method to investment projects which do not have the simple pattern of cash flows of the above examples, but we regard these problems as beyond the scope of this text.

Taxation and other factors

In order that DCF calculations should lead to correct results, it is important that all factors affecting the calculations of cash flows should be taken into account. The most important of these factors is, of course, taxation. Indeed, we have assumed from the outset that the cash flow figures were net after tax. Apart from the direct effects of taxation, we should also adjust our figures for indirect aspects of taxation, such as investment grants, and the reader will recall that in calculating the net investment outlay, any recoveries in the form of investment incentives must be deducted from the amount brought into the DCF calculation. The effects of these incentives vary from project to project.

The cost of capital

The evaluation of an investment project by DCF analysis requires a firm to calculate its cost of capital. This is true in selecting the discount rate for appraisal by means of the net present value method, or for establishing the acceptability of the internal rate of return.

A full discussion of the concept of the 'cost of capital' is beyond the scope of this book; indeed, the subject is perhaps the most difficult and controversial topic in the Theory of Finance. Our discussion will be a very elementary one so as to provide the reader with some understanding of investment planning.

The first problem in discussing the cost of capital lies in different meanings which the term has acquired. From a lender's point of view, the cost of capital represents the cost to him of lending money which may be equated to the return which he could have obtained by investing in a similar project having similar risks. This concept of the cost of capital is founded on its 'opportunity cost'. The opportunity cost approach to the assessment of the cost of capital is one which a firm must always consider when evaluating an investment project. A firm may find, for example, that investing funds outside the firm may produce higher returns than an internal project. The main obstacle to a more widespread use of the opportunity cost concept is that of identifying investment of equal risks and hence measuring the opportunity cost.

Another concept in use is the actual cost incurred by a firm in borrowing money. A firm may obtain funds in a variety of ways: and each way has a different cost attached to it. Thus, a firm may issue shares and will pay a dividend on those shares, which must represent the cost of raising funds in that way. It may also borrow money, either by the issue of debentures, bank or other methods of borrowing, and in these cases interest is payable. The fact that the firm may have raised its finance in several different ways makes it more realistic to use the 'average cost of capital' which is based on an analysis of its capital structure.

Example

The Keystone Corp Ltd has a capital structure distributed as to 80 per cent share capital and 20 per cent loan capital. The dividend rate is 10 per cent and the interest payable on the loan capital is 8 per cent. Calculate the average cost of capital.

Source of funds	Proportion of total funds %	Cost of capital %	Product
Share capital	80	10	800
Loan capital	20	8	160
	100		960

The weighted average cost of capital is: $\dfrac{960}{100} = 9.6\%$

The average cost of capital so calculated would in the case of this firm represent the minimum acceptable rate of return.

Gearing and the cost of capital

It will be recalled from Part 2 that the distribution of a firm's capital structure as between share capital (equity capital) and fixed interest stock (preference shares and debentures) is known as the gearing. A firm which is highly geared has a higher ratio of fixed interest stock to equity capital. By changing its gearing, a firm may alter its average cost of capital.

Example

The firm in the above-mentioned example increases its gearing by raising the proportion of loan capital to share capital from 20 per cent to 40 per cent. Its average cost of capital, as a result, is reduced to 9.2 per cent:

Source of funds	Proportion of total funds %	Cost of capital %	Product
Share capital	60	10	600
Loan capital	40	8	320
	100		920

The average cost of capital is $\dfrac{920}{100} = 9.2\%$

It should be noted that financial theorists have argued that it is due only to the influence of a corporation tax system which allows loan interest as a tax deductible expense that gearing is of any significance.

Financial planning requires a firm to give very serious consideration to its capital structure and to its gearing. Very complex issues are involved in planning an appropriate capital structure. Circumstances may make it advantageous to attempt to increase the proportion of loan capital, that is, increase the gearing, such as the tax deductibility of loan interest which we have already mentioned. There is an upper limit to debt finance, however, for not only are there obvious dangers in the presence of large fixed interest charges against corporate income, but there are practical limits to the amount of funds which may be borrowed for long-term purposes.

Investment appraisal and inflation

As the cash flows associated with a particular project may span a considerable period of time, it is evident that the level of inflation during that time will affect considerably the profitability of the project. We pointed out in Chapter 27 that estimates of future events should take inflation into account, and in Part 3, the distinction between general price level and specific price changes was discussed. We indicated the need to adjust cash-flow forecasts for specific price changes which would affect the enterprise, so as to maintain its operating capability. Accordingly, it is the inflating cost of specific items which are to be taken into account in investment appraisal. The cost of these specific items will exhibit different rates of change, as will the prices of the products containing elements of the specific items of costs. In effect, the existence of a lag between increases in costs and increases in prices may considerably reduce the profitability of a project under conditions of inflation. As the rate of inflation increases, so this problem becomes more acute. For this reason, firms entering into fixed-price contracts extending over a long period of time should arrange for cost-escalation clauses to mitigate the impact of inflation.

The most appropriate method of incorporating the effects of inflation into DCF calculations is to adjust cash-flow forecasts for specific price increases (Scapens, 1977). Such adjusted cash flows are then discounted by the monetary cost of capital. According to some authors, a suitable choice for this purpose is the company's overdraft rate (Cox and Hewgill, 1976).

Example

In the earlier example (p. 457), Corween Ltd had annual net cash flows of £1000 for a period of 5 years, and the discount rate was given as 10 per cent. It may now be assumed that the annual net cash flows were derived as follows:

	£	£
Cash inflows from sales		5000
Cash outflows:		
Materials	3000	
Labour	1000	
		4000
Annual net cash flow		1000

The impact of inflation is considered in the following terms:

(a) Sales revenues are expected to be adjusted for price changes at the rate of 15 per cent per annum. The adjustment to the annual expected cash inflows from sales is shown below.

(b) Material costs are expected to increase at the rate of 18 per cent per annum. The adjustment for this increase is also shown below.

(c) Labour costs are expected to increase at the rate of 10 per cent per annum. The adjustment is also shown below.

	Annual rate of change	Year 1	Year 2	Year 3	Year 4	Year 5
	%	£	£	£	£	£
Sales revenue	15	5750	6613	7605	8746	10,058
Materials	18	3540	4177	4929	5816	6863
Labour	10	1100	1210	1331	1464	1610
		4640	5387	6260	7280	8473
Net cash flows (adjusted)		1110	1226	1345	1466	1585

These annual expected future net cash flows may now be discounted at the appropriate discount rate. For simplicity, if it is assumed that the discount rate is 10 per cent, these annual net cash flows have a present value of £5017, as follows:

Year	Net cash flow	Discount factor at 10%	Present value
	£	%	£
1	1110	0.9091	1009
2	1226	0.8264	1013
3	1345	0.7513	1010
4	1466	0.6831	1001
5	1585	0.6208	984
			5017
Less: Initial investment outlay			3000
Net present value of the project			2017

The foregoing example shows the manner in which inflation adds a new dimension to the problem of calculating present values. More calculations are involved, and the degree of uncertainty is increased. Many accountants feel that, under conditions of rapid and high inflation, the task of forecasting cash flows over the lifetime of a project covering several years seems somewhat academic. Research has shown that the most popular method of investment appraisal is the payback method, which emphasizes the rate of recovery of investment outlays. During periods of inflation, the payback method places emphasis on projects which have shorter payback periods (Westwick and Shohet, 1976).

Summary

Preparing the capital expenditure plan is part of the long-range planning process. The quality of managerial decisions committing the firm's resources to new investments is probably the most significant factor affecting the level of future profitability.

Capital investment decisions encompass two aspects of the long-range profit plan—first, estimating the future net increases in cash inflows or net savings in cash outlays which will result from an investment; second, calculating the total cash outlays required to carry out an investment.

There are three well-known techniques for appraising investment proposals from a financial viewpoint:

(1) the payback method, which emphasizes the length of time required to recoup the investment outlay;

(2) the accounting rate of return, which seeks to express the average estimated yearly net inflows as a percentage of the net investment outlays for the purpose of assessing the profitability of a proposed investment;

(3) discounted cash flow methods, which attempt to evaluate an investment proposal by comparing the present value of the net cash inflows accruing over the life of the investment with the present value of the funds to be invested.

Discounted cash flow techniques provide the most useful procedures for evaluating capital investment proposals. They comprise two methods—the net present value and the internal rate of return. Both methods take into account the time value of money, unlike the other methods mentioned which ignore this factor.

In many situations it is difficult to forecast the time profile of future cash flows with any degree of certainty. The next chapter considers risk analysis as a means of handling the problem of uncertainty.

References

1. Cox, B. & Hewgill, J. C. R. *Management Accounting in Inflationary Conditions*, Institute of Cost and Management Accountants, London, 1976.
2. Scapens, R. W. *Accounting in an Inflationary Environment*, Macmillan, 1977.
3. Westwick, C. A. & Shohet, P. D. S. *Investment Appraisal and Inflation*, Research Committee Occasional Paper No. 7, I.C.A.E.W., 1976.

Questions

1. Why are capital budgeting decisions so important?
2. Define for an investment project (a) the payback, (b) the net present value and (c) the internal rate of return.
3. Some recent studies of the capital budgeting process in industry have found that the less sophisticated models, such as payback, are much more prevalent in practice than the more sophisticated models based on discounted cash flows. How do you explain this?

4. Evaluate critically the accountant's rate of return method.
5. The purchase of a machine is contemplated and the relevant facts concerning two possible choices are as follows:

	Machine A	Machine B
Capital expenditure required	£50,000	£60,000
Estimated life—years	3	4
Residual value	Nil	Nil
Cash flow after taxation—		
constant each year at	£25,000	£24,000

Assume a rate of interest of 10 per cent for which the reciprocals are:

Year 1	0.9091	Year 2	0.8264
Year 3	0.7513	Year 4	0.6830

Required:

Set out calculations illustrating and comparing the following methods of evaluating the return from these investments:

(a) Payback period
(b) Accounting rate of return
(c) Discounted cash flow

Comment on the results.

6. Jazz Ltd is considering replacing three of its record-pressing machines with one machine which has just come onto the market. The three existing machines are two years old and cost £1500 each. They are being depreciated on a straight-line basis over twelve years. It was expected that their final scrap value would be £600 each. Their replacement is being considered because a fault has developed in their operation which can only be corrected at a total cost of £5000 for the three machines. The current second-hand market value of the machines is £1000 each.

The annual operating costs of the existing and new machines are as follows:

Existing machines; costs per machine:

		£
Materials		60,000
Labour: one operator at 1800 hours		1350
Variable expenses		925
Maintenance (excluding exceptional items)		2000
Fixed expenses:		
Depreciation	75	
Fixed overheads absorbed	2700	2700

New machine:

		£
Materials		162,000
Labour: two operators at 1500 hours	3000	
one assistant at 1500 hours	900	3900
Variable expenses		2275
Maintenance		4500
Fixed expenses:		
Depreciation	9550	
Fixed overheads absorbed	7800	17,350

The new machine's estimated life is 10 years and will cost £100,000. The company's cost of capital is 10 per cent.

Required:

(i) Advise the management of Jazz Ltd on the most profitable course of action to undertake.

(ii) Comment on the method which you have used and the other factors which might influence the decision.

30 Budgetary planning

The process of budgeting focuses on the short term, normally one year, and provides an expression of the steps which management must take in the current period if it is to fulfil organizational objectives. As we explained in Chapter 26, it is useful to distinguish between the two functions—planning and control. Applying a similar distinction to budgeting, we may examine in turn the functions of budgetary planning and budgetary control. In this chapter, we deal with the technical aspects of budgeting. The analysis of the budgeting problem in terms of the relationships between costs, volume and profits are discussed in Chapter 32.

The nature of budgetary planning

In Chapter 28 we found that long-range planning involved the determination of corporate objectives and the determination of a suitable plan for attaining these objectives. The budget represents the expression of this plan in financial terms in the light of current conditions. Therefore, the long-range plan is the guide for preparing the annual budgets and defines actions that need to be taken now in order to move towards long-term objectives. Indeed, the budget represents the first one-year span of the long-range budget.

The reader will recall that one important feature of planning is the co-ordination of the various activities of an enterprise, and of its departments, so that they are harmonized in the overall task of realizing corporate objectives. For example if the marketing function were to increase sales massively over a short period of time, the manufacturing function would have to increase output substantially—probably through the use of costly overtime labour, or by buying goods from an outside supplier at high prices. Conversely, excessive production may force the marketing function to sell at unrealistically low prices in order to avoid excessive investment in stock. The function of budgetary planning is to co-ordinate the various activities of an organization in order to achieve company rather than divisional or departmental objectives. Therefore it is necessary to establish objectives for each section of the organization which are in harmony with the organization as a whole.

The need for flexibility

Because business conditions are always changing, it is necessary to view the budgeting process as a guide to future action, rather than a rigid plan which must be followed irrespective of changing circumstances. The latter approach may place the manager in a strait-jacket in which he is forced to take decisions which are not in accordance with company objectives. For example, a departmental manager may find, due to changing conditions, that he has not spent all of his budget on a particular item. In order to spend all his budget allowance, so as to prevent the possibility of a cut in his allowance next year, he may squander funds which could have been put to better use in other sections of the organization.

More importantly, management must plan for changing business conditions, in order that appropriate action may be taken to deal with changes that may occur should any of the assumptions underlying plans be affected by such changes. This implies that contingency plans should be available to deal with changes which were unforeseen at the time when the budget was originally prepared. The manner in which this degree of flexibility may be introduced in budgets is discussed in Chapter 31.

Some firms relate their planning budgets to changing conditions by means of a rolling budget which is prepared every quarter, but for one year ahead. At the end of each quarter the plans for the next three-quarters are revised, if this is necessary, and a fourth-quarter is added. By this process the budgets are kept continually up to date.

Flexibility is also required if budgetary control is to be effective. Indeed the type of budget which may be suitable for planning may be inappropriate for control purposes. Therefore, budgets should be established for control purposes which reflect operating conditions which may be different from those envisaged in the planning stages. This is essential if individual managers are to be held responsible only for those deviations over which they have control. Such a requirement is called for by the use of a responsibility accounting system, which will be discussed in Chapter 36.

The organization of budgeting

The budgeting processs itself requires careful organization. In large firms, this process is often in the hands of a budget committee which acts through the budget officer whose function it is to co-ordinate and control the budgeting process for the whole organization. Departmental budget estimates are requested from divisional managers, who in their turn collate this information from estimates submitted to them by their own departmental managers. Hence, budget estimates are based on information which flows upwards through the organization to the budget committee. The budget committee is responsible for co-ordinating this information, and resolving any differences in consultations with the managers involved. The final budget proposal is presented to the board of directors, for its final approval.

Steps in budgeting

The first stage of a budgeting exercise is the determination of the 'key' factors or constraints which impose overall limits to the budget plan. Among these

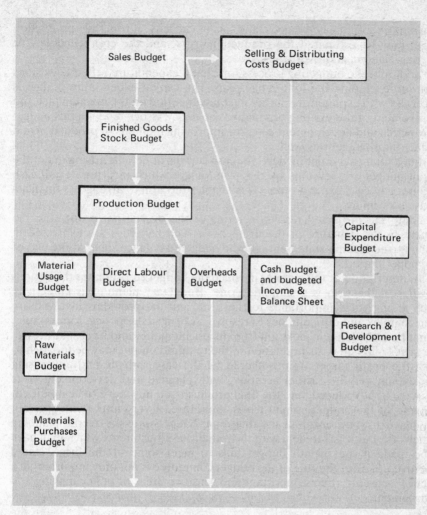

Fig. 5.9.

factors are the productive capacity of the plant, the finances available to the firm, and, of course, the market conditions which impose a total limit on the output which the firm is able to sell. Normally from a management point of view, the critical question is 'what is the firm able to sell in the budget period?', and this question summarizes all the limits to the budget plan. It is for this reason that the sales budget is at once the starting point and the fulcrum of the budgeting process.

Figure 5.9 illustrates how the various resources and activities of an enterprise are co-ordinated.

The arrows indicate the flow of relevant information. Once the level of sales is established, selling and distribution costs may be ascertained. The production budget itself is determined by the sales forecast, the desired level of inventory of finished goods and plant capacity. From the production budget may be estimated the production costs, and the cost schedules for materials, labour and overheads.

In addition, the budgeting process for capital expenditure reflects decisions taken in developing the long-range plan. The capital expenditure budget is concerned with expenditure during the budget period on the maintenance and improvement of the existing productive capacity. Associated with this budget are research and development costs for improving methods of production and product improvement as well.

From a financing point of view, the cash surplus or deficits arising out of the overall budget are revealed by the cash budget which incorporates all cash revenues and cash expenditures. This enables the firm to arrange its financial needs accordingly.

Finally, the projected results in terms of the overall net profit, and the changes in the structure of the firm's assets and liabilities are expressed in the budgeted income statement and the budgeted balance sheet at the end of the budget period.

This description of the manner in which the budget co-ordinates the various activities of the firm is a simplified one. Budgetary planning is an activity which is of critical importance to the firm, and the problems involved are often complex and difficult ones to resolve. A firm's sales policy, for example, cannot be considered in isolation from its pricing policy and its cost structure. The firm's planned costs in relation to the required output may be too high to reach the profit target. If this should be the case, pricing and advertising policies may require further scrutiny, both planned and development costs may have to be reduced, and the final product itself may have to be modified. The role of the budget committee is, therefore, a very important one: not only has it to harmonize all the divisional budgets into an overall planning framework, but it has to deal with the numerous adjustments which may have to be made if the overall budget fails to meet some of the firm's stated objectives. Hence, the role of the budget committee is not only important in a practical sense: it affects important and sensitive areas of policy making and management.

Forecasting sales

A major problem in budgeting is forecasting sales, for many factors affecting sales are outside the firm's control, for example, the behaviour of the firm's competitors and the future economic climate.

The importance of an accurate sales forecast cannot be over-emphasized. If the sales forecast is too optimistic, the firm may be induced to expand its capital expenditure programme and incur costs which may not be recoverable at a later date. In the meantime, the production target may be set too high, resulting in the pile-up of inventory of finished goods, which in itself has important financial consequences. Moreover, an optimistic sales forecast may disguise a deteriorating sales position, so that the necessary economies are not made which would produce a satisfactory profit. If, on the other hand, the sales forecast is pessimistic, the firm will miss the opportunity of larger current profit and may be misled as to its future prospects. The firm may, as a result, not undertake the necessary capital expenditure which would place it in a good position to exploit the market.

The sales forecast is the initial step in preparing the sales budget. It consists not only of analysing the market for the firm's products, but includes forecasting the levels of sales at different prices. Hence, the study of the firm's pricing policy is an integral aspect of sales forecasting. Once the sales forecast is completed, the sales budget may be derived from the target sales established both as regards price and sales volume.

There are various methods of forecasting sales, for example:

(a) The sales force composite method. This method places responsibility upon individual salesmen for developing their own sales forecast. The advantage of this method is that if participative budgeting is to be encouraged, the sales staff should assist in the preparation of the sales forecast.

(b) The analysis of market and industry factors. This method recognizes the importance of factors not within the knowledge of the sales force, such as forecasts of the gross national product, personal incomes, employment and price levels etc. The salesmen's estimates are modified by the information so obtained.

(c) Statistical analysis of fluctuations through time. Sales are generally affected by four basic factors: growth trends, business cycle fluctuations, seasonal fluctuations and irregular variations in demand. A time series analysis of sales is a statistical method of separating and analysing the historical evidence of the behaviour of sales to identify these several effects and their impact on sales. The results of this analysis are applied to the sales forecast, and are means of testing the quality of the forecast.

(d) Mathematical techniques for sales forecasting. Of recent years, mathematical techniques have been applied to the study of the relationship between economic trends and a firm's sales pattern through time, to arrive at a projection of future sales. These techniques usually involve the use of computers. One such technique is known as exponential smoothing, which is really a prediction of future sales based on current and historical sales data, weighted so as to give a greater importance to the latest incoming information.

An illustration of the budgeting process

Once the sales forecast is known, a firm may begin to prepare the budget. We believe that the reader will obtain a better understanding of budgeting if we work through a simple example. In the following example, we focus on the technical problems of budget construction, and we assume that the problem of changing price levels is not present. This assumption allows us to treat asset values as remaining constant.

Example

The Edco Manufacturing Co Ltd manufactures two products, A and B.

A formal planning system had been introduced some time ago as a means

---

The Edco Manufacturing Co Ltd
Forecast results for the year ending 31 December 19X0

Income statement

	£	£	£
Sales		135,000	
Cost of goods sold		80,000	
Gross margin		55,000	
Selling and administrative expenses		25,000	
Income before tax		30,000	
Tax at 40%		12,000	
Income after tax		18,000	

Balance sheet

	£	£	£
Shareholders' equity			
Ordinary share capital		210,000	
Retained earnings		26,000	
			236,000
Represented by			
Fixed assets			
Plant and machinery		250,000	
Less: accumulated depreciation		30,000	220,000
Current assets			
Inventories			
Finished goods		6025	
Raw materials		1650	
		7675	
Debtors		20,000	
Cash		5325	
		33,000	
Less: Current liabilities			
Sundry creditors	5000		
Tax	12,000	17,000	
Net working capital			16,000
			236,000

---

of steering the company into more profitable levels of operation. Considerable progress had already been made in streamlining production and reducing costs. The budgeting process normally began in October, prior to the end of the accounting year on 31 December.

The expected results for the current year ending on 31 December 19X0 were as shown above.

From these forecast results, the expected performance for the current year may be calculated as follows:

Return on shareholders' equity: $\dfrac{£18,000}{£236,000} = 7.6\%$

Return on capital employed: $\dfrac{£18,000}{£253,000} = 7.1\%$

The following additional information was obtained for the purpose of preparing the budget for the year ending 31 December 19X1.

(i) *The sales forecast*

	Product A	Product B
Expected selling price per unit	£11	£14
Sales volume forecast		
1st quarter	1500 units	2000 units
2nd	1000	2000
3rd	1000	2000
4th	1500	2000
Total for the year	5000	8000

(ii) *Factory costs forecast*

Two departments are concerned with production: the preparation department and the machining department. The following analysis relates to the production of these departments:

(a) Direct costs

	Direct labour required per unit of product (*in labour hours*)		Departmental wage rate (£)	Direct labour cost per unit of output (£)	
	A	B		A	B
Preparation department	1/5	1/2	£2 per hour	£0.40	£1.00
Machining department	1/2	1/2	£2 per hour	£1.00	£1.00
				£1.40	£2.00

(b) Raw material requirement forecast

The standard quantities of the two raw materials, X and Y, which should be used in the manufacture of the two products, and the prices of these raw materials have been estimated as follows:

Standard quantities
Raw material X—2 units for each unit of product A
Raw material Y—3 units for each unit of product B

Estimated costs
Raw material X—£0.50 for each unit of X
Raw material Y—£0.30 for each unit of Y

(c) Overhead costs

Factory overheads are classified into fixed and variable costs. The fixed overhead costs are deemed to be incurred in equal amounts quarterly for the purpose of allocation, whereas the variable overheads vary according to the level of production. The following estimates are available:

Fixed overheads

Depreciation	£10,000 per annum
Rates and insurances	4000
Supervisory salaries	6000
	£20,000

Variable overheads

	Cost per unit of output	
	A	B
	£	£
Indirect labour ⎫ Indirect material ⎪ Repairs and ⎬ maintenance ⎪ Power ⎭	£0.50	£1.00

(iii) *Stock forecasts*

Finished goods
Product A—estimated opening inventory: 750 units
Product B—   1000 units

It was planned that the closing stock level at the end of each quarter should be maintained at a level equal to half the expected sales for the next quarter for both products.

For the purposes of calculating the expected profit, the closing inventory is to be valued on a variable costing basis, as follows:

	A	B
Raw materials	£1.00	£0.90
Direct labour	1.40	2.00
Variable overheads	0.50	1.00
Total variable costs per unit	£2.90	£3.90

Raw materials
Raw material X—estimated opening inventory: 1500 units
Raw material Y: 3000 units

(iv) *Administrative and selling costs forecast*

(a) *Administrative costs*

Office salaries	£18,000	
Stationery	1000	
Other	1000	
		£20,000

(b) *Selling costs*

Salaries	15,000	
Advertising	5000	
		20,000
Total		£40,000

(v) Cash flow forecast

(a) Sales receipts
50 per cent of sales received in cash during month of sales
50 per cent of sales received in cash in the following month

(b) Cash expenditure
Production costs
Director labour, direct materials and variable overheads paid in the month in which incurred
Fixed overheads paid in equal amounts quarterly
Administrative and selling costs
Paid in equal amounts quarterly
Other costs
Tax outstanding amounting to £12,000 will be paid off in equal instalments quarterly over the year
Capital expenditure
Expenditure on the acquisition of fixed assets is planned as follows:

1st quarter	£10,000
2nd	15,000
3rd	8000
4th	20,000
	£53,000

(vi) Sundry creditors balance
The amount outstanding to sundry creditors will remain at a constant amount of £5000 throughout the year.

Preparing the budget for the year ending 31 December 19X1

The task of preparing the overall budget involves a sequence of steps:

Step 1.   The sales budget
2.   The production budget
3.   The direct materials usage budget
4.   The materials purchases budget
5.   The budgeted direct labour costs
6.   The overhead costs budget
7.   The closing inventory budget
8.   The selling and administrative costs budget
9.   The capital expenditure budget
10.   The cost of goods sold budget
11.   The cash budget
12.   The budgeted income statement
13.   The budgeted balance sheet

Step 1. The sales budget

The sales budget is prepared from the sales forecast as follows:

	1st quarter	2nd quarter	3rd quarter	4th quarter	Total
Units					
Product A	1500	1000	1000	1500	5000
Product B	2000	2000	2000	2000	8000
Value					
Product A(£11)	£16,500	£11,000	£11,000	£16,500	£55,000
Product B(£14)	28,000	28,000	28,000	28,000	112,000
	£44,500	£39,000	£39,000	£44,500	£167,000

Step 2. The production budget

The production budget is designed to plan the resources required to produce the output envisaged by the sales forecast. A pre-condition to an agreement as to the size of the sales budget is the adequacy of the productive capacity of the plant to provide the required output. If existing capacity is inadequate, decisions will have to be made as to the advisability of introducing overtime working, of sub-contracting production, or of hiring or purchasing additional plant and equipment. If, on the other hand, the sales forecast falls short of productive capacity, sales promotion schemes may be considered as a means of closing or reducing the gap. With the tendency of businessmen to use inventory levels as buffers to insulate an efficient rate of production from variations in sales, the production budget is also dependent upon the planned levels of closing inventory.

Using the information given in our example, the following production budget may be prepared:

	1st quarter	2nd quarter	3rd quarter	4th quarter	Year
Product A			(UNITS)		
Desired closing inventory (units)	500	500	750	750	750
Add: Sales	1500	1000	1000	1500	5000
Total required	2000	1500	1750	2250	5750
Less: Opening inventory	750	500	500	750	750
Production required	1250	1000	1250	1500	5000
Product B					
Desired closing inventory (units)	1000	1000	1000	1000	1000
Add: Sales	2000	2000	2000	2000	8000
Total required	3000	3000	3000	3000	9000
Less: Opening inventory	1000	1000	1000	1000	1000
Production required	2000	2000	2000	2000	8000

Step 3. The direct materials usage budget
The rate of usage of raw materials is known, so that the direct materials usage may be budgeted by multiplying the usage rate by the production required.

	1st quarter	2nd quarter	3rd quarter	4th quarter	Year
Material X (2 units for A)	2500	2000	2500	3000	10,000
Material Y (3 units for B)	6000	6000	6000	6000	24,000

Step 4. The direct materials purchase budget
The purpose of this budget is to determine both the quantities and the values of raw material purchases which are necessary to meet the production levels stipulated in the production budget. The information required for this budget is found in the direct materials usage budget, inventory forecasts and raw materials purchase prices.

	1st quarter	2nd quarter	3rd quarter	4th quarter	Year
Raw Material X Desired closing inventory	1000	1000	1500	1500	1500
Add: material usage (Step 3)	2500	2000	2500	3000	10,000
Total required	3500	3000	4000	4500	11,500
Less: Opening inventory	1500	1000	1000	1500	1500
Purchases required (units)	2000	2000	3000	3000	10,000
Price per unit	£0.50	£0.50	£0.50	£0.50	£0.50
Total purchases (value)	£1000	£1000	£1500	£1500	£5000
Raw Material Y Desired closing inventory	3000	3000	3000	3000	3000
Add: Material usage (Step 3)	6000	6000	6000	6000	24,000
Total required	9000	9000	9000	9000	27,000
Less: Opening inventory	3000	3000	3000	3000	3000
Purchases required (units)	6000	6000	6000	6000	24,000
Price per unit	£0.30	£0.30	£0.30	£0.30	£0.30
Total purchases (value)	£1800	£1800	£1800	£1800	£7200
Total purchases (value)	£2800	£2800	£3300	£3300	£12,200

Step 5. Budgeted direct labour costs
This budget is based upon calculations of the manpower requirements necessary to produce the planned output. The direct labour costs are

computed by multiplying the manpower requirements by the forecast of wage rates payable during the budget period.

	1st quarter	2nd quarter	3rd quarter	4th quarter	Year
Production (Step 2—units)					
Product A	1250	1000	1250	1500	5000
Product B	2000	2000	2000	2000	8000
Labour hours					
Preparation department					
Product A (1/5)	250	200	250	300	1000
Product B (1/2)	1000	1000	1000	1000	4000
Total	1250	1200	1250	1300	5000
Machining department					
Product A (1/2)	625	500	625	750	2500
Product B (1/2)	1000	1000	1000	1000	4000
Total	1625	1500	1625	1750	6500
Direct labour costs					
Preparation department					
Labour hours	1250	1200	1250	1300	5000
Wage rate/hour	£2	£2	£2	£2	£2
Direct labour cost	£2500	£2400	£2500	£2600	£10,000
Machining department					
Labour hours	1625	1500	1625	1750	6500
Wage rate/hour	£2	£2	£2	£2	£2
Direct labour cost	£3250	£3000	£3250	£3500	£13,000
Total direct labour cost	£5750	£5400	£5750	£6100	£23,000

Step 6. The overhead costs budget

Having disposed of the direct costs of production in the form of materials and direct labour, we now come to the preparation of the estimates of the overhead costs of production. These costs are divided into the two categories mentioned earlier. We are told that the fixed overheads are incurred in equal amounts quarterly, and we may calculate the total variable costs per quarter by multiplying the expected variable costs per unit by the planned quarterly output.

	1st quarter	2nd quarter	3rd quarter	4th quarter	Year
Production (Step 2)					
Product A (units)	1250	1000	1250	1500	5000
Product B (units)	2000	2000	2000	2000	8000
Variable costs					
Product A					
(£0.50 per unit)	£625	£500	£625	£750	£2500
Product B					
(£1.00 per unit)	2000	2000	2000	2000	8000
Total	2625	2500	2625	2750	10,500

contd.

	1st quarter	2nd quarter	3rd quarter	4th quarter	Year
Fixed costs					
Depreciation	2500	2500	2500	2500	10,000
Rates & insurance	1000	1000	1000	1000	4000
Supervisory salaries	1500	1500	1500	1500	6000
Total	5000	5000	5000	5000	20,000
Total overhead costs	£7625	£7500	£7625	£7750	£30,500

Step 7. *The closing inventory budget*

The closing inventory budget consists of an estimate of the value of planned closing inventory of raw materials and planned stocks of finished goods. It is arrived at by calculating the budgeted unit cost of stock and multiplying the result by the planned inventory level.

(a) *Budgeted closing raw material inventory*

Raw material	X	Y
Closing inventory (units)	1500	3000
Cost per unit	£0.50	£0.30
Value of closing inventory	£750	£900
Total		£1650

(b) *Budgeted finished goods inventory*

We are told that the accountant values the inventory of finished goods on a variable costing basis, and that the unit cost of Products A and B has been calculated to be £2.90 and £3.90 respectively. These values are applied to the budgeted closing inventory figures as follows:

Product	A	B
Closing inventory (units)	750	1000
Cost per unit	£2.90	£3.90
Value of closing inventory	2175	3900
Total		£6075

Step 8. *The selling and administrative expenses budget*

Selling expenses		
Salaries	£15,000	
Advertising	5000	£20,000
Administrative expenses		
Office salaries	18,000	
Stationery	1000	
Other expenses	1000	20,000
Total		£40,000

Step 9. The capital expenditure budget

We devoted Chapter 29 to a discussion of capital budgeting as an aspect of long-range planning. The annual capital expenditure budget must be seen, therefore, as a one-year slice of the long-term capital budget. The purpose of the annual capital expenditure is to make provision in the current budget for the planned capital expenditure in the current year. This information has been provided as follows:

Capital expenditure	
1st quarter	£10,000
2nd	15,000
3rd	8000
4th	20,000
Total for the year	£53,000

Step 10. The cost of goods sold budget

The reader will recall that all the previous budgets mentioned have dealt with the various aspects of the production process, in unit and value terms, including the expenses associated with selling and administration and the valuation of closing inventory. The purpose of this budget is to bring all these items together to arrive at an estimate of the cost of the goods sold. This estimate will be used in the budgeted income statement. It is compiled as follows:

Opening raw materials inventory (balance sheet 31/12/19X0)	£1650
Add: Materials purchases (Step 4)	12,200
Raw materials available for production	13,850
Less: Planned closing inventory of raw materials (Step 7)	1650
Cost of raw materials to be used in production	12,200
Cost of direct labour (Step 5)	23,000
Factory overhead costs (Step 6)	30,500
Cost of goods to be manufactured	65,700
Add: Opening inventory of finished goods (balance sheet 31/12/19X0)	6025
	71,725
Less: Planned closing inventory of finished goods	6075
Budgeted cost of goods sold	£65,650

Step 11. The cash budget

The cash budget consists of the estimates of cash receipts and cash payments arising from the planned levels of activities and use of resources which are considered in the various budgets we have examined. The cash budget is a complete survey of the financial implications of expenditure plans both of a current and a capital nature during the year. Moreover, by comparing the anticipated outflows of cash with the expected inflows, the cash budget enables management to anticipate any deficits so that the necessary financing arrangements may be made, and to decide upon a policy for placing any cash surpluses.

As its name implies, the cash budget deals only with 'cash' flows—it excludes expenses of a non-cash nature, such as depreciation. The cash budget is one of the last budgets to be prepared because it depends upon the other budgets which form part of the budgeting process.

	1st quarter	2nd quarter	3rd quarter	4th quarter	Total
	£	£	£	£	£
Opening cash balance	5325	10,900	11,450	15,275	5325
Receipts:					
Debtors (balance sheet)	20,000	—	—	—	20,000
50% of current sales (Step 1)	22,250	19,500	19,500	22,250	83,500
50% of previous quarter (Step 1)	—	22,250	19,500	19,500	61,250
Total receipts	42,250	41,750	39,000	41,750	164,750
Total cash available	47,575	52,650	50,450	57,025	170,075
Payments:					
Purchases (Step 4)	2800	2800	3300	3300	12,200
Direct labour (Step 5)	5750	5400	5750	6100	23,000
Factory overheads (Step 6) (excluding depreciation)	5125	5000	5125	5250	20,500
Selling and administrative expenses (Step 8)	10,000	10,000	10,000	10,000	40,000
Capital expenditure (Step 9)	10,000	15,000	8000	20,000	53,000
Tax (balance sheet)	3000	3000	3000	3000	12,000
Total payments	36,675	41,200	35,175	47,650	160,700
Closing cash balances	10,900	11,450	15,275	9375	9375

The cash budget, it will be noted, is planned through time: for the time profile of cash receipts and cash payments is critical to the analysis of a firm's cash needs at any given point of time.

In practice, determining the level of cash which is required at any point in time may not be an easy matter. The dilemma of cash management lies in the conflict of liquidity with profitability. If a firm holds too little cash in relation to its financial obligations, a liquidity crisis may occur and may lead to the collapse of the business. On the other hand, if a firm holds too much cash it is losing the opportunity to employ that cash profitably in its activities. Idle cash balances usually earn very little profit for the firm. A reasonable balance must be found, therefore, between the financial objectives of maintaining a degree of liquidity and of minimizing the level of unproductive assets. The problem of ascertaining optimal balances of physical stocks has for long attracted the attention of operational researchers, and certain of the ideas which they have developed may have applicability as regards the holding of optimal cash balances. Essentially these ideas relate the cost of holding cash with the cost of obtaining cash: total costs are minimized when the two are equated.

The effects of inflation on business enterprises are manifested in a growth in monetary terms, which may be in some direct relationship with the rate of inflation, while at the same time undergoing no growth at all in real terms, or even shrinking in profitability and value. The financing problem resulting from the monetary growth associated with inflation lies in the need to finance higher levels of inventories and debtors. If a firm is unable to finance the higher level of working capital required from adjustments to its prices and sales revenues, it must either borrow or reduce its level of activity. In effect, the rapid inflation which business firms experienced in the 1970s caused severe liquidity problems and many cases of insolvency.

The problems of cash budgeting under conditions of inflation require that special attention be given to the timing of cash inflows and outflows, which should be adjusted for changes in specific price changes affecting the firm. In this connection, adjustments to budget figures for changes in the general purchasing power of money will not reflect the impact of inflationary changes as they affect individual firms.

Among the special problems associated with budgeting under conditions of inflation is the loss of purchasing power exhibited by holdings of net monetary assets. This implies that losses in the value of net monetary items should be minimized in a manner consistent with the overall objectives of the firm by the reduction of holdings of net monetary assets. In effect, particular attention should be given to cash and debtor balances, and the impact of changes in selling prices on cash inflows should be carefully monitored. At the same time, gains resulting from the impact of inflation on creditor balances should encourage more aggressive borrowing policies.

Step 12. The budgeted income statement
The purpose of the budgeted income statement is to summarize and integrate all the operating budgets so as to measure the end result on the firm's income.

Sales (Step 1)	£167,000
Cost of goods sold (Step 10)	65,650
Gross margin	101,350
Selling and administrative expenses (Step 8)	40,000
Net income before tax	61,350
Tax (40%)	24,540
Net income after tax	£36,810

Step 13. The budgeted balance sheet
The final stage is the projection of the budgeted results on the firm's financial position at the end of the year. The following balance sheet reflects the changes in the composition of assets and liabilities as a result of the planned activities:

Capital employed		£	£
Ordinary share capital		210,000	
Retained income		62,810	
			272,810

Represented by			
		Provision	
		for	
Fixed assets	*Cost*	*depreciation*	
	£	£	
Plant & machinery	303,000	40,000	
			263,000

Current assets			
Inventories		£	
Raw materials		1650	
Finished goods		6075	
Debtors		22,250	
Cash		9375	
		39,350	

Less: Current liabilities			
Sundry creditors	5000		
Tax outstanding	24,540		
		29,540	
Net working capital			9810
			272,810

Evaluating the budget proposals

As a means of comparing the planned performance for the coming year with the results of the current year, the planned performance may be interpreted as follows:

Return on shareholders' equity: £36,810 ÷ £272,810

$$= 13.5\% \text{ (previous 7.6\%)}$$

Return on capital employed: £36,810 ÷ £302,350

$$= 12.2\% \text{ (previous 7.1\%)}$$

It is evident, therefore, that the firm is expected to make considerable improvements in the forthcoming period. If the budgeted results are considered to be satisfactory the final stage is a recommendation that the budget proposal be accepted by the Board of Directors as its policy, and as conforming with its view of the future.

Budgetary control

Planning alone does not necessarily ensure the realization of plans. It is also necessary to have control. This process necessitates the establishment of standards of performance which will act as day-to-day guidelines for the successful realization of the budget plan. In effect, the annual budget is subdivided into shorter periods for control purposes—into months and weeks. For these periods, the budget is compared with actual, the reasons for deviations are established and corrective action is taken if necessary.

As with budgetary planning, budgetary control is geared to the long-range plan. The continuous review of current progress indicates the extent to which the organization is moving towards the long-range plan.

Inflationary conditions place severe stress on budget planning and control systems. The phenomenon of rapidly changing costs distorts all the assumptions which may have shaped the budget. Thus, more importance should be attached to the latest forecasts and the analysis of changes which are occurring, if budgets are to be effective both for planning and control purposes. This difficulty has led some authors (Sizer, 1975) to emphasize effective forecasting procedures as of paramount importance to budgetary planning and control. Once effective forecasting procedures have been established, the significant comparisons are no longer between planned and actual costs, but between forecasts, as follows:

(a) Latest forecast *v* previous forecast. This comparison becomes the prime action mover, and leads to the following questions:
  (i)   Why has the forecast changed?
  (ii) How does the latest forecast affect the net cash flow?
  (iii) What actions should be taken to improve the situation?
(b) Actual *v* previous forecast. This comparison leads to the following questions being asked:
  (i)   Was the previous forecast effective as regards identifying the events now facing the firm?
  (ii) If not, why was the previous forecast wrong?
  (iii) Are the errors in forecasting due to excessive pessimism or optimism and can these errors be corrected?

Summary

Budgetary planning is an activity which should be seen as being concerned with the implementation of a yearly segment of the long-range plan. The budget expresses this plan in financial terms in the light of current conditions.

Successful budgetary planning depends on a number of other factors, for example, a sound formal organizational structure which designates clearly areas of authority and responsibility, as well as an accounting information system which allows effective financial control.

A major problem in budgetary planning is the forecasting of sales. The budget plan itself consists of some 13 stages as follows:

(1) The sales budget
(2) The production budget

(3) The direct materials usage budget

(4) The materials purchases budget
(5) The budgeted direct labour costs
(6) The overhead costs budget
(7) The closing inventory budget
(8) The selling and administrative costs budget
(9) The capital expenditure budget
(10) The cost of goods sold budget
(11) The cash budget
(12) The budgeted income statement
(13) The budgeted balance sheet

Budget plans may be evaluated by means of financial ratios such as the return on shareholders' equity and the return on capital employed.

Reference

Sizer, J. 'What we should be doing about the company liquidity and profitability crisis', *Management Accounting*, October, 1975.

Questions

1. Dafa Ltd is a trading company dealing in a single product. It is preparing its annual budget for the twelve months ending 30 June, 19X9. So far the following budgets have been prepared.

	July–Sept.	Oct.–Dec.	Jan.–Mar.	April–June
	£	£	£	£
Sales (at £3 per unit)	15,000	18,000	21,000	12,000
Purchases (at £2 per unit)	12,000	14,000	10,000	8000
Sundry expenses				
Distribution	500	800	1100	200
Administration	1000	1000	1000	1000
Depreciation	500	500	500	500
	2000	2300	2600	1700

Notes:
(1) Sales are made on one month's credit. It may be assumed that debtors outstanding on sales at the end of each quarter are equivalent to one-third of sales in that quarter, and that this is received the following quarter.
(2) All purchases are for cash. No credit is received.
(3) Distribution and Administration expenses are paid in cash as incurred.
(4) The company has no expenses apart from those given.
(5) Opening balances at 1 July, 19X8 are:

Debtors £3000
Cash £2000
Inventory 1000 units

Required: Complete Dafa Ltd's annual budget by preparing
(a) a debtors' budget
(b) a cash budget, *and*
(c) an inventory budget to show the number of units in inventory at the end of each quarter.

2. A small private company, after several years of unprofitable trading, was taken over by a new management on 31 December.

The accounts for the following year were summarized thus:

	£
Direct materials	78,000
Direct wages	31,200
Variable overheads	15,600
Fixed overheads	30,000
Profit	1200
Sales	156,000

The balance sheet as at the end of the first twelve months of trading was as follows:

	£	£	£
Capital employed			
Fixed assets			24,000
Current assets:			
Inventory	26,000		
Debtors	26,000	52,000	
less:			
Current liabilities:			
Creditors	19,500		
Bank overdraft	26,500	46,000	
Net working capital			6000
			30,000
Represented by:			
Share capital			40,000
Retained earnings			(10,000)
			30,000

The budgeted sales for the second year of trading are as follows:

	£
1st quarter	42,000
2nd quarter	45,000
3rd quarter	48,000
4th quarter	51,000

It is anticipated that the ratios of material consumption, direct wages and variable overheads to sales are unlikely to change; that the fixed overheads (incurred evenly during the year) will remain at £30,000 per annum; and that creditors can be held at three months' direct material usage. Both stocks and debtors can be maintained at two months' sales.

Bank interest and depreciation, the latter at 10 per cent per annum on fixed assets, are included in the overheads.

Required: Prepare quarterly budgets for the second year of operation to indicate to management:

(a) Whether the results are likely to be satisfactory.
(b) Whether the overdraft facilities (which are normally limited to £25,000) are sufficient, or whether further capital must be introduced.

3. Jones is considering whether to open up his own wholesaling business. He makes the following estimates about the first six month's trading:

1. *Sales on credit*	— for first two months = £50,000 per month. — thereafter £80,000 per month. — one month's credit allowed to customers.
2. *Gross margin*	— the cost of goods brought for resale is expected to be 75 per cent of the selling price.
3. *Closing inventory*	— £75,000.
4. *Purchases creditors at end*	— £50,000.
5. *Wages and salaries*	— paid for period £40,000. — owing at end of period £2500.
6. *Warehouse expenses*	— cash paid for rent, rates, lighting, heating, etc. £50,000. — in addition £5500 of warehouse expenses will be owing at end of six months. — of the cash paid, however, £3500 will be rent and rates paid in advance.
7. *Furniture, fixtures and fittings*	— amounting to £50,000 to be purchased on opening of business and will be subject to 10 per cent p.a. depreciation.
8. *Delivery vehicles*	— three vans costing £2000 each will be purchased at once and will be subject to 25 per cent p.a. depreciation.
9. *Loan interest*	— long-term loans can be raised at an interest rate of 10 per cent p.a.
10. *Jones*	— expects to draw from the business account his own 'wages' at a rate of £300 per month.

Required:

(a) A budgeted cash account for the period on the basis of the above information (see part c below).

(b) Budgeted income statement for the period and balance sheet as at the end on the basis of the above information (see part c below).

(c) Advise Jones as to how much capital should be introduced initially into the business. Jones, however, has only £50,000 available as capital. Complete the accounts on the assumption that he accepts your advice.

(d) Jones asks you whether the business appears to be a worthwhile one. Give a *brief* reply to this question.

31 Risk analysis

The process of rational decision making in organizations requires the harnessing of all the relevant facts so that the likely outcome of the different alternatives open for selection may be correctly measured. As we have seen many times so far in this book, if one were able to predict the future with complete accuracy, the problems of decision making would be largely eliminated. In a world which is characterized by change, the decision maker cannot rely entirely on the forecasts prepared for him of the likely outcome of different alternatives no matter how carefully these forecasts are prepared. By the very nature of things, predictions of future events are tentative and uncertain.

The process of decision making is fraught with risk and uncertainty. Strictly speaking, a decision problem under conditions of 'risk' is one where one knows the risk or probability attached to the outcome of the different alternatives being considered, whereas a decision problem under 'uncertainty' is one where the risk or probability attached to the outcomes is not known. The distinction between the terms risk and uncertainty is becoming quite blurred, and we shall use them interchangeably.

The purpose of this chapter is to examine the methods currently available for evaluating the risk element in business decisions.

Uncertainty and information

Uncertainty may be regarded as a deficiency of information. Under conditions of certainty, complete knowledge about the future would be available, and profit as a reward for risk bearing would not be a business phenomenon. Profits and losses occur as a result of uncertainty. The purpose of information, therefore, is to increase and improve knowledge so as to reduce uncertainty as much as possible. The greater the degree of uncertainty affecting a particular decision, the more valuable is the benefit to be derived from additional information.

The problem of the uncertainty involved in capital budgeting decisions has received much attention of recent years. Such decisions are not easily reversible, if at all, and the hazard of making wrong decisions may be minimized to a considerable extent by improving the quality and extent of the information coverage. The methods for dealing with uncertainty in capital budgeting decisions may also be applied to other types of decisions, and it is our purpose to examine these methods in this chapter.

Adjusting the discount rate for risk

In Chapter 29, we examined the usefulness of discounted cash flow techniques for making capital investment decisions. One method of allowing for uncertainty is to adjust the discount rate to take account of the expected degree of risk. Thus, whereas a discount rate of 10 per cent might be used to discount future cash flows under conditions of certainty, an organization might impose a decision rule that a higher discount rate would have to be employed for projects which face conditions of uncertainty. In calculating the internal rate of return for a project, the required rate of return, that is the 'hurdle rate', may be increased to allow for the degree of uncertainty involved in the project.

In adjusting the discount rate or increasing the hurdle rate, we are assuming a knowledge of the risk involved in the project. But the main difficulty about using a risk-adjusted discount rate lies in the problem of measuring different degrees of risk. The question really is 'how does one measure the difference between a project with a high degree of risk and one with a low degree of risk?' Furthermore, since those who are concerned with preparing the relevant information and those who will make the investment decisions are rarely the same people, means must be found of quantifying the degree of uncertainty present in the forecast of outcomes.

All in all, the risk-adjusted discount rate method of dealing with the problem of uncertainty presents a difficult measurement problem for although it recognizes the existence of uncertainty, it does not accurately evaluate it.

Sensitivity analysis and the measurement of risk

One of the ways of assessing the effects of uncertainty attached to any decision is to improve the quality of the relevant information. Sensitivity analysis is such a method. It is really a critical analysis of the factors which determine the forecasted results. Its purpose is to indicate which factors are more crucial to the predicted outcome and to provide insights into what would happen to the predicted outcome if there were subsequently any deviation from the predicted values of the key factors. For example, the estimates of the net inflows and outflows associated with a capital investment decision are based on forecasts of such factors as sales volume, selling prices, raw material costs, operating expenses, the useful life of the project and capital costs. Sensitivity analysis is directed to such questions as 'what would be the effect if capital costs turned out to be 10 per cent higher than estimated?' or 'what would be the effect if the cash inflows were 5 per cent lower than planned?' By asking such questions, it is possible to identify those factors which are likely to have proportionately a much greater impact on the planned rate of return should there be a relatively small change in their estimated value.

Sensitivity analysis is particularly useful in the study of capital investment decisions where considerable uncertainty exists or where large amounts of capital are involved, for it provides information which places management in a better position to decide whether the risks surrounding the project are too large to permit its acceptance.

Example

Spectrum Engineering Ltd is considering a capital investment project and assumes that a 15 per cent rate of return will be earned. It has undertaken a detailed sensitivity study of the effect of possible changes in the key factors on the expected rate of return as follows:

	Internal rate of return			
Estimated maximum possible change in the factors involved	Expected	Adjusted for possible change	Difference	Effect of change on the expected rate of return
	%	%	%	%
10% decrease in sales volume	15	13.0	2.0	13.4
10% decrease in sales price	15	7.3	7.7	51.4
10% decrease in project life	15	14.0	1.0	6.7
10% increase in raw material costs	15	9.1	5.9	39.3
10% increase in operating costs	15	14.5	0.5	3.3
10% increase in capital investment costs	15	14.0	1.0	6.7

This table reveals that the expected rate of return is most sensitive to possible changes in selling price and raw material costs, so that it is in respect of these estimates that errors in their forecasts are likely to be most damaging. Hence, management will be encouraged to a further investigation of the circumstances affecting the two factors in question so as to validate their estimate of their behaviour before a final decision is made.

Sensitivity analysis is subject to important limitations, which are similar in nature to those we noted in respect of the risk-adjusted rate of return method for dealing with uncertainty. First, sensitivity analysis depends on a knowledge of the chances of any deviations in the key factors from their predicted behaviour in the future. Second, sensitivity analysis also requires the effects of changes in each key factor to be isolated, whereas management is interested too in the combined effect of changes in two or more key factors and the probability of such combined changes occurring.

Risk analysis and sensitivity analysis

In order to use sensitivity analysis to full advantage, it is necessary to combine it with risk analysis which uses probability theory in the measurement of variability. Increasingly, in every aspect of accounting one sees a growing emphasis on mathematical techniques in the solution of measurement problems, and nowhere is this truer than in risk analysis.

The mathematical propositions of probability theory are relatively simple. We ascribe the number 1 to the certainty that an event will occur, and the number 0 to the certainty that it will not occur. Clearly, the chance that an event will occur depends upon the number of events which could occur. Let us take, for example, the measurement of the probability attached to the outcome of the tossing of a coin. Since there are only two events which could occur and each is equally likely, that is heads or tails, the probability of either event occurring is 1/2 or 0.5. Similarly, if throwing dice, the probability of turning up any of the numbers is 1/6 or 0.1667.

The same reasoning may be used to measure the likelihood of financial estimates and predictions turning out to be true. Since capital investment decisions require quite a long view of the future, and as uncertainty increases as the time span covered by a decision problem lengthens it is not surprising that risk analysis has a particular importance to such decisions.

Example

The Hydra International Corporation is faced with selecting one of two investment projects, both of which would require an investment of £10,000 and each of which is expected to yield £5000 annually for 5 years.

Using the investment appraisal methods described in Chapter 29 there would be no way of preferring either of the projects against the other. The firm, in effect, would have to toss a coin to decide which project to select.

If, however, it is discovered that the probabilities attached to estimated cash inflows are different, then it is clear that the two projects may be distinguished. Let us assume, therefore, that the probabilties of receiving the total net cash inflows from the two projects are as depicted in Fig. 5.10.

In terms of the risk involved, the two projects are quite different. The chances of receiving a yearly cash inflow of £5000 are much higher for Project B than they are for Project A, there being a 0.5 chance attached to the probability of receiving £5000 in Project B, whereas there is only a 0.3 chance of receiving £5000 in Project A. By contrast, the probability of receiving sums below £4600 is much higher in Project A than in Project B. The table shows, for example, that the chance of receiving less than £4000 in Project B is zero, whereas there are chances of receiving smaller sums in Project A. On the other hand, Project A offers chances of larger returns than Project B—there is no chance whatsoever of returns higher than £6000 in Project B, but there are probabilities of returns in excess of that sum in Project A. Consequently, a conservative management would prefer Project B, and would reject Project A.

The certainty equivalent method of risk appraisal

We may consider the aforementioned example in terms of the distribution of the probabilities around the mean ($\bar{X}$) so that the standard deviation (σ) may be used to represent the entire probability distribution. Students of statistics

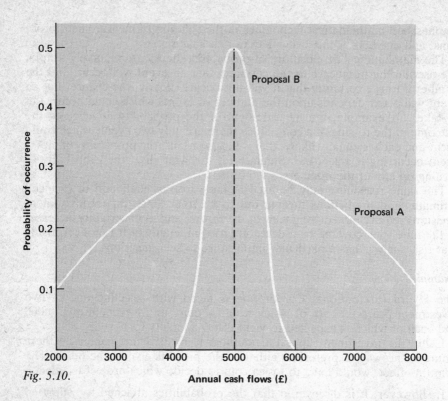

Fig. 5.10.

Annual cash flows (£)

will appreciate that the standard deviation represents a measure of dispersion around the mean. Figure 5.10 shows that the dispersion around the mean is much smaller for Project B than it is for Project A. The mean return is defined for this purpose as the expected return, that is £5000 for both projects. The standard deviation indicates the degree of risk attached to receiving the expected return, so that the higher the standard deviation the greater the risk.

We may observe that the distribution of probabilities for both projects assumes the shape of a normal curve, that is, a symmetrical curve with the shape of a bell. The normal curve is an important statistical concept, and the implications of the normal curve are well-known to students of elementary statistics. From these curves we may read off the following possibilities:

	Project A		Project B	
Cash flows £	Probability		Cash flows £	Probability
2000	0.10		4250	0.05
3500	0.25		4500	0.20
5000	0.30		5000	0.50
6500	0.25		5500	0.20
8000	0.10		5750	0.05
	1.00			1.00

The standard deviation as a measure of the risk attached to obtaining the expected return, that is £5000, is obtained by a formula which concentrates on the deviations from the expected return which are represented in the total sample taken into the probability calculations.

The formula for calculating the standard deviation is as follows:

$$\sigma = \sqrt{\frac{fd^2}{n}}$$

where σ is the standard deviation
    f is the frequency with which a value occurs (in this case the probability attached to receiving a sum)
    d is the deviation of the value of a sum from the mean $\bar{X}$
    n is the size of the sample (in this case the total probabilities represented by the number 1)

Hence, we may calculate the standard deviation for Projects A and B as follows:

Project A

Cash flow X	Probability f	fX	$\bar{X}$	(d) $X-\bar{X}$	(d^2) $(X-\bar{X})^2$	(fd^2)
£2000	0.10	200	£5000	−£3000	9,000,000	900,000
3500	0.25	875	5000	−1500	2,250,000	562,500
5000	0.30	1500	5000	—	—	—
6500	0.25	1625	5000	1500	2,250,000	562,500
8000	0.10	800	5000	3000	9,000,000	900,000
	1.00	5000			22,500,000	2,925,000

$$\text{Standard deviation} = \sqrt{\frac{2,925,000}{1}}$$

$$= 1710.265$$

Project B

Cash flow X	Probability f	fX	$\bar{X}$	(d) $X-\bar{X}$	(d^2) $(X-\bar{X})^2$	(fd^2)
£4250	0.05	212	£5000	−£750	562,500	28,125
4500	0.20	900	5000	−500	250,000	50,000
5000	0.50	2500	5000	—	—	—
5500	0.20	1100	5000	500	250,000	50,000
5750	0.05	288	5000	750	562,500	28,125
	1.00	5000			1,625,000	156,250

$$\text{Standard deviation} = \sqrt{\frac{156,250}{1}}$$

$$= 395.28$$

The significance of finding the value of the standard deviation lies in the fact that we can now estimate the degree of risk involved in a project. In a normal curve it is known that 68.27 per cent of all possible outcomes will be within plus or minus one standard deviation from the mean. Furthermore, 95.45 per cent of all possible outcomes will be within plus or minus two standard deviations from the mean, and 99.73 per cent will fall within plus or minus three standard deviations from the mean.

We can see from our calculations of one standard deviation that as regards Project A, we can be approximately 68 per cent certain that the cash flows will be within the range £3290–£6710 (that is £5000±£1710). As regards Project B, we can be 68 per cent certain that the value of the expected cash flows will fall within the range £4605–£5395 (that is £5000±£395). Clearly, we are more certain of receiving £5000 or a sum close to it from Project B than from Project A, as seen from Fig. 5.11.

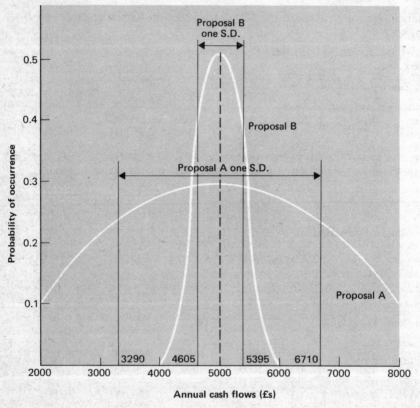

Fig. 5.11.

Project B may be preferred to Project A, therefore, because the degree of risk of receiving a sum which deviates from the expected return of £5000 is less in Project B than it is in Project A. The reason for this preference arises if we assume that decision makers are 'risk-averse', and that they will prefer smaller but more certain returns to larger and more uncertain returns. Given this assumption, we are able to relate the standard deviations and the means to give a risk percentage which may be measured as follows:

$$\text{Risk percentage} = \frac{\text{Standard deviation}}{X} \times \frac{100}{1}$$

The risk percentage for Project A would be as follows:

$$\frac{1710\ 25}{5000.00} \times 100 = 34\%$$

so that the certainty equivalent may be expressed as

$$100\% - 34\% = 66\%$$

Hence, the risk adjusted expected value of cash flows associated with Project A would be:

$$£5000 \times 66\% = £3300$$

The risk percentage for Project B would be as follows:

$$\frac{395.28}{5000.00} \times 100 = 8\%$$

and the certainty equivalent:

$$100\% - 8\% = 92\%$$

Hence, the risk-adjusted expected value of cash flows associated with Project B would be:

$$£5000 \times 92\% = £4600$$

Thus, the procedure involved in using the certainty equivalent approach is to adjust the expected cash flows for risk. The adjusted cash flows may then be discounted to their present value. In the foregoing example, the certainty equivalent is higher for Project B than for Project A and reflects the higher degree of risk attached to Project A.

The certainty equivalent approach to the measurement of risk solves the problem which we noted earlier in our analysis of the risk-adjusted discount rate, that is, the problem of determining the risk existing between projects.

Decision trees

So far we have been concerned with the problems of assessing projects with a view to making simple accept-reject decisions. However, in most cases, the values of some variables are dependent on the values of others. A decision tree illustrates this dependence by following a chain of events to some final outcome.

A decision tree consists of a series of rods and branches. Each alternative course of action under consideration is represented by a main branch which, in turn, may have subsidiary branches for related chance events that appear in chronological order. In other words, the tree diagram charts the paths that lead to possible consequences.

Let us take as a simple example the decision to launch a new product. It is very likely that sales of a new product in the second year will be influenced by the level of sales in the first year. We assume that management estimates that sales in the first year have a 0.6 probability of being excellent, let us say 7000 units, and 0.4 probability of being good, let us say 5000 units. The probability distribution of sales in the second year will vary depending on whether the first year achieved excellent or good results. Assuming that we can estimate these probabilities for either excellent or good first-year sales, we may draw a decision tree as follows:

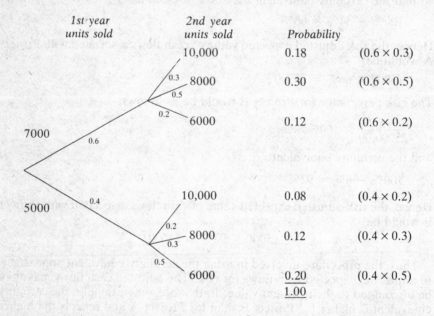

1st year units sold	2nd year units sold	Probability	
	10,000	0.18	(0.6 × 0.3)
	8000	0.30	(0.6 × 0.5)
	6000	0.12	(0.6 × 0.2)
7000			
5000	10,000	0.08	(0.4 × 0.2)
	8000	0.12	(0.4 × 0.3)
	6000	0.20	(0.4 × 0.5)
		1.00	

From this diagram it can be observed that the sum of the probabilities of each event is still the sum of the separate probabilities, but the probabilities of each of the six possible outcomes is the product of their individual probabilities. For example, if we chart the path on the topmost branch we get 0.6 × 0.3 = 0.18.

To avoid having to show each sales probability separately which is a laborious task when the number of chance events is larger and to avoid a possible confusing array of numbers, a frequency distribution may be prepared as follows:

Units sold	Probability
10,000	0.26 i.e. (0.18 + 0.08)
8000	0.42 i.e. (0.30 + 0.12)
6000	0.32 i.e. (0.12 + 0.20)
	1.00

Application of decision tree analysis

Decision tree analysis has a number of important applications to the solution of management problems. It has an important role to play in the study of investment projects which depend upon a series of events occurring in the right order, and which depend also upon the factors involved behaving according to forecast.

We shall take as our specific example the application of decision tree analysis to the problem of budgeting. In all budget planning exercises, there is a strong element of probability forecasting. It is possible to examine the probable outcome of the elements of the budget, and this process is known as *probabilistic budgeting*. As we saw in Chapter 30, the objective of budgeting is to produce an operational plan for the planning period, and if a change occurs in an important variable, such as the price of raw materials, the budget may have to be revised. Such a revision involves a laborious effort to reconstruct the budget, and in practice because of the time element required, it is normal to construct budgets on the basis of a limited number of assumptions. Traditional budgeting, therefore, does not provide a flexible instrument which may be adjusted to meet changing conditions. At best, they are flexible merely as regards varying sales and production levels. Moreover, such budgets are determined after considering only a limited number of alternative possibilities, which are aimed at attaining satisfactory rather than optimal targets.

With the advent of the computer, it is now possible to prepare in advance a number of budgets to meet all forseeable contingencies, so that if they occur it is possible immediately to select the appropriate course of action to take.

Example

Let us assume that the budget of a firm is based upon forecasts of the behaviour of three crucial elements—sales volume, material prices and operating costs. Let us assume that there is a 0.6 chance of sales volume being 90 per cent of productive capacity, and a 0.2 chance of it being 100 per cent and 80 per cent of capacity respectively. The chances of raw material costs and operating costs rising rapidly are estimated at 0.1 and 0.3 respectively. Negligible rises in these costs were also 0.1 and 0.3 with the chances of moderate rises being much higher at 0.8 and 0.4 respectively. We may tabulate these probabilities as follows:

Forecast	Sales volume	Raw material costs	Operating costs
High	0.2	0.1	0.3
Average	0.6	0.8	0.4
Low	0.2	0.1	0.3
	1.0	1.0	1.0

We may observe from these probabilities that the chances of moderate increases in raw material prices are much higher than for moderate increases in operating costs. It is possible to combine the effects of these combinations so as to produce 27 possible budgets by means of a decision tree analysis (Fig. 5.12 on p. 499).

Having worked out a total possible number of budgets, it would be too time-wasting in practice to go to the length of envisaging all the probable combinations of events which might occur and to plan budgets accordingly. It is advisable, therefore, to establish a cut-off point below which contingencies are not planned for, and in our example, we might select the probability of 0.024 as the cut-off point. Let us consider the effect of imposing such a cut-off point by reference to the frequency distribution of the probabilities.

Probability	Frequency	Pf
0.006	8	0.048
0.008	4	0.032
0.018	4	0.072
0.024	2	0.048
0.056	18	0.200
0.048	4	0.192
0.064	2	0.128
0.144	2	0.288
0.192	1	0.192
0.438	9	0.800
Total	27	1.000

As a result of selecting the cut-off point at the probability of 0.024, we can omit 18 budgets from the reckoning with a loss of coverage of only 0.2 of the total budgets which may be needed to meet all eventualities. As the table above shows, there is a probability of 0.8, or 4 chances out of 5, that the nine budgets included in part of the frequency distribution above the cut-off point will occur. Management may concentrate, therefore on the preparation of these nine budgets only.

Probabilistic budgeting increases dramatically the effectiveness of budgetary control systems, for as circumstances change the firm is ready to meet these changes. As we have noted above, probabilistic budgeting is concerned with planning for contingencies well in advance of their occurrence, so that the firm may alter its plan should these contingencies materialize. As a result, the firm is in a better position to make the best use of its resources; its plans include the possibility of shifts in resource allocations should circumstances change. Equally important is the manner in which probabilistic budgeting enables management to understand the manner in which changes affect the firm and alter the inter-relationship of its various elements.

Large-scale simulation

Our analysis of the effects of risk on decision making has been based so far on three assumptions:

(a) that the distribution of probabilities of events occurring has the characteristic of a normal curve;

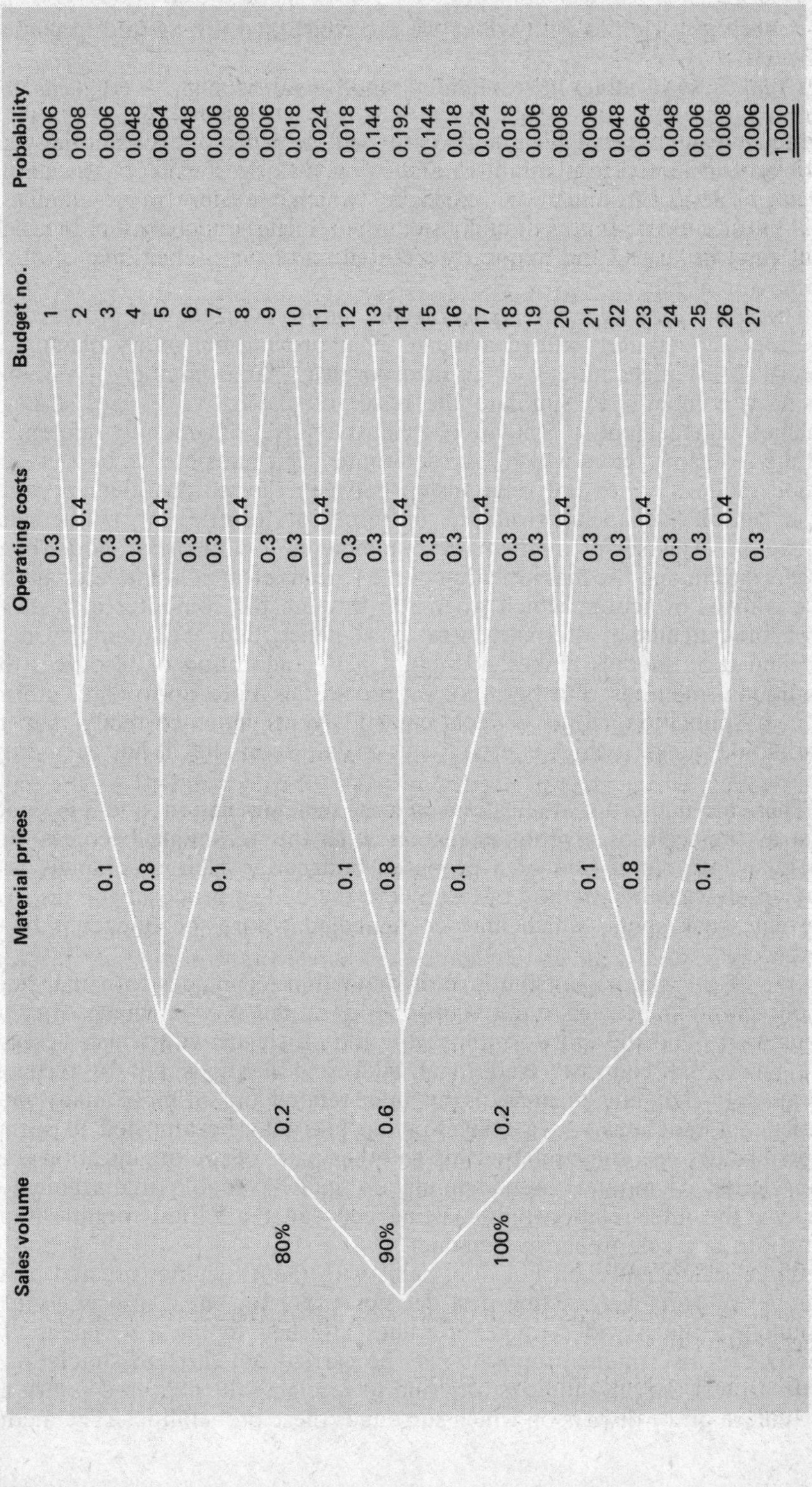

Fig. 5.12.

(b) that the variables with which we are concerned are limited in number; and

(c) that these variables have a limited range of values: high, average and low.

Modern computers have greatly extended the range of probabilities which may be considered in planning and decision making, and the application to such problems of simulation techniques which are more representative of real-life situations. It is as though the computer acts as a laboratory in which a plan may be tested and exposed to the circumstances which may probably occur in real life.

The application of mathematical techniques to management problems and the use of computers afford a means of improving budgetary planning by means of a budget model which incorporates a large number of variables. Using a computer to simulate the result of alternative budget strategies enables management to evaluate alternative courses of action by reference to all the relevant factors which may determine their outcome. A budget simulation model defines the relationship between the various elements of an organization's financial structure in terms of a series of mathematical equations. This set of mathematical statements is a financial model of the organization, and the manipulation of the various elements simulates alternative courses of action, which when run through the computer indicate the probable outcome of alternative strategies. Hence, budget planning by means of simulation models makes possible a better allocation of resources than traditional methods. Furthermore by processing more up-to-date information, a simulation model reflects current events more correctly than the traditional budget, which is usually out of date soon after it has been drawn up.

There are numerous applications of large scale simulation, and it is evident that as the scale of a problem increases, so this technique becomes more useful. Thus, simulation of a proposed budget for a large company is an immensely valuable method of testing out the budget proposal and discovering any weak spots, which may be remedied before the budget is finally agreed.

One of the major contributions of simulation techniques to management science is in improving our understanding of the way in which organizations work, and therefore in improving the efficiency with which decisions are made. By contrast, traditional budgeting methods fail to recognize adequately that any business is an inter-related organism of many interdependent functions. As a result, undue bias may be attached to specific functions because their relationship to other parts of the organization is not considered. Computer based simulation models enable management to analyse the inter-relationships existing between the various organizational functions in a comprehensive manner.

Large-scale simulation not only helps with the difficulties created by the number of variables existing in a decision problem, but it also is useful in handling a much wider range of values attached to these variables. The analysis of investment proposals may be carried out through simulation in order to test the probabilities attached to receiving the expected return and the nature of the dispersion which surrounds these probabilities. The method for calculating the dispersion is derived from what is known as the Monte Carlo technique, which, as its name implies, is concerned with the study of chance.

The assumptions underlying the Monte Carlo technique are reasonable enough, for example, if one were playing roulette one would expect that over a long sequence of games each number should come up the same number of times. Therefore, if we were to take a large enough sample of a very large number of games, the sample should represent, that is simulate, the results of all the games. This principle forms the basis of the Monte Carlo technique. The appraisal of capital investment programmed by means of the Monte Carlo method involves four stages, as follows:

(1) The determination of the factors which are important in evaluating an investment proposal. Hertz (1964), for example, considers the following factors to be relevant: market size, market growth rate, share of market, selling prices, investment required, the residual value of the investment, operating costs, fixed costs and the useful life of the investment.

(2) The determination of a frequency distribution for each of these factors showing the probability of any particular value of that factor occurring.

(3) The selection at random from each of these several distributions of a particular value which are combined so as to compute the rate of return which would result.

(4) Stage three is repeated a large number of times to ascertain the probability attaching to each possible rate of return. Although the selection made from the values of the factors on each occasion is made on a random basis, it must be remembered that the chances of any particular value for a factor being selected depends entirely on the forecast made of the probability distribution for that factor. This probability distribution will have been worked out during stage 2. The frequency distribution so obtained enables an evaluation to be made of the expected return and the degree of dispersion about the expected return. By comparing the probability distributions of one proposal with those of another, management is able to evaluate the respective merits of risky investments.

The large-scale simulation technique as a method of forecasting and eliminating risk is one of the most significant steps forward in the application of mathematical techniques to the solution of traditional accounting problems.

Utility theory and risk aversion

We have assumed in this chapter that investors are risk-averse. This statement contains an implicit assumption about the utility or satisfaction derived from money (either income or wealth), namely, that the marginal utility of money declines as the level of income or wealth rises. Thus, the utility to be derived from an additional £100 if one has only £1 is considerably greater than if one has £100,000. The utility function of money may be shown as in Fig. 5.13.

It is possible to derive the utility function of money for different individuals. Moreover, it may be postulated that the utility function of money will be different between individuals according to their degree of risk-aversion. Thus, Fig. 5.13 may be associated with a risk-averse investor, whose utility

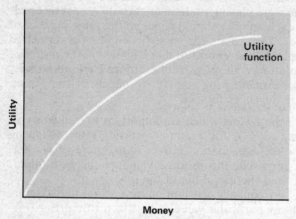

Fig. 5.13 The utility function of money.

function declines as his level of income or wealth increases. Figure 5.14 below shows the utility function of money for an investor who is 'risk neutral', that is, who regards each additional £100 as having the same value regardless of his level of income or wealth. Figure 5.15 below shows the utility function of a

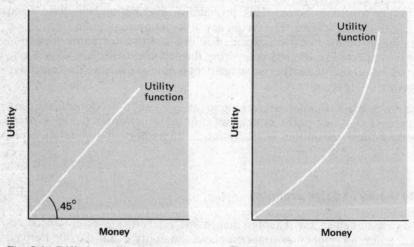

Fig. 5.14 Differing utility function   *Fig. 5.15.*
of money with Fig. 5.15.

risk-loving investor, that is, an investor whose utility function increases as his level of income or wealth rises. Thus, he derives less satisfaction from £100 when his income or wealth is low than when his income or wealth is high.

The assumption that risk-aversion represents rational investor behaviour may be validated by the following example:

Example

An investor is faced with the following alternative returns:

(a) £1,000,000 to which is attached a probability of 1
(b) £3,000,000 to which is attached a probability of 0.5 and a 0.5 probability of £0.

The expected returns may be stated as follows:

(a) £1,000,000
(b) £1,500,000   i.e. 3,000,000 × 0.5

Confronted with this choice, it may safely be assumed that the investor would prefer the certainty of receiving £1,000,000 than the gamble involved in the prospect of receiving £1,500,000.

In gambling situations, different individuals may react differently when faced with the prospect of gaining large sums to which different odds are attached. Thus, faced with a certainty of receiving £1,000,000 or sums of £1,500,000, or more to which different odds are attached, many will still prefer the certain return of £1,000,000 though others may be tempted to take a chance. Utility theory applied to the problem of risk aversion assists in understanding individual behaviour under conditions of risk. It proposes that individuals attempt to optimize the expected value of something which is defined as utility, and assumes that for each individual a relationship may be established between utility and money. Utility may be expressed in utiles* and the certainty equivalent is needed to determine the individual utility function.

Example

An individual owns a lottery ticket which offers him a 0.5 chance of winning £1 million and a 0.5 chance of winning £0. He is asked what he would accept in cash to sell the lottery ticket. If he answers £400,000, we may attach a utile value of 0.5 to £400,000, for we have determined the certainty equivalent at which he is indifferent between £400,000 and the chance of gaining the lottery prize.

The foregoing analysis may be applied to an investment decision requiring a choice between two projects, both of which involved the same initial and certain cash outlay and the same expected cash inflow, save that the cash inflow has a different dispersion for each project. Details appear on p. 504.

The discovery of the utility function attached to each possible outcome in both projects enables us to understand that the maximization of utility is

---

* The 'utile' has long featured in the literature of economics as a measure which would prove useful to the expression of utility. It is, however, purely a theoretical measure. A practical expression of a utile does not appear possible, and it has been stated that 'the search for a utile is bound to be futile'.

relevant to risk analysis. In the following example, Project B would be selected because it has a higher utility than Project A. We may deduce, therefore, that Project B would have been preferred even had it yielded a smaller expected income than Project A.

Project A

Cash inflow	Probability	Utility	Cash inflow × Probability	Utility × Probability
£			£	
−2000	0.3	−2.8	−600	−0.84
0	0.3	0	0	0
1000	0.1	0.10	100	0.01
5000	0.1	0.36	500	0.036
25,000	0.2	0.54	5000	0.108
		Expected income	5000	Expected utility 0.07

Project B

Cash inflow	Probability	Utility	Cash inflow × Probability	Utility × Probability
£			£	
3000	0.1	0.25	300	0.025
4000	0.2	0.31	800	0.062
5000	0.4	0.36	2000	0.144
6000	0.2	0.40	1200	0.080
7000	0.1	0.43	700	0.043
		Expected income	5000	Expected utility 0.354

Despite its appeal, it is unlikely that such an application of utility theory to the appraisal of risk will become operational, since it is virtually impossible to specify a reliable utility for this purpose. Attitudes towards risk are affected, moreover, by particular circumstances affecting a firm. It is doubtful also if one can talk meaningfully about the utility function of a large organization for the purpose of risk appraisal. Thus, this analysis has little usefulness other than throwing light on the nature of risk.

Portfolio risk

The preceding discussion assumed that the problem was either a single accept-reject decision or a choice between alternatives. The approaches which were discussed are feasible where the firm either has no existing investments and is making a first investment decision, or if, having already made investments, the expected returns from the existing and proposed investments are perfectly correlated. Should neither of these assumptions hold, the firm is in a situation similar to the ordinary investor. As we saw in Chapter 22, the problem facing the ordinary investor is the relationship between the investment currently under consideration and other existing or potential investment opportunities. Therefore, where a company is considering some form of diversification in its investments, the risk attached to a particular project should be considered in the context of the total risk profile of the company. Projects that are not confined to existing activities may have a higher degree of individual risk than projects already in hand, but the overall effect of accepting such projects may be to reduce the total risk profile of the company. That profile is clearly dependent on the degree of correlation between projects as well as the specific risk associated with each project.

Summary

A proper understanding of decision making is impossible unless the problem of risk is taken into account. As regards capital expenditure decisions, for example, risk implies the possibility that the actual outcome may be different from the expected outcome.

Uncertainty may be regarded as a deficiency of information, and the objective of an information system should be seen as reducing this deficiency where possible. In this respect, opportunities exist for the accountant to apply probability analysis to the problem of risk. Several approaches were considered—adjusting the discount rate for uncertainty, sensitivity analysis and the certainty equivalent method.

Methods of risk analysis have a wide-ranging usefulness. In addition to providing means of appraising investment projects, these methods offer solutions to other management problems. Decision tree analysis, for example, extends probability analysis to the study of activities which consist of a chain of dependent events. In this connection, probabilistic budgeting increases the effectiveness of budgetary control systems. The advent of computers has made possible the study of the effects of risk through simulation techniques.

Risk analysis rests on the assumption that decision makers are risk-averse. Despite its limitations in practice, utility theory is useful for providing an understanding of decision making under risk.

Reference

Hertz D. B. 'Risk analysis in capital investments', *Harvard Business Review*, 42, pp. 95–106, January–February 1964.

Questions

1. Explain the method of adjusting the discount rate to take account of risk.
2. What is meant by sensitivity analysis?

3. How does the certainty equivalent approach assist in determining the risk existing between projects?
4. What is a decision tree? How is decision tree analysis applied to the budgeting process?
5. How does large scale simulation assist in forecasting and eliminating risk?
6. What light does utility theory throw on the decision making process?

32 Cost-volume-profit analysis

Much of the discussion in the previous three chapters was concerned with the importance of the distinction between the long term and the short term for decision making, and consequently of the nature of the accounting problem of providing relevant information for decisions affecting different time periods.

The essential qualitative difference between the long term and the short term is that the long term may be defined as planning for change, whereas the short term implies adapting to change. In this sense, the firm's resources may be planned in the long term to take advantage of changing opportunities in such a way that not only its structure may be altered but its objectives as well. In the short term, however, the firm's output capacity is fixed, so that the firm's freedom of action is limited.

Short-term planning, which is the subject of this chapter, considers the most desirable course of action to take to achieve a planned profit given that the firm's output range is relatively fixed. Cost-volume-profit analysis is an important tool in short-term planning for it explores the inter-relationship which exists between the four principal variables—cost, revenue, volume of output and profit. In planning its short-term strategy management will require to know what will be the effect of changing one or more of these variables, and the effect of this change on profit.

Applications of cost-volume-profit (c-v-p) analysis

Cost-volume-profit analysis lies at the centre of short-term profit planning because it has a wider application to a whole series of decision problems. In view of the relationship between costs and volume of output, c-v-p is helpful in establishing a pricing strategy. C-v-p is also relevant to the selection of the best sales mix, where a firm produces several different products. In such a case, it is essential to select the most profitable combination of the different products having regard to their costs of production and the prices which are obtainable. A decision to produce a sales mix which is less profitable may be made, for example, in order to penetrate a market or to establish a stronger position in a particular market from a sales point of view, and in such a case c-v-p will enable management to assess the cost of that strategy in terms of lost profit. Other applications include the study of product alternatives, the acceptance of special orders, selecting channels of distribution, the strategy for entering a foreign market and changing plant lay-out.

C-v-p analysis lays emphasis on cost behaviour patterns through different volumes of output as a guide to the selection of profit targets and the adoption of an appropriate pricing policy. By uniting the behaviour of all four variables together in one short-term model, c-v-p analysis provides management with a sweeping overview of the planning process.

Cost analysis and profit planning

The response of cost to a variety of influences is invaluable to management decision making. As we saw in Chapter 27, some costs are constant, or fixed, in a given time-span, whereas other costs vary. Cost-volume-profit analysis focuses on the distinction between 'fixed' and 'variable' costs: the former being defined for this purpose as the costs which do not change over a range of output, and the latter being those which change directly with output.

C-v-p analysis requires that the fixed and variable elements be segregated and calculated so that all costs may be divided into simply fixed and variable costs.

One of the most important uses of the distinction between fixed and variable cost lies in the analysis of these costs through different levels of production.

Example

Unit sales	40,000		50,000	
	Total	Unit	Total	Unit
	£			£
Revenue	400,000	10.0	500,000	10.0
Variable costs	160,000	4.0	200,000	4.0
Contribution margin	240,000	6.0	300,000	6.0
Fixed costs	150,000	3.8	150,000	3.0
Net profit	90,000	2.2	150,000	3.0

Duofold Ltd produces an article which it sells for £10. Fixed costs of production are £150,000 per year, and variable costs are £4 per unit. The present yearly volume of output is 40,000 units, but could be increased to 50,000.

Problem: What will be the effect on total costs of the projected increase in output, and the impact of profit?

The analysis shows that total variable costs increase proportionally with output while unit variable costs are constant. Total fixed costs, however, remain constant at both levels of output so that unit fixed costs fall as output rises and vice versa. It is because unit fixed costs are falling that total unit costs are less for an output of 50,000 units than for one of 40,000 units.

If we assume that selling prices remain unaltered, costs savings themselves will lead to increased profitability. The contribution margin is an important concept in cost-profit analysis. As may be seen from the example above, the contribution margin is calculated by deducting the variable costs from revenue. It is the first stage in calculating the net profit and measures the profit which is available to cover fixed costs. Since fixed costs are incurred irrespective of sales, a firm will make a loss if the contribution margin is insufficient to cover fixed costs. At low levels of output the firm will make a loss because fixed costs are greater than the contribution margin. As output increases, so does the contribution margin which will ultimately equal and then exceed fixed costs. The relationship between fixed costs and the contribution margin may be illustrated as in Fig. 5.16. The critical point at

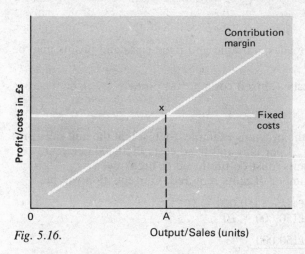

Fig. 5.16.

which the contribution margin is equal to fixed costs is known as the break-even point which indicates that level of output (OA) at which the firm makes zero profits, that is, where total costs are equal to total revenues.

Break-even analysis

Break-even analysis focuses on the measurement of the break-even point. Before we attempt any calculations, it is necessary to make certain assumptions about the behaviour of costs and revenues. Thus, we assume that costs and revenue patterns have been reliably determined and that they are linear over the range of output which is being analysed. These assumptions also imply that costs may be resolved without difficulty into fixed and variable costs; that fixed costs will remain constant, that variable costs will vary proportionally with volume of output; and that all other factors will remain constant, that is, that selling prices will remain unchanged, that the methods and the efficiency of production will not be altered and that volume is the only factor affecting costs. It is because these assumptions are difficult to maintain in a 'real life' situation that break-even analysis cannot pretend to be anything but a rough guide. Its real value to management lies in the fact that it highlights the inter-relationships between the factors affecting profits, allowing management to make certain assumptions about these factors and seeing the likely effects of changes in these assumptions. Hence, break-even analysis is useful as a management decision model.

Calculating the break-even point

There are three methods commonly employed in solving break-even problems:

(i) the equation method
(ii) the contribution margin method
(iii) the graph method.

The equation method

The relationship between sales, variable and fixed costs and profits may be expressed as an equation:

Sales = Variable costs + Fixed costs + Net profit

Example

Take the values given in the previous example, that is, that the unit sale price is £10, variable costs are £4 per unit and fixed costs £150,000 per year.
Problem 1: How many units must be produced to break-even?
Analysis: Let x be the number of units required. Our equation will be:

$$£10x = £4x + £150,000 + £0$$
$$\text{and } £10x - £4x = £150,000 + £0$$

$$\text{so that} \quad x = \frac{£150,000}{6}$$

$$= \underline{\underline{25,000 \text{ } units}}$$

Problem 2: Alternatively, the problem may be calculating the sales revenue required to break-even.
Analysis: Since net profit is zero, our formula remains:

Sales = Variable costs + Fixed costs

Let the unknown level of sales revenue be x, and knowing that variable costs are $\frac{4}{10}$th of x, we can substitute:

$$x = \tfrac{4}{10}x + £150,000$$
$$\text{and } x - \tfrac{4}{10}x = £150,000$$
$$\tfrac{6}{10}x = £150,000$$
$$x = \underline{\underline{£250,000}}$$

The break-even sales revenue can be equally derived from the break-even volume of sales (25,000 units at £10 = £250,000), but the calculations are intended to show that the results can be calculated independently.

The contribution margin method

This method makes use of the variable profit or contribution margin per unit of output which is required to cover fixed costs.

Problem 1: On the basis that the unit sale price is £10, that the variable costs are £4 per unit and that fixed costs total £150,000 a year, calculate the break-even volume of sales.

Analysis: Let x be the number of units required. We know that the unit contribution margin is the difference between unit sale price and unit variable costs. Our formula is:

$$x = \frac{\text{Fixed costs} + \text{Net profit}}{\text{Unit contribution margin}}$$

$$x = \frac{£150,000 + 0}{(£10 - £4)}$$

$$= \frac{150,000}{6}$$

$$= 25,000 \text{ units}$$

Problem 2: Using the same values calculate the break-even sales revenue.

Analysis: In this case, we make use of the contribution margin ratio to calculate the sales revenue required to cover fixed costs. The contribution margin ratio is:

$$\frac{\text{Unit contribution margin}}{\text{Revenue per unit}} \%$$

Our formula may be expressed as follows:

$$x = \frac{\text{Fixed costs} + \text{Net profit}}{\text{Contribution margin ratio}}$$

Substituting the given values we have:

$$x = \frac{150,000 + 0}{60\%}$$

$$= £250,000$$

Alternatively, the break-even revenue may be found from the following formula:

$$x = \frac{\text{Fixed costs} + \text{Net profit}}{1 - \dfrac{\text{Total variable costs}}{\text{Total sales revenue}}}$$

$$= 1 - \frac{150,000}{\dfrac{160,000}{400,000}}$$

$$= £250,000$$

It is clear that both the equation method and the contribution margin method can be applied to profit planning by the substitution of the net profit figure, which for the purpose of our analysis of the break-even point we have taken to be zero.

The graph method

This method involves using what is usually called a break-even chart. This description is not very satisfactory because it gives undue emphasis to the break-even point whereas other points on the graph are just as important.

A break-even chart is easy to compile, but the accuracy of the readings will depend on the accuracy with which the data is plotted. The output or sales in units may be drawn on the horizontal axis, and the vertical axis is used to depict money values.

Method: Using the values given for the previous examples, the stages in compiling the break-even chart are as follows:

  (i) Using suitable graph paper, draw a horizontal axis to measure total output in units (50,000 units). Draw a vertical axis representing this output at its selling price of £10 per unit (£500,000).
 (ii) Draw the variable cost curve as a straight line from zero to £200,000 at 50,000 units of output (50,000 @ £4).
(iii) Draw the fixed cost curve parallel to the variable cost curve but £150,000

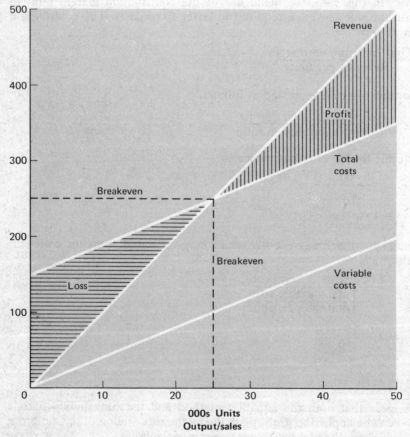

Fig. 5.17 Break-even chart.

higher, so that total costs including variable costs will be represented by the area below this curve.

(iv) Insert the total revenue curve from zero to £500,000 at 50,000 units.

Figure 5.17 vividly depicts the relationship between costs, revenues, volume of output and resultant profit. The area between the revenue curve and the variable cost curve represents the contribution to fixed costs and profit at each level of output. The point at which the revenue curve crosses the total cost curve is the break-even point. As output expands from zero, fixed costs are gradually recovered until the break-even point, and thereafter each unit of output contributes to profit.

The excess by which actual sales exceed break-even sales amounts to £250,000, so that sales could be reduced by £250,000 before losses start to be incurred. This excess is known as the margin of safety. The margin of safety ratio is the percentage by which sales revenue may fall before a loss is incurred and is expressed as follows:

$$\text{Margin of safety ratio} = \frac{\text{Margin of safety revenue}}{\text{Actual sales}}$$

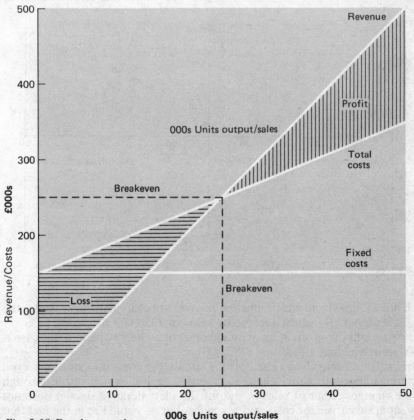

Fig. 5.18 Break-even chart.

Hence, in the example given, the margin of safety ratio is

$$\frac{£250,000}{£500,000} \text{ i.e. } 50\%$$

Clearly, the higher the margin of safety ratio, the safer the firm's position.

An alternative way of constructing the break-even chart is as in Fig. 5.18. The disadvantage of this form of presentation is that unlike Fig. 5.17, it does not emphasize the importance of the contribution margin to fixed costs.

The profit-volume chart

The profit-volume chart is a special type of break-even chart. It is concerned with analysing profit and loss at different levels of activity. As in the break-even chart, the horizontal axis is used to measure the volume of output or sales in units, but the vertical axis is employed to measure the profit or loss at any given level of output or sales.

Using the same information as above, Fig. 5.19 shows the profit-volume chart. Only three items are needed to plot this chart—the fixed costs DC,

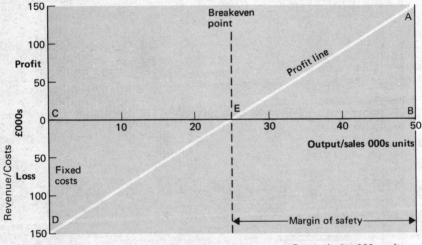

Fig. 5.19 Profit-volume chart.

which are £150,000 and which must be recovered before a profit is made, the break-even point E, which represents sales of £250,000 necessary to cover fixed costs, and the profit at an assumed level of activity (which in this case is 50,000 units yielding a profit of £150,000).

The profit-volume chart (Fig. 5.19) is simply the conventional break-even chart re-arranged to show changes in profit or loss which occur through volume changes either of sales or output. It is less detailed since it does not show separate curves for costs and revenues, but its virtue lies in the fact that it reduces any changes down to two key elements—volume and profit. For this reason, the volume-profit chart is useful for illustrating the results of different management decisions.

Insofar as the volume-profit chart focuses simply on the relationship between volume and profit, it allows for an extended analysis of this relationship. Thus, the slope of the curve DA indicates the contribution margin ratio, which may be measured by AB/BE or DC/CE—either calculation giving the same results in this case (60 per cent).

The slope of the curve DA also indicates the rate at which changes in volume assist in the recovery of fixed costs and affect profit: the greater the slope the greater will be the effect of changes in volume on profits. Equally, the steeper the slope of the profit curve the quicker will the margin of safety be eroded and the break-even point reached as the volume of output or sales falls, as may be seen from the three cases in Fig. 5.20.

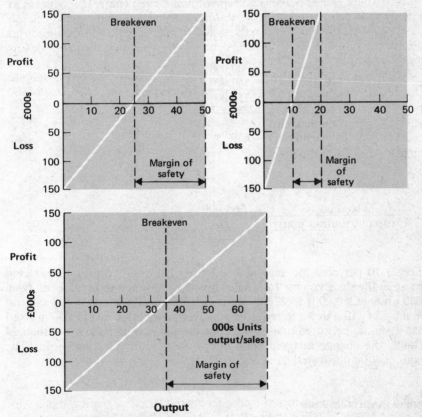

Fig. 5.20 Profit-volume charts.

Profit planning through change

Profit planning is related to a consideration of four factors—fixed costs, variable costs, selling price and sales volume. Any change in one or several of these factors will affect planning profit. Cost-volume-profit analysis enables management to consider the effects of these changes.

Changes in fixed costs

Assuming that all other factors remain unchanged, a change in fixed costs will affect only the break-even point.

Example

The consequential effect of an increase of £15,000 in head office costs on the break-even level is as follows:

	Original	After increase in fixed costs
	£	£
Sales	500,000	500,000
Variable costs	200,000	200,000
Contribution margin	300,000	300,000
Fixed costs	150,000	165,000
Net profit	150,000	135,000
Contribution margin ratio	60%	60%

The new break-even point is:

$$\frac{\text{Fixed costs}}{\text{Unit contribution margin}} = \frac{165,000}{£6} = 27,500 \text{ units}$$

Hence, a 10 per cent increase in fixed costs has resulted in a 10 per cent increase in the sales volume (and sales revenue) required to break-even from 25,000 units (£250,000) to 27,500 units (£275,000). Thus, additional sales of 2500 units at £10 a unit are required to cover an increase of £15,000 in fixed costs. It should be noted that as the contribution margin ratio has remained constant, the change in fixed costs is the only factor affecting profit. The change may be illustrated as in Fig. 5.21.

Changes in variable costs

A change in variable costs will have the immediate effect of changing the contribution margin ratio, and consequently the break-even point.

Example

It is decided to improve the quality of a product by incorporating more expensive materials. As a result, variable costs are increased by 10 per cent, and the consequential effects on the break-even level are as follows:

	Original	After increase in variable costs
	£	£
Sales	500,000	500,000
Variable costs	200,000	220,000
Contribution margin	300,000	280,000
Fixed costs	150,000	150,000
Net profit	150,000	130,000
Contribution margin ratio	60%	56%

The new break-even point will be:

$$\frac{\text{Fixed costs}}{\text{Contribution margin per unit}} = \frac{£150,000}{5.6} = 26,786 \text{ units.}$$

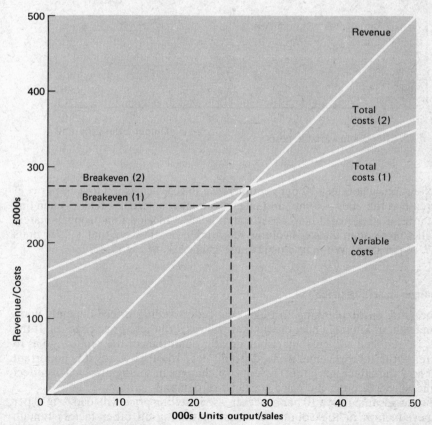

Fig. 5.21 Changes in fixed costs.

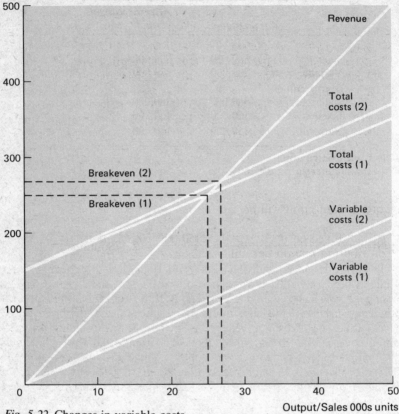

Fig. 5.22 Changes in variable costs.

Note that whereas a 10 per cent increase in fixed costs led to a 10 per cent increase in the sales volume (and sales revenue) required to break-even in this instance, a 10 per cent increase in variable costs has led to a proportionately smaller increase in the sales volume required to break-even, that is, 1786 units or 7.14 per cent. We may illustrate the change as in Fig. 5.22.

Changes in selling price

Successful profit planning through changes in selling prices depends upon management knowing how the market will react to these price changes. If the price is reduced will customers buy greater quantities of the product so as to increase the total revenue derived from sales? In other words it is important to know the effect upon total revenue of changes in selling prices. This effect is measured through the price elasticity of demand.

Let us assume that a 10 per cent increase in selling price will lead to a 10 per cent reduction in the volume of sales. Assuming all other factors remain constant, the result of the price change will be as follows:

	Original	After increase in selling price
Sales in units	50,000	45,000
Sales revenue	£500,000	£495,000 (45,000 @ £11)
Variable costs	200,000	180,000 (45,000 @ £4)
Contribution margin	300,000	315,000
Fixed costs	150,000	150,000
Net profit	150,000	165,000
Contribution margin ratio	60%	63.6%

The break-even point will, as a result, be lowered from 25,000 units to 21,429 units as follows:

$$\frac{\text{Fixed costs}}{\text{Contribution margin per unit}} = \frac{£150,000}{£7} = 21,429 \text{ units}$$

Thus, a 10 per cent increase in the selling price has led to a much greater adjustment in the sales volume required to break-even, that is, 3571/25,000 or 14.3 per cent. We have assumed, however, that the elasticity of demand for the product was unity, that is, that a percentage alteration in the price would lead to the same proportionate alteration in the volume of sales. In most situations this would be an unreal assumption to make, so that it becomes crucial to management to know the slope of the demand curve for the commodity, that is, the elasticity of demand if their analysis of the impact of a price change on the net profit is to be valid. We may compare the three different results that would be obtained by the same price change under three different demand conditions for the commodity as follows:

(1) Where demand is *elastic*, i.e., elasticity is greater than unity. In this case we assume that a 10 per cent increase in selling price will lead to a 20 per cent reduction in sales.
(2) Where the elasticy of demand is unity. In this case we assume, as in the example above that a 10 per cent increase in selling price will lead to a 10 per cent reduction in sales.
(3) Where demand is inelastic. We assume a 10 per cent increase in selling price will lead to a 5 per cent reduction in sales.

This example illustrates the importance to management of knowing the nature of the demand for their products. In the example, where demand is

	Elastic	Unity	Inelastic
Sales units	40,000	45,000	47,500
Sales revenue (£11)	£440,000	£495,000	£522,500
Variable costs (£4)	160,000	180,000	190,000
Contribution margin	280,000	315,000	332,500
Fixed costs	150,000	150,000	150,000
Net profit	£130,000	£165,000	£182,500

elastic, we witness a sharp fall in net profit from the original £150,000 to £130,000. On the other hand, a unitary or inelastic demand schedule results in an increase in net profit.

The sales mix

We mentioned at the beginning of this chapter that c-v-p was important to short-term profit planning, and that it was helpful also to the solution of other types of managerial problems. One such problem is that of selecting the best sales mix. So far in our discussion, we have assumed that the firm had only one product so that profit planning involved a consideration of only four factors, that is, fixed and variable costs, selling price and sales volume. Most firms, however, either produce or sell more than one product and management has to decide in what combination these products ought to be made or sold. It may be possible, for example, that by altering the existing sales mix by selling proportionately more of the product which has the highest contribution margin, the overall contribution margin and the break-even point may be improved.

Example

Assume that Maximix Ltd has data concerning the three products which it markets as follows:

Product	A	B	C	Total
	£	£	£	£
Sales	100,000	100,000	50,000	250,000
Variable costs	50,000	30,000	20,000	100,000
Contribution margin	50,000	70,000	30,000	150,000
Fixed costs				150,000
Net profit				Nil
Contribution margin ratio	50%	70%	60%	60%

If the firm could switch its sales so as to sell more of product B, which has a higher contribution margin ratio than the other two, it will succeed in improving its profitability. At the present moment, the firm is just breaking even. Let us assume that it maintains the present total sales of £250,000, but that the sales mix is altered as shown below:

Product	A	B	C	Total
	£	£	£	£
Sales	50,000	175,000	25,000	250,000
Variable costs	25,000	52,500	10,000	87,500
Contribution margin	25,000	122,500	15,000	162,500
Fixed costs				150,000
Net profit				12,500
Contribution margin ratio	50%	70%	60%	65%

Hence the new product mix has raised the contribution margin ratio by 5 per cent leading to a profit of £12,500 and a lowering of the break-even point from £250,000 to £230,769 as follows:

$$\frac{\text{Fixed costs}}{\text{Contribution margin ratio}} = \frac{£150,000}{65\%} = £230,769$$

The effect of the change in the product mix may be depicted graphically as in Fig. 5.23.

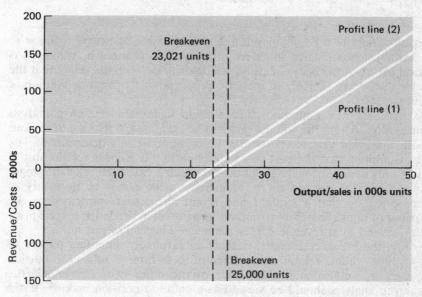

Fig. 5.23 Change in sales mix.

Cost-volume-profit analysis: some limitations

C-v-p analysis, though it is a very useful tool for decision making, is based upon certain assumptions which can rarely be completely realized in practice. Hence the fragility of these assumptions places limits on the reliability of c-v-p analysis as a tool in decision making. For example, it is assumed that fixed costs are constant, and that both the variable cost and the revenue curves are linear over the relevant volume of output. It is also assumed that volume is the only factor affecting costs, and that both the price of cost factors and of the product produced or sold remains unaffected by changes in the volume of output.

All these assumptions may be challenged. Fixed costs may not remain constant over the entire output range considered in the analysis, that being particularly true if the volume range considered is fairly extensive. Fixed costs may indeed be constant over a band of output, but then will rise sharply and remain constant for another stage, as indicated in Fig. 5.24.

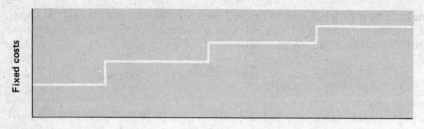

Fig. 5.24.   Volume

Equally doubtful is the assumption that the variable cost curve is linear so that variable costs change in direct proportion to changes in volume. As demand for input factors increase so will their price, with the effect that the variable cost curve is likely to increase proportionately faster as volume of output expands.

To overcome these limitations, and to retain the usefulness of c-v-p analysis it is necessary to limit the volume range to be examined so that the behaviour of both fixed and variable costs may be more accurately determined. The basic assumption that the cost-volume relationship is a linear relationship is realistic only over narrow ranges of output which is called the relevant range.

As regards the revenue curve, to increase sales it may be necessary to reduce price, so that a straight line is not an accurate portrayal of the behaviour of sales. Therefore, computations are often needed at several price levels—several total revenue curves are needed instead of just one.

Finally, the break-even chart presents an extremely simplified picture of cost-revenue-volume relationships. Each of these three is subject to outside influences as well as to the influence of the other two. Above all, the break-even analysis should be viewed as a guide to decision making, not a substitute for judgement and common sense.

Despite its limitations, the real usefulness of c-v-p is that it enriches the understanding of the relationship between costs, volume and prices as factors affecting profit, enabling management to make assumptions which will assist the decision-making process in the short-run planning period.

Summary

In the short run, the firm's output is fixed, so that its freedom of action is limited in this respect. Given this condition, short-range planning considers the most desirable action to take to achieve a planned profit. Cost-volume-profit analysis (c-v-p) has an important role to play in short-run planning by providing an insight into the relationships between costs, volume of output, revenue and profit. In particular, c-v-p analysis highlights the significance of the distinction between fixed and variable costs and the behaviour of these two types of costs through changes in the volume of output.

C-v-p analysis makes an important contribution to short-run profit planning by providing an understanding of the conditions required to break-even. It does not assist in the discovery of the conditions required to maximize profits, in sharp contrast to economic theory which pays particular attention to this aspect of profit planning. Its advantage to management is that it is a method which is operationally useful. Moreover, it deals with the most important consideration—the avoidance of losses. In this sense, c-v-p analysis reflects the assumption of risk analysis that decision makers are risk-averse.

C-v-p analysis has limitations as a result of the assumptions that it incorporates. Many of these assumptions may be challenged, for example, the linearity of the behaviour of costs and revenues over a range of output. Although some of the criticism of c-v-p analysis may be partially refuted, its real usefulness lies in the manner in which it enriches the understanding of the relationship between cost, volume of output and revenue for profit planning purposes in the short run, thereby assisting management in the making of short-run profit planning decisions.

Questions

1. 'Nobody operates to break-even, so why bother with break-even charts?' Discuss.
2. The Carbon Ink Company's income statement for the preceding year is presented below. Except as noted, the cost and sales relationship for the coming year is expected to follow the same pattern as in the preceding year.

	£
Sales (2,000,000 bottles at £0.25)	500,000
Variable costs	300,000
Fixed costs	100,000
Total costs	400,000
Profit	100,000

Required:

(a) What is the break-even point in sales value and units?
(b) An extension to the factory will add £50,000 to the fixed costs and increase production capacity by 60 per cent. How many bottles would have to be sold after the extension to break-even?
(c) The management of the company feels that it should earn at least £10,000 on the new investment. What sales volume is required to enable the company to maintain existing profits and earn the minimum required on the new investment?
(d) If the factory operates at full capacity after extension, what profit will be earned?
(e) What are the weaknesses in the use of break-even analysis?
3. An accountant and an economist were having an argument. The economist accused the accountant of using a naive over-simplified model of cost-volume-profit relationships by assuming linear patterns in variable costs. Since costs do not behave in this simplistic way the accountant, argued the economist, should be more realistic in his assumptions.

The accountant countered by saying that the economist was just as bad, if not worse, because most economic models ignore variations in fixed costs. Although the accountant agreed that in the long run all costs are variable, a firm had to make decisions in the short run in order to survive. And, argued the accountant, in the short run some costs are definitely fixed.

The economist was becoming somewhat agitated and accused the accountant of not using a dynamic analysis for solving business problems. The economist claimed, for example, that the static nature of cost-volume-profit analysis often produced misleading information. The accountant thought this a case of the pot calling the kettle black, and accused the economist of using unrealistic models which never exist in practice.

Required:
Both men turn to you for support; what would be your reply? Use the case below to illustrate your answer.

The Malplaquet Company cans fresh orange juice. The company's budget at 80 per cent capacity for 19X8 was as follows:

	£
Sales	250,000
Cost of oranges and other materials used	60,000
Cost of cans	30,000
Direct labour	60,000
Manufacturing expenses:	
Fixed	20,000
Variable	30,000
Administration, selling and other indirect expenses:	
Fixed	10,800
Variable	8000

The directors of the company anticipate the following variations in costs during 19X9:

Price of oranges and other materials used	5% increase
Price of cans	No change
Rates for direct labour	10% increase
Manufacturing expenses: fixed	£800 decrease
Administration, selling and other indirect expenses:	
Fixed	No change

Manufacturing variable expenses will maintain the same ratio to wages paid, and administration, selling and other indirect variable expenses will vary only with quantity sold.

In 19X9 sales quantity and selling price are expected to remain constant.

33 Variable costing

The cost-volume-profit relationships considered in the preceding chapter emphasize the usefulness of variable cost data for profit planning purposes. It indicates the significance of a knowledge of cost behaviour for management decision making. Nevertheless, there is considerable controversy about the use of the variable costing system for product costing and income determination purposes. In effect, the use of product costs based on variable cost only, has significant effects on the valuation of inventories, and implicitly on the measurement of periodic income. The purpose of this chapter is to examine the implication of variable costing as compared to the conventional method of product costing based on full or absorption costing.

The case for variable costing for inventory valuation

As we saw in Part 2, periodic income measurement and the matching principle constitute the core of financial accounting. According to SSAP 2 'Disclosure of Accounting Policies', 'revenues and costs are matched with one another so far as their relationship can be established or justifiably assumed.'

Different methods of matching

The logic behind the matching principle springs from a desire to provide a rule which will secure uniformity in the preparation of income statements. Investors require uniformity in accounting practices if they are to be able to evaluate the performance of one firm against another. As far as the matching principle is concerned the problem is to develop suitable methods for matching costs to revenues. Two such methods have been developed: product costing and period costing.

(a) Product costing
Accountants long ago recognized the product itself as a convenient vehicle for matching costs with revenues. Product costing involves attaching all costs, whether direct or overhead costs, to the product. In measuring the cost of goods produced and sold to be matched against revenues from sales, product costing requires the inclusion of those manufacturing costs which are incurred irrespective of production. Thus, costs such as rent, insurance and rates which are incurred on a time basis rather than on the rate of production are recovered against the units produced.

The proponents of product costing as the only method of matching costs to revenues argue that all manufacturing costs are product costs, and that there is no such thing as a period cost because 'ideally all costs incurred should be viewed as absolutely clinging to definite items of goods sold or services rendered . . . The ideal is to match costs incurred with the efforts attributable to or significantly related to such costs' (Paton and Littleton, 1940). They argue, therefore, that manufacturing costs are incurred solely to make possible the creation of a product.

(b) *Period costing*
Period costing recognizes that certain costs are incurred on a time basis, and that the benefit derived from these costs is not affected by the actual level of production during a period of time. Since rent, insurance and salaries are items which are incurred on a time basis, their deteriorating effect on a firm's cash resources are not halted by the lack of revenue.

Period costing is a method of costing which conflicts with the traditional view of costing expressed by product costing, and has given rise to the variable or marginal costing controversy. The issue between the two schools of thought revolves round the question of whether fixed manufacturing costs, that is those costs incurred irrespective of production, should be charged as the costs of the product or charged against the income of the period. According to the supporters of product costing, who employ absorption or full costing, all manufacturing costs should be absorbed by the product. Variable costing assigns only the variable costs, that is the costs which vary with the level of production, to the products, and fixed manufacturing costs are written off each year as period costs.

One advantage of variable costing over absorption costing which is often advanced by its advocates is its superiority for management decision making. Because the distinction between fixed and variable costs is 'built into' the accounting system, it assists profit planning, product pricing and control. However, the controversy which surrounds variable costing is whether or not it should be used for external reporting. The advocates of absorption costing argue that figures prepared on a variable costing basis for the use of management should be adjusted to an absorption costing basis before they are released to external users.

Both management and investors are concerned primarily with the future outcome of present decisions. Accountants who advocate the use of absorption costing for external financial statements deprive investors of a useful, analytical device and make the task of interpreting the results more difficult.

Variable costing emphasizes the behaviour of fixed and variable costs, which is of utmost importance to investors. Variable costing helps to predict cash flows in relation to volume changes; the isolation of fixed costs in the income statement permits more accurate forecasts of claims on cash in meeting current outlays on fixed expenses. Variable costing also helps to correlate fluctuations in cash flows with fluctuations in sales volume.

We argued earlier that management should not receive the credit for increasing the net worth of business before the critical event has occurred, and we conceded that in almost every case, the sale was the critical event. Since income should vary with a company's performance (which really means accomplishing the critical event) where income is related to sales, it is logical that there should be a direct relationship between the two. Variable costing should therefore be used in these cases. Absorption costing, being based on the product concept, does not provide this relationship between income and sales, because under this method, income variation is partly related to production.

Variable costing also permits more accurate income forecasts because net income will have a direct relationship with sales, instead of confusing the picture with the impact of the two activities of producing and selling (Underdown, 1971).

The treatment of overheads

The Institute of Chartered Accountants in England and Wales considered this problem in its Recommendation on Accounting Principle N.22. The Institute did not recommend one method as preferable to another, leaving the choice of the most suitable method to management, but advised that once a method has been selected it should be adhered to (ICAEW, 1970).

The matter was subsequently considered by the Accounting Standards Steering Committee in 1972, whose mandate was to consider the problem of ways of reducing the diversity of practices. SSAP 9 'Stocks and Work in Progress' restated the traditional accounting view that the aim should be to match costs and revenues 'in the year in which revenue arises rather than the year in which cost is incurred', cost being defined for this purpose as including 'all related overheads, even though some of these may accrue on a time basis'.

Absorption and variable costing compared

Let us assume the following basic data:

Total sales and production over 4 years (500 units per year)	2000 units
Direct material costs per unit	£1
Direct labour costs per unit	£1
Variable overhead costs per unit	£0.5
Fixed overhead costs	£1000 p.a.
Sales price per unit	£6

Let us further assume that the volume of sales and of production are constant in time.

The volume of production, sales and the level of stocks in units is as follows:

Year	1	2	3	4	Total
Opening inventory (units)	40	40	40	40	40
Production (units)	500	500	500	500	2000
Sales (units)	500	500	500	500	2000
Closing inventory (units)	40	40	40	40	40

The results under the two forms of costing would appear as follows:

Year	1	2	3	4	Total
Variable costing	£	£	£	£	£
Sales	3000	3000	3000	3000	12,000
Costs of goods produced	1250	1250	1250	1250	5000
Add: opening inventory	100	100	100	100	100
Available for sale	1350	1350	1350	1350	5100
Less: closing inventory	100	100	100	100	100
Cost of goods sold	1250	1250	1250	1250	5000
Contribution margin	1750	1750	1750	1750	7000
Fixed overheads	1000	1000	1000	1000	4000
Net income	750	750	750	750	3000
Absorption costing					
Sales	3000	3000	3000	3000	12,000
Cost of goods produced	2250	2250	2250	2250	9000
Add: opening inventory	180	180	180	180	180
Available for sale	2430	2430	2430	2430	9180
Less: closing inventory	180	180	180	180	180
Cost of goods sold	2250	2250	2250	2250	9000
Net income	750	750	750	750	3000

The above example illustrates the effects on income of using absorption and variable costing methods for a firm in which everything stayed exactly the same in four consecutive years. Therefore, sales and levels of production are constant in each period and both opening and closing inventory remain unchanged. Under these conditions income figures for each year remain the same under both methods of calculating income.

In reality, the effect on production of shortages of materials, or the effect on sales of credit squeezes and changes in indirect taxation distorts the relationship between sales and production and inventory levels act as buffers. Inventory levels, therefore, are not stable; they are in fact very volatile. Moreover, modern methods of production require a constant rate of production not only to maintain the efficiency of operations but also to prevent lay-offs and so assist in the preservation of good industrial relations. Flexible inventory level standards are normally established for the purpose of planning for a reasonably uniform level of production.

We shall now examine the different results obtained under variable and absorption costing under the following circumstances:

(i) where sales fluctuate but production remains constant
(ii) where sales are constant but production fluctuates.

Results where sales fluctuate but production is constant

As soon as the rate of sales begins to differ from the rate of production the use of different methods of allocating overheads to costs of production start to affect profit calculations. Let us take the figures given in the earlier example, but keeping the level of production constant against varying levels of sales as follows:

Year	1	2	3	4	Total
Opening inventory (units)	40	140	340	240	40
Production (units)	500	500	500	500	2000
Sales (units)	400	300	600	700	2000
Closing inventory (units)	140	340	240	40	40

The results under the two methods of costing would appear as follows:

Year	1	2	3	4	Total
Variable costing	£	£	£	£	£
Sales	2400	1800	3600	4200	12,000
Cost of goods produced	1250	1250	1250	1250	5000
Add: opening inventory	100	350	850	600	100
Available for sale	1350	1600	2100	1850	5100
Less: closing inventory	350	850	600	100	100
Cost of goods sold	1000	750	1500	1750	5000
Contribution margin	1400	1050	2100	2450	7000
Fixed overheads	1000	1000	1000	1000	4000
Net income	400	50	1100	1450	3000
Absorption costing					
Sales	2400	1800	3600	4200	12,000
Costs of goods produced	2250	2250	2250	2250	9000
Add: opening inventory	180	630	1530	1080	180
Available for sale	2430	2880	3780	3330	9180
Less: closing inventory	630	1530	1080	180	180
Cost of goods sold	1800	1350	2700	3150	9000
Net income	600	450	900	1050	3000

It becomes evident why there is a controversy between the two schools of thought as regards the measurement of profit for the purpose of financial reporting for under the circumstances outlined above wide differences appear in net income figures. These differences may be illustrated graphically (Fig. 5.25, p. 531), and it may be seen that the income profile fluctuates more widely when overheads are excluded, as they are under variable costing, than when they are included as under absorption costing.

Results where sales are constant but production fluctuates

Let us now keep the figures for sales constant, and compare results under the two methods of costing when levels of production vary.

Year	1	2	3	4	Total
Opening inventory (units)	40	140	340	240	40
Production (units)	600	700	400	300	2000
Sales (units)	500	500	500	500	2000
Closing inventory (units)	140	340	240	40	40

The results under the two methods would be calculated as follows:

Year	1	2	3	4	Total
Variable costing	£	£	£	£	£
Sales	3000	3000	3000	3000	12,000
Cost of goods produced	1500	1750	1000	750	5000
Add: opening inventory	100	350	850	600	100
Available for sales	1600	2100	1850	1350	5100
Less: closing inventory	350	850	600	100	100
Cost of goods sold	1250	1250	1250	1250	5000
Contribution margin	1750	1750	1750	1750	7000
Fixed overheads	1000	1000	1000	1000	4000
Net income	750	750	750	750	3000
Absorption costing					
Sales	3000	3000	3000	3000	12,000
Costs of goods produced	2700	3150	1800	1350	9000
Add: opening inventory	180	630	1530	1080	180
Available for sale	2880	3780	3330	2430	9180
Less: closing inventory	630	1530	1080	180	180
Cost of goods sold	2250	2250	2250	2250	9000
Over or (under) absorbed overhead	200	400	(200)	(400)	—
Total cost of goods sold	2050	1850	2450	2650	9000
Net income	950	1150	550	350	3000

In order to simplify the calculations under the absorption costing method we have assumed a normal level of production of 500 units a year. Since total fixed cost is £1000 per year, a recovery rate of £2 per unit is used. We have assumed also, that selling prices and costs remain unchanged over the four years. By using a normal overhead rate for recovering fixed overhead the value of opening and closing inventory per unit remains constant at £4.5 (£2.5 variable + £2.0 fixed). In the first two years the normal output level is exceeded by 100 and 200 units respectively, with shortfalls in the last two years. The cost of goods sold is adjusted by the over or under recovery of fixed overhead resulting from those differences in deriving income under absorption costing.

In this example, where sales have remained constant but production has fluctuated, we note that income results obtained under variable costing remain constant, but those based on absorption costing show wide fluctuation—£1150 in year 2 and £350 in year 4.

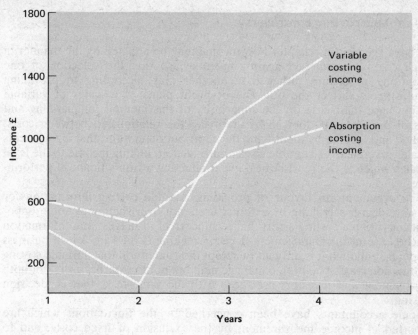

Fig. 5.25.

Variable and absorption costing: their impact on income summarized

The various examples which we have considered enable the following generalizations to be made on the impact on income of these two different methods of costing:

(i) where sales and production levels are constant through time income is the same under the two methods;

(ii) where production remains constant but sales fluctuate, income rises or falls with the level of sales, assuming that costs and prices remain constant, but the fluctuations in net income figures are greater with variable costing than with absorption costing;

(iii) where sales are constant but production fluctuates, variable costing provides for constant income, whereas under absorption costing, income fluctuates;

(iv) where production exceeds sales, income is higher under absorption costing than under variable costing for the absorption of fixed overheads into closing inventory increases their value thereby reducing the cost of goods sold;

(v) where sales exceed production, income is higher under variable costing. The fixed costs which previously were part of inventory values are now charged against revenue under absorption costing. Therefore, under absorption costing the value of fixed costs charged against revenue is greater than that incurred for the period.

The variable costing controversy

We have seen in this chapter how income may be affected by the manner in which costs are matched against revenues, so that the selection of one accounting procedure rather than another may, according to prevailing circumstances, affect the outcome of profit plans. Advocates of variable costing base their case on the superiority of this method for planning and control purposes. It does so by clarifying the relationship between costs, volume and income by identifying the contribution margin, that is the excess of sales revenue over variable costs of production, linking income to the level of sales which is the most critical event affecting a firm's financial performance.

The arguments in favour of providing variable costing information for assisting decision making by external users are overwhelming. Some opponents of variable costing assert that it is incorrect to suggest that information which is useful for management decision making is relevant for all business purposes, although it is difficult to accept the contention that variable costing information may be helpful to management but not to external users, for both management and investors are faced with the same task, that is, decision making.

Some accountants have been concerned by the fluctuations which are imported in income measurement by the exclusion of fixed costs, and to secure a certain stability in income, advocate the retention of the absorption costing method of valuing inventory. A further controversy arises from the effects of variable costing on the balance sheet of omitting fixed factory overheads from inventory values. The real argument on this issue is whether the balance sheet should show inventory at actual cost or at a value to the current period of the resources transferred from the period just ended. Variable costing is said to have an 'income statement emphasis', whereas absorption costing is said to have a 'balance sheet emphasis'.

The need for a definition of assets

The variable costing controversy stresses the need in accounting theory for a comprehensive definition of assets. Assets are not usually defined, and where they are, the definition is restricted to a vague description. Instead, considerable time is spent on discussing the classification of assets, and how one type of asset may be distinguished from another. Classifications which do not specify the tests to be applied in identifying assets are inadequate for an understanding of their basic nature.

Recently, there have been attempts to define assets as 'rights to service potentials' or 'rights to future benefits'. There remains the problem of interpreting these definitions, and some have taken the 'service potential' of an asset to mean its capacity to contribute to revenue-earning in the future. If one distinguishes unexpired and expired costs, according to whether or not they will contribute to revenue in the future, such a definition of assets would imply adherence to an absorption costing method of valuing assets.

A more recent interpretation of 'service potential' is one which considers assets as having a service potential to the extent that they avert the need to incur future costs. This 'cost obviation' interpretation has led some to believe that the variable costing method of valuing inventories is superior to the absorption costing method for the purposes of measuring inventories in terms of future benefits. The most detailed discussions of the cost obviation concept approach the problem of inventory valuation from the standpoint of relevant costs. Relevant costs are those which differ when two or more courses of action are contemplated, and they are those costs which will be avoided by not undertaking a given alternative. Irrelevant costs are those which have no influence on a decision because they remain the same under all the alternatives considered. The concept of relevant costs is not a new one. This text considers the concept fully in Chapter 35. This concept should be applied to asset valuation because the main purpose in providing accounting measurements is to influence decision making. Therefore, inventories should consist only of costs that will influence future results.

Summary

Accountants are more likely to agree on the nature of measurement if they agree on the purpose of accounting. If the central purpose of accounting is to make possible the periodic matching of costs and revenues, and if the matching principle is the 'nucleus of accounting theory', then clearly the absorption costers are correct in their view. But if, as we argue in this book, the prime objective of accounting is to provide information which is useful for decision making, then the case for variable costing seems to be very strong.

References

1. I.C.A.E.W. *Recommendations on Accounting Principles*, No. 22, 1970 edition, pp. 96–7.
2. Paton, W. A. & Littleton, A. C. *An Introduction to Corporate Accounting Standards*, Monograph 3, A.A.A., 1940.
3. Underdown, B. 'Logical principles needed for stock evaluation', *Management Accounting*, July, 1971.
4. SSAP 2.
5. SSAP 3.

Questions

1. Computer Limited was formed three years ago to produce a single product, the 'Mini'. The directors are receiving the financial results of the first three years presented by the company accountant, and are concerned with the decline in profits in the year 19X3 despite a substantial increase in sales.

Summarized results are shown below

	19X1	19X2	19X3
Production: Budget (units)	1000	1000	1000
Actual (units)	900	1100	800
Sales (units)	800	800	1000
Selling price per unit	£80	£80	£80
Variable production			
cost per unit	£10	£10	£10
Fixed production overheads	£40,000	£40,000	£40,000
Fixed selling and adminstrative			
overheads	£20,000	£20,000	£20,000
Net profit	Nil	£8000	£2000

Fixed overheads are absorbed on the basis of budgeted annual production. Under- or over-absorbed are charged to cost of goods sold.

Required:
(a) Prepare a statement showing the profit figures derived by the company accountant.
(b) Prepare income statements using a variable costing approach.
(c) Reconcile the profits calculated in parts (a) and (b) above.
(d) Explain the rationale behind the approaches adopted in parts (a) and (b).

2. The Sherwood Co Ltd is a single product manufacturing company, which uses a variable costing system for internal management purposes. The year-end external reports are converted to absorption costs. Variances are charged to the cost of goods sold.

The following data refers to the years ended 31 December 19X5 and 19X6:

	19X5	19X6
	£	£
Sale price per unit	80	90
Standard variable costs per unit:		
Direct materials	21	23
Direct labour	19	22
Variable factory overheads	8	10
Variable selling and administrative		
expenses	2	3
Fixed factory overheads	170,000	180,000
	Units	Units
Opening inventory	1500	2000
Closing inventory	2000	1500
Sales	20,000	25,000

The normal volume used for the purpose of absorption costing is 28,000 units in both years.

Required:
1. Prepare income statements for the year ended 31 December 19X6 on a variable costing and on an absorption costing basis.

2. Discuss any differences which you may find between these two income statements.
3. State what advantages and disadvantages attach to the variable costing approach for internal management purposes.

34 Pricing

It is evident from the foregoing chapters that there are many factors which are critical to the success of the firm's long-term and short-term plans. For the purpose of discussion, we have been obliged to focus upon these factors independently of each other, so as to examine their salient features more closely. As a result, the reader may have been tempted to forget that the most important point about these factors is not their independence but their inter-dependence. Indeed, successful management control is the activity of harmonizing all the elements operating within the firm.

Managers and accountants attach a great deal of importance to cost control because costs are more susceptible to control than other factors such as sales volume and profits. As we saw in Chapter 32, cost-volume-profit analysis lies at the centre of short-term planning, but we did say that given the firm's cost structure, price changes could affect both the sales volume and the profit level. How successfully management may be able to improve profits through price changes depends on its knowledge of how the market will react to such changes. Hence, management needs to formulate a pricing policy or strategy which takes into account the likely effects of price changes on the market's demand for the firm's product, so as to plan a level of operation which, given the firm's cost structure, will produce the required profit.

There is also a further dimension to the problem of pricing which the reader will readily appreciate. If the firm formulates a pricing policy which affects its relationship with the market, such a policy has long-term as well as short-term implications. Any alteration in the volume of demand for the firm's products which results directly from its own pricing policy will affect its capital budgeting programme; hence, we may say that the firm's long-range plan should reflect its pricing policy. Thus, short-term changes in that policy should be effected solely for the purpose of providing that degree of flexibility which is essential to effective long-range planning and control.

The nature of the pricing problem

By and large, it may be said that the firm's long-term survival depends on its ability to obtain prices for its products which will cover all its costs, which for this purpose may be regarded as including a reasonable rate of return to investors. Therefore, it may appear that the pricing problem is relatively easy to solve, in that the accountant may calculate unit costs of production and add a percentage for profit.

The truth is that the pricing problem is much more complex than simply estimating total costs per unit. The firm's cost structure in the short term will determine whether a given price will produce a profit or a loss on each unit sold, but the total profit may equally well be affected by changes in consumer demand and the firm's environment. Indeed, competition and economic policies which affect the level of aggregate demand are frequently more significant to the pricing decision than the firm's total unit costs. Moreover, since there are different cost concepts and measures of costs which are relevant to different decision problems, there is a variety of circumstances which call for different pricing policies.

It should be remembered, however, that pricing is only one of the ways in which the firm can influence the demand for its product. If the firm wishes to expand sales, it may do so in a number of ways, for example, by advertising, expanding its sales force, improving its selling style, improving product presentation as well as by lowering the price. Indeed, altering its pricing policy may not necessarily be the best way of expanding sales and improving total profits. Conversely, a fall in demand for the product may be remedied by improvements in selling methods rather than increasing its price competitiveness. We may say, therefore, that in analysing the pricing problem, we are concentrating on only one of the factors which may influence the level of sales.

The nature of pricing theories

Two distinct influences are seen at play on the various pricing theories which we propose to discuss. Firstly, there is the influence of classical economic theory which has been concerned to lay down guidelines for finding the best or optimum price. This school of thought does not regard the problem of pricing in isolation from other economic problems. Indeed, the pricing theory advocated by classical economists is consistent with their ideas on the manner in which resources may best be allocated throughout the economy. We do not propose to dwell on this point as most of our readers will have a knowledge of economic theory. The second influence on pricing theories stems from business traditions of conservatism or sound management which look to costs as setting a minimum point for a price. Inevitably, this school of thought focuses on the discovery of the appropriate costs for pricing decisions.

In sharp contrast to the views of classical economists, businessmen and accountants have been less concerned with finding the best price than with establishing a price which covers an agreed measure of costs and provides a sufficient profit. Hence, to the latter, pricing is an integral part of the activity of long-range and budgetary planning.

Pricing theory in economics

Classical theorists hold that the firm should seek to discover the best or optimum price, which they argue is that price which will maximize the firm's profits. From their point of view, the price which maximizes profits implies the most efficient use of the economic resources held by the firm. Furthermore, such a pricing policy is necessary if capitalist enterprise is to reflect correctly the tenets of classical philosophy of capitalism, that is, that the objective of the firm is to maximize the returns accruing to the owner of its capital. The efficient allocation of resources through the economy is secured by the assumption that every owner of capital has the behaviour characteristics of that celebrated fiction, the *'homo economicus'*—which was invented specially to give validity to classical theory. Since such persons will seek to maximize the return on invested capital, scarce economic resources will be distributed between competing ends in a manner which will produce the greatest national wealth.

The complete confidence which rests in the validity of these assumptions by those who still share a commitment to classical theory under other guises, is reflected in the exuberance with which the method for establishing the optimum price is taught. The price which maximizes profits is found at that level of sales where the addition to total revenue resulting from the sale of the last unit (the marginal revenue) is equal to the addition to total costs resulting from the production of that last unit (marginal cost).

It is clear that economic theory imposes very exacting conditions on the analysis of the optimum price, and in particular makes demands for information which are extremely difficult to meet. Classical theorists argue, nevertheless, that this principle is a useful guide to profit maximization.

Example

Let us assume that a firm producing Widgets in large numbers has sufficient knowledge of the revenue and cost schedules at different volume levels associated with different selling prices. The accountant is able to produce the undermentioned data:

Selling price per unit	No. of units which may be sold	Total sales revenue	Total variable costs	Fixed costs	Profit (loss)
£		£	£	£	£
30	100,000	3,000,000	1,800,000	800,000	400,000
32	90,000	2,880,000	1,620,000	800,000	460,000
34	80,000	2,720,000	1,440,000	800,000	480,000
36	70,000	2,520,000	1,260,000	800,000	460,000
38	60,000	2,280,000	1,080,000	800,000	400,000
40	50,000	2,000,000	900,000	800,000	300,000

It is clear that the price of £34 a unit yields the maximum profit, and that this is the price which the firm should establish. At this price, marginal revenue equals marginal costs.

The limitations of the classical theorists' approach arises from the failure to appreciate the many practical problems with which managers are faced. In particular, it is extremely difficult to estimate the exact shape of the demand curve, that is, how much will be sold at any particular price.

There are futher reasons for doubting the assumptions of classical theory. It is not only myopic in ignoring the information problem completely, but it assumes that the volume of sales is solely a function of price. As we mentioned earlier, expenditure on sales promotion may well affect the demand curve without the need to adjust the price of the product.

There is little doubt that businessmen are not as a general rule profit-maximizers. Not only are there too many social pressures acting against excessive profit-seeking, but their behavioural instincts do not correspond with those of the '*homo economicus*'. Indeed, the businessman is a human being, whose decisions are influenced by moral, social, political as well as by financial considerations. As we saw in Chapter 28 the required profit as a planning goal is never a theoretical ideal such as the maximum long-term profit but represents what is thought to be a possible and desirable target for the time span considered.

Economic theory makes an important contribution to pricing theory, despite the criticisms which we have just mentioned, because it draws attention to the factors which are relevant to the pricing decision, in particular the importance of the interaction of revenue and cost information for deciding upon a 'good' price, and draws attention to those cost elements which are relevant to such a price. It has most certainly encouraged the idea of variable or marginal cost pricing, and the formulation of flexible pricing strategies.

Cost-based pricing theories

Businessmen have for long been aware that pricing a product is one of the most important and complicated problems which they have to face. In attempting to resolve this problem, and in trying to find some general guidelines by which to establish a sound pricing policy, they are in agreement that cost is one of the factors which must be taken into account. Consistently selling below full costs will lead to bankruptcy, whilst if the firm is to survive it must try to sell at prices which will not only cover costs but yield a sufficient profit. No hard and fast rules may be laid down since each firm's product and market situations have features which themselves may be unique.

The influence of costs on pricing decisions varies according to circumstances. Where firms are under contract to supply on a cost-plus basis, their costs are all important in deciding the contract price. In other situations, for example a liquidation sale, costs are irrelevant because the price at which the goods are sold are not related to their costs. Normally, the importance of the firm's costs lies somewhere between these two extremes.

The relevance of costs to pricing decisions is influenced also by the firm's drive to meet certain objectives, for example, earning a specified rate of return, increasing its share of the market or penetrating a new market. Moreover, the firm's relative marketing strength in a particular market may be a more dominant influence on pricing than its costs. Thus, a firm may be so strong as to be a price-maker, so that it is able to fix a price which other producers will have to follow. Conversely, a firm may be a price-taker, that is, its position in the market is so weak that it cannot influence the price.

In general, cost-based pricing theories are concerned with two elements of price. The first is the relevant costs which should be included in the price, and the second is the profit margin which must be added to reach the price. The profit margin will reflect a degree of caution about the likely reactions of customers or the nearness of a substitute if the firm is contemplating improving its profitability. Its relationship with near competitors may affect the firm's views on the size of its profit margin. Price cutting through the reduction of profit margins may lead to a price war, and profit margins may be safeguarded and increased by means of trading agreements. Some of these agreements in restraint of trade, which were really agreements in restraint of competition, are now illegal.

Cost-based pricing theories have a moral quality which economic theory does not evince. In the sense that cost-based pricing reflects the notion that a cost-plus formula is 'fair', it reflects that medieval notion of a 'just price' which was such an important part of the teaching of such men as St Thomas Aquinas, and which still dominates our own conception of fair trading. It is incorrect to suggest, as does economic theory, that business theories and the actions of businessmen may be divorced from the rules of morality by which their behaviour as individuals is affected. It is evident that businessmen are concerned with finding a 'fair' price, and that this 'fair price' is one, which on the one hand will cover their own costs, and on the other will contain that measure of reward which the buyer will regard as reasonable. In this sense, cost-based pricing theories do reflect the interaction of demand and supply, but unlike economic theory, do so in a way which reflects behavioural realities.

Full-cost pricing

This theory requires that all the costs both fixed and variable of bringing the product to the market be included in the selling price. Once the full costs have been established, it suffices to add the agreed profit margin.

Example

High Speeds Castings Ltd produces two castings, Type A and Type B. The total unit costs are as follows:

	Type A £	Type B £
Direct materials	4	12
Direct labour	6	4
Factory overheads: Variable	6	3
Fixed	4	1
Total manufacturing costs	20	20
Marketing and administrative costs:		
Variable	2	3
Fixed	4	3
Full costs per unit	26	26

To calculate the selling price under this method, we simply add the required profit margin, as follows:

	£	£
Full costs per unit	26	26
Add: Mark-up (50% on costs)	13	13
Selling price	39	39

Full-cost pricing appears on the surface to be an easy method. By ignoring demand considerations completely and concentrating on costs, it avoids one of the major problem areas of pricing. Nevertheless, there are problems in calculating full costs which are not easy to resolve. By and large, one may assume that the calculation of unit variable costs presents no serious measurement difficulties. By contrast, the assignment of fixed costs to units of output is an extremely complex matter.

Indirect costs and full-cost pricing

Many factory, administrative and marketing costs cannot be identified clearly with a particular cost centre. Furthermore, there is the problem of selecting an appropriate basis for assigning them to individual products. Under full-cost pricing, this problem is critical to the determination of the selling price.

Consider the previous example of High Speed Castings Ltd and let us assume that the demand for Product B is buoyant whereas the demand for Product A is slack. In these circumstances, it may be a good idea to transfer a higher proportion of fixed costs to Product B, and so enabling the price of Product A to be lowered to encourage more sales. By introducing such considerations to the problem of the allocation of fixed costs in multi-product firms, one is introducing a new principle to full-cost pricing, that is, the ability of the market to accept costs. Consequently, one is moving away from the essence of full-cost pricing.

Fixed costs and volume changes

The impact of changes in the sales volume upon unit fixed costs leads to a circular discussion, because price changes affect the volume of sales which in turn affect unit fixed costs which finally open up the possibility of further price changes. Since full-cost pricing implies flexible pricing in this sense, it is difficult to see its usefulness to those businessmen who instead of wanting a 'safe' price are looking for an aggressive price which will encourage the expansion of sales. Hence, they will tend to select a price which will be below full costs and look to the expanded volume of sales to cover total costs ultimately. It is in the nature of things that until such men are satisfied with their market position, price will always be below full costs. This is explainable in terms of the wish of businessmen to achieve market as well as profit objectives.

The following table shows the relationship of fixed costs and volume changes. Given that the percentage mark-up remains constant, there is a range of selling prices which will cover costs at a particular volume of sales.

No. of units (thousands)	100	200	300	400	500
Variable cost per unit	£4.00	£4.00	£4.00	£4.00	£4.00
Fixed cost per unit	2.00	1.00	0.67	0.50	0.40
Full cost per unit	6.00	5.00	4.67	4.50	4.40
10% mark-up	0.60	0.50	0.47	0.45	0.44
Selling price	6.60	5.50	5.14	4.95	4.84

It is also interesting to note the resulting aggregate profits which these different prices produce.

No. of units (thousands)	100	200	300	400	500
Selling price	£6.60	£5.50	£5.14	£4.95	£4.84
Profit per unit (at 10%)	0.60	0.50	0.47	0.45	0.44
Aggregate profit (£000s)	60.00	100.00	141.00	180.00	220.00

Clearly, faced with these production possibilities, management would wish to pursue an aggressive pricing policy which would place the highest aggregate profits within the firm's reach. As explained above, full-cost pricing would stand in the way of such a pricing policy because of the decreasing nature of fixed costs per unit as output expands. A stage will be reached, of course, when the firm has reached the limit of production under existing capacity. In other words, a point exists where the firm must stabilize production or incur further capital expenditure on the expansion of productive capacity. This would involve the firm in a capital investment decision and a complete reconsideration of its pricing policy.

The price which the firm would wish to establish under full-cost pricing, therefore, is that price which will not only be the best price from a profit point of view, but one which is related to the best output capacity which the firm can maintain. It is for this reason that a 'normal volume' of output must be established so that the firm may decide the appropriate full costs which are to form the basis of the price. This is a most important consideration for customers do not like frequent price changes.

Full-cost pricing and the mark-up percentage

Having gone through the complicated process of ascertaining the full cost per unit, one moves to the final problem of determining the mark-up percentage which, when added to full costs, will yield the price.

We have already mentioned that there are a number of influences which bear upon the size of the percentage mark-up. First, there is the notion of the 'fair price', and businessmen will argue strongly that such-and-such a percentage is a 'fair profit' for a given trade. There is a connection between the rate of turnover and the mark-up percentage, for example, it is quite normal to expect jewellers to impose a higher mark-up percentage on their goods than butchers. Second, the mark-up is influenced by the elasticity of demand for the product, and market conditions generally. Third, as we have already mentioned the mark-up is influenced by the nature of the firm's long-term strategy. Fourth, although businessmen argue that they seek a reasonable profit, it is evident that they mean the highest profit which they can 'reasonably' make. Finally, there is evidence also in the pricing policies of large firms, and particularly State corporations, that the need to generate capital to finance expensive capital projects influences the profit mark-up, and hence the price.

Conversion-cost pricing

Unlike full-cost pricing, conversion-cost pricing takes into account only the costs incurred by the firm in converting raw materials and semi-finished goods into finished products. One of the limitations of full-cost pricing is that where the firm is selling two products which require different degrees of effort to convert to a marketable state, no distinction is drawn between them.

Conversion-cost pricing, therefore, excludes direct materials and may be calculated easily from the example given on page 540 which is repeated below.

	Product A		Product B	
	£	£	£	£
Direct materials		4		12
Conversion costs				
Direct labour	6		4	
Factory overheads	10		4	
		16		8
Total factory costs		20		20

Under full-cost pricing, both products were priced at £39 as follows:

	Product A	Product B
	£	£
Total factory costs	20	20
Selling and administrative costs	6	6
Full costs	26	26
Mark-up at 50%	13	13
Selling price	39	39

The objective of conversion-cost pricing is to provide a pricing policy which will relate the cost or effort required by the firm to convert raw material into a marketable product to the selling price of the product. From the foregoing example, it is evident that Product A takes twice the effort to produce (£16) as Product B (£8). Hence, the firm should wish to formulate a pricing policy which will encourage the expansion of Product B, two units of which may be produced for the same production effort as Product A. This may be achieved by conversion-cost pricing, which will establish a lower price for Product B than for Product A. Under conversion-cost pricing, the mark-up is calculated on the conversion costs, as shown below.

It will be recalled from Chapter 32 that in selecting an appropriate sales mix from a profit planning point of view, the firm is attempting to plan production in such a way as to have that mix of product which will produce the best aggregate profit situation. Conversion-cost pricing will assist the firm which is faced with such a problem. If the demand for Product B were such that the firm could switch entirely to that product, the firm would simply cease manufacturing Product A. It is the fact that the firm is compelled to produce both products because demand is limited that the sales-mix problem arises. It is equally for this reason that conversion-cost pricing is useful in such situations.

	Product A £	Product B £
Conversion costs		
Direct labour	6	4
Factory overheads	10	4
	16	8
Mark-up at 100%	16	8
	32	16
Other costs		
Direct materials	4	12
Selling and administrative costs	6	6
Selling price	42	34

Return on investment pricing

The cost-based pricing theories which we have examined so far focus on costs of production. Although such costs will include depreciation, they exclude any consideration of the capital employed by the firm. The firm has profit expectations, of course, and these are stated in terms of a percentage mark-up on costs of production. Return on investment pricing attempts to link the mark-up to the capital employed, and so set a price which includes a return on capital employed. Research has shown that many firms have pricing policies which reflect a target rate of return. The formula used is as follows:

$$\text{Selling price} = \frac{\text{Total costs} + (\text{Desired \% return on capital} \times \text{Capital employed})}{\text{Volume of output}}$$

Example

Let us assume that High Speeds Castings Ltd, which produces the two products Type A and Type B, has a 'normal' output of Product A amounting to 20,000 units a year. Let us assume, also, that the capital employed by the firm is £1½ million, of which £1 million is employed in the production of Product A. The desired rate of return which the firm has imposed on all its capital investment decisions is 20 per cent. Accordingly, the firm seeks a profit mark-up which reflects this objective. The selling price may be calculated as follows:

	Product A £
Total costs of production (20,000 × £26)	520,000
Desired return on capital employed (20% of £1 m.)	200,000
Expected sales revenue	720,000
Selling price per unit (£720,000 ÷ 20,000)	£36

The attraction of this method of establishing a mark-up to costs is that it relates the problem of pricing to financial objectives and criteria, and integrates pricing decisions with the firm's overall planning objectives. It is clearly superior from a rational point of view to simply deciding upon a percentage mark-up on the basis of what is considered to be 'fair'. At the same time, return on investment pricing has all the tendencies to rigidity which are the features of full-cost pricing policies.

Since pricing decisions are generally short run in nature, their effects on long-range objectives require that these objectives be considered. A firm which has a long-range target rate of return may find that, in attempting to apply such a target to short-run pricing policies, it may be forced from the market by competition. Thus, the firm may be compelled to price below its target rate of return to retain its share of the market, and thereby ensure the attainment of its long-range objectives in the broad sense.

Return on investment pricing may, in practice, invert the relationship of costs to price, in that costs are tailored to fit selling policies. This means that more complete knowledge of the market is known, for example the likely size of the market, its sensitivity to quality and packaging. In these circumstances, a firm may ensure that a specific rate of return on investment is obtained by selling a commodity at a price not exceeding a pre-determined cost.

Variable-cost pricing

Sometimes referred to as the contribution method of pricing or marginal pricing, this method of pricing is related to the ideas which we discussed in Chapter 32. No one seriously disputes that in the long-term a firm's pricing policy must cover full costs, whether these are interpreted as full-production costs or the replacement of the capital invested, as well as providing an acceptable margin of profit. As we saw earlier, this is the main argument put forward by the supporters of full-cost pricing. For short-term decisions, however, no one can doubt the usefulness of variable cost pricing.

There are many situations in which a price which covers variable cost but not full costs will nevertheless make a contribution to profits. Thus, if a firm has spare capacity and has covered its fixed costs in the price set for its regular customers, and no further sales can be made to this market, the firm may attempt to reach another market by selling the article at a lower price with a slight alteration to the product presentation. Price discrimination, as this practice is known, enables the firm to sell the same product in different markets at different prices. The firm's total profits will be much greater as a result. This aspect of imperfect competition is commonly treated in economic textbooks. Similarly, where the firm is facing a fall in demand for its product due to a temporary market recession with the result that it is operating at a loss, any sales at a price which is above variable costs will contribute to the recovery of fixed costs.

Variable-cost pricing enables the firm to pursue special marketing policies, such as the penetration of a new market, or the development of an export market, by imposing upon the home market a price which recovers fixed costs so as to permit sales at variable costs in the new market. Some call this practice 'dumping', and it was successfully carried out in Germany, notably, in the 1930s. Variable-cost pricing is useful, therefore, because it indicates the lowest limit for a price decision. For example, the variable costs of the two products of High Speed Castings Ltd are as follows:

	Product A £	Product B £
Direct materials	4	12
Direct labour	6	4
Variable factory overheads	6	3
Variable selling and administrative overheads	2	3
Minimum price—Variable costs	18	22

Although variable-cost pricing is useful for dealing with temporary market difficulties or for exploiting new marketing strategies, there may be a danger that variable-cost pricing becomes the established method of pricing. The firm should therefore try to evolve both long-term and short-term pricing strategies, and return to a long-term pricing strategy once the short-term situation has been cleared.

In this section we have discussed the advantages of variable-cost pricing for short-term situations. It has also advantages for the long term. Full-cost pricing, as we have already suggested, may inhibit the firm from developing sales and production strategies which management considers to be desirable from a profit planning point of view. Variable-cost pricing takes account of the relationship between price, volume and costs, and in this sense it enables better profit planning decisions to be made.

Going-rate pricing

Where the price for a product is determined by the market, so that the firm is faced with a 'going rate', the major problem for the firm is how much to produce. In such situations, the volume produced is determined by the firm's costs and its profit planned accordingly. The classic examples where firms are faced with the going rate are the various commodity markets. Producers try to solve the price uncertainty by selling in the 'future markets', that is, contracting now to supply say in three months' time at an agreed price.

Summary

Pricing decisions form an integral part of the firm's planning process, and are related directly to its objectives. The nature of the firm's product, the market situation and the firm's short-term and long-term objectives are all factors which are relevant to pricing decisions.

Pricing policies must be examined in terms of the particular objectives which they seek to achieve, and we have already said that occasions may arise where a short-term objective requires a policy which would be unacceptable in the long-term. Numerous examples may be given of business objectives which require their own tailor-made pricing policies. The introduction of a new product may require a 'skimming price policy', that is, setting a high price initially and lowering the price as the product gains acceptance and popularity and permits the firm to expand the scale of production, so reducing its costs. Ball-point pens, nylons, television sets have all undergone this process. 'Penetration price policies' on the other hand have been a popular way of entering a foreign market and call for low prices to encourage rapid acceptance of the product.

For all these reasons, the only general rule that can be laid down is that unit costs provide a means of determining the lowest limit of an acceptable short-term price, whilst in the long-term the price should cover all costs and provide the margin of profit required by management.

Questions

1. 'Since prices are determined by supply and demand, accounting data is irrelevant in determining a firm's pricing policy'. Discuss.
2. Schlutz and Co Ltd manufactures a product which it distributes through its own branches in England and Wales. The managing director was recently approached by McTosh and Co. Ltd, a Glasgow based company interested in obtaining sole distributor rights in Scotland. McTosh proposes to purchase the product from Schlutz at a price of £32.50 and to offer it for sale to retailers in Scotland at £42.50 and would pay the transport charges to Scotland averaging £3.50 per unit. No commission would be payable to McTosh on these sales. Schlutz and Co undertook to consider this offer. Given the undermentioned information, would you advise Schlutz and Co to accept the offer?
   (a) The product is now sold to retailers in England and Wales at a price of £44 inclusive of delivery charges.

(b) Sales commission paid to retailers are computed at 5 per cent of sales.

(c) Transport costs average £1.50 per unit.

(d) Other selling and administrative costs are regarded as fixed and amount to £4.50 per unit.

(e) Manufacturing costs amount to £29.50 per unit as follows:

Materials	£18.70
Labour	3.00
Variable overheads	3.30
Fixed overheads	4.50
	£29.50

(f) Manufacturing capacity is adequate to handle the increased volume which is estimated to amount to 1000 units a month, but fixed factory overheads would probably increase by £1500 a month.

3. A standard unit of the Whitmore Manufacturing Company contains the following variable costs:

	Per Unit
Direct materials	£5.60
Direct labour cost	1.50
Variable factory overhead	0.40
	£7.50

Fixed factory overhead is budgeted at £280,000 for a normal sales volume of 400,000 units. Factory capacity is 500,000 units. Distribution and administrative expenses are budgeted at £180,000.

Capital employed is considered to consist of 50 per cent of net sales for current assets and £450,000 for fixed assets.

Additional analysis indicates:

(a) Direct material prices will increase £0.40 per unit.

(b) An unfavourable direct labour variance of approximately 6 per cent has been experienced for the past two years.

(c) Customers' discounts average to about 2 per cent of the gross sales price.

Required:

Determine a sales price which will yield 16 per cent return on capital employed.

35 Short-run tactical decisions

We discussed in Chapter 32 the importance of the relationship between cost and volume of output for profit planning purposes. Cost behaviour is a crucial element in profit planning, but a knowledge of the behaviour of future costs is equally important for a whole range of other decisions which management has to make.

We may divide the accountant's task of providing information as to costs for decision making into two parts. First, when planning the volume of output in the short term, the accountant has to provide information as to the behaviour of fixed and variable costs over the planned range of output. Second, for a number of 'special decisions' relating to alternative courses of action, such as the acceptance or rejection of a special order, he has to provide cost information which will guide management towards making the best, that is, the most profitable decisions.

The nature of relevant costs

The nature of the costs which are relevant for short-run tactical decisions will depend on the type of decision problem for which they are required. We shall examine several different types of decision problems, and in this way ascertain the type of cost information which ought to be supplied by the accountant. In general, however, the relevant costs have two important characteristics:

(a) They are future costs, that is, they are costs which are not yet incurred. This is a most important point, for it is easy to fall into the error of believing that costs which have already been incurred must be recovered. Past cost, that is, sunk costs are irrelevant costs: their only usefulness is the extent to which they may help the accountant to estimate the trend of future costs.

Example

Excelsior Ltd has spent £5000 on developing a new process. A revised estimate of further expenditure required to complete the development work shows an increase of 20 per cent on the original total estimate of £10,000. The cost which is relevant to the decision to continue with the development work is £7000, that is, the future cost which will be incurred, and not the new estimate of total costs of £12,000. Hence, the costs already incurred are irrelevant to the decision to be made concerning the completion of the development work.

(b) Relevant costs are differential costs. Not all future costs are relevant costs: differential costs will be different under the alternative courses of action under examination.

Example

John Brown has decided to go to the cinema, and he is considering whether to go by bus or by car. The price of the cinema ticket is not a relevant cost, for it is not affected by the manner in which he travels to the cinema. Likewise, since cars tend to depreciate over time, the additional mileage on the car is also not a relevant cost. Although Brown's decision on his mode of travel will be influenced by his individual preference, the relevant cost is the cost difference between the cost of using the car, that is, petrol and parking, and going by bus. This cost difference is the differential cost.

From the foregoing examples, it might appear that only variable costs will be relevant costs, and that fixed costs cannot be relevant costs, since by definition they are not susceptible to change. The examples show that not all variable costs are relevant costs, for this depends on whether in the circumstances under review they are also differential costs.

In the long term, of course, fixed costs do become variable costs, so that in decisions affecting the long term, fixed costs may be differential costs and so will become relevant costs.

For short-run tactical decisions, however, it is possible, as we shall see, for fixed costs to be relevant costs. Thus, if a decision affects the short-run activity level, requiring further capital expenditure, the extra fixed costs so incurred will be relevant costs as regards that decision.

The importance of the contribution margin

Usually, short-run tactical decisions are aimed at making the best use of existing facilities. The contribution margin is an important concept in this analysis. It is defined as the excess of the revenue of any activity over its relevant costs, which is available as a contribution towards fixed costs and profits. Profits, of course, will not be made until all fixed costs have been covered, but under certain circumstances the expectation of a contribution margin will be sufficient to justify a particular decision.

One decision problem with which a businessman is frequently faced is the acceptance of a special order, which may be a large order at a price below the usual selling price, and sometimes below total manufacturing costs.

Example

Minnies Kurt Ltd manufactures a garment which is sold under the trade name of Withitog. Its total productive capacity is 100,000 units in the current period, and actual production is running at 80 per cent of productive capacity. The product sells at £1.00 per unit, and the firm's costs of production are as follows:

Fixed costs	£25,000
Variable costs	£0.50 per unit

The firm receives a special order for 10,000 Withitog from a mail order firm, subject to the firm agreeing to sell the product at £0.60 per unit. The Managing Director is reluctant to accept the order because the selling price is well below the manufacturing costs, which he has calculated as follows:

Fixed costs per unit (allocated over 90,000 units)

$$\frac{£25,000}{90,000} \qquad £0.28$$

Variable costs per unit	0.50
Total manufacturing costs per unit	£0.78

The contribution margin approach to the solution of this decision problem leads to a different conclusion. The revenue per unit is £0.60, and the relevant costs associated with the decision are the variable costs of production only, that is, £0.50, per unit. Hence, there is a unit contribution margin of £0.10 per unit, and on that basis, the firm should accept the special order. The fixed costs are not relevant costs for two reasons, firstly, they are sunk costs, that is they are not future costs and secondly, they are not affected by the decision to accept the special order, that is they are not differential costs.

The result of accepting the special order on the firm's total profit may be seen as follows:

		Without the special order		*With the special order*	*Contribution margin*
		(80,000 units)		(90,000 units)	—
Sales revenue		£		£	£
80,000 units					
@ £1.00		80,000		80,000	
10,000 units					
£0.60		—		6000	
		80,000		86,000	6000
Manufacturing costs					
Fixed costs	25,000		25,000		—
Variable costs					
@ £0.50 per unit	40,000		45,000		
		65,000		70,000	5000
Net profit		£15,000		£16,000	£1000

It is clear, therefore, that it is advantageous to the firm to accept the special order, since overall profits will be improved by £1000, which is the amount of the contribution margin resulting from the acceptance of that order.

It is evident, too, that the widespread belief that all costs should be covered may influence businessmen in considering special offers. Absorption costing is useful in determining the full costs of production, but leads to erroneous conclusions if indiscriminately applied.

Example

Speedo Engineering Ltd manufactures an electrical component widely used in the motor industry. It is currently producing 5000 units selling at £10 a unit. Its total productive capacity is 8000 units, and budgeted costs at different levels of output have been estimated as follows:

Output (units)	5000	6000	7000	8000
Variable costs	£30,000	£36,000	£42,000	£48,000
Fixed costs	10,000	10,000	10,000	10,000
Total costs	£40,000	£46,000	£52,000	£58,000
Total costs per unit	£8.00	£7.67	£7.43	£7.25

The firm receives three offers for three lots of 1000 units at selling prices of £8, £7 and £6.50 per unit respectively. Should these offers be accepted or rejected?

The unit costs of production under the absorption costing method may be calculated and compared with the respective offers, as shown below:

Output (units)	6000	7000	8000
Total costs per unit	£7.67	£7.43	£7.25
Selling price per unit	8.00	7.00	6.50
Profit (loss) per unit	£0.33	£(0.43)	£(0.75)

From these calculations one might deduce that the firm should accept the order at £8 per unit, which will produce a profit of £0.33 per unit, but should reject the other two offers of £7 and £6.50 since they would result in losses.

An examination of the relevant costs leads to a different conclusion. The fixed costs are not relevant costs, since they will be incurred irrespective of the level of output. By comparing the relevant costs with the three offers, we may calculate the differential profits as under:

Output (units)	6000	7000	8000
Differential units	1000	1000	1000
Differential selling price	£8.00	£7.00	£6.50
Differential unit cost	6.00	6.00	6.00
Differential profit per unit	2.00	1.00	0.50
Differential total profit	£2000	£1000	£500

These figures illustrate the misleading effect of using absorption costing methods for decision making, and the necessity for using the relevant cost analysis. Using this latter method, it is clear that all three offers should be accepted, for in each case they provide a contribution margin towards fixed costs and profits.

Opportunity costs

Opportunity costs are not recorded in the accounting process, and although they are favoured by economists as appropriate costs for decision making, they are difficult to identify and to measure in practice. Hence, accountants prefer to record and use more objective measures of costs, such as past costs or budgeted future costs as guidelines for decision making. There are a number of decision problems, however, in which the only relevant cost is the opportunity cost. The opportunity cost may be defined as the value of the next best opportunity foregone, or of the net cash inflow lost as a result of preferring one alternative rather than the next best one. In cases where it is clear that only the opportunity cost will assist in making the decision, the accountant is often able to attempt its measurement.

Example

The Nationwide Investment Corporation Ltd seeks to invest £1 million. It has selected two investment projects for consideration: project A which is estimated to produce an annual return of 15 per cent, and project B which is expected to yield 20 per cent annually.

On the basis of these facts, it is clear that the Corporation will select project B. The additional gain resulting from that decision may only be measured in terms of the opportunity costs of sacrificing project A, as follows:

Estimated annual return from project B	£200,000
Less: Opportunity cost (the sacrifice of the estimated	
annual returns from project B)	150,000
Advantage of project B	£50,000

The opportunity cost is always a relevant cost concept when the problem facing the firm is a problem of choice: the measure of the cost of the decision is the loss sustained by losing the opportunity of the second best alternative. It is the opportunity cost which must be taken into account in calculating the advantage of choosing one alternative rather than the other.

The use of the opportunity cost concept is illustrated in the following situations:

(a) dropping a product line
(b) selling or further processing a semi-manufactured product
(c) operate or lease
(d) make or buy a product.

Dropping a product line

Invariably the reason for wishing to drop a product line is that it is unprofitable, or it is less profitable than another product line to which the firm could switch resources.

Example

Mechanical Toys Ltd manufactures three products, whose contributions to total profits for the year just ended are as under:

Products				
	A	B	C	Total
	£	£	£	£
Sales	200,000	100,000	150,000	450,000
Variable costs	100,000	70,000	80,000	250,000
Contribution	100,000 (50%)	30,000 (30%)	70,000 (47%)	200,000 (44%)
Fixed costs	60,000	40,000	50,000	150,000
Net profit (loss)	40,000	(10,000)	20,000	50,000

The company is considering dropping product B as it is showing a loss. By dropping product B, fixed costs could be reduced by £10,000, though the remaining balance of fixed costs of £30,000 being overhead fixed costs allocated to the product would have to be re-allocated to products A and C.

The only choice facing the company is to continue or to cease making product B, and the financial consequences of that choice may be shown as follows:

	Keep product B £	Drop product B £
Sales	450,000	350,000
Variable costs	250,000	180,000
Contribution	200,000	170,000
Fixed costs	150,000	140,000
Net profit	50,000	30,000

It is clear that although an overall loss appears to result from producing product B, the contribution which product B makes to the firm's fixed costs would be lost if the decision were made to drop product B. The net cost of dropping product B would be £20,000, that is, the contribution margin less the fixed costs of £10,000 incurred solely as a consequence of its production.

Expressed in terms of opportunity cost analysis, the company has the choice between a profit of £50,000 associated with a decision to keep product B, and a profit of £30,000 associated with a decision to drop product B. Clearly, it cannot have both: hence the cost of selecting the profit of £50,000 is the sacrifice of the opportunity of the alternative profit of £30,000. Hence, the opportunity cost of the decision to keep product B is £30,000, and the advantage of this decision over the alternative of dropping product B is £20,000.

There may be other alternatives open to the firm, of course, besides the two alternatives which we have discussed, such as replacing product B by a more profitable product. In such a case, all the available alternatives must be examined and their outcomes accurately estimated if the best decision is to be made.

Selling or further processing

On occasions, it is possible for a firm to bring a product to its semi-finished state and then to sell it, rather than proceed to complete the production process and sell the finished article.

Example

Product A, which cost £4.8 per unit to produce, is sold as a refined petroleum product at £8 a unit. It could be put through a further processing stage after which it may be sold for £12 a unit. The costs associated with the further processing stage are estimated at £2 per unit.

The outcome of the two alternatives facing the firm, to sell or to further process the product may be stated in the following terms:

	To sell	To process further
Revenues associated with the decision	£8	£4
Costs associated with the decision	4.8	2
Differential profit per unit	£3.2	£2

It is clear that if the firm decides to sell rather than to process further, it will lose the additional profit of £2 per unit. Hence, the opportunity cost of the decision to sell is £2 and the advantage of selling over further processing is £1.2.

Operate or lease

The decision as to whether to operate or lease assets is another example of the importance of opportunity costs for decision making.

Example

Betashoes Ltd owns a desirable freehold in Puddingford High Street, which it uses as a selling outlet. The Managing Director receives an offer to lease the property to a local company willing to pay an annual rent of £30,000. The net contribution of the selling outlet in Puddingford to the group profits of Betashoes Ltd is £40,000, after deducting the expenses attributable to it. The information which is relevant to the decision to continue to use the selling outlet may be set out as under:

Contribution to group profits	£40,000
Opportunity cost (rent)	£30,000
Net advantage of operating	£10,000

In the absence of other factors which may induce Betashoes to sell the site, the offer to lease the premises should be rejected and Betashoes should continue to use them as a selling outlet.

Make or buy

It is quite common for firms to subcontract the making of components to specialist firms. This practice does increase their dependence on outside suppliers and reduce to some extent their control on the quality of the components. The opportunity cost approach to this type of decision enables the firm to consider the advantages which could be obtained from alternative uses of the productive capacity released as the result of subcontracting the making of components.

Example

Highperformance Motors Ltd specializes in the manufacture of sports cars, making some of the components which are required and buying others. Alparts Ltd offers to supply a part currently made by Highperformance Motors Ltd at a price of £7. The costs incurred by Highperformance Motors in making the part are as follows:

Variable costs	£4
Traceable fixed costs	2
Allocated fixed costs	3
Total unit costs	£9

Let us assume for the moment that the productive capacity released as a result of accepting the offer will remain idle. On the basis of a monthly production of 5000 units a month, the relevant monthly costs, that is, those which would be affected by the decision to buy the units, are as follows:

Variable costs	£20,000
Traceable fixed costs	10,000
Relevant costs	30,000
Cost of buying	35,000
Advantage in making	5000

The allocated fixed costs are irrelevant to the decision since they are not affected, and will continue to be incurred by Highperformance Motors irrespective of whether the parts are made or bought. Since the relevant costs of making are less than the costs of buying, the firm should reject the offer and continue to make the parts.

Let us now consider the possibility that if the firm accepted the offer, the productive capacity released as a result will not remain idle, and will be used to extend the production line of motor cars. It is calculated that an additional four cars a month could be produced, leading to an increase in profits of £10,000. The opportunity costs of not accepting the offer, therefore, amount to £10,000. Hence, the information which is now relevant to the decision as to making or buying the part is as under:

Cost of making	
Relevant manufacturing costs	£30,000
Opportunity cost	10,000
	40,000
Cost of buying	35,000
Advantage of buying	£5000

The introduction of the opportunity cost of not accepting the offer has altered the nature of the decision completely, and reversed the previous conclusion that it was advantageous to make the part.

Decision making in the face of limiting factors

In the examples which we have examined so far, the selection of alternative courses of action has been made on the basis of seeking the most profitable result. Business enterprises are limited in the pursuit of profit by the fact that they have limited resources at their disposal, so that quite apart from the limitation on the quantities of any product which the market will buy at a given price, the firm has its own constraints on the volume of output. Hence at a given price, which may be well above costs of production, the firm may be unable to increase its overall profit simply due to its inability to increase its output.

The limiting factors which affect the level of production may arise out of shortages of labour, material, equipment and factory space to mention but a few obvious examples. Faced with limiting factors of whatever nature, the firm will wish to obtain the maximum profit from the use of the resources available, and in making decisions about the allocation of its resources between competing alternatives, management will be guided by the relative contribution margins which they offer. Since the firm will be faced with limiting factors, however, the contribution margins must be calculated not in terms of units of product sold which fail to reflect constraints on the total volume of output, but should be related to the unit of quantity of the most limited factor. A simple example will serve to explain this point.

Example

Multiproduct Ltd manufactures three products about which is derived the following data:

Product	Machine hours required per unit of product	Contribution margin per unit	Contribution margin per machine hour
A	3 hours	£9	£3.0
B	2 hours	£7	£3.5
C	1 hour	£5	£5.0

The three products can be made by the same machine, and on the basis of this information, it is evident that product C is the most profitable product yielding a contribution of £5 per machine hour, as against product A, which shows the smallest contribution per machine hour. Hence, in deciding how to use the limiting factor the firm should concentrate on the production of product C, rather than products A and B. If there were no limits to the market demand for product C, there would be no problem in deciding which product to produce—it would be product C alone.

Firms undertake the manufacture of different products because the market demand for any one product is limited, so that firms seek to find that product-mix which will be the most profitable. Let us assume that the maximum weekly demand for the three products and the total machine capacity necessary to meet this demand is as follows:

Product	Maximum demand in units	Machine hours equivalents
A	100	300
B	100	200
C	100	100
		600

Machine capacity is limited to 450 hours per week, so that the most profitable product-mix is a function of both machine capacity and market demand. The following product-mix would maximize profits:

Product	Output units	Machine hours	Contribution per machine hour	Total contribution
C	100	100	£5.0	£500
B	100	200	£3.5	£700
A	50	150	£3.0	£450
		450		£1650

This product-mix reflects the order of priority in allocating machine use to the products with the highest contribution margin per hour. Product C receives the highest priority, then product B, and lastly product A. If machine hours were further limited to 300 hours, the firm would cease to make product A.

Linear programming and decision making

Linear programming is a mathematical technique which seeks to make the best use of a firm's limited resources to meet chosen objectives, which in accounting terms may take the form of the maximization of profits or the minimization of costs. In those situations, for example, where a manufacturer has a limited plant capacity, the level and cost of output will be determined by such capacity.

Example

Blackamoor Steels Ltd manufacture two high-quality steel products in respect of which the following information is available:

	Product A £	Product B £
Selling price per unit	30	20
Variable costs per unit	15	10
Contribution margin	15	10

Milling and grinding machines are used in the manufacturing process, and the total machine hours necessary to produce one unit of each product are:

	Product A	Product B
Milling	5 hours	1½ hours
Grinding	2	2
	7	3½

Both products are in great demand, and the only constraint on expanding output is machine capacity. The total machine hours available per month are:

Milling (3 machines at 200 hours a month)	600 hours
Grinding (2 machines at 200 hours a month)	400 hours.

On the basis of the facts given above, the problem facing management is to ascertain that combination of output of products A and B which will maximize the total contribution margin to overheads and profits. This problem is similar to the example discussed in the previous section (see p. 557). At first glance, it would appear that the firm should maximize the production of product A since that product yields the highest unit contribution margin. Analysed in terms of the machine capacity limit, the total number of units of *either* product A *or* product B which could be manufactured is as follows:

Product A	600 hours ÷ 5 hours = 120 units
Product B	400 hours ÷ 2 hours = 200 units

These output limits are derived in the case of product A by the fact that output is limited to the capacity of the milling machines, for product A requires 5 hours of milling as against only 2 hours of grinding. Product B, however, is limited in output by the capacity of the grinding machines of which it requires 2 hours per unit, as against 1½ hours of milling time.

By relating the calculation of the contribution margin to the machine capacity limits, the total contribution to overhead costs and profits which will be obtained by the production of *either* A *or* B is as follows:

Product A: 120 units × £15 = £1800
Product B: 200 units × £10 = £2000

It follows, therefore, that given the option of making either product A or product B the firm should concentrate on the making of product B.

The approach to the solution of this problem under linear programming consists, firstly, of formulating the problem in simple algebraic terms. There are two aspects to the problem, the first being the wish to maximize profits and the second being the need to recognize the production limits. The two aspects may be stated algebraically as follows:

(a) The objective is to maximize the contribution to fixed overheads and profit. This objective is called the objective function, and may be expressed thus:

$$\text{Maximize } C = 15A + 10B$$

where C is the total contribution and A and B being the total number of units of the two products which must be manufactured to maximize the total contribution. This equation is subject to the limits that:

$$A \geq 0$$

$$B \geq 0$$

for it is not possible to produce negative quantities of either A or B.

(b) The constraints on production arising from the machine capacity limits of the Milling Department (600 hours) and of the Grinding Department (400 hours) may also be expressed in algebraic terms as follows:

$$5A + 1\tfrac{1}{2}B \leq 600$$

$$2A + 2B \leq 400$$

The first inequality states that the total number of hours used on milling must be equal to or less than 600 hours; the second inequality states that the total hours used on grinding machines must be equal to or less than 400 hours.

The problem may now be summarized in the form:

$$\text{Maximize } C = 15A + 10B$$

subject to the constraints:

$$5A + 1\tfrac{1}{2}B \leq 600$$

$$2A + 2B \leq 400$$

$$A \geq 0$$

$$B \geq 0$$

It is possible to solve the problem by means of a graph (Fig. 5.26) showing the manufacturing possibilities for the two departments, viz:

Milling department		
Product A	$600 \div 5 = 120$ units	
or Product B	$600 \div 1\tfrac{1}{2} = 400$ units	
Grinding department		
Product A	$400 \div 2 = 200$ units	
or Product B	$400 \div 2 = 200$ units	

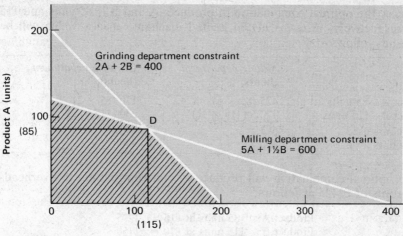

Fig. 5.26.   **Product B (units)**

The shaded region contains all the combinations of products A and B which are feasible solutions to the problem, hence its name—the feasibility region. The optimal solution, that is, the product combination of A and B which is the best of all the feasible solutions lies at the intersection of the lines at point D, and may be read off as 85 units of A and 115 of B. It will be observed that the optimal solution lies on a tangent which is the furthest away from the point of origin. The graphical method of solving the problem is susceptible to error unless carefully plotted, and a more reliable answer may be obtained by solving the problem mathematically.

The optimal combination of products A and B may be found by solving the simultaneous equation given above, that is,

(1) $5A + 1\frac{1}{2}B = 600$

(2) $2A + 2B = 400$

The solution is obtained by multiplying (1) by 4 and (2) by 3 to give us the value of A, as follows:

$$20A + 6B = 2400$$

$$-6A + 6B = 1200$$

$$\overline{14A \qquad = 1200}$$

$$A \qquad = 85\tfrac{5}{7}\text{ths}$$

Since we are concerned only with completed units of A, the optimal production of product A is 85 units. The optimal number of units of B may be calculated by inserting the known value of A into the equation, as follows:

$$6 \times 85 + 6B = 1200$$

i.e., $510 + 6B = 1200$

$$6B = 1200 - 510$$

$$B = 115.$$

Hence, the optimal combination of products A and B is 85 units and 115 units respectively, in terms of the limited machine capacity which will be utilized as follows:

	Milling department (hours)	Grinding department (hours)
Product A—85 units	425 (85 × 5)	170 (85 × 2)
Product B—115 units	172.5 (115 × 1½)	230 (115 × 2)
Total hours used	597.5	400
Total hours available	600	400

The optimal combination will produce a total contribution to overheads and profits of £2425 as follows:

$$
\begin{array}{lll}
\text{Product A:} & \text{85 units at £15} = & 1275 \\
\text{Product B:} & \text{115 units at £10} = & 1150 \\
& & \overline{£2425}
\end{array}
$$

We may verify that this combination of products is the optimal one in terms of profits and available machine capacity, as follows:

(a) Altering the product combination from 85 units of A and 115 units of B to 84 units of A and 116 units of B, which would affect machine use as follows:

	Milling department (hours)	Grinding department (hours)
Product A—84 units	420 (84 × 5)	168 (84 × 2)
Product B—116 units	174 (116 × 1½)	232 (116 × 2)
Total hours used	594	400
Total hours available	600	400

Hence, this combination is as efficient in the utilization of the grinding department but less efficient in the utilization of the milling machines. It is less profitable also yielding a contribution of only £2420 as against £2425 as follows:

$$
\begin{array}{lll}
\text{Product A:} & \text{84 units at £15} = & 1260 \\
\text{Product B:} & \text{116 units at £10} = & 1160 \\
& & \overline{£2420}
\end{array}
$$

(b) Altering the product combination from 85 units of A and 115 units of B to 86 units of A and 113 units of B, which would affect machine use as under:

	Milling department (hours)	Grinding department (hours)
Product A—86 units	430 (86 × 5)	172 (86 × 2)
Product B—113 units	169½ (113 × 1½)	226 (113 × 2)
Total hours used	599½	398
Total hours available	600	400

Hence, whereas this combination is more efficient in the use of the milling machines than the optimal combination, it is less efficient in the use of the grinding machinery. Moreover, to keep within the capacity limits of the milling department we have had to forgo the production of 2 units of product B to expand the manufacture of product A by one unit. The consequential contribution to profits is also only £2420 as against the optimal contribution of £2425, which may be calculated as follows:

Product A: 86 units at £15 =   1290
Product B: 113 units at £10 =   1130
                                    £2420

It is noteworthy, also, that the linear programming approach to the best product combination mix gives a solution which is more profitable than the one which relates the contribution margin to the machine capacity limits, which we discussed on page 559, and which suggested that only product B should be made so that 200 units of B would be manufactured to yield a contribution of £2000.

We have so far only discussed simple cases involving at the maximum only two resource constraints. In real life, a firm may be faced with more than two constraints, but mathematical techniques exist for coping with larger numbers of limits. The Simplex Method, for example, which is based on matrix algebra may be employed in such cases and it is ideally suited for solutions using a computer.

Summary

In addition to providing information for short-run profit planning purposes, the accountant also often has to provide information for a number of short-run tactical decisions such as dropping a product line or choosing between selling or further processing a semi-manufactured product. As in other areas of accounting, cost information plays an important role in short-run tactical decisions. The costs which are relevant for such decisions are future differential costs.

As in the case of c-v-p, short-run tactical decisions are aimed at making the best use of existing facilities. Particular use is made of the contribution margin, which is the excess of the expected revenue resulting from a decision over the expected relevant costs of that decision which is available as a contribution towards fixed costs and profits.

Although opportunity costs are not recorded in the accounting process, there are a number of decision problems where opportunity costs are the only relevant costs. Opportunity costs may be defined as the value of the next best opportunity foregone, or of the net cash inflow lost as a result of preferring one alternative rather than the next best one. Opportunity costs are useful and relevant costs for the following decisions:

(a) dropping a product line;
(b) selling or further processing a semi-manufactured product;

(c) operating or lease assets;
(d) making or buying a product.

Limits placed on resources have to be recognized in decision making. Product-mix decisions illustrate the nature of this problem and the manner in which the best use of limited resources may be made. In this connection, linear programming affords a useful technique for maximizing profits or minimizing costs in the face of constraints on resources.

Questions

1. Heating Products Ltd has a division which manufactures radiators. The standard radiator is the Radwarm, but the company also produces radiators to customer specifications. Such radiators are described in the firm as Specials. The forecast results of the division for the year ending 31 December 19X0 are shown below:

	Radwarm £	Specials £	Total £
Sales	50,000	100,000	150,000
Materials	16,000	20,000	36,000
Labour	18,000	40,000	58,000
Depreciation	7200	12,600	19,800
Power	800	1400	2200
Rent	2000	12,000	14,000
Heat & light	200	1200	1400
Miscellaneous costs	1800	800	2600
	46,000	88,000	134,000
Net income	4000	12,000	16,000

The expenses have been arrived at as follows:
(1) Depreciation is calculated on the book value of machinery used during production of each of the two groups of products.
(2) Rent is based on the space occupied in the division by each of the product lines. The building housing this division is rented at £14,000 p.a. on a ten year lease.
(3) Heat and light for the building is apportioned on the basis of area occupied by the two groups of products.
(4) All other costs are traced directly to the product lines.

The divisional manager has received an order to supply 1000 Special radiators. To accommodate this order, the division would have to switch half of its Radwarm production capacity. The customer has offered a price of £70 per radiator for these Specials and each radiator would take £20 of materials and £36 of labour.

A special press would need to be purchased for this order at a price of £4000. There would be no further use for this once this order is finished and it would be discarded.

Required:
(a) Calculate (i)   the differential cost of the special order;
                (ii) the full cost of the order; and
                (iii) the opportunity cost of accepting this order.
(b) Write a report explaining whether Heating Products Ltd should accept the special order.

2. It is three months since William Wright was appointed accountant at Broomhill Manufacturing Company. During this period he has become increasingly dissatisfied with the company's accounting system. In particular overheads are not analysed into fixed and variable elements. Wright believes that profit planning requires an understanding of the characteristics of cost and their behaviour at different operating levels. He resolved to write to the managing director and explain his new approach. To support his case Wright searched for examples which could be used to illustrate his arguments. One such example is given below.

Example
The income statement for 31 December 19X7, Wright believed, could be improved for making the predictions implied in the profit planning process. This showed the following results:

	£
Sales revenue	100,000
Cost of sales:	
Materials	15,000
Labour	20,000
Factory overheads	20,000
	55,000
Gross margin	45,000
Selling and administrative expenses	35,000
Net income	10,000

Wright estimated that fixed factory overheads amounted to £5000 and fixed selling and administrative expenses to £25,000.

The accountant of Broomhill Manufacturing, previous to Wright's appointment, had analysed the results for 19X7 by product groups and this had led the managing director to consider eliminating Product B, a loss-making product. The analysis by product is given below:

	A	B	C
	£	£	£
Sales revenue	60,000	15,000	25,000
Cost of sales:			
Materials	10,000	2000	3000
Labour	11,000	4000	5000
Factory overheads	11,000	4000	5000
	32,000	10,000	13,000
Gross margin	28,000	5000	12,000
Selling and administrative	20,000	8000	7000
	8000	(3000)	5000

Factory overheads were allocated to products at a rate of 100 per cent direct labour cost. Wright estimated that fixed factory overhead elements of the assigned costs were as follows:

A £3000
B £1000
C £1000

Selling and administrative expenses had been assigned to products on an arbitrary basis. Wright estimated the fixed elements as below:

	£
A	15,000
B	6000
C	4000

Required:
To what extent is Wright justified in seeking a reappraisal of the situation?

Section 3 Control

36 Organizing for control

The integration of planning and control

We mentioned in the introduction to Part 5, that control may be related to planning by defining the purpose of control as being to ensure that the organization's activities conform with its plans. Control is itself an activity, therefore, and it should and does affect every aspect of the organization. We may depict the control cycle in the form of a generalized model as shown in Fig. 5.27.

The control cycle illustrated thereon shows that the origin of control is in the objectives of the organization from which plans are developed. These plans, as we saw in Section 2, consist of both long-range and annual plans. It is evident from the model depicted on p. 568 that the control cycle integrates both the long-range and the annual plan. Information feedback enables actual performance to be compared with the planned performance required by the annual plan, thus enabling management to control operations and the resources allocated to those operations. At the end of the year, the results may be compared with those envisaged in terms of the long-range plans, thereby providing information feedback for the purposes of reviewing the long-range plan. Finally, the control process allows achievements to be compared with the organization's desired objectives, thereby enabling new goals and new objectives to be formulated.

The control model illustrates the multi-dimensional nature of the control process, and the coincidence of the control process with the planning processes. It is this coincidence which allows the planning and the control process to be integrated into one model which is focused on organizational objectives and the goals derived from those objectives. Overall control is concerned with measuring progress towards the realization of organizational objectives and the strategic goals defined in the strategic plan. This aspect of control is exercised by top management. Using the terminology adopted in Chapter 26, management control is a subordinate activity concerned with the efficient use of resources committed to the realization of organizational goals. Finally, operational control is concerned with ensuring that the tasks defined in the operational plan are carried out effectively. Specific performance standards are attached to these tasks, and information feedback allows actual performance to be compared with the required performance.

From the foregoing, it follows that control standards are designed in the planning process. They are used as indices by which the effectiveness and the

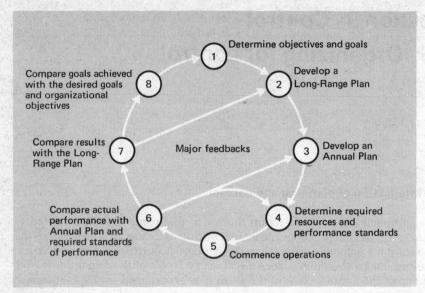

Fig. 5.27.

result of organizational activities are to be assessed, for they provide the basis by which actual and planned performance are to be compared. Moreover, since organizational activities emanate from the planning process, plans themselves also constitute performance standards.

There remains, however, a perceptible distinction between planning and control in the sense in which we consider these terms in this text. A plan reflects the expectations and the means of achieving stipulated goals during a specified period. If such a plan is to be useful for control purposes as well, it should reflect adequately the extent to which those expectations and those means are subject to organizational control. Hence, it should provide the basis for the system of responsibility accounting which requires a clear definition of the controllable elements at every level of responsibility.

Responsibility accounting

Control depends on the existence of an organizational framework which will define the responsibility for securing the performance of individual tasks. This is achieved by establishing responsibility centres throughout the organization, and defining the responsibilities of managers accordingly.

A responsibility centre may be defined as a segment of the organization where an individual manager is held responsible for the segment's performance.

The nature of the organizational framework and the kinds of responsibility centres established will depend partly on the size of the organization and partly on the style of management adopted.

As organizations grow, top management faces two continuing problems:

(a) how to divide activities and responsibilities
(b) how to co-ordinate sub-units.

Inevitably, authority for decision making has to be allocated to various managers, and as soon as this occurs, the result is the decentralization of the decision-making process. In essence, therefore, decentralization is the process of granting the freedom to make decisions to subordinate managers. In theory, there are two extreme states: total decentralization meaning a minimum of constraint or control on managers and a maximum of the freedom to make decisions even at the lowest level of the management hierarchy and total centralization implying the maximum of constraint or control on managers and the minimum freedom to make independent decisions. In practice, total centralization and total decentralization rarely occur. Total centralization is not feasible because it is impossible for top management to attend to all the decisions which are required to be made. Equally, total decentralization is rarely found because the degree of freedom which it implies would result in an organizational structure consisting of a collection of completely separate units all aiming at their own individual goals. The extent to which an organization will be decentralized depends upon the philosophy of its top management, and the benefits and costs associated with decentralization.

Having decided to decentralize to a greater or lesser extent, the problem of control nevertheless remains. It may be resolved by establishing new responsibility centres called 'divisions'. These divisions may take the form of profit or investment centres. We shall consider these responsibility centres later in this chapter.

The problem of controlling divisional operations is more complex than that of controlling a single activity within an organization. Where decision making is centralized, for example, it is possible to establish expense centres and to control their activities by means of budgetary control. Some of these expense centres may be cost centres, which are smaller segments of activity or areas of responsibility in respect of which costs are accumulated. Control may be exercised, therefore, by means of information feedback about the level of costs arising from the activities of these responsibility centres. Indeed, cost control has been the traditional means of securing the control of operations, though as we shall see later, the failure to recognize behavioural factors affecting performance has implications for the effectiveness of cost control. Where decision making is decentralized, however, the control of divisional performance is made more difficult for a number of reasons. The range of decisions over which divisional managers have authority is much more extensive. Thus, they may have authority over the determination of the pricing of products, make or buy decisions and some investment decisions. The problem goes beyond the control of costs, therefore, to the control of profits and to ensuring that there is a high degree of goal congruence between the various divisions and the organization's top management.

Our analysis of the problem of control through responsibility accounting should recognize the problems created by the degree of centralization and decentralization of authority. The first category of responsibility centre which we shall examine, namely expense centres, are appropriate to highly centralized organizations or units. The second and third categories of responsibility centres, namely profit and investment centres, are appropriate to those organizations where the authority for decision making has been decentralized to some extent, and where the problem of control is necessarily more complex. We shall deal with the behavioural aspects of control which such a degree of decentralization creates in Chapter 39. For the time being, we shall focus attention on the accounting problems stemming from the establishment of these various types of responsibility centres.

Expense centres

An expense centre may be defined as a responsibility centre in which the manager has no control over revenue but is able to control expenditure. It will be recalled that in Chapter 27, we drew a distinction between the accumulation of costs for product costing purposes and for control purposes. In product costing, we noted that costs are first allocated and apportioned to service departments and production departments; next, that service department costs are apportioned to the production departments; finally, overhead recovery rates are computed to enable overhead costs to be absorbed into product costs. Since the production departments are the focal points on which the process of cost accumulation converges, these departments are known as 'cost centres'.

From the foregoing, we may distinguish an expense centre from a cost centre. An expense centre is a department which incurs expenditure. A cost centre is a production department in which product costs are accumulated.

As we stated earlier, a prerequisite for an effective responsibility accounting system is the establishment of an organizational framework which will define the formal relationships which link the different executive roles in the organization. Levels of responsibility may be delineated for foremen, departmental managers, works managers and upwards to director level. Figure 5.28 is an organizational chart applied to a centralized organization and shows that the three foremen are responsible to the manager of department B, who in turn reports to the works manager. The works manager is responsible to the Board.

An important facet of a comprehensive planning and control programme is a system of performance reports incorporating comparisons of actual performance against planned performance for individual responsibility centres throughout the enterprise. These reports provide a means of instituting responsibility accounting, which is a method of cost control in which the cost of responsibility centres are identified with individual managers who are given authority over such costs and responsibility for them. The nature of the relationship existing between various levels of management and the flow of information between these levels may be illustrated as in Fig. 5.29 (p. 572).

Responsibility budgets deal only with the costs for which each manager is to be held responsible, and their performance as managers is evaluated by reference to the succes with which they have managed their own area of responsibility. It is important, therefore, to make a distinction between those costs which are under the control of a particular manager and those for which other managers are responsible. For example, the foreman of the assembly department may be responsible for the amount of direct labour used, but he will certainly not be responsible for the wage rate which is paid to these

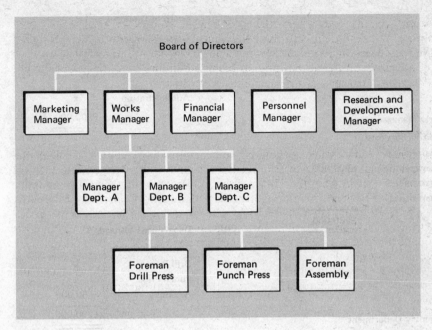

Fig. 5.28.

workers. This is determined by collective bargaining and is outside his sphere of influence. In assessing managerial performance under systems of responsibility accounting, a manager should not be held responsible for costs which are outside his control. An inference which may be drawn from our diagram is that the higher one ascends the pyramid of control, the greater is the proportion of total costs which is defined as controllable costs: at board of directors level all costs are by definition controllable as the board is ultimately responsible for all costs.

There are conflicting views as to whether non-controllable costs should be included in performance reports. One view is that, if they are included, managers will be informed of all the costs affecting their departments. Their inclusion also enables department managers to appreciate the size and the costs of the organizational support upon which his department depends. If non-controllable costs are included in performance reports, they should be distinguished from the costs which fall within the manager's responsibility, that is, those costs which are defined as controllable.

The manager in charge of an expense centre has the responsibility for seeing that the expenditure incurred by his department should not exceed the limits contained in his budgeted expenditure. Clearly, his ability to control expenditure will be an important consideration in the evaluation of his effectiveness as a manager. If follows, therefore, that the use of budgets for evaluating the performance of managers has implications for the manner in which budgets are organized. We shall discuss this problem in the next chapter.

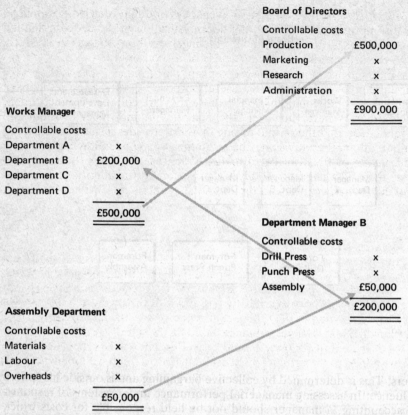

Board of Directors

Controllable costs

Production	£500,000
Marketing	x
Research	x
Administration	x
	£900,000

Works Manager

Controllable costs

Department A	x
Department B	£200,000
Department C	x
Department D	x
	£500,000

Department Manager B

Controllable costs

Drill Press	x
Punch Press	x
Assembly	£50,000
	£200,000

Assembly Department

Controllable costs

Materials	x
Labour	x
Overheads	x
	£50,000

Fig. 5.29 Levels of responsibility reporting.

Profit centres

In recent years, there has been a tendency for organizations to grow in size, and the problem of control which this growth has created has encouraged the devolution of authority in large organizations by the creation of organizational structures based upon the concept of 'divisions'. The rationale underlying this process of decentralization is founded on the belief that divisionalization enhances overall corporate profitability. Several reasons are adduced for this belief. Firstly, the responsibility for decision making is transferred to executives who are 'on the spot', and who are directly concerned with the particular problems of manufacturing and marketing divisional products. Hence, they are able to devote all their energies to these problems, whereas under systems of centralized control, top management is able to devote less time to the problems of individual divisions. Secondly, it is considered that the greater degree of freedom enjoyed by divisional executives increases their motivation towards the attainment of organizational goals, and in particular the profit goal. Thirdly, the opportunity which divisionalization affords of using accounting information to measure the contribution of each division towards the profit goal, also reveals areas of weakness and may suggest possibilities for profit improvement. Finally, the decentralization of the decision-making process provides a training ground for managers as they progress successively through the organization to higher levels of responsibility.

Conventional accounting measurements of performance, such as the return on capital employed, may serve a useful purpose in evaluating the financial performance of individual divisions, where they are completely independent of each other. Where, however, the activities of individual divisions are inter-related, so that the output of one division provides a substantial part of the input of another division, the usefulness of conventional accounting measurements of financial performance is less clear. Under these circumstances, there is a need to establish a price for transferring these so-called intermediate products between the divisions, and this price will clearly affect their profits.

Transfer pricing

From the foregoing, the use of profit centres for the control of divisional performance may give rise to the problem of determining the price at which the product of one profit centre should be transferred to another profit centre. The transfer price is critically important to the profit of both centres, being at once revenue to the selling centre and cost to the buying centre. The evaluation of managerial performance based on the size of the divisional profit requires that the transfer price should be so calculated as to reflect accurately the value-added to the product by the selling centre. If it is set too high, it will reflect too favourably upon the selling centre and too unfavourably upon the buying centre, and vice-versa. Hence, financial results may be heavily biased by the prices adopted for the transfer of intermediate goods. Defects in the transfer price mechanism may frequently invalidate the conclusions which divisional profit figures might seem to suggest. In such cases, these figures may not merely fail to produce the right decisions, they may actively promote wrong ones.

In Chapter 34, we examined pricing as a means of regulating the exchange of the firm's products with the outside world. In this chapter, we shall examine transfer pricing as a method of controlling the activities of profit centres within the firm. Hence, we shall see that the distinction between pricing and transfer pricing lies in their different purposes.

Transfer prices should satisfy the following three criteria:

(a) They should promote goal congruence within the organization by harmonizing the interest of individual divisions with the interest of the organization as a whole, by preventing divisional managers from optimizing divisional profits by policies which are harmful to the rest of the organization.
(b) They should make possible reliable assessments of divisional performance for the following purposes:
    (i) making predictions for decision-making purposes
    (ii) appraising managerial performance
    (iii) evaluating the divisional contribution to corporate profits.

(c) They should ensure that the autonomy of the individual divisions is respected, and that their profits are not dependent upon the actions of other divisions.

Transfer pricing methods

There are three main methods for establishing transfer prices:

(a) market-based transfer pricing
(b) cost-based transfer pricing
(c) negotiated pricing.

Market-based transfer pricing

Where external markets do exist for the selling centre's products, it is preferable to use market prices rather than cost-based prices. This is because market price is a better guide to the value added to products than a cost-based price which incorporates a profit element. If the external market is competitive and divisional inter-dependence is minimal, the market price generally leads to optimal decisions within the organization, that is, decisions which satisfy the three criteria stipulated above. Where market prices can be used with a large measure of success, the divisions are effectively separate business entities.

When using market prices, it is essential that the transfer price should be no higher than the buying centre would have to pay on the market. Otherwise, it is evident that an imbalance will be created between the interests of the selling and the buying centres. The existence of an independent market price imposes an upper limit to the transfer price, for given that the selling centre is able to sell at that price, the buying centre should be compelled to buy internally rather than to purchase from external suppliers.

A number of problems arise from the use of the market price as the basis for the transfer price. Thus, changes in supply may lead to large price changes, and the recognition of these changes will cause large variations in the transfer price. As a result, a degree of instability will be introduced in the control mechanism. Further problems are associated with the weight which should be attached to different market price rulings during the transfer period, and to such other factors affecting market prices, such as quantity discounts, area and trade channel differentials, transportation and delivery allowances and service factors. The market price also reflects the result of a bargain, and a reconciliation between what one has to accept to effect a sale, and what one has to pay to effect a purchase. The effects of relative bargaining positions on the market price have implications for the transfer price selected—should it favour the selling or the buying division?

Hence the determination of a fair market price for establishing a viable transfer pricing system which will satisfy the three criteria which have been stipulated, calls for a solution to the various problems mentioned above. In many cases, the solution may be arrived at only by an independent arbitrator. This process immediately undermines the third criterion—the preservation of the autonomy of individual divisions—and results in the establishment of a negotiated price.

Cost-based transfer pricing

In many cases, the transfer of products between profit centres involves intermediate goods in respect of which an external market does not exist. In such cases, it is necessary to use cost-based transfer prices.

A common problem which may arise in employing cost-based transfer prices is that they may conceal inefficiencies in the activities of the selling centre. It is essential, therefore, that the transfer price should be based on standard costs rather than actual costs. As we shall see in the following chapter, the standard cost represents what an item should cost to produce rather than what it does cost, that is, it excludes inefficiences which have arisen in production. Hence, the use of standard costs prevents inefficiencies which have occurred in one profit centre from being transferred to another profit centre.

As we mentioned in Chapter 34, there are different kinds of cost-based prices. Two commonly used cost-related prices are full-cost and variable- (or marginal-) cost prices.

Full-cost transfer pricing

The major disadvantage of using full cost, or rather full cost plus a profit percentage, as a transfer price is that this method may encourage managers to make decisions which are not in the interest of the firm as a whole.

(Negative)

Example

The following data relates to profit centre A which sells to profit centre B at full cost plus a profit percentage:

Profit centre	A	B	
	£	£	£
Variable costs	10	30 +	10
Fixed costs	10		10
Mark-up (50%)	10		25
Total unit cost	30		75

Profit centre B treats the input of £30 from profit centre A as a variable cost. Hence, before profit centre B is able to have a contribution margin (defined, it will be remembered, as the excess of sales revenue over variable costs which contributes to fixed costs and profits) it must be able to sell its own output at £40 a unit. It is clear, however, that as far as the firm as a whole is concerned, total variable costs per unit are only £20. Given that both profit centres have spare capacity, it is in the firm's interest that profit centre B should produce and sell if it can obtain a price of £20 or over per unit for its output. If it regards £40 as its minimum acceptable price, the firm will lose the benefit of a contribution margin which otherwise it would have had.

In addition to the limitations of full-cost transfer pricing illustrated by the previous example, the use of full costs as a basis for transfer pricing may import a rigidity in an organization which contradicts the rationale for establishing profit centres. Managers should be able to control all the determinants of profits (selling price, volume, fixed and variable costs) if they are to be held responsible for profits. Thus, in the example given above, the manger of profit centre A may feel that his output is constrained by the obligation to sell to profit centre B at a transfer price of £30 a unit. Furthermore, his production is also dependent upon the sales volume attained by profit centre B. This volume may be too low to enable profit centre A to achieve a satisfactory profit, and the manager of that profit centre may well wish to sell his output outside the firm, if he is able to, at varying prices.

Therefore, the rigidity imposed on a firm by virtue of the inflexibility of an agreed full-cost transfer pricing system does not provide a sound basis for the delegation of decisions to profit centres.

Variable-cost transfer pricing

Transfer prices based upon variable cost are designed to overcome some of the problems stemming from the use of full-cost measurement. Thus, in the aforementioned example, profit centre A would have transferred to profit centre B at a unit price of £10. In the short run, when both profit centres have surplus capacity, this would enable centre B to adopt a more realistic pricing policy to the benefit of the organization as a whole. Such a decision, however, applies only in special circumstances. In the long run, transfer prices based upon variable costs are of little value for the purpose of performance evaluation, for they result in a loss to the selling division, and would impair the degree of motivation which is one of the reasons for decentralizing.

As we saw in Chapter 34, pricing policies should be based on differential costs and revenues of the company as a whole in order that better profit planning decisions may be made. This implies that decisions about the output volume of divisions cannot be determined independently, thereby undermining the autonomy of individual divisions.

Negotiated pricing

Whatever method the firm adopts for determining transfer prices, it is evident that some form of negotiated price must be agreed between the managers of profit centres if the transfer pricing system is to operate satisfactorily. It is assumed that independent negotiations between managers will produce results which are beneficial to the firm as a whole, and that the resolution of conflicts of interests will not reflect any bias in favour of any particular groups. These assumptions are probably questionable for a number of reasons. First, transfer price negotiations are very time consuming, and may lead to a diversion of managerial interest from their own work as they get more involved in the negotiations. Second, conflicts which undoubtedly will occur may lead to recriminations and the involvement of top management as arbitrators may be required.

The advantages of transfer pricing

The various transfer pricing systems which we have examined seem fraught with problems and drawbacks. Nevertheless, these difficulties should be weighed against the advantages which may be derived from setting up profit centres. Equally, these difficulties do not amount to a substantial case for abandoning the practice of assigning transfer prices to inter-divisional products. Some value must be found and attached to each element of input and output for the purpose of effective organizational control. Without some form of transfer pricing, the whole structure of intra-departmental analysis and control would collapse.

Very few aids for planning and control are perfect. This is certainly true of transfer pricing. It should be recognized that no available transfer pricing system is likely to serve all the purposes for which it is needed. The limitations found present in any transfer pricing system should be recognized, and any results obtained should be interpreted in the full knowledge of those limitations.

Investment centres

Investment centres represent the ultimate stage in the decentralization of the decision-making process. Divisional managers are made responsible not only for cost goals (expense centres), profit contribution goals (profit centres), but also for elements of the capital invested in the division.

Investment centres extend the principles underlying profit centres by associating divisional profits with the capital invested in the divisions. The criterion most commonly employed for assessing the financial performance of investment centres is the return on capital employed (ROCE). It is a comprehensive measure of financial performance which enables comparisons to be made between companies and divisions for the purpose of evaluating the efficiency with which assets are utilized. The ROCE is calculated as follows:

$$\text{ROCE} = \frac{\text{Net profit before interest and tax}}{\text{Average capital invested}} \times 100$$

This formula may be extended so as to incorporate the ratio of net profit to sales, and the ratio of sales to capital employed (the rate of asset turnover).

$$\text{ROCE} = \frac{\text{NP PBIT}}{\text{Sales}} \times \frac{\text{Sales}}{\text{Average capital invested}} \times 100$$

The expanded formula is useful for focusing attention on the important elements which affect the ROCE. It implies that profitability may be improved in the following ways:

(a) by increasing the volume of sales
(b) by reducing total assets
(c) by reducing costs
(d) by improving the profit mark-up, for example by raising selling prices or improving the product mix.

The asset turnover will be improved by (a) and (b), and the profit margin by (c) and (d).

Example

The following table compares the sales, profit and capital employed for three divisions of a large organization. Their profit contribution is £50,000 in each case.

	Division A	Division B	Division C
Sales	£500,000	£500,000	£1,000,000
Net profit PBIT	£50,000	£50,000	£50,000
Capital employed	£250,000	£500,000	£500,000
Return on sales	10%	10%	5%
Asset turnover	2	1	2
ROCE	20%	10%	10%

It is clear that division A has the most effective financial performance since its ROCE of 20 per cent is higher than the ROCE of the other two divisions. Division B's return on sales, that is its profit margin, is equal to that of division A, but its asset turnover is half as high as A's, implying that it employs twice as much capital as A to earn the same profit. This position indicates that either sales could be improved or that excessive capital is being carried by division B, and that an investigation of asset use may reveal that plant and stocks could perhaps be reduced. Division C has the same ROCE as division B. Its margin on sales, however, is inferior to that of both other divisions, thereby indicating that selling prices may be too low or that operating costs may be too high.

The foregoing example shows that a ROCE analysis may isolate factors requiring investigation. These factors are illustrated in Fig. 5.30.

Problems associated with ROCE measurements of performance
Three major problems arise as a result of employing ROCE measures for assessing divisional performance. They stem from the following factors:

(a) the measurement of profit and capital employed
(b) the appropriation of costs and assets as between divisions
(c) the limitations inherent in ROCE.

The measurement of profit and capital employed
The use of ROCE measures of performance for comparing the performance of similar divisions requires measurements of profit and capital employed which are free from any accounting bias. Thus, uniform accounting procedures should be established for valuing inventory, and charging against profit such costs as depreciation, research and development and advertising costs. If comparisons are to be meaningful, the effect of price level changes should also be eliminated from accounting measurements. Moreover, profit and capital employed as measured by conventional accounting methods tend to reflect a much better rate of return than is the case. The valuation of assets on a historic cost basis means that the assets forming the capital investment base is a composite of assets of different monetary dimensions. It follows that the same problem applies to the measurement of costs applied to current revenues for profit calculation.

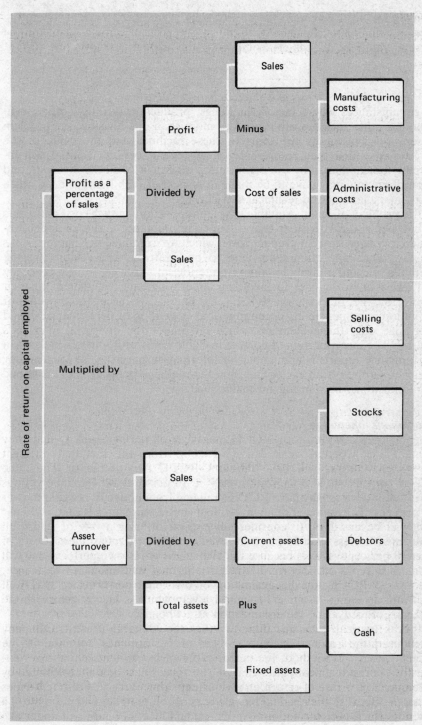

Fig. 5.30 Relationship of factors influencing the rate of return on capital employed.

In order to overcome these problems, therefore, current operating revenues should be associated with the current costs of earning them, and the current value of the assets comprising the capital employed in current operations.

The appropriation of costs and assets as between divisions
In circumstances where factory buildings, production facilities, office, canteen and other facilities are shared by more than one division, the problem arises of apportioning the costs of these facilities and the value of the investment which they respresent. In any event, certain facilities will invariably be conducted by the·organization on behalf of all the divisions, and apportionments may have to be made in respect of such items as head office costs, management and technical services, etc.

The problem of finding suitable bases for apportioning such costs and assets as between several divisions bears a strong resemblance to that of apportioning factory overheads to product costs, which we examined in Chapter 27. As we saw, such apportionments tend to be arbitrary, and seldom are the methods selected entirely immune from criticism.

There is a strong case for avoiding apportionments, whether of costs or assets for the purpose of ROCE calculations. In accordance with our definition of responsibility accounting, the evaluation of performance should recognize only those elements which are under the divisional manager's control. The incorporation of non-controllable items with controllable ones in performance reports is admissible for information purposes, so long as they are distinguished from each other, and the fundamental principles enshrined in responsibility accounting are maintained.

Limitations inherent in ROCE
The main disadvantage of ROCE measures of performance is that they contain a conceptual weakness. This stems from the fact that different investment centres will have different ROCE measurements. Thus, the ROCE for the whole organization may be 10 per cent, whereas the various investment centres may have ROCE's ranging from under 10 per cent to over 10 per cent. The manager of an investment centre enjoying a ROCE of 15 per cent will be unwilling to consider any project offering a rate of return on investment of less than 15 per cent, even though it offers a rate of return of over 10 per cent. This is because the evaluation of his own performance will be made in terms of the current ROCE for his own investment centre. Hence, the use of ROCE for the evaluation of divisional performance may well motivate divisional managers to act in a way which is inconsistent with the financial objectives of the organization as a whole.

It was to deal with this difficulty that the General Electric Company introduced the residual income method of performance appraisal in the 1950s. Under this method, the performance of investment centres is evaluated by the residual profit after charging an appropriate amount calculated by reference to the rate of return on investment being earned by different types of assets. Because the residual income is an absolute figure and not a ratio, a division which is trying to improve its residual income figure will undertake investment programmes even where the expected rate of return is less than the current ROCE.

Example

The net assets (total assets — current liabilities) of a division are valued at £1000. The company has decided that a return of 10 per cent on these net assets is an appropriate target. The division's income statement for the current year is given below:

Revenue	£1000
Less costs	700
	300
Less taxes	150
Income after taxes	150
Capital charge (10%)	100
Residual income	£50

If the manager of this division were evaluated on the ROCE basis, he would not invest in a project which produced a return of below 30 per cent, i.e.

$$\frac{£300}{£1000} \times 100$$

However, if he were evaluated on residual income he would invest in a project which gives a return above 10 per cent because this will increase residual income. This action will be beneficial to the company.

Summary

Control and planning are integrated processes which affect every aspect of organizational activity, including the determination of objectives and the development of long-range and short-range plans. The comparison of actual performance with the goals stipulated in these plans discloses the extent to which they have been attained.

Responsibility accounting underpins the control process, and requires the establishment of responsibility centres throughout an organization. A responsibility centre is a segment of an organization where an individual manager is held responsible for the segment's performance.

Responsibility centres may take three forms:

(i) expense centres in which the manager has no control over revenue but is able to control expenditure;

(ii) profit centres where the manager has control over both revenue and costs;

(iii) investment centres where the manager has responsibility not only for revenues and costs but also for the capital invested.

The control problem is made more complex by the size of business organizations and the occurrence of transactions between various divisions of such organizations. In order that divisional performance should be accurately assessed for control purposes, transfer prices should be established which will be useful in this respect. If transfer pricing systems are to operate satisfactorily, some form of negotiated pricing must be agreed by divisional managers. Investment centres pose additional problems as regards the assessment of financial performance. The ROCE is a comprehensive measure of performance, but its limitations should be understood.

Questions

1. Electrical Products Company consists of four operating divisions. Divisional managers are granted considerable discretion in setting employment, sales and production policies. For some time the Chairman, Ronald Jackson, has been concerned with the method of evaluating divisional performance. On 1 June 19X2, he wrote the following letter to Miles French, a management consultant:

Dear Mr French,
   We have been trying to develop a system which will provide an incentive to our division managers and act as a basis for evaluating their effectiveness. Originally we used profit as an index for evaluation. Then we realized that, in order to be meaningful, profit should be related to another index such as profits of prior periods. After giving the matter much thought I have now become convinced that only a composite index, as shown below, will give equal weights to the three principal objectives of a division.

Composite index for evaluating division performance

Objective	Criterion	Last year	This year	% Change
Minimize capital	Capital turnover	1.5	1.7	+ 13
Profitability	Return on sales	10.0%	9.0%	− 10
Growth	Share of market	15.0%	15.6%	+ 4
	Net composite change			+ 7%

I propose to offer each division manager a bonus of £200 for each one per cent increase in the composite index. I aim to present this proposal to the board at the October meeting, and, if approved, start the system next year.
   Please let me have an evaluation of this plan in writing.
                              Yours sincerely,
                              Ronald Jackson.

Required:

   Assuming you are the consultant, write a letter to Mr Jackson evaluating the proposal.

2. The Akroid Corporation Ltd is a divisionalized enterprise manufacturing specialized equipment for the construction industry. Division A makes one of the basic components—the Spikron—which is used by Division B in the manufacture of the Akroid Scraper, which is then sold as a final product. Division B absorbs about three-quarters of the total output of Division A. The Spikron has other applications, and Division A has been selling the remaining 25 per cent of its output to outside firms. The annual output of Spikrons is 16,000 units. The Spikron is transferred at £350 to Division B, and is sold at £400 to outside firms.

The following costs are associated with the Spikron produced in Division A:

	£
Variable costs at £300 per unit	4,800,000
Fixed costs	200,000
Total costs	5,000,000

A German company makes a similar product to the Spikron, which could be adapted for integration into the Akroid Scraper, and has offered to supply Divison B with the adapted product at a cost of £320 per unit.

The Manager of Division B wishes to buy the German product as this will substantially reduce his costs, and make his own product more competitive on the market. The Manager of Division A argues that he would not be able to expand his sales of the Spikron to outside firms, and that, as a result, the profitability of his division would be seriously affected.

Required:

Discuss the implications of the German offer from the point of view of the Akroid Corporation Ltd and of both divisions.

37 Standard costs and variance analysis

We turn now to a consideration of an important method of establishing standards of performance by the use of standard costs. The difficulty about using data recorded in the financial accounting system for planning purposes is that it relates to the past and although managers are interested in the results of previous decisions, they are primarily concerned with decisions which will affect the future.

For control purposes, historical costs are of little use. Particularly in times of inflation, past experience will not inform management whether an operation, a job or a department costs too much. Indeed, what management wishes to know is not what costs were in the past but what they ought to be, in the present. Once it has been determined what these costs ought to be, actual costs can be compared with them, and any difference may be analysed.

Standard costing has been evolved as a method to meet this need. It relies upon predetermined costs which are agreed as representing acceptable costs under specified operating conditions.

In Chapter 21, it was seen that the existence of a standard costing system could facilitate the system of current cost accounting for a manufacturing company. In effect, if standard costs are revised regularly to reflect current conditions, they are—to all intents and purposes—current costs. A company that bases its cost accounting system on standard costs will be able to obtain the cost of sales directly from the addition of variances to the standard costs.

Standard costs and budgeted costs

The principal differences between standard costs and budgeted costs lie in their scope. Whilst both are concerned with laying down cost limits for control purposes, budget costs impose total limits to costs for the firm as a whole, for departments or for functions for the budget period, whereas standard costs are attached to products and to individual manufacturing operations or processes. For example, the production department's budget for the period ahead may envisage a total production of 100,000 units at a cost of £10 a unit, so that the production department will be allocated an expenditure ceiling of £1 million. The unit cost of £10 will have been based upon the established standard costs relating to material usage and price, labour usage and labour costs as well as allocated overhead costs. Standard costs are revised when it is clear that they have ceased to be realistic in terms of current costs.

The relationship between budgeted costs and standard costs is clear: the setting of standard costs as performance standards for control purposes implies that they must be used as a basis for drawing up budget statements and calculating budget costs, for otherwise there can be no confidence in their use as a basis against which actual performance may be measured.

Applications of standard costing

Standard costing is a useful method of control in a number of ways. First, the process of evaluating performance by determining how efficiently current operations are being carried out may be facilitated by the process of management by exception. Very often the problem facing management is the time lost in sifting large masses of feedback information and in deciding what information is significant and relevant to the control problem. Management by exception overcomes this problem by highlighting only the important control information, that is the variances between the standard set and the actual result. This process allows management to focus attention on important problems so that maximum energy may be devoted to correcting situations which are falling out of control.

Second, a standard costing system may lead to cost reductions. The installation of such a system demands a re-appraisal of current production methods as it necessitates the standardization of practices. This examination often leads to an improvement in the methods employed which is reflected in a reduction of the costs of the product. One example of cost reductions through increased efficiency may be seen in the simplication of the clerical procedures relating to inventory control. All similar items of inventory may be recorded in the accounts at a uniform price; this eliminates the need which arises under historical costing for re-calculating a new unit price whenever a purchase of inventory is made at a different price.

Third, standard costs are used as a basis for determining selling prices. Standard costs represent what the product should cost, and are a much better guide for pricing decisions than historical costs which may contain purchasing and production inefficiencies which cannot be recouped in competitive markets.

Finally, perhaps the most important benefit which may be derived from a standard costing system is the atmosphere of cost consciousness which is fostered among executives and foremen. Each individual is aware that the costs and output for which he is responsible are being measured, and that he will be called on to take whatever action is necessary should large variances occur. As we concluded earlier in this chapter, if the philosophy of top management is positive and supportive, standard costing may act as an incentive to individuals to act in the best interest of the firm. Moreover, a standard costing system which allows subordinates to participate in setting the standards fosters a knowledge of costing down to shop floor level, and assists in decision making at all levels. Thus, if there should occur spoilt work necessitating a decision from the foreman in charge on whether to scrap or rectify the part involved, a knowledge of costs will enable him to make the best decision.

Setting cost standards

The setting of cost standards is no easy task. If they are set too high, for example, large variances will appear and in the degree that production managers consider them to be unrealistic so they will tend to ignore them. If standards are set too low, however, they will not act as incentives to efficiency and production efficiency may fall. The best standards are those which are set at levels which though high are nevertheless attainable, so that they will encourage efficient performance.

The process of setting cost standards requires the standardization of all the elements affecting a product so that specific standards for these elements may be established prior to its actual production. There are two component parts of this process: the determination of a physical standard and the selection of an appropriate value to be attached to the physical standard. This problem may be examined in the context of establishing standard costs for raw materials and labour, which are the two major direct costs of production.

Standard costs for raw materials

Most companies rely on engineering studies for calculations of the quantities of raw materials required for each unit of the product. If different types of raw materials are required, a bill of materials is drawn up which itemizes the standard quantities of each type of raw material required for a specific unit of the product. The computation of the quantities required should include an allowance for inevitable (i.e., normal) wastage in production, for example, those which arise due to machining, evaporation or expected breakages.

The purchasing manager should bear the responsibility for providing information regarding the prices of raw materials. These prices are not the historical prices which have been recorded as costs in the books: they are forecasts of expected prices during the period for which the standard costs are to apply, and they are essentially predetermined prices.

Standard costs for direct labour

Standard labour costs also consist of two components—quantity and price. Firstly, standard labour grades are established which take into account the various skills required to perform the operations involved in production. Time and motion studies are employed to set labour standards which reflect the labour hours which should be spent by each grade of labour in each department to manufacture the finished product. If there are several types of product, these calculations must be made for each product.

Secondly, wage rates must be applied to the labour hours in order to calculate a unit cost of labour for each unit of product. Once again, these wage rates are not the current or past wage rates but the forecast of the expected wage rates which will prevail during the period when the standard costs are to be valid.

Variance analysis

As we mentioned earlier in this chapter, the use of standard costs simplifies the control of performance for if standard costs are correctly set one needs only to be concerned with the differences or variances between actual costs and standard costs. We mentioned in this connection the method of management by exception as the appropriate means of controlling operations by variance analysis. In a general sense, the aim of variance analysis is to investigate variances to ascertain whether they are justified or unjustified. If they are justified either because estimates of quantities of input resources or input prices are wrong, clearly the standard costs must be adjusted. If, however, they are unjustified, the causes for these variances must be investigated and corrective action taken.

It is the accountant's function to assist in the evaluation of performance where a standard costing system is in operation, and he will calculate the variances by comparing actual costs of production with their standard costs. As the standard costs are made up of two components—quantity and price, so too does variance analysis seek to ascertain whether the variances are due to quantity differences or price differences. Let us consider in turn the calculation of direct material and direct labour variances.

Direct material variances

Example

A firm manufactures decorative plates from aluminium. The standard costs for raw materials in respect of each plate were estimated as follows:

Quantity	3 lb
Price	£0.50 per lb

During the period under review, 4000 plates were produced, and the following information was obtained:

Quantity used	11,000 lb
Quantity purchased	15,000 lb
Purchase price	£0.55 per lb

The following points are immediately brought to our attention:

(a) *Price*. The purchase price turned out to be 5 pence per lb higher than estimated.

(b) *Quantity*. An output of 4000 plates should have required a consumption of 12,000 lb of aluminium, according to the standard usage on which the standard cost of £1.50 per plate was estimated. As only 11,000 lb were actually used, a saving in material usage of 1000 lb was realized.

The accounting analyses of these differences are made in terms of a material price variance and a material usage variance, as follows.

Material price variance
This variance shows the difference between the actual cost of materials and

their standard cost, and is best calculated when raw materials are purchased and before they are committed to production. In this way, the variance is highlighted at the earliest possible stage so that action may be taken immediately to deal with future purchases should it turn out to be necessary. For example, the buyer may have purchased at a high price, while alternative sources may be available at the old price. A further advantage of this method is that it enables inventory to be valued in the accounts at standard cost, thereby reducing the clerical effort which is necessary if inventory is valued at actual cost. The material price variance results, therefore, from a comparison of the price of raw materials purchased with an estimate of what these purchases should have cost. The material price variance is calculated as follows:

Actual quantity of material purchased × price variance per lb,
i.e., 15,000 lb × £(0.55 − 0.50)

$$= £750$$

Since material purchase costs were greater than estimated by the standard, the variance is an unfavourable one.

Material usage variance
This variance expresses the difference between the actual quantities used to manufacture the actual output and the standard quantities envisaged for that output. For the reasons stated above, price variances are normally calculated first and this eliminates the influence of price variations from the calculation of the material usage variance. The variance is calculated after production has occurred when the difference between the amount of material used, and what should have been used in manufacturing the output produced is known. The material usage variance is expressed as follows:

Variance in quantity used × standard price per lb
i.e., 1000 lb × £0.50
= £500.

Since the material usage is less than anticipated it is a favourable usage variance.

Direct labour variances

Example

The standard costs for labour in respect of each plate were determined as follows:

Standard time per plate	0.25 hour
Standard rate for labour	£1.00 per hour

The actual output of 4000 plates was conducted under the following conditions:

Labour hours worked	900 hours
Actual rate	£1.10 per hour

Analysis. As in the calculation of direct material variances, this analysis is concerned with a price variance and a usage variance. The wage rate variance expresses the difference between standard wage set and the actual wage paid. The labour usage variance relates to the amount of labour required to produce the output as against the standard, and it is called the labour efficiency variance. The following differences appear immediately:

(a) The actual rate of pay turned out to be higher than the standard rate to the extent of 10 pence per hour.
(b) The standard labour costs were based on a standard time of 0.25 hour per plate, so that the output of 4000 plates should have taken 1000 hours. As only 900 hours were taken, there has been a more efficient use of labour.

We may calculate the wage rate and labour efficiency variances as follows.

Wage rate variance
This variance shows the impact of an increase in the wage rate over the rate which should have been incurred in relation to the output. We note, therefore, a similarity between the material price variance and the wage rate variance in that both are concerned with the net impact of price changes. In this instance, we are concerned with calculating the effect of the higher wage rate on the number of labour hours actually used.

$$\text{Actual labour hours} \times \text{Wage rate variance per hour}$$
$$\text{i.e., } 900 \times £(1.10 - 1.00)$$
$$= £90$$

The wage rate variance is an unfavourable one in the sense that had the output been obtainable at the standard wage, the total wage cost would have been £90 less.

Labour efficiency variance
The labour efficiency variance is calculated by finding the difference between the actual number of hours worked and that estimated by the standard, and multiplying this difference by the standard wage rate. The formula is as follows:

$$\text{Labour variance} \times \text{Standard wage rate per hour}$$
$$\text{i.e., } 100 \text{ hours} \times £1.00 \text{ per hour}$$
$$= £100$$

This variance is a favourable one, since it took fewer hours to produce the output.

The control of overheads

We have so far examined the control problem in two different senses. Firstly, we have looked at the annual budget as laying down the targets of performance in the short-term in respect of the activities of departments and functions. In providing a short-term planning framework, budget plans place limits upon the expenditure which the different departments may undertake or in other words the costs which they may incur. The objective of budgetary control systems is to control these costs. Secondly, we examined standard costing as a means of controlling the unit costs of production. We stressed, however, that because budget plans are based upon these standard costs, adherence to standards is necessary if budgeted plans are to be realized.

In Chapter 30, we drew a distinction between budgetary planning and budgetary control. We stressed that the two management processes of planning and control demanded the construction of different types of budgets, because the type of budget which may be suitable for planning may be inappropriate for control purposes. Earlier in the present chapter, we noticed that the higher one ascends the hierarchy of management, the greater the proportion of total costs which is defined as controllable cost. Therefore, at the Board level it is possible to use a planning budget as a control device, because at this level all costs are controllable. Below this level, management will be interested in only those deviations over which they have control. It is necessary that a measure of flexibility is built into control budgets which will reflect operating conditions which may be different from those envisaged in the planning stages.

In this section we analyse the control problem created by changes in the planned volume of production during the budget period. In Chapter 32, we classified all costs as falling into two categories—fixed costs and variable costs. The characteristics of these costs are such that changes in the total volume of production affect them, but affect them in a different way. Thus, variable costs vary with the volume of output, and if the volume of production should rise or fall so will variable costs. Therefore, we may say that changes in the volume of output will affect budgeted costs in the sense that the total budgeted variable costs will be affected by volume changes. The control problem regarding fixed costs is the reverse. In the short term, we assume that fixed costs will remain constant: this implies that budgeted fixed costs will not vary irrespective of variations in the volume of output which may not, of course, exceed the productive capacity.

For these various reasons, the control of overheads requires a method of control which takes into account the possibility of changes in the volume of production during the planning period. It is very rare that actual output equals budgeted output, and ideally one would wish to devise a system which, taking into account changes in the volume of production, will enable a comparison to be made between the actual overhead costs of production at that level of output and the budgeted costs which have been allowed for the level of output attained. The accounting method for dealing with this problem is flexible budgeting.

Flexible budgeting

As a means of controlling costs at fluctuating levels of output, the aim of flexible budgeting is to answer the question we posed for calculating direct material and direct labour variances: 'What should this output have cost to produce?' The determination of this amount enables appropriate variances to be calculated by comparing this cost with the actual cost incurred.

Example

An assembly department produced 5000 units of output during a period, and the budgeted factory overhead costs at that level of output were as follows:

Indirect material	£5000
Indirect labour	2500
Repairs and maintenance	5000
Insurance	1500
Rates	3000
Depreciation	3000
	£20,000

The overhead costs per unit are:

£20,000 ÷ 5000 = £4

These costs added to the direct material standard costs and the direct labour standard costs would indicate what costs of production should be incurred in a situation where the actual volume of production is the same as the planned volume of production.

If it were possible to contemplate in the budget plan different levels of output so as to meet possible changes in market demand during the planning period, we could not say that the departmental overhead costs per unit would remain at £4. We could not assume that departmental overhead costs would be as follows:

6000 units	£24,000
7000 units	28,000
8000 units	32,000

Overhead costs of production do not behave in this way, for they consist of fixed elements as well as variable elements; in the above computations we have assumed that all the costs are variable.

Therefore, an analysis is needed of the fixed and variable elements. We will assume that this revealed the following:

	Fixed costs	Variable costs per unit
Indirect materials		£1.0
Indirect labour		0.5
Repairs and maintenance	£2000	0.6
Insurance	500	0.2
Rates	3000	
Depreciation	3000	
	£8500	£2.3

This analysis enables us to calculate the total overhead costs which should be incurred at different levels of output, by means of a budget allowance the formula for which is:

Budget allowance = Total fixed costs + (Unit variable costs × Units produced)

Hence, for an output of 4000 units, the cost control budget would be calculated as follows:

	Total variable costs	Fixed costs	Total budget allowance
Indirect materials	£4000		£4000
Indirect labour	2000		2000
Repairs and maintenance	2400	£2000	4400
Insurance	800	500	1300
Rates		3000	3000
Depreciation		3000	3000
	£9200	£8500	£17,700

It follows that it may be possible to establish budget allowances for a range of output, assuming that the same fixed and variable cost information is valid for that range of output, as follows:

Output (units)	3000	4000	5000	6000
Indirect material	£3000	£4000	£5000	£6000
Indirect labour	1500	2000	2500	3000
Repairs and maintenance	3800	4400	5000	5600
Insurance	1100	1300	1500	1700
Rates	3000	3000	3000	3000
Depreciation	3000	3000	3000	3000
	£15,400	£17,700	£20,000	£22,300
Overhead costs per unit	£5.1	£4.4	£4.0	£3.7

These calculations illustrate the nature of overhead cost behaviour over a range of output: variable overhead costs increase as output increases but fixed costs remain constant. As a result, total overhead costs per unit fall as output expands.

The advantage of flexible budgets over fixed budgets for control

In circumstances where changes in the volume of output are likely to occur, a fixed budget will be irrelevant to a solution of the control problem. The failure to recognize and provide for the different behaviour of fixed and variable overhead costs would be reflected in faulty comparisons being employed.

Consider the case where the planning budget called for the production of 5000 units, but that only 4500 units were produced during the period. Actual costs of production are those shown in column 1 in the table on p. 593. If we use a fixed budget for control purposes, we would compare the original budget (column 3) with the actual costs of production (column 1). This is shown in column 4, where an overall gain of £850 is disclosed. One might conclude from these computations that the control of costs had been better than planned.

Our previous discussion would lead us to compare the actual costs with the budget allowance for the level of output attained. The allowance is shown in column 2, and the comparison between the budget allowance and the costs of production shows that what appeared to be a gain of £850 is in fact a loss of £300. The use of fixed budgets therefore for control purposes, conceals changes in cost due to volume changes.

	(1) Actual cost of production	(2) Total budget allowance	(3) Original budget	(4) Variation from original budget	(5) Variation from budget allowance
Units produced	4500	4500	5000	(1 − 3)	(1 − 2)
Indirect materials	£4700	£4500	£5000	£300F	£200U
Indirect labour	2400	2250	2500	100F	150U
Repairs and maintenance	4600	4700	5000	400F	100F
Insurance	1450	1400	1500	50F	50U
Rates	3000	3000	3000	—	—
Depreciation	3000	3000	3000	—	—
	£19,150	£18,850	£20,000	£850F	£300U

The analysis of overhead variances

An important conclusion which emerges from the previous section is that the flexible budget alone does not supply all the answers which are necessary for evaluating performance. For example, does the unfavourable variance for indirect labour represent higher wage rates or an inefficient use of labour? If realistic responsibilities for variances are to be established it is necessary to analyse overhead variances in greater detail. The use of overhead variances enables us to extend the analysis of variations from the budget.

In Chapter 27 we considered the problem of choosing a suitable volume base for recovering overheads. So far in this chapter we have conducted our analysis in terms of units of output. However, most concerns manufacture several products and this creates difficulties with regard to the recovery of overheads. As we noted in the earlier chapter, if products are different a uniform overhead charge such as the unit of production method may result in incorrect costing. This problem may be overcome by the use of standard hours. A standard hour is a unit of output which measures the amount of work which should be performed in one hour. Therefore, the output of many products is reduced to a common denominator, and from now on we will consider output in standard hours rather than units.

Variable overhead variance analysis

In Chapter 27 we noted that two overhead rates are usually established—a variable overhead rate and a fixed overhead rate. This distinction is important with regard to variance analysis, and makes the analysis of overhead variances somewhat more complicated.

Example

Let us assume that the assembly department is budgeted for an output of 5000 standard hours. Actual hours worked were 4800 and the variable costs incurred were as follows:

Indirect materials	£5200
Indirect labour	2400
Repairs and maintenance	3200
Insurance	800
Total variable costs	£11,600

There are two variances for variable overheads which must be ascertained; firstly the difference between the budget allowance based upon the actual hours worked and the actual expenses incurred, which is called the spending variance. Secondly, an efficiency variance must be calculated to show the difference between the standard hours allowed and the actual hours worked, multiplied by the standard overhead rate.

The formulae for these variances are as follows:

Spending variance: (Actual hours at actual cost) − (Actual hours at the standard cost)
Efficiency variance: (Standard hours at the standard cost) − (Actual hours at the standard cost)

Example

We may calculate these variances for the assembly department given that the variable costs per standard hour is £2.3 at a budgeted output of 5000 standard hours, as follows:

Spending variance:
(4800 hours at £11,600) − (4800 hours at £2.3 per hour)
= £11,600 − £11,040
= £560

As overhead costs were higher than the budget allowance, the variance is an unfavourable one.

Efficiency variance:
(5000 hours at £2.3 per hour) − (4800 hours at £2.3 per hour)
= £11,500 − £11,040
= £460

As the number of hours worked was less than the standard hours allowed, the efficiency variance is a favourable one.

It is possible to extend this analysis to the breakdown of all the individual items of overhead costs represented in the total overhead costs analysed above. The variances for the individual items may be calculated as follows:

	(1) Actual costs	(2) Actual hours at standard cost	(3) Standard hours at standard cost	(4) Spending variance (1 – 2)	(5) Efficiency variance (3 – 2)
Indirect materials	£5200	£4800	£5000	£400 U	£200 F
Indirect labour	2400	2400	2500	—	100 F
Repairs and maintenance	3200	2880	3000	320 U	120 F
Insurance	800	960	1000	160 F	40 F
	£11,600	£11,040	£11,500	£560 U	£460 F

The breakdown of the total spending variance over the individual elements of overhead variable costs discloses how much expenditures on these elements have varied from the budgeted amounts. For some items, the variance may include both usage and price elments.

The efficiency variance, on the other hand, does not represent efficiency in the use of overhead costs. Instead, it measures efficiency in the use of the factor used to recover overhead, in this case direct labour.

Fixed overhead variance analysis

Our discussion of flexible budgeting illustrated that it is the variable cost element which necessitates the computation of allowances over various ranges of output; and that fixed costs remain constant over a relevant range.

The difference between budgeted fixed costs and actual fixed costs gives the fixed overhead budget variance (also called spending variance). Using again the example of our assembly department, and assuming that actual fixed costs incurred are those shown in the table on p. 591, we may prepare a variance report as follows:

	Actual	Budget	Variance
Repairs and maintenance	£2100	£2000	£100 U
Insurance	600	500	100 U
Rates	3200	3000	200 U
Depreciation	3000	3000	
	£8900	£8500	£400 U

Another fixed overhead variance occurs when absorption costing methods are employed. As we discussed in Chapter 27, the use of an absorption costing system necessitates the recovery of fixed overheads by a predetermined rate. In that chapter we examined also the problem of choosing an activity level to enable the recovery of fixed overheads to be made. In our present example the normal (or standard) level of activity is 5000 hours and the standard rate for recovering fixed overheads is £1.7 per standard hour (£8500 ÷ 5000). If in a period, the standard hours allowed for the output were

4800, the fixed overhead for the period would be under-absorbed by 200 standard hours multiplied by the standard rate, viz.

$$200 \times £1.7 = 340$$

This is an unfavourable volume variance.

Sales variance analysis and the control of revenue

In general terms, the procedures appropriate for the control of revenue are similar to those applied to the control of costs, and may be summarized as follows:

(a) The establishment of a sales plan.
(b) The prompt determination and reporting of variances between actual and planned performance.
(c) The investigation and analysis of variances so as to ascertain their causes and those responsible for them.
(d) The implementation of appropriate corrective action.

The determination of the sales plan has both long-range and budgetary aspects. Long-range planning will be concerned with establishing revenue objectives and goals, from which may be derived specific sales targets and prices for the budget planning period. Since the level of demand for most products exhibits a seasonal pattern, the annual sales plan should be divided into smaller periods so as to make possible a system of responsibility accounting based on a meaningful comparison of actual and planned performance.

So far, we have discussed the control of revenue in terms of analysing the difference between actual and planned sales. It should be apparent, however, that management is not really so much concerned about sales themselves as the profit from sales. It is for this reason that sales variance analysis has been developed to measure the effects on profits of variances between actual sales and planned sales, and not the effect of such variances merely on revenue.

Three different variances are commonly applied to the analysis of sales:

(a) Sales price variance
(b) Sales volume variance
(c) Sales mix variance.

Sales price variance

It is quite common for actual selling prices to differ from the planned selling price. Numerous factors may be responsible for sales price variances, such as the need to adjust prices to meet competition, or to provide a new marketing strategy. By far the largest factor is the discretion allowed to individual sales managers to adjust prices to meet particular circumstances, such as price reductions for slightly spoiled goods or to secure the goodwill of a client.

The sales price variance is an ordinary price variance of the type which we have already discussed. It may be calculated from the following formula:

Sales price variance = Units sold × (Actual contribution per unit less the standard contribution)

It indicates, therefore, the total effect on profit of differences between set prices and the prices at which goods were actually sold.

Sales volume variance

This variance discloses the effect on profits of differences between the planned sales volume and the actual volume of sales. It is calculated as follows:

Sales volume variance = Standard contribution per unit
× (Actual number of units sold − Budgeted units of sales)

Sales mix variance

As we saw in Chapter 32, a change in the product mix may change the profitability of the total mix if the contribution margin of the different products is different. In these circumstances, changes in the product mix will lead to a variance between planned and actual profits. The dimension of this variance may be computed as follows:

Sales mix variance = Standard contribution per unit of each product ×
(Actual quantities of units sold − Actual total sales of units in budgeted mix proportions)

Example of all 3 variances

The following data relates to products X and Y sold by Biproducts Ltd during the quarter ended 31 December 19X0
Budgeted sales: X 5000 units at £10 (standard contribution margin £4)
Y 5000 units at £5 (standard contribution margin £2)

Actual sales: X 4000 units for £44,000 (i.e. £11 per unit)
Y 8000 units for £32,000 (i.e. £4 per unit)

These data may be tabulated as follows:

	(a) Actual contribution	(b) Actual quantity	(c) Standard contribution margin	(d) (b) × (c) Value	(e) Actual quantity in standard proportions	(f) Standard contribution margin	(g) (e) × (f) Value	(h) Budgeted margin
	£	Units	£	£	Units	£	£	£
X	20,000	4000	4	16,000	6000	4	24,000	20,000
Y	8000	8000	2	16,000	6000	2	12,000	10,000
	28,000	12,000		32,000	12,000		36,000	30,000

Notes
1. Column (a) is derived from the following formula:
   Actual contribution
   = Actual sales less (Actual units × Standard cost)

   $$= £44,000 - (4000 × £6)$$
   $$= \underline{\underline{£20,000}}$$

2. Column (e) is derived by taking total actual sales of 12,000 units and applying the budgeted mix proportions. According to the budget, 50 per cent of X and 50 per cent of Y should be sold. Total sales were 12,000 units, which expressed in budgeted mix proportions amount to 6000 units of X and 6000 units of Y.

The variances which may be extracted from these data are as follows:

(a) *Sales price variance*
   x = Units sold × (Actual contribution per unit less standard contribution)
   = Column (a) − column (d)
   = £28,000 − £32,000
   = £4000 U

   The sales price variance is unfavourable to the extent of £4000 because 3000 units of Y were sold at a price which was £1 lower than the standard, whilst only 1000 units of X were sold at a price which was £1 higher than the standard price.

(b) *Sales volume variance*
   X = Standard contribution per unit × (Actual number of units sold less budgeted units of sales)
   = Column (g) − column (h)
   = £36,000 − £30,000
   = £6000 F

   This variance reflects the fact that 12,000 units were actually sold as against a budgeted volume of only 10,000 units. Its value is the contribution which the extra 2000 units would have brought if they were at standard price and mix.

(c) *Sales mix variance*
   = (Standard contribution per unit of each product × The actual quantities of units sold) − (Standard contribution per unit of each product × Actual total sales in budgeted mix proportions)
   = Column (d) − Column (g)
   = £32,000 − £36,000
   = £4000 U

   This variance discloses the reduction in budgeted profits caused by selling a greater proportion of units having a lower contribution margin than the standard.

Responsibility for variances

We have stressed that under responsibility accounting only those costs incurred by a responsibility centre over which it can exercise control may be used as a basis for evaluation. Therefore, in variance analysis it is necessary that the precise cause of a variance be determined and that the cause be traced to the individual responsible. It is the function of the individual in charge of each responsibility centre to act promptly upon reports of variances which are within his control. Therefore, variances are not ends in themselves. Rather, they raise the questions why did the variance occur? What must be done to eliminate them? Obviously the importance of these questions depends on the significance of the deviations. We shall see how the significance of a variance is determined in the next section.

The material usage and labour efficiency variances respectively reveal that the quantities of material and labour used in production are either more or less than planned, depending on whether the variances are unfavourable or favourable. If more material is being used than planned, the cause may lie elsewhere than in the production department, for example in the purchase of inferior materials by the purchasing department. The fault, however, may lie in the production department and may be found to be attributable to careless supervision, or the use of untrained staff, or faulty machines. An unfavourable labour efficiency variance may be due to poor control by the foreman, bad labour relations, health factors, production delays, inferior tools and badly trained staff. Again the responsibility for the variance should be located. For example, if due to badly trained staff this may be caused by inefficiency on the part of the personnel department; but if, on the other hand the variance is caused by the economic conditions prevailing at the time which had produced a shortage of specialized labour, the variance is considered to be uncontrollable.

Price and wage rate variances may not be controllable by the firm, and this is particularly true of raw material prices and wages agreed nationally with trade unions. On the other hand variances may occur in the negotiation of contracts for materials which are the responsibility of the purchasing department. Purchasing department controls prices by getting several quotations, taking advantage of economic lots and securing cash discounts. Inefficiency in these areas will reveal unfavourable variances for which that department should be held responsible.

With regard to overhead variances, spending variances are usually the responsibility of the departmental head, because they are usually controllable by him. The volume variance is not normally controllable by the departmental manager; it is usually the responsibility of the sales department or production control.

The investigation of variances

Managerial time is too valuable to be wasted on the unnecessary checking of performance. When standard costs are properly established, they provide an automatic means of highlighting performance variances upon which management may concentrate its attention. Thus, the investigation of variances is concerned only with exceptional variances and not those which are minor deviations from the established standards.

The investigation of a variance is a three stage process consisting of:

(a) an investigation to determine whether the variance is significant;
(b) if it proves to be significant, its causes are investigated;
(c) if the variance can be corrected, action is taken to ensure that it will not occur in the future.

The determination of the significance of a variance in itself may be problematic. If its definition is left to managerial judgement and experience, inconsistencies may arise in the treatment of different variances solely by reason of behavioural factors affecting a manager's judgement of a situation. Thus, pressure of work in itself may lead him to perceive the significance of a variance as less important than it really is. Moreover, there is unlikely to be complete agreement between different managers about the investigation of borderline cases.

It is necessary, also, to distinguish 'chance' or 'random' variances from significant variances requiring investigation. By viewing the standard as an arithmetical mean about which fluctuations will occur, it is possible to eliminate random variances from significant variances. Experience of the investigation of variances shows that random variances are inherent in standard costing systems. Such variances assume the shape of a 'normal distribution' about the standard, and they are not controllable. It follows that a statistical control chart may be utilized to enable a manager to determine whether a variance is significant or not. It will define the limits within which random or normal variances occur, so that those variances which fall outside these limits may be assumed to be abnormal and, therefore, significant variances.

Statistical control charts have been used for many years for the purpose of quality control, but it is only recently that this technique has been applied to the control of standard cost variances. Statistical control charts permit the elimination of random variances whilst providing a high probability that non-random variances will be revealed.

The use of statistical control charts requires that upper and lower limits of random variance tolerance be laid down with precision. Setting these limits requires an analysis of the pattern of sample variances, and the standard deviation of the sample may be used to determine the acceptable limits of tolerance. These limits are illustrated in Fig. 5.31.

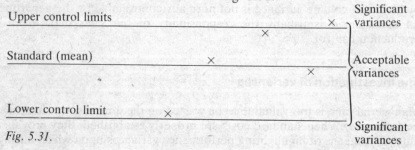

Fig. 5.31.

Opportunity cost variances

Developments in management science, in particular mathematical programming and computer science, have presented accountants with a considerable potential for extending the scope of standard costing by means of 'opportunity cost variances'. In this context, the opportunity cost variance is the variance which results from the failure to optimize profit by taking into consideration post-budget environmental changes. For example, if the price of a material used in the production process increases, the original plan may become sub-optimal, and losses may be incurred by adhering to the old (and no longer optimal) plan. As Demski (1968) points out, 'because of its emphasis on comparison between actual and planned results, and consequent disregard of changes in these planned results, the traditional accounting model does not act as an opportunity cost system'.

Linear programming affords a method of dealing with the opportunity cost problem, as defined above, but it does require changes in the traditional accounting information systems so that relevant information is made available. Thus, the detection of opportunity cost variances requires not only information about actual transactions, but also transactions which could have been made but were not made. Salkin and Kornbluth (1973) have stated this problem as follows:

'The standard costing system fails to account for opportunity losses because it is constructed without reference to the best possible plan or its alternative. . . . If we want to devise a system that recognizes opportunity losses in its control process, we must use an economic costing and control system, of which the linear programming model is a good example.'

The discussion of such a system is beyond the scope of this book, but interested readers should refer to the literature described in the bibliography.

Summary

Standard costing underlies most business activities. The cost of a product must be ascertained prior to production for pricing and control purposes. Standard costing may also lead to cost reductions. Perhaps the most important benefit which results from a standard costing system is the atmosphere of cost consciousness which is fostered among managers.

Standard cost data are compared with actual cost data for the purpose of ascertaining variances. Such variances are normally broken down into two basic components—quantity variances and price variances. The control of overhead costs as distinct from direct costs requires a method which takes into account the possibility of changes in the level of production during the planning period. Flexible budgeting affords such a method, and provides for each department a series of budget allowance schedules for various volume levels within the normal range of operations.

The ascertainment of variances is only the first stage in assessing results. Variances should be analysed in depth in order to establish whether they are significant, whether they are controllable and if so where responsibility lies.

At the same time, the analysis of variances enables established standards to be validated and methods for establishing standards in the future to be improved.

Standard costing not only provides a means of controlling costs but also monitoring revenue through the analysis of sales variances. Linear programming may allow the control process to be improved, providing that future developments in accounting information systems allow opportunity costs to be recorded.

References

1. Demski, J. S. 'Variance analysis using a constrained linear model', *in* Solomons, D. (ed.), *Studies in Cost Analysis*, 2nd ed., Sweet and Maxwell, London, 1968.
2. Salkin, G. & Kornbluth, J. *Linear Programming in Financial Planning*, Accountancy Age Books, 1973.

Questions

1. Some companies make comparisons of costs incurred in one period with those incurred in previous periods and interpret the deviations as evidence of favourable or unfavourable results of cost control. Discuss the usefulness of this practice.
2. For March 19X6 the master budget and actual results for Dept. A of a firm are as follows:

	Master budget	Actual
Output—Units A	600	500
Units B	400	500
	£	£
Costs: Materials	13,200	13,300
Direct labour	7000	8400
Machining	9600	9450
Overhead costs	4400	4400
	£34,200	£35,550

The master budget was constructed on the following production specifications:

1 Material required per unit—A, 4 lb; B, 5 lb.
2 Direct labour hours required per unit—A, 1 hour; B, 2 hours.
3 Machining costs include a variable element of £4 per machine hour. Machining time required per unit—A, 0.5 hours; B, 0.25 hours.
4 Overhead costs include a variable element of £1 per direct labour hour worked.

Required:
(a) Construct a flexible budget for the actual output and show any variances.
(b) If it is known that in fact 1400 direct labour hours were worked in January what further information about the direct labour variance can be given?

3. The Vitrox Manufacturing Co Ltd is a single product company and employs a standard absorption costing system. The standard cost per unit is calculated as follows:

	£
Direct labour 4 hrs at £3.00	12.00
Direct materials 10 lb at £1.00	10.00
Overhead costs at 25% of direct labour	3.00
Total standard cost per unit	25.00

The standard volume of output is 10,000 units per month. The variable overhead cost component is £1.00 per standard direct labour hour.

The following information is available for the month of December 19X1:

	£
Units completed	8,000
Direct materials used 83,000 lb at £1.05	87,150
Direct labour hours recorded 33,000 hrs at £3.10	102,300
Variable overhead costs incurred	32,500
Fixed overhead costs incurred	65,000

Required:
(*a*) Analyse the following variances:
   Direct material variances
   Direct labour variances
   Variable overhead variances
   Fixed overhead variances
(*b*) Explain possible reasons for the appearance of these variances.

38 The control of managed costs

Traditionally, cost accountants have been concerned with the control of manufacturing costs. In recent years, the rising proportion of non-manufacturing costs as a percentage of total costs has led to an increasing interest in the control of such costs. Non-manufacturing costs may be divided into three categories—administrative, marketing, and research and development costs. Because such costs are incurred at the discretion of management, they are often referred to as 'managed' or 'discretionary' costs.

As we saw in Chapter 37, it is possible to apply standards to estimates of manufacturing costs as a means of controlling them. In the case of direct labour costs, for example, engineering time studies determine the amount of labour time required for each operation, and the application of appropriate wage rates to labour time results in a monetary value for labour costs at a given level of output. Consequently, it is possible to establish a clear relationship between output levels and direct labour costs.

By contrast, the problem of controlling managed costs is made difficult by the absence of a method for determining appropriate cost levels since the benefits associated with these costs cannot always be measured in financial terms. Research and development costs, for example, may ultimately lead to the development of better products or production processes, but there is little if any direct connection between the costs incurred in any one year and the financial benefits attributable to such costs in that year. Similarly, advertising costs incurred in any one year are difficult to relate to any financial benefits directly attributable to such costs in that year.

This chapter is devoted to the consideration of the problem of controlling managed costs.

The control of administrative costs

We examined the nature of administrative costs in Chapter 27, and we noted that such costs are relatively fixed in the short run irrespective of short-term changes in the level of business activity.

As yet, the stricter costing procedures applied to manufacturing activities have not been applied generally to administrative activities. Management would certainly argue that administrative functions are not susceptible to work study methods. Nevertheless, certain tasks such as clerical ones are susceptible to work study, and some organizations have attempted to establish standards of efficiency by which to determine staff requirements. Examples of some of the control factors which have been employed are:

Activity	*Control factors*
Purchasing	No. of orders placed
Typing	No. of letters typed
Receipting cheques	No. of cheques received

Generally, however, administrative services are rendered indirectly to many different departments, and it is practically impossible to establish input-output relationships which would enable overall evaluations to be made. Hence, the control of administrative costs is one of the most difficult areas of management control.

To some extent, budgets can assist in exercising control over administrative costs. The budgetary control of such costs requires that accounting responsibility be clearly identified with particular managers. Financial requirements must be submitted as budget requests by individual managers, and should be scrutinized, modified as necessary and should be incorporated subsequently into an overall administrative budget. The administrative budget becomes the standard against which expenditure is to be assessed.

The difficulty in using this method of controlling administrative costs lies in determining whether the initial budget is reasonable for the proposed level of activity, for there is no way of establishing an acceptable standard of administrative expenditure in relation to particular activity levels. Hence, decisions regarding administrative cost budgets must be based largely on executive judgement and experience.

The control of research and development costs

There are two main reasons why research and development costs are difficult to control. First, since there is little connection between research costs and their benefits, research spending is no indicator of the effectiveness of a research department, or indeed, of a research project. Secondly, there is a long lead time between costs incurred and benefits received.

We noted in Chapter 28 that research and development is an activity directly related to long-range planning. The effectiveness of research and development expenditure may be assessed only in relation to the attainment of goals specified in the long-range plan. These goals should be selected by top management as crucial areas to which major research effort should be directed. In this connection, research expenditure should be concentrated on specific projects which form part of the research effort in a particular area. The control of such expenditure may be exercised by reference to the progress made towards the completion of such projects.

The control of marketing costs

Marketing costs have become significant elements in total costs, due to the rising burden of such costs as advertising and market development. It follows that attention should be directed towards developing the most efficient cost control methods in this area, so as to provide marketing managers with information which will enable them to make the best decisions from the firm's point of view.

Marketing costs cover a wide range of activities, including obtaining sales orders, warehousing and distribution, handling returns and after-sales service. They may be analysed on three different bases—the nature of the cost, the function performed and the appropriate sector of the firm's business, as follows:

(a) *Classification as to costs*
Salesmen's salaries and commission
Travelling
Advertising

(b) *Classification as to function*
Selling
Advertising
Transportation
Credit collection
Warehousing
Invoicing

(c) *Classification as to business sector*
Territory
Product
Marketing channels
Operating divisions
Customers

The analysis of marketing costs is helpful in providing information which is useful for a number of purposes, such as:

Determining the profitability of sales territories
Evaluating the profitability of product lines
Setting selling prices
Selecting from among alternative channels of distribution
Evaluating salesmen's performance
Determining the importance of individual customers
Analysing order size profitability.

It is evident from the description of the range of decisions for which information is required that the analysis of marketing costs is concerned essentially with profitability, which is a function both of revenue control and cost control.

Determining the profitability of sales territories

Most marketing activities are organized on a territorial basis. As a first stage in the analysis of territorial profitability, it is necessary to distinguish direct and indirect marketing costs. Direct costs are those incurred in respect of a territory: indirect costs are those incurred for all the various sales territories.

Direct costs will be controllable by territorial sales managers: indirect costs are beyond their control. Nevertheless, we have mentioned already that despite difficulties in effecting accurate apportionments of indirect costs, such apportionments serve the useful purpose of providing regional managers with information of the back-up services which support their own activities and should be made, provided that they are distinguished from controllable items on reports.

Table 5.1. *Income analysis by territories*

Sales	Terri-tory 1 £500,000	Terri-tory 2 £300,000	Terri-tory 3 £100,000	Total £900,000
Direct costs by territories:				
Cost of goods sold	250,000	160,000	40,000	450,000
Transport & outside warehousing	30,000	20,000	10,000	60,000
Regional office expenses	50,000	30,000	20,000	100,000
Salesmen's expenses	25,000	15,000	6000	46,000
Other regional expenses	15,000	10,000	5000	30,000
Total direct cost by territories	370,000	235,000	81,000	686,000
Contribution to headquarters' overheads and profit	130,000	65,000	19,000	214,000
Indirect costs:				
Central administration	50,000	22,000	8000	80,000
Central warehousing	20,000	8000	2000	30,000
Advertising	30,000	15,000	5000	50,000
Total indirect costs	100,000	45,000	15,000	160,000
Net profit	30,000	20,000	4000	54,000
Percentage of net profit	56%	37%	7%	100%
Percentage of sales	56%	33%	11%	100%
Contribution/sales %	26%	22%	19%	23%

Table 5.1 shows how the analysis of the profitability of sales territories may be made. Its purpose is to locate territories where weaknesses and problems exist. Once they have been located, prompt and intelligent managerial action is required, which may include such decisions as an increase in the number of salesmen operating in the area, or an improvement of the services provided. The contribution margin analysis which is applied in this context has already been discussed in Chapter 35, and it will be recalled that the existence of a contribution margin warrants the continuance of operations in the short-run even though conventional calculations indicate a loss.

Determining the profitability of products

The analysis of the profitability of different products is useful to management in a number of ways. Not only does it indicate the relative profitability of different products, but also areas of strength and weakness which should be noted in the development of corporate strategy. The application of techniques such as contribution margin analysis may assist in deciding whether or not to drop a product line. Pricing decisions may also be based on profitability analysis.

As we explained in Chapter 27, the selection of appropriate bases for determining profitability is problematical, as it is for other management purposes which require the apportionment of indirect costs.

Table 5.2 below shows how the analysis may be conducted. It indicates that product C is the least profitable product in the product range, for although it makes a contribution of £78,000 to fixed expenses and profit, a net loss of £28,000 is associated with its manufacture. Hence, the analysis implies that action should be taken to improve its profitability in the future.

	Products A	B	C	Total
Sales	£350,000	£300,000	£250,000	£900,000
Variable costs of goods sold	90,000	85,000	125,000	300,000
Gross contribution	260,000	215,000	125,000	600,000
Variable marketing costs:				
Transport and warehousing	15,000	12,000	13,000	40,000
Office expenses	30,000	30,000	20,000	80,000
Salesmen's salaries	20,000	15,000	10,000	45,000
Other expenses	6000	5000	4000	15,000
Total variable marketing costs	71,000	62,000	47,000	180,000
Contribution to fixed expenses and profit	189,000	153,000	78,000	420,000
Fixed expenses:				
Manufacturing	55,000	50,000	45,000	150,000
Administration	30,000	25,000	25,000	80,000
Marketing	50,000	50,000	36,000	136,000
Total fixed costs	135,000	125,000	106,000	366,000
Net profit (loss)	£54,000	£28,000	£(28,000)	£54,000
Contribution/Sales %	51%	51%	31%	47%

Controlling marketing costs

Marketing costs may be classified into order-getting and order-filling costs. The former are associated with such activities as advertising, sales promotion and other selling functions: the latter are incurred after the order has been obtained, and cover such costs as packing, delivering, invoicing and warehousing finished products.

(a) *Order-getting costs*
The effectiveness of such costs may only be satisfactorily assessed by relating them to sales revenue. Many factors which affect sales, however, are outside

the control of the sales department, and for this reason, it is difficult to establish standards of performance which are relevant to the problem of maintaining and increasing the effectiveness of order-getting activities. Budgetary control may be used to determine the limits of expenditure but it is not possible to use such budgetary control methods as flexible budgeting in respect of some items, particularly advertising. Flexible budgeting is designed to control expenditure through changing levels of activity: advertising is incurred in order to increase the level of activity. It would be nonsense, therefore, to attempt to apply flexible budgeting to the control of advertising expenditure.

The search for suitable methods of controlling order-getting costs continues. Objective measures may be too limited in their scope to be useful. Firms are using such objective measures of selling costs per order, selling costs per call, or calls per day to control selling costs. These measures should be used with care, for they do not necessarily reflect difficulties in selling to different markets at different times.

Advertising costs, in particular, involve such a large financial commitment that it is necessary that the effectiveness of such costs should be assessed. Market research departments are better equipped than accountants to assess the effectiveness of advertising, since its effects go beyond the expansion of immediate sales.

(b) *Order-filling costs*
It is comparatively easier to control order-filling costs than order-getting costs, since order-filling costs are associated with internal procedures. These procedures are of a standard form and of a repetitive nature making them susceptible to standard control methods: the costs of invoicing, packaging and despatching can be controlled by reference to such objective standards as number of invoices dealt with, number and size of packages, etc. Moreover, unlike order-getting costs, flexible budgeting may be applied to the control of order-filling costs.

Example

Bloxwich Ltd has a sales budget which envisages the sales of 100,000 units of its product in the current year. Budgeted delivery costs are based on standard delivery costs of £1 per unit. If only 80,000 units were sold and delivered by the end of the year at a cost of £90,000, it would be evident that the unfavourable delivery costs variance of £10,000 would require investigation.

Summary

There are two main cost classifications—manufacturing and non-manufacturing costs. Non-manufacturing costs may be sub-divided into three categories—administrative, research and development and marketing costs. These costs are frequently referred to as 'managed' or 'discretionary costs' since they are incurred at the discretion of management.

The difficulty of controlling managed costs is created by the absence of a method for determining appropriate cost levels since it is not possible to relate accurately and in financial terms the benefits associated with such costs. Moreover, it is not possible to determine whether a change in managed costs represents an improvement in performance. For example, providing product specifications are maintained, a reduction in manufacturing costs represents an improvement in performance. No such inference may be drawn from a reduction in managed costs.

In view of the rising proportion of managed costs as a percentage of total costs, the analysis and control of such costs is important and means should be found of overcoming the problems caused by the inability to establish rigorous standards.

Questions

1. What are managed or discretionary costs? How do they differ in character from the costs considered in Chapter 27?
2. What are the problems inherent in controlling administrative and research and development costs?
3. Name three bases on which marketing costs may be analysed.
4. Distinguish between order-getting and order-filling costs.

39 Behavioural aspects of performance evaluation

In recent years, the behavioural aspects of decision making have assumed an increasing importance in management literature. Traditionally, accountants have followed economists in assuming the main organizational problem to be the maximization of profit and allocation of resources necessary to this end. Consequently, accountants have tended to regard organizations from a technical viewpoint, treating men as adjuncts to or as substitutes for machines, to be hired and employed for the purpose of maximizing productivity and profits. The growing realization that the importance of accounting is related to decision making has highlighted the need to understand human behaviour in organizations. This development was well summarized by a committee of the American Accounting Association which reported:

> 'To state the matter concisely, the principal purpose of accounting reports is to influence action, that is, behavior. Additionally, it can be hypothesised that the very process of accumulating information, as well as the behavior of those who do the accumulating, will affect the behavior of others. In short, by its very nature, accounting is a behavioural process.' (The Accounting Review, Supplement, 1971.)

Therefore, accountants should have an understanding of human behaviour and a knowledge of the work of behavioural scientists in this connection. This chapter is concerned, therefore with the behavioural aspects of performance evaluation.

The objectives of performance evaluation

The objectives of performance evaluation may be stated as follows:

(a) to assess how effectively the responsibilities assigned to managers have been carried out;
(b) to identify areas where corrective actions should be taken;
(c) to ensure that managers are motivated towards organizational goals;
(d) to enable comparisons to be made between the performance of different sectors of an organization, to discover areas where improvements may be made.

In our analysis of the process of control, we have so far discussed two important prerequisites for performance evaluation. In Chapter 36, we discussed the problem of identifying areas of responsibility over which individual managers exercise control (responsibility accounting), and in Chapter 37, we discussed the setting of standards of performance to be used as yardsticks for the evaluation of performance. In this chapter, we address ourselves to some of the behavioural problems of budgets as measures for evaluating performance.

Leadership styles and the problem of control

There is a tendency for firms to expect desired results merely from the use of appropriate techniques, thereby failing to recognize that success in organizational control depends upon the actions of responsible individuals and their appreciation of the importance of sound interpersonal relationships. The manner in which the budgeting process is viewed depends on the leadership style adopted by management. McGregor has characterized the two extremes of management styles as 'Theory X' and 'Theory Y' (McGregor, 1960). According to McGregor, these extreme views are conditioned by the manager's view of man.

Theory X

The Theory X view of man, as summarized below, is supportive of an authoritarian leadership style:

(1) Management is responsible for organizing the elements of productive enterprise—money, materials, equipment and people—in activities directed to economic ends.
(2) As regards people, management is concerned with directing their efforts, motivating and controlling their actions, and modifying their behaviour to fit the needs of the organization.
(3) Without this active intervention by management, people would be passive—and even resistant—to organizational needs. Therefore, they must be persuaded, rewarded, punished, controlled. In short, their activities must be directed, and therein lies the function of management. This view is often summed up by the assertion that management consists of getting things done through other people.

Theory Y

By contrast, Theory Y is supportive of a more democratic and participative leadership style:

(1) Management is responsible for organizing the elements of productive enterprise—money, materials, equipment and people—in activities directed to economic ends.
(2) People are not by nature passive or resistant to organizational needs. They appear to have become so as a result of negative experiences of organizational needs.
(3) The motivation, the potential for development, the capacity for assuming responsibility, the readiness to direct behaviour towards organizational goals are all present in people. Management does not put these qualities

in people. It is the responsibility of management to make it possible for people to recognize and develop these human characteristics.

(4) The essential task of management is to arrange organizational conditions and methods of operation so that people can achieve their own goals best by directing their efforts towards organizational objectives.

There is evidence that the Theory X leadership style is widely prevalent and is clearly operational. Those who prefer the assumptions of Theory Y claim that the Theory X leadership style has a human cost in the frustration and the lack of personal development which results from its application to people. The trend in behavioural research suggests that benefits may be derived from leadership and organizations based on the assumptions of Theory Y. These assumptions recognize, in particular, that the basic motivating forces affecting people at work include biological, egoistic and social factors.

As a person, the employee at whatever organizational level, has certain needs which condition his own objectives. He is seeking *compensation* for his efforts to enable him to provide some desired standard of life for himself and his family. He needs outlets for his physical and intellectual energies which provide both *stimulation* and *satisfaction*. He seeks *self-realization* in a sense of his own worth and usefulness. He is pursuing further *growth* and greater *personal effectiveness*. He seeks the *recognition* of his fellows, whether his organizational equals, superiors or subordinates. He appreciates his *identification* with a worthwhile and successful undertaking.

In order to maximize the employee's contribution to organizational activities, it follows that these personal needs and goals should be capable of realization in the task in which he is employed. An awareness of the nature of personal needs, therefore, is an important aspect of control.

The effects of budgets on people

Research suggests that there is a great deal of mistrust of the entire budgetary process at the supervisory level (Argyris, 1953). There is a tendency for traditional budgets to provide the following responses.

Reactions to pressure

The evaluation of a manager's performance in terms of his departmental budget is one of the few elements in performance appraisal which is based on concrete standards. There is little room for manipulation or escape if results are not going to turn out as expected in the budget. If budget pressure becomes too great, it may lead to mistrust, hostility and eventually to poorer performance levels as reaction sets in against budgetary control.

The problem of distinguishing between controllable and non-controllable costs is an important cause of tension among managers. The task of the manager of a department or expense centre, for example, is to attain his goals with the minimum cost. One of the initial difficulties which arises in evaluating his performance applies to all levels of management, namely, the treatment of factors beyond his control. This problem is aggravated when the responsibility for an activity is shared by two or more individuals or functions. Labour inefficiency, for example, may be due to excessive machine breakdowns (maintenance function), inferior materials (purchasing function), defective materials (inspection function) or poor calibre personnel (personnel function). Establishing standards of performance in itself is not an easy task. It demands the clear definition of goals and responsibilities, the delegation of authority, the use of satisfactory surrogates for the activities concerned, effective communication of information and an understanding of the psychology of human motivation.

Over-emphasis on the short run

One of the dangers facing organizations which evaluate the effectiveness of managers in profit terms is that too much emphasis is given to achieving short-term profitability, and measures taken to improve short-term profitability may be detrimental to the organization's long-term prospects. Short-term increases in profits gained at the expense of reductions in research and development and the failure to maintain adequate standards of maintenance are two examples of short-term cost savings which are detrimental to the firm in the long term.

Poor quality decision making by top management

Excessive reliance on the profit performance of divisions may also affect the quality of decisions made by top management. If the managerial competence of divisional managers is assessed solely on the basis of the profit performance of their respective divisions, serious errors of judgement may result. Moreover, if profit results are used as part of an early warning system, action may be taken by top management which may not be warranted. Therefore, although profit budgets are indispensable for planning purposes, great care should be taken in utilizing them for control purposes. The attainment of profit targets is dependent on many factors, some of which are entirely outside the control of a divisional manager. The uncertainty attached to profit forecasts, in particular, limits the usefulness of profit targets for the evaluation of the performance of a divisional manager. The process of formulating the divisional profit forecast also introduces bias in the evaluation of performance. Divisional profit targets are usually based on the divisional manager's forecast of future events. Therefore, it is his ability to forecast the future successfully rather than his ability to manage successfully, which form the basis on which his performance is evaluated. This consideration also affects the validity of comparisons between the performance of different divisions. For example, it is easier to determine an attainable profit goal for a division whose major constraint is productive capacity, where sales are limited only by output, than for a division which sells in a highly competitive market.

Another problem arising from the use of profit budgets in evaluating divisonal performance stems from the fact that an annual budget covers too short a period in which to obtain a realistic picture of managerial performance. The effects of decisions in some instances may take several years before being reflected in profit performance. Thus, the decision to introduce a new product is one of several decisions whose impacts on divisional profits take some years before they are fully realized. The more complex and innovative the division the longer will be the time period necessary for the evaluation of performance. In the light of these considerations, the use of an annual profit result may give a completely inaccurate view of divisional performance.

Poor communication

Where a Theory X style of management exists, negative attitudes may be generated against organizational goals which may lead to faked budget results and the unwillingness to transmit information. Managers will feel that their own survival justifies these tactics.

The prevalence of negative behaviour in an organization which practices management by domination may be aggravated by the response of top management, when it is realized that information which is needed for decision making is not transmitted. Their immediate reaction may be to impose even tighter controls, which will reinforce the negative attitudes held by subordinate managers leading to the transmission of even less accurate and useful information. The progressive tightening of the managerial reins may well result, therefore, in a progressive deterioration of the information flow.

The communication of information is of central importance to the processes of planning and control, as it provides the link between various levels of management and the various decision points. Any reluctance on the part of subordinate managers to communicate information is a serious impediment to the efficiency with which planning and control decisions are made. It is not a sufficient condition for success that an organization should have accounting control systems and that it should have stipulated standards of performance. These control methods will not operate successfully and standards of performance will not be attained if the style of management adopted fails to secure a high degree of motivation and goal congruence within the organization.

Departmental self-centredness

The budget process which involves defining areas of responsibility, measuring and comparing performance accordingly, concentrates the manager's entire attention on his own department. The tendency to departmental self-centredness which is thus encouraged obscures the important relationships between departments, so that inter-departmental dependencies may be ignored or overlooked in the quest for optimizing departmental results. Consequently, economies which would result from greater inter-departmental collaboration may be lost to the organization.

The stifling of initiative

The planning and control aspects of budgeting may be over-emphasized within an organization with the result that opportunities for the exercise of personal initiative may be excluded. Budgets which appear to be strait-jackets discourage managers from deviating from budget stipulations even when circumstances indicate that individual action should be taken. It has been noted, for example, that employees who were subject to audit procedures conformed closely to company policy even when more efficient alternatives were available (Churchill, Cooper and Sainsbury, 1964).

Bias in budgeting

In the last analysis, the process of setting budget targets may be said to be a matter of making subjective judgements, and as a result, bias may inevitably be found in the budgeting process in a conscious or unconscious form. Managers may inflate costs and reduce revenue expectations when setting budget targets, thereby ensuring that they are more readily achievable. In this way, the introduction of conscious bias is a deliberate means of ensuring that their performance as managers will be highly evaluated.

The introduction of bias into estimates that find their way into budget standards typifies the behavioural responses of individuals to organizational pressures. Take the example of a salesman threatened with the possibility of redundancy as a result of falling sales. In such circumstances, he may well find it to his advantage to make optimistic forecasts of sales expectations in his area. By contrast, he may make pessimistic forecasts of achievable sales if his bonus and his performance is evaluated in terms of the extent to which he improves upon the budget target.

The presence of bias in setting budget targets may be met either through the process of counter-biasing, which leads to gamesmanship in budgeting, or by reducing ignorance or fears about the objectives of the firm in relation to personnel. The reduction of conflict between the firm's objectives and the objectives of managers and personnel is discussed later in this chapter, when the system known as Management by Objectives is discussed.

Budget information and performance evaluation

According to Hopwood (1973, 1974), budget information may be used in three different ways for the purposes of assessing managerial performance, as follows:

(1) Budget constrained evaluation, where the manager's performance is primarily evaluated on the basis of his ability to continually meet budget targets on the short-term basis,
(2) Profit-conscious evaluation, where the manager's performance is evaluated on the basis of his ability to increase the general effectiveness of the operations of his unit in relation to the long-term objectives of the firm. In this case, budget information will be used with a degree of flexibility.
(3) Non-accounting evaluation, where budget information plays a relatively small part in the evaluation of the manager's performance.

A summary of the effects of these different styles of managerial evaluation on managerial behavioural is given below:

	Budget constrained	Profit conscious	Non-accounting
Involvement with costs	High	High	Low
Job-related tension	High	Medium	Medium
Manipulation of accounting reports	Extensive	Little	Little
Relations with supervisor	Poor	Good	Good
Relations with colleagues	Poor	Good	Good

The need for several measures of performance

Whilst the use of standard costs and variable budgets play an important role in the control of activities and in the evaluation of performance, undue attention to cost control tends to diminish the importance of other goals. For example, a factory manager is expected to maintain a high level of productive efficiency, to maintain the quality of the product, to meet production schedules on time, to minimize expenses and to maintain satisfactory relations with employees.

The evaluation of performance, therefore, requires both quantitative and qualitative measures of performance. It is evident that some organizational and departmental goals may conflict, such as for example the need to minimize costs and to maintain product quality. Emphasis on specific goals, therefore, will mean that other goals may not be attained. The objectives of performance evaluation, which we have stipulated, require a balanced view of performance covering the various areas of managerial responsibility. If management uses only conventional measurements of revenues, expenses, profit, cost variances and output, it is possible that short-run economic gains may be achieved at the expense of long-run goals. The failure to appreciate the impact of control techniques on individuals responsible for organizational activities may adversely affect employee morale, loyalty, trust and motivation.

The importance of participation

The active participation by managers in the planning process not only enhances their personal sense of involvement in the organization, but improves the efficiency of the planning process. Moreover, such participation establishes a common understanding of purpose, and promotes the acceptance of organizational objectives and goals at all levels. Likewise, the control process is aided by the active participation of managers in the investigation of variances, the evaluation and selection of appropriate solutions and the development of related policies.

The degree of effort expended by members of an organization in attempting to achieve designated goals is particularly dependent upon their personal aspiration level. The aspiration level may.be defined as that level of future performance in a familiar task, which an individual explicitly undertakes knowing his past performance level (Stedry, 1960). For example, a manager's aspiration level as regards costs is the spending level which he accepts as realistic and with which he will strive to comply. Hence, we may identify three potential levels of cost performance (Welsch, 1971):

(1) the budgeted level
(2) the aspiration level
(3) the actual level.

Since the aspiration level is the real inner goal acceptable to the manager, the purpose of participation is to bring the aspiration level in harmony with the budgeted level (or vice-versa). Clearly, a budgeted level which is significantly at variance with the aspiration level will have a negative effect on managerial behaviour.

It follows that managers should be motivated and not pressurized into achieving their budgetary goals. This may be achieved by recognizing the importance of aspiration levels in the planning stage and the timely communication of results as a basis for improving performance, where necessary. The purpose of participation in the control process, therefore, is to motivate managers and to generate in each participant the desire to accomplish or even improve his level of performance.

Management by objectives

From the foregoing discussion of the problem of controlling the activities of an organization and evaluating managerial performance, it follows that several conditions must be satisfied if the accounting function is to play a useful role.

(a) Divisional and departmental goals must be clearly identified and defined, and appropriate measurements selected by which to express them and evaluate managerial performance. Where objectives are too vague or too ambiguous to be susceptible to clear definition in conventional terms, surrogates should be sought which will enable them to be defined and measured.

(b) There should be participation by all levels of management in the control process, thereby ensuring good communication between supervisor and subordinate.

(c) A style of management is required which pays particular attention to the human element in organizations, and in so doing, provides an environment conducive to the employment of all resources.

The aim of management by objectives is to provide a framework for administering a control system which embraces the above-mentioned three conditions. By translating organizational objectives and goals in such a way that they become the personal objectives and goals of all management personnel, whether they be divisional or departmental managers, management by objectives seeks to create a high degree of goal congruence within an organization. The unity of personal and organizational objectives encourages managers to take actions which are in the best interest of the organization.

Some organizational goals are too remote from individual managers, and therefore, have little significance for them, for example, goals relating to the return on capital employed or overall growth targets envisaged in the long-range plan. Management by objectives seeks to establish personal targets at all levels as a means of overcoming this problem. By relating personal goals to departmental and divisional goals and thence to organizational goals, an integration is achieved between them which may be depicted as follows:

Personal goals→Divisional goals→Organizational goals

In Chapter 26, we examined the meaning of control in an administrative context. Management by objectives gives rather a different slant to the meaning of control, which is discussed by Drucker in the following terms:

"Control' is an ambiguous word. It means the ability to direct oneself and one's work. It can also mean domination of one person by another. (Management) objectives are the basis of 'control' in the first sense; but they must never become the basis of 'control' in the second, for this would defeat their purpose. Indeed, one of the major contributions of management by objectives is that it enables us to substitute management by self-control for management by objectives.' (Drucker, 1954).

It would seem that most of the problems which researchers have discovered in relation to the budgeting process have arisen where a Theory X view of man has been reflected in management by domination as a method of control. Man has always rebelled against coercion and domination. By contrast, his most significant achievements have been attained when he has acted as a free agent, exercising self-control in his ability to direct himself and his work.

Management by objectives involves the following processes:

(1) The review of long-term and short-term organizational objectives and goals.

(2) The revision, if necessary, of the organizational structure. An organizational chart is required to illustrate the titles, duties and the relationships between managers.

(3) Standards of performance necessary to fulfil key tasks are set by the job-holder himself in agreement with his immediate supervisor. Unless the job-holder participates in setting performance standards, he will not feel committed to them. The standards of performance which result from systems of management by objectives are not 'ideal', nor are they minimum acceptable levels of performance. They indicate what are agreed to be 'satisfactory' levels of performance. As far as possible, they should be expressed in quantitative terms.

Management controls are operated so that supervisors do not act as watchdogs but rather as sources of help and guidance to their subordinates. A divisional profit goal in this sense is not only a target for the divisional manager, for it may also act as a means whereby top management may help to solve divisional problems should they become apparent through the failure to reach a stipulated figure.

(4) Results are measured against goals. An important aspect of this stage is the use of periodic performance appraisal interviews, in which supervisor and

subordinate jointly discuss results and consider their implications for the future. The performance appraisal interview is essentially a discussion between manager and subordinate about objectives and their achievement. Performance appraisal should evaluate the manager not merely in terms of current performance as expressed in tangible results; it should also enable his performance as a manager, his personal qualifications and character and his potential for advancement to be assessed. It is an integral part of the process of managing by results by which both parties to the interview assess their efficiency as managers. The manager himself assesses his role as tutor to the subordinate; the subordinate considers his role in supporting the manager.

(5) Long- and short-term organizational goals are reviewed in the light of current performance.

These stages in management by objectives are illustrated in Fig. 5.32.

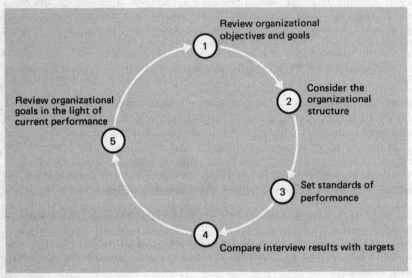

Fig. 5.32.

Organization theory

Some of the assumptions upon which we have so far relied have been necessary for the purpose of facilitating the examination of the basic aspects of accounting for planning and control. If an accounting system is to be effective in providing information for planning and control purposes, it should be capable of adapting to organizational and environmental factors peculiar to individual enterprises. Different enterprises may require different methods of control depending on the internal and external influences affecting their own activities. Hence, some of our assumptions may be more applicable to some organizations than to others. In this respect, organization theory attempts to provide a framework for understanding the influences which bear upon organizations and is important, therefore, for clarifying issues of importance to the accountant.

Approaches to organization theory

By regarding the organization as a logical and rational process, the classical approach focuses in some detail on the organizing function of management. Hence, the classical theory is concerned with the structure of organizations and the determination of the tasks necessary to attain organizational objectives. By contrast, the human relations approach stresses people rather than structures, their motives and behaviour rather than the activities which need to be harnessed for achieving organizational goals. This approach originated in the Hawthorne experiments of the 1920s, which revealed that social and human factors in work situations were often more important than physical factors in affecting productivity. The human relations theory asserts that since the most important factors are individual needs and wants, the structure of organizations should be geared to individuals rather than the individual being geared to the structure.

Finally, there has developed the contingency approach which starts with the premise that there is no single organizational design that is best in all situations. According to Sketty and Carlisle (1972), there are four factors or forces of particular significance in the design of an organizational structure, namely: (1) forces in the manager; (2) forces in the environment; (3) forces in the task; (4) forces in the subordinates.

(1) *Forces in the manager.* This refers to factors relating to the personalities of managers and their influence on the design of the organizational structure. Managers tend to perceive organizational problems in a unique way, which is a function of background, knowledge, experience and values. These factors shape organizational decisions in such areas as strategy, organizational structure and style of management. Accordingly, organizations do not have objectives—only people have objectives. In this analysis, these objectives will differ from manager to manager.

(2) *Forces in the environment.* Some studies suggest that the most effective pattern of organizational structure is that which enables the organization to adjust to the requirements of its environment (Burns and Stalker, 1961). These studies indicate that organizations with less formal structures are best able to cope with uncertain and heterogeneous environmental conditions. Conversely, highly structured organizations will be more effective in stable environmental conditions. Hence, bureaucratic structures as implied in classical theory are more appropriate to stable conditions, whereas more democratic structures are required to enable organizations to adapt to a changing environment.

(3) *Forces in the task.* Empirical studies indicate that technology has an important impact on the design of an organizational structure. For example, Woodward (1965) has found that organizational structures varied according to the technology involved. According to Woodward, fewer managers are required under systems of unit production than under systems of mass production. The technology associated with unit production systems may also

require relatively higher levels of operative skill, and there is evidence to suggest that skilled workers feel more involved in their jobs and are more anxious for an opportunity to participate in decision making relating to their jobs than unskilled workers. This makes it possible to delegate more authority to lower levels in an organization and has important implications for devising schemes based on 'management by objectives'.

(4) *Forces in the subordinates.* This refers to the psychological needs such as the subordinate's desire for a measure of independence, for the acquisition of skills and the motivation for assuming responsibility. The desire to participate in decision making is not uniform among employees, and as implied earlier it is much stronger among skilled workers and employees with a professional background than it is among unskilled workers. Hence, organizations employing relatively more skilled than unskilled employees will be faced with a greater desire for a democratic structure.

Summary

The budget process alone is not sufficient to maintain adequate management control. Too often, organizations tend to expect results from budgetary control and fail to recognize its behavioural implications. As a result, pressures are created leading to mistrust, hostility and actions detrimental to the long-term prospects of an organization. It follows that accountants should work more closely with behavioural scientists and that they should learn more about the behavioural implications of organizational control.

Participation schemes may be introduced into organizations with due consideration for the psychological problems entailed. One such scheme is management by objectives. Management by objectives differs from the conventional budgetary control theory in that it enables the precepts of Theory Y to be put into practice by creating an environment which allows employees to develop as individuals and to exercise responsibility through self-control. Self-control is found to induce stronger work motivation, for by giving individual managers greater freedom of action, it affords them in greater measure the satisfaction and pleasure which a sense of accomplishment confers.

Being concerned with the provision of information for planning and control, the accountant should find a knowledge of organization theory particularly useful in understanding the internal and external influences which affect the nature of organizational activities and the environment in which decisions are made. These influences have implications for the design of control systems, and the significance of contingency theory lies in the identification of their sources.

References

1. Argyris, C. 'Human problems with budgets', *Harvard Business Review,* January-February, 1953.
2. Burns, T. & Stalker, G. M. *The Management of Innovation*, Tavistock Publications Ltd, London, 1961.

3. Churchill, N. C., Cooper, W. E. & Sainsbury, T. 'Laboratory and field studies of the behavioural effects of audits', *in* Bonini, E. C., Jaedicke, R. K. & Wagner, H. M. (eds), *Management Controls,* McGraw-Hill, 1964.
4. Drucker, P. F. *The Practice of Management*, p. 131, Heinemann, London, 1963.
5. Hopwood, A. *Accounting and Human Behaviour*, Accountancy Age Books, London, 1974.
6. Hopwood, A. *An Accounting System and Managerial Behaviour*, Saxton House/ Lexington Books, 1973.
7. McGregor, D. M. *The Human Side of the Enterprise,* McGraw-Hill, 1960.
8. 'Report of the Committee on the Behavioural Science Context of the Accounting Curriculum', *The Accounting Review*, Supplement to Vol. 46, 1971.
9. Sketty, Y. K. & Carlisle, H. M. 'A contingency model of organization design', *California Management Review,* Vol. 15, No. 1, 1972.
10. Stedry, A. C. *Budget Control and Cost Behaviour*, Prentice-Hall, 1960.
11. Welsch, G. A. 'Some behavioural implications in profit planning and control', *Management Adviser*, July-August, 1971.
12. Woodward, J. *Industrial Organization: Theory and Practice*, Oxford University Press, 1965.

Questions

The following extract is taken from a conversation between the Chairman of Westway Engineering Company and James Brown, accountant, on the day Brown took up his appointment with the company.

Chairman: 'We apply a system of payment by results to foremen as well as to operatives. For each department, budgeted allowances are set for the expenditure which should be incurred over varying levels of output. The greater the saving on budgeted expenditure for a department, the greater the bonus received by the foreman concerned. For example, this report shows how the bonus the foreman of our Assembly Department had built up, suffered a severe jolt last month'.

He hands the following report to Brown.

Westway Engineering Co.—Assembly Department
Foreman: W. Rodgers

	Budget allowance	Actual	For month (Over) under budget	Year to date (Over) under budget
Direct material	4000	5000	(1000)	(3000)
Direct labour	10,000	12,000	(2000)	(3500)
Indirect labour	5000	4500	500	1000
Indirect material	2000	1700	300	(1000)
Power	6000	6500	(500)	(2000)
Maintenance	7000	10,000	(3000)	4000
Depreciation	5000	4000	1000	2000
Insurance	100	80	20	500
General expense	10,000	8500	1500	4500
			(3180)	2000

Chairman: 'Since the new accounting system was installed a year ago, there appears to have been a general deterioration in morale. The relations between a number of staff certainly need improving. Two months ago an error was made on an order, and the goods were returned for correction, a process which cost £700. None of the departmental foremen were prepared to accept the cost of the error which was finally charged to general factory loss. Because of the incident two foremen stopped talking to each other'.

Required:

Discuss what improvements should be made in the accounting system in operation at Westway's.

Index